JAVA
Developer's Reference

Mike Cohn
Bryan Morgan
Michael Morrison
Michael T. Nygard
Dan Joshi
Tom Trinko

sams
net

201 West 103rd Street
Indianapolis, Indiana 46290

Copyright © 1996 by Sams.net Publishing

FIRST EDITION

International Standard Book Number: 1-57521-129-7

Library of Congress Catalog Card Number: 96-68243

99 98 97 96   4 3 2 1

Interpretation of the printing code: the rightmost double-digit number is the year of the book's printing; the rightmost single-digit, the number of the book's printing. For example, a printing code of 96-1 shows that the first printing of the book occurred in 1996.

Composed in AGaramond and MCPdigital by Macmillan Computer Publishing

Printed in the United States of America

President, Sams Publishing	*Richard K. Swadley*
Publishing Team Leader	*Greg Wiegand*
Managing Editor	*Cindy Morrow*
Director of Marketing	*John Pierce*
Assistant Markerting Managers	*Kristina Perry,* *Rachel Wolfe*

Acquisitions Editor
Christopher Denny

Development Editor
Anthony Amico

Software Development Specialist
Brad Myers

Senior Editor
Kristi Hart

Production Editor
Bart Reed

Copy Editors
Margaret Berson, Fran Blauw, Lisa Lord, Marla Reece, Kris Simmons

Indexer
Tom Dinse

Technical Reviewer
Karen Clere, Vincent Mayfield

Editorial Coordinator
Bill Whitmer

Technical Edit Coordinator
Lynette Quinn

Resource Coordinator
Deborah Frisby

Editorial Assistants
Carol Ackerman, Andi Richter, Rhonda Tinch-Mize

Cover Designer
Jay Corpus

Book Designer
Alyssa Yesh

Copy Writer
Peter Fuller

Production Team Supervisor
Brad Chinn

Production
Charlotte Clapp, Jeanne Clark, Merry Dankanich, Mike Dietsch, Mike Henry, Tim Osborn, Shawn Ring, M. Anne Sipahimalani, Becky Stutzman

Overview

33   Package `java.net`   1025

Acknowledgments

A book of this size is clearly a team effort. We would like to thank Chris Denny, our acquisitions editor, for getting the ball rolling. Thanks also to Tony Amico, our development editor, who, once the ball was rolling, made sure we all rolled in the same direction. Thanks also to Vincent Mayfield and Karen Clere, our technical editors, who had the difficult job of making sure that what we wrote remained accurate as the Java language continued to evolve.

Much of what we've written would be less useful without the work of Alyssa Yesh, who designed the icons used throughout the book. Similarly, our thanks go to Brad Myers, who converted the reference section into HTML files for inclusion on the CD. Fittingly, these two have helped make this book more than the sum of its words.

Finally, special thanks to Bart Reed, our production editor, who pulled everything together and who taught us why "production editor" starts with "prod."

Special Thanks from Mike Cohn:

I would like to thank Jim Kearns and Jim Steeb of Access Health for their encouragement and for providing a cutting edge environment that needs products like Java. Thanks also to the two teachers who taught me how to write—John Dale, formerly of Rancho Alamitos High School, and my mother, Carlene. Special thanks to my daughter, Savannah, for just being who you are. Finally, nothing would be possible without the love and encouragement I receive from my wife, Laura. I love you. Thanks for being my kid's mom.

Special Thanks from Michael Morrison:

I'd like to thank my faithful and now legal accomplice, Mahsheed, for all your love and support.

Special Thanks from Tom Trinko:

Special thanks to the good Lord for all His blessings, especially my wife Colleen and the kids—Kate, Peter, Ted, Mary, and Therese.

About the Authors

Mike Cohn is the Director of Information Technology at Access Health, Inc., the leading provider of personal health management. Before that he was with Andersen Consulting and the Adler Consulting Group in New York. He holds a Masters degree in Computer Science from the University of Idaho and has been programming for 16 years. Mike lives in Cameron Park, California with his wife, Laura, and their daughter, Savannah.

Bryan Morgan is a software engineer with TASC, Inc. in Fort Walton Beach, Florida. He holds a B.S. in Electrical Engineering from Clemson University and is currently using Java to build Web applications as well as to perform Web-based distributed interactive simulations. Bryan and his wife, Becky, are expecting their first child in November 1996. Bryan is the co-author of *Teach Yourself SQL in 14 Days* and *Teach Yourself ODBC in 21 Days* for Sams Publishing.

Michael Morrison is the author of *Teach Yourself Internet Game Programming with Java in 21 Days*, co-author of *Windows 95 Game Developer's Guide, Using the Game SDK*, and is a contributing author of *Tricks of the Java Programming Gurus* and *Java Unleashed*.

Michael Nygard received his B.S. from the California Institute of Technology in 1994. He is currently employed by TASC, Inc. in Fort Walton Beach, Florida, where he is a Member of Technical Staff in the Simulation Technologies Department. Michael investigates leading-edge technologies and is currently focusing on Java, Delphi, and Windows NT.

Dan Joshi is a professional developer working for several Fortune 100 companies. He currently owns his own Internet-based consulting company, The Joshi Group. Dan is also a co-author of *Teach Yourself Java in Cafe in 21 Days*.

Tom Trinko, Mad Scientist. Born human. Unclear if he's stayed same. Worked on just about every type of computer since 1972. Expert on the world's only user-friendly computers, the Macintosh and Newton, with a couple of books on Mac scripting on his resume. When coherent, he can be reached at trinkos@aol.com, 72147,3723 on CompuServe, or via his Web page at http://members.aol.com/trinkos/basepage.html, which features some nice (in his unbiased opinion) Java stuff, including a cellular automata engine.

Tell Us What You Think!

As a reader, you are the most important critic and commentator of our books. We value your opinion and want to know what we're doing right, what we could do better, what areas you'd like to see us publish in, and any other words of wisdom you're willing to pass our way. You can help us make strong books that meet your needs and give you the computer guidance you require.

Do you have access to CompuServe or the World Wide Web? Then check out our CompuServe forum by typing **GO SAMS** at any prompt. If you prefer the World Wide Web, check out our site at http://www.mcp.com.

> **NOTE**
>
> If you have a technical question about this book, call the technical support line at (800) 571-5840, ext. 3668.

As the team leader of the group that created this book, I welcome your comments. You can fax, e-mail, or write me directly to let me know what you did or didn't like about this book—as well as what we can do to make our books stronger. Here's the information:

Fax: (317) 581-4669

E-mail: programming_mgr@sams.mcp.com

Mail: Greg Wiegand
            Comments Department
            Sams Publishing
            201 W. 103rd Street
            Indianapolis, IN 46290

Conventions Used in This Book

This book uses the following conventions:

- New terms appear in *italic.*

- Placeholders (words that stand for what you actually type) in regular text appear in *italic.*

- All code appears in monospace, as do filenames and directory names.

- Placeholders in code appear in *italic monospace.*

- When a line of code is too long to fit on only one line of this book, it is broken at a convenient place and continued to the next line. The continuation of the line is preceded by a code continuation character (➡). You should type a line of code that has this character as one long line without breaking it.

- An ellipsis (...) indicates that the remaining or intervening code required to complete a statement or code structure has been omitted for the sake of brevity.

I

The Java
Development System

In this section of the book you are introduced to the operation of the Java development environment. A number of authors have each brought their individual expertise to these topics. To begin, Mike Cohn introduces Java, and Bryan Morgan explains how the Java Developer's Kit (JDK) is installed. Then Mike and Bryan examine in detail the way developers in other languages such as C++, Delphi, and Visual Basic can leverage their knowledge as a transition into this new and exciting language.

Many people believe that Java is only applicable to Web operation. While the Web is a very important part of Java and one that offers the greatest promise, it also can be used to develop full-blown applications that are not dependent on a Web browser. First, Bryan shows how to develop applets that are downloaded from a Web server; then Dan Joshi joins these authors and provides details on the use of Java to develop stand-alone applications.

At this point the Java development environment is covered in earnest. Michael Morrison, Michael Nygard, and the other authors delve into the components of the JDK, and show how to write, compile, and execute your applets and applications. When things start going wrong, Java has some built-in debugging capabilities, which Bryan and Michael Morrison cover in detail.

In other languages, documentation is a separate process. Often overlooked, this subsidiary requirement rapidly loses accuracy as the development heats up. Realizing the importance of good documentation, the SunSoft folks have included a way to generate online documentation from the comments that you embed in your Java code. Mike Cohn examines this process in detail and provides hints on making the process much more effective.

1

Introduction to Java

by Mike Cohn

This chapter introduces Java and points out some of its strengths. It describes how programming in Java is different from programming in any other language and how you can take advantage of these differences to create exciting new applications. Also included in this chapter are high-level overviews of the Java language and the Java runtime environment. By the time you complete this chapter, you will have a good introduction to what Java is and what it can do for you.

What Is Java?

Java was developed at Sun Microsystems. Work on Java originally began with the goal of creating a platform-independent language and operating system for consumer electronics. The original intent was to use C++, but as work progressed in this direction, the Java developers realized that they would be better served by creating their own language rather than extending C++. The effort toward consumer electronics led the Java team, then known as FirstPerson, Inc., toward developing hardware and software for the delivery of video-on-demand with Time-Warner.

Unfortunately (or perhaps fortunately, depending on your perspective), Time-Warner selected Silicon Graphics as the vendor for its video-on-demand project. This setback left the FirstPerson team with an interesting piece of software (Java) but no market in which to place it. Eventually, the natural synergies of the Java language and the World Wide Web (WWW) were noticed, and Java found a market.

What we know today as Java is both a programming language and an environment for executing programs written in the Java language. Unlike traditional compilers, which convert source code into machine-level instructions, the Java compiler translates Java source code into instructions that are interpreted by the runtime Java Virtual Machine. So, unlike languages like C and C++, on which Java is based, Java is an interpreted language.

Although most of the current excitement and anticipated use of Java are related to the Internet, and the World Wide Web in particular, Java did not begin as an Internet project. Because of this, Java is suitable for many general-purpose programming tasks and, in fact, many of the Java tools themselves are written in Java. It is a compiler development custom that a language has come of age when its compiler can be written in the language. According to this custom, the Java language has come of age.

Java as an Internet Language

The excitement over Java as an Internet development language is related to its capability to solve two key problems with Internet content:

- Currently, the WWW content is passive and static.
- Delivery of WWW content is dependent on the configuration of each user's Web browser.

Although these two problems are related, each warrants independent consideration.

Passive and Static Content

Current WWW pages are very good at conveying some types of information but are inadequate for conveying other types. In particular, WWW pages excel at conveying passive, static information. This type of information changes infrequently (static) and doesn't change in response to user interactions with it (passive).

For example, many Web pages enable you to enter a company's name or stock ticker symbol and receive current price quotes. One of the best is the APL Quote Server located at `http://qs.secapl.com/cgi-bin/qs` and shown in Figure 1.1. This page is static because it isn't automatically updated with new quotes while the page is being browsed. It is passive because the user cannot interact with the page, other than to request to see a similar page.

FIGURE 1.1.

Retrieving passive, static stock prices.

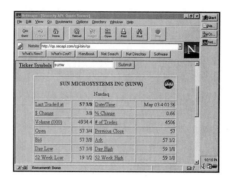

Current Web development technologies excel at displaying this type of page. Much of human communication is passive, static, or both. A highway billboard is a perfect example of a conventional means of communication that is both passive and static. Just as not all billboards will go the way of Burma Shave, not all passive, static WWW content needs to become active and dynamic (the opposites of passive and static).

However, Java is an enabling technology that allows for the creation of more powerful pages. Continuing with the example of a page that shows the price of a stock at a given point in time, you could use Java to create a page that shows a graph of a stock's price over time and have that graph continue to update in real time while you browse the page. This is where Java comes in—because Java is a full-featured programming language, Web pages like this become much more feasible. Sun Microsystems has created a page that does exactly this. It is located at

`http://java.sun.com/java.sun.com/applets/applets/StockDemo/index.html`

and is shown in Figure 1.2.

FIGURE 1.2.

A Java version of a stock price Web page.

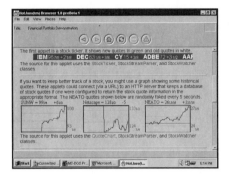

On the Java WWW page shown in Figure 1.2, there is a line of stock ticker symbols and prices that scrolls across the top of the screen. Below that are graphs for three different companies' stocks. Each of these graphs is updated every five seconds based on the latest trades. (The page shown in Figure 1.2 is just an illustration and the prices of the NEATO company are randomly generated.)

Freedom from Browser Configuration

In the pre-Java world of the Web, as a developer of Web content and pages, you could not count on your users having a specific browser configuration. You could create a Web page with leading edge graphics, sound, and real-time multimedia. Unfortunately, if any of the visitors to your Web site did not configure a browser add-on to handle the latest whiz-bang features, these users wouldn't get the full impact of your site.

Just as the prior section showed that Java enabled applications to go beyond passive, static content, Java again serves as an enabling technology. In this case, Java enables you, as a Web developer, to create Web pages that will be delivered consistently to all users with a Java-enabled browser.

Not only does Java free you from concerns about how users have configured their Web browsers, it also frees you from concerns about which hardware and operating system platform they are using. Because Java source code is interpreted, if a Java interpreter exists for a specific hardware and operating system platform, you can write programs with the knowledge that they will be usable on that platform.

How It Works

Now that you've read about some of the benefits of using Java for World Wide Web applications, it's time to take a quick look behind the scenes at how this is accomplished. Figure 1.3 shows how Java source code is transferred over the Internet. This figure shows a host computer that is storing the source code to a Java program. When a user on a local computer uses the Internet to connect to this host with a Java-enabled browser, the source is transferred from the host computer to the local computer.

FIGURE 1.3.

Transfer of Java source code over the Internet.

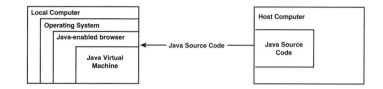

Implemented within the Java-enabled browser is the Java Virtual Machine, which interprets the Java source code. The Java Virtual Machine acts on an input byte stream and converts it into the desired program actions. In the case of Java, the byte stream is a sequence of opcodes (operation codes) and operands. Each pair of opcode and operand is read by the interpreter, and the specified action is performed. This is illustrated in Figure 1.4.

FIGURE 1.4.

Program behavior is created by the Java Virtual Machine's interpretation of a byte stream.

Java as a General-Purpose Language

Of course, the use of Java extends beyond the Web, and there is much to recommend Java as a general-purpose development language. You've already seen that Java is completely portable to a variety of hardware platforms and operating systems. In this section, you'll learn about some of Java's attributes that make it a desirable general-purpose language.

For example, because Java borrows much of its syntax and many of its concepts from C and C++, there is a preexisting pool of programmers who could quickly learn Java. However, Java goes far beyond being a mere derivative of C++. It adds to C++ in the areas of automatic memory management and language-level support for multithreaded applications. On the other hand, Java remains easier to learn and simpler to use than C++ because of those C++ features that were left out of Java: multiple inheritance, pointers, and the goto statement, among others.

Because implementations of the Java Virtual Machine can be very efficient, it is possible for Java programs to run almost as quickly as C++ programs. This is a key feature in convincing developers that Java is a viable language for non-Internet development. Because of Java's strengths as an Internet language, many of these same strengths apply when Java is used as a language for client-server development. It is very likely that as corporations do more and more Internet development in Java, they will begin to apply these same Java developers to their client-server projects. Java's strengths in terms of network awareness, security, portability, and performance make it ideally suited for corporate client-server development, as well as Internet development.

Applications and Applets

In discussing Java programs, it has become standard to refer to Java programs that are embedded in another language as *applets* and to stand-alone programs as *applications*. For example, when you use Java to augment a World Wide Web page, the Java code is embedded within HTML code. Therefore, this is referred to as an applet. On the other hand, a Java program that is not embedded within HTML or any other language and can stand on its own is referred to as an application.

Of course, there is a subtle implication here that applications are larger (and, therefore, presumably more complex) than applets. However, this is not necessarily true. Applications and applets alike can range from simple one-class programs to programs with hundreds of classes. The implication that an applet is somehow less than an application is unfortunately a connotation it is necessary to live with in an otherwise valid distinction.

Features of the Java Language

Having seen that Java is equally suited as a language for development both on and off the Internet, it's time to look more closely at the Java language itself. The creators of Java at Sun Microsystems have defined the Java language as "a simple, object-oriented, distributed, interpreted, robust, secure, architecture-neutral, portable, high-performance, multithreaded, and dynamic language." Well, they managed to fit all of the important 1990s buzzwords into one sentence, but we need to look more closely at Java to see if they managed to fit all of these concepts into one language.

Simple

If you have experience with any object-oriented language, especially C++, you probably will find Java to be easier than your high school prom date. Because Java started out as C++ but has had certain features removed, it is certainly a simpler language than C++.

The simplicity of Java is enhanced by its similarities to C and C++. Because many of today's current programmers, especially those likely to consider using Java, are experienced in at least C and probably C++, Java is instantly familiar to these programmers.

Java has simplified C++ programming by both adding features beyond those found in C++ and by removing some of the features that make C++ a complicated and difficult language to master. Java is simple because it consists of only three primitive data types—numbers, Boolean types, and arrays. Everything else in Java is a class. For example, strings are true objects, not just arrays of characters. Similarly, arrays in the Java language are first-class objects, not just memory allocations and runtime representations.

Java offers additional simplifications over C++. The ubiquitous `goto` statement has been removed. Operator overloading, a frequent source of confusion during the maintenance of C++ programs, is not allowed in Java. Unlike C and C++, Java has no preprocessor. This means that the concepts behind `#define` and `typedef` are not necessary in Java. Java reduces the redundancy of C++ by removing structures and unions from the language. These are both just poor cousins of a full-fledged class and are superfluous in a cohesively designed language. Of course, they were necessary in C++ because it was important for early C++ translators and then compilers to be able to correctly interpret the existing C code that relied on these features.

The most important C++ feature left out of Java is the capability to directly manipulate memory addresses through the use of pointers. Pointers are one of the cornerstones of the C and C++ languages, and it would be difficult to write many programs in these languages without using pointers. However, as any C or C++ programmer will admit, pointers are also a significant source of problems and debugging time in C and C++ programs. Pointers can accidentally be set to point to the wrong thing, causing unexpected behavior including crashes. Pointers also can be used to store allocated memory. If the allocated memory isn't freed, or released back to the operating system, then the program will gradually leak memory, until it eventually runs out. An entire set of commercial products, such as the Bounds Checker products, has come into existence to help programmers identify these types of pointer-related problems. Java simplifies this by completely removing pointers from the language and using a handle-based solution instead.

Of course, if all Java did was remove syntax from C++, it would be a poor compiler instead of an exciting new language. Java goes well beyond C++ by adding some important features. One of the most important is automatic memory management, usually known as *garbage collection*. Garbage collection is really just a blue-collar term that means that you don't need to free memory that you allocate—the Java Virtual Machine takes care of doing this for you. If you're a C or C++ programmer, or have ever had to track down memory leaks in another language, just imagine how nice your life could be if you never have to do it again. You would have time for walks on the beach, barbecued turkey burgers on holiday weekends, and romantic evenings with your spouse.

Java goes beyond C++ in a variety of other ways, as well. For example, Java includes language-level support for writing *multithreaded* programs. A multithreaded program is one that is written such that it performs more than one task at a time. For example, consider the stock price Web page shown earlier in Figure 1.2. One thread in the program to create this page may be constantly retrieving quotes from the stock exchange while another thread searches various news databases for breaking stories about the stocks being monitored. Although you can definitely write this program in a traditional single-threaded manner, the ability to use multiple threads can make it simpler to write and maintain.

Object-Oriented

Of course, Java is object-oriented. In fact, in the mid-1990s, it's hard to imagine someone developing a new language and declaring it the greatest new thing without it being object-oriented. In its approach to object-orientation, Java follows more closely along the lines of languages such as SmallTalk than C++. Except for its primitive data types, everything in Java is an object. In contrast, C++ is much more lax in that you are entirely free to mix and match object-oriented code (classes) and procedural code (functions). In Java, this is not the case. There are no global functions in Java: all functions are invoked through an object.

Java's support for object-orientation does not include multiple inheritance. The designers of the language felt that the complexity introduced by multiple inheritance was not justified by its benefits.

Java classes are comprised of methods and variables. *Class methods* are the functions that an object of the class can respond to. *Class variables* are the data that define the state of an object. In Java, methods and variables can be declared as *private*, *protected*, or *public*. Private methods and variables are not accessible outside of the class. Protected members are accessible to subclasses of the class, but not to other classes. Finally, public methods and variables are accessible to any class.

Classes in Java can be defined as abstract. An abstract class is a class that collects generic state and behavioral information. More specific classes are defined as subclasses of the abstract class and are used to define actual, specific entities. For example, software in use at a pet store may have an abstract class named `Pet`. This class would store information that is common to all pets—birthdate, cost, sale price, date received, and so on. Derived from the abstract `Pet` class could be classes such as `Dog`, `Cat`, `Bird`, and `Fish`. Each of these classes can augment the abstract class as necessary. For example, a member variable called `WaterType` (salt or fresh) would be necessary in `Fish`. Because `WaterType` would be meaningless for `Dogs`, `Cats`, and `Birds`, it is not part of the abstract implementation of `Pet`.

Distributed

Java facilitates the building of distributed applications by a collection of classes for use in networked applications. By using Java's URL (Uniform Resource Locator) class, an application can easily access a remote server. Classes also are provided for establishing socket-level connections.

Interpreted

Because Java is interpreted, once the Java interpreter has been ported to a specific machine, that machine can instantly run the growing body of Java applications. As an example of the usefulness of this, imagine a hypothetical chip manufacturer, Outtel, that has just finished its newest CPU chip. This new chip, named the Zentium, serves as the foundation of a new line of computers being marketed toward Zen Buddhist monasteries. Once Outtel ports the Java interpreter to work on the Zentium, the new machine will be able to run all of the Java development utilities—the compiler, the debugger, and so on. Contrast this with a traditional language. If Outtel wants to release a C++ compiler with its new computer it must port, or create from scratch, the compiler, the debugger, the runtime library, and so on.

Also, when using an interpreter, programmers are freed from some of the concerns of intermodule dependencies. You no longer have to maintain a "make" file that is sometimes as complicated as the hardest part of your program.

Another advantage is that the time-consuming edit-compile-link-test cycle is broken. Without the compile and link steps, working in an interpreted environment is a much simpler edit-test cycle. Even with today's quick C++ compilers, it is not uncommon for a complete recompile and relink of a large program to be measured in hours and take the better part of a day. Without having to wait for lengthy compiles and links, Java promotes prototyping and easier debugging.

Robust

The designers of Java anticipated that it would be used to solve some very complex programming problems. Writing a distributed, multithreaded program that can run on a variety of operating systems with a variety of processors is not a simple task. To do it successfully, you need all the help your programming language can offer you. With this in mind, Java was created as a strongly typed language. Data type issues and problems are resolved at compile-time, and implicit casts of a variable from one type to another are not allowed.

Memory management has been simplified in Java in two ways. First, Java does not support direct pointer manipulation or arithmetic. This makes it impossible for a Java program to overwrite memory or corrupt data. Second, Java uses runtime garbage collection instead of explicit freeing of memory. In languages like C++, it is necessary to delete or free memory once the program has finished with it. Java follows the lead of languages such as LISP and SmallTalk by providing automatic support for freeing memory that has been allocated but is no longer used.

Secure

Closely related to Java's robustness is its focus on security. Because Java does not use pointers to directly reference memory locations, as is prevalent in C and C++, Java has a great deal of control over the code that exists within the Java environment.

It was anticipated that Java applications would run on the Internet and that they could dynamically incorporate or execute code found at remote locations on the Internet. Because of this, the developers of Java hypothesized the existence of a hostile Java compiler that would generate Java byte codes with the intent of bypassing Java's runtime security. This led to the concept of a byte-code verifier. The byte-code verifier examines all incoming code to ensure that the code plays by the rules and is safe to execute. In addition to other properties, the byte code verifier ensures the following:

- No pointers are forged.
- No illegal object casts are performed.
- There will be no operand stack overflows or underflows.
- All parameters passed to functions are of the proper types.
- Rules regarding private, protected, and public class membership are followed.

Architecture-Neutral

Back in the dark ages of the early 1980s, there was tremendous variety in desktop personal computers. You could buy computers from Apple, Commodore, Radio Shack, Atari, and eventually even from IBM. Additionally, every machine came with its own very different operating system. Because developing software is such a time-consuming task, very little of the software developed for use on one machine was ever ported and then released for use on a different machine.

In many regards, this situation has improved with the acceptance of Windows, the Apple Macintosh, and UNIX variations as the only valid personal computer options. However, it is still not easy to write an application that can be used on Windows NT, UNIX, and a Macintosh. And it's getting more complicated with the move of Windows NT to non-Intel CPU architectures.

A number of commercially available source code libraries (for example, Zinc, ZApp, and XVT) attempt to achieve application portability. These libraries attempt this by focusing on either a lowest common denominator among the operating systems or by creating a common core API (Application Programming Interface).

Java takes a different approach. Because the Java compiler creates byte code instructions that are subsequently interpreted by the Java interpreter, architecture neutrality is achieved in the implementation of the Java interpreter for each new architecture.

Portable

In addition to being architecture-neutral, Java code is also portable. It was an important design goal of Java that it be portable so that as new architectures (due to hardware, operating system, or both) are developed, the Java environment could be ported to them.

In Java, all primitive types (integers, longs, floats, doubles, and so on) are of defined sizes, regardless of the machine or operating system on which the program is run. This is in direct contrast to languages like C and C++ that leave the sizes of primitive types up to the compiler and developer.

Additionally, Java is portable because the compiler itself is written in Java and the runtime environment is written in POSIX-compliant C.

High-Performance

For all but the simplest or most infrequently used applications, performance is always a consideration. It is no surprise, then, to discover that achieving high performance was one of the initial design goals of the Java developers. A Java application will not achieve the performance of a fully compiled language such as C or C++. However, for most applications, including graphics-intensive ones such as are commonly found on the World Wide Web, the performance of Java is more than adequate. For some applications, there may be no discernible difference in performance between C++ and Java.

Many of the early adopters of C++ were concerned about the possibility of performance degradation as they converted their programs from C to C++. However, many C++ early adopters discovered that, although a C program will outperform a C++ program in many cases, the additional development time and effort don't justify the minimal performance gains. Of course, because we're not all programming in assembly language, there must be some amount of performance we're willing to trade for faster development.

It is very likely that early experiences with Java will follow these same lines. Although a Java application may not be able to keep up with a C++ application, it will normally be fast enough, and Java may enable you to do things you couldn't do with C++.

Multithreaded

Writing a computer program that only does a single thing at a time is an artificial constraint that we've lived with in most programming languages. With Java, we no longer have to live with this limitation. Support for multiple, synchronized threads is built directly into the Java language and runtime environment.

Synchronized threads are extremely useful in creating distributed, network-aware applications. Such an application may be communicating with a remote server in one thread while interacting with a user in a different thread.

Dynamic

Because it is interpreted, Java is an extremely dynamic language. At runtime, the Java environment can extend itself by linking in classes that may be located on remote servers on a network (for example, the Internet). This is a tremendous advantage over a language like C++ that links classes in prior to runtime.

In C++, every time member variables or functions are added to a class, it is necessary to recompile that class and then all additional code that references that class. Of course, the problem is exacerbated by the fact that you need to remember to recompile the files that reference the changed class. Using make files reduces the problem, but for large, complex systems, it doesn't eliminate it.

Java addresses this problem by deferring it to runtime. At runtime, the Java interpreter performs name resolution while linking in the necessary classes. The Java interpreter is also responsible for determining the placement of objects in memory. These two features of the Java interpreter solve the problem of changing the definition of a class used by other classes. Because name lookup and resolution are performed only the first time a name is encountered, only minimal performance overhead is added.

The Java Tools

Of course, in order to write Java applications or applets, you need more than a language—you need the tools that let you write, test, and debug your programs. This section gives a very high-level overview of the various Java tools that come with the Java Developer's Kit. (For instructions on downloading the Java Developer's Kit from Sun Microsystems, see Chapter 2, "Installing Java.")

Compiler

There is, of course, a Java compiler, named javac. The Java compiler takes input source code files (these files typically have the extension .java) and converts them into compiled byte code files. The Java compiler is discussed in more detail in Chapter 9, "javac: The Java Compiler."

Interpreter

The Java interpreter, known eponymously as java, can be used to execute Java applications. The interpreter translates byte codes directly into program actions.

Debugger

The Java debugger, jdb, enables you to debug your Java classes. Unfortunately, the Java debugger is a throwback to the pre-GUI debugger dark ages of programming. The Java debugger is a command-line debugger that is enough to make you wish for even the 1988 version of CodeView. However, you can use the jdb to set breakpoints, inspect objects and variables, and monitor threads.

The Java debugger is discussed in more detail in Chapter 15, "jdb: The Java Debugger."

Disassembler

One of the basic tenets of object-oriented programming is that programmers unfamiliar with a class need only concern themselves with the public interface of that class. If you want to use a Queue or Stack class, you shouldn't be concerned with (or need to be concerned with) how this class has been written. Whether it uses a linked list, a statically sized array, or a dynamic array shouldn't influence whether and how you use the class.

Because you should be interested only in the public interface of a class, the Java Developer's Kit includes a disassembler, javap, that can be used to display the public interface, both methods and variables, of a class. Additionally, the Java disassembler includes options to display private members or to display the actual byte codes for the class's methods. This last option can be particularly useful if you want to achieve a greater understanding of the byte codes used by the Java interpreter.

Header File Generator

Because Java is a new language and must fit in a world dominated by C and C++, included in Java is the capability to use native C code within a Java class. One of the steps in doing this is using the Java header file generator, javah. The process for doing this is fully described in Chapter 19, "Extending Your Programs with Native Methods."

JavaDoc

As programmers, we've fought it in every way possible. Unfortunately, there is no longer any excuse for not documenting our source code. Using the JavaDoc utility provided with the Java Developers Kit, you can easily generate documentation in the form of HTML files. To do this, you embed special comments and tags in your source code and then process your code through JavaDoc. All of the on-line Java API documentation was created with JavaDoc.

JavaDoc is described in detail in Chapter 16, "Using JavaDoc to Document Your Program."

Applet Viewer

If you will be writing Java applets, you will definitely want to become familiar with the Applet Viewer. This small program provides a real Java environment for testing applets. It loads the HTML file in which the applet has been embedded and displays the application in a browser-like window, as shown in Figure 1.5.

FIGURE 1.5.
A bar chart applet being run in the Applet Viewer.

In Figure 1.5, the Java class Chart.class has been loaded by the Applet Viewer and is displayed on the screen. This is a simple applet for displaying a four-line bar chart. One nice feature of the Applet Viewer is that you can easily view the HTML tags or parameters that control the applet. By selecting Tag from the Applet menu, you can see all of the tags, as shown in Figure 1.6.

FIGURE 1.6.
HTML tags used to create the bar chart applet.

In this illustration, you can see that the c1 value was set to 10 and the c2 value was set to 20. By looking back at Figure 1.5, you can see that these were the values used to draw the top two bars. The Applet Viewer is described in more detail in Chapter 11, "Using the Applet Viewer."

Java-Enabled Browsers

Of course, if you plan to use Java to develop Internet content, you need to have a Java-enabled browser. Not only do you need a Java-enabled browser, so will your prospective users if your project is to be a success. Fortunately, you (and your prospective users!) are in luck. Java-enabled browsers are available from both Sun Microsystems and Netscape.

HotJava

HotJava is the name given by Sun Microsystems to its Java World Wide Web browser. HotJava is written entirely in Java. Although HotJava's purpose is to view applets embedded in HTML documents, it serves as the best example to date of what can be done in a Java application. The main screen for HotJava appears in Figure 1.7.

FIGURE 1.7.

*The main screen of the
HotJava browser.*

HotJava presents the user with a very clean and simple interface. It has a series of menus across the top and a single set of six buttons that can be used for navigation. In order, these buttons will move to the prior page, move to the next page, move to the home page, reload the current page, stop loading a page, and view HTML errors.

As an example of the type of Web content that Java enables, consider Figure 1.8. This figure shows a Web page with two adjacent illustrations. The illustration on the left is an x-ray with a horizontal indicator through it. The illustration on the right is a cross-section through the left illustration at the position indicated by the horizontal line. The 14 enclosed in a circle and connected to the line indicates that the line is at position 14.

FIGURE 1.8.

*Sample Java Web content
viewed through HotJava.*

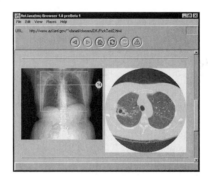

This page is both active and dynamic because a user can select the line and move it to a different location on the left illustration. This will cause a different cross-section to be displayed, as shown in Figure 1.9.

Because HotJava includes a full Java Virtual Machine, it is possible to create Web pages with active, dynamic content as shown in this example.

FIGURE 1.9.

Moving the selection line to view a different cross-section in HotJava.

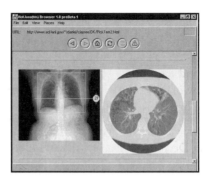

Netscape

Of course, HotJava is not your only choice for a Java-enabled Web browser. Beginning with version 2.0 of its Navigator browser, Netscape includes Java compatibility. The inclusion of Java support in a Netscape browser is significant because Netscape is the dominant browser vendor. With Java support included in Navigator, Java applets are within reach of most World Wide Web users. An example of using Netscape Navigator to view a Java Web page is shown in Figure 1.10.

FIGURE 1.10.

A Java-enabled stock quote page viewed with Netscape Navigator.

For comparison purposes, Figure 1.10 is the same page that was displayed by HotJava in Figure 1.2.

Summary

By now, you've gotten a good overview of what Java is and what you can do with it. You've learned how it can be used to create Web-based applets that move beyond the passive, static content of current Web pages. You've also learned that Java is a general-purpose language that can be used for stand-alone applications that have nothing to do with the Internet.

In this chapter, you also examined Sun Microsystems's claim that Java is "a simple, object-oriented, distributed, interpreted, robust, secure, architecture-neutral, portable, high-performance, multithreaded, and dynamic language." Each of these characteristics was examined and found to be more than just marketing hype. Finally, this chapter gave you a high-level overview of the tools that are included with the Java Developer's Kit and of two Java-enabled Web browsers.

In the next chapter, you will learn how to install Java, including how to download the latest version of the Java Developer's Kit from the World Wide Web.

2

Installing Java

by Bryan Morgan

Before writing a single line of code, the software application developer must first make sure that the best tools for the job are at his or her disposal. This universal truth also applies to Java programming. As discussed in Chapter 1, "Introduction to Java," Java was designed from the ground up as a cross-platform, object-oriented programming language. These two features (cross-platform and object-oriented) combined with the power of the Java language enable the developer to build flexible, powerful applications that were previously difficult or impossible to build with conventional toolsets.

Because of the huge amount of interest generated by the introduction of Java, new tools are being introduced daily that will provide the developer with greater flexibility and ease of use. However, the very availability of these tools can be extremely confusing to a new Java developer. Common questions include:

- What do I need to develop a Java application?
- What Web browsers (if any) do I need to run my applets?
- How do I acquire these necessary Java development tools?
- Do I need to purchase GUI development tools (such as Symantec Café, Borland Latte, or Microsoft Jakarta)?
- What do my clients need on their end to run my Java applets?

This chapter attempts to answer all of these questions and provide the reader with all of the tools necessary to build Java applications. By the end of this chapter, you should be able to answer these questions with ease.

Getting Started with the Java Developer's Kit

We will assume that you, the reader, have nothing on your local computer available for Java development. Where should you start? In terms of getting started, becoming a Java programmer is easy. Sun Microsystems decided some time ago to make Java an open standard. This means that it would release its language specification for public view and take comments and suggestions on how to improve that language. In addition to the language specification, Sun also provided implementations of the Java Virtual Machine for 32-bit Windows (Windows 95 and Windows NT) and Sun's Solaris operating system. Now, instead of simply professing that Java was cross-platform and vendor-neutral (as many other unnamed technologies have professed for years), Sun can back up what it was saying. Soon, hundreds of applets and applications across the Internet will be able to run unaltered on the most popular operating platforms available.

All of this is fine for compiler writers, but how does all of this help you, the developer? Here's the good news. Sun also decided to give away (give, as in free) a Java Developer's Kit (JDK) that would provide the basic tools needed for Java programming. The JDK provides the beginning developer with all the tools needed to begin writing powerful Java applications or applets.

It contains a compiler, an interpreter, a debugger, sample applications, and an applet viewer that you can use to test your code.

A quick visit to Sun's JavaSoft Web site (`http://java.sun.com`) will allow you to download the JDK to your local machine. (See Figure 2.1.)

FIGURE 2.1.

The JavaSoft products page on the World Wide Web.

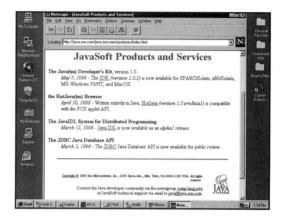

Figure 2.1 shows the type of information and tools that can be retrieved from the JavaSoft Web site as of June 1996. This site will undoubtedly have changed by the time this book is published. Therefore, make sure to check the JavaSoft Web site to download the latest version of the JDK! Clicking on the JDK link will take you to a screen that will enable you to download the JDK directly to your local machine. (At the time of this writing, the latest version of the JDK was Version 1.0.2.) Three operating system choices are then presented for your selection:

1. Sun Solaris 2.3, 2.4, or 2.5 on SPARC-based machines or Solaris 2.5 on *x*86-based machines
2. Microsoft Windows NT and Windows 95
3. Apple Macintosh System 7.5

The JDK is also available by FTP from `ftp.javasoft.com`. All of the operating system choices are available, and the JDK can be found in the `\pub` directory.

Remember that the availability of the JDK for these platforms simply means that Sun has implemented the Java Virtual Machine and development tools for these platforms. This does not mean that any Web browser on these platforms will now run Java applets! Each browser vendor still must supply the "hooks" to display Java applets within their individual windows.

> **NOTE**
>
> Although it appears that Java may soon be running on everything from mainframes to cellular telephones, at the current time the Java Virtual Machine is available from Sun only on these three platforms. To determine whether a Java Virtual Machine is available for the platform of your choice, contact the operating system vendor directly.

You may wonder why Sun chose to develop only 32-bit Windows versions of the Java Developer's Kit. Although there are several technical reasons for the omission of 16-bit support, the primary reason appears to be Java's reliance on a multitasking OS. Although Windows 3.1 originally was marketed as a multitasking operating system, it quickly became apparent that it was not "industrial-strength." Java enables the programmer to break off pieces of applications and run them as separate threads. This is handled best at runtime by a multitasking OS. At this time, IBM has expressed support for the development of a Java Virtual Machine (JVM) for Windows 3.1 and OS/2.

JDK Installation Notes

Although you may be extremely eager to display your head spinning on your World Wide Web home page, there is still a little more setup work to be done. Because the installation instructions vary depending on which platform the JDK is being installed on, this section breaks these instructions up into three groups: Solaris, Windows, and Macintosh.

I have downloaded the Windows NT version, and the resulting file is named JDK-1_0_2-win32-x86.exe. (And to think that only a short time ago, we were limited to eight characters for the filename!) After you run this file to decompress it, the Java Developer's Kit will be installed on your system. See the installation notes following to determine the necessary steps you must undertake before actually using the JDK. After the JDK is properly installed on your system, we will take a look at what tools are now at your disposal.

If Java is truly a cross-platform language, why are there separate files to download for each platform? Actual Java source code, when compiled, does result in bytecode that can be run on any platform with a Java Virtual Machine installed. Keep in mind, however, that the Java Developer's Kit contains a number of executable files (the compiler, the interpreter, the debugger, and so on) that are compiled for your specific platform. If the resources are available to you, download another version of the JDK (for Macintosh, for instance) and look through the example code. You will notice that the .java files are identical to those in the Windows and Solaris JDKs.

> **NOTE**
>
> No matter what platform you are on, it is advised that you remove all older versions of the JDK before installing the latest version.

Sun Solaris Installation Notes

1. After you acquire the tarred version of the JDK, you must unpack it before use. The following command will unpack the file:

   `/usr/bin/zcat JDK-1_0_2-solaris2-sparc.tar.Z | tar xf -`

   (Keep in mind that the current filename at the time of this writing was `JDK-1_0_2-solaris2-sparc.tar.Z`. Substitute the correct filename at the time you download this file.)

2. A directory will be created named `/java`. Add the `java/bin` directory to your path. This directory contains the compiler and other tools needed to build your applications.

Windows 95 and Windows NT Installation Notes

1. Run the self-extracting file `JDK-1_0_2-win32-x86.exe`. It will create a main directory `\java` in whichever directory you have the downloaded file stored. (Running the file from `C:\` will result in the `C:\java` directory being created.)

2. Add the `\java\bin` directory to your path.

   Windows 95: This can be done by editing the PATH variable in your AUTOEXEC.BAT file (stored in the `C:\` root directory). You must reboot the system for this change to take effect.

   Windows NT: You can change the path by editing the environment variable PATH in the Control Panel "System" application.

Apple Macintosh System 7.5 Installation Notes

1. The file downloaded (`JDK-1.0.2-MacOS.sea.bin` or `JDK-1.0.2-MacOS.sea.hqx`) must first be unpacked. Depending on which file you downloaded, this can be done using different tools. If the file is in MacBinary format, use Stuffit to decompress the file. If the file is in hqx format, use DeHQX or BinHex4 to decompress the file.

2. Run the installation program to create a folder named `JDK-1.0.2-mac`.

> **NOTE**
>
> Although environment variables are not required to be set at this point, you should be aware that there are a number of environment variables that the JDK uses to compile classes. Here's a list of them:
>
> ■ PATH—The preceding install instructions should have led you to set the PATH variable correctly.
>
> ■ JAVA_HOME—This variable is used to store the Java root directory.
>
> ■ CLASSPATH—Used to store the directory location of additional class files that will be needed to compile your project. On UNIX, this list is colon-separated; on the PC, this list is semicolon-separated.

After installing, do not unzip the classes.zip file without updating the CLASSPATH environment variable. Notice that none of the .class files actually appear (outside of the classes.zip file) on your local drive. One neat feature of Java is that classes can be read from within a ZIP file. Because of the huge amount of potential classes on each local machine, this cuts down on local file system usage without causing much of a performance penalty.

Testing the Installation

The applet viewer application can be used to run the sample applications included with the JDK. This application will be located in the \bin directory of your installation. It is at this time that you will start to appreciate your GUI-based development tools for languages such as C++, Visual Basic, and Delphi. All of the tools included with the JDK are command-line *only*. To run the applet viewer from within Windows 95/Windows NT, go to your MS-DOS prompt, and then follow these steps:

1. Change to the \demo\fractal directory. If you installed the JDK into the c:\java directory, type the following command:

   ```
   cd demo\fractal
   ```

2. The applet viewer can take as its input an .HTML source file that "contains" a Java applet (more information on HTML and Java can be found in Chapter 12, "HTML for Java Programmers"). Enter the following command to run the Fractal example:

   ```
   appletviewer example1.html
   ```

You should see output to the applet viewer that looks something like Figure 2.2.

If you still aren't convinced your installation is set up correctly, try loading any of the sample .HTML files containing applets into a Web browser that supports Java applets. At the time of this writing, this includes Netscape's Navigator 2.0 (see Figure 2.3) and Sun's HotJava Web browsers.

FIGURE 2.2.

The applet viewer running the JDK Fractal example.

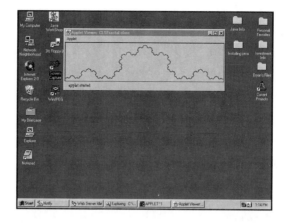

FIGURE 2.3.

Netscape 2.0 running the JDK Fractal example.

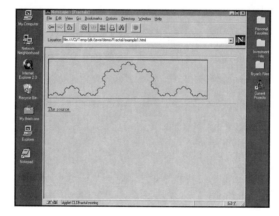

Exploring the Java Developer's Kit

What exactly did the JDK just put onto your local drive? Let's explore the contents of the Java Developer's Kit more fully. Here are the main directories that contain the JDK files:

bin\ This directory (like most development kits) contains all of the applications to compile, link, and run Java applications and applets. The most widely used applications within the bin directory include the following:

■ **java** This is the interpreter that is used to run stand-alone Java applications (see Chapter 10, "java: The Java Interpreter").

■ **javac** This is the compiler used to convert .java source code files into java .class files (see Chapter 9, "javac: The Java Compiler").

■ **javadoc** JavaDoc can be used to produce documentation for java classes (see Chapter 16, "Using JavaDoc to Document Your Program").

■ **jdb**   This is the Java debugger. It is similar to the UNIX-style dbx debugger and is command-line oriented (see Chapter 15, "jdb: The Java Debugger").

■ **appletviewer**   The applet viewer tool can be used as a test bed for java applets (see Chapter 11, "Using the Applet Viewer").

demo\   The demo directory contains a large group of sample java applets that can provide an excellent starting point for many typical java applets. Included in this set are the following applets:

Animator	GraphLayout
ArcTest	ImageMap
BarChart	JumpingBox
Blink	MoleculeViewer
CardTest	NervousText
Clock	SimpleGraph
DitherTest	SortDemo
DrawTest	SpreadSheet
Fractal	TicTacToe
GraphicsTest	WireFrame

include\   The include directory contains a set of C and C++ header files. These can be used to interface java classes to the C and C++ languages.

lib\   The primary file contained in this directory is the classes.zip file. This file contains all of the classes that together make up the JDK. Here are the primary packages (more on packages can be found in Chapter 3, "The Java Language"):

■ java.lang   Contains basic language functionality (see Chapter 32, "Package java.lang").

■ java.applet   Base class for all applets (see Chapter 27, "Package java.applet").

■ java.awt   *AWT* stands for Abstract Windowing Toolkit. This class is used for most GUI development at this time (see Chapter 30, "Package java.awt").

■ java.io   Used for file I/O operations (see Chapter 31, "Package java.io").

■ java.net   Used for all networking operations (see Chapter 33, "Package java.net").

■ java.util   Utility package that contains a number of useful functions (see Chapter 34, "Package java.util").

rc\   The rc directory contains the source files for the JDK classes. Windows 95/NT users will not see this directory, but the directory can be restored by unzipping the src.zip file found in the root directory of the JDK.

Distributing the Java Virtual Machine

Although most users think of Java applets when they think of Java, the JDK also can be used to develop stand-alone Java applications. All that is required on the user's machine is the Java Virtual Machine. The following list details the minimum required files for Windows 95/NT setup:

```
java.exe
javaw.exe
javai.dll
net.dll
awt.dll
mmedia.dll
jpeg.dll
mfc30.dll
msvcrt20.dll
classes.zip
```

Other Development Environments

Software developers have become accustomed to fully graphical development environments. Rapid application development (RAD) tools such as Powersoft Powerbuilder, Microsoft Visual Basic, and Borland Delphi have drastically increased programmer productivity and ease of use. Then along came Java! The JDK was designed to be a "basic" development toolkit that could be used on virtually any platform on which the Java Virtual Machine existed. For some developers, the toolset that comes prepackaged with the JDK will be perfectly fine. However, the industry as a whole is currently clamoring for more powerful Java tools, and where there is money, there will be products. Although many forthcoming Java products were still in development at the time of this writing, several will be discussed here. Web site addresses will be given, where possible, so you can acquire the most up-to-date information.

Not surprisingly, the most eagerly anticipated tools come from established software development tool manufacturers Sun, Borland, Symantec, and Microsoft. Although it remains to be seen which kits will be more successful than others, it is important to remember that Java development can occur on virtually every popular operating system platform available today. This in itself is a feat that must not be taken for granted. A developer using Sun Solaris can instantly test his application on Windows, Macintosh, and UNIX machines running side by side. Quite exciting! Now let's take a look at some popular tools.

SunSoft Java Workshop for Sun Solaris and Microsoft Windows 95/NT

Perhaps the most novel development platform comes from the creator of Java, Sun Microsystems. An evaluation copy can be downloaded from Javasoft's Web site at

```
http://www.sun.com/sunsoft/Developer-products/java/Workshop/
```

The Java Workshop is interesting because it is entirely written in Java. The Workshop enables the developer to organize work into projects and compile and run Java applications using a set of visual tools. At the current time, it has no capability to manage database-oriented projects, and it does not allow the user to visually edit class properties and methods. Because it was written in Java, however, the Workshop runs almost identically across the platforms it is available for. An example of its interface is shown in Figure 2.4.

FIGURE 2.4.

SunSoft Java Workshop.

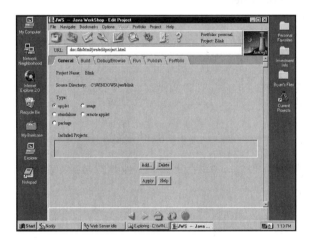

Symantec Café for Microsoft Windows 95/NT and Apple Macintosh

Symantec Café (`http://café.symantec.com`) was the first GUI-based development environment for Java on the Windows platform. The development environment is based on the popular Symantec C++ compiler but has been customized for Java applet/application development. Features include the following:

- GUI-based debugger
- Object-oriented class editor
- Drag-and-drop resource editing
- App Express, a tool used to build default Java applets and applications

- An optimizing Java compiler, which is billed as providing up to 10 times faster application performance
- An optimized Java Virtual Machine, which is billed as providing double the performance of the JVM supplied by the JDK

Borland Latte for Microsoft Windows 95/NT

Borland Latte is the long-awaited, GUI-based development environment for Java. Much of the look-and-feel of Latte (see Figure 2.5) is based on the award-winning Windows IDE Borland Delphi. Like Symantec's Café, Latte will include a GUI debugger (available as of February 1996) and a complete GUI-based IDE. Also included with Latte will be the Borland InterBase InterClient. This software, written entirely in Java, will allow InterBase databases to be connected using Java applets. Borland plans to continue to roll out Java-based development tools to meet corporate demands in areas such as database access and GUI development.

FIGURE 2.5.

Prerelease screen shot of Borland Latte.

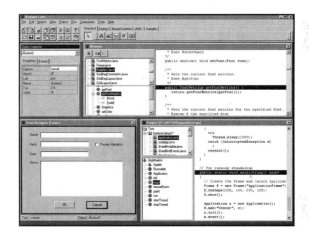

Microsoft Visual J++ for Microsoft Windows 95/NT

Microsoft Visual J++ is the name for Microsoft's Java development platform. This includes a GUI-based development environment in addition to a Java Virtual Machine implementation for the Windows platform. Microsoft plans to augment standard Java functionality with its ActiveX component object technology. Although the ActiveX framework is outside of the scope of this book, it appears that Microsoft plans to wrap Java applets with ActiveX. This will allow applets to be scripted using languages such as JavaScript and VBScript, but all of these features will obviously affect the cross-platform viability of these Java applets. Microsoft is currently readying copies of its ActiveX-enabled browser, Internet Explorer, for the Macintosh and UNIX platforms.

Summary

The Java Developer's Kit contains all of the tools necessary to begin any Java software development project. Of course, the World Wide Web contains a vast amount of information and tools not mentioned here, so any Java development project would be incomplete without constant monitoring of the Java newsgroup (`comp.lang.java`) and the JavaSoft home page (`http:\\java.sun.com`). In addition to the JDK, a wide variety of Java development platforms is available, each of which has features worth exploring further. Upcoming chapters will explore the Java language as well as the individual tools included with the Java Developer's Kit.

3

The Java Language

by Mike Cohn

This chapter outlines the core syntax and constructs of the Java language. You will learn how to declare Java variables and write Java functions. You will see how Java's minimal set of primitive types can be combined with its rich object model to fulfill the goals of object-oriented programming. If you are an experienced C++ programmer, you will find many similarities between Java and C++. As you read this chapter, you will see many areas in which C++ has been improved upon and which will influence how you program, both in C++ and in Java.

Comments

Undoubtedly, you want to start your Java career off on the right foot, so let's dive right in and start with the important stuff—comments. Java supports three types of comment delimiters—the traditional /* and */ of C, the // of C++, and a new variant that starts with /** and ends with */.

The /* and */ delimiters are used to enclose text that is to be treated as a comment by the compiler. These delimiters are useful when you want to designate a lengthy piece of code as a comment, as shown in the following:

```
/* This is a comment that will span multiple
source code lines. */
```

The // comment delimiter is borrowed from C++ and is used to indicate that the rest of the line is to be treated as a comment by the Java compiler. This type of comment delimiter is particularly useful for adding comments adjacent to lines of code, as shown in the following:

```
Date today = new Date();       // create an object with today's date
System.out.println(today);     // display the date
```

Finally, the /** and */ delimiters are new to Java and are used to indicate that the enclosed text is to be treated as a comment by the compiler, but that the text is also part of the automatic class documentation that can be generated using JavaDoc. JavaDoc is fully described in Chapter 16, "Using JavaDoc to Document Your Program." These delimiters can be used to enclose multiple lines of text, identically to how /* and */ behave, as follows:

```
/** The NeuralNetwork class implements a back-propagation
network and ... */
```

The Java comment delimiters are summarized in Table 3.1.

Table 3.1. Java comment delimiters.

Start	End	Purpose
/*	*/	The enclosed text is treated as a comment.
//	(none)	The rest of the line is treated as a comment.
/**	*/	The enclosed text is treated as a comment by the compiler but is used by JavaDoc to automatically generate documentation.

CAUTION

You cannot nest comments in Java source code. Therefore, /* and */ appearing within a // comment are ignored as is the pattern // appearing within /* or /** comments. Comments cannot be placed within quoted strings, and if comment delimiters occur within a quoted string, they will be considered part of the quoted string.

Java Keywords

The following is a list of Java keywords:

Java Keywords

abstract	float	public
boolean	for	return
break	if	short
byte	implements	static
case	import	super
catch	instanceof	switch
char	int	synchronized
class	interface	this
continue	long	throw
default	native	throws
do	new	transient
double	null	try
else	operator	void
extends	package	volatile
final	private	while
finally	protected	

Additionally, the Java specification reserves additional keywords that will be used in the future but are not part of Java 1.0. The following is a list of reserved Java keywords that are not currently used:

Reserved Java Keywords

byvalue	generic	outer
cast	goto	rest
const	inner	var
future	operator	

> **CAUTION**
>
> You may have noticed that true and false are missing from the list of Java keywords. These are actually Boolean literals but can be thought of as keywords.

Primitive Types

Primitive types are the building blocks of the data portion of a language. Just as matter is composed of atoms clinging together, more complex data types can be made by combining a language's primitive data types. The Java language contains only a small set of primitive types: integer, floating-point, character, and Boolean.

In Java, as in C and C++, you declare a variable by giving its type followed by its name, as in the following examples:

```
int x;
float LifeRaft;
short people;
long TimeNoSee;
double amountDue, amountPaid;
```

In the preceding code, x is declared as an int (integer), `LifeRaft` is declared as a floating-point variable, `people` is declared as a short integer, `TimeNoSee` is declared as a long integer, and `amountDue` and `amountPaid` are declared as double-precision, floating-point values.

Integer Types

Java consists of four integer types: `byte`, `short`, `int`, and `long`, which are defined as 8-, 16-, 32-, and 64-bit signed values as summarized in Table 3.2.

Table 3.2. The Java integer primitive types.

Type	Bit Size	Minimum Value	Maximum Value
byte	8	-256	255
short	16	-32,768	32,767
int	32	-2,147,483,648	2,147,483,647
long	64	-9,223,372,036,854,775,808	9,223,372,036,854,775,807

The operations that may be performed on integer primitives are shown in Table 3.3. A more detailed discussion of the Java operators is deferred until later in this chapter.

Table 3.3. Operators on integer primitives.

Operator	Operation
=	Equality
!=	Inequality
>	Greater than
<	Less than
>=	Greater than or equal to
<=	Less than or equal to
+	Addition
-	Subtraction
*	Multiplication
/	Division
%	Modulus
++	Increment
--	Decrement
~	Bitwise logical negation
&	Bitwise AND
¦	Bitwise OR
^	Bitwise XOR
<<	Left shift
>>	Right shift
>>>	Right shift with zero fill

If either or both of the operands is of type `long`, then the result of the operation will be a 64-bit `long`. If either operand is not a `long`, it will be cast to a `long` prior to the operation. If neither operand is a `long`, then the operation will be performed with the 32-bit precision of an `int`. Any `byte` or `short` operands will be cast to `int` prior to the operation.

CAUTION

In Java, you cannot cast between an integer type and a Boolean type.

Floating-Point Types

Support for floating-point numbers in Java is provided through two primitive types—`float` and `double`, which are 32- and 64-bit values, respectively. The operators available for use on these primitives types are shown in Table 3.4.

Table 3.4. Operators on floating-point primitives.

Operator	Operation
=	Equality
!=	Inequality
>	Greater than
<	Less than
>=	Greater than or equal to
<=	Less than or equal to
+	Addition
-	Subtraction
*	Multiplication
/	Division
%	Modulus
++	Increment
--	Decrement

Java floating-point numbers will behave as specified in IEEE Standard 754. Java variables of type `float` and `double` can be cast to other numeric types but cannot be cast to be of the `boolean` type.

If either or both of the operands is a floating-point type, the operation is considered to be a floating-point operation. If either of the operands is a `double`, then each will be treated as a `double` with the necessary casts being performed. If neither operand is a `double`, then each operand will be treated as a `float` and cast as necessary.

Floating-point numbers can take on any of the following values:

■ Negative infinity

■ Negative, finite values

■ Negative zero

■ Positive zero

- Positive, finite values
- Positive infinity
- NaN, or "not a number"

This last value, NaN, is used to indicate values that do not fit within the scale of negative infinity to positive infinity. For example, the following will produce a value of NaN:

```
0.0f / 0.0f
```

The inclusion of NaN as a floating-point value can cause some unusual effects when floating-point values are compared with the relational operators. Because NaN does not fit within the scale of negative infinity through positive infinity, comparing against it will always result in `false`. For example, both `5.3f > NaN` and `5.3f < NaN` are `false`. In fact, when NaN is compared to itself with ==, the result is `false`.

On the other hand, although negative and positive zero may sound like different values, comparing them with == will result in `true`.

Other Primitive Types

In addition to the integer and floating-point primitive types, Java includes two additional primitive types—Boolean and character. Variables of type `boolean` can hold either `true` or `false`, while variables of type `char` can hold a single Unicode character.

CAUTION

Remember, a Java Boolean variable is not a 1 or 0 in disguise as it is in other languages, in particular C and C++. Because of this, you cannot cast between Boolean and numeric types.

Default Values

One common source of programming errors is the use of an uninitialized variable. Frequently, this type of bug shows itself in a program that behaves erratically. Sometimes the program does what it's supposed to; other times it reformats your hard drive, overwrites your CMOS, declares war on a foreign country, or manifests some other undesirable side effect. It does this because an uninitialized variable may take on the value of whatever random garbage is in its memory location when the program runs. Java circumvents this problem, and possibly prevents World War III, by assigning a default value to any uninitialized variables. Default values are assigned based on the type of the variable, as shown in Table 3.5.

Table 3.5. Standard default values for Java primitive types.

Primitive	Default
byte	0
short	0
int	0
long	0L
float	0.0f
double	0.0d
char	null
boolean	false
all references	null

NOTE

It's certainly convenient and beneficial that Java will take care of assigning default values to uninitialized variables, but it is not wise to rely on this. Good programming practice suggests that you should initialize every variable you declare, without relying on default values. Although it is very unlikely that the default values would change (for example, the Boolean default of `false` is unlikely to change to `true`), other side effects are possible.

In a C program, I once spent hours tracking down a bug that was caused by my reliance on the compiler defaulting a global integer to 0. The compiler did its job correctly; unfortunately, another programmer saw my bad practice of using an uninitialized global and corrected it by initializing it for me—to 1. When I was reassigned to the maintenance of the program, I had no idea the change had been made.

Casting Between Primitive Types

Sometimes you have a variable that is of one type, and you want to use it as another. For example, one of the first programs I wrote was used to predict the final scores in baseball games based on a huge number of input statistics. It would come up with results like the Chicago Cubs beating the San Diego Padres with scores like 3.2 to 2.7. Since it was clearly impossible in real life to score a partial run, the results needed to be converted from floating-point to integer values. This is known as *casting* a variable. In Java, you can cast a variable of one type to another as follows:

```
float fRunsScored = 3.2f;
int iRunsScored = (int)fRunsScored;
```

In this case, the floating-point value 3.2 that is stored in `fRunsScored` will be cast into an integer and placed in `iRunsScored`. When cast into an integer, the non-whole portion of the `fRunsScored` will be truncated so that `iRunsScored` will equal 3.

This is an example of what is known as a *narrowing conversion*. A narrowing conversion may lose information about the overall magnitude or precision of a numeric value, as you saw in this case. You should always be careful when writing a narrowing conversion because of this potential for data loss.

The other type of conversion is called a *widening conversion*. A widening conversion may lose information about precision in the least significant bits of the value, but it will not lose information about the magnitude of the value. In general, widening conversions are much safer. Table 3.6 shows the widening conversions that are possible between Java primitive types.

Table 3.6. Available widening conversions among Java primitive types.

From	*To*
byte	short, int, long, float, or double
short	int, long, float, or double
char	int, long, float, or double
int	long, float, or double
long	float or double
float	double

Literals

A literal is an explicit value that is used by a program. For example, your program may include a literal value of 3.1415 that is used whenever the value of *pi* is necessary, or it may include 65 as the mandatory retirement age. These values, 3.1415 and 65, are both literals.

Integer Literals

Integer literals can be specified in decimal, hexadecimal, or octal notation. To specify a decimal value, simply use the number as normal. To indicate that a literal value is a long, you can append either "L" or "l" to the end of the number. Hexadecimal values are given in base 16 and include the digits 0–9 and the letters A–F. To specify a hexadecimal value, use 0x followed by the digits and letters that comprise the value. Similarly, an octal value is identified by a leading 0 symbol.

For examples of specifying integer literals, see Table 3.7.

Table 3.7. Examples of integer literals.

Integer	Long	Octal	Hexadecimal
0	0L	0	0x0
1	1L	01	0x1
10	10L	012	0xA
15	15L	017	0XF
16	16L	020	0x10
100	100L	0144	0x64

Floating-Point Literals

Similar to integer literals are Java's floating-point literals. Floating-point literals can be specified in either the familiar decimal notation (for example, 3.1415) or exponential notation (for example, 6.02e23). To indicate that a literal is to be treated as a single precision float, append either "f" or "F". To indicate that it is to be treated as a double precision value, append either "d" or "D".

Java includes predefined constants, POSITIVE_INFINITY, NEGATIVE_INFINITY, and NaN, to represent the infinity and not-a-number values.

The following list shows some valid floating-point literals:

```
43.3F
3.1415d
-12.123f
6.02e+23f
6.02e23d
6.02e-23f
6.02e23d
```

Boolean Literals

Java supports two Boolean literals—true and false.

Character Literals

A character literal is a single character or an escape sequence enclosed in single quotes, for example, 'b'. Escape sequences are used to indicate special characters or actions, such as line feed, form feed, or carriage return. The available escape sequences are shown in Table 3.8. For examples of character literals, consider the following:

```
'b'
'\n'
\u15e'
'\t'
```

Table 3.8. Escape sequences.

Sequence	Purpose
\b	Backspace
\t	Horizontal tab
\n	Line feed
\f	Form feed
\r	Carriage return
\"	Double quote
\'	Single quote
\\	Backslash
\uxxxx	Unicode character

String Literals

Although there is no string primitive type in Java, you can include string literals in your programs. Most applications and applets will make use of some form of string literal, probably at least for error messages. A string literal consists of zero or more characters (including the escape sequences shown in Table 3.8) enclosed in double quotes. As examples of string literals, consider the following:

```
"A String"
"Column 1\tColumn 2"
"First Line\r\nSecond Line"
"First Page\fSecond Page"
""
```

Because Java does not have a string primitive type, each use of a string literal causes an object of the String class to be created behind the scenes. However, because of Java's automatic memory management, your program doesn't need to do anything special to free or release the memory used by the literal or string once you are finished with it.

Arrays

In Java you declare an array using enclosing square bracket symbols ([]). For example, consider the following array declarations:

```
int intArray[];
float floatArray[];
double [] doubleArray;
char charArray[];
```

Notice that the brackets can be placed before or after the variable name. Placing the [] after the variable name follows the conventions of C, and if you are coming to Java from C or C++, you may want to continue that tradition. However, there is an advantage to placing the brackets before the variable name. By placing the brackets in front of the variable name, you can more easily declare multiple arrays. For example, consider the following declarations:

```
int [] firstArray, secondArray;
int thirdArray[], justAnInt;
```

On the first line both `firstArray` and `secondArray` are arrays. On the second line, `thirdArray` is an array but `justAnInt` is, as its name implies, a lone integer. The ability to declare singleton variables and arrays in the same statement, as on the second line in the preceding example, is the source of many problems in other programming languages. Java helps prevent this type of problem by providing an easy, alternative syntax for declaring arrays.

Allocation

Once an array is declared, it must be allocated. You probably noticed that the size of the arrays has not been specified in the examples so far. This is because, in Java, all arrays must be allocated with `new`. Declaring the following array would have resulted in a compile-time error:

```
int intArray[10];    // this is an error
```

To allocate an array you use `new`, as shown in the following examples:

```
int intArray[] = new int[100];
float floatArray[];
floatArray = new float[100];
long [] longArray = new long[100];
double [][] doubleArray = new double[10][10];
```

Initialization

An alternative way of allocating a Java array is to specify a list of element initializers when the array is declared. This is done as follows:

```
int intArray[] = {1,2,3,4,5};
char [] charArray = {'a', 'b', 'c'};
String [] stringArray = {"A", "Four", "Element", "Array"};
```

In this case, `intArray` will be a five-element array holding the values 1 through 5. The three-element array `charArray` will hold the characters `'a'`, `'b'`, and `'c'`. Finally, `stringArray` will hold the strings shown.

Array Access

Items in a Java array are known as the components of the array. You can access a component at runtime by enclosing the component number you want to access with brackets as shown in the following:

```
int intArray[] = {100, 200, 300, 400, 500};

int a = intArray[0];        // a will be equal to 100
int b = intArray[1];        // b will be equal to 200
int c = intArray[2];        // c will be equal to 300
int d = intArray[3];        // d will be equal to 400
int e = intArray[4];        // e will be equal to 500
```

Java arrays are numbered from 0 to one less than the number of components in the array. Attempting to access an array beyond the bounds of the array (for example, `intArray[42]` in the preceding example) will result in a runtime exception, `ArrayIndexOutOfBoundsException`. Exception handling is discussed in detail in Chapter 22, "Exception Handling."

CAUTION

In many languages, especially C and C++, a string is really just an array of characters. This is not the case in Java. When working with Java strings, you should remind yourself that Java strings are instances of the Java `String` class and are not simply arrays of characters.

Operators

A language's operators can be used to combine or alter a program's values. Java contains a very rich set of operators. The complete list of Java operators is as follows:

A Complete List of Java Operators

=	>	<	!	~
?	:	==	<=	>=
!=	&&	||	++	- -
+	-	*	/	&
|	^	%	<<	>>
>>>	+=	-=	*=	/=
&=	|=	^=	%=	<<=
>>=	>>>=			

Operators on Integers

The bulk of the Java operators work on integer values. The binary operators (those that require two operands) are shown in Table 3.9. The unary operators (those that require a single operand) are shown in Table 3.10. Each table gives an example of the use of each operator.

Table 3.9. Binary operators on integers.

Operator	Operation	Example
=	Assignment	a = b
==	Equality	a == b
!=	Inequality	a != b
<	Less than	a < b
<=	Less than or equal to	a <= b
>=	Greater than or equal to	a >= b
>	Greater than	a > b
+	Addition	a + b
-	Subtraction	a - b
*	Multiplication	a * b
/	Division	a / b
%	Modulus	a % b
<<	Left shift	a << b
>>	Right shift	a >> b
>>>	Right shift with zero fill	a >>> b
&	Bitwise AND	a & b
¦	Bitwise OR	a ¦ b
^	Bitwise XOR	a ^ b

Table 3.10. Unary operators on integers.

Operator	Operation	Example
-	Unary negation	-a
~	Bitwise logical negation	~a
++	Increment	a++ or ++a
--	Decrement	a-- or --a

In addition to the operators shown in Tables 3.9 and 3.10, Java also includes an assortment of assignment operators that are based on the other operators. These operators will operate on an operand and store the resulting value back in the same operand. For example, to increase the value of a variable x, you could do the following:

```
x += 3;
```

This is equal to the more verbose x = x + 3. Each of the specialized Java assignment operators performs its normal function on the operand and then stores the value in the operand. The following assignment operators are available:

Integer Assignment Operators

+=	-=	*=
/=	&=	¦=
^=	%=	<<=
>>=	>>>=	

Operators on Floating-Point Values

The Java operators on floating-point values are a subset of those available to Java integer types. The operators that may operate on operands of type float and double are shown in Table 3.11, which also gives examples of their uses.

Table 3.11. Binary operators on integers.

Operator	Operation	Example
=	Assignment	a = b
==	Equality	a == b
!=	Inequality	a != b
<	Less than	a < b
<=	Less than or equal to	a <= b
>=	Greater than or equal to	a >= b
>	Greater than	a > b
+	Addition	a + b
-	Subtraction	a - b
*	Multiplication	a * b
/	Division	a / b
%	Modulus	a % b
-	Unary negation	-a
++	Increment	a++ or ++a
--	Decrement	a-- or --a

Operators on Boolean Values

The Java Boolean operators are summarized in Table 3.12. If you are coming to Java from a C or C++ background, you are probably already familiar with these. If not, however, the conditional operator will be a new experience.

Table 3.12. Operators on Boolean values.

Operator	Operation	Example
!	Negation	!a
&&	Conditional AND	a && b
¦¦	Conditional OR	a ¦¦ b
==	Equality	a == b
!=	Inequality	a != b
?:	Conditional	a ? expr1 : expr2

The conditional operator is Java's only ternary (three-operand) operator and has the following syntactic form:

```
booleanExpr ? expr1 : expr2
```

The value of `booleanExpr` is evaluated and if `true`, the expression `expr1` is executed; if `false`, expression `expr2` is executed. This makes the conditional operator a convenient shorthand for the following:

```
if(booleanExpression)
    expr1
else
    expr2
```

Controlling Your Program

The Java keywords for controlling program flow are nearly identical to C and C++. This is one of the most obvious ways in which Java shows its legacy as a derivative of these two languages. In this section, you will see how to use Java's control flow commands to write methods.

Selection

The Java language provides two alternative structures—`if` statements and `switch` statements—for selecting among alternatives. Although it would be possible to spend your entire Java programming career using only one of these at the expense of the other, each has its definite advantages.

The `if` Statement

A Java `if` statement is a test of any Boolean expression. If the Boolean expression evaluates to `true`, the statement following the `if` is executed. On the other hand, if the Boolean expression evaluates to `false`, the statement following the `if` is not executed. For example, consider the following code fragment:

```
import java.util.Date;
Date today = new Date();
if (today.getDay == 0) then
    System.out.println("It is Sunday.");
```

This code uses the `java.Util.Date` package and creates a variable named `today` that will hold the current date. The `getDay` member method is then applied to `today` and the result compared to `0`. A return value of `0` for `getDay` indicates that the day is Sunday, so if the Boolean expression `today.getDay == 0` is `true`, a message is displayed. If today isn't Sunday, no action occurs.

If you are coming to Java from a C or C++ background, you may have been tempted to rewrite the preceding example as follows:

```
import java.util.Date;
Date today = new Date();
if (!today.getDay) then
    System.out.println("It is Sunday.");
```

In C and C++, the expression `!today.getDay` would evaluate to `1` whenever `today.getDay` evaluated to `0` (indicating Sunday). In Java, the expression used within an `if` statement must evaluate to a Boolean. Therefore, this code doesn't work because `!today.getDay` will evaluate to `0` or `1`, depending on which day of the week it is. And, as you learned earlier in this chapter, integer values cannot be cast to Boolean values. This is, of course, an example where Java's nuances may take a little getting used to for C and C++ programmers. Once you're accustomed to the change, however, you will find your code more readable, reliable, and maintainable.

Of course, an `if` statement without an `else` is as incomplete as a Labrador Retriever without a bandanna around his neck. Not wanting to be accused of cruelty to animals or programmers, the Java developers included an `else` statement that can be executed whenever an `if` statement evaluates to `false`. This can be seen in the following sample code:

```
import java.util.Date;
Date today = new Date();
if (today.getDay == 0) then
    System.out.println("It is Sunday.");
else
    System.out.println("It is NOT Sunday.");
```

In this case, the same message will be displayed whenever it is Sunday, but a different message will be displayed whenever it is not Sunday. Both examples so far have only shown the execution of a single statement within the `if` or the `else` cases. By enclosing the statements within curly braces, you can execute as many lines of code as you'd like. This can be seen in the following example that makes some suggestions about how to spend each day of the week:

```java
import java.util.Date;
Date today = new Date();
if (today.getDay == 0) then {
    System.out.println("It is Sunday.");
    System.out.println("And a good day for golf.");
}
else {
    System.out.println("It is NOT Sunday.");
    System.out.println("But still a good day for golf.");
}
```

Because it's possible to execute whatever code you desire in the else portion of an if...else block, you may have already reasoned that it is possible to execute another if statement inside the else statement of the first if statement. This is commonly known as an if...else if...else block, an example of which follows:

```java
import java.util.Date;
Date today = new Date();
if (today.getDay == 0) then
    System.out.println("It is Sunday.");
else if (today.getDay == 1) then
    System.out.println("It is Monday.");
else if (today.getDay == 2) then
    System.out.println("It is Tuesday.");
else if (today.getDay == 3) then
    System.out.println("It is Wednesday.");
else if (today.getDay == 4) then
    System.out.println("It is Thursday.");
else if (today.getDay == 5) then
    System.out.println("It is Friday.");
else
    System.out.println("It must be Saturday.");
```

The switch Statement

As you can see from the previous code sample, a lengthy series of if...else if...else statements can get convoluted and hard to read as the number of cases increases. Fortunately, you can avoid this problem by using Java's switch statement. Like its C and C++ cousins, the Java switch statement is ideal for testing a single expression against a series of possible values and executing the code associated with the matching case statement, as shown in the following example:

```java
import java.util.Date;
Date today = new Date();
switch (today.getDay) {
    case 0:    // Sunday
        System.out.println("It is Sunday.");
        break;
    case 1:    // Monday
        System.out.println("It is Monday.");
        break;
```

```
    case 2:     // Tuesday
        System.out.println("It is Tuesday.");
        break;
    case 3:     // Wednesday
        System.out.println("It is Wednesday.");
        break;
    case 4:     // Thursday
        System.out.println("It is Thursday.");
        break;
    case 5:     // Friday
        System.out.println("It is Friday.");
        System.out.println("Have a nice weekend!");
        break;
    default:    // Saturday
        System.out.println("It must be Saturday.");
}
System.out.println("All done!");
```

You should have noticed that each day has its own `case` within the `switch`. The Saturday case (where `today.getDay = 6`) is not explicitly given but is instead handled by the `default` case. Any switch block may include an optional `default` case that will handle any values not caught by an explicit `case`.

Within each `case`, there can be multiple lines of code. The block of code that will execute for the Friday `case`, for example, contains three lines. The first two lines will simply display informational messages, but the third is a `break` statement. The keyword `break` is used within a `case` statement to indicate that the flow of the program should move to the first line following the `switch` block. In this example, `break` appears as the last statement in each case except the default and will cause program execution to move to the line that prints "All done!" The `break` statement was left out of the default block because by that point in the code, the `switch` block was ending, and there was no point in using an explicit command to exit the `switch`.

If, as the previous example seems to imply, you always need to include a `break` statement at the end of each block, why not just leave `break` out and have Java assume that after a block executes, control should move outside the `switch` block? The answer is that there are times when you do not want to break out of the `switch` statement after executing the code for a specific case value. For example, consider the following code that could be used as a scheduling system for physicians:

```
import java.util.Date;
Date today = new Date();
switch (today.getDay) {
    case 0:     // Sunday
    case 3:     // Wednesday
    case 6:     // Saturday
        System.out.println("It's Golf Day!");
        break;
    case 2:     // Tuesday
        System.out.println("Tennis at 8:00 am");
    case 1:     // Monday
    case 4:     // Thursday
```

```
case 5:      // Friday
    System.out.println("Office Hours: 10:00 - 5:00");
    break;
}
System.out.println("All done!");
```

This example illustrates a couple of key concepts about switch statements. First, you'll notice that it is possible to have multiple cases execute the same block of code, as follows:

```
case 0:      // Sunday
case 3:      // Wednesday
case 6:      // Saturday
    System.out.println("It's Golf Day!");
    break;
```

This code will result in the message "It's Golf Day" being displayed if the current day is Wednesday, Saturday, or Sunday. If you collect the three cases together without any intervening break statements, each will execute the same code. But consider what happens on Tuesday when the following code executes:

```
case 2:      // Tuesday
    System.out.println("Tennis at 8:00 am");
```

Certainly a reminder about the message match will be displayed, but this case doesn't end with a break statement. Because Tuesday's code doesn't end with a break statement, the program will continue executing the code in the following cases until a break is encountered. This means that Tuesday's code flows into the code used for Monday, Thursday, and Friday as shown in the following:

```
case 2:      // Tuesday
    System.out.println("Tennis at 8:00 am");
case 1:      // Monday
case 4:      // Thursday
case 5:      // Friday
    System.out.println("Office Hours: 10:00 - 5:00");
    break;
```

This will result in the following messages being displayed every Tuesday:

```
Tennis at 8:00 am
Office Hours: 10:00 - 5:00
```

On Monday, Thursday, and Friday, only the latter message will display.

In addition to writing switch statements that use integer cases, you can use character values as shown in the following example:

```
switch (aChar) {
    case 'a':
    case 'e':
    case 'i':
    case 'o':
    case 'u':
        System.out.println("It's a vowel!");
        break;
```

```
    default:
        System.out.println("It's a consonant!");
}
```

Iteration

Iteration is an important concept in any computer language. Without the ability to loop or iterate through a set of values, our ability to solve real-world problems would be severely limited. Java's iteration statements are nearly identical to those found in C and C++ and include `for` loops, `while` loops, and `do...while` loops.

The `for` Statement

If Java programmers turn out to be anything like C or C++ programmers, many of them will be partial to the `for` statement because of its syntactic elegance. The first line of a `for` loop enables you to specify a starting value for a loop counter, specify the test condition that will exit the loop, and indicate how the loop counter should be incremented after each pass through the loop. This is definitely a statement that offers a lot of bang for the buck. The syntax of a Java `for` statement is as follows:

```
for (initialization; testExpression; incremement)
    statement
```

For example, a sample `for` loop may appear as follows:

```
int count;
for (count=0; count<100; count++)
    System.out.println("Count = " + count);
```

In this example, the initialization statement of the `for` loop sets count to 0. The test expression, count < 100, indicates that the loop should continue as long as count is less than 100. Finally, the increment statement increments the value of count by one. As long as the test expression is true, the statement following the `for` loop setup will be executed, as follows:

```
System.out.println("Count = " + count);
```

Of course, you probably need to do more than one thing inside the loop. This is as easy to do as using curly braces to indicate the scope of the `for` loop, as shown in the following:

```
int count;
for (count=0; count<100; count++) {
    YourMethod(count);
    System.out.println("Count = " + count);
}
```

One nice shortcut that can be taken with a Java `for` loop is to declare and initialize the variable used in the loop. For example, in the following code, the variable count is declared directly within the `for` loop:

```
for (int count=0; count<100; count++)
    System.out.println("Count = " + count);
```

It may look like an inconsequential difference whether you declare a variable before a for loop or within the loop. However, there are advantages to declaring the variable within the loop. First, it makes your intention to use the variable within the loop clear. If the variable is declared above the for loop, how will you remember (and how will future programmers know) that the variable was intended for use only *within* the loop? Second, a variable declared within the for loop will go out of scope at the end of the loop. This means you could not write the following code:

```
for (int count=0; count<100; count++)
    System.out.println("Count = " + count);
System.out.println("Loop exited with count = " + count);
```

The last line cannot find a variable named count because count goes out of scope when the for loop terminates. This means that, in addition to making the intended purpose of the variable more clear, it is also impossible to accidentally bypass that intent and use the variable outside the loop.

You can also leave out portions of the first line of a for loop. In the following example, the increment statement has been left out:

```
for (int count=0; count<100; ) {
    count += 2;
    System.out.println("Count = " + count);
}
```

Of course, leaving the increment statement out of the for loop declaration in this example doesn't achieve any useful purpose since count is incremented inside the loop.

It is possible to get even fancier with a Java for loop by including multiple statements or conditions. For example, consider the following code:

```
for (int up=0, down = 20; up < down; up++, down -= 2 ) {
    System.out.println("Up = " + up + "\tDown = " + down);
}
```

This loop starts the variable up at 0 and increments it by 1. It also starts the variable down at 20 and decrements it by 2 for each pass through the loop. The loop continues until up has been incremented enough that it is equal to or greater than the variable down.

The test expression portion of a Java for loop can be any Boolean expression. Because of this, it does not need to be a simple test (x < 10), as shown in the preceding examples. The test expression can be a method call, a method call combined with a value test, or anything that can be phrased as a Boolean expression. For example, suppose you want to write a method that will display a message indicating the first year since World War II that the Chicago Cubs appeared in the World Series. You could do this as follows:

```
public boolean DidCubsPlayInWorldSeries(int year) {
    boolean retval;

    switch(year) {
        case 1907:              // these are years the Cubs won
        case 1908:
```

```
                retval = true;
                break;
        case 1906:              // these are years the Cubs lost
        case 1910:
        case 1918:
        case 1929:
        case 1932:
        case 1935:
        case 1938:
        case 1945:
                retval = true;
                break;
        default:
                retval = false;
    }
    return retval;
}

public void FindFirstAfterWWII() {
    for (int year=1946; DidCubsPlayInWorldSeries(year)==false; year++) {
        System.out.println("The Cubs didn't play in " + year);
    }
}
```

The method `DidCubsPlayInWorldSeries` is passed an integer value indicating the year and returns a Boolean value that indicates whether or not the Cubs made it to the World Series in that year. This method is an example of the `switch` statement shown earlier in this chapter.

The method `FindFirstAfterWWII` uses a `for` loop to find a year in which the Cubs played in the World Series. The loop starts `year` with 1946 and increments `year` by one for each pass through the loop. The test expression for the loop will allow the loop to continue as long as the method `DidCubsPlayInWorldSeries` returns `false`. This is a useful example because it shows that a method can be called within the test expression of a `for` loop. Unfortunately, it is a bad example in that the Cubs haven't won the World Series since the goose step was popular in Berlin, and there is no sign of that changing in the near future. In other words, a loop that looks for a Cubs World Series appearance after 1945 is an infinite loop.

The `while` Statement

Related to the `for` loop is the `while` loop. The syntax for a `while` loop is as follows:

```
while (booleanExpression)
    statement
```

As you can tell from the simplicity of this, the Java `while` loop does not have the built-in support for initializing and incrementing variables that its `for` loop does. Because of this, you need to be careful to initialize loop counters prior to the loop and increment them within the body of the `while` loop. For example, the following code fragment will display a message five times:

```
int count = 0;
while (count < 5) {
    System.out.println("Count = " + count);
    count++;
}
```

The do...while **Statement**

The final looping construct in Java is the do...while loop. The syntax for a do...while loop is as follows:

```
do {
    statement
} while (booleanExpression);
```

This is similar to a while loop except that a do...while loop is guaranteed to execute at least once. It is possible that a while loop may not execute at all depending on the test expression used in the loop. For example, consider the following method:

```
public void ShowYears(int year) {
    while (year < 2000) {
        System.out.println("Year is " + year);
        year++;
    }
}
```

This method is passed a year value, then loops over the year displaying a message as long as the year is less than 2000. If year starts at 1996, then messages will be displayed for the years 1996, 1997, 1998, and 1999. However, what happens if year starts at 2010? Because the initial test, year < 2000, will be false, the while loop will never be entered. Fortunately, a do...while loop can solve this problem. Because a do...while loop performs its expression testing after the body of the loop has executed for each pass, it will always be executed at least once. This is a very valid distinction between the two types of loop, but it can also be a source of potential errors. Whenever you use a do...while loop, you should be careful to consider the first pass through the body of the loop.

Jumping

Of course, it is not always easy to write all of your for, while and do...while loops so that they are easy to read and yet the loops terminate on exactly the right pass through the loop. Java makes it easier to jump out of loops and to control other areas of program flow with its break and continue statements.

The break **Statement**

Earlier in this chapter, you saw how the break statement is used to exit a switch statement. In a similar manner, break can be used to exit a loop. This can be seen in Figure 3.1.

As Figure 3.1 illustrates, if the break statement is encountered, execution will continue with *statement4*. As an example of this, consider the following code:

```
int year = 1909;
while (DidCubsWinTheWorldSeries(year) == false) {
    System.out.println("Didn't win in " + year);
    if (year >= 3000) {
```

```
        System.out.println("Time to give up. Go White Sox!");
        break;
    }
}
System.out.println("Loop exited on year " + year);
```

FIGURE 3.1.
Flow of control with a
break *statement.*

```
While (boolean expression) {
    statement1
    statement2
    if(boolean expression)
        break; ─────────┐
    statement3           │
}                        │
statement4 ◄─────────────┘
```

This example shows a while loop that will continue to execute until it finds a year that the Chicago Cubs won the World Series. Because they haven't won since 1908 and the loop counter year starts with 1909, it has a lot of looping to do. For each year they didn't win, a message is displayed. However, even die-hard Cubs fans will eventually give up and change allegiances to the Chicago White Sox. In this example, if the year is 3000 or later, a message is displayed and then a break is encountered. The break statement will cause program control to move to the first statement after the end of the while loop. In this case, that will be the following line:

```
System.out.println("Loop exited on year " + year);
```

The continue Statement

Just as a break statement can be used to move program control to immediately after the end of a loop, the continue statement can be used to force program control back to the top of a loop. This can be seen in Figure 3.2.

FIGURE 3.2.
Flow of control with a
continue *statement.*

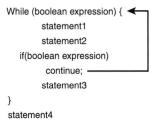

```
While (boolean expression) { ◄──┐
    statement1                   │
    statement2                   │
    if(boolean expression)       │
        continue; ───────────────┘
    statement3
}
statement4
```

Suppose you want to write a method that will count and display the number of times the Cubs have won the World Series this century. One way to do this would be to first see if the Cubs played in the World Series and then see if they won. This could be done as follows:

```
int timesWon = 0;
for (int year=1900; year <= 2000; year++) {
    if (DidCubsPlayInWorldSeries(year) = false)
        continue;
```

```
    if (DidCubsWinWorldSeries(year)) {
        System.out.println("Cubbies won in " + year + "!");
        timesWon++;
    }
}
System.out.println("The Cubs won " + timesWon + " times.");
```

In this case, a for loop is used to iterate through the years from 1900 to 2000. The first line within the loop tests to see if the Cubs played in the World Series. If they didn't, the continue statement is executed. This moves program control back to the for loop. At that point, year is incremented and the expression year <= 2000 is retested. If year is less than or equal to 2000, the loop continues. If, however, DidCubsPlayInWorldSeries equals true, then the continue statement is skipped, and the next test is performed to see if the Cubs won that year.

Using Labels

Java does not include a goto statement. However, the fact that goto is a reserved word indicates that it may be added in a future version. Instead of goto, Java allows you to combine break and continue with a label. This has an effect similar to a goto in that it allows a program to reposition control. In order to understand the use of labels with break and continue, consider the following example:

```
public void paint(Graphics g) {
    int line=1;

    outsideLoop:
    for(int out=0; out<3; out++) {
        g.drawString("out = " + out, 5, line * 20);
        line++;

        for(int inner=0;inner < 5; inner++) {
            double randNum = Math.random();
            g.drawString(Double.toString(randNum), 15, line * 20);
            line++;
            if (randNum < .10) {
                g.drawString("break to outsideLoop", 25, line * 20);
                line++;
                break outsideLoop;
            }
            if (randNum < .60) {
                g.drawString("continue to outsideLoop", 25, line * 20);
                line++;
                continue outsideLoop;
            }
        }
    }
    g.drawString("all done", 50, line * 20);
}
```

This example includes two loops. The first loops on the variable out, and the second loops on the variable inner. The outer loop has been labeled by the following line:

```
outsideLoop:
```

This statement will serve as a placeholder and as a name for the outer loop. A random number between 0 and 1 is generated for each iteration through the inner loop. This number is displayed on the screen. If the random number is less than 0.10, the statement break outsideLoop is executed. A normal break statement in this position would break out of the inner loop. However, since this is a labeled break statement, it has the effect of breaking out of the loop identified by the name. In this case, program control passes to the line that displays "all done" since that is the first line after outsideLoop.

On the other hand, if the random number is not less than 0.10, the number is compared to 0.60. If it is less than this, the statement continue outsideLoop is executed. A normal, unlabeled continue statement at this point would have the effect of transferring program control back to the top of the inner loop. Because this is a labeled continue statement, program control is transferred to the start of the named loop. A sample run of this method, as captured in the Java Applet Viewer, is shown in Figure 3.3.

FIGURE 3.3.

Sample results demonstrating the use of labels.

As you can see in Figure 3.3, the first pass through the outer loop resulted in four passes through the inner loop. When the value 0.518478 was generated, it caused the continue outsideLoop to execute because the number is less than 0.60. The next pass through the outer loop was similar except that it did a continue of the outer loop after only one iteration through the inner loop. Finally, on the third pass through the outer loop, the program generated a value lower than 0.10, which caused the program to break to the outer loop. You can see that, at this point, the next line of code to be executed was the first line of code after the outer loop (the line that prints the message "all done").

Java Classes

Now that you've seen most of the low-level details of the Java language, it's time to turn your attention to Java classes and see how Java is able to live up to its claim of being an object-oriented language. A Java class is a compile-time concept that represents a runtime object. In other words, a class is a definition or template for an object that will exist within the program. For example, if you have a class called Car, you may have a particular instance of that class that is a 1966 Volkswagen Beetle. The instances (1966 Volkswagen Beetle) of a class (Car) are known as objects. In order to define a class in Java, you would do something similar to the following:

```
class Car {
    // member variables
    // member methods
}
```

Field Declarations

Car is now an empty class. In order to make it usable and useful, you need to add some fields to the class. A field can be either a member variable or a member method. To declare member variables, all you need to do is identify the variable by type and name in the class definition, as shown in the following:

```
class Car {
    // these are member variables
    String manufacturer;
    String model;
    int year;
    int passengers;
}
```

In this example, Car has been extended to include String variables for manufacturer and model, and integer variables for the year it was built and the number of passengers it can hold. From this class definition, it is then possible to create instances, or objects, at runtime, as shown in Figure 3.4.

FIGURE 3.4.

The Car *class and objects.*

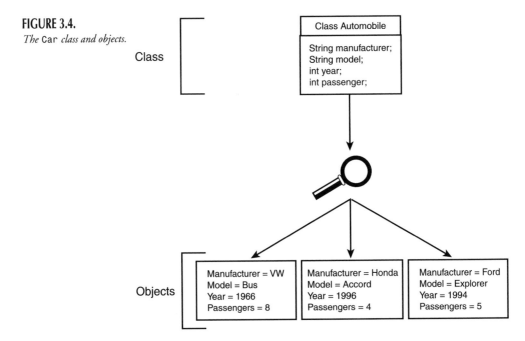

Field Access

One of the principal advantages of object-oriented programming is *encapsulation*. Encapsulation is the ability to define classes that hide their implementation details from other classes, exposing only their public interfaces to those other classes. Support for encapsulation in Java comes from three keywords: `public`, `private`, and `protected`. When you are defining a class, these field access modifiers are used to control who has access to each field in the class. By declaring a field as `public`, you are indicating that it is entirely accessible to all other classes. Continuing with the `Car` example, to declare all of the fields as `public`, do the following:

```
class Car {
    public String manufacturer;
    public String model;
    public int year;
    public int passengers;
}
```

Of course, declaring everything as public doesn't exactly achieve the goal of encapsulation because it lets other classes directly access variables in the `Car` class. Consider what would happen if you needed to create an instance of this class for a 1964-and-a-half Mustang. Because `year` only holds integer values, it would have to be changed to a `float` so that it could hold 1964.5. If code in other classes directly accessed `year`, that code could conceivably break.

To restrict access to a field, use the keyword `private`. A class cannot access the private fields of another class. Suppose the `Car` class is intended for use in a used car sales application. In this case, you may want to define `Car` as follows in order to hide your cost for a car from potential buyers:

```
class Car {
    public String manufacturer;
    public String model;
    public int year;
    public int passengers;
    private float cost;
}
```

Finally, the keyword `protected` is used to indicate that fields are accessible within the current class and all classes derived from the class, but not to other classes. The ability to derive a class from another class will be discussed later in this chapter.

Setting Initial Values

One extremely nice aspect of Java class declarations that is a deviation from C++ is the ability to specify initial values for member variables in the variable declaration. For example, because most cars will hold four passengers, it may be reasonable to default the `passengers` member variable to 4, as shown in the following code:

```
class Car {
    public String manufacturer;
    public String model;
```

```
    public int year;
    public int passengers = 4;
    private float cost;
}
```

Static Members

In addition to `private`, `protected`, and `public` members, a Java class can also have static members. A *static member* is one that belongs to the class itself, not to the instances of the class. Regardless of how many instances of a class have been created by a program at runtime, there will exist exactly one instance of each static member. Declaring a static member is done by adding the keyword `static` to any of the other field access modifiers, as shown in the following:

```
class Car {
    public String manufacturer;
    public String model;
    public int year;
    public int passengers = 4;
    private float cost;
    public static int tireQty = 4;
}
```

In this case, the variable `tireQty` has been added and is set to 4. Because every car will have four tires, `tireQty` was declared as `static`. Also, because we want `tireQty` to be accessible to other classes, it has been declared `public`.

It is also possible to declare member methods as `static`, as will be shown later in this chapter.

Member Methods

In addition to member variables, most classes will also have member methods. Because member methods, like member variables, are fields, access to them can be controlled with the `public`, `protected`, and `private` modifiers. A member method is declared according to the following syntax, in which elements enclosed in square brackets "[…]" are optional:

```
[methodModifiers] resultType methodName [throws exceptionList] {
    // method body
}
```

The `methodModifiers` are the familiar `public`, `protected`, and `private` keywords you've already seen as well as some additional modifiers. The method modifiers are described in Table 3.13.

Table 3.13. Method modifiers.

Modifier	Purpose
public	Accessible outside the class in which it is declared.
protected	Accessible by the class in which it is declared and by subclasses of that class.
private	Accessible only by the class in which it is declared.

Modifier	Purpose
static	A method of the class rather than of a particular instance of the class.
abstract	Not implemented in this class.
final	Cannot be overridden in subclasses.
native	A platform-dependent implementation of the method in another language, typically C or assembly.
synchronized	Used to indicate a critical method that will lock the object to prevent execution of other methods while the synchronized method executes.

The `resultType` of a method declaration can be one of the primitive types (for example, `int`, `float`, `char`), another class, or `void`. A `resultType` of `void` indicates that no result is passed back to the caller of the method. After the method name is given, a list of exceptions throwable by the method is given. If no exceptions are thrown by the method, this list is not necessary. Exception handling is discussed in full in Chapter 22.

As an example of adding a method to the `Car` class, consider the following sample code:

```
class Car {
    public String manufacturer;
    public String model;
    public int year;
    public int passengers;
    public float CalculateSalePrice() {
        return cost * 1.5;
    }
    private float cost;
}
```

In this case, the `Car` class has had a public member method, `CalculateSalePrice`, added. The method returns a `float`, and the body of the method calculates this return value. To calculate the sale price of a car, the private member variable `cost` is multiplied by 1.5, reflecting a markup of 50% over the amount the car was purchased for.

Overloaded Methods

The ability to overload methods is one of the biggest advantages to working in an object-oriented language, and Java certainly doesn't disappoint. Overloading a method means to use the same method name for more than one method. For example, the `Car` class can include two `CalculateSalePrice` methods, as follows:

```
public float CalculateSalePrice() {
    return cost * 1.5;
}
```

```
public float CalculateSalePrice(double margin) {
    return cost * (1 + margin);
}
private float cost;
```

In this case, the first version of CalculateSalePrice is not passed any parameters and bases the sale price on the cost plus 50% (cost * 1.5). The second version is passed a margin by which the car should be marked up in determining the car's sale price.

At runtime, Java is able to distinguish between these methods by the parameters passed to each. Because of this you can overload a method as many times as you want as long as the parameter lists of each version are unique. In other words, you could not do the following:

```
public float CalculateSalePrice() {
    return cost * 1.5;
}

public float CalculateSalePrice(double margin) {
    return cost * (1 + margin);
}

// this method declaration conflicts with the preceding method
public float CalculateSalePrice(double multiplier) {
    return cost * margin;
}
private float cost;
```

In this situation, the last two declarations are in conflict because each is passed a double. Different parameter names are insufficient to distinguish between two versions of the same overloaded function. They must differ by at least one parameter type.

Constructors

A special type of member method is known as a *constructor*. A constructor is used to create new instances of a class. You can identify a constructor because it will have the same name as the class. Like any other method, a constructor can be overloaded as long as the versions are distinguishable by the parameter types passed to each. Typically, a constructor will set the member variables of an object to values appropriate for that instance. As an example, consider the following variation on the Car class:

```
public class Car {
    String manufacturer;
    String model;
    int year;
    int passengers;
    float cost;

    // calculate the sale price of a car based on its cost
    public double CalculateSalePrice() {
        return cost * 1.5;
    }
```

```
    // a public constructor
    public Car(String madeBy, String name, int yr, int pass,
            float cst) {
        manufacturer = madeBy;
        model = name;
        year = yr;
        passengers = pass;
        cost = cst;
    }

    // create and return a string with the basic details about
    // this particular car
    public String GetStats() {
        return new String(year + " " + manufacturer + " " + model);
    }
}
```

A constructor, `Car`, has been added to this version of the `Car` class. The constructor is passed five parameters that will be used as initial values for the instance variables `manufacturer`, `model`, `year`, `passengers`, and `cost`. The code for the constructor simply sets the five instance variables. The `Car` class has also received a new public member, `GetStats`, that creates a string that contains the basic facts about the car. By using the constructor and the new `GetStats` method, you can now display some information about a car. For example, the following code will display "1967 VW Bug":

```
Car myCar = new Car("VW", "Bug", 1967, 4, 3000);
String str = myCar.GetStats();
System.out.println(str);
```

The new instance of the class `Car` was created with the following line:

```
Car myCar = new Car("VW", "Bug", 1967, 4, 3000);
```

The use of the Java keyword `new` instructs Java to create a new object of type `Car` by allocating memory for it and to invoke the constructor for `Car` whose signature matches the parameter list. In this case, `Car` has only one constructor, so it is invoked and will set the instance variables to the values of the parameters. Once the variable `myCar` goes out of scope at the end of the function in which it is declared, the automatic memory management features of Java will detect that the memory that was allocated by `new` is no longer referenced and it will be released.

TIP

If a class does not specifically include a constructor, Java will provide a default constructor that takes no parameters. This constructor will allow you to create new instances of a class and will set all member variables to their Java system default values. However, it is a dangerous and unwise practice to rely on the existence of a Java default constructor. In general, you should always provide at least one constructor for each class you define.

The this Variable

All Java classes contain a hidden member variable named this. The this member can be used at runtime to reference the object itself. One excellent use of this is in constructors. It is very common to have a set of instance variables in a class that must be set to values that are passed to a constructor. When you are doing this, it would be nice to have code that was similar to the following:

```
year = year;
```

Ideally the variable on the left could be the instance variable, and the variable on the right could be the parameter passed to the constructor. Unfortunately, I don't know of any languages that would be able to make this distinction. The typical solution most programmers have settled on is similar to the following:

```
public class Car {
    String manufacturer;
    String model;
    int year;
    int passengers;

    // a public constructor
    public Car(String madeBy, String name, int yr, int pass,
            float cst) {
        manufacturer = madeBy;
        model = name;
        year = yr;
        passengers = pass;
        cost = cst;
    }
}
```

Here, we've had to come up with two names for each concept: the best variable names (manufacturer, model, and so on) are used as the instance variables in the class declaration. The less satisfactory names are passed as parameters so as to distinguish them from the instance variables. The assignment statements are then very readable by Java but seem a little contrived to human readers. Java's this keyword provides a very effective solution to this problem in that the constructor can be written as follows:

```
public class Car {
    String manufacturer;
    String model;
    int year;
    int passengers;
    float cost;

    // calculate the sale price of a car based on its cost
    public double CalculateSalePrice() {
        return cost * 1.5;
    }
```

```
      // a public constructor
      public Car(String manufacturer, String model, int year,
            int passengers, float cost) {
         this.manufacturer = manufacturer;
         this.model = model;
         this.year = year;
         this.passengers = passengers;
         this.cost = cost;
      }
}
```

In this case, the variables like this.year refer to the instance variables, whereas the unqualified variables like year refer to the constructor's parameters.

Of course, this is only one example of how you can use this. It is also frequently used as a parameter to other functions from within member methods.

Class Inheritance

In Java, every class you declare will be derived from another class. You can specify the class to derive from by using the extends keyword as follows:

```
public class ClassicCar extends Car {
   // member methods and variables
}
```

As you probably noticed, extends was left out of all the prior examples in this chapter. This is because if a class is not declared as being derived from a specific class, then it is assumed to be derived from the Java base class, Object. This means that the following two class declarations are equivalent:

```
public class Car {
   // member methods and variables
}

public class Car extends Object {
   // member methods and variables
}
```

Because Object is the class from which all other Java classes are ultimately derived, this provides a common set of functionality among all Java classes. Most notably, garbage collection is possible because all classes will ultimately trace their lineage back to Object as shown in Figure 3.5.

A derived class is commonly referred to as a *subclass*, while the class it is derived from is commonly referred to as a *superclass*. The term *immediate superclass* is used to describe the class from which a subclass is directly derived. In Figure 3.5, for example, ClassicCar is a subclass of both Car and Object. Car and Object are both superclasses of ClassicCar, but only Car is the immediate superclass of ClassicCar.

FIGURE 3.5.
*Everything is (eventually)
derived from* Object.

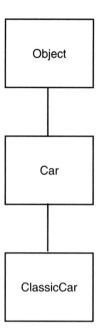

Overriding Member Methods

When you create a subclass, you inherit all of the functionality of its superclass, and then you can add or change this functionality as desired. As an example of this, consider the altered declaration of a Car class in the following code:

```java
public class Car {
    private int year;
    private float originalPrice;

    // calculate the sale price of a car based on its cost
    public double CalculateSalePrice() {
        double salePrice;
        if (year > 1994)
            salePrice = originalPrice * 0.75;
        else if (year > 1990)
            salePrice = originalPrice * 0.50;
        else
            salePrice = originalPrice * 0.25;
        return salePrice;
    }

    // a public constructor
    public Car(int year, float originalPrice) {
        this.year = year;
        this.originalPrice = originalPrice;
    }
}
```

This version of the Car class holds information about the year and the original purchase price of the car. It has a member method, CalculateSalePrice, that determines the price for which to sell the car based on its age. Depending upon the age of the car, it can sell for either 75%, 50%, or 25% of its original price.

Although very simplistic, this is a good start for most cars. However, it is completely inadequate for classic, old cars. This algorithm would indicate that a 1920 Model T would be worth only 25% of its original 1920 price. A slight improvement on this would be to assume that every ClassicCar is worth $10,000. To do this, ClassicCar is derived from Car, as follows:

```java
public class ClassicCar extends Car {
    // calculate the sale price of a car based on its cost
    public double CalculateSalePrice() {
        return 10000;
    }

    // a public constructor
    public ClassicCar(int year, float originalPrice) {
        super(year, originalPrice);
    }
}
```

Because ClassicCar is derived from Car, it inherits all of the functionality of Car, including its member variables year and originalPrice. The function CalculateSalePrice appears in both class declarations. This means that the occurrence of this function in ClassicCar overrides the occurrence of it in Car for object instances of ClassicCar. As an example of how this works, consider the following:

```java
ClassicCar myClassic = new ClassicCar(1920, 1400);
double classicPrice = myClassic.CalculateSalePrice();

Car myCar = new Car(1990, 12000);
double price = myCar.CalculateSalePrice();
```

The variable myClassic is of type ClassicCar and is constructed using that class's constructor, which is passed an original price for the car of $1,400. The sale price of this car is calculated and stored in classicPrice. Because myClassic is a ClassicCar, the sale price will be $10,000. Next, myCar is constructed as a new object of type Car with an original cost of $12,000. Its sale price is determined and stored in price. Because myCar is a Car, its sale price will be based on the year it was made (1990) and will be 25% of $12,000, or $3,000.

The super Variable

In the preceding declaration for ClassicCar, you may have noticed that the constructor made use of a variable named super. Just as each object has a this variable that references itself, each object (other than those of type Object itself) has a super variable that represents the parent class. In this case, super(year, originalPrice) invokes the constructor of the superclass Car.

Class Modifiers

Classes that are created in Java can be modified by any of three class modifiers. The Java class modifiers are public, final, and abstract. If no class modifier is used, then the class may only be used within the package in which it is declared. A public class is a class that can be accessed from other packages. A class that is declared as final cannot be derived from, meaning it cannot have subclasses.

Abstract Classes

Sometimes you may want to declare a class and yet not know how to define all of the methods that belong to that class. For example, you may want to declare a class called Mammal and include in it a member method called MarkTerritory. However, you don't know how to write MarkTerritory because it is different for each type of Mammal. Of course, you plan to handle this by deriving subclasses of Mammal, such as Dog and Human. But what code do you put in the MarkTerritory function of Mammal itself?

In Java you can declare the MarkTerritory function of Mammal as an abstract method. Doing so allows you to declare the method without writing any code for it in that class. However, you can write code for the method in the subclass. If a method is declared abstract, then the class must also be declared as abstract. For Mammal and its subclasses, this means they would appear as follows:

```
abstract class Mammal {
    abstract void MarkTerritory();
}

public class Human extends Mammal {
    public void MarkTerritory() {
        // mark territory by building a fence
    }
}

public class GangMember extends Mammal {
    public void MarkTerritory() {
        // mark territory with graffiti
    }
}

public class Dog extends Mammal {
    public void MarkTerritory() {
        // mark territory by doing what dogs do
    }
}
```

With the preceding declarations, the Mammal class contains no code for MarkTerritory. The Human class could contain code that would mark territory by building a fence around it, while the GangMember class could contain code that would mark territory by spray-painting graffiti. The Dog class would mark territory by raising the dog's leg and doing what dogs do to mark territory.

NOTE

A method that is private or static cannot also be declared abstract. Because a private method cannot be overridden in a subclass, a private abstract method would not be usable. Similarly, because all static methods are implicitly final, static methods cannot be overridden.

Implementing Interfaces

Typically, an abstract class will have some methods that are declared as abstract and some that are not. If you find yourself declaring a class that is entirely abstract, you are probably declaring what is known in Java as an *interface*. An interface is an entirely abstract class. You can derive subclasses from an interface in a manner completely analogous to deriving a subclass from another class.

As an example, suppose you are building an application that must display the hour of the day. Users will have two options for getting this information. They can get it from either a watch or a cuckoo clock. This could be implemented as follows:

```
interface Clock {
    public String GetTime(int hour);
}

class Cuckoo implements Clock  {
    public String GetTime(int hour) {
        StringBuffer str = new StringBuffer();
        for (int i=0; i < hour; i++)
            str.append("Cuckoo ");
        return str.toString();
    }
}

class Watch implements Clock  {
    public String GetTime(int hour) {
        return new String("It is " + hour + ":00");
    }
}
```

In this example, Clock is an interface that provides a single function, GetTime. What this means is that any class that is derived from (or, in other words, *implements* the Clock interface) must provide a GetTime function. Cuckoo is an example of a class that implements Clock, and you'll notice that instead of the class Cuckoo extends Clock syntax that would have been used if Clock were an abstract class, it is instead declared with class Cuckoo implements Clock.

Because Cuckoo implements the Clock interface, it provides a GetTime function. In this case, a string is created that will hold as many Cuckoos as specified by the hour parameter. The class Watch also implements Clock and provides a GetTime function. Its version is a simple message stating the hour.

Interfaces and superclasses are not mutually exclusive. A new class can be derived from a super-class and one or more interfaces. This could be done as follows for a class that implements two interfaces and has one superclass:

```
class MySubClass extends MySuperClass implements FirstInterface,
        SecondInterface {
    // class implementation
}
```

Because it is possible for one class to implement more than one interface, interfaces are a very convenient method for implementing a form of multiple inheritance.

Summary

This chapter covered a great deal of information. You were introduced to Java's primitive types and the operators that are available for these types. Next, you learned how to control the flow of a Java program through selection statements (`if`, `switch`, and `case`), iteration statements (`for`, `while`, and `do...while`), and jumping (`break` and `continue`). Finally, you learned how to put all of this together and create new classes by deriving them from existing classes or interfaces.

4

Java for C++ Programmers

By Mike Cohn

If you are coming to Java from a C++ background, you are off to a great head start. In fact, you already know most of the Java syntax. This chapter will take you through a whirlwind tour of Java, pointing out the key differences between Java and C++. You'll read about C++ features that were left out of Java and about features that were added to Java to take it beyond C++. You'll see how Java has done away with the C++ preprocessor and multiple inheritance but makes up for those through a cleaner object model and interface inheritance. This chapter doesn't attempt to teach you everything you need to know to be a Java programmer, but it will help you put Java in perspective relative to your knowledge as a C++ programmer.

Data Types

Because Java was based on C and C++, the data types supported by Java are very similar to those of C and C++. This section describes the key differences between Java types and C++ types.

Primitive Types

A language's primitive types are the building blocks from which more complicated types (such as classes) are built. Java supports a set of eight primitive types, which are shown in Table 4.1.

Table 4.1. Java primitive types.

Type	*Description*
byte	8-bit signed integer
short	16-bit signed integer
int	32-bit signed integer
long	64-bit signed integer
float	32-bit floating-point number
double	64-bit floating-point number
char	16-bit Unicode characters
boolean	Can hold true or false

From this list, you can tell that Java adds both the byte and boolean types. Some recent C++ compilers have added support for the new C++ boolean type, so you may already be using it in your code. Because Java provides Unicode support, you should notice that its char type is 16 bits wide. This is also why the 8-bit byte type is included as a primitive type. In C++, you probably have been emulating a byte type with something similar to the following:

```
type unsigned char byte;
```

There are a couple of other extremely important differences between the Java and C++ primitive types. The Java primitives are each of a known and guaranteed size. This is critical to Java because of its goal of portability across hardware and operating systems. If an int is 16 bits on one platform and 32 bits on another platform, a program is asking for trouble if it expects to be run on both platforms. C++ guarantees certain relationships among its primitive types. For example, a C++ long is guaranteed to be at least as big as a C++ int. Java takes this further and prescribes an exact size for each primitive.

Because most of the machines that will run Java programs will do so in a 32-bit environment, the sizes of the primitive types have been defined with 32-bit optimization in mind. This means that some Java primitives may use more storage space than you are accustomed to with their C++ equivalents. In particular, you should notice that a Java int is 32 bits and a Java long is 64 bits.

A final difference worth pointing out is that all Java primitive types are signed. This means that C++ declarations like the following are not allowed in Java:

```
unsigned long bigLong;      // not legal in Java
unsigned double salary;     // not legal in Java
```

The Java boolean primitive can be set to a value of true or false. In traditional C and C++ programming, true and false were defined by using the preprocessor to be equal to 1 and 0, respectively.

Casting

In both Java and C++, it is possible to cast a variable from one type to another. However, because Java is a more strongly typed language than is C++, Java protects you and prevents you from making some casts. For example, because Java's boolean type is not a disguised int in Boolean clothing, you cannot cast between a Boolean and a numeric type. This means that you cannot do the following:

```
boolean aBool = false;      // not legal in Java
int anInt = (int)aBool;     // not legal in Java
```

Because Java doesn't rely on programming conventions that indicate false equals zero, Java cannot cast aBool to anInt in this example.

Automatic Coercions

Related to casting is the concept of *automatic coercion.* Automatic coercion occurs when a compiler *coerces,* or casts, a variable of one type into another automatically. For example, consider the following C++ code:

```
long aLong = 65536L;
unsigned int justAnInt;
justAnInt = aLong;
printf("%d", justAnInt);
```

In this example, the 65,536 stored in aLong is also placed into justAnInt. Because no explicit cast is performed, an automatic coercion from a long to an unsigned int is performed. Unfortunately, on a 16-bit platform, this will result in an error because the value in aLong is too large to fit in justAnInt. The automatic coercion will place 0 into justAnInt instead of the desired 65,536.

Because Java does not perform automatic coercions, you may need to slightly alter your thinking about some of your C++ programming habits. For example, in C++ you could write the following loop:

```
int count=10;
while (count) {
    // use count to do something
    count—;
}
```

In C++, the while loop will execute as long as count is non-zero. However, a Java while loop must be formed according to the following syntax:

```
while (booleanExpression)
    statement
```

What this means is that statements like while(count) do not work in Java because there is no automatic coercion of an integer (such as count) to the boolean that a Java while loop expects. You need to rewrite the C++ code fragment to work in Java as follows:

```
int count=10;
while (count > 0) {
    // use count to do something
    count—;
}
```

This creates a Boolean expression that is evaluated on each pass through the loop. You will need to make similar adjustments with the Java for and do...while loops, as well.

Operators

The set of operators supported by Java is nearly identical to the set supported by C++. Although the operators perform nearly identical operations in the two languages, there are several relevant differences. Table 4.2 shows the Java operators on Boolean values. The contents of this table should be instantly recognizable because each operator is also available in C++.

Table 4.2. Operators on Boolean values.

Operator	*Operation*	*Example*
!	Negation	!a
&&	Conditional AND	a && b
||	Conditional OR	a || b
?:	Conditional	a ? expr1 : expr2

These operators are worth singling out because they operate only on Java boolean types. For example, consider the following C++ fragment:

```
int x = 1;
int y = 7;
if (x && y) {
    // do something
}
```

This same statement is illegal in Java. Because the && operator expects two boolean operands and there is no automatic coercion from an integer, the Java compiler does not know how to interpret this statement. In Java, it needs to be rewritten as follows:

```
int x = 1;
int y = 7;
if (x != 0 && y != 0) {
    // do something
}
```

In this case, the two integer values have been converted into explicit tests. Because these tests are Boolean expressions, the code can now be compiled.

Java also introduces two new operators, >>> and >>>=. Each of these performs a right shift with zero fill. The latter also will perform an assignment after the shift.

Another difference between operators in Java and C++ is that Java operators cannot be overloaded. Initially, operator overloading was an exciting feature of C++ that promised to allow programmers to treat all data types, whether primitive or not, equivalently. The reasoning went that if there was a logically intuitive action that should be performed by an operator, then the language should support overloading the operator to perform that action. Unfortunately, reality intervened, and many uses of operator overloading in C++ have led to unnecessary bugs. Because of the potential for introducing bugs through operator overloading, the developers of Java wisely chose to leave it out.

Pointers

If you've been programming in C or C++ for any significant amount of time, you probably mastered pointers a long time ago. You know how to use pointers to characters, integers, structures, classes, and probably even functions. Mastering the concept of pointers has long been a rite of passage in C and C++ programming. Pointers are behind much of the power and flexibility of C++. Unfortunately, pointers are also behind much of the complexity and bugs in C++ programs. So, with both regret and rejoicing, you can say farewell to pointers.

Java does not have a pointer type of any sort. When an object or array is passed to a method, it is passed by reference, rather than by value. However, a Java program still cannot access it as a pointer or memory location.

By removing pointers from Java, the language has been greatly simplified over C and C++. However, an additional benefit is that removing pointers is consistent with the design goals of Java that it be a secure environment. By removing the ability to create a pointer directly into a system's memory, a language goes a long way toward preventing the use of the language for writing deviant programs such as viruses.

Structures and Unions

One of the unfortunate problems with C++ has been its support for compiling legacy, or pre-existing, C code. Of course, this probably also has been the key reason that C++ has gained the widespread acceptance that it has. The drawback to continuing to provide support for pre-existing code is that it muddies the language, allowing and sometimes forcing programmers to create new code that is more difficult to understand than would otherwise be necessary.

Because C++ added to C the ability to define classes, it made superfluous the need to define structures and unions. Because Java is a new language with no requirement to support an existing base of code, its object model is much cleaner. In Java, you define classes. The C concepts of struct and union have been removed.

Arrays

Like C and C++, Java uses square brackets ([]) to declare and access arrays. However, when declaring an array in Java, there are two important differences from declaring an array in C or C++, as follows:

■ The square brackets ([]) can be placed either before or after the variable name.

■ The size of the array is not specified within the square brackets at the time the array is declared.

To see the effect of these differences, consider the following array declarations:

```
int intArray[];
float floatArray[];
double [] doubleArray;
char charArray[];
```

In these examples, there is no difference between these arrays based on where the brackets are located. As a C++ programmer, you may be inclined to continue placing them after the variable name. However, there is an advantage to changing your habits and placing the brackets *before* the variable name. Placing the brackets in front of the variable name allows you to more easily declare multiple arrays. For example, consider the following declaration:

```
int [] firstArray, secondArray;
```

This statement will declare two arrays of integers. Depending on your perspective, you may find it more intuitive and readable than the following more C-like version:

```
int firstArray[], secondArray[];
```

Allocation

Of course, in C++ you must specify the size or dimension of the array. In Java, this is not necessary (or even allowed) because Java requires that all arrays be allocated with new. It is not possible in Java to allocate the equivalent of a C automatic array. To allocate an array using new, you would use code similar to that shown in the following examples:

```
int intArray[] = new int[100];
float floatArray[];
floatArray = new float[100];
long [] longArray = new long[100];
double [][] doubleArray = new double[10][10];
```

From these examples, you can see that memory can be allocated on the same line on which the array is declared, as was done with intArray. Or, the array can be declared and allocated on two separate lines, as with floatArray. The variable doubleArray shows how to declare and allocate a multidimensional array in Java. In this case, a two-dimensional array is allocated. This is really an array of arrays in which each of 10 first dimension arrays contains its own array of 10 items.

An alternative way of allocating a Java array is to specify a list of element initializers when the array is declared. This is done as follows:

```
int intArray[] = {1,2,3,4,5};
char [] charArray = {'a', 'b', 'c'};
String [] stringArray = {"A", "Four", "Element", "Array"};
```

In this case, intArray will be a five-element array holding the values 1 through 5. The three-element array charArray will hold the characters 'a', 'b', and 'c'. Finally, stringArray will hold the four strings shown.

Array Access

You can access items in an array in the same way you would do in C++, as shown in the following:

```
int ages[] = {16, 18, 21, 65};

int canDrive = intArray[0];    // can drive at 16
int canVote = intArray[1];     // can vote at 18
int canDrink = intArray[2];    // can drink at 21
int canRetire = intArray[3];   // can retire at 65
```

In C++, you could even take this further and access elements outside the bounds of the array. Most of the time when you did this, however, it was accidental and caused unexpected program behavior like crashes and rebooting. Fortunately, Java protects you against this by only allowing access to allocated array elements. Java will throw the `ArrayIndexOutOfBoundsException` exception if you try to access an element beyond the bounds of the array.

Automatic Memory Management

Unless you're the manufacturer of one of the many debugging aids targeted at helping programmers find memory leaks, you have to be excited at the prospect of automatic memory management. Java's automatic memory management features mean that you no longer have to keep track of allocated memory and then explicitly free that memory.

Although memory for an object is still allocated with `new`, there is no corresponding `delete` that must be used to release memory. What happens instead is that the Java memory manager keeps track of which memory is in use, and once there are no objects referencing a particular area of memory, that memory is automatically released and available for reuse. This is very similar to the way C++ automatic variables are released once they go out of scope.

With automatic memory management (usually known as *garbage collection*), you will find yourself able to write programs more quickly and with fewer bugs.

Classes

The design of Java's object model and its support for classes was certainly influenced by C++. However, Java classes borrow less from C++ than do many other aspects of Java and its syntax. Although classes are undeniably important in C++, classes are mandatory and central to all that you will do in Java. In Java, there are no free-standing variables or functions. Everything must be encapsulated within a class. Further, every class in Java can trace back through its inheritance hierarchy and find itself a descendant of the `Object` class. In order to understand Java classes, consider the following class definition:

```
class Employee {
    public String firstName;
    public String lastName;
    protected int age;
    private float salary;
    public boolean CanVote() {
        return age >= 21;
    }
    public boolean CanDrink(int legalAge) {
        return age >= legalAge;
    }
}
```

You'll notice from the definition of Employee that Java classes support the familiar concepts of private, protected, and public members. However, in Java, members are not grouped into private, public, or protected sections as they typically are in C++. In the Employee class, each member had its access control modifier specified right with the type and name of the member. Although you may consider this a little more typing, it definitely makes the code more readable, and therefore easier to maintain, if you don't have to read backwards through the file to find out if a class member is accessible.

Each of the familiar private, protected, and public access control modifiers has the same meaning in Java that it has in C++. Additionally, however, Java has a fourth level of access control that is used as the default. If no access control modifier is specified for a member, that member is accessible throughout the package in which it is defined, but nowhere else.

A Java package shares attributes of a C++ library, a C++ source file, and a C++ header file. Java code is shared at the package level and a package contains the definitions and source code implementations of one or more classes.

Member Methods

Returning to the definition of the Employee class, you can also see that both the CanVote and CanDrink methods were written directly in the class definition without using the C++ inline keyword. In Java, there is no concept that is analogous to the C++ header file. Each class is defined, and its methods are written in the same place. Because of this, Java does not need an inline keyword, yet all methods are written as you would write a C++ inline function.

Setting Default Values

It's always the little things that make a difference. One little thing that makes a tremendous convenience improvement in Java over C++ is the ability to set a default value for a member variable at the time it is declared. For example, consider the following definition of the Employee class:

```
class Employee {
    ...
    protected int age = 21;
    ...
}
```

In this example, the member variable age is declared and is given a default value of 21. In C++, this would have been done in the constructor. There are two advantages to setting a default value at the point where the variable is declared:

- The code becomes more readable because the default value cannot be missed when reading the code.
- If the class uses more than one constructor that would have set the variable to its default, these constructors are simplified by not having to set the default value.

Static Members

In addition to class methods and variables that are associated with each instance of a class, a Java class can contain members that are associated with the class itself. Just as in C++, these are known as static members and are identified with the static keyword as follows:

```
class Employee {
    ...
    static double maxSalary = 1000000D;
    ...
}
```

In this example, the member variable maxSalary will exist once in the entire program, as opposed to once per instance of the class. Additionally, maxSalary has been set to an initial value of $1,000,000.

Constructors and Destructors

Each Java class you define may include one or more constructors. Just as in C++, the constructor is given the same name as the class. Java class constructors have no return value and are declared in the same manner as any other class method. This can be seen in the following example:

```
class Employee {
    public String firstName;
    public String lastName;
    protected int age;
    private float salary;
    public Employee(String fName, String lName) {
        firstName = fName;
        lastName = lName;
    }
```

```
    public boolean CanVote() {
        return age >= 21;
    }
    public boolean CanDrink(int legalAge) {
        return age >= legalAge;
    }
}
```

Because Java includes a garbage collection feature for the automatic release of unreferenced memory, the role of destructors is much smaller than it is in C++. In C++, a destructor is necessary so that it can free any memory allocated by the object. Because of Java's automatic memory management, destructors are no longer needed to perform this job.

For these reasons, Java classes do not include C++ style destructors. Instead, each Java class can include a finalize method that can be used to perform any object cleanup. The finalize method is declared in the Object class, but because Object is the ultimate base class of all Java classes, finalize is available to every Java class. There is one danger, however, to consider when using finalize. It is possible for a Java program to terminate without this method being invoked on every object. If a program terminates with objects that are still referenced, the garbage collection process will never be used to release those objects, and finalize will never be called.

Inheritance

Inheritance in Java is indicated by the use of the extends keyword, as shown in the following example:

```
public class Employee extends Person {
    // member methods and variables
}
```

If a class is derived directly from Object, then the extends keyword is optional. The following two class declarations are equivalent:

```
public class Person extends Object {
    // member methods and variables
}

public class Person {
    // member methods and variables
}
```

Like C++, Java includes a this keyword that can be used by an object to reference itself. Additionally, Java includes a super keyword that an object can use to reference its parent, or superclass. The use of super is frequently seen in the constructor of a subclass, as shown in the following:

```
public class Person {
    String firstName;
    String lastName;
    Person() {}
    Person(String fName, String lName) {
        firstName = fName;
        lastName = lName;
    }
}

public class Employee extends Person {
    float salary;
    Employee(float sal, String fName, String lName) {
        super(fName, lName);
        salary = sal;
    }
}
```

In this example, the `Person` class includes a constructor that is passed a first name and a last name. The `Employee` class is derived from `Person` and includes a constructor that is passed salary, first name, and last name. The constructor for `Employee` first sets the internal `salary` member and then uses `super` to invoke the constructor for Person.

Abstract Classes

The Java version of a pure, virtual class is an abstract class. Instances of Java abstract classes cannot be created with `new`. An abstract class is identified by the use of the `abstract` keyword, as shown in the following:

```
abstract class Species {
    ...
    abstract void GiveBirth();
    ...
}
```

A class is considered abstract if it has one or more methods that are abstract. In the case of the `Species` class, the method `GiveBirth` is specified as `abstract` because some species have live births and others lay eggs. Because the method is abstract, no method body is given.

Interfaces and Multiple Inheritance

If you design a class that is entirely abstract, then that class is what Java refers to as an *interface*. A Java interface is similar to a class in that it defines a new type that contains both methods and variables. However, because an interface is completely abstract, its methods are not implemented within the interface. Instead, classes that are derived from an interface implement the methods of the interface.

An interface is declared in the same manner as a class except that instead of `class`, the keyword `interface` is used. For example, the following code will declare an interface named `Clock`:

```
interface Clock {
    public String GetTime(int hour);
}
```

To derive a class from an interface, use the keyword `implements` (similar to how `extends` is used when a class is derived from another class). To derive the classes `Cuckoo` and `Watch` from the `Clock` interface, you would do the following:

```
class Cuckoo implements Clock  {
    public String GetTime(int hour) {
        StringBuffer str = new StringBuffer();
        for (int i=0; i < hour; i++)
            str.append("Cuckoo ");
        return str.toString();
    }
}

class Watch implements Clock  {
    public String GetTime(int hour) {
        return new String("It is " + hour + ":00");
    }
}
```

Java does not support multiple class inheritance. In other words, a class may have only one immediate superclass because only a single class name can follow `extends` in a Java class declaration. Fortunately, class inheritance and interface inheritance can be combined when deriving a new Java class. And, a subclass can implement more than one interface. For example, you can do the following:

```
class MySubClass extends MySuperClass implements FirstInterface,
        SecondInterface {
    // class implementation
}
```

The Preprocessor

The Java language does not include a preprocessor. Much of the complexity of C and C++ can be traced back to the preprocessor. How many times have you read a C++ function and then needed to trace a defined value or macro back through a hierarchy of headers in order to understand the function? The preprocessor brought a lot of flexibility to C and C++, but it also added artificial complexity.

Java's removal of the preprocessor means that you will need to unlearn a couple of old habits. For example, you will no longer be able to use `typedef` and `#define`. In Java, you would instead use classes and constants.

Other Changes

There are a number of additional differences between Java and C++ beyond those already mentioned in this chapter. This section will briefly describe some additional differences.

Comments

In addition to the / / and /*...*/ comments of C++, Java introduces a new comment delimiter. Java's new comment delimiter begins with /** and ends with */. A comment that is enclosed within these delimiters can be extracted from the source code and used to create documentation for the class with the JavaDoc utility. JavaDoc is fully described in Chapter 16, "Using JavaDoc to Document Your Program."

Command-Line Arguments

In a C or C++ program, the program is passed command-line arguments in the familiar `argc` and `argv` parameters to the program's `main` function. These parameters represent a count of the number of parameters and an array of parameter values, respectively. There will always be at least one parameter passed to a C or C++ program because the first parameter is the program name.

In a Java application, the command-line arguments are based in an array of `String` objects. The signature for `main` is as follows:

```
public static void main(String args[]);
```

Each component of the array args is one of the command-line arguments. A difference between C++ and Java is that the program name is not passed to the program as the first command-line argument in Java. Consider two programs that are invoked in the following manner:

For C++: `program 100 200`

For Java: `java program 100 200`

The command lines of these two programs will be interpreted by C++ and Java as shown in Table 4.3.

Table 4.3. Command-line arguments in C++ and Java.

Argument	*C++*	*Java*
program	argv[0]	(none)
100	argv[1]	args[0]
200	argv[2]	args[1]

Character Arrays and Strings

Because Java does not allow direct manipulation of pointers, it does not support C-style, null-terminated strings. For its string support, Java utilizes a `String` class. Although it is possible to allocate an array of type `char` to emulate a C++ string, the two types are not the same.

`goto`, `break`, **and** `continue`

You probably won't shed any tears, but the `goto` statement is not part of Java. On the other hand, it is still part of the reserved word list so it may come back at any time. Java does replace `goto`, however, with the ability to use `break` and `continue` with labels. You can still use `break` and `continue` as you are used to from C++, but you can now use them to pass control flow in other ways. For example, consider the following code:

```
int line=1;

outsideLoop:
for(int out=0; out<3; out++) {
    for(int inner=0;inner < 5; inner++) {
        if (foo(inner) < 10))
            break outsideLoop;
        else if (foo(inner) > 100)
            continue outsideLoop;
    }
}
```

In this example, if the `foo` method returns a value less than 10, the code `break outsideLoop` will execute. A normal `break` here would break out of the inner loop. However, because this is a named `break` statement, it will break out of the named outer loop. This example also demonstrates the use of `continue` with a label.

Runtime Type Identification

Runtime Type Identification (RTTI) is a relatively new feature to C++, or at least to many C++ compilers. A form of RTTI is included in Java through its `instanceof` keyword.

Missing Features

As you begin programming in Java, you will notice that it is missing a couple of other aspects of C++ that you may use. In most cases, there is either no need for the feature in Java, due to its simplified model for object-oriented programming, or there is an alternative way of accomplishing the goal.

Features left out of Java that you may rely on in C++ include templates, name spaces, friend functions, and default parameters. In many cases, you will find that these old friends are no longer necessary in Java, or, at least, that their removal is justified by how much doing so simplifies the rest of your code.

Summary

This chapter covered quite a lot of territory. Building on your background in C++, you learned how Java differs from C++ in regard to data types, operators, memory management, and classes. You learned how Java simplifies programming by removing those features of C++ that are likely to introduce bugs. You also learned how Java enables you to continue creating the powerful programs you are used to in C++.

5

Java for Delphi Programmers

By Mike Cohn

In many ways, a background in Delphi programming is ideal for making the move to Java. Although Java is based on C++ and borrows much of its syntax from C++, in some respects Java is more similar to the Object Pascal language of Delphi. Although you will have to adjust to some new syntactic conventions (such as using curly braces instead of begin and end), the object-oriented programming model of Delphi has a great deal in common with Java. This chapter will take you through a whirlwind tour of Java, pointing out the key differences between Java and Object Pascal. On the way, you'll learn how to translate your Delphi knowledge to Java. You'll also be exposed to new concepts such as *multiple inheritance*. This chapter doesn't attempt to teach you everything you need to know to be a Java programmer, but it will help you use your Delphi experience as a first step toward Java.

Comments

In order to make the code samples in this chapter as understandable as possible, it is useful to include comments. So, this chapter starts right off with an overview of Java comments. Java supports three comment delimiters, as shown in Table 5.1.

Table 5.1. Java comment delimiters.

Start	End	Purpose
/*	*/	The enclosed text is treated as a comment.
//	(none)	The rest of the line is treated as a comment.
/**	*/	The enclosed text is treated as a comment by the compiler but is used by JavaDoc to automatically generate documentation.

If you've been exposed to C or C++ at all, you may already be familiar with the first two comment styles. The third is new to Java. The // comment delimiter is very useful when placed to the right of a line of code. The /* and */ delimiters are most frequently used to indicate that a block of lines is a comment. As examples of how these comment delimiters can be used, consider the following:

```
print("hello");    // this is a comment to the end of the line
/* this is a comment also */
/* this is a comment that
takes up multiple lines */
/** this is a comment that generates documentation.
It can be as many lines as desired. */
```

The End of begin and end

With Java, you will say good-bye to your old friend keywords begin and end. They are replaced by the more C-like curly braces, as shown in the following:

```
if (x == y) {
    // do something
    // do something else
}
```

As with Object Pascal, if a block is comprised of only a single line, then the curly braces are optional, as follows:

```
if (x == y)
    // do something

if (x == y) {
    // do something
}
```

Data Types

Built into Delphi's Object Pascal language is a very broad set of data types. Many of Delphi's data types exist to provide compatibility with either prior versions of Borland's Turbo Pascal predecessor to Delphi or with Microsoft Windows. This section describes the Java primitive types and discusses the differences between them and their Delphi equivalents.

Declaring Variables

Variable declarations in Java are the complete opposite of what you are used to in Delphi. A Java declaration consists of the variable type followed by its name. For example, consider the following declarations:

```
int anInt;
int anotherInt = 42;
long thisIsALong = 100, secondLong;
float myFloat = 3.49f;
double myDouble = 3.1416D;
```

As you can see from these examples, more than one variable can be declared on a line. Additionally, an initial value can be assigned to a variable as was done, for example, by assigning 42 to anotherInt. In the case of float or double variables, the type of the variable can be specified by appending an upper- or lowercase F (for float) or D (for double) to the initial value.

The best news about declaring a variable in Java is that it does not need to be done in a special var section. Anywhere you need a new variable, you simply declare it. It can be at the start of a method or even in the middle of a method.

Primitive Types

A language's primitive types are the building blocks from which more complicated types (such as classes) are built. Java supports a set of eight primitive types, which are shown in Table 5.2.

Table 5.2. Java primitive types.

Type	*Description*
byte	8-bit signed integer
short	16-bit signed integer
int	32-bit signed integer
long	64-bit signed integer
float	32-bit floating-point number
double	64-bit floating-point number
char	16-bit Unicode characters
boolean	Can hold true or false

From Table 5.2, you can see that Java uses a shorter version of the type names than does Delphi. For example, Delphi has shortint and longint, whereas Java has short and long. However, behind these cosmetic changes are some substantive changes. For example, each of the similarly named integer types in Delphi is bigger in Java. A Delphi Integer is a 16-bit signed value and corresponds to a Java short. Table 5.3 is useful for converting between Delphi and Java integer variables.

Table 5.3. Delphi primitive types and their Java equivalents.

Delphi	*Java*
ShortInt	byte
Integer	short
LongInt	int
Byte	byte
Word	int

All variables in Java are signed. Because of this, the Delphi unsigned types (Word and Byte) are replaced with Java signed types large enough to hold their largest values. Because Java provides Unicode support, you should notice that its char type is 16 bits wide. This is also why the 8-bit byte type is included as a primitive.

The Java and Delphi `boolean` types are similar. However, with Delphi it is possible to perform some operations on Boolean values that are not possible in Java. For example, in Delphi the following comparison will evaluate to true, but will be a compile error in Java:

```
false < true
```

The Object Pascal language of Delphi also includes a `String` primitive type. Although Java does not include a `String` primitive, it does include a full-featured `String` class that will provide many of the same capabilities you are used to from Delphi's `String` primitive. An important difference between strings in Java and Delphi is that Java strings are enclosed in double quotes ("), not single quotes ('). In Java, a single character is enclosed within single quotes. For example, consider the following valid Java declarations:

```
String str = "This is a string";
char ch = 'a';
```

Casting

In both Java and Delphi, it is possible to cast a variable from one type to another. Both languages are strongly typed, but Java is more restrictive and doesn't allow some casts that Delphi does. For example, in Java you cannot cast between a `boolean` and a `numeric` type. This means you cannot do the following:

```
boolean aBool = false;    // not legal in Java
int anInt = (int)aBool;   // not legal in Java
```

Delphi assumes that a Boolean value `false` can be translated to zero and `true` can be translated to one. This is not true in Java. In Java, a Boolean is a Boolean and it cannot be cast into an integer value.

Automatic Coercions

Related to casting is the concept of *automatic coercion*. Automatic coercion occurs when a compiler *coerces*, or casts, a variable of one type into another automatically. For example, consider the following Delphi code:

```
var
    anInt : integer;
    aLong : longint;
begin
    aLong := 65536;
    anInt := aLong;
    MessageDlg('anInt is ' + IntToStr(anInt), mtInformation, [mbYes, mbNo], 0);
end;
```

In this example, the `65536` stored in `aLong` is also placed into `anInt`. Because no explicit cast is performed, an automatic coercion from a `longint` to an `integer` is performed. Unfortunately, this will result in an error because the value in `aLong` is too large to fit in `anInt`. The automatic coercion will place `0` into `anInt` instead of the desired `65536`. Java avoids the problems caused by automatic coercion by not allowing it.

Operators

The Java language contains a richer set of operators than does Delphi. Fortunately, many of the Java operators correspond to similar operators in Delphi. Table 5.4 shows each of the Java operators, the operation it performs, and an example of its use.

Table 5.4. Operators on Boolean values.

Operator	Operation	Example
=	Assignment	`a = b`
>	Greater than	`a > b`
<	Less than	`a < b`
<=	Less than or equal to	`a <= b`
>=	Greater than or equal to	`a >= b`
==	Equal to	`a == b`
!=	Not equal to	`a != b`
!	Boolean negation	`!a`
~	Bitwise logical negation	`~a`
?:	Conditional operators	`a ? expr1 : expr2`
&&	Conditional AND	`a && b`
¦¦	Conditional OR	`a ¦¦ b`
++	Increment	`a++ or ++a`
--	Decrement	`a-- or --a`
+	Addition	`a + b`
-	Subtraction	`a - b or -b`
*	Multiplication	`a * b`
/	Division	`a / b`
%	Modulus	`a % b`
&	Bitwise AND	`a & b`
¦	Bitwise OR	`a ¦ b`
^	Bitwise XOR	`a ^ b`
<<	Left shift	`a << b`
>>	Right shift	`a >> b`

Operator	Operation	Example
>>>	Right shift with zero fill	a >>> b
+=	Assign result of addition	a += b
-=	Assign result of subtraction	a -= b
*=	Assign result of multiplication	a *= b
/=	Assign result of division	a /= b
&=	Assign result of bitwise AND	a &= b
¦=	Assign result of bitwise OR	a ¦= b
^=	Assign result of bitwise XOR	a ^= b
%=	Assign result of modulus	a %= b
<<=	Assign result of left shift	a <<= b
>>=	Assign result of right shift	a >>= b
>>=	Assign result of right shift with zero fill	a >>>= b

One of the biggest adjustments you'll need to make will be getting used to using a lone equal sign for assignment instead of the := of Delphi. Because = is used for assignment, two equal signs (==) are used for testing equality in Java. You can see this in the following Java example:

```
int x, y;    // declare two integer variables
x = 43;      // assign a value to x
y = 42;      // assign a different value to y
if (x == y)  // do something
```

In Delphi, the four keywords not, and, or, and xor each had two meanings. Each could function as a bitwise operator as well as a Boolean operator. This had a tendency to make code more difficult to read and maintain than it needed to be. Java simplifies this by having each operator perform a unique operation. To find the Java equivalent for the Delphi not, and, or, and xor operators, see Table 5.5.

Table 5.5. The Java equivalents of Delphi's not, and, or, and xor operators.

Delphi	Java	Operation
and	&	Bitwise AND
or	¦	Bitwise OR
xor	^	Bitwise XOR
not	~	Bitwise negation
and	&&	Conditional AND
or	¦¦	Conditional OR
not	!	Boolean negation

Java includes increment and decrement operators that are extremely useful. In order to increment a variable, use the ++ operator. In order to decrement a variable, use the - - operator. These operators can be used in either prefix or postfix mode, as shown in the following examples:

```
x++;
--y;
int z = 100;
MyMethod(z++);
```

In the case of x, the code x++ is equivalent to the more verbose Delphi x := x+1 or Inc(x). The example of the call to MyMethod is illustrative because it shows a unique aspect of the increment and decrement operators. The increment of z will happen after the call to MyMethod. This means that z will be passed with a value of 100. Once MyMethod returns, z will be incremented. If you want to increment z prior to calling MyMethod, the method should have been invoked as follows:

```
int z = 100;
MyMethod(++z);
```

Special Assignment Operators

A special assignment operator sounds like something out of a 1960s spy movie. Unfortunately, a Java special assignment operator isn't anything that glamorous. However, special assignment operators are extremely useful.

In addition to the usual operators, Java includes a set of operators that perform an operation and then assign the result of that operation to one of the operands. Each of these operators is listed in Table 5.4 where you'll notice that each is composed of a different operator token with an equal sign (=) appended. Most likely, you will use the +=, -=, *=, and /= operators more frequently than the others, so consider the following examples:

```
int a, b, c, d;
a = 5;
b = 2;
a += 3;    // a now equals 8
a *= b;    // a now equals 16
a -= 4;    // a now equals 12
a /= b;    // a now equals 6
```

From this example, you can see that a += 3 is shorthand for the Delphi statement a := a + 3.

Pointers

Just your luck. You've finally mastered pointers and then you decide to learn Java—a language that doesn't use pointers. Pointers can be a very powerful aspect of a language. Unfortunately, pointers are also frequently behind much of the complexity of the languages that use them.

The Object Pascal language of Delphi took a big step toward removing the complexity of pointers by hiding them in many cases. However, Java goes even further by not having a pointer type at all. When an object or array is passed to a method, it is passed by reference, rather than by value. However, a Java program still cannot access it as a pointer or memory location.

By removing pointers from Java, the developers have greatly simplified the language. However, an additional benefit is that removing pointers is consistent with the design goal of keeping Java a secure environment. By removing the ability to create a pointer directly into a system's memory, a language goes a long way toward preventing the use of the language for writing deviant programs such as viruses.

Records

Although the Object Pascal language of Delphi is undeniably object-oriented, it just as undeniably shows its lineage as a non-object-oriented language. Because Object Pascal is a descendant of the Pascal language, it includes support for all of the traditional Pascal constructs, including `record` types. However, because Object Pascal allows for the definition of classes, records are superfluous but remain in the language to provide backward compatibility. Because Java is a new language with no need for backward compatibility, its object model is much cleaner. In Java, you define classes. There is no concept of a separate but similar `record` type.

Arrays

Like Delphi, Java uses square brackets ([ ]) to declare and access arrays. However, when declaring an array in Java, there are three important differences from declaring an array in Delphi, as follows:

- The syntax to declare an array is less verbose and does not include the use of an `array` keyword.
- All Java arrays begin with element zero, unlike Delphi in which the range can be specified.
- The size of the array is not specified within the square brackets at the time the array is declared.

To see the effect of these differences, consider the following array declarations:

```
int intArray[];
float floatArray[];
double [] doubleArray;
char charArray[];
```

As you'll notice from these examples, the square brackets ([ ]) can be placed either before or after the variable name. There is no difference based on where the brackets are placed. It is largely a matter of personal preference whether you place brackets before or after a variable name. However, as you settle on a personal preference, you should be aware of the difference that bracket placement can make when declaring more than one array in a single statement. For example, consider the following array declarations:

```
int [] firstArray, secondArray;
int thirdArray[], fourthArray[];
```

Each of these lines declares two arrays. In the first case, the brackets are required only once because they follow the type name. In the second case, the brackets are required after each variable name. Some programmers prefer the explicitness of such declarations, and others prefer the succinctness of the first case.

Allocation

Of course, in Delphi you must specify the dimension of the array by specifying low and high index values into the array. In Java, this is not necessary (or even allowed) because Java requires that all arrays be allocated with new. To allocate an array using new, you would use code similar to that shown in the following examples:

```
int intArray[] = new int[100];
float floatArray[];
floatArray = new float[100];
long [] longArray = new long[100];
double [][] doubleArray = new double[10][10];
```

From these examples, you can see that memory can be allocated on the same line on which the array is declared, as was done with intArray, or the array can be declared and allocated on two separate lines as with floatArray. The variable doubleArray shows how to declare and allocate a multidimensional array in Java. In this case, a two-dimensional array is allocated. This is really an array of arrays in which each of 10 first-dimension arrays contains its own array of ten items.

An alternative way of allocating a Java array is to specify a list of element initializers when the array is declared. This is done as follows:

```
int intArray[] = {1,2,3,4,5};
char [] charArray = {'a', 'b', 'c'};
String [] stringArray = {"A", "Four", "Element", "Array"};
```

In this case, intArray will be a five-element array holding the values 1 through 5. The three-element array charArray will hold the characters 'a', 'b', and 'c'. Finally, stringArray will hold the four strings shown.

Array Access

The initial element in a Java array is stored in index zero. Therefore, a Java array consists of elements 0 through one less than the number of items in the array. You can access items in an array in the same way you do in Delphi, as shown in the following:

```
int ages[] = {16, 18, 21, 65};

int canDrive = ages[0];    // can drive at 16
int canVote = ages[1];     // can vote at 18
```

```
int canDrink = ages[2];    // can drink at 21
int canRetire = ages[3];   // can retire at 65
```

Like Delphi, Java protects you against attempting to access an element outside the bounds of the array. Java will throw the `ArrayIndexOutOfBoundsException` exception if you try to access an element beyond the bounds of the array.

Memory Management

Like in Delphi, an instance of a Java class is allocated with the keyword `new`, as follows:

```
Label myLabel = new Label("This is a label.");
```

Although there is a Delphi function called `new`, the Java version of `new` is more similar to the `Create` method (the constructor) that can exist for a Delphi class. In Delphi, `new` is used to allocate a block of memory and set a pointer to it. In Java, `new` is used to create an instance of a class.

In Delphi, an instance that has been allocated with the `Create` method must eventually be released by a call to the `Free` method. For some instances in a Delphi program, the call to `Free` is performed automatically when the owner of an object is freed.

Garbage Collection

Although memory for an object is still allocated with `new`, there is no corresponding `free` method that must be used to release memory. What happens instead is that the Java memory manager keeps track of which memory is in use, and once there are no objects referencing a particular area of memory, that memory is automatically released and available for reuse.

With automatic memory management (usually known as *garbage collection*), you will find that you can write programs more quickly and with fewer bugs.

Classes

Java's support for classes has a great deal in common with Delphi. Although classes are undeniably important in Delphi, they are mandatory and central to all that you will do in Java. In Java there are no freestanding variables or functions. Everything must be encapsulated within a class. Further, every class in Java can trace back through its inheritance hierarchy and find itself a descendant of the `Object` class, similar to the way every Delphi object is derived from `TObject`. In order to understand Java classes, consider the following class definition:

```
class Employee {
    public String firstName;
    public String lastName;
    protected int age;
```

```
    private float salary;
    public boolean CanVote() {
        return age >= 21;
    }
    public boolean CanDrink(int legalAge) {
        return age >= legalAge;
    }
}
```

You'll notice from the definition of `Employee` that Java classes support the familiar concepts of `private`, `protected`, and `public` members. However, in Java, members are not grouped into `private`, `public`, or `protected` sections as they are in Delphi. In the `Employee` class, each member has its access control modifier specified right with the type and name of the member. Although you may consider this a little more typing, it definitely makes the code more readable, and therefore easier to maintain, because you don't have to read backwards through a file to find out if a class member is accessible.

Each of the familiar `private`, `protected`, and `public` access control modifiers has the same meaning in Java that it has in Delphi. Because Java does not have a concept analogous to Delphi's Visual Component Library (VCL), there is no `published` access control modifier in Java. However, Java does have a fourth level of access control that is used as the default. If no access control modifier is specified for a member, that member is accessible throughout the package in which it is defined, but nowhere else.

A Java package is similar to a Delphi unit but without the structure of interface, implementation, and initialization sections. Java code is shared at the package level, and a package contains the definitions and source code implementations of one or more classes.

Member Methods

Returning to the definition of the `Employee` class, you can also see that both the `CanVote` and `CanDrink` methods were written directly in the class definition. This is different from Delphi where the method prototype is given in the interface section, and the code for the method is actually written in the implementation section. The Java approach of combining a method's interface and its implementation simplifies maintenance because there is no need to duplicate method prototypes between implementation and interface sections.

Setting Default Values

It's always the little things that make a big difference. One little thing that makes a tremendous convenience improvement in Java over Delphi is the ability to set a default value for a member variable at the time it is declared. For example, consider the following definition of the `Employee` class:

```
class Employee {
    ...
    protected int age = 21;
    ...
}
```

In this example, the member variable age is declared and is given a default value of 21. In Delphi, this would have been done in the constructor. There are two advantages to setting a default value at the point where the variable is declared:

■ The code becomes more readable because the default value cannot be missed when reading the code.

■ If the class uses more than one constructor that would have set the variable to its default, these constructors are simplified by not having to set the default value.

Static Members

In addition to class methods and variables that are associated with each instance of a class, a Java class can contain members that are associated with the class itself. These are known as static members and are identified with the static keyword, as follows:

```
class Employee {
    ...
    static double maxSalary = 1000000D;
    ...
}
```

In this example, the member variable maxSalary will exist once in the entire program, as opposed to once per instance of the class. Additionally, maxSalary has been set to an initial value of $1000000.

Constructors and Destructors

Each Java class you define may include one or more constructors. In Delphi, the constructor for a class is named Create and is identified by the constructor keyword, as follows:

```
constructor Create(Owner: TComponent); override;
```

In Java, a constructor is given the same name as the class. It is also not necessary to specify constructor and override as is done in Delphi. This can be seen in the following example:

```
class Employee {
    public String firstName;
    public String lastName;
    protected int age;
    private float salary;
    public Employee(String fName, String lName) {
        firstName = fName;
        lastName = lName;
    }
```

```
    public boolean CanVote() {
        return age >= 21;
    }
    public boolean CanDrink(int legalAge) {
        return age >= legalAge;
    }
}
```

In this example, the constructor is named `Employee` and is passed two `String` parameters—one for the employee's first name and one for his last name.

In Delphi, each class can have a destructor named `Destroy`. You call `Destroy` when you are done with an object and want to free memory or any other resources the instance allocated. Because Java includes a garbage collection feature for the automatic release of unreferenced memory, the role of destructors is much smaller than it is in Delphi. In Delphi, a destructor is necessary so that it can free any memory allocated by the object. Because of Java's automatic memory management, destructors are no longer needed to perform this job.

For these reasons, Java classes do not include Delphi-style destructors. Instead, each Java class can include a `finalize` method that can be used to perform any object cleanup. The `finalize` method is declared in the `Object` class, but because `Object` is the ultimate base class of all Java classes, `finalize` is available to every Java class. There is one danger, however, to consider when using `finalize`. It is possible for a Java program to terminate without this method being invoked on every object. If a program terminates with objects that are still referenced, the garbage collection process will never be used to release those objects, and `finalize` will never be called.

Inheritance

Inheritance in Java is indicated by the use of the `extends` keyword, as shown in the following example:

```
public class Employee extends Person {
    // member methods and variables
}
```

This is the equivalent of the Delphi statement `Employee = class(Person)`. If a class is derived directly from `Object`, then the `extends` keyword is optional. The following two class declarations are equivalent:

```
public class Person extends Object {
    // member methods and variables
}

public class Person {
    // member methods and variables
}
```

Where Delphi uses `self` to allow an object to reference itself, Java uses `this` for the same purpose. Similarly, Delphi uses `inherited` to reference the immediate superclass of an object, but

Java uses super. The use of super is frequently seen in the constructor of a subclass, as shown in the following:

```java
public class Person {
    String firstName;
    String lastName;
    Person() {}
    Person(String fName, String lName) {
        firstName = fName;
        lastName = lName;
    }
}

public class Employee extends Person {
    float salary;
    Employee(float sal, String fName, String lName) {
        super(fName, lName);
        salary = sal;
    }
}
```

In this example, the Person class includes a constructor that is passed a first name and a last name. The Employee class is derived from Person and includes a constructor that is passed salary, first name, and last name. The constructor for Employee first uses super to invoke the constructor for Person and then sets the internal salary member.

Abstract Methods and Classes

Exactly like Delphi, Java supports the declaration of abstract methods. Additionally, Java takes this a step further and introduces the concept of an abstract class. Instances of Java abstract classes cannot be created with new. Abstract members and classes are identified by the use of the abstract keyword, as shown in the following:

```java
abstract class Species {
    ...
    abstract void GiveBirth();
    ...
}
```

A class is considered abstract if it has one or more methods that are abstract. In the case of the Species class, the method GiveBirth is specified as abstract because some species have live births and others lay eggs. Because the method is abstract, no method body is given.

Interfaces and Multiple Inheritance

If you design a class that is entirely abstract, then that class is what Java refers to as an *interface*. A Java interface is similar to a class in that it defines a new type that contains both methods and variables. However, because an interface is completely abstract, its methods are not implemented within the interface. Instead, classes that are derived from an interface implement the methods of the interface.

An interface is declared in the same manner as a class except that instead of `class`, the keyword `interface` is used. For example, the following code will declare an interface named `Clock`:

```
interface Clock {
    public String GetTime(int hour);
}
```

To derive a class from an interface, use the keyword `implements`, similar to the way `extends` is used when a class is derived from another class. To derive the classes `Cuckoo` and `Watch` from the `Clock` interface, you would do the following:

```
class Cuckoo implements Clock  {
    public String GetTime(int hour) {
        StringBuffer str = new StringBuffer();
        int i = 0;
        while(i < hour) {
            str.append("Cuckoo ");
            i++;
        }
        return str.toString();
    }
}

class Watch implements Clock  {
    public String GetTime(int hour) {
        return new String("It is " + hour + ":00");
    }
}
```

Java, like Delphi, does not support multiple class inheritance. In other words, a class may have only one immediate superclass because only a single class name can follow `extends` in a Java class declaration. Fortunately, class inheritance and interface inheritance can be combined when deriving a new Java class, and a subclass can implement more than one interface. For example, you can do the following:

```
class MySubClass extends MySuperClass implements FirstInterface,
        SecondInterface {
    // class implementation
}
```

Other Changes

There are a number of additional differences between Java and Delphi beyond those already mentioned in this chapter. This section will briefly describe some additional differences.

Command-Line Arguments

In Delphi, the program's command-line arguments are accessed through the functions `ParamCount` and `ParamStr`. These functions can be used to retrieve the number of command-line arguments and the text of each argument, respectively. The value returned by `ParamCount` will always be at least 1 because the first argument on the command line to a Delphi program is the name of the program. In a Java application, the command-line arguments are based in an array of String objects. The signature for main is as follows:

```
public static void main(String args[]);
```

Each component of the array args is one of the command-line arguments. A difference between Delphi and Java is that the program name is not passed to the program as the first command-line argument in Java. Consider two programs that are invoked in the following manner:

For Delphi: program 100 200

For Java: java program 100 200

The command lines of these two programs will be interpreted by Delphi and Java, as shown in Table 5.6.

Table 5.6. Command-line arguments in Delphi and Java.

Argument	Delphi	Java
program	ParamStr(0)	(none)
100	ParamStr(1)	args[0]
200	ParamStr(2)	args[1]

Parentheses Are Required

Delphi allows you to use a shorthand notation and invoke a procedure or function that received no parameters by leaving off the parentheses. For example, in Delphi you can invoke a parameterless procedure as myFunc. In Java, however, the parentheses are required and you need to use myFunc().

The Java for Statement

Java shows its C++ influence with its for statement. Fortunately, the C++ and now Java for statements are very powerful and easy to use. The first line of a for loop allows you to specify a starting value for a loop counter, specify the test condition that will exit the loop, and indicate how the loop counter should be incremented after each pass through the loop. The syntax of a Java for statement is as follows:

```
for (initialization; testExpression; incremement)
    statement
```

For example, a sample `for` loop may appear as follows:

```
int count;
for (count=0; count<100; count++)
    System.out.println("Count = " + count);
```

In this example, the initialization statement of the `for` loop sets count to 0. The test expression, count < 100 indicates that the loop should continue as long as count is less than 100. Finally, the increment statement increments the value of count by one. As long as the test expression is true, the statement enclosed in the loop will be executed.

`goto`, `break`, **and** `continue`

You probably won't shed any tears, but the `goto` statement is not part of Java. On the other hand, it is still part of the reserved word list, so it may come back at any time. Java does replace `goto`, however, with the ability to use `break` and `continue` with labels. You can still use `break` and `continue` as you are used to in Delphi, but you can now use them to pass control flow in other ways. For example, consider the following code:

```
int line=1;

outsideLoop:
for(int out=0; out<3; out++) {
    for(int inner=0;inner < 5; inner++) {
        if (foo(inner) < 10))
            break outsideLoop;
        else if (foo(inner) > 100)
            continue outsideLoop;
    }
}
```

In this example, if the `foo` method returns a value less than 10, the code `break outsideLoop` will execute. A normal `break` here would break out of the inner loop. However, because this is a named `break` statement, it will break out of the named outer loop. This example also demonstrates the use of `continue` with a label.

Summary

This chapter covered quite a lot of territory. Building on your background in Delphi, you learned how Java differs from Delphi in regards to data types, operators, memory management, and classes. You've been introduced to some new operators that don't exist in Delphi, and you've learned how to use Java to create new classes. You learned that Java, like Delphi, supports only single class inheritance, but that Java's introduction of interfaces takes Java well beyond Delphi in supporting multiple interface inheritance. Finally, you learned that by removing pointers and incorporating automatic memory management in the form of garbage collection, Java programming is greatly simplified.

6

Java for Visual Basic Programmers

by Bryan Morgan

At first glance, the Java language may seem entirely foreign to Visual Basic programmers, but both languages share a number of features. This chapter is provided as a resource for experienced Visual Basic programmers who are interested in learning to develop applications using Java. After a short period of time, Visual Basic developers will see that the language provides them with a new wealth of information and tools that were previously unavailable to them. However, there are tradeoffs (as there always are!). Special attention will be paid to major differences between Java and Visual Basic in order to provide the Visual Basic developer with the skills needed to begin programming in Java.

Visual Basic versus Java, or Object-Based versus Object-Oriented

To compare these two powerful languages, we must first make a decision: what should we look at first? Obviously, the syntax of every programming language is completely different. However, because these two languages implement different methodologies, a study of syntax will be delayed until later on in the chapter.

The argument can be made that most modern programming languages can be separated into several major groups. These range from object-oriented to what will be called "object-based" to standard procedural languages. Figure 6.1 shows some popular languages and which groups they roughly conform to.

FIGURE 6.1.
Scale of modern programming languages.

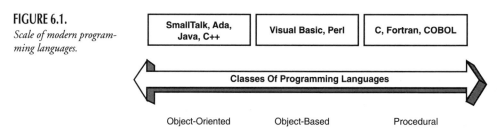

Because syntax (where to put semicolons, and so on) is a relatively minor issue, the initial emphasis will be placed on understanding exactly what the term "object-oriented" means.

Object-oriented languages enable the programmer to create programming objects that can be reused within a single application or across multiple applications. Java refers to these objects as a *class*. Classes are user-defined data types that contain both data and methods. Listing 6.1 shows a sample pseudo-class named Auto.

Listing 6.1. A sample Java class named `Auto`.

```
class Auto
{
    int Number_Of_Doors;
    int Number_Of_Seats;
    boolean Radio;
    int    Year;
    String  Model;
    float GetGasMileage();
    void Accelerate();
    void Stop();
}
```

As you can see, this class `Auto` contains data (`Number_Of_Doors`, `Number_Of_Seats`, `Radio`, and `Year`) as well as methods (`GetGasMileage`, `Accelerate`, and `Stop`). Some people like to think of these as "nouns" and "verbs." Visual Basic enables the programmer to create objects that mix data and member functions. For example, by building a form with a text field and a button on it, the programmer has just built an object. This object can be referenced by other objects and reused across multiple applications. This is why Visual Basic is said to be object-based and not procedural. So, what does it take to qualify as object-oriented?

For a language to be object-oriented, it is generally accepted that it should have several primary features:

- ■ Encapsulation
- ■ Inheritance
- ■ Polymorphism

Encapsulation

Encapsulation is the process of encapsulating data and operations within a manageable interface. The class `Auto` meets this description fully. If a programmer wanted to instantiate (create) a new `Auto` for use in his program, he would simply add a member variable of type `Auto`. Object-oriented languages also allow the class creator to limit access to data and operations within the class. Some data and operations within each class are considered *private* or "for internal use only." This allows the interface of that class to be controlled for outside use.

Inheritance

Inheritance is the process of deriving new objects from existing objects. This allows the class developer to reuse code that has already been created for the parent (or base) class. Here object-based and object-oriented languages begin to differ. In Visual Basic, for example, once an "object" within the program is created, the programmer is severely limited if he would like to inherit from it. However, in Java we can extend classes as much as necessary. Unlike C++, however, Java will only allow a class to have one parent. This is known as "single inheritance." As an example, the class `Truck` shown in Listing 6.2 demonstrates inheritance in Java.

Listing 6.2. The `Truck` class inherits from `Auto`.

```
class Truck extends Auto
{
    boolean Four_Wheel_Drive;
    Color   color;
}
```

This code means that class `Truck` was designed to be a "child" of class `Auto`. Therefore, it will inherit all of the public data and methods that exist in the `Auto` class.

Polymorphism

Polymorphism is defined as "the occurrence of different forms, stages, or types in individual organisms or in organisms of the same species." This essentially means that although the `Truck` class now inherited all of the data and methods from `Auto`, it is free to reimplement them as it chooses. You could extend `Truck` as shown in Listing 6.3.

Listing 6.3. Adding to the `Truck` class.

```
class Truck extends Auto
{
    boolean Four_Wheel_Drive;
    Color   color;
    void Accelerate();
}
```

The purpose of the `Accelerate` function in the `Truck` class might be different (for instance, the acceleration speed might be affected if `Four_Wheel_Drive` is on). Therefore, any time that any other class or method calls the `Truck.Accelerate` method, the `Truck`'s `Accelerate` method will be called, *not* `Auto`'s. (This is true even if class `Auto`'s method `GetGasMileage()` called `Accelerate()`.)

Comparing ActiveX to Java Classes

When Microsoft introduced the VBX for use within the Visual Basic programming environment, it created an entire industry of component manufacturers. The VBX standard was straightforward and allowed developers to implement encapsulation of distributable programming tools.

Each VBX/OCX implements its own properties and methods and allows the programmer to trap events. Although OCXs (now called ActiveX controls) are implemented using Microsoft OLE, these controls still appear to the developer as a set of properties, methods, and events encapsulated in one single programming object.

A Java class allows developers some advantages over an ActiveX control. Ignoring for the moment various features built into the language such as threading and exception handling, Java classes fully support inheritance and polymorphism. How important is this? Currently, hundreds of Java class source files are freely available on the World Wide Web. This list grows daily, and it is growing quickly. Java developers envision a world where Java class clearinghouses are available to quickly download classes that can be extended by individual developers. In addition to this, various third-party Java class libraries are already appearing for the support of various operations such as multimedia, networking, and database access. All of this code is completely reusable and extensible (not to mention platform-independent!).

When a Java class is downloaded from a Web server, it is able to communicate freely with the server that it was downloaded from. This is extremely useful for database access, running CGI scripts, or retrieving additional classes. ActiveX controls, meanwhile, are allowed to communicate with any machine containing Distributed Component Object Model (DCOM) objects. ActiveX controls are also basically allowed full access to the user's system, unlike Java applets, which are restricted.

ActiveX controls do have some distinct advantages, however. Any ActiveX container application can communicate with and display an ActiveX control within its window. This means that Web browsers that are ActiveX-enabled (such as Microsoft Internet Explorer 3.0) will be able to display Excel spreadsheets directly on an HTML page. ActiveX controls uploaded to a user's Web browser can also communicate with any application that supports COM (Component Object Model) interfaces.

Currently, it appears that Microsoft intends to wrap Java classes with an ActiveX layer to allow Java developers to take advantage of the features mentioned here. This will be done through the magic of the Microsoft Windows Virtual Machine for Java and the underlying Component Object Model.

Understanding Java Program Flow

One of the biggest hurdles for non-object-oriented developers to clear is simply understanding exactly what is going on within an object-oriented application. At times, it appears that methods are being called by some invisible force within your computer. GUI environments such as Windows, Macintosh, and Motif just add to this apparent state of confusion because operating system events are constantly being funneled to the application responsible for trapping those events.

The Applet Life Cycle

Think about what is actually required to create a simple Visual Basic form. The form is first created, and any controls that need to be added to it are done at this time. By default, this form is automatically created and shown when the application is run. How does this happen? As you might expect, there is a lot more going on in the background than meets the eye.

The first thing you must understand is how applications run in multitasking operating environments. The Windows environment continually handles messages from a variety of hardware and software sources. It then in turn "forwards" these messages on to each application that is currently "listening." Your application actually has a single entry point that Windows first calls. The basic operations that go on inside this entry point look something like this (please pardon the extreme pseudo-code!):

```
Entry Point HEY_WINDOWS!(int MESSAGE)
{
/* Process all of the messages your application needs */
if MESSAGE = FORM_CREATE then...
else if MESSAGE = FORM_SHOW then...
else if MESSAGE = FORM_DESTROY then...
...
}
```

As you can see, Visual Basic provides an easy-to-use GUI over the top of these low-level events. By clicking on a form's events screen, you will see a simple column of events that the Visual Basic designers chose for your form to handle. Experienced Visual Basic programmers know that you can actually process any Windows event you choose to handle, but this set of events is the most commonly used.

C++, Delphi, and Visual Basic programs all use this message-passing system in the exact same ways. What is interesting about all three of these is the way that the respective languages allow designers to hide implementation details from application developers. The Java language is an extension of this methodology. However, instead of the Windows operating system handling messages and passing them directly to a Visual Basic application, programmers in Java receive their GUI messages from something called the Advanced Windowing Toolkit (AWT). For more detailed information on what is contained in the AWT, see Chapters 7, "Developing Java Applets," 8, "Developing Java Applications," and 28, "Package `java.awt`." The AWT is a set of Java classes that use data and methods to encapsulate common GUI functionality.

Java applets and applications inherit from the AWT directly. Each Java applet can implement what are known as *lifecycle methods* to control the starting, stopping, and ending of the applet's "life."

The flow of a Java application can best be understood by stepping through one line by line. Listing 6.4 shows the entire contents of the MouseTrack sample application provided with the JDK. Figure 6.2 shows this applet running within the Netscape Web Browser. MouseTrack notifies the player if the mouse-click missed the square, and plays a tune if the player was successful. As can be seen in the following short amount of code, there is quite a bit of work being done here, including screen drawing, mouse-click handling, and the playing of sound files.

FIGURE 6.2.

The MouseTrack application.

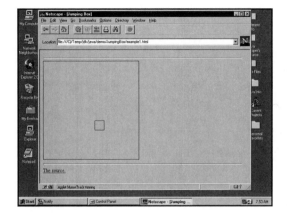

Listing 6.4. The JDK sample application MouseTrack.

```
1:  import java.awt.Graphics;
2:  import java.lang.Math;
3:
4:  public class MouseTrack extends java.applet.Applet {
5:
6:      int mx, my;
7:      int onaroll;
8:
9:      public void init() {
10:         onaroll = 0;
11:         resize(500, 500);
12:     }
13:
14:     public void paint(Graphics g) {
15:         g.drawRect(0, 0, size().width - 1, size().height - 1);
16:         mx = (int)(Math.random()*1000) % (size().width -
➡ (size().width/10));
17:         my = (int)(Math.random()*1000) % (size().height -
➡ (size().height/10));
18:         g.drawRect(mx, my, (size().width/10) - 1, (size().height/10) - 1);
19:     }
20:
21:     /*
22:      * Mouse methods
23:      */
24:     public boolean mouseDown(java.awt.Event evt, int x, int y) {
25:         requestFocus();
26:         if((mx < x && x < mx+size().width/10-1) &&
➡ (my < y && y < my+size().height/10-1)) {
27:             if(onaroll > 0) {
28:                 switch(onaroll%4) {
```

continues

Listing 6.4. continued

```
29:                 case 0:
30:                     play(getCodeBase(), "sounds/tiptoe.thru.the.tulips.au");
31:                     break;
32:                 case 1:
33:                     play(getCodeBase(), "sounds/danger,danger...!.au");
34:                     break;
35:                 case 2:
36:                     play(getCodeBase(), "sounds/adapt-or-die.au");
37:                     break;
38:                 case 3:
39:                     play(getCodeBase(), "sounds/cannot.be.completed.au");
40:                     break;
41:                 }
42:                 onaroll++;
43:                 if(onaroll > 5)
44:                     getAppletContext().showStatus("You're on your way to
➥ THE HALL OF FAME:" + onaroll + "Hits!");
45:                 else
46:                     getAppletContext().showStatus("YOU'RE ON A ROLL:"
➥ + onaroll + "Hits!");
47:                 }
48:                 else {
49:                     getAppletContext().showStatus("HIT IT AGAIN! AGAIN!");
50:                     play(getCodeBase(), "sounds/that.hurts.au");
51:                     onaroll = 1;
52:                 }
53:             }
54:             else {
55:                 getAppletContext().showStatus
➥ ("You hit nothing at (" + x + ", " + y + "), exactly");
56:                 play(getCodeBase(), "sounds/thin.bell.au");
57:                 onaroll = 0;
58:             }
59:             repaint();
60:             return true;
61:     }
62:
63:     public boolean mouseMove(java.awt.Event evt, int x, int y) {
64:         if((x % 3 == 0) && (y % 3 == 0))
65:                 repaint();
66:         return true;
67:     }
68:
69:     public void mouseEnter() {
70:         repaint();
71:     }
72:
73:     public void mouseExit() {
74:         onaroll = 0;
75:         repaint();
76:     }
77:
78:     /**
79:      * Focus methods
80:      */
81:     public void keyDown(int key) {
```

```
82:          requestFocus();
83:          onaroll = 0;
84:          play(getCodeBase(), "sounds/ip.au");
85:      }
86: }
```

As can be seen by examining the code listing for this applet, there is quite a bit of work going on here. Events are being trapped, multimedia work is being done, and objects are being painted on the screen. Examining each section of code should allow the reader to gain an appreciation for the power of the Java language.

In lines 1 and 2, MouseTrack imports the AWT's Graphics class and a Math class for calculation purposes. This operation is never done in Visual Basic because inheritance is not allowed. In other words, when an object is declared as type Form, the Visual Basic compiler automatically knows what code to go grab in order to compile. In an object-oriented system, MouseTrack could be the child of any number of classes. However, because it is an applet, it must inherit directly, or indirectly, from Applet.

In line 4, MouseTrack is declared to inherit from the java.applet.Applet class. By default, this identifies this class as the main class of this application.

In lines 6 and 7, member variables are declared. These variables are visible to everything inside the class. In addition, any other application that created a MouseTrack class within it could have access to these variables.

In line 9, the init() method is declared. By inheriting from the Applet class, each applet inherits four "life-cycle" functions: init(), start(), stop(), and destroy(). Init() is called once after an applet is initially loaded.

In lines 10 and 11, the applet is initialized. Note the resize() member call. Don't be confused just because this method isn't declared within this class. The Resize method is inherited from the Applet class.

In line 14, there is another "magic" method call. Where is this coming from? Notice that nowhere in this entire class is the paint() method actually invoked. However, the repaint() method is called in several situations. The paint() method is called whenever the AWT thinks the window needs to be redrawn, or when a repaint() is requested.

Lines 15 through 18 are used to draw the square at random locations on the screen. Note the use of the Math.random() method here. This is why the java.lang.Math class was imported on line 2.

In line 24, the mouseDown method is called whenever the AWT detects a mouse click over this applet's screen area.

In line 25, the requestFocus() method is called. This method is equivalent to Visual Basic's SetFocus().

In lines 26 through 42, some checks are done to determine whether the user successfully clicked inside the square. What is especially interesting is the `play()` call in lines 30, 33, 36, and 39. At first glance, this call simply plays a sound file depending on the frequency of the user's hits. However, note the call `getCodeBase()`. This instructs the play function to retrieve the sound file from the applet's base location. In other words, if the applet was retrieved from a Web server in Tokyo, play the sound file located there. In one function call, you have reached across the world, retrieved a sound file, and played it on a user's computer…platform notwithstanding. This type of functionality would have been unimaginable a couple of years ago, but such is the pace of change.

In lines 43 through 61, depending on the user's hit count, several messages are displayed. The `showStatus()` method will print the message in the appletContext's status window. With most Web browsers, this message will be displayed in the lower-left corner status window (see Figure 6.2 where the text "Applet MouseTrack running" is displayed).

In line 63, `mouseMove()` is called whenever a `MouseMove` message is generated.

In lines 64 through 66, the `mouseMove()` method forces a repaint every three units (probably pixels). By examining the contents of the `paint()` method, you can see that this will redraw the square on the screen.

In line 69, the `mouseEnter()` method is called whenever the mouse cursor enters the screen area of this applet. This function also forces a repaint.

In line 73, the `mouseExit()` method is called whenever the mouse leaves the screen area of the applet. This function will force a repaint and reset the user's score.

In lines 81 through 86, the `keyDown()` method is called whenever any key is hit. The applet will request focus and, once again, a sound will be played to notify the user.

This applet may be much simpler than a typical Visual Basic form, but it provides some useful illustrations. Hopefully, the Visual Basic developer will see that the overall development goal remains the same. GUI events still need to be handled, and many of the user interface elements remain the same. Object-oriented programming is a skill that Visual Basic developers will need to acquire, but Windows application development skills do provide valuable insight into the Java AWT.

Language Features and Syntax

It is now time to compare basic features of the Java language versus features of the Visual Basic language. The first item to be examined is data types.

Data Types

Java contains a small set of basic language types. (Ignore for now the fact that each new object declared in Java is a new "temporary" data type.) Here are the types:

boolean—Can be true or false

byte—8-bit signed quantity

short—16-bit signed quantity

int—32-bit signed quantity

float—32-bit floating-point value

double—64-bit floating-point value

long—64-bit signed quantity

char—16-bit Unicode character

Listed next are the Visual Basic basic data types. Next to each VB data type is the equivalent (if any) Java data type:

Integer—16-bit signed quantity; equivalent to short.

Long—32-bit signed quantity; equivalent to int.

Single—32-bit floating-point value; equivalent to float.

Double—64-bit floating-point value; equivalent to double.

Currency—64-bit floating-point value limited to four decimal places; there is no Java equivalent, although a Currency class could be defined (and undoubtedly will be with a full set of properties and methods).

String—8-bit character; although the Java char type appears to be equivalent, caution should be used here. Note that the Java char type is actually a Unicode character, whereas the Visual Basic String makes use of the ASCII characters. There are Java functions that can be used to convert Unicode characters to their ASCII values, and vice versa.

Byte—8-bit unsigned quantity; no Java equivalent.

Boolean—16-bit value used to store True or False; equivalent to boolean.

Date—64-bit value; Visual Basic automatically converts this number to represent a date between January 1, 100 and December 31, 9999. There is no Java basic type equivalent, although as with Currency, it would be relatively easy to build a date class.

Object—32-bit Object reference value; no Java equivalent, unless the class keyword is considered.

Variant—16 bytes (8 bits/byte) plus 1 byte for each character; no Java equivalent.

Declaring Variables

Variables are declared in Visual Basic using the `dim` keyword. To declare an `Integer` variable within a function, the following syntax is used:

```
dim x As Integer
```

Java has no keyword that designates a variable being defined. Instead, the following syntax is used:

```
<data type> <variable_name>;
```

To repeat this example, an integer variable would be declared in Java as follows (keep in mind that Java is case sensitive!):

```
int x;
```

What is completely different about Java, however, is the fact that there are no global variables. Every variable and method in Java must be declared inside some class. This forces everything to be stored and referenced as an object, thus enforcing the object-oriented paradigm.

Any object in Java can be stored as an array of that object. This can be done in three steps:

1. Declaring the array of objects using the syntax `<data type> <variable_name>[]`;
   Example: `int group[];`
2. Creating a new array object. Although the preceding statement declared a new array object, it must actually be initialized in memory using the `new` operator:
   `Int[] group = new int[50];`
3. Filling the array with values. This can be done using standard array notation:
   `Group[15] = 304;`

Programming Constructs

All modern programming languages contain programming constructs such as `for` and `while` loops and `if...then` branches. Visual Basic and Java are no exception. This section provides a comparison of the primary differences between the control structures of the two languages.

Visual Basic supports the following decision structures:

```
If...Then
```

```
If...Then...Else
```

```
Select Case
```

The If...Then Structure

The syntax for producing a Visual Basic If...Then structure is the following:

For a single-line statement:

```
If condition Then statement
```

For multiple statements:

```
If condition Then
  statements
End If
```

To add an additional Else block to the preceding structure, the syntax looks like this:

```
If condition1 Then
  [statementblock1]
[ElseIf condition2 Then
  [statementblock2]]...
[Else
  [statementblock3]]
End If
```

Java greatly simplifies this construct with the following syntax:

```
if condition1 {
  [statementblock1]
}
else if condition2 {
  [statementblock2]
}
else {
  [statementblock3]
}
```

The Select Case (or switch) Structure

To provide an alternative to many multiple If...Then structures, most languages provide a mechanism of selectively executing blocks of code depending on the value of some variable.

In Visual Basic, you can do this by creating a Select Case structure. Here's the syntax:

```
Select Case testexpression
  [Case expressionlist1
    [statementblock1]
  [Case expressionlist2
    [statementblock2]
  .
  .
  .
  [Case Else
    [statementblockn]
End Select
```

In Java, this construct is known as a `switch` statement (similar to C/C++). The `testexpression` must be a `byte`, `char`, `short`, or `int`. Its syntax is just like C's:

```
switch (testexpression) {
  [case expressionlist1:]
    [statementblock1]
   break;
  [case expressionlist2:]
    [statementblock2]
   break;
   .
   .

   .
  default:
    [statementblockn]
   break;
}
```

The for Loop

For loops are used to execute a group of statements a set number of times. Both Visual Basic and Java provide a `for` loop, but there are differences between the two. In Visual Basic, the `for` loop has the following properties:

```
For counter = start To end [Step increment]
   statements
Next [counter]
```

Visual Basic allows the programmer to set the start and ending value of the variable `counter` as well as set the `Step` increment. Here is the Java `for` loop:

```
for (counter = start; booleanexpression; expression) {
   statements
}
```

There are several subtle differences between the Java `for` loop and that of Visual Basic. The Java `for` loop allows the programmer to provide an expression as opposed to the Visual Basic increment. This expression could be a call to a method or, as in VB, the programmer could simply increment or decrement a value. In addition to that, Java allows a variable to be declared in the `for` loop. (See Listing 6.5 for an example.)

Listing 6.5. Example of variable initialization in a Java for loop.

```
for (int counter = 1; counter < 99; counter ++) {
    /* statements */
}
```

The variable declared in the `for` loop cannot be used outside of that loop, however. (This is yet another example of a potential error-causing language feature that the Java designers have removed!)

The while and do...while Loops

Visual Basic and Java provide nearly identical while and do...while loops. The do loop is used to execute a group of statements an unknown amount of times (until the condition returns true). The do...while loop executes the group of statements at least once before testing the condition. The syntactical differences will be shown here.

In Visual Basic:

```
Do While condition
  statements
Loop

Do
  statements
Loop While condition
```

In Java:

```
while (condition) {
  statements
}

do {
  statements
} while (condition);
```

Language Features Missing from Visual Basic

There is some similarity between Visual Basic and Java (particularly in the area of GUI programming), but there are some language features in Java that just are not available using Visual Basic. All of these topics will be discussed in greater detail later in this book; however, they will be touched on now so that the Visual Basic programmer is aware of the differences.

Threads

32-bit Windows developers are perhaps familiar with the concept of multithreaded programming. A thread is a single self-contained set of states of execution of a program. A multithreaded environment (or language) allows multiple threads to run simultaneously (in parallel). In other words, threads allow applications to execute simultaneous operations at the same time. This is most often seen in applications where the display is being updated with some type of graphics while the application is performing some type of computation in the background. (See the JDK's Animator example.) Java applets and applications that take advantage of threading can be identified easily because they implement the Runnable interface. Implementing the Runnable interface can be thought of as opening a window into Java's threading capabilities.

It should be noted that on single-processor machines, both threads are not actually executing concurrently. The execution of the threads will switch between the two at regular intervals. Using a machine with multiple processors, it is possible to split the threads off and run them at the same time. This type of operation is operating-system dependent.

Networking

The `java.net` package (see Chapters 26, "Network-Aware Programming," and 33, "Package `java.net`") provides the Java programmer with a full complement of networking capabilities using both HTTP (the World Wide Web protocol) and sockets. Sockets were originally implemented for UNIX. They allow the programmer to open a pipe to another machine (or to their own machine, if so desired) for passing data back and forth. Entire books have been written on socket programming, so we won't go into much detail here. Suffice it to say, however, that the Java networking classes are platform-independent and will continue to support open, standards-based protocols. These classes also allow Java applets to do things like call Web pages up in a browser and stream data to and from the client computer over the Internet.

Exception Handling

The ability to handle application exceptions is a powerful feature that is common to many languages including C++, Ada, and Object Pascal. An exception is any type of condition that prevents a program from continuing in its current state. Without exception handling, the program would either crash or exit at that point. Java allows this exception to be "caught" and handled appropriately. More information on exception handling can be found in Chapter 22, "Exception Handling."

Summary

Obviously, the overall programming paradigm for Java is entirely new. A vision of a highly networked, message-handling programming language is (even for software!) a relatively new idea. Therefore, the idea of applets and networking built into the core language is something new for developers of all languages, not just Visual Basic. Visual Basic developers should not look at Java as some new technology that is leaving them behind. Because the language is so new (and its potential unrealized), Visual Basic developers will undoubtedly soon find tools that allow these two languages to interact. James Gosling, creator of Java and a Sun Microsystems vice-president, has even mentioned the possibility of a Java Virtual Machine that understands the Visual Basic language. Basically, it is important that all software developers understand what Java is and how it could affect their current day-to-day work.

7

Developing Java Applets

by Bryan Morgan

This chapter focuses on the development of a type of Java program known as an *applet.* Chapter 8, "Developing Java Applications," discusses the development of Java *applications.* Although there are some inherent differences between an applet and an application, many beginning developers are unaware of these differences. After explaining exactly what an applet is, this chapter will present the Java applet in more detail. By the end of the chapter, the Java developer should have a good knowledge of the Java applet security model, the Java applet life cycle, and basic applet capabilities such as multithreading and I/O.

What Is an Applet?

Java applets are actually compiled Java class files that are run on a page within a Web browser. Because the Web browser supplies the framework for retrieving and loading an applet and also supplies the main window holding the applet, Java applets are somewhat simpler than a true Java application. A Java application does not require any additional software, such as a Web browser, other than the typical Java runtime files included in the Java Developer's Kit. Java applications are designed to be run in stand-alone mode on a client machine and therefore can be thought of as a known entity. Java applets, meanwhile, can be loaded from anywhere on the Internet, and therefore are subject to severe security restrictions. These security restrictions will be discussed in greater detail later on in this chapter.

Almost every person's first exposure to Java was in the form of a Java applet running within a Web page. Java applets currently are being used for advertising purposes because they provide the capability to include simple animation and sound in a Web advertisement. Many client/server developers currently are looking at the company intranet as an excellent platform on which to finally deliver true cross-platform corporate applications. Because of this, Java applets are certain to quickly progress from "neat" status to true business use status.

What Is Required to Run an Applet?

Java applets are typically run within a Web browser. As of July 1996, most of the popular Web browsers on the market support embedded Java applets in HTML pages. These browsers include:

■ Sun HotJava 1.0

■ Netscape Navigator 2.0 (or greater)

■ Microsoft Internet Explorer 3.0

■ Oracle PowerBrowser 1.5

Of course, the *Applet Viewer* tool included with the Java Developer's Kit can be used to test and run Java applets as well. However, it will not be included on all client machines; therefore, it is not really an option to applet developers. Many beginning Java developers wonder how an applet can run within a browser if the Java runtime libraries are not installed on the client system. To run a simple Java applet, as explained in Chapter 2, "Installing Java," it was first necessary to download the JDK from the JavaSoft Web site. After installing the JDK on the system, the reader could then run any sample Java applet included with the JDK. However, someone installing the Netscape Navigator, for instance, has not downloaded the JDK, right? In fact, they partially have. Take a look at the actual Navigator installation to find out what was actually placed on your system.

After installing Navigator 3.0 in the `C:\Program Files\Netscape\Navigator` directory, examine the contents of that directory under Windows 95. Under the `.\Program\java` directory, you will find a set of directories and files that look suspiciously like the JDK installation. This is how Web browsers are able to run Java applets. They basically install a customized version of the JDK in their runtime directories so that they can load Java applets and their own set of customized Java classes. This results in somewhat of a Catch-22 situation. Because Netscape, for instance, provides a customized version of the JDK, subtle changes in the underlying code could result in an applet running differently in the Navigator browser than, say, the Internet Explorer browser. Be sure to test completed Java applets in a wide variety of browsers on a variety of operating systems, if possible, in order to ensure that the applet you will be displaying to the world does what you think it should.

Capabilities and Limitations of Applets

Java applets obviously have many potential capabilities. Many things can be done using these applets that, until now, were impossible to implement on such a broad scale. Java applets can be used to build full-featured graphical user interfaces, communicate over the Internet to a host server, and even communicate with other applets on a form. All of this can be done in an operating-environment-neutral manner, which is what makes this such a great technology. For Java to be truly successful, however, the client security has to be completely assured. Because of this, security measures place some limitations on Java applets. By default, applets cannot communicate with any server other than the originating server. Applets also cannot read or write files to the local file system. The following section discusses the Java security model and focuses on how this applies to Java applets.

The growth of technologies such as Web-based client/server application development and electronic commerce has been severely limited by the lack of "industrial-strength" security. Because the underlying Internet was never designed to handle secure transactions (the Department of Defense has a separate net for this purpose), the entire infrastructure of the Internet was somewhat unprepared for the phenomenal growth of the World Wide Web over the last few years. The concept of applets (or related technologies such as software agents) has been discussed in academic circles for years, yet most theoreticians realized the security shortcomings of the current programming languages such as C and C++.

Programming languages that allow manipulation of pointers (memory addresses) allow programmers to overrun memory boundaries and find "trap doors" into unsuspecting users' systems. Operating systems such as UNIX have continually struggled to patch well-documented security holes. Because the designers of Java were well aware of these problems, security measures were designed into Java at nearly every layer. The Java language's lack of support for pointers also leads to simpler, easier-to-read code. (Many programming errors by C programmers can be traced to improper manipulation of pointers to memory.)

The basic security model for Java treats all Java applets and applications as unknown, unsecured objects running within a secure environment. What this means is that a clever developer can produce subversive code to his heart's content, but the underlying Java runtime environment is designed to trap any problems. When the media publicizes a Java security "bug," this generally means that a team of researchers isolated a security flaw in the underlying runtime environment that hackers could capitalize on. An example of an early Java bug allowed a Web server to track all Web sites a user visits after the Web server itself has been visited. Although Java applets will never be used in the near future to implement truly secret applications, the Java security model makes security exceedingly difficult to circumvent.

The Java designers handled security at three levels:

■ The *elimination of pointers* from the language eliminates an entire class of security problems. Programmers in C, for instance, can fake objects in memory because it is loosely typed and allows pointers.

■ The *bytecode verification* process forces uploaded Java applets to undergo a rigorous set of checks in order to run on the local system. In other words, this will foil "bad" users who decided to write a hostile compiler. Keep in mind that no matter what features are built into the language, a rogue compiler could still produce Java applets capable of circumventing the Java security model. Bytecode verification will be explained later in the chapter.

■ *Client-side precautions* add another layer of security. Most Web browsers (more on this later) preclude Java applets from doing file access or communicating with any computer on the Internet other than the computer that the applet was uploaded from. The Java class loader assists in this process.

Bytecode Verification

Language security features are simply not enough to prevent an applet from reformatting your hard drive or some other unspeakable act. (Keep in mind that file I/O is allowed and even provided using the JDK class libraries.) Features needed to be built into the entire runtime system to prevent specially compiled applets from invading remote systems. Java is an interpreted language. This means that actual memory management for the application is put off until runtime (it is not built into the compiled Java classes). This feature allows Java to run on many different platforms thanks to the installed Java Virtual Machine. However, it also allows the Java runtime engine to verify that the bytecodes being loaded are, in fact, good bytecodes. This is done using a part of the Virtual Machine known as the *verifier*. The verifier has the unenviable task of checking each bytecode before it is executed (interpreted) to make sure that it is not going to perform an illegal operation. After the bytecode has been verified, the applet is guaranteed to do the following:

■ Obey access restrictions such as public, protected, private, and friendly. No class will be allowed to access data that goes against these restrictions.

■ Never perform illegal data conversions. Because Java is a strongly typed language, automatic conversions from arrays to pointers, for instance, are not allowed.

■ Conform to all return, parameter, and argument types when calling methods.

■ Live within its allocated stack. An applet that overruns its memory will not be loaded.

The verification process checks many of the things that a good Java compiler will check, but it is important to recognize that the verification process takes place on the *client's* computer. Security on the server side is virtually meaningless to Internet clients because of the unknown nature of most servers.

Client-Side Precautions

The set of precautions enforced by the client Web browser (or other applet loader) is done by a part of the Java runtime engine known as the *class loader*. The class loader does what its name says: it loads classes.

> **NOTE**
>
> The class loader can vary from browser to browser. Security features in the HotJava Web browser allow the user to control security restrictions and even remove them altogether. The Netscape Navigator browser, however, offers no user-controlled security measures. Instead, applets are forced into a very rigid set of rules. Therefore, it is probably wise if applets are written to conform to the most restrictive case because then they will run on every user's computer.

Three possible worlds are recognized by the class loader:

■ The local system (highest level)

■ The local network within a firewall (middle level)

■ The Internet at large (lowest level)

The class loader implements defined rules that allow it to intelligently prevent an applet from wreaking havoc on your system. It does this by never allowing a class loaded from a lower level to replace a class existing on a higher level. The following example illustrates what this means.

An applet located on a Web server across the Internet imports the `java.awt.Button` class so that it can display a button on the screen. The developer on the remote machine changed some of the button's internal functionality but kept the class interface without changing anything. Fortunately for you (and unfortunately for the developer across the Internet), the `java.awt.Button` class is included with the Java Virtual Machine installed on your system. Therefore, when the applet is uploaded to your machine, the class loader will always retrieve your local `Button.class` file.

In addition to this, classes cannot call methods from other classes in other security levels unless those methods are explicitly declared to be public. This means that Java applets loaded from a remote machine cannot call file system I/O methods. If those methods were called, the class loader would catch the error, and the applet load would fail.

Java Class Loading Rules (`Example1.html`)

Although much of the information presented on Java has stated that applets cannot write to a local hard drive or connect to remote computers other than the originating host, this is in fact not necessarily correct. The HotJava Web browser allows users to configure these security restrictions (see Figure 7.1).

FIGURE 7.1.

The Java applet security screen in HotJava 1.0.

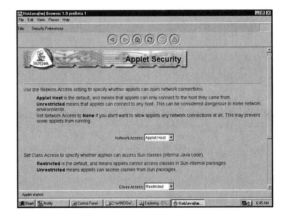

Figure 7.1 shows how the HotJava user can loosen or even drop all security restrictions so that applets can do whatever they want when uploaded to his or her machine. This may be useful in an intranet setting where machines are never connected directly to the Internet, but be very careful otherwise. Undoubtedly, devious applets will be written to do damage to unsuspecting systems. This is why the Netscape Navigator developers left configurable security features completely out of their product.

Are Java Applets Safe?

Java handles security at several different levels. The language is designed in a manner that removes many security holes because it does not allow pointer manipulation. The bytecode verifier is used to verify each uploaded Java class to ensure that it obeys all Java language rules. The class loader enforces security on another level by controlling applet operations at runtime. It is important to realize that the bytecode verifier and class loader both exist on the local system and are part of the Java Virtual Machine. Because these two components are critical to the success of the Java security model, the user must rely on these components to ensure that Java applets are secure. At the current time, Sun, Netscape, Microsoft, IBM, and others are all working on implementations of the Java Virtual Machine for a host of operating platforms. As the number of "third-party" virtual machines increases, it is critical that these virtual machines be verified by some independent source to ensure that they operate according to the JVM specification. Sun is currently working on a test suite to do just this. In short: Yes, the Java environment is safe and secure. Vendor-specific implementations, however, must be validated to ensure that they comply with the Java specifications.

Building a Java Applet

This section focuses on the construction of Java applets. The previous section discussed in some detail the process required to load an applet over the Internet to the local machine, and this section will explain what is necessary for the applet to actually run on that local machine.

Java applets are subclassed from the `Applet` class in the `java.applet` package.

> **NOTE**
>
> For more information on subclassing, see Chapter 3, "The Java Language." For more information on the `java.applet` package, see Chapter 27, "Package `java.applet`."

Each applet has four major events in its lifetime:

- Initialization
- Starting
- Stopping
- Destroying

These four events correspond directly to four methods within the `Applet` class: `init()`, `start()`, `stop()`, and `destroy()`. The following discussion provides some information on each of these methods.

```
public void init()
```

The init() method is called when the applet is initially loaded. This method is used to do one-time setup features such as add components to the layout manager, set screen colors, and connect to a host database.

```
public void start()
```

The start() method is called after the applet has been initialized, and also each time the applet is restarted after being stopped. Applets can be stopped when the user changes to another Web page. If the user returns at a later time to the page with the applet on it, the applet will be restarted by the browser. Therefore, the start() method can be called many times during an applet's life cycle. Common operations that occur during an applet's start() method are the initialization of threads within the applet and the updating of the screen display.

```
public void stop()
```

The stop() method is called whenever the user leaves the current page. Note that by default when the user leaves a page, the applet will continue to run. This can result in an enormous consumption of system resources if many applets have been loaded and these applets are performing some resource-intensive task such as animation. (In fact, it is quite common to see poorly written applets loaded from the Internet that obviously did not implement this method. They never stop running!) The stop() method is used to temporarily suspend the execution of the applet until the start() method is called again.

```
public void destroy()
```

The destroy() method is called whenever it is time to completely finish the applet's execution. This method is generally called when the browser is exiting or the applet is being reloaded from the host server. The destroy() method is used to free up allocated resources such as threads or database connections.

Listing 7.1 shows a simple applet that implements all four life cycle methods: init(), start(), stop(), and destroy(). This applet updates the screen as well as the browser status bar with some information indicating which method is being called.

Listing 7.1. An applet illustrating the life cycle methods.

```
import java.awt.Graphics;
import java.awt.Font;
import java.awt.Color;

public class LifeCycleApplet extends java.applet.Applet
{
  Font theFont = new Font("Helvetica", Font.BOLD, 20);
  int  i;
  String String1, String2;
```

```
public void paint(Graphics g)
{
  g.setFont(theFont);
  g.setColor(Color.blue);
  g.drawString(String1 + String2, 5, 30);
}

public void init()
{
  i = 0;
  String1 = "";
  String2 = "The applet is initializing!";
  repaint();
  showStatus("The applet is initializing!");
}

public void start()
{
  i = 1;
  String1 = String2;
  String2 = "The applet is starting!";
  repaint();
  showStatus("The applet is starting!");
}

public void stop()
{
  i = 2;
  String1 = String2;
  String2 = "The applet is stopping!";
  repaint();
  showStatus("The applet is stopping!");
}

public void destroy()
{
  i = 3;
  String1 = String2;
  String2 = "The applet is being destroyed!";
  repaint();
  showStatus("The applet is being destroyed!");
}
}
```

The previous example will always show the last two life cycle events on the screen. Because of the speed at which Java executes, you were probably unable to see the init() method's results all by themselves. We could have added a counter loop just to stall the applet, so feel free to do so if you're interested. Using threads, we also could have called a wait() method to stop program execution for a specified amount of time. However, threads are a topic for a later time (see Chapter 20, "Working with Threads"). Figure 7.2 shows the LifeCycleApplet loaded into a Web browser using the Example2.html file.

FIGURE 7.2.

Example2.html
*containing the LifeCycle
applet.*

HTML and Java Applets

The last example took advantage of a file named Example2.html to display the applet within a Web browser. The actual Java code used to display the applet was examined in the last section, but you may be wondering where the additional text on the screen came from. Currently, Java applets can only be displayed within a Web browser by being embedded in a standard HTML page. This does not mean that the actual bytecode or source code of the applet is included within the HTML file. Instead, the HTML text contains a reference to the Java applet known as a *tag*. Each element within an HTML file to be displayed by a Web browser is referenced using different types of these tags. Listing 7.2 shows the contents of the HTML file used to load the LifeCycleApplet applet.

Listing 7.2. The Example2.html file contents.

```
<HTML>
<HEAD>
<TITLE>This is the LifeCycle applet!</TITLE>
</HEAD>
<BODY>
<H1>Prepare to be amazed!</H1>
<BR>
<APPLET CODE="LifeCycleApplet.class" WIDTH=600 HEIGHT=50>
If you can see this, your browser does not support Java applets.
</APPLET>
</BODY>
</HTML>
```

NOTE

This chapter is not intended to be an HTML tutorial. For much more information on HTML and Java, see Chapter 12, "HTML for Java Programmers."

A quick examination of Listing 7.2 shows three primary elements:

■ The <TITLE> tag—Used to display the title caption for this page.

■ The <H1> tag—Used to represent the main heading for the page.

■ The <APPLET> tag—Used to represent a Java applet to be loaded.

If you are new to HTML, the most important point to realize is that nothing in this file specifies actual screen layout. The TITLE tag, for instance, does not specify that the title appear at (x,y) coordinates (150, 200) and that it should be set apart from the heading by ¼". HTML only specifies the markup that tells browsers *what* information to display. The page designer is somewhat at the mercy of Web browser developers, although keep in mind that it is in the best interest of browser developers to provide a standardized "look-and-feel" to most Web pages. It is still common, however, to load pages side by side in Netscape Navigator and Microsoft Internet Explorer and notice slight layout differences. Fortunately, for the Java developer, the actual screen layout *within the applet* is completely controllable down to the pixel level. Graphics and Java are discussed briefly later in this chapter, and then in detail in Chapter 17, "Programming the User Interface." The remainder of this section presents the <APPLET> tag.

The <APPLET> Tag

The syntax for using the <APPLET> tag is the following:

```
<APPLET attributes>
applet_parameters
alternate_content
</APPLET>
```

The APPLET attributes are standard values that all applets accept and are a standard part of HTML. The applet_parameters are applet-specific parameters that are read by the applet at runtime. This is a handy way of passing arguments to an applet to allow the applet to be more generic.

<APPLET> Tag Attributes

ALT—Alternate text that can be displayed by text-only browsers.

ALIGN—The ALIGN attribute designates the alignment of the applet within the browser page.

CODE—(Required) The CODE attribute is used to indicate the .class file that loads the applet.

CODEBASE—The CODEBASE attribute is used to indicate the location of the .class file that loads the applet.

HEIGHT—(Required) The HEIGHT attribute is used to set the applet's bounding rectangle height.

HSPACE—The HSPACE attribute sets the amount of horizontal space to set off around the applet.

NAME—The NAME attribute sets the symbolic name of the applet.

VSPACE—The VSPACE attribute sets the amount of vertical space to set off around the applet.

WIDTH—(Required) The WIDTH attribute is used to set the applet's box width.

Passing Parameters to Java Applets

Parameters are an easy way to configure Java applets without actually changing the source file. In the previous applet example, the text drawn on the screen was drawn using the blue color. This was "hardwired" into the applet's code. However, just as easily, we could have passed a parameter to the applet specifying that it use the blue tag. Listing 7.3 shows the Example2.html file modified to do just this.

Listing 7.3. Passing parameters to the applet using HTML parameters.

```
<HTML>
<HEAD>
<TITLE>This is the LifeCycle applet!</TITLE>
</HEAD>
<BODY>
<H1>Prepare to be amazed!</H1>
<BR>
<APPLET CODE="LifeCycleApplet.class" WIDTH=600 HEIGHT=50>
<PARAM NAME=color VALUE="blue">
If you can see this, your browser does not support Java applets.
</APPLET>
</BODY>
</HTML>
```

The only question left to be answered is this: how does the Java applet determine the value of the parameters? (Excellent question!) The answer is that the applet has to call the getParameter() method supplied by the java.applet.Applet parent class. Calling getParameter("color") using the previous Java applet example would return a String value containing the text "blue". It is then left up to the applet to take advantage of this information and actually paint the text blue on the screen.

Here are three methods commonly used by applets:

■ String getParameter(String name)—Returns the value for the specified parameter string

■ URL getCodeBase()—Returns the URL of the applet

■ URL getDocumentBase()—Returns the URL of the document containing the applet

Listing 12.9 in Chapter 12 shows a detailed example (with Java code) of using parameters to pass values to an applet using HTML parameters. For more detailed information on parameters and the <APPLET> tag, see Chapter 12.

Simple Graphics and GUI Techniques

This section presents an introduction to the graphical user interface capabilities provided in the Java Abstract Windowing Toolkit (AWT). The AWT is actually a package named java.awt included with the JDK. (For a complete documentation of the java.awt package, see Chapter 28.) Although there are many user interface classes contained in package java.awt, Table 7.1 lists the most commonly used classes with a brief description of each class.

Table 7.1. Commonly used user interface classes in package java.awt.

Class Name	Description
Button	A standard pushbutton user interface component
Canvas	A canvas that is used as a graphics drawing context
Checkbox	A standard checkbox user interface component
CheckboxGroup	A user interface component used to group checkboxes
CheckboxMenuItem	A checkbox that is displayed as a menu item
Choice	A menu component that displays the currently selected choice
Color	A class used to encapsulate colors in Java
Component	The base class of all user interface components
Container	A base class for all container/grouping components
Dialog	A standard dialog screen that can be either modal or nonmodal
FileDialog	A standard file selection dialog that is OS-dependent
Font	A class used to encapsulate fonts in Java
Frame	A frame that can contain window objects
Graphics	The base class used for all graphics and drawing operations
Image	A class used to encapsulate images in Java
Label	A standard label user interface component
List	A standard list box user interface component
Menu	A menu component that resides on a menubar
MenuBar	The menubar that contains menus and menu items
MenuItem	Menu selection items that trigger program events
Panel	A user interface component used to surround other components
Scrollbar	A standard scrollbar user interface component
TextArea	A multiline text editing window
TextField	A single-line text editing window
Window	A window inside a frame that contains multiple objects

By examining this table, you can see that three primary classes of components exist within the AWT: drawing objects, containers, and user interface components. If you have ever done any type of GUI programming before, you are probably familiar with all of the components listed here.

Laying Out Components on the Screen

Before you dive into GUI programming with Java, there is one type of class contained in the AWT (not listed in Table 7.1) that may be new even to experienced programmers. This type of class is known as a *layout manager*. Layout managers allow components to be added onscreen without specifying exact coordinate locations for the components. This type of class makes working with onscreen components much easier. Because advanced "drag-and-drop" Java Developer's environments are not currently available, Java developers currently must either use layout managers or give specific screen coordinates to locate components onscreen. This will remain true in the future for developers coding on platforms that do not support advanced development environments. Here are some examples of layout managers:

- FlowLayout—The default layout manager. This class lays out components from left to right, wrapping onto the next row when necessary.
- GridLayout—Breaks the screen up into a rectangular grid and then places a component within each grid element.
- BorderLayout—Adds components to the screen using some specified geographic direction (north, south, east, west, and center).
- CardLayout—Adds components onto a stack of cards, where only one card is visible at a time. Specific methods need to be called to switch cards and show a different set of components.

Although the FlowLayout is the default layout manager used in the applet class, the following example (Listing 7.4) illustrates the use of the BorderLayout class. All this simple applet does at the current time is add a text box, a list, and a push button. Don't worry about the actual functionality now. This will be added when we discuss events in the next section.

Listing 7.4. The contents of `EditList1.java`.

```
import java.awt.TextField;
import java.awt.List;
import java.awt.Button;
import java.awt.BorderLayout;
import java.applet.Applet;

public class EditList1 extends java.applet.Applet
{
  TextField theText;
  List      theList;
```

```
Button     theButton;

public void init()
{
   setLayout(new BorderLayout()); // sets the layout manager to be a
➡ BorderLayout

   theText = new TextField();
   theList = new List();
   theButton = new Button("Add text to list!");

   add("North", theText);
   add("Center", theList);
   add("South", theButton);
}
}
```

The EditList1 applet uses the BorderLayout Manager to automatically lay out a TextField, List, and Button. Figure 7.3 shows the EditList1 applet running within a Web browser using the Example3.html file.

FIGURE 7.3.
*The EditList1 applet
running within Netscape
Navigator.*

This is an exciting step, but this applet would be incomplete without some sort of functionality. We can use Java events to force some work to be done when the user clicks on a button, double-clicks the list, or edits the text. The next section will briefly discuss event handling. At the end of the section, the EditList1 applet will be modified so that when a user clicks the button, whatever text has been typed into the text field gets added to the list.

Handling Events

Event handling is one of the primary features of graphical user interface programming. It is so important that this type of interface is also commonly called an *event-driven interface*. If you stop to think about it, there are many events going on constantly within a standard user interface. Key presses, button clicks, and even voice activation can cause processing to occur on your computer. (In addition to common user events, the operating system itself commonly sends events to applications such as when a window is dragged over another window, or when the system itself is preparing to shut down.) To take advantage of this rich model, it is necessary to be able to "handle" or respond to these events in some way. Of course, Java provides this functionality, but it is up to the programmer to implement it. In the previous example, EditList1.java, the user can click on the button continuously, yet no text will ever be added to the list. This is because the default button-click event for the Button class does nothing except change the look of the button while the user is actually clicking it. It is up to the user to provide some type of functionality.

To trap an event sent from any user interface component, the programmer must define an action() method. By examining the documentation in Chapter 28 for the java.awt.Component class, you can see that this method is part of the Component class, which is the base class for all onscreen elements.

NOTE

There are two ways to trap events:

■ Override the applet's action() method and trap the events for all components within the applet. If this is done, the action() method's Event object will need to be examined so that the object that sent the event can be determined.

■ Create a new class for each component on the screen that needs to have its events handled. Then override the individual component's action methods.

Listing 7.5 (EditList2.java) uses the Applet class's action() method to trap the button-click event. When this event has been trapped, the contents of the edit control are added to the list box.

Listing 7.5. The contents of EditList2.java.

```
import java.awt.TextField;
import java.awt.List;
import java.awt.Button;
import java.awt.BorderLayout;
import java.applet.Applet;
import java.awt.Event;

public class EditList2 extends java.applet.Applet
{
  TextField theText;
  List      theList;
  Button    theButton;
```

```
public void init()
{
  setLayout(new BorderLayout()); // sets the layout manager to be a
➡ BorderLayout

  theText = new TextField();
  theList = new List();
  theButton  = new Button("Add text to list!");

  add("North", theText);
  add("Center", theList);
  add("South", theButton);
}

public boolean action(Event evt, Object arg)
{
  if (evt.target instanceof Button)
    theList.addItem(theText.getText());

  return true;
}
}
```

Running the `Example4.html` file within a Web browser will show that the event handling implemented above actually works. Figure 7.4 shows `Example4.html` running within the Netscape Navigator browser.

FIGURE 7.4.

The EditList2 applet running within Netscape Navigator.

Inter-Applet Communication

In the previous example, the button component was used to add items to the list component. All of these operations occurred inside a single applet. However, imagine a case where a button-click in one applet could update a database and trigger update messages to another applet running within the same Web page or even running on a remote computer. This type of communication is known as *inter-applet communication*. Since the early days of Java, this feature has been requested by developers wanting to push the envelope of Java's capabilities. This section briefly discusses several methods for communicating between applets, but you should note that these methods are browser-dependent and are subject to change.

Java Beans

Recently, a technology known as Java Beans has been introduced by JavaSoft. Java Beans is a component object model that will allow Java applets to be integrated with other applets and applications using multiple component architectures, including COM, OpenDoc, LiveConnect, and CORBA. This component model is supposed to compete heavily with Microsoft's Component Object Model (COM, which is the basis of ActiveX) and should be released in late 1996. Until then, however, developers who want to provide inter-applet communication must resort to other methods.

Possibilities of Inter-Applet Communication

There are several interesting possibilities that will be available when applets are truly enabled to communicate among themselves. Here are possible types of communication:

- Applets that share the same Web page within the same browser
- Applets loaded in completely different browser windows
- Applets loaded on different client's browsers
- Applets loaded from different servers

Using a technology such as Java Beans or ActiveX will also allow developers to "wrap" their applets with code that will expose an applet's methods and properties in some standardized way. Using the component model, the applet could potentially be dropped onto a Visual Basic form or used to communicate with applications written in other programming languages.

Some Inter-Applet Communication Methods

Once again, keep in mind that currently, the only way to implement this type of communication is to take advantage of specific browser features. The following examples focus on capabilities using the Netscape Navigator browser.

> **NOTE**
>
> Throughout this book, there has been and will be little mention of operating system-specific problems. This is because Java is truly a cross-platform development tool. However, it is interesting to note that there are many *browser*-specific tendencies. Perhaps those who say the Web browser is an operating system are somewhat correct. This is certainly true in the case of Java programming.

Using the AppletContext

Calling the `getApplets()` or `getApplet()` method is the easiest way to reach applets running within the same Web page. Although this feature appears to be relatively foolproof, there are some gotchas to watch out for. By examining the documentation on the `getApplets()` method in Chapter 27, you can see that this method returns an `Enumeration` containing all applets located within the current AppletContext. This works fine on browsers that treat a single Web page as an AppletContext; however, some browsers (including an earlier version of Sun's HotJava) break each applet up into a separate AppletContext. Be careful to really check out the browser your users will be using (in the intranet case) to make sure you really understand how this method actually works.

Using a Web Server

A somewhat more difficult, and less reliable, method of inter-applet communication is the use of socket-based communication between applets using the originating Web server. At the current time, any desired type of messaging service can be set up on the server, although it has been mentioned that Sun may discontinue this feature and limit communications to the server's HTTP port only.

Using JavaScript

The Netscape Navigator 3.0 browser implements a technology known as LiveConnect to allow an applet to expose its methods and data to the outside world. Using the scripting language known as JavaScript, the Web page developer can access and change an applet's internal data.

Netscape Navigator 3.0 will also allow the use of *cookies*. Cookies are basically text files that can contain messages. At the current time, only JavaScript can actually access cookies, but this feature could be useful to script together applets that were loaded at different times.

These features are truly browser-dependent. HTML files containing these features can only be displayed correctly using the Netscape Navigator 3.0 browser.

Using Static Variables

If both applets doing the communication share the same class, a common inter-applet communication mechanism is the use of static variables. Static variables can be thought of as global variables that apply to all instances of the class within an applet. However, the Netscape implementation of this feature allows static variables to be shared within an AppletContext's boundaries. This, then, is yet another method for "passing" data between applets within the same AppletContext.

Summary

The widespread use of Java applets is one of the most exciting software development technologies in recent memory. Applets offer the promise of truly platform-independent software that will allow developers to add interesting interactive content to their Web pages. Although the Java language itself is platform-independent, developers should be warned that vendor-specific additions such as Microsoft's ActiveX extensions could render Java applets unusable on non-Windows platforms. Before pursuing technologies such as this or inter-applet communication, be sure that the needs of users are clearly understood so that your applet development project will not be hindered in the future.

The next chapter discusses Java application development. At the current time, much of the development world has focused solely on Java applets, but Java applications are sure to see widespread growth in the near future as development tools become more powerful.

8

Developing Java Applications

by Dan Joshi

The last chapter introduced you to Java applets. This chapter is devoted to a term most programmers should already be familiar with: the application. Applications are the more traditional type of programs that are used in less recent programming languages like C and Pascal. You learned in the last chapter that applets are a new strain of Java programs designed with an Internet readiness built into them. In this chapter, you will learn about Java applications and how they differ from Java applets.

In general, most Java enthusiasts have seen a Java applet on the Net in one place or another. If you are not in this category, then point your Java-capable browser to the following site for an example of a Java applet animation: `http://cafe.symantec.com`. The two coffee mugs are animated based on the animation applet that comes with the Java Developer's Kit (see Figure 8.1).

FIGURE 8.1.

An example of animation on the Net (the coffee cups are animated with Java).

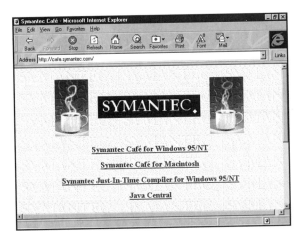

Probably one of the most powerful (but as yet untapped features) of the Java programming language is that applets are only half of the entire Java language picture. Applets are the celebrated way of creating Java programs, leaving regular Java applications in the minority. There are probably only a few Java enthusiasts who have hands-on experience using Java applications. This is the result of the extreme exposure of the Internet and not of deficiencies in the applications themselves. The Internet is not a place from which applications are designed to be accessed. Nevertheless, Java applications are no less powerful—and in some situations much more versatile—than their applet counterparts. Java applications are just like applets in that they are multiplatformed and bytecode-verified. However, as you learn in this chapter, because Java applications are designed to exist inside a secure environment, they are not as restricted as applets typically are.

Java applications can be used as client/server solutions or in an Intranet environment—pretty much in any already secure environment. Anatomically, Java applications are based on a more traditional program design model, very similar to that of C/C++.

> **NOTE**
>
> An intranet is a smaller, self-contained Internet that is mostly employed by corporations as a way of connecting people to information. The advantage of intranets for Java applications is that they have an already secure internal environment from which Java applications can be used without having to impose all sorts of restrictions on your application.

Topics covered in this chapter include the following:

■ Applications versus applets: Understanding the differences and similarities between the two. Reviewing some of what you already learned in the last chapter.

■ Understanding the anatomy of Java applications. Dealing with the `main()` method and the `argv[]` array.

■ Learning about the `Date` and `System` classes in the Java class library.

■ Designing sample runnable applications, including one example to pass parameters to applications.

The next section covers the similarities and differences between applets and applications.

Applications versus Applets

In essence, applets and Java applications share many of the same resources and features. As you will learn in the next section, the major anatomical difference between an applet and an application that makes both of them unique is that an applet extends the `java.applet.Applet` class, and an application utilizes the `main()` method. On a higher level, an application is not as restricted as an applet in terms of what it can access. On the other hand, applications cannot be embedded into HTML pages for any Internet user to view with a Java-capable browser. Applets and applications overlap in many areas, but they are specifically designed for different environments. Figure 8.2 shows a visual interpretation of the differences and similarities between applications and applets. Basically, in many core respects they are the same, but they are unique in the audiences they are trying to reach.

FIGURE 8.2.

Venn diagram of Java applications and applets.

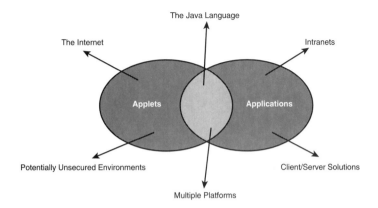

Review of Java Applets

In the preceding chapter, you were introduced to the java.applet.Applet class. In order to tell Java that this program is going to be an applet, all that you basically need to do is create a subclass of the Applet class. Everything that makes up an applet is inherited from the superclass java.applet.Applet. Included in this inheritance are the basic user interface, methods for accessing parameters from an HTML page, and several methods known as life-cycle methods that are called directly by the system you use to organize your program. Another method that is part of the java.awt.Component class (which would be a super-super-super class to the class containing your applet) is the method paint(), which is used to draw various things in your applet's pane. The following shows an example of what the structure of a typical applet might look like:

```
import java.awt.Graphics;
class ABClass extends java.applet.Applet {
    public void init() {
        /* Initialize any variables, images, etc here.
        Any initialization that only needs to be done once should be
        included here because this method is called only once. */
    }
    public void start() {
        /* This method can also be used for initialization.
        However, the difference for this one is that it is used for
        components in your applet that need to be initialized more
        than once, or if the reader leaves the applet and then
          returns. This method can be called more than once. */
    }

    public void stop() {
        /* This life cycle method is the counterpart to start().
        Any code to suspend execution should be retained here. */
    }
```

```
public void destroy() {
    /* This method is used to clean up the applet before it is
    finished. This method is called only once. */
}
public void paint(Graphics g) {
    /* Any code to draw, write, or color things on the
    applet pane belongs here */
}
}
```

In the preceding pseudo-applet, each method is called by the system at a particular moment, under specific circumstances, or in a special order. Some of the methods can be called more than once depending on how the user engages the applet and the environment in which the applet is being run.

To review more closely the logistics of an applet, the fact that an applet is designed to run in the heterogeneous and possibly unsecured environment of the Internet has imposed several restrictions on it. Most of this is review from the last chapter, so this explanation highlights an applet in its strictest sense, pointing out potential differences with that of applications. Also, note that in certain situations, there are exceptions to the following restriction, even in applets. In some cases, these restrictions can be lowered depending on the type of Internet browser running the applet and its configuration.

Applets cannot read or write to the user's file system. This means that the applet cannot access anything locally or place anything locally either. For example, many Windows-based applications written in C utilize an initialization file (an .INI file) in 16-bit Windows or the Registry in 32-bit Windows to store information about the application and any user preferences. This is not possible in the current applet model and imposes a challenge to traditional programming techniques. This limited access can also include just checking to see if a file even exists on the user's system.

Applets cannot utilize native methods, load shared libraries, or run any programs that may be on the user's system. The major security concern here is that native methods and local shared libraries (such as DLLs) can facilitate a loophole in the Java security model described in the previous paragraph.

Applets cannot communicate with any server other than the one from which they originated. In some cases, an encrypted key can be used to verify a particular applet to a server, or a server accessed due to a configuration with the Internet browser, but access to any server on the Net cannot be assumed.

Overall, applets provide a different format for program execution and a very tight security model, which is necessary in the very open environment of the Internet.

Introduction to Java Applications

Java applications are different from Java applets in several ways. On the inside (that is, the source code level), you do not need to extend any class in the Java class library when creating an application. As a result, you do not have a set of basic methods that you override to execute your program. Instead, you create a set of classes that contain various parts of your program, and then you attach a main() method that will contain the code used to execute your code. The main() method is very similar to that of the C/C++ model; it is here that Java will start the actual execution of your application. The following shows what the structure for a typical Java application would look like this:

```
public class TheClass {
    /* variables and methods specific to the class TheClass
    are located here. */
    class ABClass {
        /* The body of the class ABClass
        is located here */
    }

    public static void main(String argv[]) {
    /* The actual execution of the application
    is located here. **/
    }
}
```

NOTE

The modifiers before the main() method—public, static, and void—must be present every time you use the main() method. public lets it have maximum exposure inside the current class. static causes this method to no longer need instancing in order to be available to all of the other methods in the current class. void means that there is no returning value coming from this method.

The main() method shown in the preceding code is the system method that is used to invoke the application. As mentioned earlier, any action code should be located in main(). The main() method is more than just another method in a Java application. If you do not include a main() method in your application when you attempt to run it, you will receive a message similar to the following error message:

```
In the class TheClass: void main(String argv[]) is undefined
```

Looking at a higher level in Java application topology, the major point to note is that in a typical Java application security model, an application can use native methods and access the user's file system. If the application and the user's environment are configured properly, it can also access all kinds of stuff from the Net. Of course, the price for all of this built-in versatility is that an application cannot be embedded in an HTML page and downloaded from a Java-capable browser.

In most cases, a Java application should look very similar to a typical C/C++ application. In this chapter, you are going to create several applications to exemplify some of the features and methods specific to a Java application. All of these will be based solely on console-based Java applications, because at this point you will not cover the AWT (Abstract Window Toolkit) until Part II, "Using the Java Packages," in this book. So remember that all Java applications can be used to create Windows-based applications complete with dialog boxes and an event handler.

Java Applications: An Example

Start by creating an application that you can execute at the command prompt. Using the Java Developer's Kit and a text editor, start by creating a new file called `First.java` and enter the code from Listing 8.1 into it.

Listing 8.1. The code for `First.java`.

```
1:public class First {
2:
3:      //variables for class First
4:      String name;
5:      int accountNumber;
6:      float balance;
7:
8:      //Method to print information on the screen
9:      void Printout() {
10:         System.out.println("Name:              " + name);
11:         System.out.println("Account Number: " + accountNumber);
12:         System.out.println("Balance:
➥ $XXXXXX, Sorry that is classified");
13:      }
14:
15:      public static void main(String argv[]) {
16:         //Create an instance of First
17:         First f = new First();
18:
19:         //Add data to the variables in class First
20:         f.name = "John Smith";
21:         f.accountNumber = 235412345;
22:         f.balance = 25;
23:
24:         //Draw the top border
25:         for (int i = 0; i < 40; i++)
26:             System.out.print("--");
27:
28:         //Title
29:         System.out.println("      INFORMATION");
30:
31:         //Call method to print the information
32:         f.Printout();
33:
34:         //Draw bottom border
35:         for (int i = 0; i < 40; i++)
```

continues

Listing 8.1. continued

```
36:                System.out.print("--");
37:
38:         //Ending remark
39:         System.out.println("End of printout");
40:
41:     }
42:}
```

Looking at Listing 8.1, you should notice some things that are familiar to you. Basically, the class First has three variables: name, accountNumber, and balance (lines 4, 5, and 6); and one method called Printout() (lines 9 through 13). However, no action takes place until line 15, which is the first line of the main() method. On line 17, an instance of class First is constructed. Then, in lines 25 and 26, the top border is an algorithm that scrolls through and draws dashes across the screen. On line 32, Printout() is invoked. Method Printout() uses the method System.out.println() (lines 10, 11, and 12). Lines 35 and 36 draw a lower border, and line 39 puts in a closing remark.

The system methods of print() and println() may be something you have seen before. However, take a closer look at System.out.print(). The class System comes from the package java.lang that is automatically imported in any Java program (be it application or applet). Table 8.1 shows a list of variables and methods that belong to the System class.

Table 8.1. The System class.

Variable index

Variable Name	Usage
public static PrintStream err	The output stream for error messages.
public static InputStream in	The standard input stream for reading data.
public static PrintStream out	The standard output stream for printing messages.

Method Index

Method Name	Usage
arraycopy (Object src, int src Position, Object dst, dstPosition, int len)	Copies an array.
currentTimeMillis()	Returns a long that holds the value in milliseconds since January 1, 1970.
exit(int status)	Exits the application with the specified status code (0 if successful).

Method Name	Usage
gc()	Manually invokes the garbage collector. Note that unless garbage collection is manually enabled or disabled, it is done automatically by the Java virtual machine.
getProperties()	Returns a Properties class with the system properties.
getProperty (String key, String default)	Returns a String with a value for the specified property. Or, returns the default if the specified property is not set.
runFinalization ()	Runs the finalization methods of any object pending finalization.
setProperties (Properties props)	Sets the system properties based on the specified properties.

Table 8.1 shows only a partial list of all of the methods available for the System class; for a complete review, reference Chapter 32, "Package java.lang."

So where are the println() and print() methods for the System class? If you noticed in Listing 8.1, you are using the variable out that belongs to the System class. The variable out is an instance of the class PrintStream. PrintStream is part of the set of stream classes that are used in Java.

Now go ahead and compile the code for First.java by running the javac.exe on the file at the command prompt. If the executable is in the same directory as the source file, or the directory where javac.exe is located is specified in the environmental path, then you can type the following at the command prompt. Otherwise, you will need to include the directory where the javac executable is located:

```
javac First.java
```

If you typed everything correctly, then you should see something like Figure 8.3.

NOTE

When compiling a source code file, the executable compiled file will retain the same name as the source file but have an extension of .class. The compiled file, unless otherwise specified, will be dropped in the same directory where the source file is located.

FIGURE 8.3.

Compiling the First *application.*

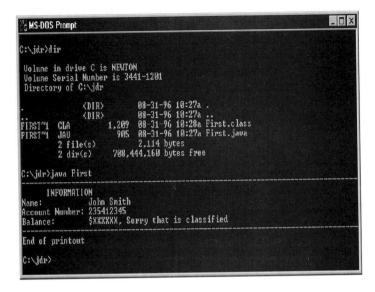

Now you can run the application by using the Java interpreter (called java.exe) from the command prompt in a very similar fashion to which you compiled it:

```
java First
```

When the execution is finished, you should see something similar to Figure 8.4.

> **NOTE**
>
> When interpreting files, you do not need to specify the extension of the source code file, which is always .class.

FIGURE 8.4.

Running the First *application.*

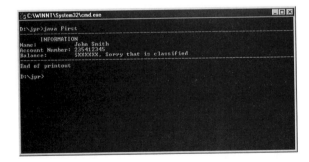

> **NOTE**
>
> Now that you have compiled your first Java application, you may be wondering what you need to distribute it. Basically, all that you need to distribute a Java application is the compiled class file (that is, the file javac creates with the `.class` extension) and an interpreter.

Importing Other Packages to Your Java Applications

Looking back at Table 8.1, imagine that you wanted to create a very simple Java application that would display the date. One method available to you is the `currentTimeMillis()`. The `currentTimeMillis()` returns a 64-bit integer long representing the number of seconds since January 1, 1970. In your text editor, go ahead and key in Listing 8.2 and save it as `DisplayDate.java`.

Listing 8.2. The code for `DisplayDate.java`.

```
1:public class DisplayDate {
2:
3:    public static void main(String argv[]) {
4:
5:        //Draw the top border
6:        for (int i = 0; i < 40; i++)
7:            System.out.print("--");
8:
9:        //Display the time
10:            System.out.println("Milliseconds since January 1, 1970:
➥ " + System.currentTimeMillis());
11:
12:        //Draw the bottom border
13:        for (int i = 0; i < 40; i++)
14:            System.out.print("--");
15:
16:        //Closing remark
17:        System.out.println("End of printing");
18:
19:    }
20:}
```

Reviewing Listing 8.2, you see that, just as in the first example, there is a top border created in lines 6 and 7. The actual method `currentTimeMillis()` is located inside `System.out.println()` on line 10. A bottom border is drawn on lines 13 and 14 with a closing remark on line 17.

Compile this example by typing the following at the command prompt (or something similar):

```
javac DisplayDate.java
```

Once it has successfully compiled, run it by typing the following at the command prompt, and you should see something similar to Figure 8.5:

```
java DisplayDate
```

FIGURE 8.5.
Running the
`DisplayDate`
application.

Obviously, this is not very useful for figuring out what today's date is. You would need to write several fairly complex algorithms to turn that huge number into a more useful format—something not very practical in the real world.

NOTE

The number displayed in Figure 8.5 is very large and growing at a fast rate. One might guess that it will overflow and become inaccurate. However, the integer data type that holds it is a `long`, which is a 64-bit signed integer and should be accurate well past the year 200,000,000, so there is no immediate cause for worry.

This number is used as an internal clock by the system, and it may not be useful for giving you the date. However, it is useful in some cases for time-driven software. For example, imagine you had a piece of software that you wanted to expire in 30 days. You would stamp that number inside your program with the date it was installed on the user's system, and calculate 30 days worth of milliseconds before shutting off your program.

Returning to a more common issue: What if you wanted to display today's date to the user of your application? Java has a built-in class in the package `java.util` called `Date` that gives you this functionality. However, if you tried to use the class `Date` now, you would immediately notice that `java.util` is not one of the default packages automatically imported to your application. Hence, you will need to import it manually. The syntax for importing a package or class is the same for applications and applets alike and by this point should not be anything new to you. At the very beginning of your source code class file, you state the class, classes, or packages you want to have imported and precede each one of them by the keyword `import`:

```
import java.util.Date;
```

Now, based on this snippet of code, your class will have access to all the non-private members of the `Date` class. Once again, this should be nothing new to you, and you will definitely have a chance to work with it more in the coming chapters.

Listing 8.3 shows the `DisplayDate2.java` application that has imported the `java.util.Date` class and uses some of the methods contained in it. For more information on all of the methods available to you in the `Date` class, see Chapter 34, "Package `java.util`."

Listing 8.3. The code for `DisplayDate2.java`.

```
 1:import java.util.Date;
 2:
 3:public class DisplayDate2 {
 4:
 5:     Date todaysDate = new Date();
 6:
 7:     public static void main(String argv[]) {
 8:
 9:          //Draw the top border
10:          for (int i = 0; i < 40; i++)
11:              System.out.print("--");
12:
13:          //Create an instance of DisplayDate2
14:          DisplayDate2 d = new DisplayDate2();
15:
16:          //Display the Date
17:          System.out.println("Today's Date: " + d.todaysDate);
18:
19:          //Draw the bottom border
20:          for (int i = 0; i < 40; i++)
21:              System.out.print("--");
22:
23:          //Closing remark
24:          System.out.println("End of printing");
25:
26:     }
27:}
```

Looking at the preceding code, you can see that in line 5 you are declaring a variable called `todaysDate` from `Date`, and by using the constructor in this format, you are in fact retrieving the date and time. Once again in lines 10, 11, 20, and 21, you are building the upper and lower borders for the application. Then, in line 14, you are creating an instance `d` of the `DisplayDate2` class; and on line 17 using `System.out.println()`, you are actually printing it out. Overall, this application is fairly simple and the date being printed out is much easier to understand. Compile and run the program, and you should see something similar to Figure 8.6.

FIGURE 8.6.

Running the `DisplayDate2` *application.*

Importing is an integral part of the Java experience whether it is with applications or applets— it's something which with every Java developer should become familiar.

Using `argv[]` to Pass Command-Line Arguments

One of the attributes of an application is the ability to pass a command-line argument to it. For example, imagine you had a program to which you wanted to pass a word. The following shows what you would type when you run the application:

```
java ABClass test
```

Where does the argument go? It goes to the array of strings you declared in the `main()` method, in this case, `argv[]`.

> **TIP**
>
> You can name the array of strings anything you want. Typically, the most common names used are `argv[]` (which comes from C), `arg[]`, or even `args[]`.

Basically, the input parameter will put each of the arguments passed to it in a separate index in the array. Hence, you can have more than one argument passed in a single session:

```
java ABClass test 2
```

In the preceding example, there are two arguments. The first argument, `test`, in this case will go into `argv[0]`, and the second `2` will be placed in `argv[1]`.

> **NOTE**
>
> Unlike C/C++, the name of the application is not stored as the first item in the argv[] array.

The last thing to note about passing arguments is what to do if you want to pass two or more items as one argument. This can be accomplished by putting the entire argument into quotation marks. In the following snippet of code, you have only two arguments, Ford Mustang and Honda Civic:

```
java ABClass "Ford Mustang" "Honda Civic"
```

Now move forward and create a runnable example of how to pass parameters to a Java application.

Listing 8.4. The code for SayHello.java.

```
 1:public class SayHello {
 2:
 3:    public static void main(String argv[]) {
 4:
 5:        //Draw the top border
 6:        for (int i = 0; i < 40; i++)
 7:            System.out.print("--");
 8:
 9:        //Check to see if no argument was passed
10:        if (argv.length == 0) {
11:            System.out.println("Please enter your name!");
12:            System.out.exit(0);
13:        }
14:
15:        // Loop through and say hello to everyone
16:        for (int i = 0; i < argv.length; i++)
17:        System.out.println("Hello " + argv[i]);
18:
19:        //Draw the bottom border
20:        for (int i = 0; i < 40; i++)
21:            System.out.print("--");
22:
23:        //Closing Remark
24:        System.out.println("End of printing");
25:    }
26:}
```

When you look at Listing 8.4, nothing should be new to you except for the argv.length used in line 10 and line 16, and System.out.exit(). The argv.length variable contains the value for the number of elements utilized in the specified array, which in this case is argv[]. The

`System.out.exit()` is used to end execution of the application. Other than that, lines 10 to 13 check to see if the length of the array is 0; if `true`, then there were no arguments passed to it. The `for` loop located in lines 16 through 17 loops through the length of the array and then prints it out.

Now go ahead and compile it by typing the following at the command prompt:

```
javac SayHello.java
```

Next, go ahead and run it by typing the following:

```
java SayHello Dan Bill "John Smith"
```

Figure 8.7 shows the command prompt displaying the output for the preceding command. As you can see in the figure, it says hello to each of the three arguments passed to it.

FIGURE 8.7.

Running the SayHello *application.*

Now, experiment by not passing any parameters to the application by typing the following:

```
java SayHello
```

Figure 8.8 shows what you should see as the output of the application.

FIGURE 8.8.

Running the SayHello *application without arguments.*

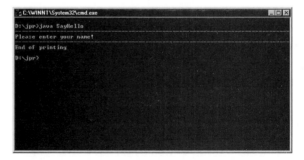

Summary

In this chapter, you learned about the similarities and differences between applets and applications and where applications reside in the overall Java paradigm. Applications provide the advantages of being able to link native code, as well as more flexibility with security than their applet counterparts. Also, the anatomy of Java applets is vastly different, with applications being designed around the more traditional (that is, C/C++) format of utilizing the main() method. The other half of the chapter gave several examples of passing arguments to Java applications.

Probably the last topic to note before leaving this chapter is the fact that all of the examples in this chapter were based strictly on console-based applications. In Chapter 17, "Programming the User Interface," when you are introduced to the AWT (Abstract Window Toolkit), you will be able to create applications that contain windows, dialogs, text fields, and all of the other components that make up a modern GUI-based program.

9

javac: The Java Compiler

by Michael Morrison

The Java compiler (javac) is the component of the Java Developer's Kit used to transform Java source code files into bytecode executables that can be run in the Java runtime system. In this chapter, you learn all about the Java compiler and how it is used, including the different compilation options it supports. You also learn about an alternate version of the compiler that ships with some versions of the JDK. Toward the end of the chapter, you get a glimpse of a few of the bugs in the current version of the Java compiler.

Overview

In Java, source code files have the extension .java. Java source code files are standard ASCII text files, much like the source code files for other popular programming languages like C++. It is the job of the Java compiler to process Java source code files and create executable Java bytecode classes from them. Executable bytecode class files have the extension .class, and they represent a Java class in its useable form.

Java class files are generated on a one-to-one basis with the classes defined in the source code. In other words, the Java compiler generates exactly one .class file for each class you create. Technically, it is possible to define more than one class in a single source file; it is therefore possible for the compiler to generate multiple class files from a single source file. When this happens, it means that the source file contains multiple class definitions.

You may have heard something about *just-in-time compilers* in reference to Java. It's important not to get these compilers confused with the Java compiler and the role it plays. The Java compiler is responsible for turning Java source code into Java bytecodes that can be executed within the Java runtime system. The Java Virtual Machine, which is a component of the runtime system, is responsible for interpreting the bytecodes and making the appropriate system-level calls to the native platform. It is at this point where platform independence is achieved by Java; the bytecodes are in a generic form that is only converted to a native form when processed by the Virtual Machine. Figure 9.1 shows how the Java compiler and runtime system relate to each other.

FIGURE 9.1.

The relationship between the Java compiler and runtime system.

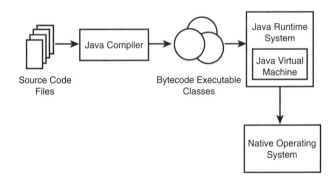

Source Code Files   Java Compiler   Bytecode Executable Classes   Java Runtime System / Java Virtual Machine → Native Operating System

Just-in-time compilers remove the role of the runtime interpreter by converting Java bytecodes to native code on the fly before executing a Java program. In this way, just-in-time Java compilers work more like the back end of traditional language compilers in that they generate code for a native platform. Similarly, the Java compiler works more like the front end of a traditional compiler in that it parses Java source code and generates internally useful bytecode classes. Figure 9.2 shows the relationship between the Java compiler and just-in-time compilers.

FIGURE 9.2.
The difference between the Java compiler and just-in-time Java compilers.

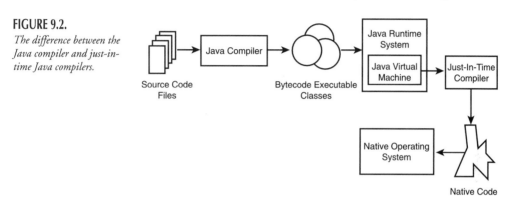

Keep in mind that Java executables are still centered around the bytecode class format. Even with just-in-time compilers in the picture, all you must be concerned with as a developer is generating the appropriate bytecode classes using the Java compiler. If no just-in-time compiler is present on a user's system, the bytecode classes will be processed and executed by the runtime interpreter. On the other hand, if a just-in-time compiler happens to exist on the system, the bytecode classes will be converted to native code and then executed. Either way, the key to executing Java programs is the bytecode classes, which are created by the Java compiler.

Usage

The Java compiler is a command-line tool, meaning that it is invoked from a command prompt, such as the MS-DOS shell in Windows 95. The syntax for the Java compiler follows:

```
javac Options Filename
```

The `Filename` argument specifies the name of the source code file you want to compile. The compiler will generate bytecode classes for all classes defined in this file. Likewise, the compiler also will generate bytecode classes for any dependent classes that haven't been compiled yet. In other words, if you are compiling class A, which is derived from class B, and class B has not yet been compiled, the compiler will go ahead and compile both classes.

Options

The *Options* compiler argument specifies options related to how the compiler creates the executable Java classes. Following is a list of the compiler options:

```
-classpath Path

-d Dir

-g

-nowarn

-O

-verbose
```

The -classpath option tells the compiler to override the CLASSPATH environment variable with the path specified by *Path*. This causes the compiler to look for user-defined classes in the path specified by *Path*. *Path* is a semicolon-delimited list of directory paths taking the following form:

`.;<your_path>`

An example of a specific usage of -classpath follows:

`javac -classpath .;\dev\animate\classes;\dev\render\classes A.java`

In this case, the compiler is using a user-defined class path to access any classes it needs while compiling the source code file A.java. The -classpath option is sometimes useful when you want to try compiling something without taking the trouble to modify the CLASSPATH environment variable.

The -d option determines the root directory where compiled classes are stored. This is important because many times classes are organized in a hierarchical directory structure. With the -d option, the directory structure will be created beneath the directory specified by *Dir*.

The -g compiler option causes the compiler to generate debugging tables for the Java classes. Debugging tables are used by the Java debugger, and they contain information such as local variables and line numbers. The default action of the compiler is to only generate line numbers. If you are going to be using the Java debugger, you must use the -g option. Additionally, for debugging, make sure you don't use the -O option, which optimizes the code.

The -nowarn option turns off compiler warnings. Warnings are printed to standard output during compilation to inform you of potential problems with the source code. It is generally a good idea to keep warnings enabled, because they often signal problem areas in your code. However, you may run into a situation where warnings are getting in the way, in which case the -nowarn option might be useful.

The -O option causes the compiler to optimize the compiled code. In this case, optimization simply means that static, final, and private methods are compiled inline. When a method is compiled inline, it means that the entire body of the method is included in place of each call to the method. This speeds up execution because it eliminates the method call overhead. Optimized classes are usually larger in size, to accommodate the duplicate code. The -O optimization option also suppresses the default creation of line numbers by the compiler. Keep in mind that the -O option should not be used when you plan on debugging the compiled code using the Java debugger.

The -verbose option has somewhat of an opposite effect as the -nowarn option—it prints out extra information about the compilation process. You can use -verbose to see exactly what source files are being compiled and what class files are being loaded.

The Non-Optimizing Compiler

Some distributions of the Java Developer's Kit include an alternate Java compiler called javac_g. This version of the Java compiler generates code without some of the internal optimizations performed by the standard javac compiler. If this compiler is in your JDK distribution, be sure to use it when you are compiling code for debugging. Otherwise, stick with the javac compiler for all release code.

Bugs

As of this writing, the latest release of the Java Developer's Kit is 1.02, which contains some known bugs. More specifically, the following Java compiler bugs have been documented and acknowledged by the JavaSoft development team:

- The compiler doesn't distinguish between the same class names in different packages.
- The compiler doesn't distinguish between class names that are only differing by case (Windows 95/NT version only).
- The compiler will not compile a method with more than 63 local variables.

The first bug is only a problem if you are using different packages containing classes with the same name. Generally speaking, most programmers probably won't develop two packages with same-named classes in each. However, the problem can easily arise without your even realizing it; suppose you are using someone else's package that has a bunch of classes already defined, and a class name conflicts with one of your own. Or, for example, suppose you had your own package including the following source code:

```
package stuff;
import java.util.*;

public class Hashtable
{
  public Hashtable() {
    // initialize the hashtable
  }
}
```

A class called Hashtable already exists in the java.util package, so your Hashtable class would conflict with it upon compilation thanks to the compiler bug.

The second compiler bug also is related to class names, and this bug rears its head whenever you have two classes with names that differ only by case, as shown in the following code:

```
// File EncryptIt.java
class EncryptIt
{
  // encrypt something
}

// File encryptit.java
class encryptit
{
  // encrypt something else
}
```

Notice that the second class, which is defined in a different source code file, has the same name as the first class, with the exception of the case on two of the characters. The Java compiler will give an error while attempting to compile this code, although technically the class naming is legal. Keep in mind that this bug exists only on the Windows 95/NT platform.

Finally, the last bug deals with the number of local variables defined in a method. If a method defines more than 63 local variables, the Java compiler will not be able to compile the method. The Java language specification has yet to set a specific upper limit on the number of local variables allowed, so you can think of the number 63 as the working limit until a formal decision has been made.

Admittedly, none of these bugs are all that likely to occur, simply because most programmers give their classes unique names and typically use less than 63 local variables in each method! However, just in case you ever find yourself pulling your hair out over a strange compiler problem, these bugs might be good to keep in mind.

Summary

In this chapter, you learned all about the standard Java compiler that ships with the Java Developer's Kit. You learned its role in generating executable Java code, along with how it differs from just-in-time Java compilers. You then learned how to use the compiler and what options are available for generating executable Java classes. You finished up with a quick look at an alternate non-optimizing Java compiler that ships with some versions of the JDK, along with a few bugs that made their way into the compiler.

10

java: The Java Interpreter

by Michael Morrison

The Java runtime interpreter (java) is the component of the Java Developer's Kit used to run executable Java bytecode classes. The Java interpreter provides a means to run Java programs outside of a conventional Web browser. In this chapter, you learn about the Java interpreter, including how to use it and what options it provides for executing Java classes.

Overview

The Java runtime interpreter is a stand-alone version of the Java interpreter built into Java-compatible Web browsers, such as Netscape Navigator. The runtime interpreter provides the support to run Java executable programs in the compiled bytecode class format. Because the interpreter doesn't directly provide any means to view graphical output, you are limited to using it to execute purely textual Java programs and applications that manage their own graphics. If you want to run graphical Java applets, you need to use either the Java applet viewer or a Java-compatible Web browser. The Java applet viewer is covered in the next chapter, "Using the Applet Viewer."

You can think of the runtime interpreter as exposing the bare essentials of the Java runtime system. Even though I use the term "bare essentials," the interpreter actually lets you do quite a lot. Essentially, you can run any Java programs that don't rely on the Applet class. In fact, the statement earlier about not being able to run graphical programs isn't entirely true; you can run graphical Java applications—you just can't run Java applets. The difference between a Java application and a Java applet is that an application is responsible for creating and maintaining its own window if it requires the need for graphical output, whereas an applet relies on a Web browser to provide a window on which to display graphics. So, the Java interpreter is capable of executing both textual Java programs and graphical Java applications.

Usage

The runtime interpreter is a command-line tool for running Java programs and applications; Java applets require the graphics and display support of a Web browser. The syntax for using the Java runtime interpreter follows:

```
java Options Classname Arguments
```

The *Classname* argument specifies the name of the class you want to execute. If the class resides in a package, you must fully qualify the name. For example, if you want to run a class called SolveIt that is located in a package called Equations, you would execute it in the interpreter like this:

```
java Equations.SolveIt
```

When the Java interpreter executes a class, what it is really doing is executing the `main` method of the class. The interpreter exits when the `main` method and any threads created by it are finished executing. The `main` method accepts a list of arguments that can be used to control the program. Following is the definition of the `main` method as specified by the Java language:

```
class DoIt {
  public static void main(String argv[]) {
    // do something
  }
}
```

Notice that `main` has a single parameter, `argv`, which is an array of `String` objects. This brings us to the *Arguments* argument for the runtime interpreter, which specifies the arguments passed into the `main` method. Any arguments passed to the runtime interpreter by *Arguments* are accessible from the `argv` parameter in `main`. The following interpreter call passes two numeric arguments to the `main` method in the `DoIt` class:

```
java DoIt 8 24
```

Options

The *Options* argument specifies options related to how the runtime interpreter executes the Java program. Following is a list of the most important runtime interpreter options:

    -debug

    -checksource or -cs

    -classpath *Path*

    -mx *x*

    -ms *x*

    -noasyncgc

    -noverify

    -ss *x*

    -oss *x*

    -t

    -verbose or -v

    -verbosegc

    -verify

    -verifyremote

    -D*PropertyName=NewValue*

The -debug option starts the interpreter in debugging mode, which enables you to use the Java debugger (jdb) in conjunction with the interpreter. To learn more about using the Java debugger, check out Chapter 15, "jdb: The Java Debugger."

The -checksource option causes the interpreter to compare the modification dates of the source code files and executable class files. If the source file is more recent, the class is automatically recompiled and the new bytecode executable is loaded.

The Java interpreter uses an environment variable, CLASSPATH, to determine where to look for user-defined classes. The CLASSPATH variable contains a semicolon-delimited list of system paths to user-defined Java classes. Actually, most of the Java tools use the CLASSPATH variable to know where to find user-defined classes. The -classpath option informs the runtime interpreter to override CLASSPATH with the path specified by *Path*.

The -mx option enables you to modify the maximum size of the memory allocation pool, or garbage collection heap, used by the interpreter. By default, the pool has a maximum size of 16 megabytes (-mx 16m). x specifies the new maximum size of the pool, and it is measured in bytes by default. You also can specify x in either kilobytes or megabytes by appending the letter k or m respectively onto the value. Also, x must be greater than 1,000 bytes, meaning that the pool must have a maximum size of at least 1,000 bytes.

The -ms option is similar to the -mx option, except that it enables you to modify the initial size of the memory allocation pool rather than the maximum size. By default, the size of the pool is initially set to 1 megabyte (-ms 1m). x specifies the new initial pool size and is measured in bytes by default. As with the -mx option, you also can specify x in either kilobytes or megabytes by appending the letter k or m respectively onto the value. Additionally, x must be greater than 1,000 bytes.

The Java runtime system typically performs garbage collection automatically to make sure unneeded memory stays freed up. This takes place in an asynchronous thread that runs alongside other threads in the runtime system. The -noasyncgc option alters this behavior by turning off asynchronous garbage collection. The result is that no garbage collection takes place unless it is explicitly called upon or the Java program runs out of memory. Incidentally, an explicit garbage collection can be forced by calling the gc method in the System class.

The -noverify option turns all code verification off, meaning that no bytecodes are processed by the bytecode verifier. Typically, the verifier verifies code loaded into the system using a class loader.

Every thread in the Java runtime system is given two stacks, one for Java code and one for C/C++ code. The presence of two stacks reflects the native code support in Java. The -ss option enables you to alter the maximum stack size used by C code in a thread. The default C stack size is 128 kilobytes (-ss 128k). The x parameter specifies the new maximum size in bytes of the C stack, which must be greater than 1,000 bytes. You also can specify x in either kilobytes or megabytes by appending the letter k or m onto the value, respectively. Keep in mind that this option applies to all threads created during program execution.

Similar to the -ss option, the -oss option enables you to set the maximum stack size that can be used by the Java code in a thread. The default Java code stack size is 400 kilobytes (-oss 400k). The x parameter specifies the new maximum size in bytes of the Java stack, which must be greater than 1,000 bytes.

The -t option prints a trace of the bytecode instructions executed. This option works only with the non-optimized version of the Java interpreter, java_g. You learn about the non-optimized interpreter in a moment. The -t option generates a great deal of information that can give you a lot of insight into what is happening within a program. Of course, it would help if you had some understanding of Java bytecodes.

The -verbose option causes the interpreter to print a message to standard output each time a Java class is loaded. Similarly, the -verbosegc option causes the interpreter to print a message each time a garbage collection is performed. A garbage collection is performed by the runtime system to clean up unneeded objects and to free memory.

The opposite of the -noverify option, the -verify option causes the interpreter to run the bytecode verifier on all code loaded into the runtime environment. The default function of the verifier is to only verify code loaded into the system using a class loader. This default behavior also can be explicitly specified using the -verifyremote option.

The -D option enables you to redefine property values. *PropertyName* specifies the name of the property you want to change, and *NewValue* specifies the new value you want to assign to it.

The Non-Optimized Interpreter

Some distributions of the Java Developer's Kit include an alternate Java interpreter called java_g. This is a non-optimized version of the Java interpreter that executes Java bytecodes in a manner more suitable for debugging. If this interpreter is in your JDK distribution, be sure to use it when you are executing code within the Java debugger.

Bugs

The latest release of the Java Developer's Kit, which as of this writing is 1.02, contains some known bugs. More specifically, the following Java runtime interpreter bugs, which apply only to the Windows 95/NT platform, have been documented and acknowledged by the JavaSoft development team:

- Programs using multiple threads never exit.
- Ordered comparisons with NaN don't return `false`.
- Conversion from `Double.MAX_VALUE` to an integer doesn't produce `Integer.MAX_VALUE`.
- Conversion from `Double.MAX_VALUE` to a long doesn't produce `Long.MAX_VALUE`.

The first bug is a pretty big problem and occurs whenever a program starts or creates multiple threads; any program that starts multiple threads will not exit. Fortunately, there is a workaround for this bug: either call `System.exit` when the last running thread is finished, or monitor the threads by calling `Thread.join` and force an exit yourself. Keep in mind that this problem, along with all the interpreter bugs, is apparent only on the Windows 95/NT platform.

The NaN constant defined in the `Float` and `Double` classes represents a result that isn't a number. Because NaN isn't a number, any numeric comparisons made with it should always return `false`. However, the second bug causes the runtime interpreter to evaluate NaN as less than `NEGATIVE_INFINITY`, which allows for comparisons with it to return `true`.

The last two bugs listed deal with converting doubles to integer numbers. More specifically, `Double.MAX_VALUE` doesn't result in `Integer.MAX_VALUE` or `Long.MAX_VALUE` when converted to an integer or long, respectively.

Summary

In this chapter, you found out what the Java runtime interpreter is used for, along with what kind of Java programs can be executed with it. You learned about the `main` function, which is where execution begins in a Java program. You then learned how to use the interpreter and how to specify different options to custom-tailor the execution of Java programs to fit your needs. The chapter finished up by taking a look at some of the bugs present in the current release of the Java interpreter, and how you can get around them.

11

Using the Applet Viewer

by Michael Morrison

The Java applet viewer (`AppletViewer`) is a tool used to run applets without the need for a Web browser. In this chapter, you learn how the applet viewer works, as well as how to use it to run Java applets. You then learn how to use the applet viewer to debug programs, along with how to use it in conjunction with the runtime interpreter to profile executing Java code in an applet. You finish up the chapter by taking a look at the documented bugs in the current release of the applet viewer.

Overview

The typical method of executing a Java applet is from within a Web browser that has a Web page loaded containing the applet. This is the typical scenario in which most Web users come into contact with Java applets. As a Java developer, you have another option for running Java applets that doesn't involve the use of a Web browser. This option involves using the Java applet viewer, which is a tool that serves as a minimal test bed for Java applets. At times, you may not want to hassle with using a full-blown Web browser to test an applet, in which case the applet viewer is an ideal alternative.

Even though the applet viewer logically takes the place of a Web browser, it functions very differently than a Web browser. The applet viewer operates on HTML documents, but all it looks for is embedded applet tags; any other HTML code in the document is ignored. Each time the applet viewer encounters an applet tag in an HTML document, it launches a separate applet viewer window containing the respective applet.

The only drawback to using the applet viewer is that it won't show you how an applet will run within the confines of a real Web setting. Because the applet viewer ignores all HTML codes except applet tags, it doesn't even attempt to display any other information contained in the HTML document. So, once you've tested your applet using the applet viewer, be sure you also test it using a Web browser, just to make sure that it works OK in the context of a real Web page.

Usage

The Java applet viewer is a command-line tool, meaning that it is invoked from a command prompt. The syntax for the applet viewer follows:

```
appletviewer Options URL
```

The *URL* argument specifies a document URL containing an HTML page with an embedded Java applet. The applet viewer launches a separate window for each applet embedded in the HTML document. If the document doesn't contain any embedded applets, the applet viewer will simply exit. Figure 11.1 shows the applet viewer in action.

FIGURE 11.1.

The Animator applet running in the Java applet viewer.

Figure 11.1 shows the Animator demo applet that comes with the Java Developer's Kit running in the applet viewer. The applet was launched in the applet viewer by changing to the directory containing the Animator bytecode class and embedded HTML file, and then executing the following statement at the command prompt:

```
appletviewer example1.html
```

example1.html is the HTML file containing the embedded Java applet. As you can see, there's nothing complicated about running Java applets using the applet viewer. The applet viewer is a useful and easy-to-use tool for testing Java applets in a simple environment.

Options

The Options argument to the applet viewer specifies how to run the Java applet. There is currently only one option supported by the applet viewer, -debug. The -debug option starts the applet viewer in the Java debugger, which enables you to debug applets. For more information about debugging Java programs using the Java debugger, refer to Chapter 15, "jdb: The Java Debugger."

Commands

The applet viewer has a drop-down menu called Applet containing a group of commands, as shown in Figure 11.2.

FIGURE 11.2.

*The Java applet viewer
with commands available
in the drop-down menu.*

The `Restart` command restarts the currently loaded applet, resulting in a call to the `start` method for the applet. The `Restart` command does not reload the applet. Similar to `Restart`, the `Reload` command reloads the applet and then starts it. `Reload` is often a better command to use to restart applets because it ensures that an applet is completely reinitialized.

The `Clone` command launches another instance of the applet viewer executing the same applet. This command is useful when you want to run multiple copies of an applet. For example, a multiuser network applet might support multiple instances that can communicate with each other. You could load one instance of the applet and then use the `Clone` command to start other instances.

The `Tag` command displays a window showing the HTML applet tag for the executing applet. The Applet HTML Tag window is shown in Figure 11.3.

FIGURE 11.3.

*The Applet HTML Tag
window displayed by the
`Tag` command.*

The `Info` command displays a window showing information about the executing applet, including general applet information and information relating to the parameters used by the applet. This information is returned by the `getAppletInfo` and `getParameterInfo` methods of the `Applet` class. The Applet Info window is shown in Figure 11.4.

FIGURE 11.4.

The Applet Info window displayed by the Info *command.*

The Edit command is disabled in the current release of the applet viewer. Presumably, it will be activated in a future release of the applet viewer, in which case it will probably provide a way to alter the applet parameters in the HTML document containing the applet tag.

The Properties command displays a window with access options relating to HTTP and firewall proxies and servers, along with network and class access options. The applet viewer Properties window is shown in Figure 11.5.

FIGURE 11.5.

The applet viewer Properties window displayed by the Properties *command.*

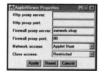

Finally, the Close and Quit commands perform the same function, which is shutting down the applet viewer. It's not clear why there are two different commands for closing the applet viewer—it's presumably an oversight.

Profiling Java Applets

In the previous chapter, "java: The Java Interpreter," the profiler built into the Java runtime interpreter was discussed. This profiler can be used to profile Java applets by running it in conjunction with the applet viewer. In this case, the applet viewer is launched from within the runtime interpreter, like this:

```
java -prof sun.applet.AppletViewer URL
```

URL specifies the name of the HTML file containing an applet tag (or tags). Notice that the applet viewer is referenced using its fully qualified class name, AppletViewer. When you finish running the applet, the interpreter writes a text file named java.prof to the current directory. This file contains profile information for the applet you just ran. Please refer to the previous chapter for more information regarding the meaning of the contents of this file.

Bugs

The latest release of the Java Developer's Kit as of this writing is 1.02, which contains some known bugs. More specifically, the following Java applet viewer bugs have been documented and acknowledged by the JavaSoft development team:

- Transparent images draw incorrectly using ATI video cards (Windows 95/NT version only).
- The Applet HTML Tag window does not display the HTML Applet tag width and height correctly.
- File URLs can only be debugged in local directories.

The first bug applies only to Windows 95/NT systems with ATI video cards. On these systems, transparent images are drawn with their colors reversed. This problem is related to the ATI Windows video driver, for which a fix will no doubt appear in the near future.

The second bug has to do with the applet width and height shown in the Applet HTML Tag window. Rather than displaying the applet width and height as specified in the HTML tag, the window displays the actual applet width and height, which can potentially be different.

The last bug appears when running the applet viewer in debug mode and accessing file URLs that aren't in the current working directory. The bug causes these URLs to throw exceptions when they are referenced. For now, the solution is to set the current working directory to the directory containing the class to be debugged or to reference the applet by an HTTP URL (rather than a file URL).

Summary

This chapter covered the Java applet viewer, which allows you to run Java applets without the help of a Web browser. You learned how to use the applet viewer, along with which options and commands are available to tweak the execution of applets and obtain extra information. You then learned how to use the runtime interpreter profiler in conjunction with the applet viewer to profile Java applets. The chapter finished up by taking a look at the bugs present in the JDK 1.02 release of the applet viewer.

12

HTML for Java
Programmers

by Bryan Morgan

At the current time, it is almost impossible to separate the Java programming language from its use on the World Wide Web (WWW). Java applets were initially the most visible use of Java, and they continue to be the most widespread implementations of the language. Although stand-alone Java applications are possible, runtime speed is the limiting factor to a wider deployment of this type of application. As "just-in-time" and native code compilers become available for the Java platform, perhaps these applications will become more widespread. However, for the time being, Java applet developers will rely on current technologies to display and distribute their applets. These technologies include HTTP (the HyperText Transport Protocol), HTML (HyperText Markup Language), and World Wide Web browsers such as Netscape Navigator, Microsoft Internet Explorer, and Sun HotJava.

Other than the applet itself, the most visible of these technologies to the end-user will be the HTML page in which the applet is embedded. This chapter will attempt to provide the Java programmer with the knowledge needed to create interesting, visually appealing HTML pages to surround the Java applet(s) used.

Welcome to the Internet

The World Wide Web is an enormous collection of computing and information resources connected together in a computer network known as the Internet. It is important to understand that the World Wide Web lies "on top of" the Internet. The collection of networks known as the Internet can be used for standard intercommunication and file transfer between computers. Essentially, it is a vast number of computers (most of which run the UNIX operating system) that communicate among each other using the TCP/IP protocol. Virtually every operating system today currently supplies this protocol, thereby making it the de facto non-proprietary standard for computer intercommunication.

The World Wide Web was invented (by CERN in Switzerland) to provide a more visual means of linking these computing resources together. Using a technology known as hypertext, users can click on highlighted links and automatically jump to that topic. The actual text for this topic can reside within the current file, on the current computer, or on a computer anywhere else in the world. The requestor of information is commonly referred to as the *client*. The holder (and sender) of the information is known as the *server*. The requirements are as follows:

- Both computers must pass information using the TCP/IP protocol. This means that both computers must be assigned addresses (known as IP addresses).

- Both computers must create connections to each other using the HTTP protocol. This protocol essentially uses the pipe (created by TCP/IP) between the two computers to process send and request commands. HTTP will also enable the client to post information to the server.

- Both computers must be visible to each other.

To determine whether you can "see" another computer across the Internet, you can execute the ping command. If you are using Windows 95/NT or UNIX, this command can be executed by simply typing **ping**. Figure 12.1 shows the Sun Web server being pinged. The user will be notified if the server could not be located.

FIGURE 12.1.

Using the ping *command to locate* www.sun.com.

What Exactly Is HTML?

Once this connection is established, the magic of the World Wide Web begins. A type of data file known as HTML (HyperText Markup Language) is transferred to the client machine. If the client is using what is known as a Web browser, the HTML file will be translated and displayed on the screen. The first popular Web browser was distributed freely by the National Center for Supercomputer Applications (NCSA). This browser was known as Mosaic. Other popular browsers include Netscape Navigator, Microsoft Internet Explorer, Spyglass Mosaic, Cello, and many others.

The format of HTML is standards-based. A consortium of organizations (including representatives from the banking, healthcare, government, and computer business sectors) known as the World Wide Web Consortium collectively vote on and manage the official HTML syntax. The World Wide Web Consortium, or W3C as it is also known, can be located at http://www.w3.org. At the time this book was published, the latest version of HTML, known as HTML 3.2, was being finalized.

When browser manufacturers (such as Netscape) add proprietary features to HTML, they press extremely hard for these features to be added to the next release of the HTML specification. Such was the case when Netscape 2.0 announced support for tables and Java applets. At that time, no other browser supported these two features, so the popularity of the Netscape browser increased dramatically. Partly because of this popularity and partly because these two items were truly good ideas, HTML 3.2 will support both tables and Java applets. Therefore, from this point on, if a browser manufacturer announces support for HTML 3.2, Java developers can be sure that their applet will run unmodified within that browser.

Diving into the HTML Format

Many first-time users think that HTML files are actually programs that run within the browser. This could not be further from the truth. An HTML file is simply a text file containing a number of special codes (known as *tags*). These tags are used by browsers to display text, graphics, multimedia, and you guessed it, applets on the browser screen.

> **NOTE**
>
> Because of the way HTML was designed, it is becoming more common to find fantastic Web pages created by desktop publishing gurus and artists than it is to find good pages created by software developers. (As a Java developer, however, you will be able to add a whole new level of interactivity that the less technically minded will find impossible to duplicate!)

All of this would have been a fantastic technology had the Web creators stopped there…but they didn't. They also allowed "links" to other locations to be included as normal text, graphics, and so on. These locations are collectively known as *Uniform Resource Locators (URLs)*. The format for designating a URL is the following:

```
URLType://Internet Node/File Path/File?Arguments
```

Some sample URLs include:

```
http://www.tasc.com (My company's home page)
ftp://ftp.sun.com (Sun's ftp site used to transfer files to your machine.
The JDK can be obtained here as well as from a Sun web page).
news://comp.lang.java (the Java language newsgroup.
An absolute must-visit for serious Java developers!)
```

The following types of URLs currently recognized include:

- `http`—HyperText Transport Protocol.
- `https`—Secure version of HTTP.
- `file`—Used to access files on the user's local drive.
- `ftp`—File Transfer Protocol. FTP is used to transfer files to and from computers that can act as FTP servers.
- `mailto`—Used to generate an e-mail form. This is a non-standard URL that is supported by most Web browsers.
- `news`—USENET news group.
- `wais`—Wide Area Information Server.

■ gopher—Gopher is a method used to search the Internet for file information. This search method has fallen out of favor due to the vast amount of information stored at Web sites such as Yahoo! (http://www.yahoo.com) and AltaVista (http://altavista.digital.com).

■ telnet—Opens a telnet session at a remote computer.

Listing 12.1 shows the contents of the HTML file that makes up the text-only (http://www.sun.com/960601/index.textonly.html) home page of Sun Microsystems (in June 1996). There is also a graphical home page and, of course, a Java version as well. Figure 12.2 shows how this HTML file is interpreted by the Netscape Navigator 2.0 browser.

Listing 12.1. Contents of the Sun Microsystems home page.

```
<HTML>
<HEAD>
<TITLE>Sun Microsystems</TITLE>
</HEAD>
<BODY BGCOLOR=#FFFFFF>
<!-- HEAD_END -->
<H2>Sun Microsystems<br>
    June 1996</H2>
<P>
<ul>
<font size=+2><strong>Scott says... <A HREF="/960601/cover/">
➡ kick butt and have FUN"</a></strong></font><br><em>Sun's feisty
➡ CEO Scott McNealy discusses Java, the Internet, his son Maverick,
➡ and more...</em>
<p>
<font size=+1><strong>Rapid, Reliable <A HREF="/960601/feature1/">
➡ Web Services</a></strong></font>
<p>
<font size=+1><strong>Sun's <A HREF="/960601/feature2/">Intranet</a>
➡ Boosts Productivity</strong></font>
<p>
<font size=+1><strong><A HREF="/960601/feature3/">Infoseek</a>
➡ Spiders Index the Web</strong></font>

</ul>
<UL>
<ul>
<LI><h3>Check out <A HREF="/960416/pbs_facts.html">&quot;Life on the
➡ Internet&quot; </A><br><strong> A 13-week PBS series underwritten
➡ by Sun.</strong></h3>
<LI><h3>Visit <A HREF=/sunworldonline/index.html>SunWorld Online
➡ </A> magazine - it's hot!</h3>
<LI><h3> <A HREF=whatshappening.html>What's New!</A></h3>
<LI><h3> <A HREF="/sunsoft/Developer-products/java">Develop Web
➡ Applications that Sizzle !</A></h3>
</ul>
</ul>
<HR>
<ul>
```

continues

Listing 12.1. continued

```
<h3><A HREF="/products-n-solutions/index.html">Products and Solutions</A></h3>
<h3><A HREF="/sales-n-service/index.html">Sales and Service</A></h3>
<h3><A HREF="/tech/index.html">Technology and Developers</A></h3>
<h3><A HREF="/corporateoverview/corp.html">Corporate Overview</A></h3>
</ul>
<HR>
<ul>
<h3><A HREF="/sun-on-net/index.html">Sun on the Net</A></h3>
<h3><A HREF="/search/search.html">Search</A></h3>
<h3><A HREF="/backissues.html">Back Issues</A></h3>
</ul>
<HR>

A version of this page with nice <A HREF="index.html">graphics</A> is available.
<P>

<!-- FOOT_START -->
<HR>
<FONT SIZE=2> Questions or comments regarding this service?
<A HREF="/cgi-bin/comment-form.pl"><EM>webmaster@sun.com</EM></A>
</FONT>
<P>
<H5><A HREF="/share/text/SMIcopyright.html">Copyright</A> 1996
➥ Sun Microsystems, Inc., 2550 Garcia Ave., Mtn. View, Ca 94043-1100 USA.
➥ All Rights Reserved
</H5>
</BODY></HTML>
```

FIGURE 12.2.

index.textonly.html
*displayed in the Netscape
Navigator browser.*

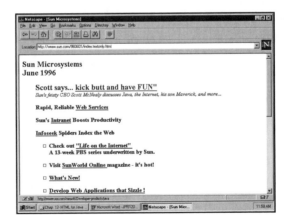

This file is included on the companion CD-ROM to this book as index_textonly.html. If the pages still exist on the Web servers that this document points to, the document should be able to be loaded at any point in the future and still allow the reader to connect to any of its links. You can see, therefore, that the content of HTML pages is independent of where these pages reside.

The remainder of this chapter will focus on two topics:

- Embedding Java applets within HTML pages
- HTML document creation

Java and HTML: The Basics

Most new Java programmers probably had their first exposure to Java through an applet embedded within a World Wide Web page. Although the actual complex coding resides within the Java applet (a .class file residing on the Web server), HTML provides a tag that enables the developer or Web publisher to "embed" the applet within the page. This tag is known as the APPLET tag. Before the APPLET tag can be used, however, it is necessary for the developer to understand the absolute basics of HTML. This section will cover the bare minimum set of tags necessary for your applet to be displayed within the browser. These tags will be examined in more detail later in this chapter.

> **NOTE**
>
> Before continuing, please note the format of HTML tags. All tags begin with a "<" character and end with a ">" character. Tags that contain a group of information also are denoted by a closing tag (</tag>) similar to the start tag with a forward slash. This format is known as a begin-end pair. For example, an applet begins with <APPLET> and ends with </APPLET>. For more information on HTML publishing, see *Teach Yourself Web Publishing with HTML in 14 Days* from Sams.net.

Starting the Document: The <HTML> Tag

The very first tag that should appear in your HTML file is the HTML tag. This tag has no attributes. Simply add the following to the beginning of your document:

```
<HTML>
```

It simply denotes that this file is an HTML file for browsers that are reading in the file.

To end your document, use the ending HTML tag.

```
</HTML>
```

> **NOTE**
>
> Another tag that is rarely used at the beginning of documents, but is supported by the HTML standard, is the doctype tag. The doctype tag denotes, to systems that use

SGML (Standard Generalized Markup Language), that this file is to use the HTML DTD (Document Type Definition). For more information on SGML, see `http://www.sil.org/sgml/sgml.html`.

Its format is

```
<!doctype html public "-//IETF//DTD HTML//EN">
```

Setting Up the Title: The `<HEAD>` and the `<TITLE>` Tags

After it sees the `<HTML>` tag, your browser is ready to process this HTML document. The HEAD tag is used after the HTML tag to contain information that will not appear directly on the page (also see the META tag later on in this chapter). The most important of these tags is the TITLE tag. The information inserted in the TITLE tag will be displayed at the top of most Web browsers. Adding these tags to the HTML tag would result in the following:

```
<HTML>
<HEAD>
<TITLE>This is my applet's first home!</TITLE>
</HEAD>
</HTML>
```

The preceding text represents a complete HTML file that could be loaded into any application that displays HTML markup. Unfortunately, at this point, it would only display a blank screen with the title on the top bar of the application. A little bit more information is needed to get an applet on the screen.

The Center of Attention: The `<BODY>` Tag

As mentioned already, the HEAD tag is used to contain header information for the HTML document. (It will be shown later that the HEAD tag can also contain several other items besides the TITLE tag.) The BODY tag is used to contain the information to be displayed on the browser screen. Using the HTML lines you entered earlier for the HEAD tag, now add the BODY tag.

```
<HTML>
<HEAD>
<TITLE>This is my applet's first home!</TITLE>
</HEAD>
<BODY>
</BODY>
</HTML>
```

Now it's time to make this page display something besides a blank screen. Text can be displayed using a number of HTML tags. The two most commonly used tags are the heading tags and paragraph tags.

Displaying Text on the Page: Headings, Paragraphs, and Line Breaks

Because by definition, headings appear at the top of a paragraph, they will be examined first. In HTML, there are six levels of headings, known as Heading 1 through Heading 6. These six different levels (denoted as <H#>...</H#>) are typically displayed using the same type of font with smaller point sizes as the heading number increases.

NOTE

Like Java, HTML was designed to be completely platform- and browser-independent. HTML in no way dictates *which* fonts or colors applications should be used to view it.

`Example1.html`, shown in Listing 12.2, illustrates the use of all six headings within Netscape Navigator (see Figure 12.3).

Listing 12.2. `Example1.html`: Displaying the six heading types using HTML.

```
<HTML>
<HEAD>
<TITLE>This is my applet's first home!</TITLE>
</HEAD>
<BODY>
<H1>This is Heading 1</H1>
<H2>This is Heading 2</H2>
<H3>This is Heading 3</H3>
<H4>This is Heading 4</H4>
<H5>This is Heading 5</H5>
<H6>This is Heading 6</H6>
</BODY>
</HTML>
```

FIGURE 12.3.

Displaying the six heading types using Netscape's default settings.

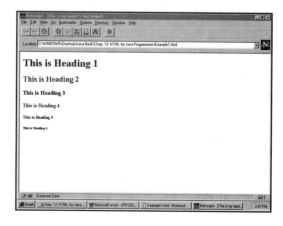

The paragraph tag is one of the most commonly used tags in HTML. It is used to contain regular text. Its format is

```
<P> Insert your text here... </P>
```

All text can be formatted using a large number of text formatting tags, but these will be saved for later in the chapter (see the section titled "Text Formatting").

Line breaks are used to insert blank lines within HTML pages without beginning a new, blank paragraph. Because line breaks do not actually *contain* anything, they have no ending tag. The format for a line break is

```
<BR>
```

Before adding an applet to a page, run `Example2.html` in Listing 12.3 to make sure that you fully understand these tags. You should see a result similar to that in Figure 12.4.

Listing 12.3. `Example2.html`: A simple HTML file complete with onscreen display.

```
<HTML>
<HEAD>
<TITLE>This is my applet's first home!</TITLE>
</HEAD>
<BODY>
<H1>Welcome to the brave new world!</H1>
<BR>
<P>This page represents a first try at creating a fully functional
➡ HTML page.</P>
<BR>
<P>More exciting concepts will be visiting this page in a short time
➡ ...Stay tuned!</P>
</BODY>
</HTML>
```

FIGURE 12.4.

`Example2.html` *file displayed in Netscape Navigator.*

Adding a Java Applet

At this point, all that is left is to add an actual Java applet to the screen. To do this, several steps are required:

1. The Java language .java source file must be created.
2. The .java source file must be compiled into a .class file.
3. The .class file must be referenced from within the HTML page using the <APPLET> tag.

Creating the Java Applet

This chapter is not intended to cover the specifics of Java applet development, but at this point we will demonstrate a simple Java applet for display within a browser so that you can traverse the process of creating HTML pages containing Java applets. For additional information on Java applets, see Chapter 7, "Developing Java Applets." The sample applet that will be created here is the now familiar HelloWorld applet. Listing 12.4 shows the Java source code necessary to print a string to the screen.

Listing 12.4. The HelloWorld applet: HelloWorld.java.

```
import java.awt.Font;
import java.awt.Graphics;

/* The following class prints the text "Hello World!" to the screen */

public class HelloWorld extends java.applet.Applet
{
 Font tempFont = new Font("Helvetica", Font.PLAIN, 20);

  public void paint(Graphics g)
  {
    g.setFont(tempFont);
    g.drawString("Hello world!", 10, 25);
  }
}
```

Compiling HelloWorld.java with the javac compiler will result in the creation of a HelloWorld.class file. Example3.html, shown in Listing 12.5, shows the Example3.html file with the APPLET tag for HelloWorld added to it. The text "If you can see this…" outside of the APPLET tag itself will be displayed to browsers that are not capable of hosting Java applets. The APPLET tag will be covered in more detail in the next section, but for now it may be useful to run this example to prove to yourself that it really is this simple. The results are shown in Figure 12.5.

Listing 12.5. `Example3.html`: A simple HTML file containing the HelloWorld applet.

```
<HTML>
<HEAD>
<TITLE>This is my applet's first home!</TITLE>
</HEAD>
<BODY>
<H1>Welcome to the brave new world!</H1>
<BR>
<P>This page represents a first try at creating a fully functional HTML
➥ page.</P>
<BR>
<P>Below you will find my HelloWorld applet.</P>
<BR>
<APPLET CODE="HelloWorld.class" WIDTH=150 HEIGHT=30>
If you can see this, your browser does not support Java applets.
</APPLET>
</BODY>
</HTML>
```

FIGURE 12.5.

`Example3.html` *file displayed in Netscape Navigator.*

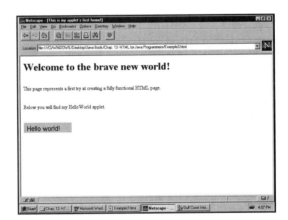

The <APPLET> Tag in Detail

Now that a simple Java-enabled Web page has been demonstrated, it is time to explore the APPLET tag in more detail. The basic description of this tag is as follows:

```
<APPLET attributes>
applet_parameters
alternate_content
</APPLET>
```

What you are concerned with here are the `attributes` and the `applet_parameters`.

<APPLET> Tag Attributes

The APPLET tag supports a number of standard attributes. The majority of these attributes are nearly identical to the attributes of the IMG tag (to be discussed later in this chapter). The three *required* attributes are CODE/CODEBASE, WIDTH, and HEIGHT. The following list describes each attribute and its meaning.

ALT—Alternate text that can be displayed by text-only browsers. Some browsers also show this text when the applet is loading.

ALIGN—The ALIGN attribute designates the alignment of the applet within the browser page. Here are the possible choices for alignment:

- left—Aligns the applet at the left margin. The left and right values allow text to flow around the applet. (For spacing around the applet, see the VSPACE and HSPACE attributes.)

- right—Aligns the applet at the right margin.

- top—Aligns the applet with the topmost item on the current line in the HTML file.

- texttop—Aligns the applet with the top of the tallest text in the current line of the HTML file.

- middle—Aligns the applet with the middle of the baseline of the text in the current line of the HTML file.

- absmiddle—Aligns the middle of the applet with the middle of the largest item (text or otherwise) in the current line of the HTML file.

- baseline—Aligns the bottom of the applet with the baseline of the current line of the HTML file.

- bottom—Equivalent to baseline.

- absbottom—Aligns the bottom of the applet with the lowest item (text or otherwise) in the current line of the HTML file.

CODE—(Required) The CODE attribute is used to indicate the .class file that loads the applet. This file must be in the same directory location as this HTML file. To load an applet located in a different directory, use the CODEBASE attribute.

CODEBASE—The CODEBASE attribute is used to indicate the location of the .class file that loads the applet. This attribute can contain either a directory name or a URL.

HEIGHT—(Required) The HEIGHT attribute is used to set the applet's box height.

HSPACE—The HSPACE attribute sets the amount of horizontal space to be set off around the applet. Both the HSPACE and VSPACE attributes are used only when the ALIGN attribute is equal to LEFT or RIGHT.

NAME—The NAME attribute sets the symbolic name of the applet. This attribute is useful when multiple applets present on a page need to locate each other.

VSPACE—The VSPACE attribute sets the amount of vertical space to be set off around the applet. Both the HSPACE and VSPACE attributes are used only when the ALIGN attribute is equal to LEFT or RIGHT.

WIDTH—(Required) The WIDTH attribute is used to set the applet's box width.

Examples Using <APPLET> Attributes

This section presents some examples detailing the use of the APPLET tag's attributes. Because the most commonly used attributes are the ALIGN, HSPACE, and VSPACE attributes, special attention will be paid to them.

Example4.html, shown in Listing 12.6, makes use of the APPLET tag's ALIGN attribute. The HelloWorld applet is loaded several times onto one form to show the use of the ALIGN attribute. Listing 12.7 is Example5.html, which expands on Example4.html by including the VSPACE and HSPACE attributes. The resulting pages are shown in Figures 12.6 and 12.7.

Listing 12.6. Example4.html: Various uses of the APPLET tag's ALIGN attribute.

```
<HTML>
<HEAD>
<TITLE>This is my applet's first home!</TITLE>
</HEAD>
<BODY>
<H1>Welcome to the brave new world!</H1>
<BR>
<P>This page represents a first try at creating a fully functional HTML
➥ page.</P>
<BR>
<P>Below you will find my HelloWorld applet.</P>
<BR>
<P>Note the clever use of the ALIGN attribute to move the applet around
➥ on the screen.</P>
<BR>

<P><APPLET CODE="HelloWorld.class" WIDTH=150 HEIGHT=30 ALIGN=LEFT>
If you can see this, your browser does not support Java applets.
</APPLET>
To the left you will notice the HelloWorld applet
</P>
<BR>

<P><APPLET CODE="HelloWorld.class" WIDTH=150 HEIGHT=30 ALIGN=RIGHT>
If you can see this, your browser does not support Java applets.
</APPLET>
To the right you will notice the HelloWorld applet
</P>
<BR>

</BODY>
</HTML>
```

FIGURE 12.6.

Example4.html *showing the use of the* ALIGN *attribute.*

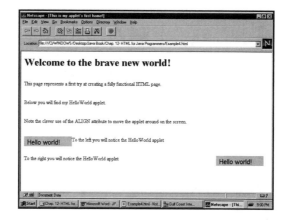

Listing 12.7. Repeats Example4.html, but it now includes the VSPACE and HSPACE attributes.

```
<HTML>
<HEAD>
<TITLE>This is my applet's first home!</TITLE>
</HEAD>
<BODY>
<H1>Welcome to the brave new world!</H1>
<BR>
<P>This page represents a first try at creating a fully functional HTML
➥ page.</P>
<BR>
<P>Below you will find my HelloWorld applet.</P>
<BR>
<P>Note the clever use of the ALIGN, VSPACE, and HSPACE attributes to set the
 applet's location on the screen.</P>
<BR>

<P><APPLET CODE="HelloWorld.class" WIDTH=150 HEIGHT=30 ALIGN=LEFT HSPACE=25>
If you can see this, your browser does not support Java applets.
</APPLET>
To the left you will notice the HelloWorld applet
</P>
<BR>

<P><APPLET CODE="HelloWorld.class" WIDTH=150 HEIGHT=30 ALIGN=RIGHT VSPACE=50>
If you can see this, your browser does not support Java applets.
</APPLET>
To the right you will notice the HelloWorld applet
</P>
<BR>

</BODY>
</HTML>
```

FIGURE 12.7.

Illustrates the use of the VSPACE *and* HSPACE *attributes to offset text around the applet.*

<APPLET> Tag Parameters: The <PARAM> Tag

The APPLET parameters stored in the PARAM tag actually have little directly to do with HTML. Instead, they are parameters passed directly to a Java applet. It is the responsibility of the applet to check the parameter values and respond accordingly.

There are two steps to passing parameters to applets:

1. Add the PARAM tag (with values) to the HTML source file.
2. Add necessary code to the applet to retrieve these parameter values.

Passing Parameters to the Applet

The syntax required to pass these parameters is

```
<PARAM NAME=param_name VALUE=param_value>
```

In this syntax, *param_name* and *param_value* are the values passed to the Java applet.

Retrieving Parameters Within the Applet

Java applets retrieve these parameter values using the getParameter() method. Although this function can be called anywhere, the most common case occurs when this function is called in the applet's init() method. (For more on applet initialization, see Chapter 7.) The method syntax is the following:

```
String getParameter(String name);
```

> **NOTE**
>
> When passing parameters to applets, keep in mind that the parameter names are case-sensitive! Also note that all parameter values are converted to strings.

It is now time to revisit the HelloWorld class created earlier in Listing 12.4. A new class entitled FancyHelloWorld will be created (see Listing 12.8) that will take a parameter named "COLOR" and draw the text on the screen according to the value of that parameter.

Listing 12.8. Class FancyHelloWorld reacts to the COLOR parameter.

```java
import java.awt.Font;
import java.awt.Graphics;
import java.awt.Color;

/* The following class prints the text "Hello World!" to the screen      */
/* It also accepts a font color as input and draws the text in that color */
public class FancyHelloWorld extends java.applet.Applet
{
  Font tempFont = new Font("Helvetica", Font.PLAIN, 20);
  Color tempColor;
  String tempString;

  public void init()
  {
    tempString = getParameter("COLOR");

    if (tempString.equals("WHITE"))
      tempColor = new Color(255, 255, 255);
    else if (tempString.equals("BLACK"))
      tempColor = new Color(0, 0, 0);
    else if (tempString.equals("GRAY"))
      tempColor = new Color(128, 128, 128);
    else if (tempString.equals("RED"))
      tempColor = new Color(255, 0, 0);
    else if (tempString.equals("GREEN"))
      tempColor = new Color(0, 255, 0);
    else if (tempString.equals("BLUE"))
      tempColor = new Color(0, 0, 255);
    else if (tempString.equals("YELLOW"))
      tempColor = new Color(255, 255, 0);
    else if (tempString.equals("MAGENTA"))
      tempColor = new Color(255, 0, 255);
    else if (tempString.equals("CYAN"))
      tempColor = new Color(0, 255, 255);
    else if (tempString.equals("PINK"))
      tempColor = new Color(255, 175, 175);
    else if (tempString.equals("ORANGE"))
      tempColor = new Color(255, 200, 0);
    else
      tempColor = new Color(0, 0, 0);
  }

  public void paint(Graphics g)
  {
    g.setFont(tempFont);
    g.setColor(tempColor);
    g.drawString("Hello world!", 10, 25);
  }
}
```

Example6.html, shown in Listing 12.9, modifies the HTML file built in Example3.html by passing in several COLOR parameters. Figure 12.8 shows the Example6.html loaded in Netscape.

Listing 12.9. Example6.html passes several COLOR parameters to FancyHelloWorld.class.

```
<HTML>
<HEAD>
<TITLE>This is my applet's first home!</TITLE>
</HEAD>
<BODY>
<H1>Welcome to the brave new world!</H1>
<BR>
<P>This page represents a first try at creating a fully functional HTML
➥ page.</P>
<BR>
<P>Below you will find my HelloWorld applet.</P>
<BR>

<APPLET CODE="FancyHelloWorld.class" WIDTH=150 HEIGHT=30>
<PARAM NAME=COLOR VALUE="BLUE">
If you can see this, your browser does not support Java applets.
</APPLET>
<BR>

<APPLET CODE="FancyHelloWorld.class" WIDTH=150 HEIGHT=30>
<PARAM NAME=COLOR VALUE="RED">
If you can see this, your browser does not support Java applets.
</APPLET>
<BR>

<APPLET CODE="FancyHelloWorld.class" WIDTH=150 HEIGHT=30>
<PARAM NAME=COLOR VALUE="CYAN">
If you can see this, your browser does not support Java applets.
</APPLET>
<BR>

<APPLET CODE="FancyHelloWorld.class" WIDTH=150 HEIGHT=30>
<PARAM NAME=COLOR VALUE="YELLOW">
If you can see this, your browser does not support Java applets.
</APPLET>

</BODY>
</HTML>
```

FIGURE 12.8.

`Example6.html` *loaded into Netscape Navigator.*

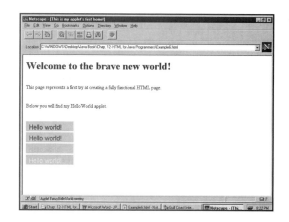

HTML Document Creation

The preceding section contains all the information needed to embed Java applets within HTML pages. However, it is only a tiny subset of the information needed to create complete HTML documents. Though there are hundreds of tags that make up the entire HTML specification, the remainder of this chapter will focus on the topics needed to provide a thorough introduction to HTML for Java programmers.

So far, the following tags have been introduced:

- `<HTML>` HTML tag
- `<HEAD>` Header tag that can contain document information
- `<TITLE>` Header title tag that contains the document title
- `<BODY>` Body tag
- `<H1>–<H6>` Body heading tags
- `<P>` Body paragraph tag
- `<BR>` Body line breaks
- `<APPLET>` Java applet tag

If you have much experience browsing World Wide Web documents, you probably realize that HTML allows a great deal more flexibility than what has been covered thus far. Features to be covered throughout the rest of this chapter include the following:

- Additional header information
- Complete text formatting (including lists, effects, and character entities)
- Hyperlinks to remote documents or files
- Images

Additional Header Information

Earlier in this chapter the HEAD tag was introduced. It is generally used to store data that does not directly affect the appearance of the HTML document. To review, the TITLE tag was used to display the document's title and is contained within the document header. Two more additional tags are commonly used to stamp information into the HTML file should someone choose to view the source at a later date.

The <META> Tag

In addition to the title, the header can also contain what is known as *metadata*. This data is essentially miscellaneous information that may be of use to someone that views the HTML source at a later date. Each document can contain an unlimited number of META tags (use discretion here). <META> has three allowed attributes:

NAME—This attribute is used to define what information is stored in the current META tag. If NAME is used, HTTP-EQUIV should not be.

CONTENT—The CONTENT attribute defines the actual contents of the META tag.

HTTP-EQUIV—This attribute exists for the primary use of Web server administrators. This enables the HTML author to tie the contents of a META tag to an HTTP server's response header. If HTTP-EQUIV is used, NAME should not be.

Some examples that demonstrate the use of the META tag are as follows:

```
<HTML>
<HEAD>
<TITLE>Sample Meta Information</TITLE>
<META NAME="Creation_Date" CONTENT="June 9, 1996">
<META NAME="Author" CONTENT="Bryan Morgan">
</HEAD>
</HTML>
```

The <BASE> Tag

HTML also provides a tag that furnishes a self-referencing URL for the document. This allows the remaining URLs within the document to contain relative location information instead of continually "hard-wiring" themselves. This is especially useful if a document is mirrored at several locations. Use of the BASE tag allows the document's links to still point to valid addresses (if all of the additional files, and so on were mirrored with the main document). The BASE tag has one attribute:

HREF—The HREF attribute stores the URL of the document containing the BASE tag.

Overall Document Formatting

Several tags provided by HTML allow the document to provide a more visually appealing appearance (as opposed to black text on a gray screen!). This section discusses these tags briefly.

Modifying the BODY Tag

The BODY tag (<BODY>) has already been introduced in its simplest form—that of a container for the body of the document. However, it does have several attributes that allow the publisher to edit its visual appearance. These attributes include the BGCOLOR, BACKGROUND, TEXT, LINK, VLINK, and ALINK attributes.

- ■ BGCOLOR—Sets the background color of the document.
- ■ BACKGROUND—Designates the URL of the background image to be used.
- ■ TEXT—Sets the color of regular text (overrides browser defaults).
- ■ LINK—Sets the color of hyperlinks (overrides browser defaults).
- ■ VLINK—Sets the color of visited links (overrides browser defaults).
- ■ ALINK—Sets the color of active links (overrides browser defaults).

The colors available can be viewed in Figure 12.9.

FIGURE 12.9.
Allowed colors in HTML.

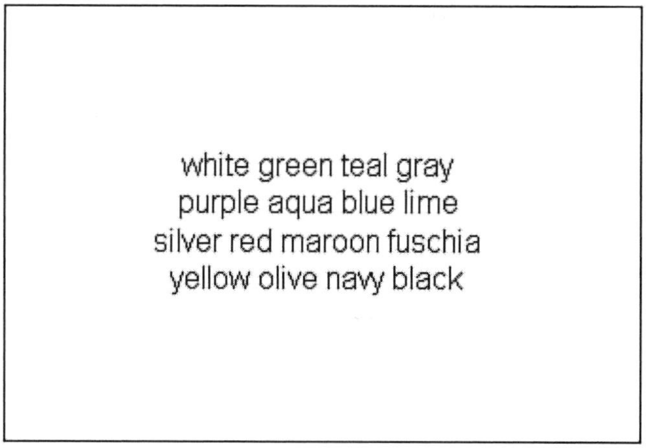

```
white green teal gray
purple aqua blue lime
silver red maroon fuschia
yellow olive navy black
```

Complete Text Formatting

The previous section dealt with "invisible" information that is placed into the HTML header section. The remainder of the topics that will be discussed directly affect the onscreen display of HTML.

HTML allows the publisher to completely format text output on a screen. This includes the ability to change the size, type, and color of fonts, modify the highlighting of characters to show emphasis, and add onscreen visual effects such as horizontal lines and background coloring.

Text Tags

One of the most common operations on text in a document is the modifying of various character styles to add effects to a document. The following paragraphs cover the most popular of these styles, and `Example7.html`, shown in Listing 12.10, gives an HTML file that demonstrates the use of many of these styles.

Making Text Bold

The `<B>...</B>` and `<STRONG>...</STRONG>` tags are used to boldface text. For these tags (and all of the remaining tags in this section), simply place the text to be made bold within these tags.

Italicizing Text

The `<I>...</I>` and `<EM>...</EM>` tags are used to italicize text.

Setting the Base Font

The `BASEFONT` tag forces the size of all text within the page. It has one attribute, `SIZE`.

The syntax is

```
<BASEFONT SIZE=25>
```

Using Comments

Comments can be used in HTML but they also have a special tag to contain them. The format of this tag is a normal tag that begins with an exclamation point (no ending exclamation point is needed).

Here is the syntax:

```
<!...comments...>
```

Font Color and Size

One of the most visually appealing effects, if used properly, can be the modification of text's font size and color. To do this, HTML supplies the publisher with the `FONT` tag. The `FONT` tag has two attributes: `COLOR` and `SIZE`. These attributes have the following properties:

■ `COLOR`—The `COLOR` attribute can be any of the values illustrated in Figure 12.10.

■ `SIZE`—The `SIZE` attribute can range from 1 to 7, with 1 being the smallest and 7 representing the document's `BASEFONT`.

Listing 12.10. `Example7.html`: A simple HTML file demonstrating various text tags.

```
<HTML>
<HEAD>
<TITLE>Sample HTML Page</TITLE>
</HEAD>
```

```
<BODY>
<H1>Examples of HTML Character Formatting</H1>
<BR>

<P>
<!Show default font size first>
BASEFONT = Default<BR>
<B>Bold Text</B><I>Italic Text</I>
<BR><BR>

<!Now change the font size to 20>
BASEFONT = 20<BR>
<BASEFONT SIZE=20>
<B>Bold Text</B><I>Italic Text</I>
<BR><BR>

<!Let's play with the Font!>
<B><FONT COLOR=RED>Happy </FONT><FONT COLOR=WHITE>Fourth </FONT>
<FONT COLOR=BLUE>Of </FONT><FONT COLOR=RED>July!</FONT></B>
<BR><BR>
<!Now change the size>
<B><FONT COLOR=RED SIZE=7>Happy </FONT><FONT COLOR=WHITE SIZE=5>Fourth </FONT>
<FONT COLOR=BLUE SIZE=3>Of </FONT><FONT COLOR=RED SIZE=1>July!</FONT></B>
<BR><BR>
</P>
```

FIGURE 12.10.

Example7.html
*demonstrating various text
tags.*

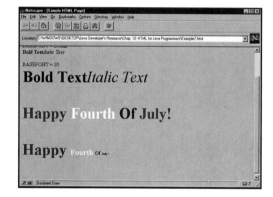

Using Anchors to Create Hyperlinks

There are many advantages to creating documents using the HTML format. Arguably, one of the greatest advantages is the ability to create hyperlinks to other documents and embed these hyperlinks as part of the current document with the implementation hidden from the reader. HTML allows the creation of these hyperlinks through the use of the Anchor (<A>...</A>) tag.

NOTE

The <A>...</A> tag by itself does nothing. To create hyperlinks, the <A>...</A> tag must be used in conjunction with one of its attributes such as HREF or NAME.

Linking to Another URL

To link to another URL from the current document, the HREF attribute is provided. The <A> tag is called an anchor because it "anchors" text to a URL. You can see this by examining the syntax:

```
<A HREF="URL">LocationNameInText</A>
```

The actual location name displayed to the user is not an actual attribute. Instead, it is "anchored" to the HREF attribute.

Modify the phrase "Happy Fourth Of July!" in Example7.html (see Listing 12.11 and corresponding Figure 12.11) to point to the White House Web site (http://www.whitehouse.gov). When you run the example, you should see a result like that in Figure 12.12.

Listing 12.11. Example8.html: Adding a link to the White House web site using the Anchor tag.

```
<HTML>
<HEAD>
<TITLE>Sample HTML Page</TITLE>
</HEAD>
<BODY>
<H1>Examples of HTML Character Formatting</H1>
<BR>

<P>
<!Show default font size first>
BASEFONT = Default<BR>
<B>Bold Text</B><I>Italic Text</I>
<BR><BR>

<!Now change the font size to 20>
BASEFONT = 20<BR>
<BASEFONT SIZE=20>
<B>Bold Text</B><I>Italic Text</I>
<BR><BR>

<!Let's go to the White House!!>
<B><A HREF="http://www.whitehouse.gov">Happy Fourth Of July!</A></B>
<BR><BR>
</P>

</BODY>
</HTML>
```

NOTE

The URL used with the HREF attribute does not have to be an HTTP address. It could be FTP, e-mail, or any other URL qualifier.

FIGURE 12.11.

`Example8.html` *with the White House link.*

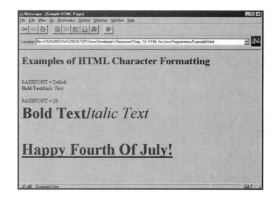

FIGURE 12.12.

The White House Web Page (note the Java Flag applet!)

Linking within the Page

What if your document has no reason to point to a remote URL, but you would like to jump to a location at the end of the document? As you may have guessed by now, the designers of HTML thought of that also. This can be accomplished through the use of the NAME attribute. Using the NAME attribute actually requires two steps:

1. Using an anchor to set a link to the NAMED location.
2. Setting the NAMED location through the use of the # character.

The syntax is

```
<A HREF="#named_location">named_location_text</A>
.
.
.
<A NAME="named_location">link_name_text</A>
```

`Example9.html` (see Listing 12.12) illustrates the use of the NAME tag.

Listing 12.12. `Example9.html`: Using the `NAME` attribute to jump through a document.

```
<HTML>
<HEAD>
<TITLE>Sample HTML Page</TITLE>
</HEAD>
<BODY>
<H1>Examples of HTML Anchoring</H1>
<BR>

<P>
<!>To test this, make your browser height really small. Otherwise,
   you won't notice the jump.  Now, let's make a named link!>

<B><A HREF="#jumphere">Jump Back Jack!</A></B>
<BR><BR>

Text<BR>
Text<BR>
Text<BR>
Text<BR>
Text<BR>
Text<BR>
Text<BR>
Text<BR>
Text<BR>

<B><A NAME="jumphere">Take a leap!</A></B>

</P>
</BODY>
</HTML>
```

HTML and Images

Adding images to an HTML document can greatly improve the document's visual appeal. You can do this through the use of the HTML IMAGE tag. The basic syntax for using the IMAGE tag is the following:

```
<IMG SRC="graphic_URL">
```

The IMAGE tag actually has several attributes in addition to the SRC attribute. The following list gives more information on IMAGE tag attributes.

- ■ SRC—Used to set the URL of the image being loaded.

- ■ ALT—Contains text that will be displayed in text-only browsers (or browsers that have image-loading turned off).

- ■ ALIGN—Can be one of two possible values: TOP or MIDDLE. These values behave the same as the APPLET tag's ALIGN attribute.

CAUTION

It is imperative that the image format included in your HTML document be viewable by all popular browser types. At the current time, the most common image formats are JPEG and GIF (with GIF being the most commonly accepted format).

Summary

HTML is an open specification that enables anyone with a text editor to create dynamic, visually interesting documents that can be read on any computer in widespread use today. It is essentially comprised of a set of tags that enable the file creator to lay out the document in an implementation-neutral manner. (Details such as font type and screen resolution are of no concern to the HTML publisher.) Java applets can be embedded within an HTML page through the use of the <APPLET> tag. Tags that have attributes enable the HTML developer to customize the layout and display of the form.

One of the most exciting aspects of the World Wide Web is that it gives individuals the ability to publish information that can be viewed by the entire world. Although many programmers tend to ignore the publishing aspects of Web development, the appearance and functionality of Web pages are just as important as GUI screen layouts are. The time you spend planning out an HTML page and its interaction with Java applets will be time well spent if the application is deployed and met with success.

13

HotJava and Other Java-Enabled Browsers

by Bryan Morgan

For users and developers new to the Java world, the great amount of new terminology tends to be a little confusing. Questions often asked are

■ What separates a Java applet from a Java application?

■ Can any Web browser run a Java applet?

■ What is the difference between Java, JavaScript, and HotJava?

The answer to the first question can be found by reading Chapters 7 and 8, "Developing Java Applets" and "Developing Java Applications." This chapter will focus on the second question— Web browsers that support Java applets. By demonstrating the capabilities of these Web browsers, the differences between Java, JavaScript, and HotJava should become apparent.

Currently, three Web browsers support Java applets: Sun HotJava, Netscape Navigator 2.0 (or greater), and Microsoft Internet Explorer 3.0. This chapter will explore these three products and illustrate differences between them. The first browser to be examined will be Sun's HotJava.

The HotJava 1.0 Browser

The HotJava Browser is a product of Sun Microsystems' JavaSoft. It is the only Web browser that not only supports Java applets but also is actually written in Java. Although the browser market is dominated at the present time by Netscape's Navigator and Microsoft's Internet Explorer, the HotJava 1.0 release will run as a platform-independent application. This means that if devices such as Oracle's Network Computer become widely used, HotJava will undoubtedly be the first browser available for these platforms. Because the beta versions of HotJava were written using a special version of the JDK, however, pre-1.0 releases are platform-dependent.

What is now known as the HotJava product actually was introduced as a stand-alone Web browser back in the spring of 1995. As Java's potential was recognized by the public and its popularity skyrocketed, HotJava came to be much more than a Web browser. The HotJava product now refers to a set of Java class libraries that simplifies the creation of Internet-aware applications. The HotJava browser is provided as a showcase of these class libraries' capabilities. The HotJava class library will be available from JavaSoft as a licensable product at a later date. At this time, HotJava can best be explored by downloading and installing the HotJava Web browser.

Installing the HotJava Browser

Like the JDK, HotJava can be downloaded for free by visiting the following location:
`http://www.javasoft.com/java.sun.com/HotJava`.

> **NOTE**
>
> Unlike the JDK, HotJava does not currently support the Apple Macintosh operating system. However, Sun Solaris and Microsoft Windows 95/NT are supported. Apple Macintosh support is planned to coincide with the release of the JDK V1.1.

These installation instructions will be split into separate listings for Solaris and Windows. To install HotJava, follow the instructions that apply to your platform.

Sun Solaris 2.4+ SPARC-Based Machines

The HotJava browser can be obtained by FTP at `ftp://ftp.javasoft.com/pub/`. At the time this book was written, the current version of the browser was the pre-Beta1 release. The filename to download is `hotjava-1_0prebeta1-solaris2-sparc.tar.Z`. (To retrieve the latest version, visit the HotJava home page at `http://www.javasoft.com/java.sun.com/HotJava`.)

This file is in the TAR format, so once it has been downloaded, you need to "untar" the file. Use the following command to untar the file:

```
% zcat hotjava-1_0prebeta1-solaris2-sparc.tar.Z ¦ tar xf -
```

This will create a `/HotJava` directory in the directory where the file was unzipped. This directory should contain all of the HotJava files including the `classes.zip` file that contains the HotJava class library (more on this later).

> **CAUTION**
>
> As with the JDK's `classes.zip` file, do not unzip the HotJava `classes.zip` file.

If you previously have installed Alpha or earlier Beta versions of HotJava, you may need to unset the environment variables `HOTJAVA_HOME`, `JAVA_HOME`, or `CLASSPATH`. You can do this by executing the following command:

```
% unsetenv JAVA_HOME HOTJAVA_HOME CLASSPATH
```

Microsoft Windows 95/NT

The HotJava browser can be obtained by FTP at `ftp://ftp.javasoft.com/pub/`. At the time this book was written, the current version of the browser was the pre-Beta1 release. The filename to download is `hotjava-1_0prebeta1-win32-x86.exe`. (To retrieve the latest version, visit the HotJava home page at `http://www.javasoft.com/java.sun.com/HotJava`.)

This file is in a self-extracting zip format, so once it has been downloaded, all you need to do is execute the file. This will create a `\HotJava` directory in the directory where the file was unzipped. This directory should contain all of the HotJava files including the `classes.zip` file that contains the HotJava class library (more on this later).

> **CAUTION**
>
> As with the JDK's `classes.zip` file, do not unzip the HotJava `classes.zip` file.

If you previously have installed Alpha or earlier Beta versions of HotJava, you may need to unset the environment variables `HOTJAVA_HOME`, `JAVA_HOME`, or `CLASSPATH`. You can do this by removing these lines from the `AUTOEXEC.BAT` file (under Windows 95) or by making these changes using Control Panel's System tool (under Windows NT).

Installation Tips

If you followed the preceding steps, the HotJava browser should be ready to run. Test the installation by running the `HOTJAVA.EXE` application. If the browser returns an error or is unable to run, read on for a list of potential problems:

1. Under Windows 95, the HotJava browser requires the Microsoft Windows 95 TCP/IP drivers. If your system is using anything but these drivers, HotJava will be unable to run.

2. HotJava will not run under Windows 3.1. Do not confuse Windows 3.1 with Windows 95/NT because they are actually very different platforms.

3. Don't forget to delete the downloaded file after its contents have been extracted. This will free up file system space.

4. If you were unable to extract the downloaded files, make sure that they were downloaded using binary format, not ASCII.

HotJava Features

The HotJava Web browser supports many of the most popular browser features. Most importantly, of course, it fully supports the running of Java applets (see Chapter 7 for more information on applets). It also has the following features, some of which are unique to HotJava:

■ **Security**   Because HotJava was written using the Java language, it provides a secure environment for Java applets to run in. Later in this chapter, HotJava's security options will be examined in detail.

■ **HTML 2.0+ Support**   HotJava will correctly display all HTML pages that support the HTML 2.0 standard. In addition, HotJava provides support for tables, forms, and client-side image maps (see Chapter 12, "HTML for Java Programmers," for more information on HTML).

■ **External Viewers**   Although the HotJava browser will natively display a number of file formats such as HTML, GIF, and JPEG, its designers realized the need to occasionally view documents of other types. HotJava allows the user to configure viewers based on the file's MIME (Multipurpose Internet Mail Extensions) type.

■ **Configurable User Interface**   The HotJava user interface is completely contained within files included with the HotJava installation. These files can be changed or replaced, allowing users to completely modify their HotJava browser's appearance.

Using HotJava

HotJava can be run by executing the HOTJAVA application located in your installation's bin directory. Figure 13.1 shows the HotJava browser loaded and running under Windows 95.

FIGURE 13.1.

The HotJava Browser running in Windows 95.

The browser will initially load a page that was included in the HotJava installation (in this case `./lib/hotjava/whats-hot.html`). To enter another address, simply click on the current document's title. When this is done, a URL text entry box will be displayed. HotJava supports the following Internet transfer protocols:

■ `http`   HyperText Transport Protocol. Example: `http://www.javasoft.com`.

■ `ftp`   File Transfer Protocol. Example: `ftp://ftp.sun.com/pub`.

■ `mailto`   Used to send e-mail to a recipient using the HotJava sendmail form. Example: `mailto:java@java.sun.com`.

■ `file`   Loads a file on the current file system (does not access a remote Web server). File extensions that HotJava will recognize include `.text`, `.txt`, `.java`, `.c`, `.cc`, `.c++`, `.h`, `.pl`, `.el`, `.html`, `.htm`, `.gif`, and `.jpeg`.

■ `gopher`   Archival system that at one time was widely used on the Internet, but has fallen out of favor with new users due to the popularity of Web search sites such as Yahoo! and AltaVista.

Navigating in HotJava

Figure 13.2 shows the navigation buttons available to the HotJava user.

FIGURE 13.2.
The HotJava navigator buttons.

These buttons are used, from left to right, to

■ go back a page

■ go forward a page

■ go to home page

■ reload a page

■ stop a page's loading

■ show HTML errors

The last button bears some special mention because this feature is unique to the HotJava Web browser. HotJava features a sophisticated HTML parser that can detect errors in HTML pages. The last button on the HotJava toolbar is used to display any HTML errors located within a page.

The File Menu

The File menu contains the usual suspects: Open, Save, Print, Send, Close, and Quit. The following list explains the File menu options in more detail:

Clone Window   Opens a new HotJava window displaying the page that is currently loaded in HotJava. (This feature seems to be a little buggy in the pre-Beta1 release of HotJava.)

Open Page   The equivalent of clicking on the Document Name field to display a URL text field. This feature is useful if a mouse isn't handy.

Open Document   Displays a file open dialog, which allows the user to select a file on the local system.

Save   Saves the current page to an HTML file on the local system.

Print   Displays the print dialog for setting print options before printing the current document.

Send   Loads the Send Mail form. (Note that this form is actually `maildoc.html`. This means that this form, like most other forms within HotJava, can be completely customized by the HotJava user.)

Close   Iconizes the HotJava application according to the HotJava documentation; however, this feature in the pre-Beta1 release seems to serve the same function as the Quit option.

Quit   Shuts down the HotJava browser.

The Edit Menu

The Edit menu contains normal Edit options such as Cut, Copy, and Paste. In addition, it contains more detailed environment editing options as well. The following list explains each menu item briefly:

Undo, Cut, Copy, Paste, Clear   Currently disabled. These items will be operational by the release of version 1.0.

Find   Enables the Find text entry field. Any text entered into this field will be used to search the current document.

Use Index   Enables the Index text entry field. Any text entered into this field will be used to search the current document's server. This option is only enabled for documents containing the `ISINDEX` HTML tag.

Preferences   This menu item contains several submenus: Display, Proxies, Mail, and Applet Security.

Display   This option will load a form that contains several entry fields (see Figure 13.3). This form will allow the user to change default font sizes, set a home page, and control the display of the HotJava welcome screen.

FIGURE 13.3.

Contents of the Preferences/Display form.

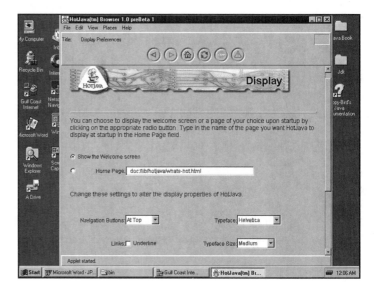

Proxies   The Proxies option will load a form in HotJava that allows the user to set HTTP, gopher, FTP, caching, and SOCKS proxy server for users accessing the Internet from within a firewall.

Mail   Loads the Mail Preferences form containing fields for entering a default e-mail address and the name of your SMTP Mail server. If you are unsure of the name of your mail server, check with your Internet Service Provider (ISP) or your system administrator.

Applet Security   This is the most interesting of these options. Although the security limitations of applets have been described in some detail throughout this book, those in fact were the *default* security limitations. HotJava actually allows you to disable (or weaken) security precautions and allow applets complete file access on your local machine, as well as the ability to communicate with other computers across the Internet (in addition to the server the applet was sent from). Unless you have good reason for not doing so, these security settings should be set to the following:

```
Network Access = Applet Host
Class Access = Restricted
```

If, for some reason, you would like to configure your HotJava browser to allow applets to read and write files on your local drive, you can do so by modifying the Access Control List in the HotJava properties file. This file is located in the ./.hotjava directory. Although the Access Control List is blank by default, it can be modified by adding the `acl_read` and `acl_write` properties, using the following syntax:

```
acl_read=[directory_name1 or file_name1]:[directory_nameN or file_nameN]
acl_write=[directory_name1 or file_name1]:[directory_nameN or file_nameN]
```

NOTE

These security settings are completely browser-dependent and not reliant in any way on Java or the Java Virtual Machine. Developers who complain that Java is too restrictive are generally misinformed (or underinformed). In general, it is the Java *default* implementations that are designed to be restrictive (for good reason!).

The View Menu

The View menu contains a set of options that apply specifically to the current page that is being viewed. The following list explains each menu item briefly:

Reload Page   This option is equivalent to hitting the Reload button (refer to Figure 13.2). It is used to reload a page when the current HTML page may have changed.

Stop Loading   Equivalent to hitting the Stop button (refer to Figure 13.2). This will stop the loading of all applets and pictures, but will not stop applets that have already begun running.

Flush Cache   This option will remove all files from the HotJava cache. If a page has recently been loaded in HotJava, it will have been stored in the cache for speedier access. However, if that page has changed on its Web server and you would like to load the most up-to-date version, the cache will need to be flushed.

HTML Source...   Allows the user to view the HTML source of the current HTML page.

HTML Errors...   Equivalent to selecting the HTML Errors button. Shows form detailing all HTML style or tag errors.

Show Tags   Shows all HTML tags on the current page. Useful for beginning HTML developers.

Monitor   The Monitor menu contains the following submenus: Progress, Memory, and Thread. These submenus load HTML pages that can be used to see the current state of various operations. Remember to hit the Shift key when selecting any of these options to load a separate HotJava window. Otherwise, these pages will replace the current HTML page you are viewing.

Monitor Progress   This submenu selection will load a form that shows the progress of the current form load process. Note that a miniature version of the progress bar is located in the right corner of the HotJava browser window. When the progress bar is completely filled, the loading process has been completed.

Monitor Memory   This selection will load a form that shows a bar graph illustrating the amount of total free memory and the amount that HotJava is currently using. At the bottom of this page is a button that will clean up memory previously allocated by HotJava.

Monitor Thread   This submenu selection will load a form showing all active threads in HotJava with their priorities and thread groups. Available options allow the user to Raise/Lower thread priorities as well as kill active threads (see Figure 13.4).

FIGURE 13.4.
The HotJava Monitor
Thread page.

The Places Menu

The Places menu contains a set of operations that is used to navigate to different Web pages. A "place" in HotJava refers to a saved link to a chosen Web site. This is similar to the "Favorites" list in Netscape Navigator or Microsoft Internet Explorer. The following list explains each menu item briefly:

Back   The Back menu item is equivalent to the Back button (refer to Figure 13.2). It returns the main screen to the previous document loaded in HotJava.

Forward   The Forward menu item is equivalent to the Forward button (refer to Figure 13.2). It returns the main screen to the next document loaded in HotJava.

Home   The Home menu item is equivalent to the Home button (refer to Figure 13.2). It returns the main screen to the home page (also see the preceding section on the Edit/Preferences menu selection to find out how to set the default home page).

Add Current To Places Menu   Selecting this item will add the current page to the HotJava Places menu. This menu is used to retain a list of "favorite" locations that will be accessed often.

Show All Places   Displays a page showing the "Remembered" and "Places" lists together. The Remembered list can only be reached by this page and is used to store locations that won't be accessed often (unlike the Places list, which will appear on the bottom of the View menu). Options exist on this page to import and export lists from/to HTML and to move locations from the Remembered list to and from the Places list.

Show History   Shows a list of all locations visited during the current HotJava session.

Planned Features for HotJava 1.0

The following feature set is planned for the 1.0 release of HotJava:

- HotJava class library (Java class library that will allow developers to build Internet-aware applications that go beyond the basic power of the classes provided by the JDK)
- Full HTML 2.0 (and some HTML 3.0) support including tables
- Performance improvements (most noticeably, scrolling!)
- Improved hotlists
- User interface for setting up external viewers for unsupported file types
- HTTP KEEPALIVE support
- Disk caching
- Improved installation process

The Netscape Navigator 2.0 Browser

If you are like the average user of the World Wide Web, the chances are extremely good that you currently use the Netscape Navigator Web browser. Surveys have shown that Netscape currently controls over 70 percent of the Web browser market. Currently, versions of this browser are available for Windows 3.1, Windows 95/NT, Apple Macintosh System 7, and Sun Solaris 2.3 or greater. Because Netscape has nearly all of the features included in the HotJava Web browser, we will not spend a great deal of time discussing each individual feature of the Navigator (or Microsoft's Internet Explorer, for that matter). Instead, particular attention will be applied to these browsers' support of Java, and in particular Java applets. Netscape supports a scripting language called JavaScript (which is not related to Sun's Java—more on this later).

Java versus JavaScript

The release of the Netscape Navigator 2.0 browser for Solaris and 32-bit Windows marked the first time a browser (outside of Sun's HotJava) supported the running of Java applets. Because of Netscape's astounding growth and the popularity of its browser, Java received a great boost in name recognition and availability on the desktop. Netscape uses a special version of the Java Virtual Machine to run Java applets within the browser. You can see this by visiting your Navigator installation directory (if you have installed Netscape Navigator). In the `.\Program\java\classes` directory, the file `moz2_02.zip` resides, containing the Java `.class` files used by Netscape. (Moz refers to Mozilla—a code name for the Navigator project at Netscape.) These class files resemble the classes included in the current release of the JDK, but some may have been modified by Netscape for specialized display, performance, and so on. What is important, however, is that Netscape had the vision to support Java in its infancy, and is now positioned, with its LiveConnect strategy, to provide developers with just about everything needed to build industrial-strength Web applications on the client side.

Both new and experienced developers are confused when forced to differentiate between Java, HotJava, and JavaScript. By now, the reader of this book should have a firm understanding of what Java and HotJava are. However, JavaScript may remain somewhat of a mystery.

JavaScript was initially introduced by Netscape as a feature known as LiveScript. It is fully incorporated into Netscape's Navigator 2.0 browser. JavaScript is a scripting language that is used primarily to build dynamic forms. Because Java applets generally do not interact with other elements on HTML pages, JavaScript can be used to tie the various elements together. Although much of the syntax is similar to Java, there are some major differences. Most notably, JavaScript does not allow the author to define new types of objects. Inheritance also is not allowed. JavaScript is not compiled. Instead, it is embedded within the `<SCRIPT>…</SCRIPT>` tag in an HTML form. See the Netscape home page (`http://home.netscape.com`) for more information on JavaScript.

Netscape and Java

The Netscape browser V2.0 includes complete support for Java applets on the Sun Solaris and Microsoft Windows 95/NT operating systems. A later version was released that added Java applet support for the Apple Macintosh. Currently, Java support has not been added for Windows 3.1 because the Java Virtual Machine has not been ported to that platform, although IBM apparently plans to do so in the near future.

The way Netscape handles applet security is what separates its Java support from the HotJava browser (besides sheer performance, which appears to be better in HotJava). HotJava allows the user to set security options, but Netscape does not. With Netscape, Java applets are not allowed to read or write to the local file system, and they are restricted to communicating only with the computer from which they came. In addition, unlike HotJava users, users of the Netscape browser can turn off applet support altogether. This was provided to pacify users who were initially concerned over reported Java security holes. See Figure 13.5 for Netscape's Java options.

FIGURE 13.5.

Netscape's Preferences dialog box.

The Netscape Navigator has one nice feature not found in many other Web browsers. That feature is the Java console (see Figure 13.6).

FIGURE 13.6.

The Java console in Netscape Navigator.

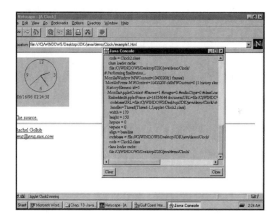

The Java console allows the user to see exactly what is being loaded in his or her display without having to examine the HTML source directly. This feature can come in handy when trying to debug Java and HTML forms.

Microsoft's Internet Explorer 3.0

Fortunately for Microsoft, "Web-mania" hit before the release of its Windows 95 operating system. This gave Microsoft developers the time to create their own Web browser, named Internet Explorer, and include it for free within their Windows 95 operating system installation. Unfortunately for Java aficionados, neither Internet Explorer 1.0 nor Internet Explorer 2.0 supported Java applets (nor JavaScript, but as we've seen, that's another topic entirely!). Internet Explorer 3.0 is promising Java applet support as well as support for a host of other semi-related technologies such as Visual Basic Script (VBScript), JavaScript, and Microsoft's ActiveX controls (see Figure 13.7 to view the Internet Explorer application).

FIGURE 13.7.

Microsoft's Internet Explorer 3.0.

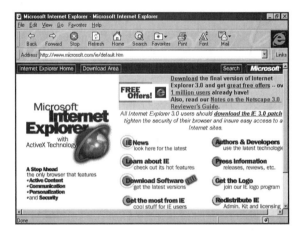

Although the current beta of Internet Explorer 3.0 does not yet support Java applets, we assume that this support will be provided by the final release. What is more interesting with this product is the ActiveX technology and how it applies to Java programmers.

Java and ActiveX

For developers who thought that following the Java technologies alone was bewildering enough, ActiveX is sure to add an entirely new level of decision-making complexity. In a nutshell, Microsoft's ActiveX technology may be more familiar to developers when called by its old name: OLE (Object Linking and Embedding). OLE was renamed to ActiveX to more accurately represent the active, Internet-aware, distributed OLE that will soon be upon us. For Web developers, the most important ActiveX subset to understand may be ActiveX controls (formerly known as OCX controls). ActiveX controls are programming objects that encapsulate an object's properties, methods, and events. These controls currently are supported by nearly all popular Windows development tools including Visual Basic, Visual C++, Borland C++, Borland Delphi, Powersoft PowerBuilder, and many others. (ActiveX also is being ported to other platforms including the Apple Macintosh.)

What is new about the ActiveX control technology is that the Microsoft Internet Explorer 3.0 browser will allow these controls to be run within a Web page just as Java applets are. In fact, these controls could actually be running side by side with other Java applets. How is this done? Microsoft is developing a special Java Virtual Machine that will expose Java applets running within a browser as ActiveX controls. Any application using the Microsoft Java Virtual Machine will acquire this capability.

Microsoft envisions an environment where scripting languages such as VBScript and JavaScript will be used to tie all of these components together into dynamic, fully functional Web pages. Sounds great, right? Because Internet-aware ActiveX controls are so new, it remains to be seen whether developers will get excited and support them with the fervor currently directed toward Java. The remainder of this section will point out some differences between Java and ActiveX and leave it to the software market to sort out the better of the two.

Security

Because of the nature of the Internet, no large-scale development effort can be undertaken that does not take security into account at every level. The designers of Java and ActiveX have both provided security features in their technologies. However, they have arrived at very different results. As explained throughout this book, Java applets are treated as untrusted programs running within trusted environments (a restriction known as "sand boxing"). They can only be written using the Java language, which was designed from the ground up to be a secure language. ActiveX controls, on the other hand, are primarily created using C++, although Visual Basic 5.0 is rumored to provide support for ActiveX control creation. Whatever way they are created, obviously the languages used give programmers a way around Java's strict security limits. Microsoft is attempting to solve this problem through the use of secure digital signatures.

Because they recognize that the momentum behind Java is somewhat unavoidable, Microsoft plans to provide Java applets with the capability of calling remote ActiveX objects throughout the Internet, which violates Java applets' security rules. Microsoft realizes this and is promoting the concept of "code signing" to verify the authenticity and security of downloaded ActiveX controls and Java applets. Developers should realize that these extensions have advantages and disadvantages. In the meantime, Sun is encouraging developers to avoid all proprietary extensions to Java.

NOTE

Extending the base Java class libraries with new classes is not considered a proprietary extension. This is what object-oriented programming is all about! However, customizations of the Java Virtual Machine and Java `.class` file formats are considered proprietary extensions. Developers undertake these extensions at the risk of losing Java's platform independence and flexibility.

Platform Independence

At the time this book is being written, the Internet Explorer 3.0 (Windows-only) browser is the only application that will support the running of ActiveX controls within an HTML page. This means that any ActiveX controls you create will be restricted to a 32-bit Windows-only audience. In smaller corporate intranet settings where the audience is limited and known, this restriction may not be a limiting factor. However, if your product will be displayed on the Web to a wide audience, platform independence is a huge bonus.

Summary

Within a year of Java's introduction in 1995, it has seen unprecedented growth. The three Web browsers studied in this chapter all have the capability of running Java applets. It is interesting to note the difference in philosophies behind the creation of each of these three products. In the near future, the HotJava 1.0 product should be released with a complete class library of reusable Java components. This library will include components capable of displaying Web pages and will greatly ease the creation of "Internet-aware" applications. Also due for release is Netscape Navigator 3.0. This application will provide improved performance for Java applets (including a just-in-time compiler licensed from Borland). The release of the Microsoft Internet Explorer 3.0 will mark the availability of the first browser to support both Java and ActiveX.

Although this chapter provides a good introduction to Web browsers for Java programmers, it is recommended that you visit the Web sites for the respective companies for the latest and greatest information on their browsers. Here are the addresses:

`http://www.javasoft.com/HotJava` (Sun's HotJava)
`http://home.netscape.com` (Netscape Navigator)
`http://www.microsoft.com/ie` (Microsoft Internet Explorer)

14

Using javah

by Michael T. Nygard

One of the lesser known tools provided in the JDK is *javah*. This specialized tool creates two C files from your Java classes. These C files can be used to implement *native methods*. Native methods are discussed fully in Chapter 19, "Extending Your Programs with Native Methods." javah creates a header file and a "stub" file for the native methods of a class. The header file declares the functions that will implement the class methods. The stub file provides the glue that binds the Java method invocation and object references to the C code. It is up to you to provide another C file (called the *implementation file*) with the functions declared in the header. These three C files allow a Java class to call C functions. In turn, the C functions can reference the object's instance variables. Ultimately, these files (possibly with others) are compiled into a dynamically loadable library. This process is shown pictorially in Figure 14.1.

FIGURE 14.1.

Using javah to create native method files.

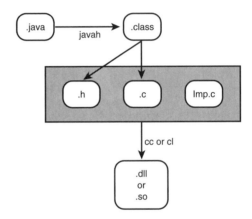

SHOULD I USE NATIVE METHODS?

Before you decide to use native methods, there are some things you should consider carefully. First of all, the native methods are in pure C code, not C++. The function prototypes provided by javah are in an object-oriented style of C, but they are still not really object methods. You will lose the benefits of inheritance and polymorphism. The stubs create some data structures that provide weak encapsulation, but it is up to you to enforce it.

Second, native methods can only be called from applications. Applets are prevented from calling native methods for security reasons.

Third, and most importantly, native methods are inherently platform-specific. You will have to build the dynamically loadable library for each platform your application targets. Of course, that means any system-specific code has to be ported, too. (I know, C is *supposed* to be a portable language, but isn't that why you are using Java?)

On the other hand, native methods are the only way to use any system features not provided by the Java Virtual Machine.

The Header File

When you create a header file from a Java class, the header contains two things: declarations for the C implementation functions and a structure definition. The layout of the structure matches the layout of the Java class. A pointer to an instance of the structure is passed to the implementation functions. By using the fields of the structure, the C functions can access the instance variables of the Java class.

Because of this mapping, whenever you change the instance variables of the Java class, you should regenerate the header file. Of course, that also means it will be best if you do not modify the header manually.

The Java class name determines the header filename and the name of the structure declaration. javah appends ".h" to the class name for the header filename. For the structure name, javah uses the class name with the word "Class" prepended. For example, if you run javah on a class named HelloWorld, it will produce a header file named HelloWorld.h with a structure in it called ClassHelloWorld.

The Stub

The stub filename is just the class name with ".c" appended. For the sample class HelloWorld, javah would create a stub file named HelloWorld.c. At this point, just think of the stub functions as glue between the C implementation functions and the Java method invocations.

javah creates the stub functions directly from the class native methods, just as it creates the structure declaration in the header file from the instance variables. So, be sure to regenerate the stub file any time you change a native method in the class.

In this case, it is not just inconvenient to modify the stub file—it's a bad idea. Any changes you might want to make are probably best done in the Java code or in the implementation file, anyway. It really is best if you put the stub file aside because any changes you make here are likely to break the Java-to-C linkage.

Usage

The synopsis for javah is as follows:

```
javah [ options ] classname …
```

```
javah_g [ options ] classname …
```

javah uses slightly different options for the two platforms. In all cases, javah accepts multiple class names on the command line. javah_g produces files suitable for use with debuggers like jdb. It accepts identical options to javah.

Here are the command-line options for the Windows 95/NT version of javah and javah_g. (These are from version 1.0.2 of the JDK.)

Windows 95/NT Option	Description
-o *outputfile*	This option will force all of the headers or stubs for all of the classes to be placed into *outputfile*. Without this option, javah will create a separate file for each class.
-d *directory*	Tells javah to put all output files in *directory*.
-td *directory*	Tells javah to use *directory* for temporary files. Otherwise, javah checks the environment variable %TEMP%. If %TEMP% is not set, then javah checks %TMP%. If %TMP% is not set, javah falls back on C:\tmp, creating it if necessary.
-stubs	Tells javah to create the stub files. By default, javah creates the header files.
-verbose	Tells javah to print messages to stdout regarding the output files.
-classpath *path*	Overrides the default class path and the environment variable %CLASSPATH%. Path uses the same syntax as the CLASSPATH environment variable.

Windows 95/NT Environment Variable	Description
CLASSPATH	You can set the environment variable CLASSPATH to provide the JDK a path to your user-defined classes. You can specify multiple directories separated by semicolons. Use the DOS-style backslash as the path component separator. Under JDK 1.0.2 and higher, the class path can include an archive file classes.zip, which will be searched for the classes given on the command line. It is a good idea to always start the class path with the current directory (for example, set CLASSPATH=.;C:\Java\Lib\classes.zip).
TEMP, TMP	If you do not use the -td option, javah uses %TEMP% and %TMP% to determine where to store temporary files. See the discussion of the -td option.

SPARC Solaris

Option	Description
-o *outputfile*	This option will force all of the headers or stubs for all of the classes to be placed into *outputfile*. Without this option, javah will create a separate file for each class.
-d *directory*	Tells javah to put all output files in *directory*.
-td *directory*	Tells javah to use *directory* for its temporary files, instead of /tmp.
-stubs	Tells javah to create the stubs files. By default, javah creates the header files.
-verbose	Tells javah to print messages to stdout regarding the output files.
-classpath *path*	Overrides the default class path and the environment variable $CLASSPATH. path uses the same syntax as the CLASSPATH environment variable.

Here are the command-line options for the Solaris version of javah and javah_g. (These are from version 1.0.2 of the JDK.)

SPARC Solaris

Environment Variable	Description
CLASSPATH	You can set the environment variable CLASSPATH to provide the JDK a path to your user-defined classes. You can specify multiple directories separated by colons. Under JDK 1.0.2 and higher, the class path can include an archive file classes.zip, which will be searched for the classes given on the command line. It is a good idea to always start the class path with the current directory "." (for example, CLASSPATH=".:/ java/lib/classes.zip").

Example

Now create a class and see how javah translates it into a header and stub file. For now, disregard the implementation file. (See Chapter 19 for details on creating implementation files.) Listing 14.1 shows a class that might be used as part of a stock portfolio charting application. The exact output may vary slightly depending on your target platform and the version of the JDK you use.

Listing 14.1. Initial `PortfolioEntry` class.

```
class PortfolioEntry {
   String  TickerSymbol;
   int        NumberOfShares;
   float   LastQuote;
   float   BoughtAtPrice;
   float   LastDividends;
   float   LastEPS;

   public native void  FetchQuote();
   public native float CurrentValue();
   public native float NetGain();
   public native float Yield();
};
```

The `PortfolioEntry` class has attributes for the current stock quote, number of shares owned, the buy price for these shares, the dividends paid last quarter, and the earnings per share reported for last quarter. It has methods to calculate the current value of the shares, the net profit or loss based on the current value, and the yield of the lot (net profit or loss per share as a percentage). It also has one crucial method to retrieve the latest quote for this stock. (For the sake of this example, assume that the dozens of Web-based quote services do not exist.) Notice the use of the `native` keyword. Without this modifier, this class will not compile, because we have not provided any method bodies.

USE AND ABUSE OF THE `native` KEYWORD

The keyword `native` modifies a method declaration. It indicates to javac that the body of the method will be provided by code native to the current platform. You can compose `native` with other method declaration modifiers such as `static` and `abstract`. How does javac interpret an abstract, native method? Not very well. Although you can provide a method body for an abstract native method, that body will never be called. A static native method behaves exactly as you would expect. Be careful about the object instance pointer passed to the native method, however. A static, native method is always passed a `NULL` for its argument.

Native methods that are overridden in a subclass work just as you would expect. In fact, you can override a native method with a Java method, or a Java method with a native method, or a native method with a native method. (Whew!)

You cannot make a constructor native, but then again, you cannot make a constructor static, synchronized, abstract, or final.

All commands in this example follow the syntax for the Windows 95/NT JDK version 1.0.

First, compile the Java code:

```
>javac PortfolioEntry.java
```

This will create the usual `PortfolioEntry.class` file. Now, use javah to create the header file:

```
>javah PortfolioEntry
```

Note that javah only expects class names, not filenames. Therefore, you do not need to add `.java` or `.class` to the command-line arguments. (If your CLASSPATH environment variable does not include the current directory, you will need to use a command line like

```
javah -classpath .;C:\Java\lib\classes.zip PortfolioEntry)
```

Now take a look at the output file `PortfolioEntry.h`. You should see something like Listing 14.2.

Listing 14.2. First `PortfolioEntry.h` file.

```
/* DO NOT EDIT THIS FILE - it is machine generated */
#include <native.h>
/* Header for class PortfolioEntry */

#ifndef _Included_PortfolioEntry
#define _Included_PortfolioEntry
struct Hjava_lang_String;

typedef struct ClassPortfolioEntry {
    struct Hjava_lang_String *TickerSymbol;
    long NumberOfShares;
    float LastQuote;
    float BoughtAtPrice;
    float LastDividends;
    float LastEPS;
} ClassPortfolioEntry;
HandleTo(PortfolioEntry);

#ifdef __cplusplus
extern "C" {
#endif
extern void PortfolioEntry_FetchQuote(struct HPortfolioEntry *);
extern float PortfolioEntry_CurrentValue(struct HPortfolioEntry *);
extern float PortfolioEntry_NetGain(struct HPortfolioEntry *);
extern float PortfolioEntry_Yield(struct HPortfolioEntry *);
#ifdef __cplusplus
}
#endif
#endif
```

You can see how the class `PortfolioEntry` maps directly to the structure `ClassPortfolioEntry`. The class methods map directly to the C function declarations.

WHERE DID HPortfolioEntry COME FROM?

The structure HPortfolioEntry, which is passed to each of the C functions, is declared as a result of the HandleTo() macro, which is defined in \java\include\oobj.h as

```
#define HandleTo(T) typedef struct H##T { Class##T *obj; \
                     struct methodtable *methods;} H##T
```

So, HandleTo(PortfolioEntry); expands to

```
typedef struct HPortfolioEntry {
   ClassPortfolioEntry *obj;
   struct methodtable *methods;
} HPortfolioEntry;
```

This structure provides the bookkeeping that will allow C functions to behave like class methods. To access an instance variable from your native method, follow the obj pointer to the instance variable structure declared by the header file. For example, one of the native methods for PortfolioEntry would access the NumberOfShares attribute by dereferencing hPortfolioEntry->obj->NumberOfShares.

The methods pointer also allows your native method to get information about, and even invoke, the other methods of your class. Until you are quite conversant with the Java object model, you should probably avoid this feature.

Now, create the stub file:

```
>javah -stubs -classpath .;C:\JAVA\LIB\CLASSES.ZIP PortfolioEntry
```

This creates the rather obfuscated file in Listing 14.3. You should never need to modify the stub file. In fact, it is best to ignore it completely after you have created it.

Listing 14.3. Stub file for PortfolioEntry class.

```
/* DO NOT EDIT THIS FILE - it is machine generated */
#include <StubPreamble.h>

/* Stubs for class PortfolioEntry */
/* SYMBOL: "PortfolioEntry/FetchQuote()V",
          Java_PortfolioEntry_FetchQuote_stub */
__declspec(dllexport) stack_item *
 Java_PortfolioEntry_FetchQuote_stub(stack_item *_P_,
                                     struct execenv *_EE_)
{
   extern void PortfolioEntry_FetchQuote(void *);
   (void) PortfolioEntry_FetchQuote(_P_[0].p);
   return _P_;
}
/* SYMBOL: "PortfolioEntry/CurrentValue()F",
          Java_PortfolioEntry_CurrentValue_stub */
```

```
__declspec(dllexport) stack_item *
  Java_PortfolioEntry_CurrentValue_stub(stack_item *_P_,
                                        struct execenv *_EE_)
{
   extern float PortfolioEntry_CurrentValue(void *);
   _P_[0].f = PortfolioEntry_CurrentValue(_P_[0].p);
   return _P_ + 1;
}
/* SYMBOL: "PortfolioEntry/NetGain()F",
           Java_PortfolioEntry_NetGain_stub */
__declspec(dllexport) stack_item *
  Java_PortfolioEntry_NetGain_stub(stack_item *_P_,
                                   struct execenv *_EE_)
{
   extern float PortfolioEntry_NetGain(void *);
   _P_[0].f = PortfolioEntry_NetGain(_P_[0].p);
   return _P_ + 1;
}
/* SYMBOL: "PortfolioEntry/Yield()F",
           Java_PortfolioEntry_Yield_stub */
__declspec(dllexport) stack_item *
  Java_PortfolioEntry_Yield_stub(stack_item *_P_,
                                 struct execenv *_EE_)
{
   extern float PortfolioEntry_Yield(void *);
   _P_[0].f = PortfolioEntry_Yield(_P_[0].p);
   return _P_ + 1;
}
```

Looking back at the class definition, it seems that most of the methods could be implemented in Java alone. Suppose that the function to retrieve the latest quote used a third-party C library. Now modify the class definition to include some native and some Java methods, as shown in Listing 14.4.

Listing 14.4. Revised PortfolioEntry class.

```
class PortfolioEntry {
   String  TickerSymbol;
   int        NumberOfShares;
   float   LastQuote;
   float   BoughtAtPrice;
   float   LastDividends;
   float   LastEPS;

   public native void  FetchQuote();
   public float CurrentValue() {
      return (NumberOfShares * LastQuote);
   };
   public float NetGain() {
      return (CurrentValue() - NumberOfShares * BoughtAtPrice);
   }
   public float Yield() {
      return (100 * (NetGain() / NumberOfShares * BoughtAtPrice));
   };
};
```

Now, recompile the class and regenerate the header file. Notice the change in the declarations section of the header file in Listing 14.5.

Listing 14.5. Header file for revised `PortfolioEntry` class.

```
/* DO NOT EDIT THIS FILE - it is machine generated */
#include <native.h>
/* Header for class PortfolioEntry */

#ifndef _Included_PortfolioEntry
#define _Included_PortfolioEntry
struct Hjava_lang_String;

typedef struct ClassPortfolioEntry {
    struct Hjava_lang_String *TickerSymbol;
    long NumberOfShares;
    float LastQuote;
    float BoughtAtPrice;
    float LastDividends;
    float LastEPS;
} ClassPortfolioEntry;
HandleTo(PortfolioEntry);

#ifdef __cplusplus
extern "C" {
#endif
extern void PortfolioEntry_FetchQuote(struct HPortfolioEntry *);
#ifdef __cplusplus
}
#endif
#endif
```

Because only one method is declared as native this time, that is the only method mapped to a C function. This also implies that your C code will not be able to call any Java methods in the class, although the C functions can call each other freely. Keep in mind that the javah-generated header file only declares the C functions that the Java runtime system can call. In your implementation file, you can create as many C functions as you need. You are free to modularize your native methods as much as necessary. The C functions have access to the instance variables of the calling object. To encourage encapsulation, you should give any additional C functions you create file scope, by declaring them as `static`. That way, they cannot be called inadvertently by other C modules. Likewise, if you need to use any global variables in your implementation file, you should give them file scope, too. (Look carefully at any global variables in the implementation file. Most of the time, you will find that they should really be instance variables.)

One last thing you want to add to your Java class is a static code block to load the dynamically loadable library. Recall that the Java runtime executes a class's static block the first time that class is loaded. Think of it as an initializer for the class. Assume that the example's native methods are compiled and linked into a library called "PortfolioEntry." The static code block shown in Listing 14.6 loads the library when the class is loaded.

Listing 14.6. Final revision of the `PortfolioEntry` class.

```
class PortfolioEntry {
    String  TickerSymbol;
    int       NumberOfShares;
    float   LastQuote;
    float   BoughtAtPrice;
    float   LastDividends;
    float   LastEPS;

    static {
        System.loadLibrary("PortfolioEntry");
    }
    public native void  FetchQuote();
    public float CurrentValue() {
        return (NumberOfShares * LastQuote);
    };
    public float NetGain() {
        return (CurrentValue() - NumberOfShares * BoughtAtPrice);
    }
    public float Yield() {
        return (100 * (NetGain() / NumberOfShares * BoughtAtPrice));
    };
};
```

(See `java.lang.System` for details about the `System.loadLibrary` method.) You should know that `System.loadLibrary` will throw an exception if it cannot find the specified library. Because this exception will be thrown when the Java runtime loads the class, before your application starts, you will not be able to catch it. You do not need to explicitly unload the library—the Java runtime system will handle that for you.

Summary

javah creates C header files and C stubs for Java classes. It exists to support the use of native methods to extend Java classes beyond the capabilities built into the Java Virtual Machine. Along with the header and stub files, you must provide an implementation file to define the C functions declared in the header file. javah maps the class attributes to a C structure definition, which is passed to the methods, thus allowing a C function to access the object's instance variables. javah only creates declarations for those methods declared as `native` in the Java class.

Before deciding to implement your application's functionality as native methods, you should answer several questions:

■ Am I writing an application or an applet? Native method calls are allowed only from applications.

■ Can I tolerate losing cross-platform compatibility? Or, can I tolerate creating multiple versions of my native methods?

■ Will distribution and installation of the native methods be a problem?

15

jdb: The Java Debugger

by Bryan Morgan

Debugging is one of the necessary "evils" of software development. Very few developers on earth can routinely write large segments of error-free code on the first try. What often separates good developers from great developers is their skill at debugging complex code. To be considered truly masterful in a programming environment or language, a programmer must first master that environment's complete debugging capabilities. Modern programming environments allow the developer to set breakpoints, view function call stacks, and watch variables as program code is stepped through. This chapter will address using the JDK's debugger, jdb, so that you can take advantage of its debugging capabilities. If you are not already familiar with jdb, be sure to thoroughly cover the material in this chapter and work through the examples.

The Java Debugger API

jdb is the name of the debugger supplied by Sun in the Java Developer's Kit (JDK). It is a command-line tool (like the interpreter, compiler, and applet viewer) that you can use to step through Java code and study the code's behavior at runtime.

> **WARNING**
>
> At an early stage, avoid the temptation to ignore the jdb debugging tool! Although average developers are relying on `print` statements to the screen to examine the contents of variables, jdb allows the above-average developer to step through code line by line and examine that code's operation. This is an invaluable resource that you should not bypass.

jdb was designed to have some special capabilities not found in many other language debuggers. These include:

- An object-oriented interface similar to that of the Java language
- Java language runtime features such as threads and monitors
- Support for remote debugging (see the "Security Precautions" section later in this chapter)

The debugger was implemented using the Java Debugger API. This API was provided by Sun in order to fulfill these requirements for a full-featured Java language debugger. A key feature of the Debugger API is the capability of remote debugging. This means that a remote viewer can see into a Java Language Runtime if the security precautions have been taken care of.

The Sun documentation stresses that jdb was implemented as a "proof-of-concept" tool for the Java Debugger API. In other words, they viewed the *real* product as the API itself. (Tool developers were strongly encouraged to produce a more user-friendly tool.) More user-friendly debuggers currently exist in the form of the Symantec Café debugger and in the forthcoming Borland Latte IDE's debugger.

Security Precautions

The ability for programmers to debug Java applications and applets from remote locations is an exciting concept. Experienced developers realize that just because an application may run fine on their development platform, that does not mean it will run without flaws on other users' machines. In the Windows environment, common distribution problems include conflicting DLLs, VBXs, and OCXs, as well as an extremely large assortment of software packages that may conflict with changes being made to the system. The ability to remotely debug applications on users' machines is extremely powerful; however, it also introduces a variety of potential security problems.

One potential security "hole" could occur in the following situation. User A could be running a Java application locally on his machine. Using this application, he is entering confidential data into several edit fields before posting the data to a database. Meanwhile, across the Internet, a wily hacker sits with his Java debugger patiently viewing the contents of these edit fields' values.

The designers of the Java Debugger API (and in turn, jdb) foresaw this security problem and included mechanisms in the API to prevent security problems. Communication between the debugger and the runtime interpreter occurs using a socket-based, proprietary protocol.

> **NOTE**
>
> The communication protocol between the debugger and interpreter is neither public nor modifiable. Because it uses sockets for communication, however, developers will need a TCP/IP connection in order to use the debugger to debug Java code. Keep this in mind when developing on machines with no network connection.

When the Java Language Runtime is started in `-debug` mode, the interpreter prints out a password to be used by the debugger. At this time, the runtime also begins to monitor a dynamically chosen port for communications from the debugger. On the debugger side, a correct *hostname* and *password* must be specified to connect to the interpreter. Programmers also should be aware that only one debugger instance can connect to an interpreter at a time.

Debugging with jdb

jdb is similar in operation and functionality to the UNIX dbx-style debugger (another Sun tool, by the way). The debugger is used to debug a currently running application. jdb can be used in two different ways for debugging Java applications.

Using the Interpreter Through the Command Line

At its simplest, jdb essentially works through the Java interpreter and loads the Java class indicated on the command line. This can be done by using the following command (exactly like invoking the Java interpreter):

```
% jdb classname <arguments>
```

Listing 15.1 uses the jdb debugger to load a copy of the Java interpreter. The class specified on the command line is then run using the specified arguments.

This example creates a simple Java application that displays a screen with the text on it. This text depends on what the user gives as an argument. If no argument is given, then the text "Give argument!" is printed on the screen. The Button is added so that the application will be able to exit gracefully.

Listing 15.1. Using jdb to debug a simple Java application.

```java
import java.awt.*;

/* The following class prints the text "Hello World!" to the screen */
class HelloWorldApp
{
  public static void main(String args[])
  {
    ExitButton button;
    String     lbl;

    button = new ExitButton("Exit!");
    if (args.length == 0)
      lbl = "Give argument!";
    else
      lbl = args[0];

    Frame mainFrame = new Frame("HelloWorldApp");
    Label HelloWorldlbl = new Label(lbl, Label.CENTER);
    mainFrame.add("Center", HelloWorldlbl);
    mainFrame.add("South", button);
    mainFrame.resize(450, 450);
    mainFrame.show();
  }
}
```

```
class ExitButton extends Button
{

  public ExitButton(String buttonLbl)
  {
    setLabel(buttonLbl);
  }

  public boolean action(Event evt, Object arg)
  {
    System.exit(0);
    return true;
  }
}
```

Figure 15.1 shows the screen output with the following input:

```
c:\> java HelloWorldApp Howdy!
```

FIGURE 15.1.
Application displaying the command-line argument.

Figure 15.2 shows the screen output with no arguments given.

FIGURE 15.2.
Application display with no command-line argument.

Now that this application is apparently running, this is as good a time as any to try out the debugger for the first time.

> **NOTE**
>
> To examine local (stack) variables, the class must have been compiled using the `-g` option (`javac -g classname`).

Enter the following to begin:

```
% jdb HelloWorldApp Howdy!
```

The following output (or something similar) should appear on the debugger screen:

```
% Initializing jdb...
0x139fdf0:class(HelloWorldApp)
```

If this does appear, the debugger and interpreter have been initialized and are awaiting commands. The entire list of commands will be studied later in this chapter. For now, test out jdb's breakpoint capabilities by entering the following to set a breakpoint:

```
% stop in HelloWorldApp.main
```

The debugger should have responded with this:

```
Breakpoint set in HelloWorldApp.main
```

The next step should be to actually run the application. The `run` command is used to do this:

```
% run
```

Here is the debugger output:

```
run HelloWorldApp Howdy!
Breakpoint hit: running ...
HelloWorldApp.main (HelloWorldApp:11)
```

At this time, the breakpoint already has been hit. The actual syntax used here means that the breakpoint was hit in the `HelloWorldApp.main` method (or, alternatively, in the `HelloWorldApp` class, Line 11). Finally, to make sure that the command-line argument was processed properly, do a quick check of the `args` variable.

```
% print args
```

The value should be printed to the screen correctly if all went according to plan.

```
args = { Howdy! }
```

The final step in this debugging process is to send the application on its way using the cont command.

```
% cont
```

Attaching to a Running Interpreter

The second method available for debugging with jdb is to attach it to an interpreter that is currently running. To do this, that interpreter must have been started using the -debug option. At startup time, this interpreter should have generated a password to be used by jdb. To attach to a currently running interpreter, use the following syntax:

```
% jdb - host <hostname> -password <password>
```

To debug an application using this method when the application resides on your local machine, it is necessary to create two separate debug windows. This example repeats the steps necessary to re-create the example in the previous section. However, here we use a Java interpreter that is already running for the debugging connection.

This example reuses the HelloWorldApp class created in Listing 15.1. However, this time the application will be run using the Java interpreter and a separate jdb process.

The first step is to run the application using the Java interpreter and the -debug option.

```
% java -debug HelloWorldClass Howdy!
```

The Java interpreter responded with the following password message:

```
Agent password=k56pn
```

This password will be different each time the interpreter is run in debug mode and it is randomly generated internal to the Java interpreter. Before continuing, notice that the HelloWorldApp frame window is already showing. This is the drawback to using this method. When the debugger is actually started, the application is already running, so it is difficult to check startup initialization information. However, to track events (such as the button-click), this method still allows the powerful capability of remote debugging!

At this time, in another window, run the jdb debugger using the -password argument (and the -host <hostname> argument if you are currently debugging a remote application):

```
% jdb -password k56pn
```

Now that the debugger has been started and has initialized its link with the Java interpreter, you are free to examine all classes currently loaded into memory. For instructional purposes, type in the classes command at the jdb prompt.

```
% classes
.
.
.
0x13994a8:class(java.awt.Rectangle)
0x13994c0:class(java.awt.Insets)
0x13994d8:class(java.awt.Font)
0x1399548:class(java.awt.Color)
0x13995c8:class(sun.awt.win32.MLabelPeer)
0x13995e8:class(sun.awt.win32.MButtonPeer)
0x1399608:interface(java.awt.peer.ContainerPeer)
0x1399618:interface(java.awt.peer.FramePeer)
0x1399628:interface(java.awt.peer.WindowPeer)
0x1399638:class(sun.awt.win32.Win32FontMetrics)
0x1399648:class(java.awt.FontMetrics)
0x1399680:class(java.awt.Dimension)
0x13996a0:class(sun.awt.ScreenUpdater)
0x13996d8:class(sun.awt.ScreenUpdaterEntry)
0x13996f0:class(sun.awt.win32.Win32Graphics)
0x1399700:class(java.awt.Graphics)
0x13998b0:class(java.io.DataInputStream)
0x13998d0:class(java.net.SocketInputStream)
0x13998f8:class(sun.tools.debug.ResponseStream)
0x1399910:class(java.net.SocketOutputStream)
0x1399938:class(java.io.DataOutputStream)
0x13999a8:class(sun.tools.debug.AgentOutputStream)
0x1399a70:class(java.util.HashtableEnumerator)
0x1399a98:class(java.util.VectorEnumerator)
```

The preceding listing represents a small portion of the total amount of class information generated. Notice the extremely large number of classes that are listed. These are all of the classes currently in use by either the Java runtime environment, debugger, or the HelloWorldApp application. To explore the environment, type **help** and a list of all commands available will be shown. This same list (with descriptions of each command) appears later in this chapter.

Debugging Java Applets

The information presented so far dealt with using jdb in combination with the Java interpreter to debug Java applications. However, Java applets run within a container application such as appletviewer. As mentioned in Chapter 11, "Using the Applet Viewer," the applet viewer tool can be run in -debug mode.

This example proceeds through the steps required to properly debug a Java applet. The Java applet created takes in user-entered text and retrieves the URL entered. If this applet is being run inside a Web browser such as Netscape Navigator, the URL will be retrieved and shown. Figure 15.3 shows this applet actually being run in Netscape.

FIGURE 15.3.

The GetURL applet running in Netscape Navigator.

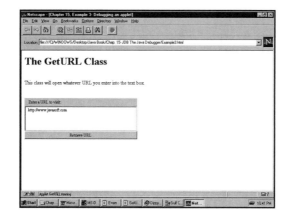

The source code used to build the GetURL applet is shown in Listing 15.2.

Listing 15.2. GetURL source code (`Example3.html`).

```
import java.awt.*;
import java.net.URL;
import java.net.MalformedURLException;
import java.applet.Applet;

/* The following class will load a URL using the URL entered by the user */
/* It also accepts a default URL as input and enters the text
➡ into the TextField */

public class GetURL extends java.applet.Applet
{
  String       tempString;
  TextField    URLText;
  GetURLButton URLbutton;

  public void init()
  {
    /* First, retrieve the default URL from the HTML file */
    tempString = getParameter("DEFAULT_URL");

    /* Now set up the applet's appearance              */
    setLayout(new BorderLayout());
    add("North", new Label("Enter a URL to visit:"));
    URLText = new TextField();
    URLText.setText(tempString);
    add("Center", URLText);
    URLbutton = new GetURLButton(this, "Retrieve URL");
    add("South", URLbutton);
  }

  public void GetURLDocument()
  {
```

continues

Listing 15.2. continued

```
    /* Use the MalformedURLException to catch incorrect entries */
    try
    {
      URL tempURL = new URL(URLText.getText());
      getAppletContext().showDocument(tempURL);
    }
    catch(MalformedURLException e)
    {
      URLText.setText("Bad URL!!");
    }
  }
}

//This button will trigger the retrieval of the URL
class GetURLButton extends Button
{
  private GetURL appHandle;

  public GetURLButton(GetURL app, String label)
  {
    appHandle = app;
    setLabel(label);
  }

  public boolean action(Event evt, Object arg)
  {
    appHandle.GetURLDocument();
    return true;
  }
}
```

Proceed through the following steps to use the applet viewer to debug this applet:

1. Compile the applet with the -g option so that the debugger can be used to examine local variables. Once again, this is done by invoking the following command: %javac -g GetURL.java.

2. Run the file Example3.html in a Web browser to test out its capabilities. By default, simply clicking the button will retrieve the JavaSoft home page.

3. Prepare to debug the applet in the applet viewer. Enter the following command to start the applet viewer in debug mode: %appletviewer -debug Example3.html.

4. Once jdb is initialized, type **run** to start the applet viewer with Example3.html.

5. Enter **classes** to see a list of all of the currently loaded classes. The class GetURL should appear somewhere in that list.

6. Notice that the prompt changed from ">" to "main[1]". This means that the *main* thread (thread #1) is currently selected. Enter the threads command and look for one that designates the GetURL class with the following text: Group group applet-

GetURL.class. Select this thread by entering: **thread #** (where # is the number of the GetURL thread). Now that this has been selected, enter **print GetURL** to reassure yourself that the GetURL class was loaded and is accessible.

7. Now dump the contents of the GetURL class. Remember that each object in Java can be printed (or dumped). Its contents should look something like this:

```
GetURL = 0x13a5338:class(GetURL) {
    superclass = 0x13a5370:class(java.applet.Applet)
    loader = (sun.applet.AppletClassLoader)0x13a51a0
    static final LayoutManager panelLayout = (java.awt.FlowLayout)0x13a4898
}
```

8. To view the actual contents of the thread that is running this class, dump that thread using the "dump t@#" syntax (where # is the thread number). Your output might appear like the following:

```
t@4 = (java.lang.Thread)0x13a4a70 {
    private char name[] = "thread applet-GetURL.class"
    private int priority = 6
    private Thread threadQ = null
    private int PrivateInfo = 7217156
    private int eetop = 85851928
    private boolean single_step = false
    private boolean daemon = false
    private boolean stillborn = false
    private Runnable target = (sun.applet.AppletViewerPanel)0x13a48c8
    private boolean interruptRequested = false
    private ThreadGroup group = (sun.applet.AppletThreadGroup)0x13a4a88
}
```

As mentioned earlier, jdb is a command-line tool that accepts a number of options. The following section details these options and their meanings.

jdb Options

The jdb debugger enables the developer to perform a variety of options while the Java class is being run. These options range from printing the class's contents to stepping through the class one line at a time. The following table explains each option briefly:

Option Name	Purpose
threads [threadgroup]	List threads
thread <thread id>	Set default thread
suspend [thread id(s)]	Suspend threads (default: all)
resume [thread id(s)]	Resume threads (default: all)
where [thread id] ¦ all	Dump a thread's stack
threadgroups	List threadgroups

continues

Option Name	*Purpose*
`threadgroup <name>`	Set current threadgroup
`print <id> [id(s)]`	Print object or field
`dump <id> [id(s)]`	Print all object information
`locals`	Print all local variables in current stack frame
`classes`	List currently known classes
`methods <class id>`	List a class's methods
`stop in <class id>.<method>`	Set a breakpoint in a method
`stop at <class id>:<line>`	Set a breakpoint at a line
`up [n frames]`	Move up a thread's stack
`down [n frames]`	Move down a thread's stack
`clear <class id>:<line>`	Clear a breakpoint
`step`	Execute current line
`cont`	Continue execution from breakpoint
`catch <class id>`	Break for the specified exception
`ignore <class id>`	Ignore the specified exception
`list [line number¦method]`	Print source code
`use [source file path]`	Display or change the source path
`memory`	Report memory usage
`gc`	Free unused objects
`load classname`	Load Java class to be debugged
`run <class> [args]`	Start execution of a loaded Java class
`!!`	Repeat last command
`help (or ?)`	List commands
`exit (or quit)`	Exit debugger

Other Debuggers

jdb provides the Java programmer with a rudimentary tool that you can use to examine threads, classes, and events. For some developers, all of the capability they could ever want is provided by the jdb tool. However, for many other programmers accustomed to graphical debugging tools such as those found in many C++ environments, Delphi, and Visual Basic, this tool is severely lacking. Because of Java's surge in popularity, tools for Java are on the way that will compare favorably with the best tools of any language. This section will examine common features of modern debuggers with the assumption that Java programmers will soon have these at their disposal. These features also can be used to evaluate new tools as they are released.

Visual Breakpoints

Nearly all GUI development environments currently allow programmers to set breakpoints using some graphical construct (a popular method is to highlight the breakpoint line in red or some other color). This allows the developer to actually see where breakpoints have been set instead of having to store these locations in their own memory. Another convenient feature is the ability to set breakpoints and have the development environment remember where these breakpoints are between sessions. As you have seen, jdb only allows the programmer to set a breakpoint while the program is being debugged. The next time the application is run, these breakpoints will need to be reset. The Symantec Visual Café toolkit includes a debugger that supports this option.

Step Into or Over

Once the breakpoint has been set, most debuggers will allow the programmer to then execute code line by line. If the source code is available for a function call, some debuggers will actually allow the developer to step "down" into the function, all the while monitoring program variables and conditions that may be critical to fixing a problem.

Evaluate and Modify at Runtime

Like jdb, nearly all debuggers allow the developer some mechanism for examining program variables and states while the application is executing. This can be done (like jdb) using `print` or `dump` commands, or it may be done using GUI tools.

One exciting feature of many newer environments such as Borland Delphi (perhaps Latte?) and the new Asymetric Java/C++ development tools is the ability to actually modify code and variables *at runtime* without stopping the application to recompile. This can save huge amounts of wasted development time, particularly in situations where the programmer knows that something is going to crash but would like to step past that point. By modifying program values, you can avoid the known crash in order to explore the unknown bug lurking around the corner.

View Call Stack

Debuggers that allow the call stack to be viewed also provide an extremely useful service, particularly in event-driven programming environments. Many times, methods can be triggered by several sources. At times such as this, it is extremely helpful to be able to see *which* method called your method. Knowing this can help you to track down otherwise untraceable method calls.

Adding Watches

The use of watches has become extremely popular since the advent of GUI debuggers. When an application is being debugged, development environments that support watches will allow the developer to open a Watch window off to the side. Within this window, any number of objects or properties can be added. As the program is stepped through, the debugger continually updates these values so that the developer can see at all times what is actually happening among several objects or variables.

All of these tools are considered absolute "must-haves" by most professional software developers today. Obviously, jdb falls short in some of these areas. However, it is important to remember that jdb is implemented using the Java Debugger API. Many third-party Java debuggers will be implemented using this same API, so any skills and terminologies learned by using jdb will not be wasted. Instead, these newer tools will simply empower developers to do more with less manual effort.

Summary

jdb is an extremely useful tool, particularly for beginning Java developers. Just as the UNIX dbx debugger remains popular today (many developers use nothing else), there will probably always be a command-line debugger like jdb supplied with the JDK. In many environments where GUI systems are not available (but the Java Virtual Machine is), jdb may be the only option available.

At the current time, no matter what the platform, jdb is probably the most widely used Java debugger. However, as time goes by and more advanced GUI tools are provided, its usage will wane somewhat. However, for beginning software developers, it is imperative that the concepts of debugging introduced here with jdb be understood. Weaker developers may feel that debugging is a necessary evil and can be avoided (by printing to the screen, and so on). The best software developers, however, know that excellent code simply cannot be developed without it.

16

Using JavaDoc to Document Your Program

by Mike Cohn

One of the problems that has faced maintenance programmers through the years has been the horrible documentation left behind by the original programmers. Usually the original programmers included comments in the source code but probably didn't comment as thoroughly as they should have. Then an ambitious project manager recognized the inadequacy of the inline comments and forced the programmers to write a lengthy document about the software. This document was handed over to the maintenance programmers who used it to continue supporting and enhancing the software. Of course, even if the maintenance programmers kept the inline comments current, the other documentation fell out of date because it was just too hard to maintain. And, besides, the maintenance programmers ask, "Why should we keep the document up-to-date if we're also documenting the code?"

This is, of course, a very good question and one the Java developers must have asked themselves. Imagine yourself on the Java team. You've been working long hours writing the hundreds of classes that comprise Java and then you wake up one morning, hands still trembling from the previous night's caffeine excesses, and realize, "Darn! Now we've got to document all that code." The solution the Java developers came up with actually made it possible for them not to write a separate document describing each class, interface, and method. Instead, they wrote a program that would extract specially formatted source code comments and create class documentation from the embedded comments. The tool they developed to do this is called JavaDoc and is included in the Java Developer's Kit.

Overview

JavaDoc reads a `.java` file and creates a set of HTML files that can be read by a Web browser. As an example, consider the documentation for the `Employee` class that is shown in Figure 16.1. At the top of the documentation shown in this figure is an inheritance tree showing that `Employee` is a subclass of `Person`, which is a subclass of `java.lang.Object`.

FIGURE 16.1.

A sample documentation page generated by JavaDoc.

Class Employee

```
java.lang.Object
    |
    +----Person
            |
            +----Employee
```

public class **Employee**
extends Person

The Employee class is used to represent employees of our company. It augments the Person class with information about an employee's salary and job title.

* **Employee**(float, String, String)
    This constructor is used to create a new employee and assign him an initial salary.

In addition to the class's inheritance tree, Figure 16.1 shows that an overall class description can be provided as well as a constructor index. Figure 16.1 shows only one screen of the documentation that will be created for the `Employee` class in this chapter. There are many more areas and types of documentation that can be generated and are described in this chapter.

Running JavaDoc

JavaDoc is a command-line program that is supplied with the Java Developer's Kit. It can be invoked in the following manner:

```
javadoc [options] PackageName ¦ FileName.java
```

For example, to use JavaDoc to create documentation on a class named `Employee`, you would do the following:

```
javadoc employee.java
```

> **NOTE**
>
> When specifying a filename, be sure to include the `.java` extension. If you forget to do so, JavaDoc will still produce HTML files as output. However, they will be essentially blank and not based on your *filename*`.java`.

Command-Line Arguments and Environment Variables

The `[options]` parameter shown as part of the JavaDoc command line can be included if desired. It can be used to specify which directories should be searched for input files, the directory in which to put the generated HTML files, and whether JavaDoc should run in a special verbose mode. These are summarized in Table 16.1.

Table 16.1. The JavaDoc command-line options.

Option	Description
`-classpath` *path*	Specifies the path to be searched for files ending with the `.java` extension. If specified, it overrides the `CLASSPATH` environment variable.
`-d` *directory*	Specifies the target directory for writing HTML files.
`-verbose`	Instructs JavaDoc to run in a special mode that displays additional information as the files are parsed. This option is most useful if you have a class for which the documentation appears incorrect.

The only environment variable used by JavaDoc is `CLASSPATH`. This variable, if set in your environment, informs JavaDoc of the directories in which it should search for `.java` files. For example, to search the current directory, `C:\CAFE\JAVA\SOURCE`, and `C:\MYJAVA\SOURCE`, you would set `CLASSPATH` to the following:

```
.;C:\cafe\java\source;C:\myjava\source
```

Adding JavaDoc Comments

Unfortunately, JavaDoc is only as smart as the information you give it. It gets its information by parsing source code files and looking for comments enclosed within the `/**` and `*/` delimiters. JavaDoc comments are placed immediately above the class or member that they are meant to describe. For example, consider the following class definition and associated comment:

```
/** This is a comment that describes MyClass in general. */
public class MyClass {
    /** The DoSomething method is used to do something. */
    public int DoSomething() {
        // method source goes here
    }
    // remaining class source code
}
```

In this example, a JavaDoc comment has been placed above the class and above the `DoSomething` member method.

Documenting Classes

When documenting a class (in the comment immediately preceding the class definition), you can add class documentation tags to enhance the usability of the documentation. Class documentation tags each begin with an `@` symbol to distinguish them. The following class documentation tags are available:

```
@author author-name
@see classname
@see fully-qualified-classname
@see fully-qualified-classname#method-name
@version version-text
```

As an example of how these tags work, consider the following definitions of an `Employee` class and a `Contractor` class:

```
/**
 * The Employee class is used to represent employees
 * of our company. It augments the Person class with
```

```
   * information about an employee's salary and job
   * title.
   * @author Mike Cohn
   * @version 1.0.0
   * @see Contractor
 */
public class Employee extends Person {
    // class body
}

/**
   * The Contractor class is used to represent
   * contract employees. Contract employees are
   * paid by the hour.
   * @author Mike Cohn
   * @version 1.0.0
   */
class Contractor extends Employee {
    // class body
}
```

The comment preceding the `Employee` class describes the class and then shows the use of three of the class documentation tags. The author and version do not get included in the generated documentation but are useful to include. The `@see Contractor` line in the `Employee` comment will inform readers that they may want to see a related class. Because the `@see` tag is used, JavaDoc will generate a link to the `Contractor` class documentation. This can be seen in Figure 16.2.

FIGURE 16.2.

Class documentation for Employee.

Class Employee

```
java.lang.Object
   |
   +----Person
        |
        +----Employee
```

public class **Employee**
extends Person

The Employee class is used to represent employees of our company. It augments the Person class with information about an employee's salary and job title.

See Also:
    Contractor

As you can see in Figure 16.2, a link is provided for all superclasses of `Employee` (`java.lang.Object` and `Person`) and the `@see` tag has created a link to `Contractor` in a See Also section. Following this link will jump directly to the `Contractor` documentation, as shown in Figure 16.3. The `Contractor` documentation does not need a `@see` tag back to `Employee` because `Employee` is a superclass of `Contractor` and already appears as a link in the inheritance hierarchy.

FIGURE 16.3.

Class documentation for
Contractor.

Class Contractor

class **Contractor**
extends Employee

The Contractor class is used to represent contract employees. Contract employees are paid by the hour.

The link from Employee to Contractor positions your Web browser at the top of the documentation for the Contractor class. Sometimes you would prefer to have a link jump to a specific place within the target class. You can link directly to a method by specifying the name of the method after the target class. For example, the following tag would jump directly to the GetHourlyRate method in the Contractor class:

@see Contractor#GetHourlyRate

Documenting Methods

Like its class documentation tags, JavaDoc also supports method documentation tags. Method documentation tags are optional and can be placed in a JavaDoc comment directly above a method. Like class documentation tags, method tags begin with the @ symbol. The following method documentation tags are available:

```
@param parameter-name description
@return description
@exception fully-qualified-class-name description
```

To see how these tags can be used, consider the following definition of the Contractor class:

```
class Contractor extends Employee {
    public Contractor(float sal, String fName, String lName) {
        super(sal, fName, lName);
    }
    private float hourlyRate;
  /**
    * This method can be used to retrieve the hourly rate
    * paid to the contractor.
    * @return The contractor's hourly rate, excluding
    *          exceptional circumstances such as holidays
    *          and overtime.
    */
    public float GetHourlyRate() {
        return hourlyRate;
    }
  /**
    * This method calculates how much is due to
    * a contractor based on how much he's worked
    * and his hourly rate.
```

```
 * @param hours The number of hours worked by the
 *         contractor during this pay period.
 * @return The amount of money due the contractor.
 */
public float CalculatePayCheck(int hours) {
    return hours * hourlyRate;
}
}
```

The `Contractor` class includes two non-constructor methods—`GetHourlyRate` and `CalculatePayCheck`. Each of these uses the `@return` tag to describe its return value. Additionally, `GetHourlyRate` uses `@param` to describe its input parameters. The results of this documentation can be seen in Figure 16.4.

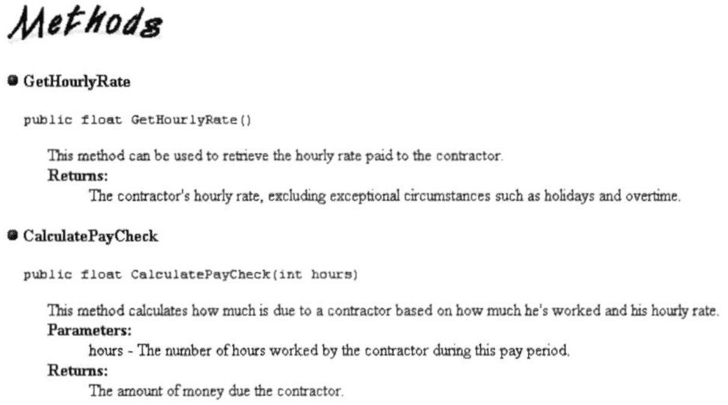

FIGURE 16.4.
Using `@param` *and* `@return` *to document* `Contractor`.

Methods

● **GetHourlyRate**

    `public float GetHourlyRate()`

       This method can be used to retrieve the hourly rate paid to the contractor.
       Returns:
           The contractor's hourly rate, excluding exceptional circumstances such as holidays and overtime.

● **CalculatePayCheck**

    `public float CalculatePayCheck(int hours)`

       This method calculates how much is due to a contractor based on how much he's worked and his hourly rate.
       Parameters:
           hours - The number of hours worked by the contractor during this pay period.
       Returns:
           The amount of money due the contractor.

As you can see from Figure 16.4, the `@return` and `@param` tags nicely format the descriptions entered in the JavaDoc comments. If a method receives more than one parameter, the `@param` tag can be repeated as often as necessary. Although the `@exception` tag is not shown in this example, it behaves identically to `@return` and `@param`.

Enhancing Your Documentation with HTML

By using the class and method documentation tags that you can embed within JavaDoc comments, you can take huge strides toward improving the way you document your code. However, because JavaDoc produces HTML (HyperText Markup Language) files, you can go much further. By embedding HTML commands within your JavaDoc comments, you have almost infinite control over how your documentation will appear when viewed in a browser.

By using HTML tags, you can enhance your documentation by drawing attention to bold or italicized text, including numbered and bulleted lists, images, preformatted text, or even links to other documentation files or Web-based resources.

Table 16.2 shows the HTML tags that you probably find most useful in documenting your Java code. Additionally, you also may want to refer to Chapter 12, "HTML for Java Programmers."

Table 16.2. Useful HTML tags for documenting Java code.

Tag	*Purpose*
`<A>…</A>`	Indicates a link anchor.
`<B>…</B>`	Formats marked text with bold font.
`<BLOCKQUOTE>…</BLOCKQUOTE>`	Formats marked text as a lengthy quotation.
`<CITE>…</CITE>`	Formats marked text as a citation.
`<CODE>…</CODE>`	Formats marked text as source code.
`<EM>…</EM>`	Adds emphasis to marked text.
`<I>…</I>`	Formats marked text in italics.
`<IMG>`	Inserts a named image file.
`<LI>`	Indicates a list item with an ordered or unordered list.
`<OL>…</OL>`	Indicates an ordered (numbered) list.
`<P>`	Indicates the end of a paragraph.
`<PRE>…</PRE>`	Indicates preformatted text. Spacing and layout is preserved by using a monospaced font.
`<STRONG>…</STRONG>`	Adds maximum-strength emphasis to marked text.
`<TT>…</TT>`	Formats marked text in a typewriter font.
`<UL>…</UL>`	Indicates an unordered (bulleted) list.

CAUTION

Because JavaDoc makes its own assumptions about how it will format text, you cannot use HTML tags like `<H1>` that are used to define headings.

An Example

This section demonstrates the use of JavaDoc, including class documentation tags, method documentation tags, and embedded HTML tags. Assume you have the following class definition that you need to document:

```
public class Employee extends Person {
    private float salary;
    private String job;
```

```
    public Employee(float sal, String fName, String lName) {
        super(fName, lName);
        salary = sal;
    }
    public void AssignJob(String newJob) {
        job = newJob;
    }
    public String GetJobTitle() {
        return job;
    }
    public static int GetMaxWorkingAge() {
        return 64;
    }
    private float GetMaxSalary() {
        return 200000f;
    }
    public boolean ChangeSalary(float newSalary) {
        if (newSalary < salary)
            return false;
        if (newSalary > GetMaxSalary())
            return false;
        salary = newSalary;
        return true;
    }
}
```

First, you need to document the class itself. You do this with the following comment:

```
/**
 * The <tt>Employee</tt> class is used to represent
 * employees of our company. It augments the <tt>Person</tt>
 * class with information about an employee's salary and
 * job title.<p>
 * This class was written by:
 * <blockquote>
 * <img src=logo.gif width=300 height=100>
 * </blockquote>
 * @author Mike Cohn
 * @version 1.0.0
 * @see Contractor
 */
public class Employee extends Person {
```

This will create the documentation screen shown in Figure 16.5. You can see that the `<tt>`…`</tt>` tags were used to set the names of other classes in a distinctive typewriter-style font. The `<p>` tag is used to indicate the end of a paragraph. If this tag had not been used, the text on the following line would have merged with the text prior to the tag. The `<blockquote>` and `<img>` tags were used to include a graphics image indicating the author of the class.

FIGURE 16.5.

Class documentation for Employee, *including embedded graphic.*

public class **Employee**
extends Person

The Employee class is used to represent employees of our company. It augments the Person class with information about an employee's salary and job title.

This class was written by:

See Also:
    Contractor

Next, you need to document the constructor. This is done with the following comment, which will produce the documentation shown in Figure 16.6:

```
/** This constructor is used to create a new employee and
 * assign him an initial salary. <EM>It does not verify that
 * salary is less than the company's maximum salary.</EM>
 * You could use this method as follows:
 * <CODE><PRE>
 * Employee Emp = new Employee(35000f,"Mike","Cohn");
 * </PRE></CODE>
 * @param sal The starting salary of the new employee.
 * @param fName The employee's first name.
 * @param lName The employee's last name.
 */
public Employee(float sal, String fName, String lName) {
```

In this case the <CODE>…</CODE> and <PRE>…</PRE> tags were used to indicate a preformatted block of source code. Also, the <EM>…</EM> tags were used to apply emphasis to the statement that the employee's salary must be less than a company maximum. Finally, because this constructor is passed three parameters, each parameter is documented with the @param method tag.

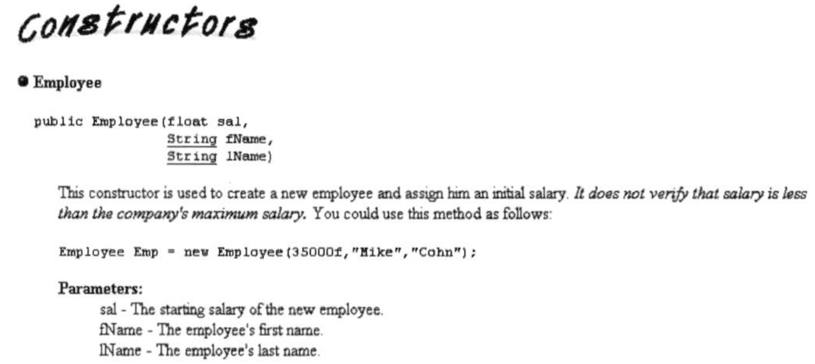

FIGURE 16.6.

Documentation for the Employee *constructor.*

Constructors

● **Employee**

    public Employee(float sal,
                      String fName,
                      String lName)

This constructor is used to create a new employee and assign him an initial salary. *It does not verify that salary is less than the company's maximum salary.* You could use this method as follows:

    Employee Emp = new Employee(35000f,"Mike","Cohn");

Parameters:
    sal - The starting salary of the new employee.
    fName - The employee's first name.
    lName - The employee's last name.

In addition to the full documentation shown in Figure 16.6, JavaDoc creates a list of constructors for the class. This appears as a separate section in the HTML document, as shown in Figure 16.7.

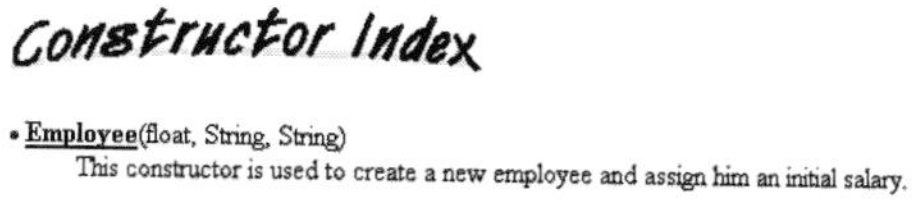

FIGURE 16.7.

The constructor index for the Employee class.

Constructor Index

• **Employee**(float, String, String)
  This constructor is used to create a new employee and assign him an initial salary.

The `AssignJob` method is documented by adding the following comment:

```
/**
 * This method assigns the employee to the
 * specified job. This method does not verify the
 * <i>job title</i> against the list of <i>approved
 * job titles</i> created by <b>Human Resources</b>.
 * Likely job titles you may want to pass include:
 * <ul>
 * <li>Programmer
 * <li>Analyst
 * <li>QA
 * <li>Tech Writer
 * <li>Project Manager
 * <li>Database Administrator
 * <li>Database Engineer
 * </ul>
 * Reminder: All positions must be approved by the
 * <b>Manager of Human Resources</b> according to
 * the company's <CITE>Employee Hiring Guidelines.
 * </CITE>
 * @param newJob This is the new job title.
 * @see #GetJobTitle
 */
public void AssignJob(String newJob) {
```

The result of this documentation can be seen in Figure 16.8. This example demonstrates the use of `<B>`...`</B>` and `<I>`...`</I>` to bold and italicize text. Additionally, the use of an unordered (bulleted) list is demonstrated. The `<UL>`...`</UL>` tags indicate the start and end of the list and the `<LI>` tags indicate each of the list items. This example also demonstrates the use of `<CITE>`... `</CITE>` to indicate a citation. Finally, the @see method tag is used. In this example, no class name appears to the left of the #. This will create a link to a method within the current class.

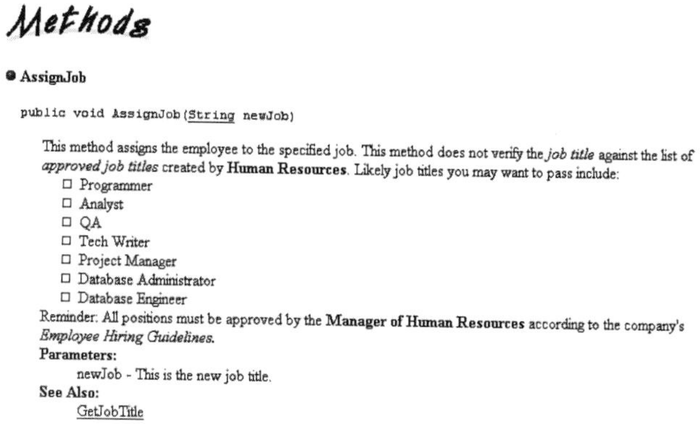

FIGURE 16.8.

Documentation for the AssignJob method.

Methods

● **AssignJob**

public void AssignJob(String newJob)

This method assigns the employee to the specified job. This method does not verify the *job title* against the list of *approved job titles* created by **Human Resources**. Likely job titles you may want to pass include:
  □ Programmer
  □ Analyst
  □ QA
  □ Tech Writer
  □ Project Manager
  □ Database Administrator
  □ Database Engineer
Reminder: All positions must be approved by the **Manager of Human Resources** according to the company's *Employee Hiring Guidelines.*
Parameters:
  newJob - This is the new job title.
See Also:
  GetJobTitle

Just as JavaDoc created a constructor index that listed each of a class's constructors, it also creates a method index that will list each of a class's non-private methods. The method index for Employee is shown in Figure 16.9.

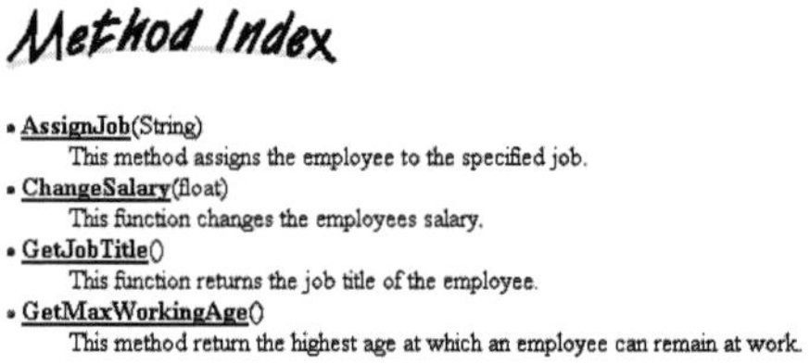

FIGURE 16.9.

The method index for the Employee class.

Method Index

- **AssignJob**(String)
  This method assigns the employee to the specified job.
- **ChangeSalary**(float)
  This function changes the employees salary.
- **GetJobTitle**()
  This function returns the job title of the employee.
- **GetMaxWorkingAge**()
  This method return the highest age at which an employee can remain at work.

Next, the following comment is written for GetJobTitle to produce the documentation shown in Figure 16.10:

```
/**
 * This function returns the job title of the employee.
 * @return A string representing the job title (for
 * example, "programmer").
 * @see #AssignJob
 */
public String GetJobTitle() {
```

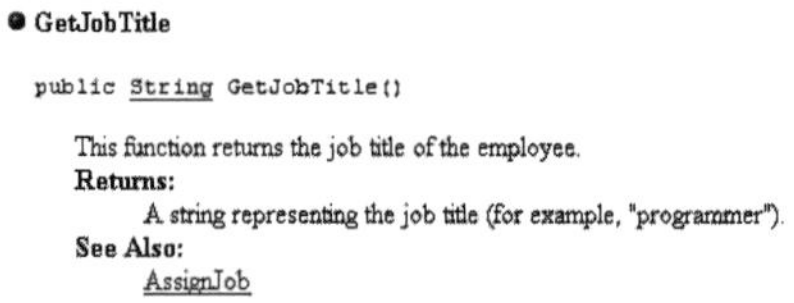

FIGURE 16.10.

Documentation for the GetJobTitle method.

● GetJobTitle

public String GetJobTitle()

This function returns the job title of the employee.
Returns:
    A string representing the job title (for example, "programmer").
See Also:
    AssignJob

The method GetMaxWorkingAge is defined as static, meaning that it is associated with the class itself, rather than with instances of the class. However, because it is a public method, it can be documented as shown in the following comment:

```
/**
 * This method returns the highest age at which
 * an employee can remain at work. <STRONG>
 * After this age, an employee must retire and
 * move to Florida.</STRONG>
 * @return The last allowable working year before
 * mandatory retirement.
 */
public static int GetMaxWorkingAge() {
```

As you can see in Figure 16.11, the use of the <STRONG>…</STRONG> tag places heavy emphasis on the need for retirees to move to Florida.

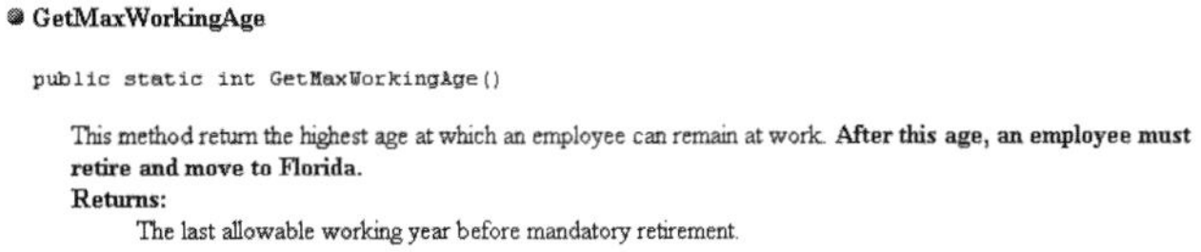

FIGURE 16.11.

Documentation for the
GetMaxWorkingAge
method.

● **GetMaxWorkingAge**

`public static int GetMaxWorkingAge()`

This method return the highest age at which an employee can remain at work. **After this age, an employee must retire and move to Florida.**
Returns:
    The last allowable working year before mandatory retirement.

Next, the method `GetMaxSalary` is documented, as follows:

```
/**
 * This comment will not show up in JavaDoc because
 * it is private.
 */
private float GetMaxSalary() {
```

However, `GetMaxSalary` is declared as `private`, so it will not be documented by JavaDoc. Because private functions are not usable outside the class in which they are declared, there is no need to document them for use by others in the same way that exists for externally visible methods.

At this point, the only method left to document is `ChangeSalary`, which is documented as follows:

```
/**
 * This function changes the employee's salary.
 * A salary change can occur only after the two following
 * tests have been applied:
 * <ol>
 * <li>The new salary is higher than the current salary.
 * <li>The new salary is less than the maximum salary.
 * </ol>
 * @return <B>true</B> if the salary change is approved,
 *         <B>false</B> otherwise.
 * @param newSalary The proposed new salary.
 */
public boolean ChangeSalary(float newSalary) {
```

The documentation for `ChangeSalary` will appear as shown in Figure 16.12. This example demonstrates the use of `<OL>`...`</OL>` and `<LI>` to introduce an ordered list and its items. Ordered lists are like unordered lists except that instead of bullets, they have numbers to the left of each item. Additionally, this example shows that some HTML tags can be embedded with class or method documentation tags. In this case, `<B>`...`</B>` is embedded within the `@return` tag.

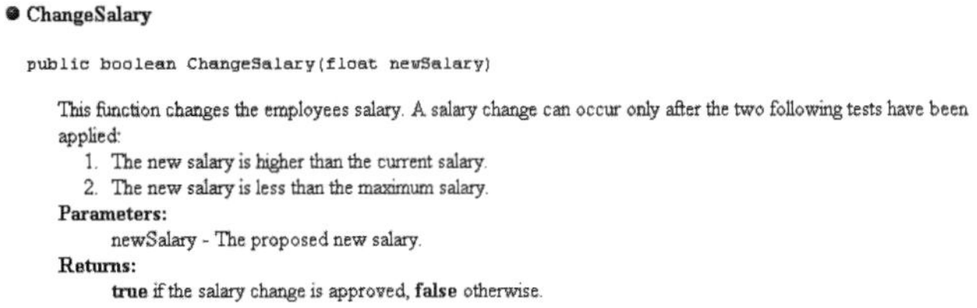

FIGURE 16.12.

Documentation for the
ChangeSalary *method.*

● **ChangeSalary**

`public boolean ChangeSalary(float newSalary)`

This function changes the employees salary. A salary change can occur only after the two following tests have been applied:
1. The new salary is higher than the current salary.
2. The new salary is less than the maximum salary.
Parameters:
    newSalary - The proposed new salary.
Returns:
    true if the salary change is approved, **false** otherwise.

Summary

In this chapter, you learned how JavaDoc can simplify the job of documenting your classes. You saw how class documentation tags can be used to link classes by providing jumps between related classes. You also learned how to use method documentation tags to document the parameters, return values, and exceptions of each method. Even with this much power and flexibility, it only scratched the surface of what can be done. By embedding HTML commands directly into your comments, you learned how to enhance your documentation by using formatted text, numbered and bulleted lists, and embedded images. Finally, you saw an extensive example that put all of these pieces together to document a single class.

II

Using the Java Packages

In this section of the book, the authors explore the capabilities of the Java system and show you how it can be used to develop serious applications and applets. Tom Trinko begins the process by discussing the user interface and how you can exploit the presentation system. Then he covers some of the security restrictions inherent in Java.

Since using an interpreted language can be slow at times, Michael Nygard shows you how to use native code in the target system to speed up the executions. Then Michael Morrison shows how to make your applets and applications even more robust by handling threads, events, and exceptions. Rounding out the development process, Mike Cohn teaches you to drive databases, and then Dan Joshi dives into the topics of network-aware programming and the use of sockets in Java.

17

Programming the User Interface

by Tom Trinko

Introduction and Basic Concepts

This chapter covers the various tools Java provides to help you build the user interface for your Java application or applet. Java provides a rich set of tools to make platform-independent, easy-to-use graphical user interfaces. Your Java project can use three groups of interface elements:

■ **Drawing**: Non-interactive interface items such as lines, rectangles, ovals, and arcs in both filled and unfilled versions.

■ **Interactive elements**: Interface elements that enable the user to interact with your project. They consist of things such as buttons, menus, and text areas.

■ **Images**: Bitmaps that can be built on-the-fly or read in as GIF or JPEG format files.

If you've ever programmed a *graphical user interface* (GUI) for the Mac, Windows, or UNIX, you'll find that the basic tools are familiar. Java is catching on because, unlike previous languages, the interface is pretty much platform independent so that you don't have to maintain multiple code bases—one for each target platform.

Platform Independence: Gone Today, Here Tomorrow

Although Java is technically platform independent, discrepancies still exist between platforms. These differences result from three different mechanisms:

■ **Implementation:** The hooks from Java to the client machine's operating system are implemented by different teams on each machine. Although they work with a single standard, they introduce different bugs at different times. A particular interface feature that works in JDK 1.0.2 for the Mac might not work in JDK 1.0.2 for Windows, for example, and the bug list for JDK 1.0.2 on Windows is different (and longer) than the bug list for the same version of the JDK on the Mac. The good news is that as Java matures, these types of differences will go away. Check http://java.sun.com/products/JDK/ to find links to the latest information on the current version of the JDK and associated bug lists.

■ **Design:** Because Java uses the operating system on each platform to provide basic GUI elements (such as buttons), applications and applets look different on each platform. On the Mac, for example, a windows menu bar is placed at the top of the screen rather than in the window. This is very different from what users see on Windows or UNIX machines, but it's what Mac users expect. Although you can control the amount of space used by an item, you can't control the detailed look and feel. These differences are there as long as different operating systems are used. This actually is nice, because your users see interfaces that are familiar to them. Imagine the uproar if you tried to make Mac users live with a Motif interface!

■ **Standards or the lack thereof:** The Java language standard strives to be complete and unambiguous. Unfortunately, defining a computer language so that everyone who implements it does so in an exactly identical fashion is very difficult. You should expect some ambiguities in the standard; it is interpreted in slightly different ways by the people who implement Java on different platforms. These discrepancies tend to be eliminated over time; the larger the discrepancy, the quicker it is stomped out.

Because you can't really do much about any of these issues, you need to test your projects on as many different platforms as you think they will run on. For applets that are used on the Internet, that means pretty much every platform, whereas for an application running on your company's intranet, it might mean only Sun and SGI. The good news is that for simple interfaces, you'll find that although everything doesn't look identical across platforms, the matchup is pretty good. If you don't have access to multiple platforms, you can be fairly sure that your interface will look pretty much the same on any platform that supports Java.

> **NOTE**
>
> If the content of the WWW site on which you're going to use the applet is machine specific, you probably don't have to worry about the applet not being pretty on other platforms. If you have a Mac software site, you probably won't get a whole lot of visits from Windows users.

Abstract Window Toolkit (AWT)

The Abstract Window Toolkit (or Alternative Window Toolkit, depending on who you talk to) is a visual interface kit that comes with all the current implementations of Java. As its name indicates, though, the intent is for other—hopefully, more powerful and easier to use—toolkits to be developed by various vendors in the future. For now, if you want to do any interface work in Java, the AWT package is the way to go.

Figures 17.1 through 17.3 show the inheritance hierarchy of the classes commonly used in building interfaces.

These class structures might seem a bit intimidating at first, but if you glance through them, you'll see that most AWT classes just inherit from `Object`. In addition, all the interactive elements (except menus) inherit from `Component`. The only other very important thing to note is that because `Applet` inherits from `Panel` (which inherits from `Container`), applets can directly contain other objects such as buttons, canvases, and so on. This section describes how you can build hierarchies of containers in applets.

FIGURE 17.1.
AWT classes that inherit from `java.lang Object`.

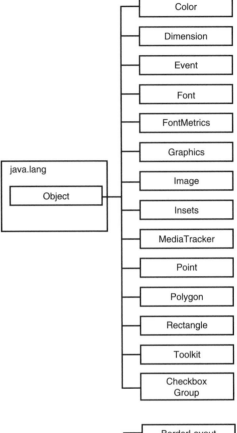

FIGURE 17.2.
All the classes that control the placement of objects on the screen inherit from the `java.lang Object` *class.*

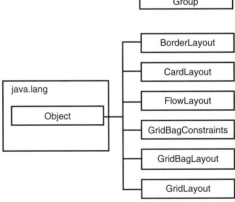

FIGURE 17.3.

The `Applet` *class inherits from* `java.awt.panel`, *so you can draw directly to an applet.*

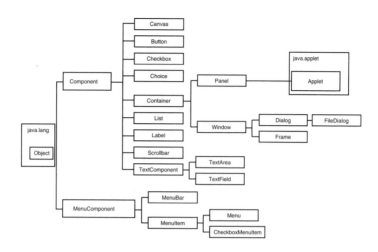

All the other classes are described as they become relevant in the following sections. Use the diagrams included in these sections as quick references when you want to find out what capabilities a class inherits.

Graphics Class

The `Graphics` class is part of the AWT. It's contained in `java.awt.Graphics`, and it's the basic class for everything you'll draw on-screen. Applets have associated `Graphics` instances, as do various components such as buttons. Drawing methods, such as `drawLine`, work on a `Graphics` instance, so you'll see many calls in this form in a typical Java applet:

```
public void paint(Graphics g) {
    g.drawLine(10,10,20,20);
}
```

The `Graphics` class uses a standard computer coordinate system with the origin in the upper-left corner, as shown in Figure 17.4.

All coordinate measurements in Java are done in pixels. The size of items, therefore, in absolute units such as inches or millimeters, differs on various machines due to differing pixels/inch values.

You'll find that whenever your program has to draw something, you'll be using `Graphics` class methods. The following sections discuss the most useful methods. Here's a listing of the methods that aren't covered later in this chapter, but that occasionally will be useful.

`clipRect(int x, int y, int width, int height)`
Changes the clipping region to the intersection of the current clipping rectangle and the one specified in the input arguments. This means that the clipping region can only get smaller.

FIGURE 17.4.

The Java Graphics *class coordinate system.*

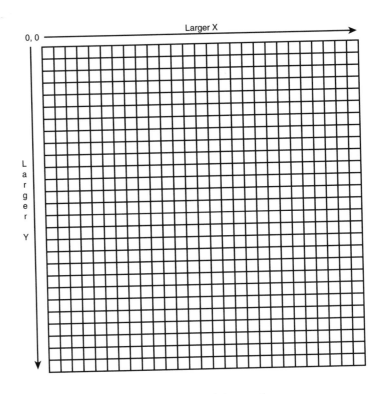

copyArea(int x, int y, int width, int height, int new_x, int new_y)
Copies the rectangular area defined by x, y, width, and height to a rectangle defined by new_x, new_y, width, and height in the same Graphics object.

Graphics, create()
Makes a clone of the Graphics object.

Graphics, create(int x, int y, int width, int height)
Makes a clone of the Graphics object, but with a clipping region defined by the intersection of the current clipping rectangle and the one specified by x, y, width, and height. In addition, the origin of the Graphics object returned by this call is set to x,y.

setPaintMode()
Sets the painting mode to draw over; it is used to undo the effects of setXORMode.

setXORMode(Color a_color)
Sets the drawing mode to exclusive OR. The color is bitwise exclusive ORed with the current color and the foreground color to produce the final color.

```
translate(int x, int y)
```
Translates the origin of the Graphics area to the specified point.

The update, paint, and repaint Methods

You'll encounter three key methods over and over again as you work with the various user interface elements.

repaint

Requests a redraw of an item or an entire interface. It then calls update.

update

Controls what happens when repaint is called; you can override this method.

paint

Determines what's done when any item is redrawn. It's called whenever something needs to be redrawn—for example, when a window is uncovered. All displayable entities have paint methods that they inherit from Component.

> **NOTE**
>
> Interactive elements, such as buttons, are redrawn automatically; you don't have to implement a paint method for them.

All these methods are defined in the Component class. This means that all the various interactive controls and applets inherit these methods. Although all these methods can be overridden, you'll find that paint and update are the ones you work with most often. Listing 17.1 shows a simple example of how paint and repaint can be used.

Listing 17.1. An example of paint and repaint.

```java
import java.awt.*;
import java.applet.Applet;

public class paint_methods extends Applet{
    int y;
    public void init() {
        y = 1;
    }
    public void start () {
        while(true) {
```

continues

Listing 17.1. continued

```
                y += 1;
                repaint();
                //wait 50 milliseconds and then call repaint again
                try {
                    Thread.sleep(50);
                    } catch(InterruptedException e) {}


        }
    }

    public void paint(Graphics g)
    {
        //draw a string to the screen
        g.drawString("Hello, World!", 25, y );
    }
}
```

After you run this code, you see the phrase Hello, World! slide down the screen. You're probably wondering why you don't see many copies of Hello, World! on-screen at the same time. The answer is the update method. Listing 17.2 shows the default update method.

Listing 17.2. The default update method.

```
public void update(Graphics g) {
    g.setColor(getBackground());  //set the drawing color to the
                                  //background color
    g.fillRect(0,0,width,height); //fill the window with the
                                  //background color
    g.setColor(getForeground());  //reset the foreground color
    paint(g); //call paint to redraw everything
}
```

The first three lines erase whatever is in the Graphics object so that anything that was drawn before it is deleted. You can change this behavior by overriding the update method. The version of the update method shown in Listing 17.3, when added to the applet in Listing 17.1, gives you the result shown in Figure 17.5 because the screen isn't erased between calls to paint.

Listing 17.3. A revised update method.

```
public void update(Graphics g) {
    paint(g); //call paint to redraw everything
}
```

FIGURE 17.5.

Overriding the update *method.*

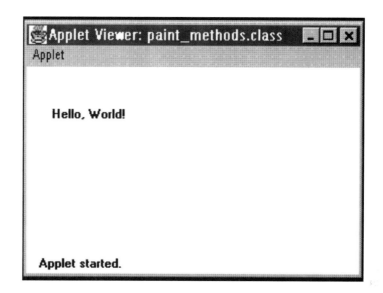

One thing to remember about calling the repaint method is that it doesn't always execute immediately. Java repaints as soon as it can, but sometimes repaints pile up because the computer is busy. Remember that your applet might be running on some fairly slow platforms; in this case, Java throws out some of the repaints, discarding the oldest repaints first. Because of this practice, three other versions of repaint are available with different input parameters.

repaint(long time_in_milliseconds)

Tries to call update for the number of milliseconds specified in the input argument. If update can't be called by the end of the specified time, repaint gives up. Note that no error is thrown if the method gives up. You will want to use this version primarily for animations, when you know that repaints will occur frequently.

repaint(int x, int y, int width, int height)

Repaints only the rectangular part of the screen defined by x, y, width, and height.

repaint(long time, int x, int y, int width, int height)

Combines the previous two repaint versions so that only a portion of the screen is updated. If it can't be done before the specified time elapses (in milliseconds), it is skipped.

When you invoke repaint on a container, such as an applet, the AWT takes care of invoking update on all the items in the container—even ones inside other containers that are in the top-level container.

Working with Color

The AWT provides very generalized color support. The abstract `ColorModel` class enables you to define how colors are represented. The AWT comes with two predefined color models: `IndexColorModel` and `DirectColorModel`. `IndexColorModel` is used when images have a lookup table of colors and each pixel's value is an index in the lookup table. The pixel's color is determined by the color value in the lookup table specified by the index. `DirectColorModel` uses a 32-bit integer to hold the data for the color. Regardless of which color model you use, you still can represent individual colors as 32-bit integers (as described later in this section). In general, you won't have to worry about the `ColorModel` class.

RGB and HSB Color Formats

The AWT's normal color model is RGB; in this model, a color is defined by its `red`, `green`, and `blue` components. Each of these three values is an `int` with a value between `0` and `255`. An RGB value can be stored in an `int` with bits 31 through 24 being unused, bits 23 through 16 for the `red` value, bits 15 through 8 storing the `green` value, and bits 0 through 7 for the `blue` component of the color. The applet in Listing 17.4 shows how to extract the color components from an `int`.

Listing 17.4. Extracting color components from an integer.

```
import java.awt.*;
import java.applet.Applet;


public class unpack_color extends Applet
{
    public void init()
    {
        //getRGB is a static method so you invoke it with the name of the
        //class. You don't need a specific instance.

        int temp = Color.white.getRGB();
        unpack_colors(temp);

    }
    public void unpack_colors(int the_color)
    {
        int red, green, blue;
        //the highest order byte is unused
        //the next highest byte is red
        red = the_color & 0x00FF0000;
        //shift the value to the right so it's in the range 0-255
        red = red >> 16;
        //the next-to-last byte is green
        green = the_color & 0x0000FF00;
        //shift the value to the right so it's in the range 0-255
        green = green >> 8;
```

```
        //the lowest byte is blue
        blue = the_color & 0x000000FF;
        System.out.println("red = " + red + " green= " + green +
            " blue= " + blue);
    }
}
```

A `Color` class is available that enables you to use a single object rather than three `int`s to define a color. Most AWT methods that use colors require you to pass them an instance of a `Color` object.

The `Color` class also has several methods for manipulating and creating colors.

> **NOTE**
>
> All of the method descriptions in this chapter start with the type of value returned by the method (if no type is shown it's void) followed by the method name and its input arguments. For example,
>
> `clipRect(int x, int y, int width, int height)`
>
> means that the `clipRect` method does not return a value.
>
> `Graphics, create()`
>
> means that the `create` method returns a value of type `Graphics`.

`Color, brighter()`
Returns a new color that is approximately 1.5 times brighter than the current color.

`Color, darker()`
Returns a color about 70 percent as bright as the original color.

`boolean, equals(Object item)`
Checks to see whether two colors are the same.

`int, getBlue()`
Returns the `blue` component of a color.

`Color, getColor(String color)`
Returns an instance of the `Color` class given a string containing a decimal or hexadecimal number. For example, `0x0000FF` produces a deep blue. This is a static method. This version and the next two versions are useful primarily when reading in parameters from HTML.

`Color, getColor(String color, Color default)`
Performs the same function as the preceding, except if the string isn't in the right format, it returns the color defined by the second parameter.

`Color, getColor(String color, int rgb)`
Performs the same function as the preceding, except you supply a default packed integer with RGB values, not an instance of `color`.

`Color, getHSBColor(float hue, float saturation, float brightness)`
Returns an instance of the `Color` class based on the supplied HSB values (`hue`, `saturation`, and `brightness`). This is a static method.

`int, getGreen()`
Returns the `green` component of the color.

`int, HSBtoRGB(float hue, float saturation, float brightness)`
Produces an integer containing the RGB values of a color—with `blue` in the lowest byte, `green` in the second byte, and `red` in the third byte—when given the three HSB values. This is a static method.

`int, getRGB()`
Returns the packed-integer version of the RGB values of a color.

`int, getRed()`
Returns the `red` component of a color.

`float[], RGBtoHSB(int r, int g, int b)`
Returns an array of floats containing the `h`, `s`, and `b` values of the equivalent color to the specified `r`, `g`, and `b` values.

Using HSB Colors

As you probably guessed from the names of some of these methods, the AWT also lets you work with the HSB model. In this model, colors are represented as hue, saturation, and brightness.

- **Hue:** The hue—red or blue, for example—portion of the color. The value runs from `0` to `1/4` `PI`, with `0` corresponding to red and `1/4` `PI` to violet.
- **Saturation:** Determines how far from gray a color is. The value runs from `0` to `1`. A value of `0` corresponds to a gray scale. By varying this parameter, you can fade out a color picture.

■ **Brightness:** Determines how bright a given color is. The value runs from 0 to 1. A brightness of 0 gives you black. A value of 1 gives you the brightest color of the given hue and saturation possible.

There are a number of reasons to use the HSB representation. You can convert a color image to black and white by just setting the saturation of all the pixels to 0. Similarly, if you want to create a continuous color spectrum, it's easy to smoothly change the hue to get a continuum— within the limits of the color support of your monitor and Web browser—of colors. The applet shown in Listing 17.5 creates the rainbow shown in Figure 17.6; trust me—even though you can see it only in black and white, it looks great in color.

FIGURE 17.6.

A Java rainbow brought to you by the wonders of HSB. Because you easily can create color objects with RGB or HSB values, you can use both in any program.

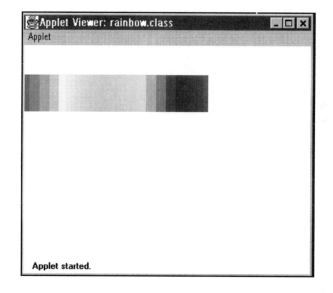

Listing 17.5. Creating a rainbow.

```java
import java.awt.*;
import java.applet.Applet;


public class rainbow extends Applet{
    int n_steps;
    int rainbow_width;

    public void init()
    {

    }
    public void paint(Graphics g)
    {
        float h,s,b;
        int x,y,i;
        Color temp_color;
```

continues

Listing 17.5. continued

```
        int patch_width,patch_height;
        float incr;

        n_steps = 256;
        //define how much the Hue will change between steps
        incr = (float)(0.25*Math.PI/n_steps);
        rainbow_width = 256;
        //figure out how wide each step would be
        patch_width = (int)(rainbow_width/n_steps);
        patch_height = 50;
        //fix the value of Saturation to the maximum value
        s = (float)1.0;
        //fix the value of Brightness to the maximum value
        b = (float)1.0;
        y = 40;
        x = 0;
        //draw a set of rectangles filled with the colors of
        //the rainbow
        for(i=0;i<n_steps;i++) {
            h = incr*i;
            //create a new color using the HSB parameters
            temp_color = Color.getHSBColor(h,s,b);
            //set the current drawing color to the new color
            g.setColor(temp_color);
            x += patch_width;
            //draw a rectangle whose upper lefthand corner is at
            //x,y and which is patch_width wide and patch_height
            //tall
            g.fillRect(x,y,patch_width,patch_height);
        }
    }
}
```

Geometric Classes

Several generally useful classes exist that are used to contain information about locations and shapes. They're used as arguments for many of the drawing-related methods.

Dimension

Stores a width and a height as attributes. You can access these attributes with this code:

```
Dimension d;
int w,h;
h = d.height;
w = d.width;
```

Point

Represents an x and y coordinate. The points x and y are accessible. Point also supports two methods.

```
move(int x, int y)
```
Sets the x and y values of the point to the input parameter values.

```
translate(int delta_x, int delta_y)
```
Adds the input parameter values to the current x and y values of the point—for example, x = x + delta_x.

Polygon

Represents an arbitrarily ordered list of vertices. You can directly access the three main attributes.

```
int x[]
```
Specifies the array of x values for the vertices.

```
int y[]
```
Specifies the array of y values. The *n*th y value and the *n*th x value define a vertex location.

Polygon has several useful methods.

```
int npoints
```
Specifies the number of vertices.

```
addPoint(int x, int y)
```
Adds a new vertex to the polygon.

```
Rectangle, getBoundingBox()
```
Returns the smallest rectangle that contains all the vertices.

```
boolean, inside(int x, int y)
```
Returns TRUE if the point defined by x and y is inside the polygon.

Rectangle

This has four public instance variables: the x and y coordinates of its upper-left corner (unless the height or width is negative, in which case the origin is in one of the other corners), its width, and its height. Rectangle has a number of methods that make working with rectangular regions easy.

```
add(int x, int y)
```
Adds the specified x,y point to a Rectangle by growing the rectangle to the smallest rectangle that contains the original rectangle and the point.

add(Point a_point)

Performs the same function as the preceding method, except the input parameter is a point rather than two integers.

add(Rectangle a_rectangle)

Grows the rectangle to the smallest one that contains the original rectangle and the rectangle supplied as the input parameter.

grow(int delta_w, int delta_h)

Grows the rectangle by the specified amount in height and width. Each side of the rectangle moves a distance delta_w so that the overall width of the rectangle increases by 2*delta_w. If the original rectangle width and height are 50,50 and the two input parameters to grow are 50,75, the new width and height would be 150,200.

boolean, inside(int x, int y)

Returns TRUE if the point x,y is inside the rectangle.

Rectangle, intersection(Rectangle rect)

Returns a rectangle that contains the intersection of the two rectangles. If the rectangles don't overlap, the resulting rectangle has 0 height and width.

boolean, intersects(Rectangle rect)

Returns TRUE if the rectangles overlap, including just a shared edge or vertex.

boolean, isEmpty()

Returns TRUE if the height or width of a rectangle is 0.

move(int x, int y)

Sets the origin of the rectangle to x,y.

reshape(int x, int y, int width, int height)

Sets the origin of the rectangle to x,y, its width to width, and its height to height.

resize(int width, int height)

Sets the width of the rectangle to width and its height to height.

translate(int d_x, int d_y)

Moves the rectangle a distance d_x in x and d_y in y.

Rectangle, union(Rectangle rect)

Returns a new rectangle that is the smallest one that contains both rectangles.

The `Toolkit`

This abstract class serves as a bridge between the platform-specific and the platform-independent parts of Java. It's the interface used to create peers for components such as buttons, and its methods let Java programs find out about platform-specific features such as the available fonts and the characteristics of the desktop. Because this is an abstract class, you don't instantiate it, but it does have a number of useful methods, including the following.

The `Toolkit` is your primary interface to machine-dependent information and interfaces. It's usable in applications and applets. Methods that are implemented by the `Applet` class, such as `getImage`, are available in applications via the `Toolkit`. You can use the static method `getDefaultToolkit()` to get the `Toolkit`, as in this snippet:

```
try {
    Toolkit current_toolkit = Toolkit.getDefaultToolkit();
} catch(AWTError e) {}
```

> **NOTE**
>
> The peer of a component is the platform-specific interface definition of the methods that the component has to support. Implementing a Java component on a new platform (Linux, for example) consists of writing native methods to fill in the peer interface definition.

`Dimension: getScreenSize()`
Returns the screen size in pixels.

`int: getScreenResolution()`
Returns the screen resolution in pixels/inch.

`ColorModel: getColorModel()`
Returns the `ColorModel`, which defines how color is represented on the platform.

`String[]: getFontList()`
Gets a list of the names of the fonts available on the platform.

`FontMetrics: getFontMetrics(Font font)`
Returns the `FontMetrics`, which provide measurements of a font's screen size, for the specified font on the desktop.

`Image: getImage(String filename)`
Gets an image from the file specified in the input argument.

```
Image: getImage(URL a_url)
```
Gets an image from a specified URL.

```
boolean, prepareImage(Image an_image, int width, int height, ImageObserver obs)
```
Forces the loading of an image, with a given width and height. You can use the image observer to monitor the progress of loading the image. If width and `height` aren't the current dimensions of the image, the image is scaled.

```
int, checkImage(Image an_image, int width, int height, ImageObserver obs)
```
Returns an integer that can be tested to determine the status of the image. `ImageObserver` constants that you can AND with the returned value are WIDTH, HEIGHT, PROPERTIES, SOMEBITS, FRAMEBITS, and ALLBITS. If the returned value ANDed with ALLBITS returns TRUE, the image is fully loaded.

```
Image: createImage(ImageProducer an_image_source)
```
Takes an image source, such as a filter, and creates an image.

Drawing

The methods and tools described in this section enable you to draw simple graphical items that are non-interactive—although you can use the Canvas component and/or the location of mouse clicks to make these items behave as though they were interactive. If you've ever written code for a modern GUI, or even Windows, you'll find most of the drawing utilities fairly familiar. All these operations are implemented as methods on the Graphics class. Because anything you can draw on has a Graphics class as an attribute, this doesn't limit the utility of these functions.

Drawing Text

You've already seen an example of drawing text using the drawString method. The general syntax for that method follows:

```
Graphics g;
g.drawString(String string_to_draw, int x_position, int y_position)
```

You also can use the drawChars method if you have an array of type char rather than a string.

Working with Fonts

Back in the dark ages, before the Mac and the desktop publishing revolution, people were used to having only a few fonts available for use on the computer. Things have changed dramatically since then; now people commonly buy CD-ROMs with more than 1,000 fonts for $50. Unfortunately, Java reintroduces a new generation to the wonders of limited fonts. This probably will change rapidly as Java and the Internet standards mature, but for right now, typographic simplicity is the order of the day.

You can create instances of the Font class using this creator syntax:

```
Font a_font = new Font(String name_of_font, int font_style, int font_size);
```

The generally available fonts follow:

> Courier
> Dialog
> Helvetica
> Symbol
> TimesRoman

Because the set of available fonts may change, you might want to use a variation of the applet shown in Listing 17.6 to check for what fonts are available; this code works in applications as well.

Listing 17.6. Checking for available fonts.

```
import java.awt.*;
import java.applet.Applet;


public class discover_fonts extends Applet
{

    public void paint(Graphics g){
        String FontList[];
        int i;
        Font a_font;

        FontList = getToolkit().getFontList();
        for(i=0;i<FontList.length;i++) {
            a_font = new Font(FontList[i],Font.BOLD,12);
            g.setFont(a_font);
            g.drawString("This is the " + FontList[i] +
                    " Font",25, 15*(i + 1));
        }
    }
}
```

This applet just gets a list of strings containing the names of the available fonts. Figure 17.7 shows the output of this applet.

The last line is Symbol font. The style for all the fonts was set to bold by using the font constant Font.BOLD. You also can use Font.ITALIC and Font.PLAIN. You can combine styles by bitwise ORing them. This line produces a font that is both italic and bold, for example:

```
Font a_font = new Font("Helvetica",(Font.BOLD ¦ Font.ITALIC),12);
```

FIGURE 17.7.

The available fonts.

Measuring Fonts, Centering Text

You'll find that you often need to precisely position text in an applet. The FontMetrics class provides an easy way to find out how much space text drawn with a given instance of Font will be. Just in case you're not a typographic expert, Table 17.1 provides some quick definitions of the key font measurement terms, illustrated in Figure 17.8.

Table 17.1. FontMetrics terms.

Height	The height of the tallest character in a font. It's therefore the maximum vertical distance you need to reserve when drawing a string with the font.
Baseline	The bottom of all characters are positioned on this imaginary line. The descent part of a character, such as the bottom curl on a g, lies below this line.
Ascent	Measures the height of the character above the baseline. This can include the amount of whitespace recommended by the font designer.
Descent	Measures the height (or, more appropriately, depth) of the character below the baseline. This can include the amount of whitespace recommended by the font designer.

FIGURE 17.8.
Font terminology.

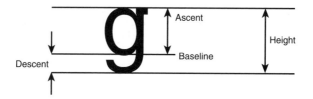

The applet shown in Listing 17.7 shows you how to access the FontMetrics information. The result is shown in Figure 17.9.

Listing 17.7. Accessing FontMetrics information.

```
import java.awt.*;
import java.applet.Applet;


public class font_metrics extends Applet
{

    public void paint(Graphics g){
        Font a_font;
        FontMetrics a_font_metric;
        String the_message;
        int string_width, font_height,font_ascent, font_descent;
        int font_ascent_no_white, font_descent_no_white;
        int y;

        the_message = "Alien Space Monsters! ";
        //Make a new font
        a_font = new Font("Helvetica",Font.BOLD,16);
        g.setFont(a_font);
        //get the metrics for the font
        a_font_metric = g.getFontMetrics();
        //get the width of the message
        string_width = a_font_metric.stringWidth(the_message);
        //get the height of the font
        font_height = a_font_metric.getHeight();
        //get the ascent of the font; this includes whitespace
        //recommended by the font designer
        font_ascent = a_font_metric.getAscent();
        //get the descent of the font; this includes whitespace
        //recommended by the font designer
        font_descent = a_font_metric.getDescent();
        //get the ascent without whitespace
        font_ascent_no_white = a_font_metric.getMaxAscent();
        //get the descent without whitespace
        font_descent_no_white = a_font_metric.getMaxDescent();
        //now show these values to the user
        y = 10;
        g.drawString(the_message, 10,y);
        y += font_height + 1;
        g.drawString("Message width is " + string_width, 10,y);
        y += font_height + 1;
```

continues

Listing 17.7. continued

```
        g.drawString("Font height is " + font_height, 10,y);
        y += font_height + 1;
        g.drawString("Font ascent is " + font_ascent +
            " without white space it's " + font_ascent_no_white , 10,y);
        y += font_height + 1;
        g.drawString("Font descent is " + font_descent +
            " without white space it's " + font_descent_no_white , 10,y);


    }
}
```

FIGURE 17.9.

Viewing FontMetrics *information.*

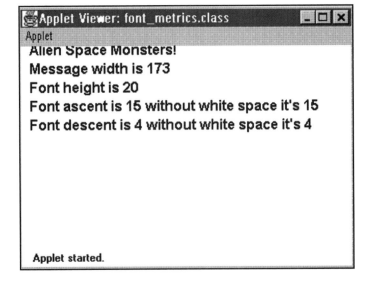

This information is useful in a number of ways. First, notice how the tops of the letters in the first line in Figure 17.9 are cut off. That's because when you specify the y coordinate for a string, you're specifying the location of the baseline—not the upper-left corner of the text that is being drawn. To figure out where to put the baseline, you just need to look at the value of the ascent. Instead of defining the first value of y as 10, just change it to this:

```
y = font_ascent + 2; //the extra 2 provides some whitespace
                     //that the font otherwise lacks
```

The first line now is completely visible, as Figure 17.10 shows.

Another common use for FontMetrics data is to center text in an area. The code in Listing 17.8 centers text in an area.

FIGURE 17.10.
Keeping your text in sight.

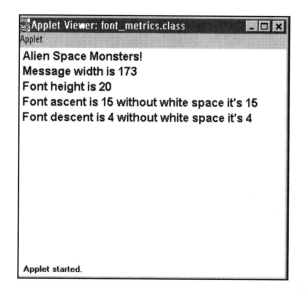

Listing 17.8. Centering text.

```
public void draw_centered_text(Graphics g, String the_msg,
                               int width, int height) {
    int x,y;
    FontMetrics fm;

    fm = g.getFontMetrics();
    //find out how much free space there is on either side of the string by
    //subtracting the width of the string from the width of the window and
    //dividing by 2
    x = (width - fm.stringWidth(the_msg))/2;
    //find out how much free space there is above
    //and below the string's baseline
    y = fm.getAscent() + (height - fm.getHeight())/2;
    //draw the string so that the baseline is centered
    g.drawString(the_msg,x,y);
}
```

NOTE

You can get the width and height of an applet's area by using the getSize method, which returns a Dimension value. The height() and width() methods of the Dimension class enable you to get the height and width values.

Figure 17.11 shows the result of centering text in a window.

FIGURE 17.11.

Centering text.

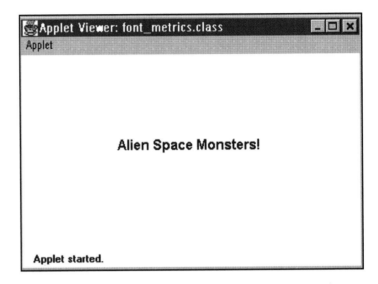

Alien Space Monsters!

Drawing Lines

Three methods for drawing lines currently are available in Java. Listing 17.9 shows a small applet that demonstrates how to draw straight lines, arcs, and a point.

> **NOTE**
>
> No special command for drawing individual pixels is available. Just use `drawLine` as shown in Listing 17.9; alternatively, you can use `drawRect` or `fillRect`, which are discussed later in this section.

Listing 17.9. Drawing straight lines, arcs, and a point.

```
import java.awt.*;
import java.applet.Applet;


public class drawpoint extends Applet{
    public void paint(Graphics g)
    {
        int x_final, y_final;
        int i;

        //this draws a line
```

```
        g.drawLine(10,10,100,100);
        //this draws a point at 10,30
        g.drawLine(10,30,10,30);
        //this draws an arc
        g.drawArc(50,50,30,30,0,180);
        //this draws a filled arc
        g.fillArc(50,100,20,40,90,90);

    }
}
```

This applet generates the picture shown in Figure 17.12.

FIGURE 17.12.

A point, a line, an arc, and a filled arc.

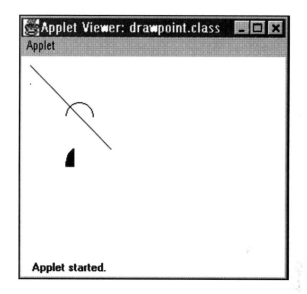

Here are the full descriptions for the three line-drawing methods.

drawLine(int x_start, int y_start, int x_end, int y_end)
This draws a line between two points.

> x_start: Starting x position
> y_start: Starting y position
> x_end: Final x position
> y_end: Final y position

drawArc(int x, int y, int width, int height, int start_angle, int delta_angle)
This routine draws an arc, a segment of an ellipse, or a circle, as Figure 17.13 shows.

FIGURE 17.13.

Parameters for drawArc *and* fillArc *methods.*

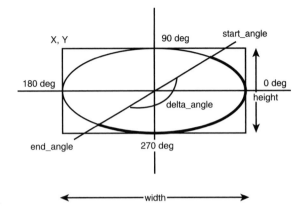

x: Upper-left corner of the rectangle that contains the ellipse the arc is from.

y: Upper-left corner of the rectangle that contains the ellipse the arc is from.

width: The width of the rectangle that contains the ellipse the arc is from.

height: The height of the rectangle that contains the ellipse the arc is from.

start_angle: The angle at which the arc starts; 0 degrees is at the 3 o'clock position, and the value increases in the counterclockwise direction.

fillArc(int x, int y, int width, int height, int start_angle, int delta_angle)

This is the same as drawArc, except that the arc is filled with the current color.

One of the key shortcomings with current Java drawing routines is that you can't specify a line width. All the drawing commands draw unit-width lines. If you want to draw thicker lines, you can follow an approach similar to the one shown in Listing 17.10.

Listing 17.10. Drawing thicker lines.

```
public void draw_thick_line(Graphics g, int x_start,
                    int y_start, int x_final,
                    int y_final, int width) {
    int i;

    for (i=0;i<width;i++) {
        g.drawLine(x_start+i,y_start + i,x_final+i,y_final+i);
    }
}
```

This method just draws several lines to make a thicker line. You can use the same approach for the shapes you'll see in the next section.

The final way to draw very complex lines is to use the drawPolygon method, which is described in the next section. With it, you can draw arbitrarily complex paths.

Drawing Shapes

Java provides a standard set of methods for drawing typical geometric shapes, such as rectangles, ovals, and polygons. It also has a method for drawing 3D rectangles (rectangles with shading to make them look 3D), but because the line widths are so narrow, it's almost impossible to see the 3D effect under normal circumstances. The syntax for the various shape-drawing methods follow.

`drawRect(int x, int y, int width, int height)`

This draws a traditional rectangle.

> x: Upper-left corner
> y: Upper-left corner
> `width`: Width of the rectangle
> `height`: Height of the rectangle

`drawRoundRect(int x, int y, int width, int height, int r_width, int r_height)`

This draws a rectangle with rounded corners. You define the amount of curvature by setting the width and height of the rectangle that contains the curved corner (see Figure 17.14).

> x: Upper-left corner
> y: Upper-left corner
> `width`: Width of the rectangle
> `height`: Height of the rectangle
> r_width: Width of the rectangle that defines the roundness of the corner
> `rectangle`: Defines the roundness of the corner
> r_height: Height of the rectangle that defines the roundness of the corner

FIGURE 17.14.

Defining the degree of roundness for rounded rectangles.

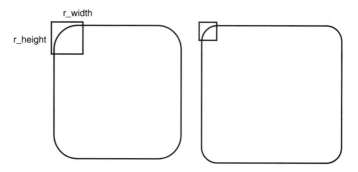

`draw3DRect(int x, int y, int width, int height, boolean flag)`

This draws a rectangle with a 3D shadow. Because the lines are so thin, you can't really see the shadow.

    x: Upper-left corner
    y: Upper-left corner
    `width`: Width of rectangle
    `height`: Height of rectangle
    `flag`: If `TRUE`, the rectangle is raised; if `FALSE`, the rectangle is indented

`drawPolygon(int x[], int y[], int n_points)`

This takes two lists—one with x and one with y coordinates—and draws a line between successive points. The polygon will not close automatically. If you want a closed polygon, you must make sure that the first and last points have the same coordinates.

    x: An array of integers with the x coordinates of the polygon's vertices
    y: An array of integers with the y coordinates of the polygon's vertices
    `n_points`: Number of vertices in the polygon

`drawOval(int x, int y, int width, int height)`

This draws an oval. If `width` and `height` have the same value, you get a circle.

    x: Upper-left corner of the rectangle that contains the oval (see Figure 17.15)
    y: Upper-left corner of the rectangle that contains the oval
    `width`: Width of the rectangle that contains the oval
    `height`: Height of the rectangle that contains the oval

FIGURE 17.15.

Defining the size of an oval with the `width` *and* `height` *parameters.*

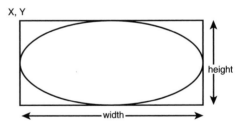

Filling Shapes

For each method starting with "draw," there is another method that starts with "fill." The "fill" methods have the same parameters and behave in the same way, except that they draw versions of the shapes filled with the current color.

The applet in Listing 17.11 shows how the draw and fill versions of the various commands work. It produces the screen shown in Figure 17.16.

FIGURE 17.16.

The various drawing functions in action.

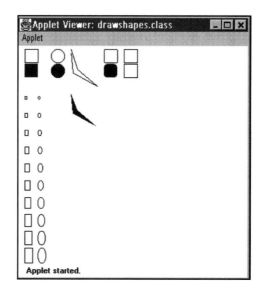

Listing 17.11. Using the draw and fill commands.

```java
import java.awt.*;
import java.applet.Applet;


public class drawshapes extends Applet
{

    public void paint(Graphics g)
    {
        int i;
        int x,y,x_o,width,height;
        //set the x coordinates for the polygon vertices
        int x_list[] = {80,90,120,83,80};
        //set the y coordinates for the two polygons
        int y_list[] ={5,35,60,40,10};
        int y_list_1[] = {70,95,120,100,70};

        g.drawRect(10,5,20,20);
        g.fillRect(10,27,20,20);
        g.drawOval(50,5,20,20);
        g.fillOval(50,27,20,20);
        g.drawPolygon(x_list, y_list, 5);
        g.fillPolygon(x_list,y_list_1,5);
        g.drawRoundRect(130,5,20,20,5,5);
        g.fillRoundRect(130,27,20,20,10,15);
        g.draw3DRect(160,5,20,20,true);
        g.draw3DRect(160,27,20,20,false);
```

continues

Listing 17.11. continued

```
        width = 2;
        height = 2;
        x = 10;
        x_o = 30;
        y = 50;
        //draw a set of ten regular and filled rectangles and ovals
        for(i=0;i<10;i++) {
            y += 25;
            width += 1;
            height += 2;

            g.drawRect(x,y,width,height);
            g.drawOval(x_o,y,width,height);
        }
    }
}
```

The 3D rectangles don't look all that three-dimensional. The effect is subtle, and you should experiment with it on different platforms and with different color combinations to find one that looks good. Figure 17.17 shows the result of an applet that draws two standard 3D rectangles—one raised and the other sunken—with white lines on a black background. It then draws two thick-sided 3D rectangles by drawing several 3D rectangles together. You can see—assuming that the print quality of the book is good enough—in the standard 3D rectangles that in both cases two sides of the rectangle are slightly darker than the other two sides. Just in case you had trouble seeing that (and I know that I did), this effect is fairly clear on the thick-sided 3D rectangles.

FIGURE 17.17.

The secret of 3D rectangles.

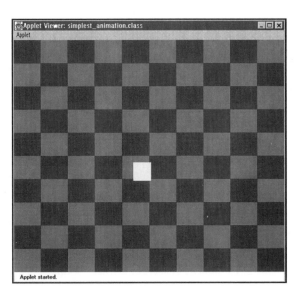

Animation

One of the keys to the success of Java is its capability to add animation and action to Web pages without requiring you to download huge video files. Even though Java is an interpreted language (assuming that your users' browsers don't have a JIT—Just In Time compiler—installed), it's more than fast enough for most animation tasks. Listing 17.12 shows a simple animation that moves a yellow square over a red and blue checkerboard pattern. Figure 17.18 shows a screen shot—unmoving, unfortunately.

Listing 17.12. A simple animation applet.

```
import java.awt.*;
import java.applet.Applet;

public class simplest_animation extends Applet implements Runnable
{
    int x_pos,y_pos;
    int n_squares;
    int dh,dw;
    Color color_1,color_2;
    Color square_color;
    int square_size;
    int square_step;
    Thread the_thread;

    public void start() {
        if (the_thread == null) {
            the_thread = new Thread(this);
            the_thread.start();
        }
    }
    public void stop() {
        the_thread.stop();
    }

    public void run() {
        while (true) {

            repaint();
            try {
                the_thread.sleep(50);
            } catch(InterruptedException e) {};
        }
    }

    public void init()
    {
        int w_height, w_width;
        //set the starting point of the moving square
        x_pos = 0;
        y_pos = 0;
```

continues

Listing 17.12. continued

```
        //set the size of the moving square
        square_size = 40;
        //set how much the square moves between screen redraws
        square_step = 2;
        //specifies the number of squares on each side of the checkerboard
        n_squares = 10;
        //get the size of the applet's drawing area
        w_height = size().height;
        w_width = size().width;
        //determine the size of the squares in the checkerboard
        dh = w_height/n_squares;
        dw = w_width/n_squares;
        //set the colors for the checkerboard.
        //Could have used Color.blue and
        //Color.red instead of creating new color instances
        color_1 = new Color(0,0,255);
        color_2 = new Color(255,0,0);
        //set the color for the moving square
        square_color = new Color(255,255,0);
    }

    public void draw_check(Graphics g) {
        int i,j,offset;
        int x,y;
        //this draws a checkerboard
        offset = 0;
        for(i=0;i<n_squares;i++) {
            y = i * dh;
            offset++;
            for(j=0;j<n_squares;j++) {
                x = j * dw;
                if (((j + offset)% 2) > 0) {
                    g.setColor(color_1);
                } else {
                    g.setColor(color_2);
                }
                g.fillRect(x,y,dw,dh);
            }
        }
    }
    public void paint(Graphics g)
    {
        //draw the blue and red checkerboard background
        draw_check(g);
        //increment the position of the moving square
        x_pos += square_step;
        y_pos += square_step;
        //set the drawing color to the square color
        g.setColor(square_color);
        //draw a filled rectangle that moves
        g.fillRect(x_pos,y_pos,square_size, square_size);
    }
}
```

FIGURE 17.18.

*Animation in action—
well, use your imagination.*

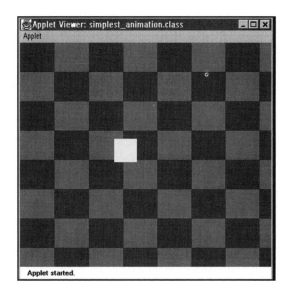

What you can't see unless you run the applet is that the whole image is flickering; you can see the background through the yellow square. All in all, the word that comes to mind is *ugly*— hardly the sort of thing that will help sell a Web page. You can reduce this flicker in several ways. A large part of the flicker occurs when repaint invokes the update method. You saw earlier in this chapter that the update method erases the applet by drawing a background colored rectangle. This erasing, followed by the drawing of the background rectangle, causes a lot of the flicker. You can avoid this by overriding the update method with this version:

```
public void update(Graphics g) {
        paint(g);
    }
```

This eliminates the flicker in most of the image, but you'll still see flicker in the region of the rectangle. That's because the background is drawn and then the square is drawn over it. Your eye sees the background and then the yellow square every time the screen is redrawn. One way to reduce the amount of drawing that has to be done is to tell the AWT to redraw only the part of the screen that has changed.

The version of the paint method shown in Listing 17.13 does just that. It creates two rectangles: one for where the square is and one for where it will be after it's moved in this call to paint. The union method on Rectangle then is used to get the smallest rectangle that contains both those rectangles. That rectangle is the one that contains all the changes between the two frames. Next, clipRect is used to tell the AWT to repaint only this rectangle.

> **NOTE**
>
> Instead of creating two new rectangles each time `paint` is called, you could save the second rectangle in an instance variable and then use it as the old rectangle in the next call to paint.

Listing 17.13. Repainting the minimal area.

```
public void paint(Graphics g)
{
    Rectangle old_r, new_r,to_repaint;

     draw_check(getGraphics());
     //Figure out where the square is now
    old_r = new Rectangle(x_pos,y_pos,square_size,square_size);
    //Figure out where the square will be after this method executes
    new_r = new Rectangle((x_pos + square_step),(y_pos +
                    square_step),square_size, square_size);
    //Find the smallest rectangle that contains the old and new positions
    to_repaint = new_r.union(old_r);
    //Tell Java to only repaint the areas that have been
   // affected by the moving square
    g.clipRect(to_repaint.x,to_repaint.y,
                        to_repaint.width,to_repaint.height);
    x_pos += square_step;
    y_pos += square_step;
    g.setColor(square_color);
    g.fillRect(x_pos,y_pos,square_size, square_size);
}
```

Although using `clipRect` reduces the amount of work the AWT has to do, it's still not fast enough to fool your eye. To do that, you need to use double buffering.

Double buffering involves doing all your drawing to an invisible, off-screen bitmap—an image, actually—and then copying that off-screen image to the applet. This is called *bitblitting* on the Mac and results in much faster drawing. Listing 17.14 shows the commented changes you need to make in the animation applet to do double buffering.

Listing 17.14. Using double buffering.

```
public class simple_animation extends Applet implements Runnable
{
    ....
    //Define an image to use for offscreen drawing
    Image offscreen;
    Graphics offscreen_graphics;
```

```
    ....
    public void init()
    {
        ....
        //create the offscreen image and get its Graphics instance
        offscreen = createImage(size().width,size().height);
        offscreen_graphics = offscreen.getGraphics();
        //draw the background checkerboard
        draw_check();
    }
....
    public void draw_check() {
        int i,j,offset;
        int x,y;

        offset = 0;
        for(i=0;i<n_squares;i++) {
            y = i * dh;
            offset++;
            for(j=0;j<n_squares;j++) {
                x = j * dw;
                if (((j + offset)% 2) > 0) {
                    offscreen_graphics.setColor(color_1);
                } else {
                    offscreen_graphics.setColor(color_2);
                }
                offscreen_graphics.fillRect(x,y,dw,dh);
            }
        }
    }
    public void paint(Graphics g)
    {
        Rectangle old_r, new_r,to_repaint;

        old_r = new Rectangle(x_pos,y_pos,square_size,square_size);
        new_r = new Rectangle((x_pos + square_step),(y_pos +
                    square_step),square_size, square_size);
        to_repaint = new_r.union(old_r);
        draw_check();
        //just draw what's needed except for the first time
        if (x_pos < 1) {
            g.clipRect(to_repaint.x,to_repaint.y,
                    to_repaint.width,to_repaint.height);
        }
        x_pos += square_step;
        y_pos += square_step;
        //same as before but now the square is drawn to the offscreen image
        offscreen_graphics.setColor(square_color);
        offscreen_graphics.fillRect(x_pos,y_pos,square_size,
                    square_size);
        //now that the offscreen image is all done draw the whole thing
        //to the screen
        g.drawImage(offscreen,0,0,this);
    }
}
```

Interactive Interface Elements

These items are the ones that enable the user to dynamically interact with your program. They range from buttons to text display areas. Although different operating systems tend to use slightly different interaction elements, the AWT provides a rich enough set that users on all platforms will feel pretty much at home. This is especially true because the visual representation of each item actually is generated by the host operating system on the machine on which the application or applet is running. In addition, freeware, shareware, and commercial widget kits already exist that extend the basic elements provided by the AWT (see the section "Extending the AWT," later in this chapter, for more details).

Component Class—Shared Features of All Active GUI Elements

As you saw in Figure 17.3, all the active components (other than menus), such as Button, inherit from the Component class. The Component methods provide a wide selection of functionality applicable to any interactive graphical element. Although you can't create an instance of Component, you'll use its methods fairly often. Component has a lot of methods, but this section lists some of the ones you'll use fairly often. These methods are invoked in response to various types of events. In all cases, if the method returns TRUE, it means that the method has handled the event. If FALSE is returned, the event is passed up the event chain. You can use these methods on multiple objects to deal with the same event.

boolean, action(Event e, Object o)
This method usually is overridden. It's called whenever an ACTION_EVENT occurs on a component. Events are discussed in Chapter 21, "Event Handling."

boolean, keyDown(Event e, int key)
This is called when a KEY_PRESS or KEY_ACTION event reaches a component. The key parameter specifies which key was involved. You can use this to have components respond to key clicks.

boolean, keyUp(Event e, int key)
This method is invoked when the component receives a KEY_RELEASE event.

boolean, lostFocus(Event e, Object o)
This is called when the object receives a LOST_FOCUS event.

boolean, mouseDown(Event e, int x, int y)
This is invoked when the component receives a MOUSE_DOWN event, caused by the user clicking the mouse inside the component. The x and y coordinates are in the coordinate system of the component, where 0,0 is in the upper-left corner.

```
boolean, mouseDrag(Event e, int x, int y)
```
This is invoked when the user drags the mouse with the mouse button down over the component, generating a MOUSE_DRAG event.

```
boolean, mouseEnter(Event e, int x, int y)
```
This is invoked each time the mouse goes over the component, generating a MOUSE_ENTER event.

```
boolean, mouseExit(Event e, int x, int y)
```
This is called when the component receives a MOUSE_EXIT event. The x and y values—which are expressed in the component's coordinates—represent the first point outside the component's bounding rectangle that the mouse goes over.

Although Component has a large selection of methods, the following are the ones you'll use most often.

```
Rectangle, bounds()
```
Returns the bounding rectangle that contains the component.

```
int, checkImage(Image img, ImageObserver iobs)
```
Monitors the status of an image as it's being composed. You can use this to wait to display a component, such as a Canvas, that uses an image until the image is ready.

```
Image, createImage(int width, int height)
```
Creates a new Image of the specified size.

```
disable()
```
Disables the component so that the user can't interact with it. (This is a synchronized method.) The AWT draws a disabled component differently than an enabled one.

```
enable()
```
Enables a disabled component. This is a synchronized method.

```
Color, getBackground()
```
Returns the color of the background for the component.

```
Font, getFont()
```
Returns the current font for the component.

```
FontMetrics, getFontMetrics()
```
Gets the FontMetrics, which contains information about the size of text on the current platform, for the component.

`Color, getForeground()`
Returns the foreground color—the one that will be used to draw lines, fill shapes, and so on.

`Graphics, getGraphics()`
Gets the `Graphics` object associated with the component. You can then use drawing methods, such as `fillRect`, that are associated with the `Graphics` object to draw on the component.

`hide()`
Makes the component invisible. This is a synchronized method.

`boolean, inside(int x, int y)`
Returns TRUE if x,y lies inside the component's bounding rectangle. x and y should be specified in the coordinate system of the container that holds the component. The container's coordinate system origin is in the upper-left corner of the container. This is a synchronized method.

`invalidate()`
Sets a flag indicating that the component has been changed in a way that requires the Layout Manager to be called to lay out the screen again. A button's name might be made longer, for example, so the button will need to be resized.

`boolean, isEnabled()`
Returns TRUE if the component is enabled to respond to user actions.

`boolean, isShowing()`
Returns TRUE if the component is visible in its parent's window. It can be visible but not showing if its height or width is 0 or if its location is outside the parent's window; for example, it might have been scrolled off-screen.

`boolean, isVisible()`
Returns TRUE if the component currently is visible. You can make a component invisible by invoking its `hide` method.

`Point, location()`
Returns a point that contains the coordinates of the component's origin.

`move(int x, int y)`
Moves the component to the specified position in the parent container's coordinate system.

`paint(Graphics g)`
Redraws the component when it needs to be redrawn. Unless you want some custom behavior, the default method ensures that the component is drawn properly.

`boolean, prepareImage(Image img, ImageObserver img_obs)`
Enables you to get an image ready for display prior to displaying it on the component. Another version enables you to specify a size for the image so that it can be scaled.

`repaint(long time)`
Repaints this component by a specified time or cancels the request.

`repaint(int x, int y, int width, int height)`
Repaints the specified part of the component.

`repaint(long time, int x, int y, int width, int height)`
Tries to repaint the specified region. If it can't do so before the specified time, it quits.

`reshape(int x, int y, int width, int height)`
Enables you to specify the position and size of the component. This is a synchronized method.

`resize(int width, int height)`
Scales the component to fit in the defined bounding rectangle maintaining the same origin. This is the same as the version below except you specify the width and height separately rather than with a `Dimension` object.

`resize(Dimension dim)`
Scales the component to fit in the defined bounding rectangle maintaining the same origin.

`setBackground(Color a_color)`
Sets the background color for a component. This is a synchronized method.

`setFont(Font a_font)`
Specifies the font that will be used for any text drawn in the component. This is a synchronized method.

`setForeground(Color a_color)`
Sets the color used for drawing lines and filling in shapes. This is a synchronized method.

`show()`
Makes the component visible if it had been hidden.

`Dimension, size()`
Returns the height and width of the component.

`update(Graphics g)`
Erases the contents of the component's graphic area every time it's called.

`validate()`
Causes the component to see whether it or any of the components it contains is invalid. If any are invalid, the Layout Manager is called to bring things up-to-date. See the section "Buttons," later in this chapter, for an example of how to use `invalidate/validate`.

Remember that all the interactive interface elements, including containers such as applets and windows, inherit from `Component`.

Containers

The AWT containers contain classes that can contain other elements. Windows, panels, dialog boxes, frames, and applets are all containers. Whenever you want to display a component such as a button or pop-up menu, you'll use a container to hold it. The base class for all containers is—surprise! surprise!—the `Container` class.

The `Container` class has a number of methods that make it easy to add and remove components as well as to control the relative positioning and layout of those components. Containers can contain other containers, for example, so a window can contain several panels.

`Container` is an abstract class, and the methods you'll use most often follow.

`add(Component a_component)`
Adds a component to the container.

`add(Component a_component, int pos)`
Adds a component at the specified z position. This is a synchronized method. Be warned that the order of clipping based on relative z position may vary between machines. This problem should be fixed eventually, though.

`int, countComponents()`
Returns the number of top-level components of a container. It doesn't count components inside components; for example, a panel with three buttons inside a window is counted only as one component for the window.

`Component, getComponent(int index)`

Returns a reference to the `index` component. The `index` value is determined when the component is added. This is a synchronized method. This throws `ArrayIndexOutOfBoundsException`.

`Component[], getComponents()`

Returns an array of references to all the components in the container. This is a synchronized method.

`insets, insets()`

Returns the `insets` object for the container. Insets define the empty space the Layout Manager reserves around the edge of the container—the minimum distance from the edge of a component to the edge of the container.

`remove(Component a_component)`

Removes the component from the container. This is a synchronized method.

`setLayout(LayoutManager lm)`

Sets the Layout Manager the container will use. If you supply NULL as the argument, no Layout Manager is used; you can use absolute positioning.

Panels

`Applet` inherits from this class, so this section examines `Panel` in detail so that you can understand how the various demonstration applets work. The other container classes are discussed later in this section.

`Panel` inherits from `Container`. It doesn't create its own window because it's used to group components inside other containers. Panels enable you to group items in a display in a way that might not be allowed by the available Layout Managers. If you have a number of entries in your interface, for example, that have a label and a text field, you can define a panel that contains a label and a text field and add the panel so that the label and the text field always stay together on the same line (which wouldn't be the case if you added the two items separately). Without the panel, the Layout Manager could put the label and the text field on different lines. Panels also are useful in Layout Managers in which only one item is allowed in an area, such as the `BorderLayout` Manager. By using a panel, you can put several components in a single `BorderLayout` area, such as `North`.

> **NOTE**
>
> A Layout Manager autopositions and sizes the various interface components, taking into account the screen resolution and the window size.

Insets

An inset object defines the amount of empty space around the edge of a panel. The creator method for insets follows:

```
Insets, new Insets(int top, int left, int bottom, int right)
```

This defines a new `Insets` instance, which defines the boundaries specified by the input arguments.

You can change the amount of empty space, which is set to 0 by default, by overriding the `Insets` method of the container. The applet in Listing 17.15 defines its own panel class that does that. It defines a plain panel and a custom version that overrides the `Insets` method. Each of the items has four buttons added. Both items have white backgrounds so that you can see the size of the item, not just where the buttons are.

Listing 17.15. Defining a panel class.

```
import java.awt.*;
import java.applet.Applet;


public class HelloWorld extends Applet
{
    public void init()
    {
        Panel a;
        my_panel b;
        GridLayout gl;
        Button buttons[];
        int i;
        //create a new GridLayout to force the 4 buttons to arrange themselves
        // in a 2 by 2 grid
        gl = new GridLayout(2,2);
        //create two panels to contain the 8 buttons
        a = new Panel();
        b = new my_panel();
        //tell the panels to use the GridLayout manager rather than the default
        //FlowLayout manager
        a.setLayout(gl);
        b.setLayout(gl);
        //Make the backgrounds of the panels white so you
        //can see them in the picture
        a.setBackground(Color.white);
        b.setBackground(Color.white);
        //add the panels to the applet
        add(a);
        add(b);
        //make the buttons and add them to the panels
        buttons = new Button[8];
        for(i=0; i< 8;i++) {
            buttons[i] = new Button("Button " + i);
            if (i <4) {
```

```
                a.add(buttons[i]);
        } else {
                b.add(buttons[i]);
        }
      }
    }
}
class my_panel extends Panel {
    //This class exists so we can override the insets method
    public Insets insets() {
        return new Insets(5,10,15,20);
    }
}
```

The applet generates the applet interface shown in Figure 17.19; look closely to see the white background for the first panel. Because the insets for the top panel default to 0, the panel background is the same size as the space required by the buttons. The custom panel is larger than the buttons because of the inset's value; the space on each side is different because the four values assigned to the inset are all different.

FIGURE 17.19.

Panels with the default insets and with custom insets.

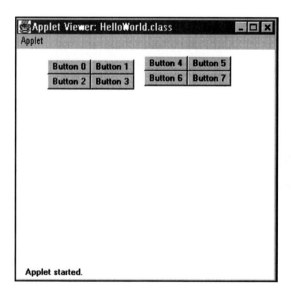

Frames

A *frame* is a full-fledged, top-level, resizable window with a menu bar. You can specify the title, an icon, and a cursor. See the "Frames" section for examples.

Windows

This class isn't used very often, but it's a top-level window without borders and a menu bar.

Labels

Labels are text items that don't really do much. By using a label instead of `drawString`, you can use the Layout Managers to control text placement in a platform- and monitor-independent manner. The code in Listing 17.16 shows how to use labels. About the only significant flexibility you have, other than the alignment of the text, is the capability to change the font used (see Figure 17.20).

Listing 17.16. Using labels.

```
import java.awt.*;
import java.applet.Applet;


public class label_example extends Applet{
    Label the_labels[];

    public void init(){
        int i;
        //set up an array of labels
        the_labels = new Label[3];
        //Create a label with the default format
        the_labels[0] = new Label("on the left");
        //these two commands show how to set the color of a Label
        //the text itself is drawn with the Foreground color
        the_labels[0].setBackground(Color.red);
        the_labels[0].setForeground(Color.white);
        //Make a new Font and then assign it to the label
        Font a_font = new Font("TimesRoman",Font.PLAIN,24);
        the_labels[0].setFont(a_font);
        //Create a centered label
        the_labels[1] = new Label("middle", Label.CENTER);
        //Make a new Font and then assign it to the label
        a_font = new Font("TimesRoman",Font.BOLD,24);
        the_labels[1].setFont(a_font);
        //Create a label aligned to the right
        the_labels[2] = new Label("on the right", Label.RIGHT);
        //Make a new Font and then assign it to the label
        a_font = new Font("Helvetica",Font.ITALIC,18);
        the_labels[2].setFont(a_font);
        //these two commands show how to set the color of a Label
        //the text itself is drawn with the Foreground color
        the_labels[2].setBackground(Color.white);
        the_labels[2].setForeground(Color.blue);
        //add the three labels to the applet
        for(i=0;i<3;i++) {
            add(the_labels[i]);
        }
    }
}
```

FIGURE 17.20.
Aligning text and modifying the fonts for labels.

The label creators and the most useful methods for the Label class follow:

```
new Label(String label)
```
Produces a label with the specified string.

```
new Label(String label,int positioning)
```
Produces a label with the string aligned according to the second value, which should be one of the three constants Label.CENTER, Label.LEFT, or Label.RIGHT.

```
String, getText()
```
Returns the label string.

```
setText(String new_label)
```
Changes the label text.

Buttons

Java buttons are just like the buttons in every other GUI. They are text surrounded by a shape, and they generate an ACTION_EVENT event—the argument is a button's label—after the user clicks them. Java uses the native operating system—Mac, Windows, UNIX, and so on—to actually draw the buttons, so the look and feel of the buttons will be what is expected by users on each platform. Listing 17.17 shows a simple example of using buttons; see Chapter 21 for more information on handling events.

Listing 17.17. Using buttons.

```
import java.awt.*;
import java.applet.Applet;


public class buttons extends Applet{
    Button a_button;

    public void init()
    {
        //make a new button called "Howdy"
        a_button = new Button("Howdy!");
        //add the button to the Applet, which extends Panel
        add(a_button);
    }
    public boolean action (Event e, Object o) {
        Dimension  d_should;
        if (e.target instanceof Button) {
            //check the button label and toggle between the two values
            if (((String)o).equals("Howdy!")) {
                a_button.setLabel("Alien Space Monster!");
            } else {
                a_button.setLabel("Howdy!");
            }
            //mark the button as having changed
            a_button.invalidate();
            //tell the applet to validate the layout
            validate();
        }
        return true;
    }
}
```

This applet starts out with a single button and then toggles the name of the button between two values every time the button is clicked. Figure 17.21 shows the applet before the button is clicked, and Figure 17.22 shows it afterward.

Notice how the invalidate method, inherited from Component, is used to mark the button as having changed in a way that would affect the layout. That isn't sufficient to force the applet to automatically lay out the screen again, although it ensures that the next time the screen is redrawn, things will look okay, so you have to invoke the validate method, inherited from Component, on the applet.

The available button creator calls and the key button methods follow.

new Button()
Creates a button with no label (see Figure 17.23).

new Button(String the_button_label)
Creates a button with the specified label.

FIGURE 17.21.
A simple button.

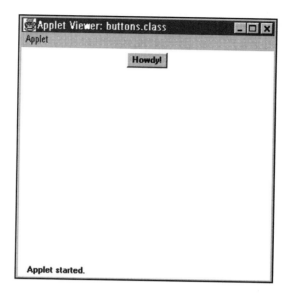

FIGURE 17.22.
A button in action.

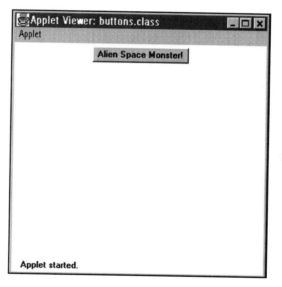

```
setLabel(String the_new_label)
```
Sets the button label to the specified string.

```
String getLabel()
```
Returns the current button label as a string.

FIGURE 17.23.
A button without a label.

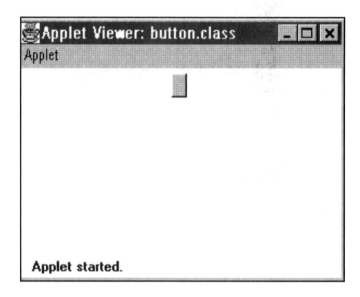

Checkboxes

Checkboxes are text items with a checkable icon next to them. They're generally used when you want the user to be able to set several options prior to making a decision. You usually don't do anything when a checkbox is checked or unchecked, you usually just read the values of the checkboxes when some other control, such as a button or menu item, is activated. Just in case you do want the code to do something when a box's state changes, checkboxes generate an ACTION_EVENT with the new Checkbox state as the argument after the user clicks on them.

> **NOTE**
>
> Radio buttons look just like checkboxes, but they are grouped and only one radio button in a group can be checked at any given time. The next section discusses how to implement radio buttons.

The code in Listing 17.18 produces the applet interface shown in Figure 17.24.

Listing 17.18. Checkboxes without a bank.

```
import java.awt.*;
import java.applet.Applet;


public class checkboxes extends Applet
{
    public void init()
    {
```

```
        Checkbox box_1, box_2, box_3;

        box_1 = new Checkbox();
        box_2 = new Checkbox("this is a labeled checkbox");
        box_3 = new Checkbox("Labeled and checked", null, true);
        add(box_1);
        add(box_2);
        add(box_3);
    }

}
```

FIGURE 17.24.

Checkboxes in action.

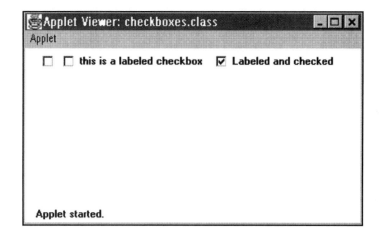

The creator's methods for `Checkbox` and the key checkbox methods follow.

`new Checkbox()`
Creates a new checkbox with no label.

`new Checkbox(String the_label)`
Creates a new checkbox with a label.

`new Checkbox(String the_label, CheckboxGroup null, boolean checked?)`
Creates a new checkbox that is labeled and checked. The middle argument is used with radio buttons.

`setLabel(String the_new_label)`
Changes the label of a checkbox.

`String getLabel()`
Returns the current label as a string.

```
boolean getState()
```
Gets the current checkbox state (checked = TRUE).

```
setState(boolean new_state)
```
Sets the checkbox state.

Radio Buttons

Checkboxes and radio buttons look different. Even though radio buttons are made up of checkboxes, they're called radio buttons because that's what they're called in most current GUIs. The only functional difference is that only one of the items in a radio button group can be selected at one time, like the buttons on your car radio. This is useful when you want your user to select one of a set of options. The AWT creates a radio button group by associating a CheckboxGroup instance with all the checkboxes in the group, as shown in Listing 17.19.

Listing 17.19. Creating a radio button group.

```java
import java.awt.*;
import java.applet.Applet;


public class radio_buttons extends Applet
{
    public void init()
    {
        CheckboxGroup group;
        Checkbox box_1,box_2,box_3;
        CheckboxGroup group_1;
        Checkbox box_1_1,box_2_1,box_3_1;
        //set up the first radio button group
        group = new CheckboxGroup();
        box_1 = new Checkbox("Yes", group, true);
        box_2 = new Checkbox("No", group, false);
        box_3 = new Checkbox("Maybe", group, false);
        //set up the second group
        group_1 = new CheckboxGroup();
        box_1_1 = new Checkbox("Yes", group_1, false);
        box_2_1 = new Checkbox("No", group_1, false);
        box_3_1 = new Checkbox("Maybe", group_1, false);
        //add the components to the applet panel
        add(box_1);
        add(box_2);
        add(box_3);
        add(box_1_1);
        add(box_2_1);
        add(box_3_1);
    }

}
```

Figure 17.25 shows the interface to this applet. The first thing to note is that the second group doesn't have any button selected. That's because none of them were created with a checked state. As soon as the user clicks one of them, though, it won't be possible to return all of them to the unchecked state. Clicking a selected item, such as Yes in the first group, does not change its state to unchecked. Selecting one of the other buttons in the first group deselects Yes and selects the button you clicked.

FIGURE 17.25.
Radio buttons (nearly the same as checkboxes).

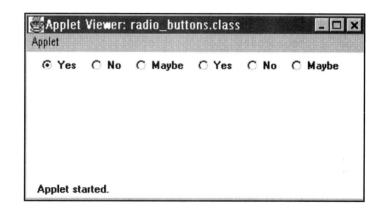

Radio buttons have only one creator method:

```
new Checkbox(String the_label, CheckboxGroup a_group, boolean checked?)
```

This creates a new `Checkbox` that is labeled and checked. The middle argument defines which radio button group the checkbox belongs to.

In order to use radio buttons, you also need to create a new checkbox group. Use this code:

```
new CheckboxGroup()
```

Because radio buttons are implemented as checkboxes, the methods described in the "Checkboxes" section are the ones you'll use to get and set information.

Choice Menus

Choice menus—often called *pop-up menus*—are designed to allow the user to select an option from a menu and see the value chosen at all times. Figures 17.26 and 27 show how this works. The label of the Choice menu is the currently selected menu item. Choice menus can be constructed as shown in Listing 17.20.

Listing 17.20. Creating a Choice menu.

```java
import java.awt.*;
import java.applet.Applet;


public class popup_menus extends Applet
{
    public void init()
    {
        Choice a_menu;

        //create the new choice item
        a_menu = new Choice();
        //add the menu items
        a_menu.addItem("Red");
        a_menu.addItem("Green");
        a_menu.addItem("Blue");
        //add the menu to the applet panel
        add(a_menu);
    }

}
```

FIGURE 17.26.

Selecting from a Choice menu.

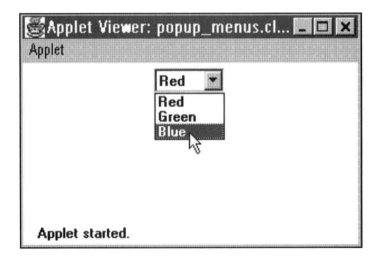

You can add any number of items to a Choice menu, but you can't add hierarchical menus as you can with regular menus. The creator method and other useful methods follow.

new Choice()

Creates a new Choice item.

addItem(String the_item_name)

Adds an item to the Choice menu. It can throw a NullPointerException. This is a synchronized method.

FIGURE 17.27.
Showing the currently selected menu item.

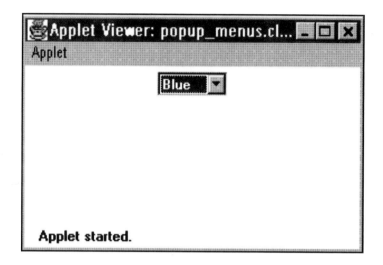

```
int countItems()
```
Returns the number of items currently in the menu.

```
String getItem(int menu_item_number)
```
Returns the text of the specified menu item (item 0 is the first item in the menu).

```
int getSelectIndex()
```
Returns the index of the currently selected item (item 0 is the first item in the menu).

```
String getSelectedItem()
```
Returns the text of currently selected menu items.

```
select(int menu_item)
```
Changes the selection to the specified item. This is a synchronized method, and it can throw `IllegallArgumentException`.

```
select(String menu_item_name)
```
Selects the menu item for which the name is the specified string.

Scrolling Lists

Scrolling lists display multiple lines of text, and each line corresponds to a selection item. Scroll bars are displayed if the text is larger than the available space. The user can select one or more of the lines. Your program can read the user's selections. Lists generate three event types:

- ■ **ACTION_EVENT:** When a list item is double-clicked. The argument is the name of the list item.
- ■ **LIST_SELECT:** When a list item is selected. The argument is the name of the list item selected.
- ■ **LIST_DESELECT:** When a list item is deselected. The argument is the name of the item deselected.

The applet shown in Listing 17.21 shows how to create single- and multiple-choice scrolling lists. Figure 17.28 shows the resulting interface elements. Note that the scrollbar for the left list is disabled because all the items in the list are visible.

FIGURE 17.28.

Single- and multiple-choice lists.

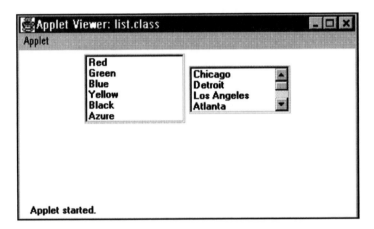

Listing 17.21. Creating single- and multiple-choice scrolling lists.

```
import java.awt.*;
import java.applet.Applet;


public class list extends Applet
{
    public void init()
    {
        List mult_choice, single_choice;

        //define a scrolling list that shows 6 elements at a time and that
        //allows the selection of multiple items at the same time
        mult_choice = new List(6,true);
        single_choice = new List();
        //define the list entries
        mult_choice.addItem("Red");
        mult_choice.addItem("Green");
        mult_choice.addItem("Blue");
        mult_choice.addItem("Yellow");
        mult_choice.addItem("Black");
        mult_choice.addItem("Azure");
```

```
            single_choice.addItem("Chicago");
            single_choice.addItem("Detroit");
            single_choice.addItem("Los Angeles");
            single_choice.addItem("Atlanta");
            single_choice.addItem("Washington");
            single_choice.addItem("Lincoln");
            single_choice.addItem("LaGrange");
            //add the lists to the applet panel
            add(mult_choice);
            add(single_choice);

    }
}
```

The key methods you'll most commonly use with lists follow.

addItem(String item_label)

Adds the specified item to the end of the current list of items in the list. This is a synchronized method.

addItem(String item_label, int location)

Adds the specified item to the list at the specified location. This is a synchronized method. Remember that the first item in the list is numbered 0. For example, addItem("a test", 3) puts "a test" into the fourth position in the list and slides the previous fourth entry and all entries after it down one.

int clear()

Removes all the entries in the list. This is a synchronized method.

int countItems()

Returns the number of items currently in the list.

delItem(int location)

Deletes the list item at the specified location. This is a synchronized method.

delItems(int first, int last)

Deletes all the items between the first and last location, inclusive. This is a synchronized method. For example, delItems(1,3)—note the s at the end of Item—deletes the second, third, and fourth entries in the list; remember that the first location is 0.

deselect(int location)

Deselects the item at the specified location. This is a synchronized method.

`String getItem(int location)`
Returns the label of the list item at the specified location.

`int getRows()`
Returns the number of rows currently visible to the user.

`int getSelectedIndex()`
Throws an `ArrayIndexOutofBoundsException` if it's invoked on a list where more than one item is selected. The method returns -1 if no items are selected. This is a synchronized method.

`int[] getSelectedIndexes()`
Returns an array of the locations of the selected items. This is a synchronized method. It works with a single selection and with single-selection lists. It returns -1 if no items are selected.

`String getSelectedItem()`
Returns the location of the currently selected item. This is a synchronized method. A runtime `Exception` is thrown if this method is called on a multiple-selection list. For that reason, and the fact that `getSelectedItems` will work with a single item, it's best to avoid this method. If no item is selected, it returns `NULL`.

`String[] getSelectedItems()`
Returns an array of `Strings` containing the names of the currently selected list items. This is a synchronized method. It returns an empty array if no items are selected. In that case, trying to access the 0th array item, as in

```
String [] picked = list.getSelectedItems()
String x = picked[0];
```

raises an `ArrayIndexOutofBoundsException`.

`makeVisible(int location)`
Forces the item at the specified location to be visible. This is a synchronized method. It comes in handy because not all choices are visible to the user if the number of visible rows is less than the number of list items. The specified location is moved to the top of the visible area.

`replaceItem(String new_label, int location)`
Changes the name of the label specified by the value of `location`. This is a synchronized method.

`select(int location)`
Selects the specified item. This is a synchronized method.

Because the `List` class has such an extensive set of methods for manipulating the list's contents, it's a good choice for displaying information that is going to change often. It would be a good choice for showing recently visited pages—with event support to rapidly return to those pages—or the list of shopping items the user wants to purchase.

The `TextComponent` Class—Invisible but Useful

This class is abstract, but it's extended by both `TextFields` and `TextAreas`. All the methods covered here are available in both those GUI elements. `TextComponent` provides the basic tools for finding out what text is in a Text item (`getText`), setting the text in an item (`setText`), and selecting pieces of text (`setSelect`). When using `TextFields` or `TextAreas`, you won't have to worry about managing the cursor location, the insertion point (the vertical cursor that tells the user where newly typed text will be inserted), or the marking of the selected text. All these functions are done for you by the AWT. The most useful `TextComponent` methods follow.

`String getSelectedText()`

Returns the text currently selected in the text item. The text may have been selected by the user or through the `setSelection` method.

`int getSelectionEnd()`

Returns the index of the last character in the selection +1. Suppose that you pick a single character such as index 3; this method returns 4. If no characters are selected, this method returns the location of the insertion point. In that case, this method and `getSelectionStart` return the same value.

`int getSelectionStart()`

Returns the index of the first character in the current selection or the location of the insertion point if nothing is selected.

`String getText()`

Returns all the text in the text item.

`select(int start, int stop)`

Selects the text specified by input arguments. As with `getSelectionEnd`, the end value should be the index of the last character you want to select +1. If `start` and `stop` are the same value, the insertion point is placed immediately before the character with that index.

`selectAll`

Selects all the text in the text item.

`setEditable(boolean state)`

Enables you to toggle between whether or not a text item is editable by the user.

`setText(String new_text)`

Enables you to set the text in the text item. This replaces all the text in the item. If you want to insert or append text, you need to use `getText`, modify the string, and then use `setText` to put the modified string back in the text item. Note that `TextArea` has `insert` and `append` methods.

The applet in Listing 17.22 shows you how the various methods work. You'll see more about the unique characteristics of `TextFields` and `TextAreas` in the next two sections. Figure 17.29 shows the applet's interface. You can use this little applet to help you understand how the various input parameters work. By selecting text and then clicking the Selection Report button, for example, you can see what input parameters you need to use in the `select` method to get that same selection.

FIGURE 17.29.

Exploring the parameters of `TextComponent` *methods.*

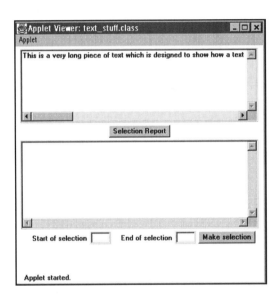

Listing 17.22. `TextFields` **and** `TextAreas` **in action.**

```
import java.awt.*;
import java.applet.Applet;


public class text_stuff extends Applet
{
    TextArea text_space;
    TextArea selection;
    Button show_selection, make_selection;
    TextField start, stop;

    public void init()
    {
        int i;
        String sample_text;
```

```
        //This string could have included \n to force returns
        sample_text = "This is a very long piece of text which is" +
        " designed to show how " +
        "a text area can hold a lot of text without you having to do a lot of" +
            "work." +
        "In general text areas are good for holding large chunks of text or for" +
        "getting " +
        "long answers back from the user.  TextAreas have lots of methods for " +
        "manipulating the their contents and for controlling how the text is " +
        "scrolled";
        //define the TextArea
        text_space = new TextArea(sample_text,8,50);
        //define the report TextArea
        selection = new TextArea("",10,50);
        //create the button to show the selection values
        show_selection = new Button("Selection Report");
        //create the text field to input the start of the selection
        start = new TextField(2);
        //create the text field to input the end of the selection
        stop = new TextField(2);
        //make the labels for the two input fields
        Label l_start = new Label("Start of selection");
        Label l_stop = new Label("End of selection");
        //define the button to make the selection
        make_selection = new Button("Make selection");
        //add everything to the applet's panel
        add(text_space);
        add(show_selection);
        add(selection);
        add(l_start);
        add(start);
        add(l_stop);
        add(stop);
        add(make_selection);
    }

    //handle mouse clicks on the two buttons
    public boolean action (Event e, Object o) {
        int start_location,stop_location;
        String report, temp;

        if (e.target instanceof Button) {
            //check the button label to decide which button was clicked
            if (((String)o).equals("Make selection")) {
                //read the text from the text field to
                //get the start of the selection
                temp = start.getText();
                //convert the text to an integer
                start_location = Integer.parseInt(temp);
                //get the text from the text field to
                //define the end of the selection
                temp = stop.getText();
                //convert the text to an integer
                stop_location = Integer.parseInt(temp);
                //set the selection to the interval defined by
                //the values in the text fields
                text_space.select(start_location,
                                        stop_location);
```

continues

Listing 17.22. continued

```
            } else {
                report = "Selection Start = ";
                //get the start of the current selection
                report = report + text_space.getSelectionStart() + "\n";
                //get the end of the current selection
                report = report + "Selection End = ";
                report = report + text_space.getSelectionEnd() + "\n";
                //get the selected text
                report = report + "Selected Text is: ";
                report = report + text_space.getSelectedText() + "\n";
                //put the report in the text area
                selection.setText(report);
            }
        }
        return true;
    }
}
```

TextField

Text fields are designed to be used to allow the user to input short pieces of text—usually no more than a few words or a single number. You also can use them to display information to the user, such as a phone number or the current sum of the costs of the items the user is going to order. Because TextField extends TextComponent, you can define whether the user can edit the contents of a TextField. The example in Listing 17.23 shows the various types of text fields you can create. Figures 17.30 and 17.31 show how changing the size of the window causes the text fields' sizes to change.

FIGURE 17.30.

Text fields with limited space.

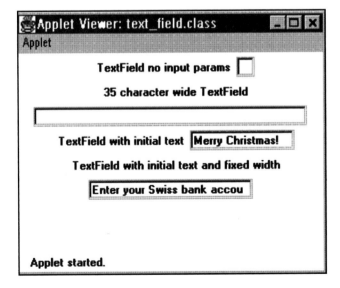

FIGURE 17.31.
With FlowLayout, *the size of* TextFields *change as the window size changes.*

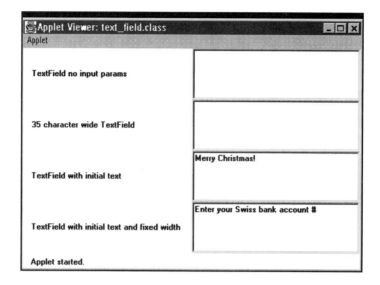

Listing 17.23. Creating TextFields.

```java
import java.awt.*;
import java.applet.Applet;


public class text_field extends Applet
{
    TextField t[];
    Label   l[];
    int n_fields;
    GridLayout gl;

    public void init(){
        int i;

        //This defines a new layout manager with 4 rows and 2 columns
        //You'll learn about layout managers in a few pages
        gl = new GridLayout(4,2);
        //tell the applet to use this new layout manager
        //rather than the default one
        setLayout(gl);

        n_fields = 4;
        t = new TextField[n_fields];
        l = new Label[n_fields];
        //set up the labels and text fields
        t[0] = new TextField();
        l[0] = new Label("TextField no input params");
        t[1] = new TextField(35);
        l[1] = new Label("35 character wide TextField");
        t[2] = new TextField("Merry Christmas!");
        l[2] = new Label("TextField with initial text");
```

continues

Listing 17.23. continued

```
        t[3] = new TextField("Enter your Swiss bank account #",20);
        l[3] = new Label("TextField with initial text and fixed width");
        //add all the components to the applet panel
        for(i=0;i<n_fields;i++){
            add(l[i]);
            add(t[i]);
        }
    }

}
```

TextArea

Text areas are designed to hold large chunks of text, where large is more than one line. `TextArea` extends `TextComponent` by adding a number of additional methods as well as automatic scrolling of the text. Listing 17.24 shows examples of the different `TextArea` creator methods displayed in Figure 17.32.

FIGURE 17.32.

Different ways to create text areas.

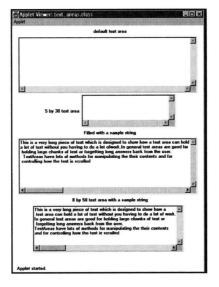

Listing 17.24. `TextArea` creator methods.

```
import java.awt.*;
import java.applet.Applet;


public class text_areas extends Applet
{
```

```
TextArea text_space[];
Label labels[];
int n_fields;

public void init()
{

    int i;
    String sample_text;

    n_fields = 4;
    labels = new Label[n_fields];
    text_space = new TextArea[n_fields];
    //This string could have included \n to force returns
    sample_text = "This is a very long piece of text which is" +
    " designed to show how " +
    "a text area can hold a lot of text without you having to do a lot of" +
        "work." +
    "In general text areas are good for holding large chunks of text or for" +
        "getting " +
    "long answers back from the user.  TextAreas have lots of methods for " +
    "manipulating the their contents and for controlling how the text is " +
    "scrolled";

    //define the TextAreas and their labels.
    labels[0] = new Label("default text area");
    text_space[0] = new TextArea();
    labels[1] = new Label("5 by 30 text area");
    text_space[1] = new TextArea(5,30);
    labels[2] = new Label("Filled with a sample string");
    text_space[2] = new TextArea(sample_text);
    labels[3] = new Label("8 by 50 text area with a sample string");
    text_space[3] = new TextArea(sample_text,8,50);
    //add everything to the applet's panel
    for (i=0;i<n_fields;i++){
        add(labels[i]);
        add(text_space[i]);
    }

}

}
```

TextArea extends TextComponent in several ways, but one of the most useful ones is its support of more powerful text-manipulation methods, such as insert and append. The most useful TextArea methods follow.

new TextArea()
Defines a default empty TextArea.

new TextArea(int rows, int columns)
Defines an empty TextArea with the specified number of rows and columns.

```
new TextArea(String the_contents)
```
Defines a TextArea that contains the specified string.

```
new TextArea(String the_contents, int rows, int columns)
```
Defines a TextArea containing the specified string and with a set number of rows and columns.

```
appendText(String new_text)
```
Appends the specified string to the current contents of the TextArea.

```
int, getColumns()
```
Returns the current width of the TextArea in columns.

```
int, getRows()
```
Returns the current number of rows in a TextArea.

```
insertText(String the_text, int where_to_add)
```
Inserts the specified string at the specified location.

```
replaceText(String new_text, int start, int stop)
```
Takes the text between start and stop, inclusive, and replaces it with the specified string.

Canvases

A *canvas* is an empty space—a starting point for complex interface elements such as a picture button. A canvas is a place to draw. You use it instead of just drawing to a panel, as in an applet, so you can take advantage of the Layout Manager's capability to keep your interface machine-independent. The applet in Listing 17.25 draws to the screen and to a canvas, as shown in Figure 17.33.

Listing 17.25. Drawing to the screen and to a canvas.

```
import java.awt.*;
import java.applet.Applet;


public class canvas_example extends Applet
{
    drawing_area drawing;
    Graphics drawing_graphics;

    public void init()
    {
```

```
        //Don't need to do this but we don't want the Canvas
        //being resized by the
        //Layout Manager. Layout Managers are discussed later in this chapter.
        setLayout(null);
        drawing = new drawing_area();
        add(drawing);

    }
    public void paint(Graphics g)
    {
        //This is just here to show that you can combine direct drawing to
        //the applet panel with Canvases
        g.drawString("Hello, World!", 25, 125 );

    }
}
//Can't have more than one public class in a source file but
//you can have several
//non-public ones
class drawing_area extends Canvas {
    Font my_font;

    drawing_area() {
        //set up a font for this Canvas to use
        my_font = new Font("TimesRoman", Font.BOLD,16);
        //set the size of the Canvas
        resize(100,100);
    }

    public void paint(Graphics g) {
        //By overriding the paint method you can control what is
        //drawn in a canvas. If you want to avoid flicker you might
        //also want to override the update method as discussed in the
        //animation section.
        //Fill a rectangle with the default color, black
        g.fillRect(0,0,100,100);
        //set the foreground color to white so we can read the text
        g.setColor(Color.white);
        g.setFont(my_font);
        g.drawString("this is a test", 10,50);
        //Be careful and reset the color or the next time paint is called the
        //rectangle will be filled with white and the text will be invisible
        g.setColor(Color.black);
    }
}
```

FIGURE 17.33.

Drawing on a canvas without being an artist.

Organizing Your Interface with Layouts

The traditional method for building a GUI has been to position various interface elements, such as buttons, at specific locations inside a window and then to allow the user to move the windows around. Java has had to explore new approaches to defining the layout of components because of the diversity of standards that it has to support. Although the AWT does let you specify the absolute location of components, it also gives you Layout Managers that let you define the relative placement of components that will look the same on a wide spectrum of display devices.

Although you can build your own Layout Manager, it's easiest to use one of the Managers that come with the AWT. In addition, freeware Layout Managers currently are available; these are discussed along with how to build your own Layout Manager, and more will be arriving in the future.

No Layout Manager

Although most containers come with a preset `FlowLayout` Manager, you can tell the AWT to use absolute positions with the following line of code:

```
setLayout(null);
```

This eliminates the default Layout Manager, or any other one that the container had been using, enabling you to position components by using absolute coordinates. Keep in mind, though, that absolute coordinates won't look the same on all platforms. Listing 17.26 shows a little applet that uses absolute coordinates and the `resize` and `reshape` methods from the `Component` class to position and size a label and a text field. Figure 17.34 shows the resulting applet. If you don't use `resize` or `reshape`, you won't see the components. This approach to layouts can run into problems when the size of a font varies between platforms. You can use the `FontMetrics` class to figure out the size of a font relative to some standard size and then scale your absolute coordinates, but it's probably easier to just implement a custom Layout Manager.

FIGURE 17.34.

A simple applet with absolute positioning.

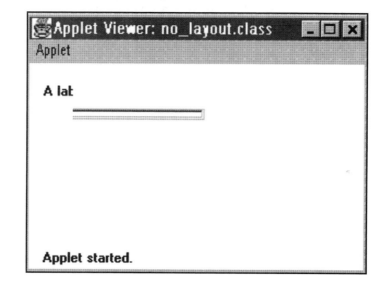

Listing 17.26. Positioning and sizing a label and text field.

```java
import java.awt.*;
import java.applet.Applet;


public class no_layout extends Applet
{
    public void init()
    {
        Label a_label;
        TextField a_textfield;

        setLayout(null);
        a_label = new Label("A label");
        add(a_label);
        //change the size of the Label
        a_label.resize(40,50);
        a_textfield = new TextField(20);
        add(a_textfield);
        //set the size and position of the TextField
        a_textfield.reshape(20,40,140,10);
    }
}
```

FlowLayout

This is the default Layout Manager that every panel uses unless you use the setLayout method to change it. It keeps adding components to the right of the preceding one until it runs out of space; then it starts with the next row. The code in Listing 17.27 shows how to place 30 buttons in an applet using FlowLayout.

> **NOTE**
>
> The creation of a new layout and the use of the setLayout method are superfluous in this case because the panel comes with a FlowLayout as a default. They're included here to show you how you create and define the Layout Manager for a panel.

Listing 17.27. Placing 30 buttons in an applet using FlowLayout.

```java
import java.awt.*;
import java.applet.Applet;


public class flowlayout extends Applet{
    Button the_buttons[];

    public void init()
    {   int i;
        int n_buttons;
        FlowLayout fl;
        String name;

        //make a new FlowLayout manager
        fl = new FlowLayout();
        //tell the applet to use the FlowLayout Manager
        setLayout(fl);
        n_buttons = 30;
        the_buttons = new Button[n_buttons];
        //make all the buttons and add them to the applet
        for(i=0;i<n_buttons;i++) {
            name = "Button " + i;
            the_buttons[i] = new Button(name);
            add(the_buttons[i]);
        }
    }

}
```

This sample applet generates the interfaces shown in Figures 17.35 and 17.36. You might be wondering how this is possible. The answer is that the FlowLayout Manager follows its rule; it places elements in a row until there isn't room for more and then goes to the next, regardless of the size of the container.

FIGURE 17.35.

FlowLayout *of 30 buttons with one window size.*

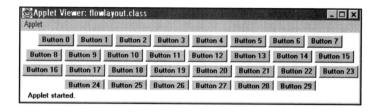

FIGURE 17.36.

Same applet, same Layout Manager, same buttons, different window size.

GridLayout

GridLayout's simple rule is to allow the user to define the number of rows and columns in the layout. GridLayout then sticks one item in each grid cell. The cells are all the same size. The size of the cells is determined by the number of cells and the size of the container. Figures 17.37 and 17.38 show how GridLayout positions the items for two window sizes in the applet shown in Listing 17.28.

Listing 17.28. Using the GridLayout Manager.

```
import java.awt.*;
import java.applet.Applet;


public class gridlayout extends Applet{
    Button the_buttons[];

    public void init()
    {   int i;
```

continues

Listing 17.28. continued

```
        int n_buttons;
        GridLayout gl;
        String name;

        //set up a grid that is 3 rows and 10 columns. There is a 10 pixel space
        //between rows and 15 pixels between columns
        gl = new GridLayout(3,10,10,15);
        setLayout(gl);
        n_buttons = 30;
        the_buttons = new Button[n_buttons];
        for(i=0;i<n_buttons;i++) {
            name = "Button " + i;
            the_buttons[i] = new Button(name);
            add(the_buttons[i]);
        }
    }

}
```

FIGURE 17.37.

GridLayout *with a*
small window.

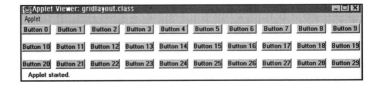

FIGURE 17.38.

The same applet with a
larger window.

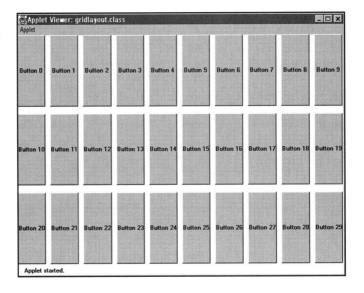

As you see in this listing, the GridLayout creator method enables you to define gaps between components.

There are two GridLayout creator methods:

```
new GridLayout(int rows, int cols)
```
Makes a GridLayout with the specified number of rows and columns.

```
new GridLayout(int rows, int cols, int horizontal_gap, int vertical_gap)
```
Makes a GridLayout with the specified rows and columns and with the specified empty space around each component.

GridBagLayout

This is the most powerful, complex, and hard-to-use Layout Manager that comes with the AWT. Although it gives you the most flexibility, you should plan to spend some time experimenting with its parameters before you get a layout that you like. The basic principle of GridBagLayout is that you associate a constraint object, an instance of GridBagConstraints, with each component in the layout. The GridBagLayout Manager uses those constraints to determine how to lay out the components on an invisible grid, where each component can occupy one or more grid cells. The creator methods for GridBagConstraints take no input parameters; you customize the instance by changing the following instance variables.

anchor
Specifies how a component is to be aligned if a component is smaller than the allocated space. The available constants follow:

CENTER: Puts the component in the middle of the area.
EAST: Aligns it with the right-middle side.
NORTH: Aligns it with the top-middle.
NORTHEAST: Puts it in the upper-right corner.
NORTHWEST: Puts it in the upper-left corner.
SOUTH: Aligns it with the bottom-middle.
SOUTHEAST: Puts it in the lower-right corner.
SOUTHWEST: Puts it in the lower-left corner.
WEST: Aligns it with the left-middle side.

fill
Determines what happens if the space allotted to a component is larger than its default size. The allowable values follow:

BOTH: Tells the component to fill the space in both directions.

HORIZONTAL: Tells the component to fill the space in the horizontal direction.

NONE: Leaves the component at its default size.

VERTICAL: Tells the component to fill the space in the vertical direction.

gridheight

Specifies the height of the component in grid cells. The constant REMAINDER specifies that the component is the last one in the column and therefore should get all the remaining cells.

gridwidth

Specifies the width of the component in grid cells. The constant REMAINDER specifies that the component is the last one in the row and therefore should get all the cells remaining in the row.

gridx

Specifies the grid position of the left side of a component in the horizontal direction. The constant RELATIVE specifies the position to the right of the previous component.

gridy

Specifies the grid position of the top of a component in the vertical direction. The constant RELATIVE specifies the position below the previous component.

insets

Enables you to set an instance of the Insets class that specifies the whitespace reserved around an object. It provides more flexibility than ipadx and ipady because it allows different whitespace on the left than on the right and different whitespace on the top than on the bottom of the component.

ipadx

Specifies the amount of padding (empty space) to put on either side of a component. This increases the effective size of the component.

ipady

Specifies the amount of padding to put above and below the component.

weightx

Specifies how extra horizontal space (space not needed for the default component sizes) is allocated between components. This is a relative value, normally chosen to be between 0 and 1, and the values of the components are compared when allocating space. If one component has a weight of .7 and another has a weight of .2, for example, the one with weight .7 gets more of the extra space than the one with .2.

weighty

Same as `weightx` but for the vertical direction.

As you play around with this Layout Manager, you'll discover that it's very powerful but not entirely intuitive. Listing 17.29 shows an example that gives you a feeling for what `GridBagLayout` can do.

Listing 17.29. Using `GridBagLayout`.

```
import java.awt.*;
import java.applet.Applet;


public class gridbaglayout extends Applet{
    Button the_buttons[];

    public void init()
    {   int i;
        int n_buttons;
        GridBagLayout gbl;
        GridBagConstraints gbc;
        String name;
        int j;
        //define a new GridBagLayout
        gbl = new GridBagLayout();
        //define a new GridBagConstraints. this will be used
        //for all the components
        gbc = new GridBagConstraints();
        //if a component gets more space than it needs don't grow
        //the component to fit the
        //available space
        gbc.fill = GridBagConstraints.NONE;
        //if a component doesn't fill the space assigned to it
        //put it in the top middle of the area
        gbc.anchor = GridBagConstraints.NORTH;
        //pad the size of the component
        gbc.ipadx = 5;
        gbc.ipady = 5;
        //if there is more width available than needed for
        //the components give this
        //component a weight of .3 when allocating the extra horizontal space
        gbc.weightx = .3;
        gbc.weighty = .1;
        setLayout(gbl);
        n_buttons = 15;
        the_buttons = new Button[n_buttons];
        j = 0;
        for(i=0;i<9;i++) {
            j++;
            //start a new row after every 3 buttons
            if (j == 3) {
                j = 0;
                //make this component the last one in the row
                gbc.gridwidth = GridBagConstraints.REMAINDER;
```

continues

Listing 17.29. continued

```
        }
        name = "Button " + i;
        the_buttons[i] = new Button(name);
        //tell GridBagLayout which constraint object to use. you can use
        //the same constraint object for many components even if you
        //change the instance variables values in the constraints object
        //for different components
        gbl.setConstraints(the_buttons[i],gbc);
        add(the_buttons[i]);
        //this sets the gridwidth to its default value. it cleans up the
        //REMAINDER value assigned to the last button in a row
        gbc.gridwidth = 1;
    }
    //change the weight for allocating extra space to subsequent
    gbc.weightx = .4;
    gbc.weighty = .2;
    name = "Button 9";
    the_buttons[9] = new Button(name);
    //if there's extra space put the component in the upper right corner
    gbc.anchor = GridBagConstraints.NORTHEAST;
    //make it the last component in the row
    gbc.gridwidth = GridBagConstraints.REMAINDER;
    gbl.setConstraints(the_buttons[9],gbc);
    add(the_buttons[9]);
    name = "Button 10";
    the_buttons[10] = new Button(name);
    //if the component has extra space assigned grow the component to
    //fill it in both the x and y direction
    gbc.fill = GridBagConstraints.BOTH;
    //this line is unnecessary because the value of gridwidth is retained
    //from when it was set for the previous button
    gbc.gridwidth = GridBagConstraints.REMAINDER;
    gbl.setConstraints(the_buttons[10],gbc);
    add(the_buttons[10]);
    name = "Button 11";
    the_buttons[11] = new Button(name);
    //if there's extra space align the component with the right hand side
    gbc.anchor = GridBagConstraints.EAST;
    //change the weights for allocating extra space
    gbc.weightx = .5;
    gbc.weighty = 0;
    //don't grow the component in either direction if there's extra space
    gbc.fill = GridBagConstraints.NONE;
    gbl.setConstraints(the_buttons[11],gbc);
    add(the_buttons[11]);
    name = "Button 12";
    the_buttons[12] = new Button(name);
    //pad the component--on the Mac the component grows
    gbc.ipadx = 20;
    //set the allocation of width to the default.
    //note that it had been set to
    //REMAINDER above
    gbc.gridwidth = 1;
    //put this component to the right and below the previous one
    gbc.gridx = GridBagConstraints.RELATIVE;
    gbc.gridy = GridBagConstraints.RELATIVE;
```

```
    gbl.setConstraints(the_buttons[12],gbc);
    add(the_buttons[12]);
    name = "Button 13";
    the_buttons[13] = new Button(name);
    //set the pad space to 0
    gbc.ipadx = 0;
    //align the component with the left hand side of the available space
    gbc.anchor = GridBagConstraints.WEST;
    gbl.setConstraints(the_buttons[13],gbc);
    add(the_buttons[13]);
  }

}
```

This applet has the interface shown in Figures 17.39 and 17.40. The two figures show how GridBagLayout behaves as the window resizes.

FIGURE 17.39.

The large window layout.

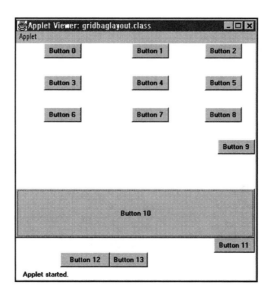

BorderLayout

The BorderLayout divides the container into five pieces; four form the four borders of the container and the fifth is the center. You can add one component to each of these five areas. Because the component can be a panel, you can add more than one interface element, such as a button, to each of the five areas. BorderLayout makes room for the items in the four border areas (referred to as North, South, East, and West), and then whatever is left over is assigned to the Center area. This layout is nice if you want to place scrollbars around a panel, place the scrollbars in the border regions, use all four scrollbars or just two, and place the panel you want to scroll in the center.

FIGURE 17.40.
The small window layout.

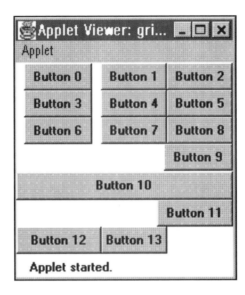

Listing 17.30 shows an example of the BorderLayout in action, which generates the screen shown in Figure 17.41.

FIGURE 17.41.
The BorderLayout.

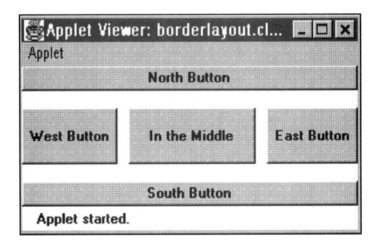

Listing 17.30. Using BorderLayout.

```
import java.awt.*;
import java.applet.Applet;


public class borderlayout extends Applet{
    Button the_buttons[];
```

```
public void init()
{    int i;
     int n_buttons;
     BorderLayout bl;
     String name;

     bl = new BorderLayout(10,15);
     setLayout(bl);
     n_buttons = 5;
     the_buttons = new Button[n_buttons];
     //add the buttons to the various "geographic" regions
     the_buttons[0] = new Button("North Button");
     add("North",the_buttons[0]);

     the_buttons[1] = new Button("South Button");
     add("South",the_buttons[1]);

     the_buttons[2] = new Button("East Button");
     add("East",the_buttons[2]);

     the_buttons[3] = new Button("West Button");
     add("West",the_buttons[3]);

     the_buttons[4] = new Button("In the Middle");
     add("Center",the_buttons[4]);
}

}
```

CardLayout

The CardLayout is different from the others because it enables you to create virtual screen real estate by defining multiple Cards, one of which is visible at any time. Each Card contains a panel that can contain any number of interface elements, including other panels. If you've ever used HyperCard on the Mac, you'll be familiar with this Rolodex™ type of interface. It's also similar to the tabbed dialog boxes that are the rage in Microsoft products, but Cards lack any built-in way to go from Card to Card; you have to provide an interface for that.

> **NOTE**
>
> Commercial widgets that implement tabbed dialog boxes are available; see the section "Extending the AWT," later in this chapter.

The example in Listing 17.31 generates a group of five cards. Each card has a button that takes you to the next card. You can tell which card you're on by looking at the button name.

Listing 17.31. Generating a group of five cards.

```java
import java.awt.*;
import java.applet.Applet;


public class cardlayout extends Applet{
    Button the_buttons[];
    Panel  the_panels[];
    CardLayout cl;

    public void init()
    {   int i;
        int n_buttons;
        String name;

        cl = new CardLayout();
        setLayout(cl);
        n_buttons = 5;
        the_panels = new Panel[n_buttons];
        the_buttons = new Button[n_buttons];
        //this loop creates the 5 panels and adds a button to each
        for(i=0;i<n_buttons;i++) {
            the_panels[i] = new Panel();
            name = "Button " + i;
            the_buttons[i] = new Button(name);
            the_panels[i].add(the_buttons[i]);
            name = "Card " + i;
            //give the panel a name to be used to access it
            add(name, the_panels[i]);
        }
        cl.show(this,"Card 2");
    }
        public boolean action (Event e, Object o) {
        Dimension  d_should;
        //when the button is clicked this takes you to the next card,
        //it will cycle around so that when you're
        //at card 4 this will take you to card 0
        if (e.target instanceof Button) {
            cl.next(this);
        }
        return true;
    }

}
```

Figure 17.42 shows the second card in the stack. Clearly, you could make a tabbed dialog box interface by using a row of buttons across the top of all the cards (one for each card in the group) or with a canvas at the top with a set of tabs drawn on it.

Custom Layouts

You can develop your own Layout Managers by creating a new class that implements LayoutManager and overrides the following five methods.

FIGURE 17.42.
Card two of a
CardLayout *Manager*
interface.

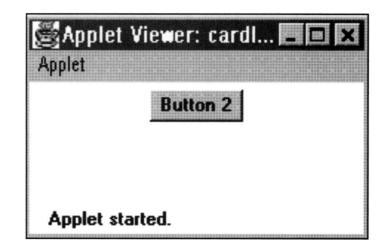

addLayoutComponent(String area_name, Component a_component)

Adds a component to the layout. If your layout has multiple named areas (such as North in BorderLayout), the name specifies which region the component should go to. If your layout doesn't keep any special information about the component, you can make this method do nothing.

removeLayoutComponent(Component c)

Removes a component from the layout. If you don't keep any special information about a component, you can make this method do nothing.

Dimension, preferredLayoutSize(Container the_parent)

Computes the preferred size for the container that holds the layout.

Dimension, minimumLayoutSize(Container the_parent)

Returns the minimum size needed for the layout.

layoutContainer(Container the_parent)

Lays out the components using the reshape method. This is where you put the logic for deciding how to position components.

Although implementing a custom Layout Manager isn't earth-shatteringly complex, the good news is that there are lots of people in the Java community—and some already are making custom Layout Managers. You can get a PackerLayout, for example, which is very similar to the layout approach used in tcl/tk—another mainly UNIX programming language. Before spending the time building your own Layout Manager, do a Web search to make sure that you can't save the time by using someone else's work.

Here are some sample Layout Managers that you can get on the Web. I haven't tried them, so don't view this as a recommendation; instead, it merely should be a starting point in your quest to avoid writing any more code than necessary.

Fractional Layout Manager

```
http://www.mcs.net/~elunt/Java/FractionalLayoutDescription.html
```

Layout Manager Launch

(a collection of links to various Layout Managers)

```
http://www.softbear.com/people/larry/javalm.htm
```

Packer Layout Manager

```
http://www.geom.umn.edu/~daeron/apps/ui/pack/gui.html
```

Relative Layout Manager

```
http://www-elec.enst.fr/java/RelativeLayout.java
```

Rule-Based Layout Manager

```
http://www.sealevelsoftware.com/sealevel/testrule.htm
```

Tree Layout Manager

```
http://www.sbktech.org/tree.html
```

> **NOTE**
>
> One problem with custom Layout Mangers is that they have to be downloaded over the network, while the AWT Layout Managers already reside on the local machine. Because a Layout Manager can be large (more than 10 KB), this is an issue if a lot of your users will be working with 14.4-Kbps or 28.8-Kbps modems. If your users have T1 lines, it's not an issue.

Images

The developers of Java knew that working with images is a critical part of any modern programming language with a goal of implementing user interfaces that meet the criteria of users. Because Java is platform independent, though, it couldn't use any of the platform-specific formats, such as the Mac's PICT standard. Fortunately, there already are two platform-independent formats: GIF and JPEG. These formats are especially nice because they are compressed so that transmitting them takes less of the limited network bandwidth. The AWT supports both these compression formats, but it uses neither of them internally. Although you can read in GIF and JPEG files, they are converted into images, which are just bitmaps. All the work you do in Java with images is based on the `Image` class. For some strange reason, even though there is a special package for image-manipulation-related classes (`java.awt.image`), the `Image` class itself resides in the top-level `java.awt` package.

`Image` is an abstract class designed to support bitmapped images in a platform-independent manner. Although this class provides just the basics for working with images, it does have several methods you'll find useful.

Java uses a model of image producers and image consumers. *Image producers* generate pixels from a file or `Image` object, and *image consumers* use and/or display those pixels. Both `ImageConsumer` and `ImageProducer` are Java interfaces. AWT comes with `ImageProducers` for reading from local files and URLs, arrays in memory, and `Image` objects. It also comes with `CropImageFilter`, `RGBImageFilter`, and `PixelGrabber`, which implement the `ImageConsumer` interface.

Graphics, getGraphics()

Returns the graphics object for this image. You can use this to draw to the image using the drawing methods discussed in the `Graphics` object section, "Graphics Class."

int, getHeight(ImageObserver imgobs)

Returns the height of the image. The `ImageObserver` class monitors the construction of the image—as it's loaded over the Internet, for example. The `ImageObserver` is notified when the image is fully loaded into memory if it isn't at the time this method is called.

Object, getProperty(String prop_name, ImageObserver imgobs)

Returns the value of one of the image properties. The specific properties depend on the original image format. Three properties are supported by Java:

> `comments`: A string full of information defined by the person who made the image file.
> `croprect`: If a Java `croprect` filter is used, this holds the boundary of the original image.
> `filters`: If Java image filters are used to make the image, they are listed here.

ImageProducer, getSource()

Returns an instance of `ImageProducer`, which serves as a source for the pixels in an image.

int, getWidth()

Returns the width of the image.

Loading Images from Files (ImageObserver)

Java makes it easy to load images from files located on the server. Security restrictions vary between browsers, but even Netscape, which tends to have the tightest security, allows you to get images from files in the same directory from which the Java classes are loaded. The simple applet shown in Listing 17.32 loads in an image, monitors the loading with an ImageObserver, and then displays the image (see Figure 17.43).

FIGURE 17.43.

Displaying a GIF file.

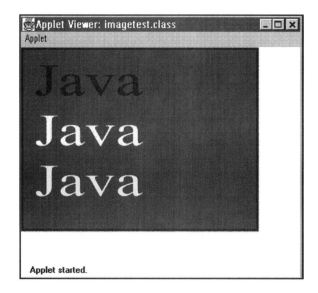

Listing 17.32. Showing a GIF image.

```
import java.awt.*;
import java.applet.Applet;
import java.awt.image.*;


public class imagetest extends Applet implements ImageObserver, Runnable{
    Image the_picture;
    boolean image_ready;
    Thread the_thread;

    public void init()
    {
        //we'll use this flag to see when the image is ready to use
        image_ready = false;
        //get the image from the same location as the
        //HTML document this applet is on
        the_picture = getImage(getDocumentBase(),"test.gif");
```

```
    }
    //overriding this method allows you to monitor the
    //status of the loading of the image
    public boolean imageUpdate(Image img,int status, int x,
                       int y, int width, int height){

        if ((status & ALLBITS) == 0) {
            //Monitor the load status
            System.out.println("Processing image " + x + " " +
                y + " width, height " + width + " " + height);
             return true;
        } else {
            System.out.println("Image fully read in");
            return false;
        }
    }

    public void start() {
        if (the_thread == null) {
            the_thread = new Thread(this);
            the_thread.start();
        }
    }
    public void stop() {
        the_thread.stop();
    }

    public void run() {
        //Give the thread that's loading the image more cycles by minimizing the
        //priority of the applet's animation thread
        the_thread.setPriority(Thread.MIN_PRIORITY);
        //cycle while you're waiting for the image to load. You could put in a
        //message telling the user what's going on as well
        while (!image_ready) {
            repaint();
            try {
                the_thread.sleep(50);
            } catch(InterruptedException e) {};
        }
    }
    public void paint(Graphics g)
    {
        //Draw the image. The "this" assigns the applet
        //as the image observer for
        //this drawing.
        image_ready = g.drawImage(the_picture,0,0,this);
    }
}
}
```

Notice that the applet itself implements the ImageObserver interface so that when an ImageObserver is called for, as in the drawImage method call, this is used. The only other change you have to make to your applet is to override the imageUpdate method with one of your own to track the image-loading process. Although the behavior of this seems to vary a bit between platforms (probably due to differences in the way thread priorities are handled), you can use it to see when an image is ready to be displayed. But there is a better way, using the `MediaTracker` class, which you'll see in the next section.

Clipping Images (`CropImageFilter`, `MediaTracker`)

If you're using Java on the Internet, you'll find that you'll want to crop images more often than you might expect. The reason for this is that there is a fairly significant overhead associated with sending a file from the server to the client. As a result, you can make your applet load faster if you send one file that is 2x pixels on a side instead of four files that are 1x pixels on a side. If you go with one large file, you'll find that the `CropImageFilter` class will make it easy to cut out pieces of the image. This is a good way to work with multi-frame animations. Put all the animations in a single file and then use `CropImageFilter` to make a separate image for each cell in the animation.

`CropImageFilter` Creator

You won't use any of `CropImageFilter`'s methods other than its creator:

```
new CropImageFilter(int x, int y, int width, int height)
```

The input parameters define the rectangular region that will be selected. The coordinates are with respect to the upper-left corner of the image, which is set to 0,0.

The applet in Listing 17.33 reads in a GIF file, creates a new image that is the upper-left corner of the original image, and then displays both images, as shown in Figure 17.44.

FIGURE 17.44.

The original and the cropped image.

Listing 17.33. Cropping an image.

```
import java.applet.Applet;
import java.awt.*;
import java.awt.image.*;


public class crop_image extends Applet implements  Runnable{
    Image the_picture, cropped_picture;
    boolean image_ready;
    Thread the_thread;
    MediaTracker the_tracker;

    public void start() {
        if (the_thread == null) {
            the_thread = new Thread(this);
            the_thread.start();
        }
    }
    public void stop() {
        the_thread.stop();
    }

    public void run() {
        the_thread.setPriority(Thread.MIN_PRIORITY);
        while (true) {
            repaint();
            try {
                the_thread.sleep(3000);
            } catch(InterruptedException e) {};
        }
    }
    public void init()
    {
        CropImageFilter c_i_filter;

        //Define a MediaTracker to monitor the completion status of an image
        //You need to supply a component as the argument.
        //In this case the applet
        // is used
        the_tracker = new MediaTracker(this);
        image_ready = false;
        the_picture = getImage(getDocumentBase(),"test.gif");
        //tell MediaTracker to monitor the progress of the image and
        //assign the image
        //the index of 0--the index value is arbitrary
        the_tracker.addImage(the_picture,0);
        //Define an image cropping filter
        c_i_filter = new CropImageFilter(0,0,32,32);
        //Apply the filter to the image and make a new image of the cropped area
        cropped_picture = createImage(new FilteredImageSource(
                the_picture.getSource(),c_i_filter));
        //Monitor the cropped image to see when it's done
        the_tracker.addImage(cropped_picture,1);
```

continues

Listing 17.33. continued

```
    }
    public void paint(Graphics g)
    {
        //Wait till both images are ready
        if(the_tracker.checkID(0,true) &
                            the_tracker.checkID(1,true)) {
            image_ready = true;
            g.drawImage(the_picture,0,0,this);
            g.drawImage(cropped_picture,70,70,this);
        } else {
            System.out.println("Waiting for image to fully load");
        }
    }
}
```

MediaTracker

The applet shown in Figure 17.44 also demonstrates how to use the MediaTracker class to monitor images that are being loaded or built. All you have to do is create a new instance of the MediaTracker class.

To create a MediaTracker instance to monitor the loading of images associated with the specified component, use this code:

```
new MediaTracker(Component a_component)
```

To track images, you'll use these MediaTracker methods:

addImage(Image an_image, int id)
Tells MediaTracker to monitor the specified image. The ID is used in other method calls to identify the image. You can use any value for the ID, and you can assign the same ID to more than one image.

addImage(Image an_image, int id, int width, int height)
Functions like the preceding method, except that it registers a scaled image where width and height are the new dimensions of the image. This is a synchronized method.

boolean, checkAll()
Returns TRUE when the images have loaded or stopped loading due to an error. Use the isErrorAny and/or isErrorID methods to check for problems.

boolean, checkAll(boolean load_flag)
Returns TRUE if all images have finished loading or encountered an error. This is a synchronized method. It forces the images to load if the input parameter is TRUE.

```
boolean, checkID(int the_id)
```
Returns TRUE if the specified image (or group of images, if more than one image has the same ID) has finished loading or stopped due to an error.

```
boolean, checkID(int the_id, boolean load_flag)
```
Returns TRUE if the images with the specified ID are loaded or have encountered an error. If load_flag is TRUE, this synchronized method starts to load the image if it isn't already loading.

```
Object[], getErrorsAny()
```
Returns an array of media objects for those images that encountered errors. This is a synchronized method. You can print these objects by using the .toString method on them.

```
Object[], getErrorsID(int id)
```
Returns an array of media objects for the images with the specified ID that encountered an error while loading. This is a synchronized method.

```
boolean, isErrorAny()
```
Returns TRUE if any image currently being tracked has a problem. This is a synchronized method.

```
boolean, isErrorID(int id)
```
Returns TRUE if any image with the specified ID has received an error while loading. This is a synchronized method.

```
int, statusAll(boolean load_flag)
```
Returns the status of the loading of all the images. ANDing the returned value with MediaTracker.ERRORED returns TRUE if there is an error. If the input parameter is TRUE, this method starts loading the images if they haven't already been loaded.

```
int, statusID(int id, boolean load_flag)
```
Functions similarly to statusAll, except for a single ID.

```
waitForAll()
```
Waits until all images are loaded or encounter an error. If this method is interrupted, it throws the InterruptedException error.

```
boolean, waitForAll(long time_in_ms)
```
Functions similarly to waitForAll, except that it will timeout after the specified time. This is a synchronized method.

`waitForID(int id)`
Functions similarly to `waitForAll`, except for a single ID.

`boolean, waitForID(int id, long time_in_ms)`
Functions similarly to `waitForAll`, except for a single ID. This is a synchronized method.

As you can see from the applet in Listing 17.33, though, you only need to use a couple of methods to monitor image loading in most circumstances.

NOTE

Java will not be able to garbage-collect images that have been monitored by `MediaTracker`, because `MediaTracker` retains references to them unless the `MediaTracker` instance itself can be garbage-collected. If you load and then delete images, make sure to set all references to the `MediaTracker` you used to `NULL` if you want Java to free up the space used by the images.

Filtering Images (`RGBImageFilter`)

Image filters provide an easy way to transform images. The `RGBImageFilter` makes it easy to execute transformations that only require information about the pixel being modified. Although that excludes a wide range of common transformations, it does support a large number, such as converting to grayscale, image fade out, and color separation. The applet in Listing 17.34 takes an image, inverts all the colors, and then displays the before and after pictures (see Figure 17.45).

FIGURE 17.45.
Inverting colors with
`RGBImageFilter`.

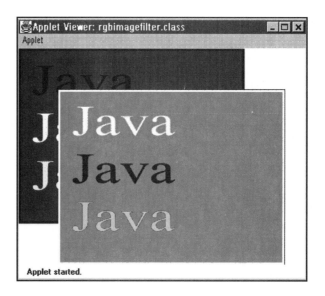

Listing 17.34. Using an `RGBImageFilter`.

```java
import java.applet.Applet;
import java.awt.*;
import java.awt.image.*;


public class rgbimagefilter extends Applet implements  Runnable{
    Image the_picture, filtered_image;
    boolean image_ready;
    Thread the_thread;
    MediaTracker the_tracker;
    //Sep is the new class that extends RGBImageFilter
    Sep image_filter;

    public void start() {
        if (the_thread == null) {
            the_thread = new Thread(this);
            the_thread.start();
        }
    }
    public void stop() {
        the_thread.stop();
    }

    public void run() {

        the_thread.setPriority(Thread.MIN_PRIORITY);
        while (true) {
            repaint();
            try {
                the_thread.sleep(3000);
            } catch(InterruptedException e) {};
        }
    }
    public void init()
    {
        the_tracker = new MediaTracker(this);
        image_ready = false;
        the_picture = getImage(getDocumentBase(),"test.gif");
        the_tracker.addImage(the_picture,0);
        //modify the image and track the process
        filter_image();
        the_tracker.addImage(filtered_image,1);

    }
    public void filter_image() {
        image_filter = new Sep();
        //create the new filtered image using the getSource method on the input
        //picture as a pixel producer
        filtered_image = createImage(new FilteredImageSource
                        (the_picture.getSource(),image_filter));
    }
    public void paint(Graphics g)
    {
```

continues

Listing 17.34. continued

```
                //wait for both images to be loaded before drawing them
                if(the_tracker.checkID(0,true) &
                                    the_tracker.checkID(1,true)) {
                    image_ready = true;
                    g.drawImage(the_picture,0,0,this);
                    g.drawImage(filtered_image,60,60,this);
                } else {
                    System.out.println("Waiting for image to fully load");
                }
            }
    }
}

class Sep extends RGBImageFilter{

    public Sep() {
        //This specifies that this class can work with IndexColorModel where
        //each pixel contains a pointer to a color in a lookup table rather than
        //a 32 bit color
        canFilterIndexColorModel = true;
    }

    public int filterRGB(int x, int y, int rgb) {
        int blue,red,green,new_color;

        //get the three color components from the rgb int
        blue = rgb & 0x000000FF;
        green = (rgb & 0x0000FF00) >> 8;
        red = (rgb & 0x00FF0000) >> 16;
        //These three lines invert the color
        blue = 255 - blue;
        green = 255 - green;
        red = 255 - red;
        //create the new color and then get the int version of the color
        new_color = (new Color(red,blue,green)).getRGB();
        return new_color;
    }
}
```

All the work is done in the `filterRGB` method, which is called for each pixel or every color in the lookup table for indexed color models. You can put any algorithm in that method that only requires information about that one color and/or pixel. If your transformation is position dependent (it's a function of x and/or y), you can't work with an indexed color model because the `filterRGB` method, in this case, is called only for the colors in the lookup table—not for every pixel.

Building Images On-the-Fly (MemoryImageSource)

The AWT provides a class, `MemoryImageSource`, that makes it easy to convert an array of data into an image. This is useful if you're building images on-the-fly—drawing the Mandelbrot set, for example. In Listing 17.35, the image is a gradient fill that's built as an array of integers and then converted to an image (see Figure 17.46).

FIGURE 17.46.

A gradient fill generated as an array of integers.

Listing 17.35. Working with pixel values.

```
import java.awt.image.*;
import java.awt.*;
import java.applet.Applet;


public class memory_image extends Applet implements Runnable
{
    Image working;
    Thread the_thread;
    MediaTracker the_tracker;
    int pixels[];
    int max_x, max_y;

    public void start() {
        if (the_thread == null) {
            the_thread = new Thread(this);
            the_thread.start();
        }
    }
    public void stop() {
        the_thread.stop();
    }

    public void run() {
        while (true) {
            repaint();
            try {
                the_thread.sleep(3000);
            } catch(InterruptedException e) {};
        }
    }
```

continues

Listing 17.35. continued

```java
public void init()
{
    max_x = 256;
    max_y = 256;
    the_tracker = new MediaTracker(this);
    //set up the pixel array that we're going to convert to an image
    pixels = new int[max_x * max_y];
    //set up the new image
    init_pixels();

}
public void init_pixels() {
    int x,y,i, j;
    double step;
    //this method does a gradient fill starting with black at the top
    //and going to blue at the bottom
    //step is used to determine how much the color changes between rows
    step = 255.0/max_y;
    i = 0;
    Color c = new Color(0,0,0);
    int ci = c.getRGB();
    j= 0;
    for (y=0;y<max_y;y++) {
        //get a new color for each row. notice that the fastest cycling
        // in the array is x. variable
        c = new Color(0,0,Math.round((float)(j*step)));
        ci = c.getRGB();
        j++;
        for (x=0;x<max_x;x++) {
            pixels[i++]= ci;
        }
    }
    //make the image and use MediaTracker to see when it's
    //done being processed
    working = createImage(new MemoryImageSource
                (max_x,max_y,pixels,0,max_y));
    the_tracker.addImage(working,0);
}
public void paint(Graphics g)
{
    //if the image is done display it, otherwise let the
    //user know what's going on
    if(the_tracker.checkID(0,true)) {
        g.drawImage(working,0,0,this);
    } else {
        g.drawString("please wait",50,50);
    }
}
}
```

After you have an image from the int array, you can use all the other image-processing tools with them.

Converting Images to Arrays (PixelGrabber)

If you're going to process images, you often want to work with the pixel data as an array. The AWT provides a class, java.awt.image.PixelGrabber, to do just that. This class has two creator methods, plus some other useful methods.

new PixelGrabber(Image img, int x, int y, int width, int height, int[] pixels, int offset, int linewidth)
Takes the region of the image defined by x, y, height, and width and puts it into the pixel's array with the specified offset and line width.

new PixelGrabber(ImageProducer img, int x, int y, int width, int height, int[] pixels, int offset, int linewidth)
Takes the region of the image produced by the image producer defined by x, y, height, and width and puts it into the pixel's array with the specified offset and line width.

boolean, grabPixels()
Throws InterruptedException if it's interrupted. It takes the image data and puts it into the pixel array. This is a synchronized method.

int, status()
Returns the status of getting the pixels from an image. The return value uses the same flag constants as the ImageObserver class. This is a synchronized method.

The applet in Listing 17.36 reads in a GIF file, fills in an array with the pixel values, applies an averaging filter to the data (which uses information about each pixel's neighbors), and then converts the pixel array back to an image. This results in the screen shown in Figure 17.47.

Listing 17.36. A filter that uses data from a pixel's local area.

```
import java.awt.image.*;
import java.awt.*;
import java.applet.Applet;


public class pixel_grabber extends Applet implements Runnable
{
    Image working;
    Thread the_thread;
    MediaTracker the_tracker;
    int pixels[];
    int max_x, max_y;
    Image the_picture;
    Image the_modified_picture;
    boolean done_flag;
```

continues

Listing 17.36. continued

```
public void start() {
    if (the_thread == null) {
        the_thread = new Thread(this);
        the_thread.start();
    }
}
public void stop() {
    the_thread.stop();
}

public void run() {
    while (true) {
        repaint();
        try {
            the_thread.sleep(3000);
        } catch(InterruptedException e) {};
        //when the original image is loaded transform it.
        //The use of the flag
        //makes sure you only transform the image once
        if(the_tracker.checkID(0,true) & !(done_flag)) {
            transform_image();
            done_flag = true;
        }
    }
}

public void init()
{
    done_flag = false;
    max_x = 64;
    max_y = 64;
    the_tracker = new MediaTracker(this);
    //set up the pixel array that we're going to
    //fill with data from the image
    pixels = new int[max_x * max_y];
    the_picture = getImage(getDocumentBase(),"test.gif");
    the_tracker.addImage(the_picture,0);

}
public void transform_image() {
    PixelGrabber pg;
    int x,y;
    double sum, temp;
    //set up the PixelGrabber to capture the full image, unscaled
    pg = new PixelGrabber(the_picture, 0,0,max_x,max_y,pixels,0,max_y);
    //fill the pixel's array with the image data
    try {
        pg.grabPixels();
    } catch(InterruptedException e) {};
    //just to show something happened apply an averaging filter.
    //This is designed to
    //work with grayscale images because it assumes all of the
    //color components are
    //equal. It takes the Blue component of a pixel and its
    //four neighbors, averages them,
    //and then sets the pixel color to that average
    for (x=3;x<(max_x - 3);x++) {
```

```
        for (y=3;y<(max_y - 3);y++) {
            temp = pixels[x + y * max_y] & 0x000000FF;
            sum = 0.2 * temp;
            temp = pixels[(x - 1) + y * max_y] & 0x000000FF;
            sum = sum + 0.2 * temp;
            temp = pixels[(x+1) + y * max_y] & 0x000000FF;
            sum = sum + 0.2 * temp;
            temp = pixels[x + (y - 1) * max_y] & 0x000000FF;
            sum = sum + 0.2 * temp;
            temp = pixels[x + (y + 1) * max_y] & 0x000000FF;
            sum = sum + 0.2 * temp;
            int gray = (int)Math.round(sum);
            Color c = new Color(gray,gray,gray);
            pixels[x + y * max_y] = c.getRGB() ;
        }
    }
    //here we use MemoryImageSource to convert the pixel array into an Image
    the_modified_picture = createImage(new
                        MemoryImageSource(max_x,max_y,pixels,0,max_y));
    the_tracker.addImage(the_modified_picture,1);
}
public void paint(Graphics g)
{
    //if the image is done display it, otherwise let
    //the user know what's going on
    if(the_tracker.checkID(0,true) ) {
        g.drawImage(the_picture,0,0,this);
        if( the_tracker.checkID(1,true)) {
            g.drawImage(the_modified_picture, 64,64,this);
        }
    } else {
        g.drawString("please wait",50,50);
    }
}
}
```

FIGURE 17.47.

An average filter applied to a grayscale image.

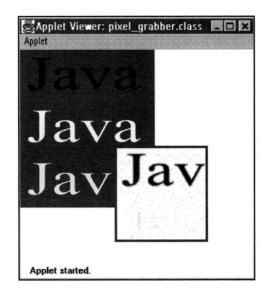

Windows

The Window class implements a window with no borders and no menu bar. This generally isn't a useful class on its own, but because Frame and Dialog—which are useful—extend it, it's useful to take a quick look at Window's methods.

dispose()
This gets rid of the window's peer. When the window is destroyed, you need to call this method. This is a synchronized method.

Toolkit, getToolkit()
Returns the Toolkit associated with the window.

show()
Displays the window, making it visible and moving it to the front. This is a synchronized method.

toBack()
Moves the window behind all other windows in the application.

toFront()
Moves the window in front of all other windows.

User interactions with a window can cause it to generate the WINDOW_DESTROY, WINDOW_ICONIFY, WINDOW_DEICONIFY, and WINDOW_MOVED events.

> **NOTE**
>
> Here's another example of how the AWT conforms to the expectations of platform users. On the Mac, the window doesn't reduce to an icon, because that is not the sort of behavior a Mac user would expect.

Frames

A Frame implements a resizable window that supports a menu bar, cursor, icon, and title.

> **CAUTION**
>
> An AWT frame has nothing to do with an HTML frame, which is a concept for defining panes inside a window and was developed by Netscape. A Java frame only

applies within an applet window or a Java application. You can't use a Java frame to set up Frames on an HTML page.

This is your basic application-type window, which looks like the windows you'll see in most programs. You can use frames with an applet; in fact, it's the only way to use dialog boxes and menu bars.

Frames generate the same events as windows, which they extend: WINDOW_DESTROY, WINDOW_ICONIFY, WINDOW_DEICONIFY, and WINDOW_MOVED.

The only parameter you can pass to the Frame constructor is a String, which will be the window title. You generally will create your own class that extends Frame and contains event-handling methods that override Component methods such as action, mouseDown, and keyDown. When you extend the class, you can make creator methods with more input parameters. One useful technique when you're using Frames with applets is to pass the applet, using this—the Java construct that refers to the object in whose scope the program line is in—to the Frame so that the Frame methods can invoke applet methods and read/write applet instance variables.

The most useful Frame methods follow.

dispose()

Enables you to free up windowing resources when you're done with a Frame. This is a synchronized method.

int, getCursorType()

Returns the integer constant that defines which cursor currently is displayed. The available Frame final static (constant) values follow:

```
CROSSHAIR_CURSOR
DEFAULT_CURSOR
E_RESIZE_CURSOR
HAND_CURSOR
MOVE_CURSOR
N_RESIZE_CURSOR
NE_RESIZE_CURSOR
NW_RESIZE_CURSOR
S_RESIZE_CURSOR
SE_RESIZE_CURSOR
SW_RESIZE_CURSOR
TEXT_CURSOR
W_RESIZE_CURSOR
WAIT_CURSOR
```

`Image, getIconImage()`
Returns the image being used when the window is reduced to an icon.

`MenuBar, getMenuBar()`
Returns the frame's menu bar.

`String, getTitle()`
Returns the frame's title.

`boolean, isResizable()`
Returns TRUE if the frame can be resized. This attribute can be toggled using the `setResizable` method.

`remove(MenuComponent mb)`
Removes the menu bar associated with the frame. This is a synchronized method.

`setCursor(int cursor_constant)`
Sets the current cursor to the one specified by the input argument.

`setIconImage(Image icon)`
Sets the icon to be used when the frame is reduced to an icon to the input image.

`setMenuBar(MenuBar mb)`
Sets the menu bar for the frame. This is a synchronized method.

`setResizable(boolean flag)`
Changes the frame size if the input parameter is TRUE. If the input is FALSE, the frame is a fixed size.

`setTitle(String new_title)`
Sets the window title.

The applet in Listing 17.37 shows you how to work with a frame. A button on the applet shows the frame. The user then can enter text in a `TextArea` on the frame. When the user closes the frame (either with the button in the frame or the one in the applet), the frame is hidden and the text in the frame's `TextArea` is put into the `TextArea` in the applet. The applet and the frame are shown in Figures 17.48 and 17.49.

FIGURE 17.48.
The applet window.

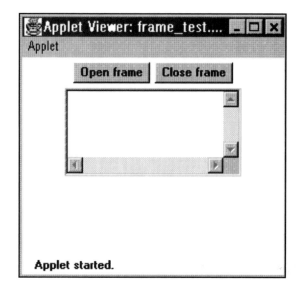

FIGURE 17.49.
The new frame.

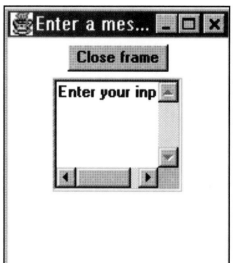

Listing 17.37. Working with frames.

```
import java.awt.*;
import java.applet.Applet;

public class frame_test extends Applet
{
```

continues

Listing 17.37. continued

```
input_frame a_frame;
Button b_open, b_close;
TextArea the_message;
boolean frame_visible;

public void init()
{
    b_open = new Button("Open frame");
    b_close = new Button("Close frame");
    add(b_open);
    add(b_close);
    the_message = new TextArea(5,20);
    add(the_message);
    frame_visible = false;
    a_frame = create_dialog("Enter a message");
    // Uncomment these next two lines if you want the frame showing
    //when the applet starts
    //a_frame.show();
    //frame_visible = true;
}

public input_frame create_dialog(String the_title) {
    //create a new frame. pass this so that the frame can
    //access the applet's
    //instance variables in order to pass information back.
    a_frame = new input_frame(the_title,this);
    //set its size to 200 by 200
    a_frame.resize(200,200);
    return a_frame;
}

public boolean action(Event the_event, Object the_arg) {
    String item_name;
    //handle mouse clicks on the two buttons
    if(the_event.target instanceof Button) {
        item_name = (String)the_arg;
        if(item_name.equals("Open frame")) {
            if(!frame_visible) {
                a_frame.show();
                frame_visible = true;
            }
        }
        if(item_name.equals("Close frame")) {
            if(frame_visible) {
                a_frame.hide();
                frame_visible = false;
            }
        }
    }
    return true;
}


}
```

```
class input_frame extends Frame {
    Button close_frame;
    TextArea text_space;
    //this has to be of type frame_test not Applet. If you use Applet
    //instead of frame_test it
    //will still compile but you won't be able to use my_
    //parent to access the instance
    //variables of the frame_test applet such as frame_visible.
    frame_test my_parent;

    input_frame(String the_title, frame_test host) {
        super(the_title);
        FlowLayout fl;

        my_parent = host;
        //have to define a layout manager for the frame
        fl = new FlowLayout();
        setLayout(fl);
        close_frame = new Button("Close frame");
        add(close_frame);
        text_space = new TextArea("Enter your input",5,10);
        add(text_space);
    }
    //By overriding the hide method we ensure that the text
    //from the dialog is sent back
    //to the applet if the frame is closed by clicking on the
    //close frame button in the
    //applet.
    public synchronized void hide() {
        String the_input;

        the_input = text_space.getText();
        //use the reference to the applet to pass data back by accessing the
        //TextArea component
        my_parent.the_message.insertText(the_input,0);
        my_parent.frame_visible = false;
        super.hide();
    }

    public boolean action(Event an_event, Object arg) {
        String button_name;
        String the_input;

        if (an_event.target instanceof Button) {
            button_name = (String)arg;
            if(button_name.equals("Close frame")) {
                //we don't have to do anything to copy the text to
                //the applet here because we overrode the
                //hide method
                hide();
            }
        }
        return true;
    }
}
```

Notice how the applet extends the Frame class and passes the applet object, using this, to the frame so the Frame methods can work with applet data. In general, creating frames is straightforward because the AWT does most of the work for you. Frames are the basic element for Java application interfaces.

Cursor Control

For some strange reason, the capability to control the cursor is in the Frame class, so when you can control the cursor, the user sees when a frame has focus. The applet in Listing 17.38 enables you to select the cursor from a pop-up menu. Figure 17.50 shows the frame that enables you to select the cursor. The actual cursor images are platform dependent. This is yet another way to make sure that users on every platform feel comfortable with the interface.

FIGURE 17.50.

A pop-up menu to pick the cursor.

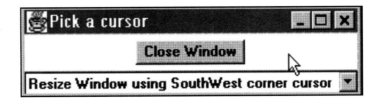

Listing 17.38. Selecting the cursor from a pop-up menu.

```java
import java.awt.*;
import java.applet.Applet;


public class cursor_test extends Applet
{
    a_frame a_window;
    Button b_open, b_close;
    boolean window_visible;

    public void init()
    {
        b_open = new Button("Open Window");
        b_close = new Button("Close Window");
        add(b_open);
        add(b_close);
        create_dialog("Pick a cursor");
    }

    public a_frame create_dialog(String the_title) {
        //create a new Frame
        a_window = new a_frame(the_title,this);
        //set its size to 300 by 80 pixels
        a_window.resize(300,80);
        return a_window;
    }
```

```java
    public boolean action(Event the_event, Object the_arg) {
        String item_name;
        //handle mouse clicks on the two buttons
        if(the_event.target instanceof Button) {
            item_name = (String)the_arg;
            if(item_name.equals("Open Window")) {
                if(!window_visible) {
                    a_window.show();
                    window_visible = true;
                }
            }
            if(item_name.equals("Close Window")) {
                if(window_visible) {
                    a_window.hide();
                    window_visible = false;
                }
            }
        }
        return true;
    }


}

class a_frame extends Frame {
    Button close_window;
    Choice a_menu;
    //this has to be of type cursor_test not Applet. If you
    //use Applet instead of cursor_test it
    //will still compile but you won't be able to use my_
    //parent to access the instance
    //variables of the dialogs applet such as window_visible.
    cursor_test my_parent;

    a_frame(String the_title, cursor_test host) {
        super(the_title);
        FlowLayout fl;

        my_parent = host;
        //have to define a layout manager for the window
        fl = new FlowLayout();
        setLayout(fl);
        close_window = new Button("Close Window");
        add(close_window);
        a_menu = new Choice();
        a_menu.addItem("Crosshair cursor");
        a_menu.addItem("Default Arrow cursor");
        a_menu.addItem("Resize Window to the Right cursor");
        a_menu.addItem("Hand cursor");
        a_menu.addItem("Move Window cursor");
        a_menu.addItem("Resize Window Upwards cursor");
        a_menu.addItem("Resize Window using NorthEast corner cursor");
        a_menu.addItem("Resize Window using NorthWest corner cursor");
        a_menu.addItem("Resize Window Downwards cursor");
        a_menu.addItem("Resize Window using SouthEast corner cursor");
```

continues

Listing 17.38. continued

```
            a_menu.addItem("Resize Window using SouthWest corner cursor");
            a_menu.addItem("Text Editing cursor");
            a_menu.addItem("Resizing Window to the left cursor");
            a_menu.addItem("Hourglass cursor");
            add(a_menu);
    }
    public boolean action(Event an_event, Object arg) {
        String button_name;
        String the_input;
        String item_name;

        if (an_event.target instanceof Button) {
            button_name = (String)arg;
            if(button_name.equals("Close Window")) {
             my_parent.window_visible = false;
                hide();
            }
        }
        if(an_event.target instanceof Choice) {
            item_name = (String)arg;
            if(item_name.equals("Crosshair cursor")){
                setCursor(Frame.CROSSHAIR_CURSOR);
            }
            if(item_name.equals("Default Arrow cursor")){
                setCursor(Frame.DEFAULT_CURSOR);
            }
            if(item_name.equals("Resize Window to the Right cursor")){
                setCursor(Frame.E_RESIZE_CURSOR);
            }
            if(item_name.equals("Hand cursor")){
                setCursor(Frame.HAND_CURSOR);
            }
            if(item_name.equals("Move Window cursor")){
                setCursor(Frame.MOVE_CURSOR);
            }
            if(item_name.equals("Resize Window Upwards cursor")){
                setCursor(Frame.N_RESIZE_CURSOR);
            }
            if(item_name.equals("Resize Window using NorthEast corner cursor")){
                setCursor(Frame.NE_RESIZE_CURSOR);
            }
            if(item_name.equals("Resize Window using NorthWest corner cursor")){
                setCursor(Frame.NW_RESIZE_CURSOR);
            }
            if(item_name.equals("Resize Window Downwards cursor")){
                setCursor(Frame.S_RESIZE_CURSOR);
            }
            if(item_name.equals("Resize Window using SouthEast corner cursor")){
                setCursor(Frame.SE_RESIZE_CURSOR);
            }
            if(item_name.equals("Resize Window using SouthWest corner cursor")){
                setCursor(Frame.SW_RESIZE_CURSOR);
            }
            if(item_name.equals("Text Editing cursor")){
                setCursor(Frame.TEXT_CURSOR);
```

```
            }
            if(item_name.equals("Resizing Window to the left cursor")){
                setCursor(Frame.W_RESIZE_CURSOR);
            }
            if(item_name.equals("Hourglass cursor")){
                setCursor(Frame.WAIT_CURSOR);
            }

        }
        return true;
    }
}
```

Menus

You can put a menu bar in a frame or window, but not an applet. Refer to the illustration in Figure 17.3 showing the five menu-related classes: MenuComponent, MenuBar, Menu, MenuItem, and CheckboxMenuItem.

All the other menu classes inherit from MenuComponent. MenuComponent is an abstract class, but you'll use these methods fairly often.

Font, getFont()
Returns the font used for the current item.

setFont(Font a_font)
Sets the font to be used to display the item on which the menu is invoked.

The MenuBar class is a container for a set of menus displayed with a frame. The key MenuBar methods follow.

Menu, add(Menu a_menu)
Adds a menu to the menu bar. The return value is a handle to the added menu. Menus are added left to right. This is a synchronized method.

int, countMenus()
Returns the number of menus currently in the menu bar.

Menu, getHelpMenu()
Returns the menu that is defined as the Help menu for the menu bar.

Menu, getMenu(int pos)
Returns the menu item at a given location in the menu bar.

```
remove(int pos)
```
Removes the menu at the specified position. This is a synchronized method.

```
remove(MenuComponent menu)
```
Removes the specified menu from the menu bar. This is a synchronized method.

```
setHelpMenu(Menu a_menu)
```
Sets the specified menu to be the Help menu, which always is placed on the right side of the menu bar. This is a synchronized method.

The Menu class implements pull-down menus. There are two constructor methods and some useful Menu methods.

```
new Menu(String a_label)
```
Creates a new menu with the specified label.

```
new Menu(String a_label, boolean tear_off)
```
Creates a new menu with the specified label, which can be torn off from the menu bar.

```
MenuItem, add(MenuItem an_entry)
```
Adds the specified menu item to the menu. You make hierarchical menus by adding menus to another menu. This is a synchronized method.

```
add(String label)
```
Adds a new entry to the menu.

```
addSeparator()
```
Adds a separating line to the menu.

```
int, countItems()
```
Returns a count of the number of items in the menu.

```
MenuItem, getItem(int position)
```
Returns the menu item at the specified location.

```
boolean, isTearOff()
```
Returns TRUE if the menu has tear off enabled.

```
remove(int position)
```
Removes the menu item at the specified location. This is a synchronized method.

```
remove(MenuComponent an_item)
```
Removes the specified menu item. This is a synchronized method.

The `MenuItem` class implements the functionality of a single entry in a pull-down menu. When you create one, you have to supply its label (as a string) as the input parameter. You use the `add` method to add `MenuItems` to menus. The most useful `MenuItem` methods follow.

```
disable()
```
Grays out a menu item and prevents the user from selecting it.

```
enable()
```
Enables a menu item so the user can select it.

```
enable(boolean some_statement)
```
Enables a menu item if the logical statement evaluates to TRUE.

```
StringgetLabel()
```
Returns the item's label.

```
boolean, isEnabled()
```
Returns TRUE if the user can select the item.

```
setLabel(String new_label)
```
Changes the label of the menu item to the specified string.

An `ACTION_EVENT` is generated whenever a menu item is selected by the user.

The `CheckboxMenuItem` class extends `MenuItem` and implements the functionality of a menu item with an associated checkbox. The two methods of this class that will come in handy follow.

```
boolean, getState()
```
Returns TRUE if the menu item is checked.

```
setState(boolean new_state)
```
Sets the state of the menu item.

The applet in Listing 17.39 shows how to use menus. It creates a new frame to support the menu bar because you can't put a menu bar in an applet itself. The two buttons in the main applet window enable you to open and close the frame. Figure 17.51 shows the applet interface. Menus are a good example of how different your interfaces can look on different platforms. Mac users expect menu bars to show up at the top of the screen as the focus changes between windows. As a result, the peer classes on the Mac put the menu bar at the top of the screen rather than inside the frame, as a UNIX or Windows user would expect. Although the functionality is the same as you would see on any other platform, the details are designed to make Mac users feel comfortable. This is one of the strong points of Java: users on any platform will see an interface that looks familiar. Unfortunately, it does mean that you, the programmer, will have to spend a little extra time thinking about the implications of these types of differences on your user interface.

FIGURE 17.51.

The menu bar.

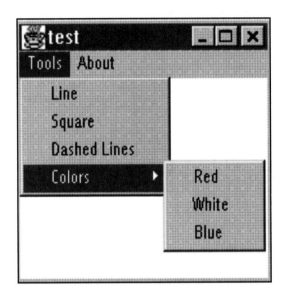

Listing 17.39. Using a menu bar.

```
import java.awt.*;
import java.applet.Applet;


public class menu_test extends Applet
{
    Frame f;
    Button b_open, b_close;
    boolean window_visible;

    public void init()
    {   Menu m_about, m_tools, m_sub;
        //these buttons will allow us to control the new window
        b_open = new Button("Open Window");
        b_close = new Button("Close Window");
        add(b_open);
        add(b_close);
```

```
        //make a new frame because the applet can't have a menu bar
         f = new Frame("test");
        //set the initial size of the frame
        f.resize(200,200);
        //make a new menu bar and attach it to the frame
        MenuBar mb = new MenuBar();
        f.setMenuBar(mb);
        //set up the various menu items
        m_about = new Menu("About");
        m_about.add(new MenuItem("Credits"));
        m_about.add(new MenuItem("Register"));
        m_about.add(new MenuItem("Help"));
        m_tools = new Menu("Tools");
        m_tools.add(new MenuItem("Line"));
        m_tools.add(new MenuItem("Square"));
        //add a checkbox menu item
        m_tools.add(new CheckboxMenuItem("Dashed Lines"));
        //create a hierarchical menu
        m_sub = new Menu("Colors");
        m_sub.add("Red");
        m_sub.add("White");
        m_sub.add("Blue");
        //Make the menu hierarchical by adding it as though it were a menu
        //item
        m_tools.add(m_sub);
        mb.setHelpMenu(m_about);
        mb.add(m_tools);
        mb.add(m_about);
        //show the new frame
        f.show();
        window_visible = true;
    }
    public boolean action(Event the_event, Object the_arg) {
        String item_name;
        //handle mouse clicks on the two buttons
        if(the_event.target instanceof Button) {
            item_name = (String)the_arg;
            if(item_name.equals("Open Window")) {
                if(!window_visible) {
                    f.show();
                    window_visible = true;
                }
            }
            if(item_name.equals("Close Window")) {
                if(window_visible) {
                    f.hide();
                    window_visible = false;
                }
            }
        }
        return true;
    }
}
```

Dialog

You can build your own dialog boxes using Frames, but the Dialog class enables you to create modal dialog boxes. A modal dialog box forces the user to deal with the dialog box before doing anything else. Although this generally isn't a good idea, certain types of actions, such as notifying a user of a problem, require user input before the program can do anything else.

Dialog boxes are containers, so you can add components to them, but their default Layout Manager is BorderLayout rather than FlowLayout. User interaction with dialog boxes can generate the WINDOW_DESTROY, WINDOW_ICONIFY, WINDOW_DEICONIFY, and WINDOW_MOVED events. As with other window-related classes, you should call the dispose method (inherited from Window) when the window is destroyed in order to free up window system resources.

The two dialog creator methods follow.

```
new Dialog(Frame a_parent, boolean modal_flag)
```
Creates a new dialog box that is modal if the second argument is TRUE.

```
new Dialog(Frame a_parent, String dialog_title, boolean modal_flag)
```
Functions like the preceding method, except that you can specify the name of the dialog box.

Unfortunately, Dialogs can be created only as children of Frames, as you can see from the arguments to the creator functions. This might make you think that you can't use Dialogs with your applets but, through the use of a minor subterfuge, you can. The secret, demonstrated in Listing 17.40, is to make a Frame but not show it. The applet extends the Dialog class and makes a simple Dialog that is shown in Figure 17.52.

FIGURE 17.52.
A dialog box in action.

Listing 17.40. Using a dialog.

```
import java.awt.*;
import java.applet.Applet;


public class dialogs extends Applet
{
```

```
        Frame a_window;
        user_dialog real_dialog;
        Button show_dialog;


        public void init()
        {
            //You need a Frame to make a dialog but you don't have to display it.
            a_window = new Frame("Testing Dialogs");
            //This is a non-modal dialog, that is the user can
            //switch between windows
            //while the dialog is active.  Change the false to true
            //to make it modal and force
            //the user to deal with and dismiss it before doing anything else.
            real_dialog = new user_dialog(a_window,"The Sky Is Falling!",false);
            show_dialog = new Button("Show Dialog");
            add(show_dialog);
        }
        public boolean action(Event the_event, Object the_arg) {
            //There's only one button so we just make sure that a button was clicked
            if(the_event.target instanceof Button) {
                real_dialog.show();
            }
            return true;
        }
}
class user_dialog extends Dialog {
    Button b_ok, b_cancel;

    user_dialog(Frame a_frame,String the_title, boolean modal) {
        super(a_frame,the_title,modal);
        FlowLayout fl;

        b_ok = new Button("Ok");
        fl = new FlowLayout();
        setLayout(fl);
        add(b_ok);
        //resize the dialog so the title, "The Sky Is Falling!"
        //shows. You should use
        //FontMetrics here to see how many pixels wide that phrase is on a given
        //platform
        resize(200,40);
    }

    public boolean action(Event the_event, Object the_arg) {
        if(the_event.target instanceof Button) {
            //Hide the dialog. If you're not going to use it again you should call
            //window.dispose to get rid of it. Hide just makes it invisible
            hide();
        }
        return true;
    }
}
```

FileDialog

This class enables you to access the user's native file opening and saving dialog boxes. It's a modal dialog box that you can create with the following two creator methods.

`new FileDialog(Frame a_parent, String title)`
Creates a file selection modal dialog box with the specified title.

`new FileDialog(Frame a_parent, String title, int mode_flag)`
Functions like the preceding method, except that you can specify, using the third parameter, whether this is a file selection or a file saving dialog box. The two constants you should use follow:

> `FileDialog.LOAD`: Open File dialog box
> `FileDialog.SAVE`: Save File dialog box

The general approach to using this class is to create the dialog box and then show it when you want the user to select or save a file. When the user finishes with the modal dialog box, you use the `getDirectory` and `getFile` methods to get a path to the file that's to be saved or loaded. The methods you'll find most useful for `FileDialog` follow.

`String, getDirectory()`
Returns the directory to the file the user has selected or the directory where the user wants to save a file. The string uses backslashes to separate directories and it doesn't end with a backslash. A file on disk Space inside folder Files, for example, would return `/Space/Files`.

`String, getFile()`
Returns the name of the file to be opened or the name the file is to be saved as.

`FilenameFilter, getFilenameFilter()`
Returns the `FilenameFilter`—an interface specification that enables you to filter which files appear in the dialog box—associated with the File dialog box.

`int, getMode()`
Returns the mode of the dialog box.

`setDirectory(String default_directory)`
Enables you to set the directory the user sees when the dialog box opens. Specify the directory with the same string format returned by the `getDirectory` method.

`setFile(String a_file)`

Sets the file in the dialog box.

`setFilenameFilter(FilenameFilter a_filter)`

Associates an instance of the `FilenameFilter` with the dialog box. The one method in the `FilenameFilter` class is called for every file, and only those that pass the test are displayed.

The applet in Listing 17.41 generates the two File dialog boxes shown in Figures 17.53 and 17.54, depending on the second parameter in the creation function.

Listing 17.41. Generating File dialog boxes.

```
import java.awt.*;
import java.applet.Applet;
import java.io.*;


public class file_dialog extends Applet
{
    Frame a_window;
    FileDialog real_dialog;
    Button show_dialog;


    public void init()
    {
        //You need a Frame to make a dialog but you don't have to display it.
        a_window = new Frame("Testing Dialogs");
        //This is a dialog that lets you save files. By changing
        //the last parameter to
        // FileDialog.LOAD you'll get a dialog that lets you open a file.
        real_dialog = new FileDialog(a_window,"Save File to:");
        show_dialog = new Button("Show File Dialog");
        add(show_dialog);
    }
    public boolean action(Event the_event, Object the_arg) {
        //There's only one button so we just make sure that a button was clicked
        if(the_event.target instanceof Button) {
            real_dialog.show();
            String a_file = real_dialog.getFile();
            String a_directory = real_dialog.getDirectory();
            System.out.println(a_directory + " " + a_file);
        }
        return true;
    }
}
```

FIGURE 17.53.

The File Open dialog box with the mode set to FileDialog.LOAD.

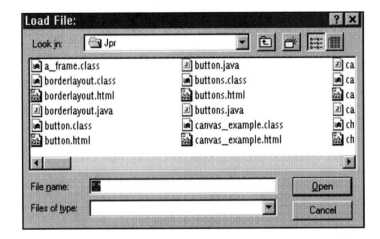

FIGURE 17.54.

The File Save dialog box with the mode set to FileDialog.SAVE.

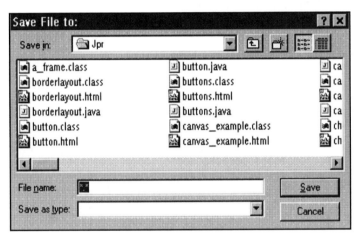

The FilenameFilter interface is very simple; it has only one method:

```
boolean, accept(File directory, String file_name)
```

This is called for each file. The input parameters are the directory the file is in and the filename. You can use this information to decide whether a file should be shown in the dialog box. If the method returns TRUE, the file is shown.

You can implement a FilenameFilter as shown in Listing 17.42.

Listing 17.42. Implementing a `FilenameFilter`.

```
public class my_filenameFilter implements FilenameFilter {

    my_filenameFilter() {
        ....
    }

    public boolean accept(File a_directory, String file_name) {

        //some code to decide if the file should be displayed
    }
}
```

`FilenameFilters` are useful in preventing a user from inadvertently picking the wrong file.

Working with Applications

Although all the examples in this chapter have been applets (a conscious choice because most of the current excitement about Java is related to its role in the WWW), you can use almost all these techniques in an application. Unless you're using applet-specific methods, you can replace `Applet` with `Panel`. So, instead of extending `Applet`, you extend `Panel`. You also can still extend the `Applet` class but put the `Applet` into a `Frame`.

> **NOTE**
>
> An example of an applet-specific method is `getImage`. In an application, you can use the `Toolkit`'s `getImage` method instead and everything else stays the same.

> **NOTE**
>
> Remember that `Applet` inherits from `Component`, so you can place an applet in a container—such as a frame—just as you would put a button in the frame.

The general approach is to add a main method to your code, create a `Frame`, add your class that extends `Applet` or `Panel` to the `Frame`, and then call the `init` and `startup` methods for the class that extends `Applet`. Make sure that the event handler for the `Frame` handles the `WINDOW_DESTROY` method properly.

Applet Methods of Interest

Most of what's covered in this chapter is independent of the `Applet` class's methods. The following are the methods that are of use when building the user interface.

`Image, getImage(URL a_url)`
Loads the GIF or JPEG image at the specified URL.

`Image, getImage(URL a_url, String relative_file_location)`
Enables you to specify a base URL, as you would get from `getDocumentBase()`, and an address relative to that address.

`showStatus(String a_message)`
Displays the specified message to the user. In the applet viewer, it's placed in the bottom edge of the applet window. The specific place where the display occurs is browser dependent.

Clearly, you can build pretty much any Java program that doesn't rely on these methods, so switching between applets and applications shouldn't be too difficult as far as your GUI is concerned.

Extending the AWT

You can add more elements to your interface toolbox in two ways: you can extend existing components yourself or you can use someone else's classes.

Extending Components (the Image Button)

One of the nice features of object-oriented programming is that you can extend existing classes and add new functionality with minimal effort. The applet in Listing 17.43 contains the code for a class called `image_button_component`, which behaves like a button but has an image for its interface rather than the regular button picture.

Listing 17.43. The `image_button_component` class.

```
import java.applet.Applet;
import java.awt.*;


public class image_button extends Applet {
    MediaTracker the_tracker;
    image_button_component  the_button;
```

```
    public void init()
    {
        Image the_picture, inverse_picture;
        //load the two images, one for the regular
        //button image and one for when the
        //mouse button is held down on the button
        the_tracker = new MediaTracker(this);
        the_picture = getImage(getDocumentBase(),"test.gif");
        the_tracker.addImage(the_picture,0);
        inverse_picture = getImage(getDocumentBase(),"invert.gif");
        the_tracker.addImage(inverse_picture,0);
        //Wait until both images are fully loaded.
        try {
            the_tracker.waitForID(0);
        } catch(InterruptedException e) {}
        the_button = new image_button_component(the_picture,inverse_picture);
        add(the_button);
    }
    public boolean mouseDown(Event e, int x, int y) {
        if (e.target instanceof image_button_component) {
            System.out.println("image_button_component clicked");
        }
        return true;
    }
}

class image_button_component extends Canvas {
    Image my_image, inverse_image;
    boolean mousedown_flag;

    public image_button_component(Image an_image,Image i_image) {
        my_image = an_image;
        inverse_image = i_image;
        //the button starts unclicked
        mousedown_flag = false;
        //make sure the canvas image is drawn
        repaint();

    }
    //override these methods to tell the layout manager
    //the size of the button which is defined by the
    //size of the image. This assumes that the two images are the same size.
    public Dimension minimumSize() {
        return new Dimension(my_image.getWidth(null),my_image.getHeight(null));
    }
    public Dimension preferredSize() {
        return new Dimension(my_image.getWidth(null),my_image.getHeight(null));
    }
    //make sure the button image is changed when the mouse is clicked
    public boolean mouseDown(Event e, int x, int y) {
        mousedown_flag = true;
        repaint();
        //return false so the event is passed on so the mouseDown
        //method in the applet can use it
        return false;
    }
```

continues

Listing 17.43. continued

```
public boolean mouseUp(Event e, int x, int y) {
    mousedown_flag = false;
    repaint();
    //return true because the applet doesn't need this
    //event but you might want to
    //return false to make this more button like
    return true;
}
public void paint(Graphics g) {
    //determine which image to draw based on the mouse state
    if (!mousedown_flag) {
        g.drawImage(my_image,0,0,null);
    } else {
        g.drawImage(inverse_image,0,0,null);
    }
}
}
```

The applet loads in two images—one for the regular button and one for when it's clicked—and then creates a new instance of the image_button_component class. The button is shown in Figure 17.55, whereas Figure 17.56 shows the button after being clicked with the mouse. Although this class doesn't do much, you can put in whatever behavior you want just as though it were a standard button.

FIGURE 17.55.

An image button.

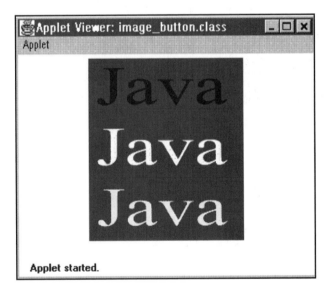

FIGURE 17.56.

The same image button after being clicked with the mouse.

One technique to note is that you can assign multiple images to the same `MediaTracker` ID and then just wait for that one ID to finish loading instead of looking for multiple IDs to load. Of course, if speed is a concern, you might want to load the basic image first, draw the interface, and then hope that the user doesn't click the button until the second image is loaded. You can use an even better solution if you're working with a `Frame`. You can load the first image, draw the interface, and then set the cursor to `WAIT_CURSOR` until the second image is loaded. Users will be able to start familiarizing themselves with the interface while the second image is loading.

Using Other People's Classes

Although you can improve the AWT by extending its classes, you're probably better off buying that sort of thing from someone else if the functionality you require is very complex. The following list is a very limited one of various commercial Java classes that bring more sophisticated interfaces to your toolbox. Inclusion in this list shouldn't be viewed as an endorsement. Java has too many bugs, and these tools run afoul of them, for anyone to make definitive statements about the quality of any given package. In addition, things are changing too rapidly to give complex software libraries like these an in-depth evaluation and still get this book out before 1998. View this list as a set of starting points for your search for work-saving classes to jazz up your Java program's interface.

> **NOTE**
>
> One thing to keep in mind when looking at these classes is that, unlike the AWT, they have to be downloaded from the server if you're using them in an applet. Because some of these files are large, it could be a problem if the people who will be viewing your applet have slow connections.

> **NOTE**
>
> In general, all the components have many more methods and adjustable parameters than I mention here. If you see a component that seems in the ballpark for meeting your requirements, check with the vendor for more details.

Microline Component Toolkit

(`info@mlsoft.com` `http://www.mlsoft.com/mct/mct.html`)

This is a commercial toolkit that comes with a nice printed manual to help you understand how to use it. Table 17.2 lists the primary components.

Table 17.2. Microline Component Toolkit components.

Component	Description
Grid	A two-dimensional scrolling array of cells, much like a standard spreadsheet. This type of interface component also can be called a *table*.
Misc	Includes methods to draw shadows and word-wrap text.
Progress	A customizable progress bar.
TabPanel	A tabbed panel that enables you to switch between window contents by clicking on tabs at the top of the window.
Tree	A hierarchical view where you can show and hide the items inside containers. If you want to show a file structure, for example, the folders would have arrows next to them. After you click on an arrow, the items in the folder are shown.

Jlibraries

(`http://www.roguewave.com/products/jlibraries/jlibraries.html`)

This is a set of three libraries: one with tools, one with financial functions, and one with widgets. Table 17.3 lists the main widgets.

Table 17.3. Jlibraries main widgets.

Widget	Description
Grid control	A spreadsheet-like widget.
Group box	Enables you to group related sets of controls.
Image button	Enables you to create an image button.
Tabbed dialog box	A dialog box with tabs on the top that enable you to switch between screens.
Toolbar	A toolbar with icons.

Connect! Widgets Pro
(`http://www.connectcorp.com/Index.html`)

This is a very extensive kit of useful widgets. Although it's expensive, if you use many of the widgets you'll save a lot of time. The lack of printed documentation is a drawback but not too horrible. Table 17.4 lists these widgets.

Table 17.4. Connect! Widgets Pro widgets.

Widget	Description
3D label	Same functionality as label, but with a 3D look and text coloring.
Calendar	Shows a calendar for a specified date.
Combo box	An editable, searchable text field with a drop-down listbox. There are some platform dependencies in this one.
Direction button	Makes a button with an arrow pointing in the specified direction.
Editable, searchable choice listbox	An enhanced choice control.
Enhanced text fields	Components that restrict the type of data that can be entered.
Grid control	An option in the multicolumn listbox.
Group box panel	A panel with a label and a visual boundary.
Image buttons	Enables you to associate different images with different button states—Normal, Pressed, and Disabled—and the position of the image with respect to the button text.
Image canvas	A picture button type of widget.

continues

Table 17.4. continued

Widget	*Description*
Image listbox	A standard listbox, but you can add images to each of the entries.
Key Press Manager panel	Extends panel and supports tabbing between components and some key accelerators.
Multicolumn listbox	A listbox with multiple columns.
Performance Animator	A class that makes an animation from a single image file that saves download time, hence improving performance.
Pop-up context menu	A better version than the one in the AWT.
Progress gauge	A 3D color progress indicator.
Scrolling panel	A panel with built-in scrolling.
Spin control	Spin control and list spin control widgets.
Splitter panel	A panel that is split into subareas, each of which can be a splitter panel. Nice for rectangular-style layouts.
Tab panel	A standard tab dialog box widget.

jKit/Grid
(`http://www.objectshare.com/`)
This is a table component.

JavaGRID
(`http://www.vincent.se/Products/JavaGRID/JavaGRID.html`)
This is another table component.

In addition to widget and utility collections such as these, a number of data display collections exist that have various charting types, such as bar and pie charts.

Summary

In this chapter, you learned how to build the user interface for Java applets and applications using the AWT. You saw how to draw pictures using the `Graphics` class and how to use the various GUI elements, such as buttons and menus, to give your project an easy-to-use interface that uses the graphical look and feel users are used to. Finally, you saw how to extend that interface and what sorts of freeware, shareware, and commercial tools are available to enhance the basic AWT repertoire of interface widgets.

18

Writing Secure Programs

by Tom Trinko

As the first new language of the network age, Java's fundamental architecture is structured to confront a wide spectrum of security issues that previously have been addressed in a stop-gap, ad-hoc manner. Java was designed from the ground up to be able to have a fighting chance at giving users sufficient confidence in a program so that they would run it—even if it appeared on I.M. Rotten's home page—because they know a Java program can't cause them any major problems. As you write Java programs, you'll find that knowing how Java deals with security will help you save time and effort as well as help you avoid trying to do things that just aren't allowed, such as having an applet write a file to a random directory on the user's computer.

A Bit of History

In ancient times, the 1970s, when programmers talked about security, it was job security through not commenting their code. The introduction of mass market computers brought about concerns of software piracy, so key disks and copy-protected disks became the weapons that programmers used to enforce security. The network revolution began with BBSs and moved on to LANs, online services such as AOL, and has so far culminated in the Internet and the World Wide Web. This progress has forced programmers to address a new spectrum of issues ranging from viruses (should my program detect when it's been infected?) to protecting users' data (how does my program protect the users' passwords?).

The expansion of the computer-using public is also a key factor in current security concerns. In the past, people using computers were usually experts who understood the details of their systems and could rapidly respond to problems. Now computers are in the hands of real people who just want to balance a checkbook or finish the boss's report. Most computer users lack the expertise to rapidly respond to security breaches. Additionally, the natural problems of complex systems tend to be blamed on viruses by a public who knows as much about how computers work as they know about the details of smog tests.

NOTE

My first contact with computer security put me on the wrong side of the law, or at least my high school administration. The high school computer used punched cards to input programs. Every deck had to be prefaced by a card you got out of a special box which determined your job's priority. Those cards didn't have anything printed on them, so I used the keypunch to print out what they "said." I discovered that they were just the numbers from 1 to 100.

I then made a new card with the number 2—I wasn't selfish enough to want the highest priority—and used it on all my jobs for the Fortran class I was taking. Well, my turn-around time sure improved. Unfortunately, one day a school official came storming into the computer classroom asking who Trinko was, a situation which I—a lowly student—didn't find to be very much fun. It turns out that the school payroll program had the number 2 card reserved. When they loaded it the computer, not the most brilliant of machines, shuffled my cards with the payroll cards. Fortunately, they were able to rerun the payroll job and no real damage was done.

Well, I learned my lesson. The point is that no security system is ever perfect, but it's very important to strive for perfection, because poor security can cause real problems. If those teachers weren't paid that week—which didn't happen—my exploitation of the security hole could have had significant impact on real people.

Java Security Issues

If Java succeeds as the Internet language, it will have to provide a workable and effective security system. The reason is simple: How many people would risk running an applet from some unknown Web site if the applet could destroy their hard disk, make it look as though they'd sent threatening mail to the President, or steal their passwords? Even if individuals would take this chance, companies would not, because a poorly secured Java applet could destroy the effectiveness of their own system's firewalls.

> **NOTE**
>
> A *firewall* is a computer that controls the flow of information between the Internet and a company's internal networks. Its mission is to let the folks on the inside access any information they need on the Internet while preventing folks on the outside from seeing what's on the company's computers. As a result, machines on the Internet can't establish connections with machines behind the firewall, but machines behind the firewall can establish connections with machines outside the firewall. Remote users can get behind the firewall if they have the appropriate security software/keycards—a daunting task even if you're authorized.

Figure 18.1 shows how a Java applet could circumvent a firewall. Local machine A runs a hostile applet that it downloads from the evil Hostile Applet Server, which resides somewhere out on the Internet—perhaps in Chernobyl. That applet opens a network connection to machine C, which contains valuable corporate secrets—like the toupée vendor the boss uses—and steals all of the data, which it sends back to the Hostile Applet Server. While it's doing all this, the poor idiot working on machine A thinks he's just playing some game.

Essentially, the firewall couldn't distinguish a Java applet running on an internal machine from a user using a browser on the same machine. As a result, the firewall wouldn't stop the applet from reading files from a company's machine and sending them to some other company's machine—not too good from a security perspective. Even worse scenarios arise if a Java applet can write files on the client system. The potential for Trojan horses and viruses would be unlimited. Clearly, people wouldn't be willing to wander around the World Wide Web as they currently do if any site could inflict this type of damage.

FIGURE 18.1.

Defeating a firewall.

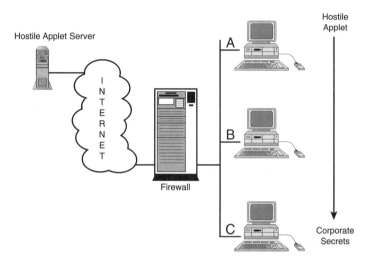

The bottom line is that, if Java weren't designed to provide security, the probability of anyone using it on the WWW would be fairly small.

> **NOTE**
>
> A *Trojan horse* is an application that pretends to be useful but actually performs some bad actions on a computer. An example might be a program that is supposed to be a freeware word processor but which actually erases your hard disk. Trojan horses are different from the products of software companies in that they are designed to cause problems.

The Differing Security Aspects of Applets and Applications

If you download applications from the Internet, you probably check them with a virus scanner before running them. In general, using applications you get from an unknown source is buyer-beware activity where you know there are risks involved. Most of the time things are fine. I've found only two infected files in all my years surfing BBSs and the Net with my trustworthy Mac—but Mac viruses are much less common than IBM ones. However, if a problem occurs and you don't fix it quickly, you can lose lots of time and money. Because a Java application is no different than any other application, it has no more purely security-related constraints than any other language. *Applets*, though, are different.

Unlike the people who frequently download applications, most folks who encounter Java applets are real people, not computer experts. When you surf to a given URL, the applets on any of its pages automatically load and execute—unless you've set your browser to keep from running applets. You don't have a chance to run a virus checker or to control the execution environment of the applet. As a result, if you didn't know that Java applets couldn't hurt you, you'd tend to set your browser to avoid running Java. But if most browsers are set not to execute Java applets, a significant part of the appeal of Java goes away. That's why there are extensive security features in Java applets that aren't there for Java applications. The next section walks you through them.

> **NOTE**
>
> When you use Java to write an application, security restrictions are pretty much the same as writing an application in C or SmallTalk.

Applets

The first thing to realize is that although Java works on every platform, it's not the same—from a security perspective—in every browser. Netscape's Navigator has much more restrictive security rules than does Sun's HotJava browser. That's probably because UNIX users—HotJava's audience—are generally more familiar with security issues and computers in general than typical Mac or PC users. As a result, the current versions of Navigator hardwire more security limitations than are required by the Java security baseline. Because the various security restrictions are rapidly changing, the following list covers the various types of restrictions your customers are likely to encounter when trying to run Java applets:

- **Cannot read or write files on the local machine.** This can be loosened by allowing the user to define a specific directory on his own machine which contains files that can be written or read. The objective is to prevent trashing of your files or the installation of a virus. Netscape currently (version 3.0) does not allow an applet to read or write any files on the local machine. You *can* use the Java/JavaScript link to write data to a cookie, though.
- **Cannot delete user files.**
- **Cannot rename files.**

■ **Cannot create new directories.**

■ **Cannot list the contents of directories**. You wouldn't want applets to be able to snoop through your files and report back.

■ **Cannot get file information** (such as modification date, size, or type).

■ **Cannot make a network connection** to any machine other than the one that originated the applet.

■ **Cannot run any programs on the user's machine.**

■ **Cannot work with any `ThreadGroup` other than its own.**

■ **Cannot load native methods**. Clearly, if an applet could load native C++ code, all security would go out the door.

■ **Cannot avoid warning banners on any windows your applet creates.** This prevents an applet window from pretending to be something else, such your AOL signon dialog asking for your password. The banner is automatically added so you don't have to worry about it.

■ **Cannot create its own `SecurityManager` subclass.**

Unless you're doing something fairly unusual, all of the security restrictions boil down to these two rules:

■ **You can't work with files on the user's machine unless he lets you.**

■ **You can't connect to anything on the network other than the machine that originated your applet.**

These restrictions are designed to ensure that an applet, no matter how malicious its developer is, can't cause you significant difficulty. The security rules prevent an applet from reading or modifying your file system and making network connections to sites other than the one that the applet came from. This prevents the sending of forged e-mail or the transfer of data from machines behind firewalls. Of course, if you use a browser that gives you more security control, you can overcome some of these protections. For example, if your browser lets you authorize writing of files and you accidentally include your root directory as an allowed place to write, an applet could then write files anywhere with potentially significant results.

One last thing is that, even with all of these restrictions, one class of attacks is still possible. Either through malicious intent or incompetent programming, an applet can execute what is called a *denial of services* attack on the user's computer. Such an attack consists of the applet using large amounts of system resources, thereby preventing you from doing anything else. This could be accomplished by opening several windows or initiating tons of threads. Although this is annoying, the worst it can do is force you to reboot your computer.

Of course, all of this assumes that Java is properly implemented. There have already been a number of bugs found in versions of Java prior to 1.0.2. Until Java settles down and the implementations are found to be bug-free on all platforms, there will always be a risk of security breaches due to implementation errors in Java itself. But since Java is designed to be secure, it's reasonable to expect that once the bugs are ironed out, Java will be very secure.

The Java Security Model

Now that you know what restrictions the Java security system enforces, you'd probably like to know how it does this. The answer is shown in Figure 18.2, which shows the four layers in the Java security model. Each layer provides a unique barrier to the construction and execution of applets with evil intent.

FIGURE 18.2.
The four-layered Java security model.

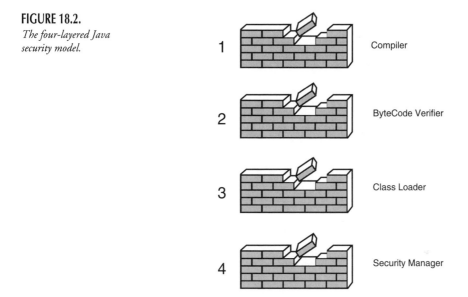

1 — Compiler

2 — ByteCode Verifier

3 — Class Loader

4 — Security Manager

Now let's examine each of the layers in Figure 18.2 in detail.

The Compiler and the Java Language

One of the first barriers to rogue applets is the design of the Java language. Because Java doesn't have pointers and is strongly *type checked*—so much so that you can't cast an integer to an object reference—many of the traditional security holes found in C and C++ are plugged. For example, because there are no pointers, Java applets can't invade the memory space of another program. These architectural features are actually beneficial in that they eliminate the most common coding errors that cause problems in C++. In fact, the lack of pointers and the automatic garbage collection will probably lead to a factor of two or more reduction in software development costs for any application that doesn't require low-level control of the machine—such as a device driver—because of the time saved tracking down pointer-related errors in the code.

The compiler plays a role in this by enforcing the rules and prohibiting various types of potentially dangerous casts.

The ByteCode Verifier

This is the heart of the Java security scheme. If someone figures out how to get past this, real trouble can arise. The basic job of this layer is to verify every program before it's run. This protects you against someone hand-coding a class file that violates the Java security rules or developing a compiler that doesn't enforce the Java security rules.

The ByteCode verifier is a very powerful guard which first verifies that the file is a properly structured Java class file. The next step is complex and involves proving certain theorems about the class. The process guarantees the following about the applet:

- It doesn't cause stack over- or underflows.
- Operators' arguments are of the proper type: An integer isn't being used with an operator that requires an object reference for example.
- Objects are only accessed according to the approved rules; for example, this refers to accessing private and protected methods.
- No casts that violate Java security rules are attempted.

This approach has a significant side benefit of making the interpreter run faster, because it doesn't have to check for any of these problems.

The `ClassLoader`

After a class has been verified, it can be loaded into the Java system. In order to prevent applets from replacing security-related classes and thereby breaking the security system, Java divides the namespace into several levels. Currently there are three levels: the local file system—most protected; the local network—middle protection; and the Internet—least protected. The class loader won't replace a class in a more protected level with a class from a less protected level. The really key classes, such as those that control I/O, are in the local level so no applet that is coming from another machine can override and replace them.

Additionally, the class loader prevents classes in one layer from accessing any non-public methods in classes in other layers. In a similar fashion, when multiple applets are loaded, they're placed in separate namespaces so that they can't interact unless they're designed to do so.

The `SecurityManager`

This is actually an abstract class that is designed to allow you to tailor the security policies that a browser or application will enforce. Applets can't modify the `SecurityManager`, but applications can extend it and define their own security policies. Your security policies, as determined by your `SecurityManager`, determine what types of dangerous operations an applet can perform. For example, the Netscape `SecurityManager` prohibits all file reading/writing, but other browser `SecurityManagers` could allow different levels of file access depending upon the source of the applet.

These four levels working together provide a nearly airtight defense against malicious applets. There are still some security problems (researchers have been finding a new problem every few months), but they are fairly difficult to exploit. In fact, the real problem is that, because the security system limits file and network I/O (a key reason for the wonderfulness of networks and computers), there are too many powerful and useful applications that can't be written.

The Future

Netscape and Sun have recognized the fact that the security model has to be extended so that users have more flexibility in controlling the privileges given to applets. After all, if you'll be able to download your next word processor as a LiveObject OpenDoc component over the Net, it's silly to restrict its access anymore than you would restrict Microsoft Word—although, given the behavior of Word 6, perhaps limiting its access wouldn't be a bad idea. According to the latest news from Netscape, the solution they're exploring is a way to certify applets via encrypted tags so that you would know that the applet is in fact one provided by someone you'd trust. Netscape has said version 4.0 will allow the browser to assign different privilege levels depending upon the level of trust an applet can have.

It's hard to know what the actual security system of the future will be; things are changing too quickly. For example, in the last beta of Netscape 3.0, a change in the security rules broke a number of applets that used applet-to-applet communications. One thing is sure: Maintaining a secure Java environment will be a critical objective that all players—Sun and the browser vendors—will assiduously pursue.

> **NOTE**
>
> As of this writing the Sun Security FAQ for Java can be found at `http://www.javasoft.com/sfaq/index.html`.

Summary

You've seen how Java is designed to protect the applet user from malicious programs. The four-tiered security system is designed to enable browsers to control the level of access to dangerous operations, while preventing problems. The future seems to hold a scheme for making trusted applets whose source is unimpeachably known. Those applets can be safely assigned more extensive privileges.

19

Extending Your Programs with Native Methods

By Michael T. Nygard

The Java Virtual Machine provides sophisticated capabilities for creating user interfaces, performing Internet and WWW accesses, and for general-purpose programming. Unfortunately, the Java Virtual Machine has some (deliberate) limitations. First and foremost, the JVM only supports functionality that applies to many platforms. That means that unaided Java applications cannot take full advantage of their host platforms. The Java development team also introduced some artificial limitations in the interest of security. For the most part, these restrictions are not onerous. In fact, users can have a relatively high degree of confidence that Java applications and applets are not malicious. Without such assurances, the World Wide Web community would surely have revolted at the notion of self-downloading, self-executing code in a Web page. Just imagine the prospect of a cross-platform virus that attaches itself to Web pages! In some cases, however, these benevolent restrictions prevent applications from making the most of Java.

Consider these situations:

■ You have a large, specialized library of C or C++ functions that you would like to use from Java applications.

■ Your application must use a non-standard (that is, non-JDBC) database access library.

■ An existing application that communicates through an operating system–specific channel (such as Windows DDE or UNIX shared memory) must be integrated with a new Java application.

■ Your application needs to automatically determine operating system–specific information, such as the user's Netware ID.

Native methods can solve all of these problems. A Java class can declare a native method to indicate that the actual code for the method is provided in another language. (At present, native methods must be implemented in C. Support for other languages is in the works.) That code is compiled to the native machine code of your particular platform, hence the name "native method." Before it can be used by the Java Virtual Machine, the compiled code must be linked into a dynamically loadable library suitable for use on the target platform. Finally, the DLL or .so file must be installed on the target computer.

There are two parts to every native method, the Java declaration and the "native" implementation. As you do with all other methods, you declare a native method inside a Java class. Native methods can be final, static, or synchronized. They can throw exceptions and be inherited (unless they are final, of course). Because the implementation is compiled for the target platform, it can take full advantage of the capabilities of that platform. Native methods provide a powerful means of extending the Java Virtual Machine.

You have probably guessed by now that native methods are not cross-platform by nature. Your native methods will be as portable as the C code in which you write them and the APIs they call. Because the most common reason for creating native methods is to use a platform-specific API, native methods tend not to be very portable.

Because the dynamically loadable library must be installed on the target machine *prior* to execution of the Java classes that need it, you will have to face all the issues of software distribution and configuration management. On the other hand, native methods can only be called from Java applications, which have to be distributed and installed themselves. So, the added difficulty of distributing multiple native-method libraries should not pose too great a hurdle.

WHEN NOT TO USE NATIVE METHODS

Here are some questions to ask yourself before you decide to use native methods:

■ Are you writing a full-blown application instead of an applet? Some Web browsers will prevent applets from calling native methods not distributed in the base classes. In some cases, the browser allows the user to enable native method calls from applets. Bear in mind that many users will be reluctant to deliberately short-circuit security features.

■ Can you manage the platform-specific code? Because the native methods are compiled for each platform, you will encounter significant configuration management hassles. More than likely, you will also have to cope with multiple versions of the native methods, one for each platform. This is particularly true when you are dealing with operating system features. (I know, C is supposed to be a portable language, but isn't that why you are using Java?)

■ Is it acceptable to mix object-oriented and procedural code? Keep in mind that the native methods will be written in an object-oriented style of C. You will be working with regular C structures instead of classes. These structures do not provide full information hiding. (No protected or private specifiers.) Ultimately, you will be working in C, with no encapsulation, no inheritance, and no polymorphism. It will require great discipline to maintain good object semantics in C. Most native methods are self-contained, so these should not be serious limitations, but you should be aware of the difficulties ahead.

If you answered "yes" to all of these questions, then feel free to proceed. If any of the questions trouble you, then you should probably think twice before implementing that class with native methods. The Java packages contain hundreds of classes, and the method you are looking for just might be there already, buried within an obscure class.

An Overview of Native Methods

All functions in Java are object methods. Even the declaration part of your native methods must be contained within a class. Therefore, the first step to creating native methods is to define one or more class interfaces. If you are dealing with a large number of functions, it will be useful for you to partition them into logical, coherent groups. These should form the nucleus of each class. There are basically two approaches for defining a class interface that will wrap the native methods. Suppose you are dealing with native methods to provide file access. Assume that your target platform's standard runtime library supports multithreading. If it does not, you will have to serialize access to all RTL functions.

One approach we could take is to create a `File` class that contains a mixture of native and Java methods that implement an abstraction of a disk file. (This is the approach used most often by the Java development team.) As an alternative design, we could create two classes: a `File` class that presents an abstract view of files, and a `FileImp` class that contains all of the native methods relevant to files. The `File` class would then contain a reference to a single global instance of `FileImp`. See Figure 19.1.

FIGURE 19.1.

Encapsulating a native interface.

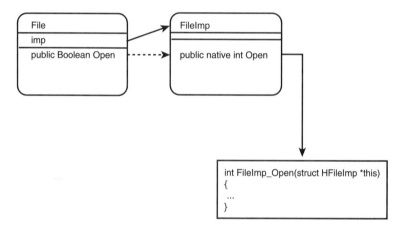

Ultimately, both techniques result in a `File` class that presents a clean abstraction of a file. The first approach (the single-class approach) has a significant drawback in terms of maintainability, however. Whenever the `File` class changes, the dynamically loadable library must be rebuilt. In fact, you would need to regenerate the C header and C stub files and recompile the library for every interface change in `File`.

With the second approach (the split interface), `FileImp` is insulated from changes to `File`. Likewise, changes to `FileImp` do not affect `File`. The methods of `FileImp` do not need to be a direct mapping from the target API. You can give them abstract names and easily define an interface, which will rarely (if ever) need to change. For example, the POSIX API defines two sets of file-manipulation functions. Roughly, the sets correspond to those which use handles returned by `open`, and those which use a structure pointer returned by `fopen`. The Win32 API defines a group of file-manipulation functions that use a `Handle` returned by `CreateFile`. Your `FileImp` class would define a single method called `Open` as illustrated by Listing 19.1. Now any client of `File` can call `Open` without regard to the underlying system-level API.

Listing 19.1. Definition of the native `Open` method.

```
class FileImp {
   ...
   public native boolean Open(String Pathname);
   ...
}
```

After you have designed your class interfaces, you will need to create the Java classes. These will be identical to any other Java class, except for the use of the keyword `native`. `Native` signals to javac that this method body will be provided by a library loaded at runtime. Therefore, you do not provide a method body for a native method. The method declaration looks the same as if you were declaring an abstract method. This is no coincidence. In both cases, you are telling javac that you want to defer the definition of this method until later. With an abstract method, you are saying that "later" means a subclass. With a native method, "later" means runtime loadable C code.

WHEN AND WHERE CAN I USE "native"?

You can put "native" on almost any method declaration. How does javac interpret an abstract, native method? Not very well. You can provide a method body for an abstract native method in C, but it will never be called. A static native method behaves just as you would expect. Its semantics are the same as they would be in a static method defined in Java. A static native method is always passed a NULL for its `this` argument.

Native methods that are overridden in a subclass work normally. In fact, you can mix native and Java methods arbitrarily when subclassing.

After creating and compiling your Java classes, you will use javah to create two C files: a header file and a stub file. (See Chapter 14, "Using javah" for usage information for javah.) The header file contains a structure definition and function declarations (prototypes) for the native methods. The stub file contains some "glue" code, which you should never need to change. Because both files created by javah are generated automatically, you should never change either of them. javah maps the instance variables and methods of the class directly into the C files. So, if you ever change the Java class, you must regenerate the C files. If you do not, strange and unpredictable behavior will result. For example, javah created the header in Listing 19.3 from the class in Listing 19.2.

Listing 19.2. This is the original `PortfolioEntry` class.

```
class PortfolioEntry {
    String  TickerSymbol;
    float   LastQuote;
    float   BoughtAtPrice;
    float   LastDividends;
    float   LastEPS;
}
```

Listing 19.3. The structure definition javah created from `PortfolioEntry`.

```
typedef struct ClassPortfolioEntry {
    struct Hjava_lang_String *TickerSymbol;
    float LastQuote;
    float BoughtAtPrice;
    float LastDividends;
    float LastEPS;
} ClassPortfolioEntry;
```

Now suppose that you add a new integer member, `NumberOfShares`, to the Java class, right after the `TickerSymbol`. If you do not recreate the header file, your C code will be using the old structure layout. Therefore, your C code would access every member from `LastQuote`. Your C code would use the offset for `NumberOfShares` (an integer) as if it were `LastQuote` (a `float`)! This mismatch can cause some of the most irreproducible and hard-to-find bugs. A similar problem can arise with the methods. In that case, you are even more likely to have problems, because any change in a method's signature means that you have to regenerate the stub and header files.

One good way to avoid this problem is to make sure that you rarely need to change your classes after you write them. Good design will help there, but changes are inevitable. Creating a makefile is the best way to ensure that you always use the most up-to-date header and stub files. Some version of "make" is available for every platform supported by the JDK. Later in this chapter, you will find sample makefiles for Java classes with native methods.

Javah creates two files for you, but it leaves the most important file up to you. Along with the header and stub files, you will need to write an implementation file. The implementation file must contain the definitions of the functions that the header file declares. All of the really interesting things happen in the implementation file. Figure 19.2 depicts the relationships among the four files—the Java source, the C header, the C stubs, and the C implementation files.

At this point, a simple example will illustrate the interaction between the Java class and the three C files.

FIGURE 19.2.

The relationship between the Java class file and the three C files.

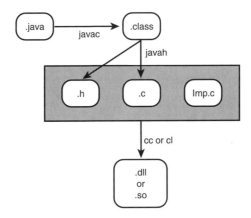

Who Am I? A Java Class to Identify the User

To demonstrate the entire process, from the Java class all the way to the implementation file, we will develop a class that can return the current user's name as a string. This example will use Windows NT native methods.

> **NOTE**
>
> There is already a mechanism in Java to do this. (See the documentation for the `java.lang.System` class.) Normally, you should not create a native method to accomplish something already available in the base packages. Because this is a simple demonstration, we will conveniently disregard the `System.getProperty` method.

The Class Definition

What do we really want to know? For now, we just want to know the user's login name. Various platforms have different API calls to get this information. Good design dictates that we should have a method name that is descriptive of *what* we want to know, not *how* we learn it. So, let's just call this method `Username`. It will return a Java string.

Remember that there are no global functions in Java. Even though we really only need one function, we have to put it in a class. At first, this might seem like a lot of trouble. After all, who wants to define a complete class just to get one method? But think about the future. Will this class always have just one method? Odds are that, like everything else, the requirements for this class will evolve over time. Perhaps there are other details about users that would be of interest to your application (or even a future application). The extra few minutes spent here in creating a class give you a framework in which to build additional functionality later.

Listing 19.4 shows the Java source for the UserInformation class.

Listing 19.4. The Java class definition of UserInformation.

```
1:  class UserInformation {
2:      static {
3:          System.loadLibrary("UserInformation");
4:      }
5:      public native String Username();
6:  }
```

Here is a line-by-line description of the code:

> **Line 1:** This line defines the class UserInformation. There is nothing fancy about this class; it inherits directly from java.lang.Object. Although this class does not show it, it is usually a good idea to make native methods—sometimes entire classes—"final." Otherwise, anyone can inherit from your native methods and possibly subvert their behavior.

> **Line 2:** This line defines a static block of code. Static blocks are executed when the *class itself* is loaded. You can think of a static block as a constructor for the class as a whole.

> **Line 3:** When this class is loaded, direct the runtime system to load the dynamically loadable library UserInformation. Exactly how the library is located and loaded varies by target platform. See the appropriate "Configuring Your Environment" section for your platform later in this chapter.

> **Line 5:** This line defines the method Username as a native method that returns a Java String object.

Now, compile this class using javac. (For details on javac usage, see Chapter 9, "javac: The Java Compiler.")

```
> javac UserInformation.java
```

This will produce the usual class file UserInformation.class. The next step is to create the header and stub files using javah. (For details on javah usage, see Chapter 14.)

```
> javah UserInformation
> javah -stubs UserInformation
```

This will produce two files, UserInformation.h and UserInformation.c. These are the header and stub files. You can disregard UserInformation.c (until it is time to compile, of course.) Listing 19.5 contains the header file UserInformation.h as created by javah. Your output file may vary in some details, depending on your platform and version of the JDK.

Listing 19.5. The header file `UserInformation.h` created from the `UserInformation.class` class file.

```
0    /* DO NOT EDIT THIS FILE - it is machine generated */
1    #include <native.h>
2    /* Header for class UserInformation */
3
4    #ifndef _Included_UserInformation
5    #define _Included_UserInformation
6
7    typedef struct ClassUserInformation {
8         char PAD;   /* ANSI C requires structures to have at least one member */
9    } ClassUserInformation;
10   HandleTo(UserInformation);
11
12   #ifdef __cplusplus
13   extern "C" {
14   #endif
15   struct Hjava_lang_String;
16   extern struct Hjava_lang_String
        *UserInformation_Username(struct HUserInformation *);
17   #ifdef __cplusplus
18   }
19   #endif
20   #endif
```

Notice the structure definition on lines 7 through 9. Because we did not define any members of the Java class, javah created this dummy structure. This will keep C compilers happy, but you should not attempt to use PAD to store information. The Java specification makes no guarantees about the contents of PAD. For our purposes, the only line of real interest is line 16, where the declaration for Username appears. This is the function that our implementation file must define. Notice that instead of taking a pointer to a ClassUserInformation structure, the C function gets a pointer to an HUserInformation structure. See the sidebar "Where Did HUserInformation Come From?" for details on this structure.

WHERE DID HUserInformation COME FROM?

The structure HUserInformation, which is passed to each of the C functions, is declared as a result of the HandleTo() macro, which is defined in \java\include\oobj.h as this:

```
#define HandleTo(T) typedef struct H##T { Class##T *obj; \
                    struct methodtable *methods;} H##T
```

So, HandleTo(UserInformation); expands to

```
typedef struct HUserInformation {
   ClassUserInformation *obj;
   struct methodtable *methods;
} HUserInformation;
```

This structure provides the bookkeeping that will allow C functions to behave like class methods. To access an instance variable from your native method, follow the obj pointer to the instance variable structure declared by the header file. For example, if the Java class `UserInformation` had a member variable `UserID`, its native methods could reference that member as `hUserInformation->obj->UserID`.

The `methods` pointer also allows your native method to get information about, and even invoke, the other methods of your class.

This structure is intended to be opaque to native methods. Because it may change in the future, the include file `interpreter.h` provides macros to hide the details of `HUserInformation`. In your native methods, you would use `unhand(hUserInformation)` to get access to the `ClassUserInformation` pointer. By using the macros, you insulate your code from future changes to Java internals. See "Using Java Objects from Native Methods" later in this chapter for details.

Finally, the time has come to write the implementation file. By convention, the implementation filename ends in "Imp". For `UserInformation`, our implementation file is named `UserInformationImp.c`. Listing 19.6 shows the implementation file for `UserInformation`, followed by a line-by-line description of the code. (We will not explore the target platform's API functions. After all, this is a book about Java, not C.)

Listing 19.6. The implementation file `UserInformationImp.c`.

```
1:  /* UserInformationImp.c                                 */
2:  /* Implementation file for Java class UserInformation   */
3:  #include <StubPreamble.h>
4:  #include "UserInformation.h"
5:  #include <winnetwk.h>
6:
7:  struct Hjava_lang_String *UserInformation_Username(
8:      struct HUserInformation *hUserInformation
9:  )
10: {
11:     char szUserName[128];
12:     DWORD cchBuffer = sizeof(szUserName);
13:     if(NO_ERROR == WNetGetUser(NULL,szUserName,&cchBuffer))
14:        return makeJavaString(szUserName, sizeof(szUserName));
15:     else {
16:        printf("UserInformation_Username: GetLastError = %x\n",
17:           GetLastError());
19:        return makeJavaString("", 0);
20:     }
21: }
```

Here is a line-by-line description of the implementation file:

Line 3: Every native method implementation file must include StubPreamble.h. Indirectly, it provides all of the macros, definitions, and declarations that enable C code to interoperate with the Java Virtual Machine.

Line 4: Include the header file created by javah. This brings in the structure definitions ClassUserInformation and HUserInformation.

Line 5: Include the Win32 header file, which defines WNetGetUser—the function we will use to find the user's name.

Lines 7–9: This function signature must be identical to the corresponding function declaration in UserInformation.h.

Lines 11–12: Declare two local variables—a character array that will hold the C string of the user's name, and a double word that will indicate the buffers size.

Line 13: Retrieve the user's login name by calling WNetGetUser and checking the return value for failure. If WNetGetUser fails because the buffer is too small, cchBuffer will contain the actual buffer length needed.

Line 14: If the call to WGetNetUser succeeded, construct a Java string object from the C string. The function makeJavaString is declared in javaString.h, along with several other functions which C code can use to manipulate Java string objects. Not all Java classes have such convenient C interfaces. In general, you will use the classes' inherent capabilities by calling the Java code from your C code.

Lines 15–19: If the call to WGetNetUser failed, print an error message on stdout and construct an empty Java string to return. Returning an empty string is more conscientious than returning a NULL. Java has garbage collection, so you do not need to worry about the eventual destruction of these strings.

Now we just need to compile and link the two C files. For complete details on building the code, see the following sections called "Building Native Methods for Solaris" and "Building Native Methods for Windows 95/NT," whichever is appropriate for your target platform. For now, the sample makefile in Listing 19.7 will make things more convenient. (It will also make sure that your header and stub files stay current with respect to your .java file.) Remember to put tabs, not spaces, at the beginnings of the action lines.

Listing 19.7. Sample makefile suitable for use on Windows 95/NT.

```
CC         = cl
LFLAGS     = -MD -LD
CLASSPATH  = .;$(JAVA_HOME)\lib\classes.zip

CLASS      = UserInformation

all: $(CLASS).dll $(CLASS).class main.class
```

```
main.class: main.java
    javac main.java

$(CLASS).class: $(CLASS).java
    javac $(CLASS).java

$(CLASS).dll: $(CLASS)Imp.c $(CLASS).class
    javah -classpath $(CLASSPATH) $(CLASS)
    javah -stubs -classpath $(CLASSPATH) $(CLASS)
    $(CC) $(CLASS)Imp.c $(CLASS).c -Fe$(CLASS).dll $(LFLAGS) mpr.lib javai.lib
```

Once you compile your native methods into a dynamically loadable library, you can create a simple class to exercise this native method from an application. When you are testing an application that uses native methods, the command-line Java interpreter "java" can be a tremendous help. In this case, the class main simply creates an instance of UserInformation and prints the results of Username(). Figure 19.2 shows the sequence of events that makes this happen.

```
>java main
Your username is: mtnygard
```

Now that you have gone through the entire process one step at a time, you can delve into the nuts and bolts. The next sections will refer back to this example from time to time as they explore the details of the interaction between native methods and pure Java code.

The Nuts and Bolts of Native Methods

Because native language methods are so closely tied to a particular platform, the difference in procedures is more pronounced than with the JDK itself. For example, the compilers for different platforms have wildly different command-line arguments. Because of the possible variations and permutations, this section cannot present an exhaustive reference on the native compilers. Therefore, you should always consider the appropriate compiler reference as the ultimate authority. The procedures in these sections worked at the time this was written, using JDK 1.0.2 on the following platforms: SPARC Solaris 2.5, *x*86 Solaris 2.5, Microsoft Windows 95, Microsoft Windows NT 3.51, and Microsoft Windows NT 4.0 Beta. The Solaris platforms use the usual "cc" compiler. The Windows platforms have been tested using Visual C++ 2.0 and 4.0.

Configuring Your Environment for Solaris

If you have not already done so, you should modify your PATH variable to include the /java/ bin directory. In addition, setting your JAVAHOME and CLASSPATH variables properly will help javah run smoothly.

When your class's static block calls System.loadLibrary, the Java runtime will search for the library in the current directory. If you intend to install your dynamic libraries in any other directory, you will need to set your library search path to include that directory. For example, if your libraries are stored in `java_lib` in your home directory, use the following command in Bourne and Korn shells:

```
$ LD_LIBRARY_PATH=$LD_LIBRARY_PATH:$HOME/java_lib
$ export LD_LIBRARY_PATH
```

In C shell, use this:

```
% setenv LD_LIBRARY_PATH "$LD_LIBRARY_PATH:$HOME/java_lib"
```

Building Native Methods for Solaris

Use the following command to compile the code and link the dynamic library:

```
$ cc -G UserInformation.c UserInformationImp.c \
> -o libUserInformation.so
```

You will probably need to use the `-I` flag to tell the compiler where to find the Java header files:

```
$ cc -G -I${JAVA_HOME}/include -I${JAVA_HOME}/include/solaris \
> UserInformation.c UserInformationImp.c \
> -o libUserInformation.so
```

The linker will create `libUserInformation.so` in your current directory. For details about the linker options, refer to the man pages for `cc` and `ld`.

To execute `System.loadLibrary("libname")`, the Solaris Java Virtual Machine will search for a library named `liblibname.so`.

Configuring Your Environment for Windows 95/NT

You should either make these changes to your `C:\AUTOEXEC.BAT` file or to a batch file you will run every session.

Setting your `JAVA_HOME` and `CLASSPATH` variables properly will help javah run smoothly. In addition, if you have not already done so, you should modify your `PATH` variable to include the `%JAVA_HOME%\bin` directory.

When your class's static block calls `System.loadLibrary`, the Java runtime will search for the library in the `PATH` variable, as well as the directory in which the executable lives. If you intend to install your dynamic libraries in any directory other than these, you will need to set your path to include that directory.

To make the compile process a little easier, you might want to set the `INCLUDE` and `LIB` variables to point to the Java files:

```
set INCLUDE=%JAVA_HOME%\include;%INCLUDE%
set LIB=%JAVA_HOME%\lib;%LIB%
```

Building Native Methods for Windows 95/NT

Use the following command to compile and link the dynamic library:

```
C:\> cl UserInformation.c UserInformationImp.c
-FeUserInformation.dll -MD -LD [other_libs] javai.lib
```

> **NOTE**
>
> You must use Visual C++ 2.0 or higher to compile the dynamically linked libraries. In particular, Visual C++ 1.52 or below produce 16-bit code, which will not work with Java.

The linker will create `UserInformation.dll` in the current directory. For details on the linker options, refer to the Visual C++ online manual.

To execute `System.loadLibrary("libname")`, the Windows 95/NT Java Virtual Machine will search for a library named `libname.dll`.

Troubleshooting Native Methods

Here are some common exceptions you might see when you run your program.

```
java.lang.UnsatisfiedLinkError no hello in LD_LIBRARY_PATH
    at java.lang.Throwable.(Throwable.java)
    at java.lang.Error.(Error.java)
    at java.lang.LinkageError.(LinkageError.java)
    at java.lang.UnsatisfiedLinkError.(UnsatisfiedLinkError.java)
    at java.lang.Runtime.loadLibrary(Runtime.java)
    at java.lang.System.loadLibrary(System.java)
    at UserInformation.(UserInformation.java:5)
    at
java.lang.UnsatisfiedLinkError: Username
    at main.main(main.java:6)
```

This exception appears on Solaris systems. It means that you have a library path set, but the particular library is not in it. You need to modify your library path to include the directory where your library lives.

```
java.lang.NullPointerException
    at java.lang.Runtime.loadLibrary(Runtime.java)
    at java.lang.System.loadLibrary(System.java)
    at UserInformation.(UserInformation.java:5)
    at
java.lang.UnsatisfiedLinkError: Username
    at main.main(main.java:6)
```

This exception also appears on Solaris systems. It indicates that you do not have a library path set at all, and that the runtime cannot find your library without it. You should either set your library path or move your library to the current directory.

```
Unable to load dll 'UserInformation.dll' (errcode = 485)
Exception in thread "main" java.lang.UnsatisfiedLinkError:
   no UserInformation in shared library path
   at java.lang.Runtime.loadLibrary(Runtime.java:268)
   at java.lang.System.loadLibrary(System.java:266)
   at UserInformation.<clinit>(UserInformation.java:3)
   at
java.lang.UnsatisfiedLinkError: Username
   at main.main(main.java:6)
```

This is essentially just the Windows version of the same problem. Again, the solution is to copy the library into a directory that *is* in the PATH, or to modify the PATH to include the library's directory.

```
java.lang.UnsatisfiedLinkError: Username
       at main.main(main.java:6)
```

If you get this exception by itself, without a larger walkback above it, then your library is missing the function being called by this native method.

As you can see, when you are using native methods, most of the problems show up when the runtime attempts to load the library. Unfortunately, there is no simple solution. This is basically an installation and configuration management problem. Worse yet, there is no way for one class to catch exceptions that occur when the JVM is loading another class.

The Method and the Function

There are two parts to every native method: the Java declaration and the native language definition. The Java Virtual Machine provides enough capabilities that the native language component can do virtually everything that a typical Java method can. This section will examine the two sides of a native method: the Java declaration and the native language definition. The next few sections will examine how the native language component works with the JVM to make all of this work.

Starting with the Java declaration, consider the method signature from the UserInformation example earlier in the chapter.

```
public native String Username();
```

It looks more or less the same as any other method. The native keyword means that the method body is not needed. (In fact, it is not permitted.) The native keyword tells the compiler that the definition (the method body) is provided in a different language.

In this example, no arguments were needed. However, you can pass arguments to native methods and get return values from them. These arguments and return values can include objects. See "Arguments and Return Values" for specifics.

We used javah to create the header file for the native side. Take a look at the function signature created by javah.

```
struct Hjava_lang_String *UserInformation_Username(struct HUserInformation *);
```

By examining this piece by piece, you can see how the Java to C linkage works. First, the return type is declared as struct `Hjava_lang_String` *. In the native language, all objects are accessed through a *handle*—a special structures that allows access to an object's instance variables and the class's methods (the object's vtable.) You can translate `Hjava_lang_String` directly to "`java.lang.String`". Handles are always passed as pointers for efficiency.

As you can see, the function name itself is comprised of the class name, an underscore, and the method name itself. If you wanted to add a new native method to find out the user's disk quota, it would be named something like `UserInformation_DiskQuota`. Because javah can generate all of the function declarations, there is rarely a need to create these names, but because the names are not "mangled" (the way early C++ to C translators did), the resulting code is very readable.

The final item in this signature is the argument struct `HUserInformation` *. It is an *automatic parameter*, which will be explained in the next section.

Arguments and Return Values

Pure Java methods can pass arguments to native methods just as they would to any other method call. Native methods can return any value that a Java method would. How does this work when two such vastly different languages are involved? It works because the Java Virtual Machine exposes some of its internals to the native language. At the same time, the header files that support native methods use features of the C preprocessor and compiler to shield you, the developer, from the guts of the Java implementation. Essentially, when you are developing a native method, you are hooking right into the most fundamental aspects of Java's implementation. As a result, you must be careful to follow the rules, or you risk writing fragile code and upsetting the JVM itself.

Simple data types map directly from Java to C. Some difficulties arise because arrays are first class objects in Java, whereas they are aggregate data types in C. Arrays appear in C code as Java objects. Table 19.1 shows the data type mapping from Java to C.

Table 19.1. Mapping some Java data types to C data types.

Java type	*C Argument*	*C Structure*
Primitive Types		
boolean	long	long
char	long	long
short	long	long
ushort	long	long
int	long	long

float	float	float
double	float	float

Complex Types

Object	struct Hjava_lang_Object	struct Hjava_lang_Object
boolean[]	long	long
char[]	unicode	struct HArrayOfChar
short[]	long	struct HArrayOfLong
ushort[]	unsigned short	unsigned short
int[]	long	struct HArrayOfLong
float[]	float	struct HArrayOfFloat
double[]	float	struct HArrayOfFloat
Object[]	HArrayOfClass	struct Hjava_lang_Object

The most important argument for any native method is the first parameter passed to all native methods. It is referred to as an automatic parameter. Look back at the example earlier in this chapter. The function UserInformation_Username was passed a struct HUserInformation * as the first (and only) argument. This pointer serves the same function as the implicit this pointer in C++. That is, the first parameter passed to a native method points to the object instance for which that method is being called. You can use this pointer to access the instance variables of the class. With it, you can even call other methods of the object. This automatic parameter takes the form of a *handle*. (See the sidebar "What are Handles, Anyway?".)

The confluence of handles, multithreading, and garbage collection leads to some interesting consequences for your C code. First of all, your C code *must* be fully re-entrant. Because a Java application can have an arbitrary number of threads, any one of those threads can call your native method—even if another thread is already executing in that method, unless you synchronize the method. See "Multithreading and Native Methods." Also, remember that the garbage collection runs in an idle thread, but another thread may request that the garbage collector run immediately.

How does this affect your native methods? The garbage collector may relocate objects in memory! As long as you maintain a reference to your arguments, particularly your this pointer, it will not be relocated. However, if you try to store the obj pointer from the object handle (for example, hUserInformation->obj) in a global variable, two very bad things will happen. First, the garbage collector may relocate or *even destroy* the object. This is because each object has a reference count—a count of the outstanding handles to that object. When the object's reference count hits zero, it is put into a pool that can be garbage collected at any time. When your method returned, the handle passed to it went out of scope and the object's reference count was decremented. Although you still have a copy of the handle, the object may get destroyed without warning. For instance, another thread may cause the reference count to hit zero, even though your variable still has a pointer. Then your variable points to deallocated memory. The second problem with this scenario comes from the multithreading itself. Any function that uses global data is suspect in a multithreaded program. It is very difficult to prove that a function using global data will behave correctly when faced with re-entrant calls. Here again, the most likely consequence is an invalid pointer. The JVM is well protected, but it can still be crashed. Never believe anyone who tells you that it is impossible to get a core dump or GPF from Java! Anytime native methods are involved, the JVM is only as robust as those native methods.

In Table 19.1, all of the Java array types appear as handles in the object instances. Java treats arrays as first-class types and implements them as objects. When passing an array to a native method, the JVM translates it into a C-like array. However, the array instance variables are still (Java) arrays when accessed from C. Therefore, the C code must treat it as an object.

Returning primitive and complex data types works exactly the same way as primitive and complex arguments. Sometimes, as in the UserInformation example, this may involve constructing new Java objects in C code. The next section explains how to accomplish this feat.

Using Java Objects from Native Methods

In native methods, all objects appear as handles. Handles are at the heart of the Java object model, but you will be shielded from directly manipulating handles. A group of C macros and functions permit you to deal with handles largely as an abstract type. So what can you do with a handle?

Accessing Instance Variables from Native Methods

For starters, you can access all of an object's instance variables—all those that are visible to your code, at least. In order for your native method to access the data members of your object, you dereference the handle with the macro unhand(). Unhand() is defined in the header file interpreter.h, which is included by StubPreamble.h. Listing 19.8 shows an example of accessing an object's instance variables from a native method.

Listing 19.8. Using unhand() to access instance variables.

```
typedef struct ClassUserInformation {
    long iUserID;
} ClassUserInformation;
HandleTo(UserInformation);
...
void UserInformation_SetUserID(struct HUserInformation *hUI,
    long newValue)
{
    unhand(hUI)->iUserID = newValue;
}
```

WHAT ARE HANDLES, ANYWAY?

In the Java implementation, a handle is used to maintain references to objects. Handles allow the use of native languages to truly be "two-way." That is, the native methods can access instance variables and call other methods, just as pure Java methods can. Handles are at the very heart of the Java object model. In code, a handle is a small structure with two pointers, which together form an object instance. One points to the instance variables, the other to the method table (the vtable in C++ parlance). Handles for your classes are created automatically when you create the header file. (See the sidebar "Where Did HUserInformation Come From?")

By using pointers to handles to pass objects around, Java attains great efficiency. Because object manipulations work through handles, there is a single item of interest to the garbage collector, and a natural mechanism for marking objects in use or discarded.

The unhand() macro returns a pointer to an ordinary C structure. (For handles to objects of your class, it returns a pointer to the structure defined in your header file.) In all cases, the members of the C structure have the same names as the members of the Java class. The types may be different, however. Check Table 19.1 for the type mapping. You can read and write to the members of the structure. In fact, you can even pass pointers to them as arguments to other functions. They behave in all ways as members of ordinary C structures, because that is exactly what they are. When you use unhand() on a handle, you are actually looking at the fundamental Java implementation of an object. The structures you see using the handle are the real structures; there is no behind-the-scenes marshalling before the call.

Accessing Class Variables from Native Methods

Class variables (static variables) do not appear in the instance variable structure generated by javah. This is because they are not stored with each instance of a class, but rather with the class structure itself. The Java runtime provides a function that you can use to get a pointer to the class variable getclassvariable.

```
long *getclassvariable(struct ClassClass *cb, char *fname);
```

Notice that this function, like many other Java runtime functions, requires a pointer to the class structure. Fortunately, every object instance carries this pointer around. The obj_classblock macro from interpreter.h takes an object handle as an argument and returns a pointer to the class structure.

Why does getclassvariable return a pointer to a long? It returns a pointer because the native language code should be able to modify the class variables, as well as see them. The return type is long, but in C, all pointers to data are the same size. So, it is safe to cast the returned pointer to a pointer to whatever type the class variable really is.

Be warned that unless your native methods are synchronized, modifying class variables can be problematic. Always remember that, even though this method is in C, it really is being called from a multithreaded environment. There may be other threads executing Java methods or native methods. They may be doing any number of things, including accessing the class variable at exactly the same time as the native method. Any time global data is involved, whether it is class-wide or truly global, synchronization is an issue. See "Multithreading and Native Methods" for more details.

Wouldn't it be nice if your native language code could also call Java code? Yes, it really would. Fortunately, we can do exactly that. It all starts with the object handle. (Where else?) You have to use a slightly more complicated mechanism than you might think at first. Calling another C function from a function pointer in a structure is something familiar to all of us, something like:

```
hUserInformation->Username();                    // DO NOT DO THIS!
```

Although this would have the net effect of transferring execution to the other function, it is not sufficient. Here's why: When calling a C function, a stack frame is created with the return address and some arguments. (Implementations vary somewhat; this is necessarily a very general description.) In Java, there is much more *context* provided for a function call. In addition to the processor stack, the JVM maintains a great deal of stack information on its own, internal stack. (Presumably, combining this stack with the processor stack, both in hardware, is one of the benefits of a "Java chip.")

In order to make the method call, we really have to ask the JVM to do the call for us. Here are the three functions declared in `interpreter.h` that will make these calls:

```
HObject *execute_java_constructor(ExecEnv *, char *classname,
    ClassClass *cb, char *signature, ...);
long execute_java_dynamic_method(ExecEnv *, HObject *obj,
    char *method_name, char *signature, ...);
long execute_java_static_method(ExecEnv *, ClassClass *cb,
    char *method_name, char *signature, ...);
```

Each function serves a specific purpose and is described separately in the following section.

Calling a Java Constructor

Native language code can construct an instance of any Java class that is currently loaded. Here again, the native code is hooking directly into the implementation of Java. Therefore, the new object will behave exactly as it would if you had constructed it in Java code. The general form of a native language constructor is this:

```
hNewObject = (HClassName *)execute_java_constructor(NULL,
    "ClassName", NULL, "ConstructorSignature", ...);
```

The first parameter here is the ExecEnv or exception environment that applies to the constructor call. You can safely pass a NULL here, and the constructor will operate with the default exception environment. If you are using sophisticated exception handling in your native code, please see the section "Native Methods and Exceptions."

The interesting pieces of this call are shown in italics. First of all, in order for the native method to use the object that gets constructed, it must know the object's class. Usually, this comes from including a header file for that class. Only a few classes have headers distributed with the JDK: ClassLoader, String, Thread, and ThreadGroup. However, by using javah, you can create header files for whatever classes you need. (See Chapter 14 for details.) If you do not need to access the object's methods or instance variables, you can cast the return value from execute_java_constructor to an HObject pointer. HObject is the handle to the base class Object.

LOADING JAVA CLASSES FROM NATIVE LANGUAGE CODE

If you need to load a class directly from native code, you can call the function:

```
int LoadFile(char *filename, char *directory, char *SourceHint);
```

It is safe to pass NULL for SourceHint. This function will cause the ClassLoader to find the file and load it into memory. Once the class is loaded, its static block is executed. Be aware that the static block can throw an exception.

The ClassLoader also provides native code for the DoImport function.

```
int DoImport(char *name, char *SourceHint);
```

This will behave exactly as if the Java code had contained an "import name;" line.

The next item of interest in this call is the class name. This is a text string that specifies what class is to be instantiated. This class must already be loaded, or reside on the class path. When you pass a class name, the Java runtime must perform a lookup on the class itself. However, if you have a pointer to the class itself, you can leave the class name argument NULL and pass the ClassClass pointer in the third argument. For example, if you wanted to clone an existing object of any class, you might use code like this:

```
struct HObject *Cloner_Clone(struct HCloner *hCloner,
                             struct HObject *hObj)
{
   HObject *hNewInst;
   hNewInst = execute_java_constructor(NULL, NULL,
               obj_classblock(hObject), "(A)", hObj);
   return hNewInst;
}
```

This native method can clone any object that has a copy constructor. The macro obj_classblock is another of the handle convenience macros. For any object, it will return a pointer to the class structure for that object. Many of the built-in functions of the Java runtime require a pointer to the class structure "ClassClass".

The constructor signature is used to select which constructor to invoke. It is a character string that specifies the number and type of arguments to follow. Table 19.2 shows the possible characters and their meanings.

Table 19.2. Signature characters and their meanings.

Character	Meaning
A	Any (object)
[	Array (object)
B	Byte
C	Char
L	Class
;	End class
E	Enumeration
F	Float
D	Double
(	Function argument list start
)	Function argument list end
I	Int
J	Long
S	Short
V	Void
Z	Boolean

By concatenating characters from this set, you specify what arguments are to follow. Two characters have special significance: the parentheses indicate the beginning and end of the argument list. For a constructor, parentheses should enclose the entire argument list. For other methods, the signature will also indicate the return type of the method. In the preceding example, the signature is "(A)", which means the constructor must simply take one argument— an object instance. This implies that our constructor could receive objects of other classes as arguments. If we knew the class name, say Foo, for example, we could write the signature as "(LFoo;)", which means the constructor must take an instance of class Foo *or its subclasses*, as an argument. Here is a revised version of the Clone method, which takes into account the class name of the argument passed in:

```
struct HObject *Cloner_Clone(struct HCloner *hCloner,
                             struct HObject *hObj)
{
```

```
    HObject *hNewInst;
    char     signature[80];

    sprintf(signature, "(L%s;)", classname(obj_classblock(hObj)));
    hNewInst = execute_java_constructor(NULL, NULL,
                  obj_classblock(hObject), signature, hObj);
    return hNewInst;
}
```

Notice that, although "name" is a simple member of struct ClassClass, we use the classname macro (from oobj.h) instead of a direct access. In general, you should never access a structure member directly. Instead, use one of the macros provided in oobj.h or interpreter.h (both included by StubPreamble.h). The macros shield you from future changes to the structures. What if there is no macro to access a particular member? Then you probably are not meant to use that member in the first place!

After the constructor signature, you can place a variable length argument list. These are the arguments that will be passed to your constructor. You should be careful to make sure that the type, number, and order of your arguments match the signature. Otherwise, your constructor may be called with garbage for arguments.

If there is an error while calling the constructor, execute_java_constructor will return NULL.

Calling a Java Method

Now for the really good part. You can call any Java method from native code. It all works through the handle to the object instance. If the method to be called is static, see the next section. For dynamic methods—including final and native methods—use the execute_java_dynamic_method function:

```
long execute_java_dynamic_method(ExecEnv *, HObject *obj,
   char *method_name, char *signature, ...);
```

The first parameter is the same as the first argument to execute_java_constructor—an exception environment. Again, it is safe to pass a NULL for this parameter. If you require more sophisticated exception handling for the native code, see "Native Methods and Exceptions."

The second parameter is the object instance itself. This can be any valid object handle, whether it was passed from Java code as an argument or constructed in the native method itself.

The next parameter is the name of the method to be invoked. If this method does not exist in the object passed, execute_java_dynamic_method will throw an exception.

Finally, the fourth argument is the signature of the instance method. Again, the signature indicates the type and number of arguments to be passed to the instance method being called. This must be the same number and type of remaining arguments in the call to execute_java_dynamic_method.

The signature for a method differs slightly from the signature for a constructor. A method signature needs to indicate the expected return type. The signature can show this with an extra character after the closing parenthesis. For example, consider a method that takes arguments of two classes and a float and returns a byte:

```
public byte[] FunkyMethod(Object fc, SecondClass sc,
                          float difference);
```

This method would have the signature "(ALSecondClass;F)B". The call to execute_java_dynamic_method would then have three arguments after the signature: a generic object, an instance of SecondClass, and a float.

The return value from execute_java_dynamic_method depends on the method being invoked. It is declared as long, however, so you will need to cast it to the appropriate type. (Because long is wide enough to hold any primitive type or a handle, it is safe to cast it to whatever the method really returns.) Be careful, though. Because you are calling the method by a function, not directly, the compiler cannot possibly notify you of any changes in the method definition.

Calling a Static Java Method

Calling a class method from native code is similar to calling a dynamic method. Use the execute_java_static_method function:

```
long execute_java_static_method(ExecEnv *, ClassClass *cb,
   char *method_name, char *signature, ...);
```

This is entirely analogous to the execute_java_dynamic_method function, with one crucial difference. Instead of taking an object instance as a parameter, execute_java_static_method requires a class structure. This class structure can come from an object instance, using the obj_classblock macro, or it can be retrieved using the FindClass function:

```
ClassClass* FindClass(ExecEnv *ee, char *classname, bool_t resolve);
```

FindClass will return a pointer to the class structure for any class name you pass in. This function may cause several things to happen. First, the named class may be loaded, which will in turn cause the named class's static block to execute. Exceptions may be thrown by FindClass itself, if it cannot find the class, or by the static block of the named class, when it is loaded.

Like the other runtime functions that can throw exceptions, FindClass can take an exception environment as an argument. As usual, it is safe to pass a NULL here, in which case FindClass will use the current exception environment.

Multithreading and Native Methods

Even though the native methods are written in C, they still execute within the context of the Java environment, including multithreading. Native methods will sometimes have sections of code that modify global (class or application) data, which modify important state variables, or which must call non-re-entrant functions. (Some platform-specific APIs fall into this category.) These sections are called *critical sections*, because it is critical that no more than one thread executes the section of code at a time. Critical sections are not unique to native methods: the same issues exist when dealing with multithreading in pure Java code.

In order to ensure that the native methods maintain the application in a consistent state, these native methods will have to be synchronized with other threads. The simplest way to accomplish this is to declare the native methods as synchronized in the Java code. Sometimes, however, this will be insufficient, either for performance reasons (for example, a method that does a long computation, but only changes the condition variable infrequently), or because a multithreaded application needs to use an existing object that does not have synchronized methods (most do not).

In these cases, your native code can perform the synchronization directly. In Java code, you could put the critical section inside a synchronized block. The native method analogue to a synchronized block directly uses a *monitor*.

Monitors prevent two threads from simultaneously executing a section of code. Monitors were first introduced in C.A.R. Hoare's seminal paper "Communicating Sequential Processes" (*Communications of the ACM*, Vol. 21, No. 8, August 1978). Typically, each condition variable has a monitor associated with it. The monitor acts as a lock on that data. Unless a thread holds the monitor, it cannot modify *or inspect* that data. Obviously, a thread should hold the monitor as briefly as possible.

> **NOTE**
>
> In Java, critical sections are usually methods. You can synchronize blocks of code smaller than methods. However, this leads to complex code, with many failure modes. Deadlock prevention at the method level is fairly straightforward, but it becomes rapidly more difficult when dealing with many small blocks of synchronized code.
>
> Even when dealing with native methods, it is best to use synchronization at the method level.

Monitors provide the Java runtime system support for thread synchronization. Every object instance has a unique monitor attached to it. In this case, the entire object is considered a condition variable. Through a trio of functions, native methods can also use monitors.

```
void MonitorWait(unsigned int, int);
void MonitorNotify(unsigned int);
void MonitorNotifyAll(unsigned int);
```

These functions are analogous to the `wait()`, `notify()`, and `notifyAll()` functions in Java:

    monitorWait   This function blocks the executing thread until the monitor is notified. If you encounter a deadlock, the first place to start is to check each occurrence of `monitorWait()`.

`monitorNotify`	This function awakens no more than one waiting thread. It signals that the monitor is now available. It must only be called from the thread that holds the monitor. If an unhandled exception occurs while a thread holds the monitor, any threads waiting on the monitor will be blocked indefinitely.
`monitorNotifyAll`	This function awakens all threads waiting on the monitor. It signals that the monitor is now available.

TIP

Monitors are re-entrant, which means that a thread that already holds a monitor will not deadlock if it calls `monitorWait` again.

Monitor operations are atomic. They are not subject to race conditions (although the code that calls them is).

The Java implementation of monitors has a nice feature that helps to prevent deadlock. Consider this scenario: a synchronized native method calls `monitorWait`, to wait for another synchronized method (native or not) to notify the monitor. Because the first method is synchronized, it already holds the monitor when `monitorWait` is called. How is the second method ever supposed to execute? The implementation of `monitorWait` makes this possible by releasing the monitor on entry. This allows the second method to execute and notify the monitor. Once the monitor is notified, the first thread awakens. On exit from `monitorWait`, the first thread acquires the monitor again.

All three of the monitor functions are declared as receiving an unsigned integer. To get the monitor for an object, use the `obj_monitor` macro on the object's handle.

Here is an example of a synchronized string. This is an example of a producer/consumer problem. (Most synchronization problems can be reduced to one of two classic examples, producer/consumer and the colorfully named "dining philosophers problem." The dining philosophers problem is discussed in Chapter 20, "Working with Threads.") In a producer/consumer problem, one thread produces data items while another consumes them. Both operations must be synchronized so that the consumer gets each item exactly once. Listing 19.9 contains the Java definition of the synchronized string class, `SyncString`. Listing 19.10 shows the native method implementations of the `SyncString.Set` and `SyncString.Get` methods. Note once again that this could easily have been accomplished without the use of native methods. You will find that native methods are only useful in a very small set of circumstances.

Listing 19.9. Java class for SyncString.

```java
class SyncString {
    String str;
    int bAvail;

    public native synchronized void Set(String s);
    public native synchronized String Get();

    static {
        try {
            System.loadLibrary("SyncString");
        } catch (UnsatisfiedLinkError e) {
            System.err.println("Cannot find library SyncString.");
            System.exit(-1);
        }
    }
}
```

Listing 19.10. Native language implementation for SyncString.

```c
#include <StubPreamble.h>
#include "SyncString.h"


void SyncString_Set(struct HSyncString *this,
                    struct Hjava_lang_String *str)
{
    while(unhand(this)->bAvail == TRUE)
        monitorNotify(obj_monitor(this));

    unhand(this)->bAvail = TRUE;
    unhand(this)->str = str;

    monitorNotify(obj_monitor(this));
}

struct Hjava_lang_String *SyncString_Get(struct HSyncString *this)
{
    Hjava_lang_String *hstrTemp;

    while(unhand(this)->bAvail == FALSE)
        monitorWait(obj_monitor(this));

    unhand(this)->bAvail = FALSE;
        hstrTemp = unhand(this)->str;

    monitorNotify(obj_monitor(this));

    return hstrTemp;
}
```

> **NOTE**
>
> There are other functions that allow native code to construct new monitors not associated with an object. Use of these functions is strongly discouraged, due to the increasing difficulty of deadlock prevention in the face of many monitors.

Native Methods and Exceptions

Native methods can throw exceptions just like a regular Java method. As with any other method that throws an exception, the native method in the Java class must declare the exceptions that it can throw. This looks exactly like the `throws` clause for any other method.

Your native code throws the actual exception using the `SignalError` function:

```
void SignalError(ExecEnv *ee, char *Exception, char *SourceHint);
```

The first argument is the exception environment to use for the exception. Generally, you will pass a `NULL` here to indicate the current environment.

The second argument is the fully specified exception name. This name includes the package in which the exception is defined. It should also be specified as a path, replacing the usual period separators with forward slashes (that is, UNIX-style path separators).

The third argument is a source code hint. You can pass a string that describes the error or provides some useful details. This string will appear on the walkback if the exception is not handled. It is safe to pass a `NULL` here.

Using Java Strings from Native Methods

Because there is an "impedance mismatch" between Java strings and C strings, there are several convenience functions that allow C code to use the Java strings. Java strings offer several advantages over C strings, including reference counting, automatic memory management, and Unicode support. On the other hand, no C runtime library function or API function will expect a Java string. The utility functions provide a bridge between Java and C strings.

These functions are defined in `javaString.h`, which will be included automatically if you include `StubPreamble.h`:

■ The following function will print a Java string on `stdout`:
```
void javaStringPrint(Hjava_lang_String *)
```
■ The following function returns the length of the Java string, in characters:
```
int javaStringLength(Hjava_lang_String *)
```

- The following function will construct a new Java string from a given C string. The second argument indicates the length of the buffer passed in the first argument:

```
Hjava_lang_String *makeJavaString(char *, int)
```

- The following interesting function allocates some temporary memory for a C string initialized from the given Java string. Once all references to this storage are eliminated, the memory is automatically deallocated. In other words, as long as you keep this pointer in a variable, the memory is valid:

```
char *makeCString(Hjava_lang_String *)
```

- The following function uses "malloc" to allocate some memory for a C string initialized from the given Java string:

```
char *mallocCString(Hjava_lang_String *)
```

- The following function will convert the characters of the given Java string into a unicode string. It assumes that the buffer passed in as the second argument already exists. The third argument specifies the buffer length. The function returns the unicode string's address:

```
unicode *javaString2unicode(Hjava_lang_String *, unicode*, int)
```

- The following function will convert the characters of the given Java string into a C string. It assumes that the buffer passed in as the second argument already exists. The third argument specifies the buffer length. The function returns the C string's address:

```
char *javaString2Cstring(Hjava_lang_String *, char *, int)
```

Summary

Native methods provide a powerful means of extending the capabilities of the Java runtime environment. Although native methods are inherently platform-specific, there are certain cases where they might be used. By tapping directly into the implementation of the Java object model, the native language functions can access instance and class variables, construct objects, and call static and dynamic methods. Native methods can be synchronized like ordinary Java methods. They can also throw exceptions. To bridge the gap between Java strings and C strings, the Java runtime environment provides a number of utility functions.

The steps to constructing native methods are as follows:

1. Define the class interface.
2. Write the Java classes.
3. Compile the Java classes.
4. Use javah to create the header and stub files.
5. Write the implementation file.
6. Compile the C files into a dynamically loadable library.
7. Install the dynamically loadable library on the target platform.

20

Working with Threads

by Michael Morrison

A key feature of the Java programming environment and runtime system is the multithreaded architecture shared by both. Multithreading, which is a fairly recent construct in the programming community, is a very powerful means of enhancing and controlling program execution. This chapter takes a look at how the Java language supports multithreading through the use of threads. You learn all about the different classes that enable Java to be a threaded language, along with many of the issues surrounding the effective use of threads.

Thread Basics

The multithreading support in Java revolves around the concept of a thread. The question is, what is a thread? Put simply, a *thread* is a single stream of execution within a process. OK, maybe that wasn't so simple. It might be better to start off by exploring exactly what a process is.

A *process* is a program executing within its own address space. Java is a multiprocessing system, meaning that it supports many processes running concurrently in their own address spaces. You may be more familiar with the term multitasking, which describes a scenario very similar to multiprocessing. As an example, consider the variety of applications typically running at once in a graphical environment. As I write this, I am running Microsoft Word along with Internet Explorer, Windows Explorer, Inbox, CD Player, and Volume Control. These applications are all processes executing within the Windows 95 environment. In this way, you can think of processes as being analogous to applications, or stand-alone programs; each process in a system is given its own room to execute.

A thread is a sequence of code executing within the context of a process. As a matter of fact, threads cannot execute on their own; they require the overhead of a parent process to run. Within each of the processes I mentioned running on my machine, there are no doubt a variety of threads executing. For example, Word may have a thread in the background automatically checking the spelling of what I'm writing, while another thread may be automatically saving changes to the document I'm working on. Like Word, each application (process) can be running many threads that are performing any number of tasks. The significance here is that threads are always associated with a particular process. Figure 20.1 shows the relationship between threads and processes.

FIGURE 20.1.

The relationship between threads and processes.

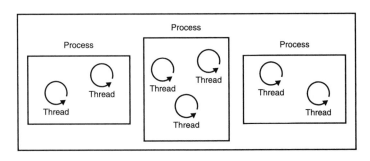

> **NOTE**
>
> Threads are sometimes referred to as *lightweight processes,* implying that they are a limited form of a process. A thread is in fact very similar to a full-blown process, with the major difference being that a thread always runs within the context of another program. Unlike processes, which maintain their own address space and operating environment, threads rely on a parent program for execution resources.

I've described threads and processes using Windows 95 as an example, so you've probably guessed that Java isn't the first system to employ the use of threads. That's true, but Java is the first major programming language to incorporate threads at the heart of the language itself. Typically, threads are implemented at the system level, requiring a platform-specific programming interface separate from the core programming language. This is the case with C/C++ Windows programming, because you have to use the Win32 programming interface to develop multithreaded Windows applications.

Java is presented as both a language and a runtime system, so the Sun architects were able to integrate threads into both. The end result is that you are able to make use of Java threads in a standard, cross-platform fashion. Trust me, this is no small feat, especially considering the fact that some systems, like Windows 3.1, don't have any native support for threads!

The Thread Classes

The Java programming language provides support for threads through a single interface and a handful of classes. The Java interface and classes that include thread functionality follow:

- ◼ Thread
- ◼ Runnable
- ◼ ThreadDeath
- ◼ ThreadGroup
- ◼ Object

All of these classes are part of the java.lang package, and they are covered in great detail in Chapter 32, "Package java.lang." For now, take a brief look at what each offers in the way of thread support.

Thread

The Thread class is the primary class responsible for providing thread functionality to other classes. To add thread functionality to a class, you simply derive the class from Thread and override the run method. The run method is where the processing for a thread takes place, and it is often referred to as the *thread body*. The Thread class also defines start and stop methods that allow you to start and stop the execution of the thread, along with a host of other useful methods.

Runnable

Java does not directly support multiple inheritance, which involves deriving a class from multiple parent classes. This brings up a pretty big question in regard to adding thread functionality to a class: how can you derive from the Thread class if you are already deriving from another class? The answer is: you can't! This is where the Runnable interface comes into play.

The Runnable interface provides the overhead for adding thread functionality to a class simply by implementing the interface, rather than deriving from Thread. Classes that implement the Runnable interface simply provide a run method that is executed by an associated thread object that is created separately. This is a very useful feature and is often the only outlet you have to incorporating multithreading into existing classes.

ThreadDeath

The ThreadDeath error class provides a mechanism for allowing you to clean up after a thread is asynchronously terminated. I'm calling the ThreadDeath an error class because it is derived from the Error class, which provides a means of handling and reporting errors. When the stop method is called on a thread, an instance of ThreadDeath is thrown by the dying thread as an error. You should only catch the ThreadDeath object if you need to perform cleanup specific to the asynchronous termination, which is a pretty rare situation. If you do catch the object, you must rethrow it so the thread will actually die.

ThreadGroup

The ThreadGroup class is used to manage a group of threads as a single unit. This provides you with a means to finely control thread execution for a series of threads. For example, the ThreadGroup class provides stop, suspend, and resume methods for controlling the execution of all the threads in the group. Thread groups can also contain other thread groups, allowing for a nested hierarchy of threads. Individual threads have access to their immediate thread group, but not to the parent of the thread group.

Object

Although not strictly a thread support class, the Object class does provide a few methods that are crucial to the Java thread architecture. These methods are wait, notify, and notifyAll.

The wait method causes a thread to wait in a sleep state until it is notified to continue. Likewise, the notify method informs a waiting thread to continue along with its processing. The notifyAll method is similar to notify except it applies to all waiting threads. These three methods can only be called from a synchronized method; don't worry, you'll learn more about synchronized methods a little later in this chapter.

Typically, these methods are used with multiple threads, where one method waits for another to finish some processing before it can continue. The first thread waits for the other thread to notify it so it can continue. Just in case you're in the dark here, the Object class rests at the top of the Java class hierarchy, meaning that it is the parent of all classes. In other words, every Java class inherits the functionality provided by Object, including the wait, notify, and notifyAll methods. For more information on the Object class, check out Chapter 32.

Creating Threads

Threads aren't much use if you don't know how to create them. Fortunately, you have two options for creating and using threads in your own programs, which have already been alluded to when discussing the thread classes:

■ Derive your class from the Thread class and override its run method.

■ Implement the Runnable interface in your class and provide an implementation for the run method.

Both of these approaches revolve around providing a run method, which is where all the actual processing takes place. After a thread has been created and initialized, its run method is called and given the opportunity to perform whatever processing the thread is designed to provide. Because it provides all the processing power, the run method is the heart of a thread. It's not uncommon for the run method to consist of an infinite loop that performs some repetitive action like updating the frames of an animation. But enough about run for now; go ahead and create some threads!

Deriving from the Thread Class

If your class isn't derived from a specific class, you can easily make it threaded by deriving it from the Thread class. The following source code shows how to add thread functionality to a class by deriving from the Thread class:

```
public class ThreadMe extends Thread {
  public run() {
    // do some busy work
  }
}
```

It's as easy as that! To use this class in a real program and set the thread in motion, you simply create a `ThreadMe` object and call the `start` method inherited from `Thread`, like this:

```
ThreadMe me = new ThreadMe();
me.start();
```

The `start` method automatically calls `run` and gets the thread busy performing its processing. The thread will then run until the `run` method exits or the thread is stopped, suspended, or killed. If for some reason you want to stop the thread's execution, just call the `stop` method, like this:

```
me.stop();
```

If stopping the thread entirely is a little too abrupt, you can also temporarily pause it by calling the `suspend` method, like this:

```
me.suspend();
```

The `suspend` method puts the thread in a wait state, very similar to the state a thread enters when you call the `wait` method. When you decide the thread has waited long enough, just call `resume` to get things rolling again, like this:

```
me.resume();
```

Implementing the `Runnable` Interface

If your class needs to derive from a class other than `Thread`, you are forced to implement the `Runnable` interface to make it threaded. A very common situation where you have to do this is when an applet class needs to be threaded. Because applet classes must be derived from the `Applet` class, and Java doesn't provide a mechanism for multiple inheritance, you have no other option but to implement the `Runnable` interface to add threading support. You implement the `Runnable` interface in a class like this:

```
public class ThreadYou implements Runnable {
  public run() {
    // do some busy work
  }
}
```

As you can see, the only syntactic difference in this approach is that you use the `implements` keyword instead of `extends`. However, notice that you can still use the `extends` keyword to derive from another class, like this:

```
public class ThreadedApp extends Applet implements Runnable {
  public run() {
    // do some busy work
  }
}
```

This is a very practical scenario involving an applet class with a `run` method that performs some type of threaded processing. Even though the definition of a class implementing the `Runnable` interface is little different than directly deriving from Thread, there is a big difference when it comes to creating the thread and getting it running. Creating and running a threaded class implementing the Runnable interface is a three-part process, as the following code shows:

```
ThreadYou you = new ThreadYou();
Thread t = new Thread(you);
t.start();
```

Unlike the previous approach involving creating a thread object and calling its start method, this approach requires you to create both an instance of your class and a separate instance of the Thread class. You pass your object into the Thread class's constructor, which gives it access to your run method. You then set the thread running by calling the thread object's start method. The thread in turn executes your object's run method. The thread knows your class has a run method because it implements the Runnable interface.

If you have no need to access the thread after you get it started, the creation and starting of the thread can be combined into one statement, like this:

```
ThreadYou you = new ThreadYou();
new Thread(you).start();
```

This approach eliminates the creation of the local variable t, which makes the code a little more efficient. Of course, you may think the original code is easier to understand, in which case you should by all means stick with the clearer technique.

Scheduling and Thread Priority

You may be wondering how any software system can be truly threaded when running on a machine with a single CPU. If there is only one physical CPU in a computer system, it's impossible for more than one machine code instruction to be executed at a time. This means that no matter how hard you try to rationalize the behavior of a multithreaded system, only one thread is really being executed at a particular time. The reality is that multithreading on a single CPU system, like the systems most of us use, is at best a good illusion. The good news is that the illusion works so well most of the time that we feel pretty comfortable in the thought that multiple threads are really running in parallel.

> **NOTE**
>
> Incidentally, this same rule applies to multiprocessing systems involving a single CPU. Even though it may look as though you're downloading a file and playing a game in parallel, under the hood the CPU is busy juggling the execution of each process.

How It Works

The illusion of parallel thread execution on a system with a single CPU is often managed by giving each thread an opportunity to execute a little bit of code at regular intervals. This approach is known as *timeslicing*, which refers to the way each thread gets a little of the CPU's time to execute code. When you speed up this whole scenario to millions of instructions per second, the whole effect of parallel execution comes across pretty well. The general task of managing and executing multiple threads in an environment such as this is known as *scheduling*. So far, I've described the most basic form of timesliced scheduling, where every thread is given equal access to the processor in small increments. In reality, this turns out not to be the best approach to managing thread execution.

Undoubtedly, there are going to be situations where you would like some threads to get more of the CPU's attention than others. To accommodate this reality, most threaded systems employ some type of prioritization to allow threads to execute at different priority levels. Java employs a type of scheduling known as *fixed priority scheduling*, which schedules thread execution based on the relative priorities between threads. It works like this: each thread is assigned a relative priority level, which determines the order in which it receives access to the CPU. High-priority threads are given first rights to the CPU, while low-priority threads are left to execute when the CPU is idle.

One interesting thing about Java's approach to scheduling is that it doesn't employ timeslicing. In other words, the currently executing thread gets to enjoy the complete control of the CPU until it yields control to other threads. Lower-priority threads must simply wait until high-priority threads give them a chance to execute. Threads with the same priority level are given access to the CPU one after the next. Figure 20.2 shows how priority impacts the order in which threads are executed.

> **NOTE**
>
> The Java runtime system itself could be merely a single process within a timesliced multiprocessing system on a particular platform. In this way, the fixed priority scheduling employed in Java applies only to Java programs executing within the Java runtime environment.

A good example of a low-priority thread is the garbage collection thread in the Java runtime system. Even though garbage collection is a very important function, it is not something you want hogging the CPU. Because the garbage collection thread is a low-priority thread, it chugs along in the background freeing up memory as the processor allows it. This may result in memory being freed a little more slowly, but it allows more time-critical threads, such as the user input handling thread, full access to the CPU. You may be wondering what happens if the CPU stays busy and the garbage collector never gets to clean up memory. Does the runtime system run out of memory and crash? No—this brings up one of the neat aspects of threads and how they work. If a high-priority thread can't access a resource it needs, such as memory, it enters a wait state until memory becomes available. When all memory is gone, all the threads running will eventually go into a wait state, thereby freeing up the CPU to execute the garbage collection thread, which in turn frees up memory. And the circle of threaded life continues!

FIGURE 20.2.

The relationship between thread priority and execution.

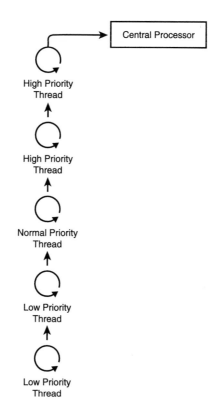

Establishing Thread Priority

When a new thread is created, it inherits its priority from the thread that created it. The Thread class defines three constants representing the relative priority levels for threads, which follow:

```
MIN_PRIORITY
NORM_PRIORITY
MAX_PRIORITY
```

The Java garbage collection thread has a priority of MIN_PRIORITY, whereas the system thread that manages user input events has a priority of MAX_PRIORITY. Knowing this, it's a good idea to take the middle road for most of your own threads and declare them as NORM_PRIORITY.

Generally speaking, this should happen without your having to do anything special because the parent thread you are creating threads from will likely be set to NORM_PRIORITY. If, however, you want to explicitly set a thread's priority, it's pretty easy—the Thread class provides a method called setPriority that allows you to directly set a thread's priority.

Incidentally, the thread priority constants are actually integers that define a range of priorities. MIN_PRIORITY and MAX_PRIORITY are the lower and upper limits of the range of acceptable priority values, while NORM_PRIORITY rests squarely in the middle of the range. This means that you can offset these values to get varying priority levels. If you pass a priority value outside the legal range (MIN_PRIORITY to MAX_PRIORITY), the thread will throw an exception of type IllegalArgumentException.

Getting back to the setPriority method, you can use it to set a thread's priority like this:

```
t.setPriority(Thread.MAX_PRIORITY);
```

Likewise, you can use the getPriority method to retrieve a thread's priority like this:

```
int priority = t.getPriority();
```

Knowing that thread priority is a relative integer value, you can fine-tune a thread's priority by incrementing or decrementing its priority value, like this:

```
t.setPriority(t.getPriority() + 1);
```

This statement moves the thread up a little in the priority list. Of course, the extents of the priority range determine the effectiveness of this statement; in the current release of Java, MIN_PRIORITY is set to 1 and MAX_PRIORITY is set to 10.

Daemons

So far, you've been learning about threads that operate within the context of a parent program. Java provides support for another type of thread, called a *daemon thread*, that acts in many ways like an independent process. Unlike traditional threads, daemon threads belong to the runtime system itself, rather than a particular program. Daemon threads are typically used to manage some type of background service available to all programs. The garbage collection thread is a perfect example of a daemon thread; it chugs along without regard to any particular program performing a very useful service that benefits all programs.

You can set a thread as a daemon thread simply by calling the setDaemon method, which is defined in the Thread class, and passing true:

```
thread.setDaemon(true);
```

You can query a thread to see if it is a daemon thread simply by calling the `isDaemon` method, which is also defined in the `Thread` class:

```
boolean b = thread.isDaemon();
```

The Java runtime interpreter typically stays around until all threads in the system have finished executing. However, it makes an exception when it comes to daemon threads. Because daemon threads are specifically designed to provide some type of service for full-blown programs, it makes no sense to continue to run them when there are no programs running. So, when all the remaining threads in the system are daemon threads, the interpreter exits. This is still the same familiar situation of the interpreter exiting when your program finishes executing; you just may not have realized there were daemon threads out there as well.

Grouping Threads

Earlier you learned a little about the `ThreadGroup` class, which is used to group threads together. Grouping threads is sometimes useful because it allows you to control multiple threads as a single entity. For example, the `ThreadGroup` class has `suspend` and `resume` methods, which can be used to suspend and resume the entire group of threads. What you haven't learned is how to actually manage thread groups, which is the focus of this section.

Every thread in the Java runtime system belongs to a thread group. You may be wondering how this is possible, considering the fact that you saw earlier how to create threads with no mention of a thread group. If you create a thread without specifying a thread group, the thread is added to the group that the current thread belongs to. The current thread is the thread where the new thread is created from. In some cases, there may not be a current thread, in which case the Java runtime system adds the thread to a default thread group called `main`.

You associate threads with a particular group upon thread creation. There is no way to alter the group membership of a thread once it has been created; in other words, you get one opportunity to specify the permanent group for a thread when you create the thread. The Thread class includes constructors for specifying the thread group for the thread:

```
Thread(ThreadGroup, String)
Thread(ThreadGroup, Runnable)
Thread(ThreadGroup, Runnable, String)
```

Each constructor takes a `ThreadGroup` object as the first parameter. The first constructor also takes a string parameter, allowing you to give the thread a name. The last two constructors take a `Runnable` object as the second parameter, which is typically an object of your own concoction that implements the `Runnable` interface. Finally, the last constructor also takes a string parameter, allowing you to name the thread.

Before you can create any threads, you need to create a `ThreadGroup` object. The `ThreadGroup` class defines two constructors, which follow:

```
ThreadGroup(String name)
ThreadGroup(ThreadGroup parent, String name)
```

The first constructor simply creates an empty thread group with the specified name. The second constructor does the same thing, but places the new thread group within the thread group specified in the `parent` parameter. This constructor allows you to nest thread groups.

Take a look at a quick example of creating a thread group and adding a few threads to it. The following code shows how to create and manage a thread group and a couple of member threads:

```
ThreadGroup group = new ThreadGroup("Queen bee");
Thread t1 = new Thread(group, "Worker bee 1");
Thread t2 = new Thread(group, "Worker bee 2");
t1.start();
t2.start();
...
group.suspend();
...
group.resume();
```

After the thread group is created, each thread is created and passed the `ThreadGroup` object. This makes them members of the thread group. Each thread is then started by calling the `start` method of each; the `ThreadGroup` class doesn't provide a means to start all the thread members at once. Sometime later the thread group suspends both threads with a call to the `suspend` method. It then gets them running again by calling `resume`.

You can find out what group a thread belongs to by calling the `getThreadGroup` method. This method returns the `ThreadGroup` object that the thread belongs to. You can then find out the name of the thread group by calling the `getName` method defined in the `ThreadGroup` class. The following code shows how to print the name of the thread group for a particular thread.

```
ThreadGroup group = t.getThreadGroup();
System.out.println(group.getName());
```

Thread States

Thread behavior is completely dependent on the state a thread is in. The *state* of a thread defines its current mode of operation, such as whether it is running or not. Following is a list of the Java thread states:

- New
- Runnable
- Not running
- Dead

New

A thread is in the "new" state when it is first created until its start method is called. New threads are already initialized and ready to get to work, but they haven't been given the cue to take off and get busy.

Runnable

When the start method is called on a new thread, the run method is in turn called and the thread enters the "runnable" state. You may be thinking this state should just be called "running," because the execution of the run method means a thread is running. However, you have to take into consideration the whole priority issue of threads having to potentially share a single CPU. Even though every thread may be running from an end-user perspective, in actuality all but the one currently accessing the CPU are in a "runnable" wait state at any particular instant. You can still conceptually think of the "runnable" state as the "running" state; just remember that all threads have to share system resources.

Not Running

The "not running" state applies to all threads that are temporarily halted for some reason. When a thread is in this state, it is still available for use and is capable of re-entering the "runnable" state at some point. Threads can enter the "not running" state through a variety of means. Following is a list of the different possible events that can cause a thread to be temporarily halted:

■ The suspend method is called.

■ The sleep method is called.

■ The wait method is called.

■ The thread is blocking for I/O.

For each of these actions causing a thread to enter the "not running" state, there is an equivalent response to get the thread running again. Following is a list of the corresponding events that can put a thread back in the "runnable" state:

■ If a thread is suspended, the resume method is called.

■ If a thread is sleeping, the number of specified milliseconds elapse.

■ If a thread is waiting, the object owning the condition variable calls notify or notifyAll.

■ If a thread is blocking for I/O, the I/O operation finishes.

Dead

A thread enters the "dead" state when it is no longer needed. Dead threads cannot be revived and executed again. A thread can enter the "dead" state through one of two approaches, which follow:

- ▪ The run method finishes executing.
- ▪ The stop method is called.

The first approach is the natural way for a thread to die; you can think of a thread dying when its run method finishes executing as death by natural causes. In contrast to this is a thread dying by way of the stop method; calling the stop method kills a thread in an asynchronous fashion.

Even though the latter approach sounds kind of abrupt, it is often very useful. For example, it's common for applets to kill their threads using stop when their own stop method is called. The reason for this is that an applet's stop method is usually called in response to a user leaving the Web page containing the applet. You don't want threads out there executing for an applet that isn't even active, so killing the threads makes perfect sense.

Synchronization

Throughout the discussion of threads thus far, you've really only learned about threads from an asynchronous perspective. In other words, you've only been concerned with getting threads up and running and not worrying too much about how they actually execute. You can only think in these terms when you are dealing with a single thread or with threads that don't interact with the same data. In reality, there are many instances where it is useful to have multiple threads running and accessing the same data. In this type of scenario, the asynchronous programming approach just won't work; you must take extra steps to synchronize the threads so they don't step on each other's toes.

The problem of thread synchronization occurs when multiple threads attempt to access the same resources or data. As an example, imagine the situation where two threads are accessing the same data file; one thread may be writing to the file while the other thread is simultaneously reading from it. This type of situation can create some very unpredictable, and therefore undesirable, results.

> **NOTE**
>
> When data objects are shared between competing threads, they are referred to as *condition variables.*

When you are dealing with threads that are competing for limited resources, you simply must take control of the situation to ensure that each thread gets equal access to the resources in a predictable manner. A system where each thread is given a reasonable degree of access to resources is called a *fair system*. The two situations you must try to avoid when implementing a fair system are starvation and deadlock. *Starvation* occurs when a thread is completely cut off from the resources and can't make any progress; the thread is effectively frozen. Where starvation can apply to a number of threads individually, *deadlock* occurs when two or more threads are waiting for a mutual condition that can never be satisfied; they are starving each other.

A Hypothetical Example

A popular hypothetical example that more clearly demonstrates the problem of deadlock is the dining philosophers. The story goes that there are five hungry philosophers sitting around a table preparing to eat. In front of each philosopher is a bowl of rice, while between each philosopher there is a chopstick. To take a bite of rice, a philosopher needs two chopsticks: one from the left and one from the right. In this situation, the philosophers are equivalent to threads, with the chopsticks representing the limited, shared resources they all need access to. Their desired function is to eat the rice, which requires access to a pair of chopsticks.

The philosophers are only allowed to pick up one chopstick at a time, and they must always pick up the left chopstick and then the right. When a philosopher gets both chopsticks, he can take a bite of rice and then put down both chopsticks. This sounds like a pretty reasonable system of sharing the limited resources so everyone can eat. But consider what happens when each philosopher goes after the chopsticks with equal access to them. Each philosopher immediately grabs the chopstick to his left, resulting in every philosopher having a single chopstick. They all then reach for the chopstick on their right, which is now being held by the philosopher to their right. They are all waiting for another chopstick, so they each just sit holding a single chopstick indefinitely. Both figuratively and literally, they are starving each other!

This is a very good example of how a seemingly fair system can easily go awry. One potential solution to this problem is to force each philosopher to wait a varying amount of time before attempting to grab each chopstick. This approach definitely helps, and the philosophers will probably get to eat some rice, but the potential for deadlock, and therefore starvation, is still there. You are counting on blind luck to save the day and keep the philosophers well fed. In case you didn't guess, this isn't the ideal approach to solving deadlock problems.

You have two approaches to solving deadlock in a situation like this: prevention or detection. Prevention means designing the system so that deadlock is impossible. Detection, on the other hand, means allowing for deadlock but detecting it and dealing with its consequences when they arise. As with a medical illness, it doesn't take a huge mental leap to realize that prevention usually involves much less pain than detection, which results in sort of a chemotherapy for deadlock. My vote is clearly for avoiding deadlock in the first place. Besides, trying to detect deadlock can often be a daunting task in and of itself.

Getting back to the famished philosophers, the root of the problem is the fact that there is no order imposed on the selection of chopsticks. By assigning a priority order to the chopsticks, you can easily solve the deadlock problem; just assign increasing numbers to the chopsticks. Then force the philosophers to always pick up the chopstick with the lower number first. This results in the philosopher sitting between chopsticks 1 and 2 and the philosopher sitting between chopsticks 1 and 5 both going for chopstick 1. Whoever gets it first is then able to get the remaining chopstick, while the other philosopher is left waiting. When the lucky philosopher with two chopsticks finishes his bite and returns the chopsticks, the process repeats itself, allowing all the philosophers to eat. Deadlock has been successfully avoided!

Synchronizing Threads

If you're thinking the dining philosophers example seems fairly simple, you're right. But don't get too confident yet—real-world thread synchronization situations can get extremely messy. Fortunately, Java provides a very powerful solution to the whole issue: the `synchronized` modifier. The `synchronized` modifier is used to flag certain parts of your code as synchronized, resulting in limited, predictable access for threads. More specifically, only one thread is allowed access to a synchronized section of code at a time.

For synchronized methods, it works like this: each synchronized method is given a lock, which determines if it can be accessed, similar to a real lock. When a thread attempts to access the method, it must first see if it is locked, in which case the thread is denied access. If the method isn't locked, the thread gets access and the method then becomes locked. Pretty simple, right?

> **NOTE**
>
> Locks can apply to both methods as well as entire classes, but not directly to individual blocks of code. You are allowed to specify an object or class that is locked for a particular block of synchronized code, but the block itself isn't locked.

Synchronized sections of code are called *critical sections*, implying that access to them is critical to the successful threaded execution of the program. Critical sections are also sometimes referred to as *atomic operations*, meaning that they appear to other threads as if they occur at once. In other words, just as an atom is a discrete unit of matter, atomic operations effectively act like a discrete operation to other threads, even though they may really contain many operations inside.

You can use the `synchronized` modifier to mark critical sections in your code and make them threadsafe. Following are some examples of using the `synchronized` modifier:

```
synchronized public void addEmUp() {
  float a, b;
  a += b;
  b += a;
```

```
}

public void moveEmOut() {
  Rectangle rect;
  synchronized (rect) {
    rect.width -= 2;
  }
  rect.height -= 2;
}
```

The first example shows how to secure an entire method and make it synchronized; only one thread is allowed to execute the addEmUp method at a time. The moveEmOut method, on the other hand, contains a synchronized block of code within it. The synchronized block protects the width of the rectangle from being modified by multiple threads at once. Notice that the rect object itself is used as the lock for the block of code. Also notice that the modification of the height of the rectangle isn't included in the synchronized block, and therefore is subject to access by multiple threads at once.

NOTE

It's important to note that even though there are legitimate situations where you will need to make a block of code synchronized, in general it is better to apply synchronization at the method level. Employing method synchronization as opposed to block synchronization facilitates a more object-oriented design and results in code that is easier to debug and maintain.

There is a subtle problem when using synchronized methods that you may not have thought about. Check out the following code sample:

```
public class countEngine {
  private static int count;
  public synchronized void decCount() {
    count--;
  }
}
```

The decCount method is synchronized, so it appears that the count member variable is protected from misuse. However, count is a class variable, not an instance variable, because it is declared as being static. The lock on the synchronized method is performed on the instance object, so the class data isn't protected. The solution is to synchronize the block using the class as the locked object, like this:

```
public class countEngine {
  private static int count;
  public void decCount() {
    synchronized (getClass()) {
      count--;
    }
  }
}
```

Notice that the getClass method is called to retrieve the class for the synchronized block. This is a perfect example of where you have to use block synchronization over method synchronization to get a desired result.

Volatile Variables

In rare cases where you don't mind threads modifying a variable whenever they please, Java provides a means of maintaining the variable's integrity. The volatile modifier allows you to specify that a variable will be modified asynchronously by threads. The purpose of the volatile modifier is to protect against variable corruption through registered storage of the variable. In an asynchronous environment, corruption can sometimes occur when a variable is stored in CPU registers. The volatile modifier tells the runtime system to always reference a variable directly from memory, instead of using a register. Furthermore, the variable is read from and written back to memory after each access, just to be safe. It's fairly rare that you'll need to use the volatile modifier, but if you feel like living on the edge, it's there for your enjoyment!

Summary

In this chapter, you learned about multithreading from both a conceptual level and a practical programming level, while seeing exactly what facilities Java provides to support multithreaded programming. You saw the two techniques for creating threads using the Thread class and the Runnable interface. You then took a look at the Java scheduler and how it affects thread priority. You moved on to daemons and thread groups, and why they are important. You finished up by tackling the issue of thread synchronization, which is something you will often have to contend with in multithreaded programming. Fortunately, you saw how Java provides plenty of support for handling the most common types of synchronization problems.

21

Event Handling

by Michael Morrison

Many of the actions that take place in the Java environment occur as events that can be handled programmatically. This chapter focuses on the types of events supported by Java, along with how to write code that responds to them. In this chapter, you learn how to handle events such as key presses on the keyboard, mouse movements and button clicks, and some more abstract events that aren't directly related to user input. You also learn about the internal makeup of the Java system that enables event processing.

Event-Driven Programming

Java is an event-driven environment, meaning that most actions that take place in Java generate an event that can be handled and responded to. In Java, an *event* is defined quite literally as something that happens that you might want to know about. For example, when a Java component gains the input focus, an event occurs because it might be important for your applet to know about the focus change.

In the event-driven world of Java, the flow of your program follows events external to your applet, as opposed to following an internally linear program flow. This is an important point, because it means that a Java applet is in a constant state of responding to events. The most visible events are things like mouse clicks and key presses, which are known as *input events*. You provide methods that respond to these events, which are called *event handlers*. Figure 21.1 shows how program flow is altered by external events.

FIGURE 21.1.

How external events impact program flow.

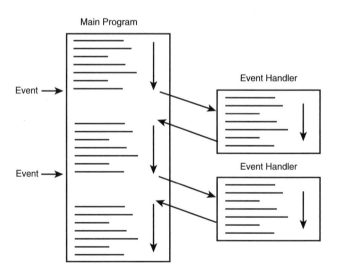

Because of the inherent graphical nature of Java applets, it will eventually become obvious to you why the event-driven programming model is not only more convenient, but downright necessary. With the potential of having multiple applets on a single Web page, along with on-the-fly system configuration changes and a multitude of other things going on, a procedural programming model would be much more difficult to manage. The event-based model provides a more sound solution to the problems inherent in a system with a graphical interface, such as Java.

All events in Java are processed within the java.awt (Advanced Windowing Toolkit) package, and are tightly linked to AWT components. A *component* is basically a generic abstraction for a Java window. If you recall, Java applets are themselves a specific type of component. This means that they inherit the same event-processing features built in to the Component superclass. For more juicy details on the Component class and the AWT package, refer to Chapter 28, "Package java.awt."

AWT Event Handling

The Java AWT is responsible for generating events in response to user actions. For example, when the user selects a button, an event of type ACTION_EVENT is generated. These events are in turn processed by applications or applets, who use the AWT to respond to the events in an *event-driven* manner.

Somewhere deep inside the AWT is an event-processing loop, which handles the dirty job of routing events to their appropriate targets. This process of routing an event to a target object is known as *posting an event*. It should come as no surprise that the method used to post events to target objects is the postEvent method, which is defined for all target objects. For target objects derived from Component, postEvent will in turn call the handleEvent method. handleEvent serves as the default handler for all events, and it has the option of responding to an event or letting it pass through. If handleEvent doesn't handle an event, it returns false, in which case the parent object's handleEvent method is called. This process continues until an event is handled or the top of the object tree is reached. Figure 21.2 shows how this event-handling process takes place.

The Java AWT provides a class for encapsulating all types of events that can occur within the system: Event. The Event class models a generic event and has constants defined within it to represent specific events. You learn more details about the Event class a little later in this chapter. The Event class is used primarily by the handleEvent method, which is defined as:

```
public boolean handleEvent(Event evt)
```

Notice that handleEvent takes an Event object as its only parameter. handleEvent uses this Event object to determine what type of event has occurred. It then calls a more specific event-handler method to deal with the specific event. For example, if a key is pressed, the Event object's id member variable is set to KEY_PRESS, which is a constant defining the key press event. handleEvent checks the value of id and upon finding it equal to KEY_PRESS, calls the keyDown handler method. Following is a section of code showing the keypress-handling portion of the handleEvent method in the 1.02 release of Java:

```
public boolean handleEvent(Event evt) {
  switch (evt.id) {
    ...
  case Event.KEY_PRESS:
    return keyDown(evt, evt.key);
    ...
  }
  return false;
}
```

FIGURE 21.2.

The Java AWT event-handling process.

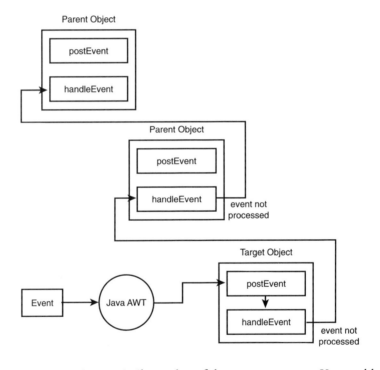

The handling of other system events is very similar to that of the KEY_PRESS event. You could easily override handleEvent to provide custom routing of event handlers, but it is rarely necessary. Although you may not ever need to intervene with the default event-handling provided by handleEvent, it is nevertheless important to understand how it works.

The Event Class

The Event class is a critical component of the Java AWT. Event objects are constructed and passed into methods such as postEvent when an event occurs. They then are used in handleEvent and other methods to encapsulate the specifics regarding a particular event. A thorough understanding of the Event class is important for the successful handling of events generated by the AWT.

Member Variables

The Event class defines a lot of member constants that represent a variety of event types and states, which you learn about in the next section. Beyond these constants, there are also member variables defined in Event that are used to store the state of a particular event. These member variables follow:

```
Object  target;
long    when;
int     id;
int     x;
int     y;
int     key;
int     modifiers;
int     clickCount;
Object  arg;
Event   evt;
```

The target variable specifies the object in which the event occurred; for example, in the case of a button press event, the target variable would contain the associated Button object. The when variable is a timestamp for the event, which specifies exactly when the event occurred. The id variable is used to store the type of event that occurred; you learn more about event types in the next section. The x and y variables are the coordinates of the event within the target graphical object. A typical usage of x and y is keeping up with the mouse position when an event occurs.

The key and modifiers variables are used for storing extra information related to keyboard input events. The clickCount variable keeps up with the number of consecutive mouse clicks, and it is only applicable to mouse events. The arg variable is a generic storage member for associating arbitrary information with an event. Finally, the evt variable is used to store the next Event object when building a linked list of events.

Types

The Event class defines a set of constants, which specify the different types of possible events (see Table 21.1). These event constants are pretty self-explanatory in that their name sufficiently describes the type of event they represent.

Table 21.1. Constant event types defined in the Event class.

ACTION_EVENT		
GOT_FOCUS	LOST_FOCUS	
KEY_ACTION	KEY_ACTION_RELEASE	KEY_PRESS
KEY_RELEASE		
LIST_DESELECT	LIST_SELECT	
LOAD_FILE	SAVE_FILE	
MOUSE_DOWN	MOUSE_DRAG	MOUSE_ENTER
MOUSE_EXIT	MOUSE_MOVE	MOUSE_UP
SCROLL_ABSOLUTE	SCROLL_LINE_DOWN	SCROLL_LINE_UP
SCROLL_PAGE_DOWN	SCROLL_PAGE_UP	
WINDOW_DEICONIFY	WINDOW_DESTROY	WINDOW_EXPOSE
WINDOW_ICONIFY	WINDOW_MOVED	

Usage

The id field is used by the AWT (and possibly your own Java code) to distinguish between event types. The information associated with an event varies depending on the type of event. For example, the MOUSE_DOWN event type is generated when a mouse button is pressed. Because the coordinates of the mouse often are used when handling a mouse button-click event, the x and y member variables of Event are filled in with the current mouse coordinates.

Some event information is meaningless in the context of other types of events, so it's important to understand which member variables of the Event class are valid in particular circumstances. Table 21.2 lists the member variables of the Event class that are valid for each different type of event. Keep in mind that the target and id variables are valid for every type. Also, some event types are never generated by the AWT, so their valid variables are all unknown.

Table 21.2. Valid member variables for different events.

Event	*Valid Fields*
ACTION_EVENT	arg*
LIST_DESELECT	arg
LIST_SELECT	arg
GOT_FOCUS	none
LOST_FOCUS	none
LOAD_FILE	never generated
SAVE_FILE	never generated
MOUSE_DOWN	when, x, y, modifiers, clickCount
MOUSE_DRAG	when, x, y, modifiers
MOUSE_ENTER	when, x, y
MOUSE_EXIT	when, x, y
MOUSE_MOVE	when, x, y, modifiers
MOUSE_UP	when, x, y, modifiers
SCROLL_ABSOLUTE	arg
SCROLL_LINE_DOWN	arg
SCROLL_LINE_UP	arg
SCROLL_PAGE_DOWN	arg
SCROLL_PAGE_UP	arg
KEY_ACTION	when, x, y, key, modifiers
KEY_ACTION_RELEASE	when, x, y, key, modifiers
KEY_PRESS	when, x, y, key, modifiers
KEY_RELEASE	when, x, y, key, modifiers
WINDOW_DEICONIFY	none
WINDOW_DESTROY	none
WINDOW_EXPOSE	never generated
WINDOW_ICONIFY	none
WINDOW_MOVED	x, y

(* For MenuItem and CheckboxMenuItem objects, the fields when and modifiers are also valid. Also keep in mind that the target and id variables are valid for all events.)

Java Input Events

As you've learned throughout the chapter, user input in Java is handled through an event-driven architecture. When the user interacts with an input device, it results in an input event being dispatched to the component with the input focus. In most cases, this component is the applet window. An input event is a special type of event that notifies an applet that something has occurred on an input device. An example of an input event is a movement of the mouse.

Input events are crucial in Java programs because they provide a means of handling user responses. If Java applets could not monitor user responses, they wouldn't be very interactive, which is one of the primary benefits of Java applets. Java user event responses come in two varieties, which correspond to the input devices supported by Java. The two types of input events supported in the current release of Java follow:

- Keyboard events
- Mouse events

Keyboard events are events generated by a key press on the keyboard. Whenever the user presses a key, a keyboard event is generated that can be trapped and handled by the applet with the input focus. Actually, a key press generates two events, a key down event and a key up event. You'll learn more about these two types in a moment.

Mouse events are generated by mouse clicks and movements. Every mouse click and mouse movement generates a corresponding mouse input event. Like key presses, mouse clicks actually come as a series of events; a mouse-click down event and a mouse-click up event. There is also a mouse event specifically targeted at mouse dragging. Mouse dragging occurs when the mouse is moved with the button down. Applets wanting to respond to mouse clicks and movement simply have to process these events and take action accordingly. You learn more about processing mouse events a little later in this chapter.

NOTE

You may have noticed in the discussion of mouse events the mention of the mouse *button*, as opposed to the mouse *buttons*. This is intentional because Java only supports a single mouse button. This may seem limiting to users on some platforms, such as Windows, but keep in mind that Java is designed to support as many platforms as possible. Considering the fact that some platforms have mice with a single button, such as Macintosh, it makes sense for Java to support only a single button.

Keyboard Events

Java keyboard events are generated when the user presses or releases a key. There are two standard keyboard event-handler methods supported by the `Component` class: `keyDown` and `keyUp`. These two methods are defined as:

```
public boolean keyDown(Event evt, int key)
public boolean keyUp(Event evt, int key)
```

The `keyDown` method is called in response to the user pressing a key, and the `keyUp` method is called in response to the user releasing a key. Both methods are passed an `Event` object and an integer key value parameter. The key value parameter, `key`, specifies which key was pressed or released. The `Event` object parameter contains extra information relating to the keyboard event, such as whether the Shift key was held down when the key was pressed.

The `Event` object contains constants representing the different keys that can be specified in the key parameter. Table 21.3 shows a list of some of the more useful key constants.

Table 21.3. Useful key constants.

Constant	Key
UP	Up arrow
DOWN	Down arrow
LEFT	Left arrow
RIGHT	Right arrow
HOME	Home
END	End
PGUP	Page Up
PGDN	Page Down

To check if the key pressed or released is one of these keys, you override `keyDown` or `keyUp` and compare the value of `key` to one of the constants. Following is an example of overriding `keyDown` to check for the user pressing one of the arrow keys:

```
public boolean keyDown(Event evt, int key) {
  switch (key) {
  case Event.LEFT:
    // left arrow key pressed
    break;
  case Event.RIGHT:
    // right arrow key pressed
    break;
```

```
  case Event.UP:
    // up arrow key pressed
    break;
  case Event.DOWN:
    // down arrow key pressed
    break;
  }
  return true;
}
```

This code shows that handling different key presses is as easy as providing a `switch` statement with `case` clauses for each key. Although the example here used the `keyDown` method for handling key presses, the `keyUp` method works in the same fashion.

If you need more details about the key that was pressed or released, you can use the `Event` object passed into the `keyDown` and `keyUp` methods. The typical usage of the `Event` object in regard to key processing is to check for *modifier keys*. Modifier keys are keys that can be pressed in conjunction with other input events, such as the Shift and Control keys. The three methods in `Event` used to check the status of modifier keys follow:

```
public boolean shiftDown()
public boolean controlDown()
public boolean metaDown()
```

All these methods return Boolean values specifying whether or not the key in question is being held down. Checking the status of the modifier keys is necessary sometimes in applets that make heavy use of the mouse. For example, you may have a drawing applet that performs a different function if the Shift key is held down and the mouse is moved.

NOTE

The `shiftDown`, `controlDown`, and `metaDown` methods actually check for the flags `SHIFT_MASK`, `CTRL_MASK`, and `META_MASK`, which are defined in the `Event` class. You can check for any of these flags yourself in lieu of using the comparable methods. There is also an `ALT_MASK` flag which specifies that the Alt key was pressed.

Mouse Events

Mouse events occur when the user moves the mouse or clicks the mouse button. There are a handful of methods for handling mouse events. These methods follow:

```
public boolean mouseUp(Event evt, int x, int y)
public boolean mouseDown(Event evt, int x, int y)
public boolean mouseMove(Event evt, int x, int y)
public boolean mouseDrag(Event evt, int x, int y)
public boolean mouseEnter(Event evt, int x, int y)
public boolean mouseExit(Event evt, int x, int y)
```

All these methods are passed an Event object and two integer parameters representing the X and Y position of the mouse pointer. The mouseUp and mouseDown methods are called when the user presses and releases the mouse button. The mouseMove method is called when the mouse is moved. The mouseDrag method is very similar to the mouseMove method; the only difference is that mouseDrag is called when the mouse is moved with the button held down. The mouseEnter and mouseExit methods are used to track when the mouse enters and exits the applet window.

You can use the x and y parameters passed into the mouse event handler methods to perform any processing based on the position of the mouse. The following code snippet contains an example of overriding the mouseMove method to output the mouse position to standard output:

```
public boolean mouseMove(Event evt, int x, int y) {
  System.out.println("Mouse position = (" + x + ", " + y + ")");
  return true;
}
```

Similar to the keyboard event handlers, you can use the Event object passed in the mouse event handlers to find out additional information such as the status of modifier keys.

Summary

In this chapter, you learned about Java events and the event-driven architecture necessary to support them. More specifically, you learned about Java input events, including the input devices capable of generating them and how they are handled by the Java AWT library. You saw examples of using the input event-handler methods to capture and respond to keyboard and mouse events.

22

Exception Handling

by Michael Morrison

A sad reality associated with being human is that we are all error prone. Because software is a human creation, it often suffers from this same weakness. As nice as the Java programming language is, software written with it will inevitably contain errors. The Java architects realized this and built a complete error-handling mechanism into the Java language and runtime environment. Runtime errors in Java are collectively known as exceptions, and the act of detecting and dealing with these errors is known as exception handling. The focus of this chapter is on understanding exceptions and how to effectively deal with them in Java programs.

What Is Exception Handling?

Although most programs include a certain degree of error-handling overhead, few programmers have the time or resources to fully cover their tracks when it comes to handling every possible type of error that can occur in a running program. For example, is it really the responsibility of the programmer to detect when a user's hard drive fills up, or when the system runs out of memory? If so, what exactly should a program do when something like this occurs? Although Java doesn't completely provide an answer to the latter question, it does address the first one head on.

The Java programming environment borrows a very powerful error-handling technique from C++ known as exception handling. An *exception* is defined as an abnormal event that disrupts the normal flow of a program. *Exception handling*, therefore, is the process of detecting and responding to exceptions in a consistent and reliable manner. The term "exception" is used instead of "error" because exceptions represent exceptional, or abnormal, conditions that aren't necessarily errors. In this way, an exception is a very general concept, meaning that any number of abnormal events could be interpreted as an exception.

So, how do you decide what constitutes an abnormal enough condition to warrant an exception? Most of the time you don't—you let Java decide! The Java API defines practically every type of exception you'll ever need. For a detailed look at exactly what exceptions are defined by the Java API, refer to Chapters 27 through 35 in Part III, "Package, Class, and Interface Reference," which contain information about the different API packages and the exceptions defined in each.

Getting back to exception handling, Java provides a mechanism for detecting and handling exceptions as they occur. More specifically, any method that is at risk of causing an exceptional event is defined as potentially generating an exception. Generating an exception at runtime is also known as *throwing* an exception. Any code that calls this method is aware that the method can potentially throw a particular exception and can include special code to handle the exception should it be thrown. This process is known as *catching* an exception. In this way, you can think of an exception as an object that is thrown containing information about an abnormal event; the exception-handling code catches the exception object and uses any information it provides to help deal with the abnormal event. This actually describes the exact way exceptions work in Java.

To get a better understanding of the practical usage of exception handling, consider the exceptional condition of the system running out of memory. An exception is thrown indicating that the system is out of memory. The exception-handling code catches the exception and in return tries to run the Java garbage collector to free up memory.

Why Is Exception Handling Important?

Obviously, programmers have been dealing with errors for a long time, so you may be wondering why exceptions are such a big deal. This curiosity is reasonable, as there is a lot of code out there working fine without ever using exception-handling facilities. However, like many recent advances in software design, exception handling is meant more as a tool for improving the management of errors by providing a better approach to attacking the problem. The problem isn't so much that programmers don't know how to deal with errors or exceptional conditions; it's that every programmer has his or her own notion of how to go about doing it. Exception handling provides a very standardized approach to something that has been home-brewed for many years now: the handling of errors.

More specifically, exception handling provides the Java programmer with three distinct advantages over traditional error-handling techniques:

- It provides a means to separate error-handling code from functioning program code.
- It provides a mechanism for propagating errors up the method call stack, meaning that methods higher up the call chain can be allowed to handle problems originating lower in the chain.
- It provides a way to organize and differentiate between different types of abnormal conditions.

The first point is significant because, all too often, error-handling code is mixed in with code that actually performs a function. This may not seem like a big deal, but if you carry this approach into a huge project, complexities abound brought on by trying to differentiate between legitimate code that is necessary versus code that is trying to handle some obscure problem condition.

The second advantage of exception handling has to do with making errors accessible to other parts of a program. Typically, you only get a chance to deal with an error at the immediate point where the error occurs. Using exception handling, the error condition itself can be passed up the method call stack so that other objects get a chance to take action based on the problem.

Finally, the last major advantage to using exception handling is that of providing a clean way to organize and differentiate between different types of exceptional conditions. Because exceptions are implemented in Java as actual objects, they are open to the same design benefits of object-oriented programming, such as inheritance. You can define general types of exceptions that deal with a particular set of problems, and then define more specific types that are derived from the general one. In fact, the Java API makes great use of inheritance in the design of its standard exception classes.

Along with the organization benefit at the design stage, you also gain from being able to respond to exceptions based on their type. For example, you may want to handle a whole class of exceptions, such as exceptions relating to indexes being out of bounds. In this case, you wouldn't care if the culprit was a string index or an array index, because the general exception type handles both.

Types of Exceptions

In the discussion thus far, I've been using the terms "exception" and "error" pretty much interchangeably. Although they are the same in a general programming sense, Java does distinguish between the two. In Java, an *exception* is simply defined as an abnormal event that interrupts the normal flow of a program. Most programs are designed to handle any exceptions that may arise during the life of the program. An *error* is a specific type of exception that a program isn't expected to be able to handle. In other words, errors are a more serious strain of exceptions, which are a superset of errors. Check out Figure 22.1, which shows a simple diagram relating exceptions and errors.

FIGURE 22.1.

The relationship between exceptions and errors.

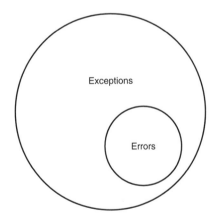

Understanding that errors are a more serious type of exception doesn't really tell the whole story in regard to exceptions. Including errors, there are three different categories of exceptions common to Java programming:

■ Normal exceptions
■ Runtime exceptions
■ Errors

Normal exceptions are exceptions that occur based on a specific piece of code. In other words, the location where a normal exception can occur is predictable, even if the exception itself is not. An example of a normal exception is a *file not found* exception, which occurs at a very specific location in a program when a file access is attempted but the file isn't found.

Unlike normal exceptions, *runtime exceptions* are exceptions whose location is much harder to nail down. For example, a *null pointer* exception can occur any time a null object is referenced, which basically includes any part of a Java program. Because this type of exception is much more general and hard to handle, it is considered a runtime exception. In actuality, all exceptions are thrown at runtime; it's just that runtime exceptions are a specialized type of exception that address problems in programs that have typically been considered runtime problems. Another example of a runtime exception is a *divide by zero* exception, which can occur in practically any mathematical calculation involving a division.

The third type of exception is *errors*, which are more serious exceptions that are aimed at handling catastrophic conditions. No, I don't mean catastrophic as in your monitor bursting into flames; I mean situations where it is very unlikely that a program could handle the problem. This brings up the big distinction between errors and the two prior types of exceptions: Java programs aren't expected to be able to handle errors. Errors are assumed to be beyond the control of a program and are used primarily within the Java system itself to deal with major problems such as running out of system memory or the runtime interpreter crashing.

Throwing Exceptions

You've already learned that the basic gist of exceptions is that an exception is thrown when an abnormal problem arises, and your program is responsible for catching the exception and somehow dealing with it. You'll learn the details of catching exceptions in the next section of this chapter. For now, let's focus on how exceptions are thrown to begin with.

Any code that is capable of throwing an exception must specifically be designed to do so. In other words, exceptions aren't just something that magically appear whenever a problem occurs; code that has the potential of causing problems must be designed to notify a program of these problems accordingly. The Java throws keyword provides the necessary mechanism to wire exception information into code that is potentially dangerous. The throws keyword is used at the method level, meaning that you declare a particular method capable of throwing a certain exception or set of exceptions, like this:

```
public void thisIsTrouble() throws anException {
  // method body
}
```

In this example, the throws keyword is used to specify that the thisIsTrouble method can generate an exception of type anException. Any code that calls this method knows immediately that the risk is there for the method to generate an anException exception. If you have a method that is capable of causing even more problems, you can define it as potentially throwing multiple exceptions, like this:

```
public void thisIsRealTrouble() throws anException, anotherException {
  // method body
}
```

In this example, the `thisIsRealTrouble` method can throw two different types of exceptions: `anException` and `anotherException`.

The whole point of throwing an exception is not to try to deal with a problem at the point where it occurs, but rather to try to allow other code to deal with the problem. In other words, a method that is declared as throwing a particular type of exception is notifying all code that calls it that it might have a problem that it needs help solving. The calling code is responsible for helping out the method by catching the exception and dealing with it as smoothly as possible. If the method itself were capable of handling the problem, it would do so quietly and never mention the problem to the calling code.

The Java programming language is pretty strict about handling exceptions. In fact, the Java compiler will generate warnings if you make calls to methods that throw exceptions without providing the necessary exception-handling code. In some cases, ignoring these warnings may be acceptable programming practice, but in general you should try to address exceptions that can be thrown at your code. Remember, whoever designed the method must have realized there was a potential for trouble, or they wouldn't have declared it as throwing an exception in the first place.

Catching Normal Exceptions

Let's look at exactly how the exception handling is carried out. You've already learned that exceptions are typically thrown relative to a particular method, so you should be able to isolate where an exception is coming from. The trick then is to look for an exception to occur right at the point where you call the method in question. Actually, the technique for handling exceptions involves both looking for the exception and providing code to deal with the exception. You carry out this technique using the `try` and `catch` keywords, like this:

```
try {
  thisIsTrouble();
}
catch(anException e) {
  System.out.println(e.getMessage());
}
```

This code makes a call to the `thisIsTrouble` method inside a `try` block. A `try` block is used to hold code that is at risk of throwing an exception. Any code executing in a `try` block is considered at risk of throwing an exception. If an exception occurs in the `try` block, the runtime system looks to the `catch` clause to see if the exception type matches the one that was thrown. If so, the code in the `catch` block is executed; this is the code that actually deals with, or handles, the exception. From this discussion, you may have guessed that there can be multiple `catch` clauses that respond to different types of exceptions. If so, you guessed right!

Take a look at the following code, which demonstrates how to handle multiple exceptions:

```
try {
  thisIsRealTrouble();
}
catch(anException e) {
  System.out.println(e.getMessage());
}
catch(anotherException e) {
  System.out.println(e.getMessage());
}
```

In this example, the `thisIsRealTrouble` method is called, which is capable of generating two different types of exceptions. Each of these exception types is handled in a separate `catch` clause, which provides a means to handle each type of exception in a unique manner.

As you just learned, the Java system matches up exception types with `catch` clauses when there is an exact match. However, it can also match exception types based on a superclass of an exception. It works like this: when an exception occurs in a `try` block, the `catch` clauses are examined by comparing the exception type to the type in each clause. If the exception type is either the same as the one in a `catch` clause or a subclass of the one in a `catch` clause, a match will occur. This allows you to sometimes provide multilevel catch handlers based on more derived exception types. If you happen to implement an exception-handling arrangement involving derived types, remember to list the more specific types first and the more general types last.

Keep in mind that the Java API defines a wide variety of exceptions that are used a great deal throughout the Java system. So, even though the discussion has been somewhat general thus far, remember that all the exception-handling techniques of trying and catching exceptions apply to standard Java exceptions as well. Check out the following code:

```
try {
  FileInputStream in = new FileInputStream("Data.txt");
}
  catch (FileNotFoundException e) {
  System.out.println("File not found : " + e.getMessage());
}
```

In this example, a file input stream is created using a constructor that takes a filename representing the file to read from. This constructor is defined as throwing a `FileNotFoundException` if the input file cannot be found. Because the constructor is capable of throwing this exception, the sample code creates the object within a `try` block and handles the exception `FileNotFoundException` in a `catch` block. Notice that this example code merely prints information about the exception to standard output. In a practical program, you would probably want to provide a more robust exception handler rather than just one that printed a message to standard output.

Catching Runtime Exceptions

So far you've focused your attention on handling exceptions that are generated by methods. If you recall from the earlier discussion on exception types, these exceptions are referred to as normal exceptions. Another strain of exception you learned about is runtime exceptions, which involve problems that aren't so easy to track down. The following code demonstrates a runtime exception and how it is handled:

```
try {
  int x = 100;
  for (int i = 10; i >= 0; i--)
    System.out.println(x / i);
}
catch(ArithmeticException e) {
  System.out.println(e.getMessage());
}
```

Although it is a little subtle, this code contains a pretty big problem that results in a runtime exception: the `for` loop results in a divide by zero exception in its last iteration. The exception is handled by encasing the problem calculation within a `try` block and providing a corresponding handler by means of a `catch` clause. If you hadn't handled this exception, the runtime system would have bailed out and exited the program with an error message. You provided a cleaner outlet by catching the exception yourself. Again, a more robust solution would probably be in order in a full-blown program, such as notifying the user of an infinite result.

The drawback to this whole approach of handling runtime exceptions is that it requires you to wrap any questionable code inside a `try` block, which can get pretty messy. The solution is to try to balance your handling of exceptions and only go after problems that are significant enough to really cause you trouble. Exceptions are only useful when used in moderation; they aren't meant as an easy out for every little problem you encounter.

Forced Execution

The structure of exception handling tends to cause parts of a program to conditionally execute based on an exception occurring. For this reason, there is a problem of code not getting called when it really should be, based on an exception occurring. For example, consider a program that needs to perform some type of cleanup, regardless of the outcome of a risky piece of code. The very nature of the `try-catch` technique of exception handling makes it difficult to ensure that a particular piece of code is always executed.

Enter the `finally` keyword. The `finally` keyword provides a means of executing a piece of code regardless of what happens within a try block. To use `finally`, you declare a `finally` block and place it after the `try` and `catch` blocks; any code inside the `finally` block is always executed no matter what happens in the try block. You use the `finally` keyword like this:

```
try {
  int x = 100;
  for (int i = 10; i >= 0; i--)
    System.out.println(x / i);
}
catch(ArithmeticException e) {
  System.out.println(e.getMessage());
}
finally {
  System.out.println("Can't get around me!");
}
```

In this example, no matter what happens in the try block, the code inside the finally block is always executed. It turns out that the try block generates an exception that results in the catch block being executed. Nevertheless, as soon as the catch block finishes, the finally block is executed, even if the try or catch blocks had code that resulted in a return from the method. Even though this example doesn't really demonstrate the finally keyword in complete context, the most common usage of it is to provide cleanup for objects that must be performed no matter what happens. Using finally, you can feel safe that a certain piece of code will always get called.

Please don't confuse the name or the usage of the finally keyword with the finalize method. Granted, in some ways they are used to perform a similar function, but finally is a keyword related to exception handling, whereas finalize is a specific method related to object destruction.

When to Use Exception Handling

Even though exception handling is a very powerful and useful facility of the Java programming and runtime environment, it doesn't aim to solve all problems relating to abnormal program execution. You will no doubt encounter many situations where an exception could be in order but where it may be more simple to just handle the problem with an if statement. This thinking doesn't apply to exceptions that are already defined in Java; you can already count on them being important enough to worry about.

The point here is that exception handling should be reserved for legitimate problems where you don't mind taking more time to define a problem and build in the necessary overhead to deal with it. Notice the usage of the term "overhead," which implies that exceptions carry with them a certain amount of baggage. Exceptions do in fact cost more to implement and work with, which is an issue you must weigh when you start thinking about exceptionizing your code.

My suggestion is to handle all the standard Java exceptions accordingly and then assess the needs of your own code carefully. Studying the use of exceptions in the Java API is a very good way to learn about when and where to use exceptions. The Java architects made a lot of tradeoffs in their usage of exceptions, which is a good indicator of how much of a judgment issue exception handling is. Ultimately, experience will be your guide as you work with exceptions in practical programs.

The best approach when designing your own code is to look at how a potential problem impacts the code around it. In other words, does the problem exist only within the confines of a particular method, or can it cause larger problems to the program at large? If the problem can be reasonably dealt with locally, there is probably no need to worry about defining or throwing an exception. However, if there is a chance that the problem can reach beyond the immediate method or object, then by all means toss that exception so other code will know about the risks.

The only other issue to consider is how often the risky code will potentially get called. Because exception handling involves more overhead than most other types of error handling, you don't want to have a bunch of exception-handling code in the middle of a routine that needs to be very efficient, such as a loop that performs some repetitive function. One solution to this problem is to throw an exception the first time a problem occurs, rather than over and over in a piece of code that gets called a lot.

Summary

In this chapter, you learned about imperfections in programming. More importantly, you learned about how Java eases the pain and allows us to be imperfect and still develop robust programs through the use of exception handling. You learned what exception handling is and why it is important in Java development. You then covered the basic kinds of exceptions, which include normal exceptions, runtime exceptions, and errors. You then progressed to how exceptions are thrown and caught, along with how to force the execution of code regardless of exceptional conditions. You finished up the chapter with a practical look at how exceptions can be leveraged alongside more traditional error-handling techniques.

23

Using Observers

by Michael T. Nygard

Introduction

Consider an applet—call it Frammitz 1.0—comprising a large data structure, a sophisticated user interface, and some complex control logic. How would you go about constructing such an applet? As a good object-oriented developer, you immediately say: "Aha! That data structure should go in its own class! While I'm at it, I'll put the logic in there too!" Uttering the battle cry of the followers of OO—"Encapsulate!"—you separate the data from the interface. You then reap the many expected benefits—increased abstraction and readability, and reduced complexity (which helps during maintenance, too). By partitioning the system into interface and behavior, you reduce the coupling between classes. You also pave the way for later reuse of either piece. By keeping the interface separate, you avoid the "event-spaghetti" code that plagues many object-oriented GUI environments. So, you have two classes: a UI in the form of an applet, and the data with its rules. Because the rules for handling the data are important, you make sure that the only way to access the data is through methods that enforce the rules. Otherwise, a malicious object could circumvent the model's logic. Now you have a full-fledged model and its user interface.

Consider the user interface a bit more closely. The user interface arbitrates between the user and the model. So, it makes sense to think of the user interface from two perspectives. First, what about the model needs to be presented? Second, what tasks will a user perform on that model? Thus, thinking in terms of a model, what does a UI really need to do? Well, it needs to present the model in a comprehensible way. Most of the time, it also needs to allow the user to interact with the model. An unspoken assumption is that the interface always accurately reflects the contents of the model. That is, the state of the interface should always be consistent with that of the model. All right then, we need two sets of methods in the user interface, a group of display methods to present the model, and a group of control methods, which can alter the model. (These usually end up being `paint` and `action` methods.) So, we code the `paint` and `action` methods to access Frammitz's associated data object. The `paint` methods read the model's state from one set of accessor methods. The `action` methods change the model's state through a different set of accessor and logic methods.

Flash forward a few weeks (or maybe days). For the most part, all went well on Frammitz version 1.0. You ran into a little sticky spot when implementing the control methods. You see, any time the model changed, you had to redisplay the new data. Because the control methods were changing the model, they had to call the display methods to update the display. So, it got a little messy—the control methods were calling the display methods all over the place—but it works. Version 1.0 is out the door (although that particular metaphor probably needs to be updated for the Webbed World).

Disaster! Frammitz 1.0 is a wild success. Your users love it, and your boss loves that your users love it. Why is that a disaster? Because your users love it so much that they are requesting all kinds of wild enhancements—things like totally new ways of looking at the model, or totally new ways of interacting with it, or new rules for the model itself. "While you're at it, how hard would it be to add multithreading?" Sound familiar? Odds are, you've been here at least once. Nothing fails like success, because now you must find a way to add new views and new rules. Suddenly, what seemed like "a little sticky spot" starts to look like exponentially proliferating methods, with all the maintenance and stability problems that that implies. Worse yet, because this applet is constantly being shipped all over the world in byte-codes, adding even a few kilobytes to your code size can turn the most loyal of users against you. Frammitz 2.0 starts to look unlikely.

Now, imagine that a simple design change in the beginning could make changing views simple. Or that it could make new interaction modes possible, without doubling the number of methods and interconnections in your class. Even better, imagine that your users could create their own views, without affecting your model! Now you're cooking with gas! Decoupling your classes is the secret. You can achieve complete decoupling in many cases by using a class and an interface defined in package `java.util`. It provides a class, `Observable`, and an interface, `Observer`, that can make it happen. `Observable`s collaborate with `Observer`s to automatically keep `Observer`s up to date. The `Observer`s can use these notifications to synchronize their state with that of the `Observable`s, or to update their display, or to trigger some other action.

This chapter will present the parts of the `Observer`/`Observable` pair and describe their interaction with the aid of a simple example. By examining `Observer`/`Observable` as a *design pattern*, it will discuss the implications of using the **Observer** pattern. It will also explore an important object-oriented architecture enabled by **Observer**, which originated in Smalltalk-80, called Model-View-Controller or MVC. A more sophisticated example will illustrate the flexibility provided by using MVC. A final section will briefly discuss other applications of **Observer**, outside of the GUI realm. (**Observer** in boldface refers to the pattern name. `Observer` in monospaced type refers to the interface defined by `java.util.Observer`, and `ConcreteObserver` refers to any class that implements `Observer`. Don't worry, each of these is discussed in detail later on.)

Interface `Observer`

The `Observer` interface is shown in Listing 23.1. It is quite simple, consisting of only one method declaration—`update`. By defining `update` within a class, you make that class an `Observer`.

Listing 23.1. The definition of interface `Observer`.

```
package java.util;

public interface Observer {
    void update(Observable o, Object arg);
}
```

NOTE

By convention, an interface name usually ends in "-able," but not this time. Here, the class name ends in "-able," but the interface name does not. Admittedly, this is not terribly consistent, but imagine how confusing it would be if the "Observable" were actually the thing doing the observing, and the "Observer" were the thing being observed!

Observers subscribe to Observables. One Observer can subscribe to many Observers, but there is only one update() method, which all of the Observables will call. The Observer can use the first argument to update() to tell which Observable sent the notification. The second argument is available for whatever use the Observable supplies. Generally, arg will be one of two things:

■ The data item within the Observable that changed.

■ An event object of whatever protocol the Observer and Observable agree upon.

Using arg for an application-specific protocol can optimize the updates greatly; however, it increases the coupling between the classes.

Remember that Java considers interfaces to be types. Suppose a class PassMe extends Applet and implements Observer. Then, an instance of PassMe can legitimately be passed to any of the following functions:

```
public void GiveMeAnApplet(Applet a);
public void GiveMeAnObserver(Observer o);
public void GiveMeAPassMe(PassMe p);
```

Moreover, GiveMeAnObserver can take an instance of any other class that implements Observer, whatever its class type or superclass may be. This first-class rank of interfaces is the key to Java's **Observer** mechanism. (For more details on interfaces and inheritance, see the sidebar "Interface vs. Implementation Inheritance" later in this chapter.)

Class Observable

The public and protected interface to class Observable is shown in Listing 23.2.

Listing 23.2. The definition of class Observable.

```
package java.util;

public class Observable {
    public synchronized void addObserver(Observer o);
    public synchronized void deleteObserver(Observer o);
    public synchronized int countObservers();
    public void notifyObservers();
    public synchronized void notifyObservers(Object arg);
```

```
    public synchronized void deleteObservers();
    protected synchronized void setChanged();
    protected synchronized void clearChanged();
    protected synchronized boolean hasChanged();
}
```

Remember that this is a class, so your data items and models will use Observable by inheriting from it. Although they are not declared as final, there is usually no reason to override the provided implementations for these methods. You can see that this class is well protected for use by multithreaded applications. Indeed, allowing changes from any thread to be immediately reflected in other threads is one of the best uses for the Observer/Observable pair.

The addObserver() and deleteObserver() methods allow an Observer to subscribe or unsubscribe to this Observable. Notice that they each take a parameter of type Observer. This implies that they can be passed instances of any class that implements Observer. Internally, Observable maintains a vector of all the Observers that have been added to it. When notifyObservers() is called, the update() method of each subscribed Observer is invoked with an optional argument to indicate what changed.

The setChanged(), clearChanged(), and hasChanged() methods allow a subclass of Observable to keep a "dirty flag" to indicate when the Observers need to be notified. Typically, an Observable will call setChanged() as soon as a state change occurs. It will not call clearChanged() until it notifies its Observers. Although these methods are protected, you may sometimes find it useful to define pass-through methods in your subclass. Allowing another object to set and clear this flag can sometimes speed up notifications.

Notice that there are two forms of notifyObservers(), one with an Object argument and one with no arguments. The simpler form of notifyObservers() just calls notifyObservers(null). (That is why the simpler form is not synchronized.) For simple data items, the first form is adequate. Sometimes it will be useful to provide the Observer with more information about *what* has changed. In a complex Observable, it may be costly to redisplay everything, so the Observer would like to optimize its redisplay. Often, this is impossible, because it can be difficult to deduce what aspect of an Observable has changed. Because you can pass any Object to notifyObservers(), your particular Observable can define a protocol for its Observers. For example, an Observable that maintained a vector of Points might pass the changed Point to its Observers. Be careful, however, that this protocol does not couple the Observer too tightly to the Observable. Your Observable should consider this argument a hint to the Observer, something which can help the Observer, but could safely be ignored.

Putting Them Together

Neither Observer nor Observable is useful by itself. Used together, Observer and Observable create a *publish-subscribe* protocol. The Observable publishes notifications, to which Observers subscribe. It sends notifications to any and all interested Observers, without knowing or caring what the concrete classes of the Observers are. Any number of Observers can subscribe to a single Observable. Also, each Observer can subscribe to more than one Observable. This creates a one-to-many dependency between objects so that when the Observable changes state, all of its dependents (Observers) are notified and can update themselves automatically.

You cannot use either the Observer interface or the Observable class as is. In order to make use of this publish-subscribe protocol, you must subclass Observable *and* implement Observer. In the rest of this chapter, Observer refers to the interface, whereas ConcreteObserver refers to a class that implements Observer. Likewise, Observable refers to the class Observable, whereas ConcreteObservable refers to a specific subclass of Observable. Figure 23.1 illustrates the relationships involved between Observer, its ConcreteObserver, the ConcreteObservable under scrutiny, and Observable.

FIGURE 23.1.

Relationships between
Observer,
ConcreteObserver,
Observable, *and*
ConcreteObservable.

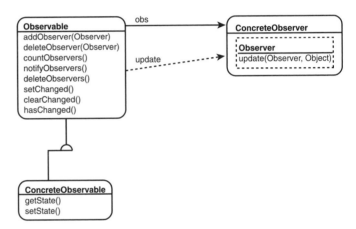

The Observable knows its Observers but does not know what they are. This important distinction arises because Observer is an interface. Each Observer can be from vastly different, unrelated classes. Because they implement the correct interface, Observable can send the notification without any regard for what each Observer does on receipt of the message.

In Figure 23.2, you can see the flow of events that occurs when an Observable's state is changed. The initial "set" message can come from an Observer or from some other controlling class. The accessor methods that cause state changes must set the "dirty" flag by calling setChanged(). At some point notifyObservers() gets called, often from within the accessor method itself. Sometimes, another object will call it. Both methods have advantages. (See the section "Observer Implementation Trade-Offs" later in this chapter.) In this case, the ConcreteObservable itself calls notifyObservers(). Within notifyObservers(), the ConcreteObservable calls the update() method on each ConcreteObserver in turn. The order in which the Observers are notified is undefined. (Even though you can look at the source code for Observable and see exactly what the order will be, that is an implementation detail, not part of Observable's contract! The abstraction of Observable does not define the notification order, so you should not rely on the implementation. After all, implementations change without warning.) After the Observers have been notified, the `ConcreteObservable` calls `clearChanged()`. It is very important that all of the crucial data items in a `ConcreteObservable` are private. If any were made public, other objects could modify the members without calling `setChanged()` or `notifyObservers()`, completely defeating the purpose of using `Observers` in the first place.

FIGURE 23.2.

Object interaction diagram.

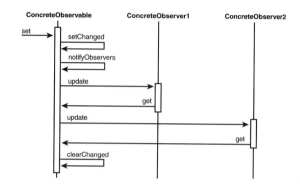

NOTE

Sometimes, it will be useful to add public methods to your `Observable` to pass through to `setChanged()` and `clearChanged()`. For example, if your controller is in the process of making several small changes to different parts of the `Observable`'s state, you may want to defer the `notifyObservers()` call until all of the changes are done. Avoiding superfluous updates can boost performance significantly. By eliminating unnecessary updates, you also eliminate the annoying display flicker from the extra updates.

On the other hand, adding that sort of knowledge to your controller increases the coupling between the controller and the `Observable`.

A Simple Example: The `SlideValue` Applet

Let's use `Observer` and `Observable` to create a simple applet. This applet will consist of a scrollbar and a text field. We want the text field to always reflect the value of the scrollbar. For this example, the relationship will be one-way. That is, changes to the text field do not need to be reflected in the scrollbar. Adding the updates in the other direction is just an application of the same techniques used here. Figure 23.3 shows the `SlideValue` applet in action.

FIGURE 23.3.

The `SlideValue` applet in action.

The most basic approach, and the one taken most often by new designers, would be to construct an applet class with a scrollbar, a text field, and a private integer. The class would have an event handler for the scrollbar changes, which would update the internal integer and call a method to put a string in the text field. Although this approach has the benefit of keeping everything in one class, there really is no way to separate the behavior from the interface. Any future changes in either presentation or behavior would require touching every part of the class that deals with presentation and behavior.

A more sophisticated approach separates the data, the view, and the controller. By using a separate data class, derived from Observable, we can implement whatever logic is necessary to maintain a consistent state. In addition, we can change that logic without having to make any corresponding changes in the user interface. Because the text field needs to update itself when the data value changes, we will derive a class from java.awt.TextField, which implements Observer.

The Observable

In this case, the ConcreteObservable is Value, shown in Listing 23.3. It mainly consists of the value itself, val, and two methods to set and return the value. Look carefully at the set() method. The extra code in this method sets the changed flag, notifies any interested Observers, and then clears the changed flag. (If the changed flag is not set, notifyObservers() will do nothing.) As an alternative to the boolean flag provided by Observable, your ConcreteObservable class can also override the hasChanged() method to perform more sophisticated detection.

When Value calls notifyObservers(), it uses the form without parameters. Because there is only one item of interest (one state variable) in this class, passing anything to the notification would be somewhat superfluous.

Listing 23.3. Value.java, **the** ConcreteObservable **for the** SlideValue **example.**

```
/*
** Value.java
**
** ConcreteObserver class for the SlideValue example
**
*/

import java.util.Observable;

class Value extends Observable {
    private float val;

    public void Value(float v) {
        val = v;
    }

    public void set(float v) {
        setChanged();
        val = v;
        notifyObservers();
        clearChanged();
```

```
    }

    public float get() {
        return val;
    }
}
```

The Observer

For this example, the only view into the data is a simple text field. For this reason, our ConcreteObserver will be derived from java.awt.TextField, which will implement Observer. Observer is an interface, so any class can implement it, whatever its heritage. Listing 23.4 shows View.java.

Listing 23.4. View.java, the ConcreteObserver for the SlideValue example.

```
/*
** View.java
**
** ConcreteObserver for the SlideValue example
**
*/

import java.awt.TextField;
import java.util.Observer;
import java.util.Observable;
import Value;

class View extends TextField implements Observer {
    public void update(Observable o, Object arg) {
        Value v = (Value)o;

        setText(Float.toString(v.get()));
    }
}
```

Because the update method is passed an Observable, View must cast the Observable to a Value. In this example, View will only be used to observe Value, so this cast is safe. In a production class, you would want to use the instanceof operator to ensure safe casting. In fact, if you have several ConcreteObservables you want to observe from a single ConcreteObserver, a good approach would be to define a protocol by which the ConcreteObserver can query the state of the Observables.

The Controller

The controller for SlideValue is embedded directly in the applet class. In general, the controller should have its own class also. In this case, however, we are primarily interested in the interaction between Value and View. Therefore, embedding the controller in the applet class helps clarify that interaction. (See Listing 23.5.)

Listing 23.5. SlideValue applet definition.

```
/*
** SlideValue.java
**
** Applet container for SlideValue example
**
*/

import java.applet.*;
import java.awt.*;
import Value;
import View;

public class SlideValue extends Applet {
    private Value      value;
    private View       view;
    private Scrollbar controller;

    public void init() {
        // Set up a layout manager
        setLayout(new BorderLayout());
        resize(200, 55);

        // Create the value, view, and controller.
        value = new Value();
        view = new View();
        controller = new Scrollbar(Scrollbar.HORIZONTAL, 0, 10, 0, 100);

        // Add the view to the model's notification list.
        value.addObserver(view);

        // Put the view and the controller into the UI.
        add("North", controller);
        add("South", view);
    }

    public boolean handleEvent(Event e) {
        if (e.target instanceof Scrollbar) {
            value.set((float)controller.getValue());
        }
        return super.handleEvent(e);
    }
}
```

This simple applet really just creates the components and defines the relationships. It uses the Border Layout Manager described in Chapter 17, "Programming the User Interface," to place the View and ScrollBar objects. For this example, the ConcreteObserver and ConcreteObservable are both created by the applet itself, and the Observer is added to the notify list right here. In general, the applet itself does not need to create all of the relationships. You can even have the constructor for the Observer take an Observable as a parameter, although you will usually not want to introduce another class dependency. By constructing the relationship outside of the two classes being related, you reduce the coupling between those classes and allow them to be related in different ways as the occasions arise.

The HTML Container

The containing page for this applet is extremely basic. Listing 23.6 shows the HTML code. It simply gives the applet a region of the page and provides links to the Java code.

Listing 23.6. HTML container page for the SlideValue example.

```
<title>SlideValue</title>
<hr>
<applet code=SlideValue.class>
</applet>
<hr>
<a href="SlideValue.java">SlideValue.java</a><br>
<a href="View.java">View.java</a><br>
<a href="Value.java">Value.java</a><p>
```

SlideValue Interaction

Figure 23.4 shows the interaction diagram for the SlideValue applet. The chain of events begins when the user acts upon the scrollbar. This results in a call to SlideValue.handleEvent(), which sets the value of Value. At this point, the controller is finished. After set is called, SlideValue leaves the picture. None of the interaction from this point on involves the main applet. Instead, everything happens between the Value and its Observers (just the single TextField view this time around).

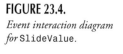

FIGURE 23.4.

Event interaction diagram for SlideValue.

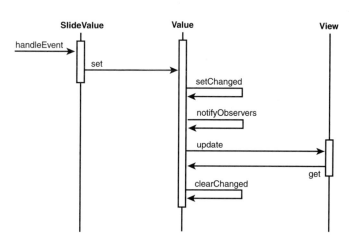

`Value` publishes its state, and `View` subscribes to it. By relating the classes this way, all changes to `Value`'s state are automatically reflected in `View`. Additional views can be added easily. Further, the applet code does not need to know anything about the state of `Value` or `Value`'s implementation. It does not need to know anything about how `View` creates its display or gets updates. By reducing the amount of knowledge one class needs about another, we have reduced the coupling. To illustrate, let's enhance `SlideValue` to include a second view, a gauge that shows the `Value` as a percentage. (See Figure 23.5.)

FIGURE 23.5.

`SlideValue` *in action,*
with a `GaugeView` *added.*

The new view will be a subclass of `Panel`, and, of course, it will implement `Observer`. Listing 23.7 shows the new class. Although `GaugeView` does maintain an integer, `lastKnownPercentage`, which is fetched from `Value`, it is not really copying the state of `Value`. It is processed after retrieving it from `Value` (a cast from `float` to `int`) and treated as read-only elsewhere. A member used this way is more like a cached value than a state variable. The cached value is guaranteed to be up-to-date, because any time the `Value` changes, `GaugeView` gets notified! An equally valid technique would be to store a reference to `Value` in `GaugeView` and get the value directly from `Value` whenever it is needed. In this case, the added overhead of the extra method calls far outweighs the added storage for the extra integer. For a more complex model, that might not be the case.

Listing 23.7. The new `GaugeView` class.

```
/*
** GaugeView.java
**
** A new ConcreteObserver for the SlideValue example
**
*/

import java.awt.Panel;
import java.awt.Graphics;
import java.awt.Dimension;
import java.awt.FontMetrics;
import java.awt.Color;
import java.util.Observer;
import java.util.Observable;
import Value;

class   GaugeView extends Panel implements Observer {
    private int lastKnownPercentage;

    public void update(Observable o, Object arg) {
        Graphics  g = getGraphics();
        Value     v = (Value)o;

        lastKnownPercentage = (int)v.get();
```

```
        repaint();
    }

    public void paint(Graphics g) {
        Dimension    d = size();
        FontMetrics  fm = g.getFontMetrics();
        int          textHeight = fm.getAscent() + fm.getDescent();
        StringBuffer s = new StringBuffer();

        s.append(lastKnownPercentage);
        s.append("%");

        g.setColor(getForeground());

        g.fillRect(0, 0,
            (int)(d.width * (lastKnownPercentage / 100.0)),
            d.height);

        g.setColor(Color.lightGray);
        g.drawString(s.toString(),
            (int)((d.width - fm.stringWidth(s.toString()))/2),
            (int)((d.height - textHeight)/2 + fm.getAscent()));
    }
}
```

Listing 23.8 shows the modifications to SlideValue in bold. Notice that the only changes required to add a new view were in the code that creates the view itself! The Value and the existing View did not change at all—not one line.

Listing 23.8. The modified SlideValue applet class with changes shown in bold.

```
/*
** SlideValue.java
**
** Applet container for SlideValue example
**
*/

import java.applet.*;
import java.awt.*;
import Value;
import View;
import GaugeView;

public class SlideValue extends Applet {
    private Value      value;
    private View       view;
    private GaugeView gauge;
    private Scrollbar controller;

    public void init() {
        // Set up a layout manager
        setLayout(new BorderLayout());
        resize(200, 55);
```

continues

Listing 23.8. continued

```
        // Create the value, views, and controller.
        value = new Value();
        view = new View();
        gauge = new GaugeView();
        controller = new Scrollbar(Scrollbar.HORIZONTAL, 0, 10, 0, 100);

        // Add the views to the model's notification list.
        value.addObserver(view);
        value.addObserver(gauge);

        // Put the views and the controller into the UI.
        add("North", controller);
        add("South", view);
        add("Center", gauge);
    }

    public boolean handleEvent(Event e) {
        if (e.target instanceof Scrollbar) {
            value.set((float)controller.getValue());
        }
        return super.handleEvent(e);
    }
}
```

No way could you add a new feature to a monolithic applet that easily! Because we used
Observers, the new view dropped right in without disturbing the existing classes.

INTERFACE VERSUS IMPLEMENTATION INHERITANCE

Java supports several advanced object-oriented constructs, including interfaces. An
interface is a collection of method signatures, without actual implementations. A class
can declare that it implements one or more interfaces. Think of an interface as a
contract between your class and other objects. By implementing interfaces, your class
commits to providing methods with the same signatures as in the interface. Java treats
interfaces as first class types; you can declare variables of interface types just as you
would declare variables of class types. Although a class can only inherit from one base
class, it can implement several interfaces. The main distinction is that interfaces do not
override implementations. (In other words, you cannot call "super" methods in an
interface method.)

Interfaces are useful when you need to require certain behavior from client objects, but
do not necessarily want all of the client objects to share a common parent. For example, it is impractical to require that all Observers inherit from a common base class.
That would preclude you from subclassing TextField, Panel, Thread, and so on as
Observers.

There are two situations that become somewhat confusing. First, what happens when a class implements two interfaces with the same method? Because no implementation comes with either interface, there is no conflict. The class simply provides one actual method that can be called from either interface. Second, what happens when you subclass a class that implements an interface? The subclasses automatically implement the interface, through the parent class's method. In fact, you can override the parent class's method (even calling the "super" method). Your class will still legally implement the interface. (For an example of this usage, see the classes TwoDView and XYView in the AppletCAD example later in this chapter.)

Flexible Object-Oriented Design

Designing flexible, reusable object-oriented software is difficult in any language. Balancing the needs of the problem at hand with the desire for reuse is difficult, even for the most seasoned designer. In fact, most of the thought involved in creating any software goes toward solving problems during design. With a good design, the actual coding becomes largely mechanical. So, how can we create good designs, designs that can evolve with the requirements of a project?

Experienced object-oriented designers know better than to solve every problem from scratch. Rather, when faced with a problem, experienced designers will compare it to similar problems they have faced in the past and apply a solution that worked before. They tend to work with a group of tried-and-true designs, adapting them to the problem at hand. This is not the same as code reuse. Actual code reuse is rare and vastly overstated. Instead, they reuse designs by extracting recurring patterns of classes, relationships, and interaction. These *design patterns* solve specific problems that occur over and over again across a wide variety of domains. By recognizing and identifying a design pattern, you become able to reuse that design by applying it to new problems. Design patterns make it easier to take a successful architecture of classes, communicating objects, and relationships to a new problem.

In general, design patterns are not code. Instead, they collect a common interaction and a common set of objects at an abstract level. The actual coding depends on the particular problem. Design patterns are not a template mechanism, like the templates in C++. They are also not classes that you can directly apply. Moreover, design patterns are not language-specific. The pattern itself is completely abstract. It is the kernel of a solution, not the solution itself. In the case of Java, there are classes and interfaces that allow you to apply some patterns easily, but this is an instance of a pattern. This distinction—between the pattern and one implementation of the pattern—is the same as the distinction between a class and an instance of that class. One is abstract, describing *how* to construct something. The second is the product of that construction.

The designers of the Java classes collectively represent decades of experience with object-oriented designs. Not surprisingly, the built-in Java classes include instantiations of several design patterns. One particularly well-known design pattern is **Observer**. Also not surprisingly, the instantiation of the **Observer** pattern comprises the Observer interface and the Observable class. From here on, this chapter will refer to the aggregate of Observer, Observable, and their interaction as **Observer**. (Remember, **Observer** in boldface refers to the pattern name, while Observer in monospaced type refers to the interface defined by java.util.Observer. ConcreteObserver refers to any class that implements Observer.)

Observer as a Design Pattern

The need to partition an object-oriented system into a collection of interdependent classes leads to a common difficulty. Often, related classes must maintain a consistent state. A label must reflect the contents of a string, or a choice box must only display the choices allowed by a policy determined by another object. Tight coupling between classes is one (poor) way to achieve coherence. Many early object-oriented designs relied upon classes having such carnal knowledge of each other. This approach works. It is easy to design and code. On the other hand, the tight coupling severely limits—or eliminates—their reusability. Such systems do not grow or evolve well.

Many GUI toolkits solve this problem by separating the interface classes from the underlying model. As in the earlier example, classes defining the application data and the interface can each be reused or replaced independently. Multiple views of the application data can coexist. For all intents and purposes, the views will behave as if they have full knowledge of each other. Changes to one view are automatically reflected in the others. Figure 23.6 shows a conceptual example of this partitioning. In this example, three views into the application data need to be kept synchronized with the data itself. Such a system will behave as if the views are tightly coupled, when, in fact, quite the opposite is true.

FIGURE 23.6.

Conceptual model of the model/interface partitioning and interaction.

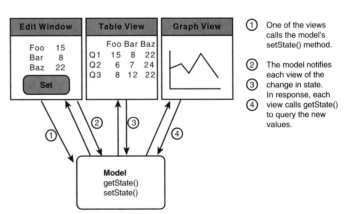

① One of the views calls the model's setState() method.

② The model notifies each view of the change in state.

③ In response, each view calls getState() to query the new values.

④

This type of interaction is characteristic of the **Observer** design pattern. As described earlier, the key parts of **Observer** are the Observer and the Observable. The Observable may have any number of Observers, drawn from any number of potentially unrelated classes. Whenever the Observable's public state changes, all of its Observers are notified of the change. All Observers are notified. If an Observer initiated the state change, it will still receive the notification and should postpone its update until it receives the notification. When an Observer receives a notification, it queries the Observable in order to synchronize its state with that of the Observable.

This pattern is sometimes referred to as Publish-Subscribe or Dependents. Each of the three names reflects a different perspective on the interaction. (Chris Warth, the Java developer who implemented this pattern, evidently preferred Observer.) The Observable publishes notifications, to which the Observers subscribe. Or, looking at it another way, the Observers are dependent on the Observable.

Whatever name you prefer, there are several situations in which this pattern is applicable:

■ When two or more objects need to remain synchronized, without making assumptions about the objects themselves. (This is the essence of decoupling.)

■ When a change to one object can trigger actions in an unspecified number of other objects. The change can come from an external object or agent, or from an internal event, such as a clock tick. These notifications can cascade.

■ When an abstraction has more than one interdependent part. By separating the pieces of the abstraction into multiple objects, you can reuse or replace the pieces independently. (This follows the maxim: "If it changes, encapsulate it. If it doesn't change, encapsulate it anyway.")

Some Implications of Using Observer

This pattern allows you to independently reuse or replace Observers and Observables. This tremendous level of flexibility does not come without a cost, however. The most obvious cost is complexity. By using **Observer**, you do add a certain degree of complexity to your system. There will be at least one additional class, if nothing else. For anything other than a small system, the added complexity is a small price to pay, both in terms of code size and development time. Furthermore, to anyone familiar with the **Observer** pattern, the intent of your code will be immediately obvious. (This is a bonus awarded for using a well-known pattern!)

Observer carries a more insidious cost you must be aware of. Because the notification protocol is very generic, an Observer often has no details on what part of the Observable's state changes, or who made the change. Without adding to the protocol, it can be difficult for an Observer to deduce the nature and origin of a change. Adding such a protocol can improve performance, sometimes dramatically, by eliminating unnecessary work in the Observers and by allowing Observers to ignore notifications in which they have no interest. At the same time, however, adding the extra protocol increases the coupling between the classes.

Another possible solution to this problem would be to allow an Observer to subscribe to specific parts of an Observable. The Java team evidently decided that the benefits of that approach were outweighed by the added conceptual and code complexity required. It would not be difficult, however, to create your own implementation of the **Observer** pattern that did allow partial subscriptions.

Because multiple Observers do not know about each other's existence, they may be ignorant of the ultimate cost of a simple state change. A small, relatively harmless-seeming change can trigger many updates, even a cascade of updates, because an Observer of one item may be an Observable to its own Observers. Observers do not know the implementation details of the Observable, so a particular Observer cannot predict which changes will trigger notifications.

The coupling between Observables and their Observers is minimal. The Observers do need a little more information about the Observable, but still relatively little. Because an Observable knows nothing about the concrete class of an Observer, Observers can be modified or added long after the initial design.

An added bonus that Java awards you for using **Observer** is that there is often no need to download some of the Observers. If your applet includes ten potential views, but the user only calls for two of them, there is no need to download the other eight classes. This kind of runtime customization can really improve the perceived performance of your applet.

Interactions

The publish-subscribe interaction is depicted in Figure 23.7. This basically follows the interaction you observed in the SlideValue example. Several questions arise about this diagram. First, how are these relationships created? Also, when should notifyObservers() be called? **Observer** does not specify the answers. Instead, when you implement the pattern, you decide what is the best option for this application. (This tailoring is a fundamental characteristic of a design pattern, and it is one of the things that distinguish a pattern from an actual design. A pattern describes the core of a solution to a problem—you can use it a million times over and never do it the same way twice.)

FIGURE 23.7.

Basic Observer/ Observable *interaction during a* notifyObservers.

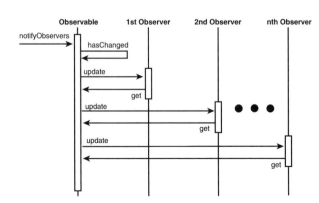

Figure 23.8 depicts a cascaded notification, in which ConcreteObserver2 is also an Observable for ConcreteObserver3. You might use an arrangement like this when dealing with a layered system. Because the coupling between Observers and Observables is very loose, you can span architectural layers without violating the system layering. In Figure 23.8, for example, ConcreteObservable might be at the data access layer, ConcreteObserver2 at the logic layer, and ConcreteObserver3 at the interface layer.

FIGURE 23.8.

Cascaded notification when an Observer *is also* Observable.

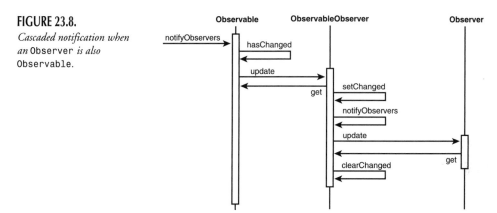

It is possible to have mutually dependent Observables that are both also Observers. These objects would interact exactly as in Figure 23.7. This time, however, the classes each need some knowledge about the other. They must be careful not to trigger a notification during their update methods, or a vicious cycle of notifications will ensue. (This can really be a problem in multithreaded applications, because one thread will go completely out to lunch and eat processor cycles, but everything else will seem to work fine. In fact, other Observers will often still behave correctly.) Such a storm of notifications can be exceedingly difficult to detect.

Observer Implementation Trade-Offs

This section discusses some of the decisions made by the Java team. It also explores some of the implementation choices you will need to make when using **Observer**.

Observables need to know about their Observers. Observables could maintain a simple array, an associative array (a hash table), a linked list, and so on. The Java team chose to use a subclass of Vector to maintain the Observers. Strictly speaking, this is part of the implementation details of Observable, and we should ignore such details. However, because we are inheriting from Observable, implementation details such as this have some direct implications. By using Vector to contain the Observers, we can have an arbitrary number of them, while still maintaining a good memory/speed balance. Thus, an Observer with no Observables incurs minimal overhead. Sequential and random access to the Observer list allows good performance when adding or deleting Observers. Therefore, we can create Observables with many Observers with confidence that performance will not degrade unduly.

In some implementations of **Observer**, Observers maintain references to their Observables. This leads to a number of additional synchronization problems, especially when deleting Observables. To avoid this problem, the Java implementation of Observer has no reference to the Observable. One consequence of this decision is that Observers cannot access their Observable's state outside of the update method. As in the GaugeView class in the SlideValue example, the Observer must cache any information it needs in methods like paint. An alternative approach would have update in your ConcreteObserver store the Observable reference passed to it, at which point we come full circle to the problem of dangling references.

Sometimes, it makes sense for a single Observer to depend on multiple Observables. For example, a complicated form may incorporate data from multiple data sources, or a three-dimensional rendering may include multiple models. For situations like this, the Observable reference passed to update can disambiguate *what* is being updated. If each Observable of interest is from a separate class, the instanceof keyword can provide enough information. If some of the Observables are from the same classes, your Observer may need to keep references to all of its Observables and compare the object references.

Does it seem as if many of these issues imply that Observers should keep references to their Observables? You may ask why the Java team did not incorporate these references into Observer. Well, first of all, Observer is an interface—it has no data members. More importantly, however, the Java implementation is the most basic and generic one. Nothing in the Java implementation precludes adding an Observable reference in your Observers. If the implementation already had such references, you would not be able to remove them from your Observers. In other words, you can embellish the existing classes at will, but it is impossible to delete items from parent classes. This philosophy is apparent in much of the Java class architecture. Wherever possible, the Java developers have provided enough of a framework to allow the embellishment, but not require it.

One of the questions you must answer when using Observers is "Who calls notifyObservers()?" There are basically two options:

■ Have the Observable itself call notifyObservers() when it changes its own state. The advantage of this approach is that the objects that request the state changes do not need to know that the object is an Observable. It is impossible to subvert the publish-subscribe mechanism, whether intentionally or accidentally. The developers of the client classes do not need to remember to call notifyObservers(). In the face of multiple, rapid updates, this approach will cause several notifications, which may degrade performance.

■ Have the client object call notifyObservers() when it is finished making state changes. Although this approach can provide dramatically improved performance by not triggering unnecessary updates, it is not as safe. Client objects have an additional responsibility, making errors more likely. Client may forget to call notifyObservers(), or they might deliberately avoid the call. In the Java environment, you can never really guarantee that your class will be used only in the intended manner.

If you decide to have client objects call notifyObservers(), your Observable will need pass-through methods for the setChanged() and clearChanged() methods. The notifyObservers() methods in Observable check hasChanged(). If hasChanged() returns false, notifyObservers() does nothing.

An issue of consistency relates to this question of responsibility. It is very important that Observables publish notifications only when their internal state is consistent. Otherwise, Observers may update their state from an inconsistent Observable. Intentional violations of this rule are not a big problem—they are easily caught—but inherited operations can lead to violations. For example, consider the following code fragment:

```
public class ParentClass extends Observable {
...
    public void setState(float value) {
        m_ParentState = value;
        setChanged();
        notifyObservers();
        clearChanged();
    }
}

public class ChildClass extends ParentClass {
...
    public void setState(float value) {
        super.setState(value);      // notifyObservers gets called.
        setChanged();
        m_ChildState += value;      // Too late!
        clearChanged();
    }
}
```

By the time m_ChildState is updated, the notifications have already been sent, while the state was inconsistent. Sending another notification will not help, because there is no telling what the Observer did with the bogus values in the meantime. If making all state-changing methods in your Observable final is an option, you should do so. If not, you can use another technique that is more or less bulletproof. The trick is to remove the notification code from the methods that get inherited. Or, stated another way, inherit only the state modification code. The following code fragment illustrates this technique:

```
public class ParentClass extends Observable {
...
    public final void setState(float value) {
        internalSetState(value);
        notifyObservers();
        clearChanged();
    }
    protected void internalSetState(float value) {
        m_ParentState = value;
        setChanged();
    }
}
```

```
public class ChildClass extends ParentClass {
...
    protected void internalSetState(float value) {
        super.internalSetState(value);
        m_ChildState += value;
    }
}
```

MULTITHREADED OBSERVERS

A multithreaded application is an ideal environment for using **Observer**. Often, controllers and views execute in separate threads. Using an Observable allows the controller object, in its thread, to make changes in a synchronized manner. At the same time, the Observers automatically get notified. Be careful, because update() gets called in the context of the controller that made the changes. If you intend to use Observers in a multithreaded application, all of your update() methods should be synchronized. In addition, if your Observer needs to do a lot of work in response to an update, it should do it in the context of the Observer's thread and not tie up the controller's thread. Take a look at the following code fragment for an idea of how this would work.

```
public class MyObserver implements Observer {
    boolean bUpdateNeeded;
    ...
    public void update(Observable o, Object arg) {
        updateSync(o, arg);
    }

    private synchronized void updateSync(Observable o, Object arg) {
        wait();
        bUpdateNeeded = true;
        notify();
    }
    ...
    public void RunsInThread() {
        /* Wait for notice that an update is needed. */
        while(bUpdateNeeded == false) {
            try {
                wait();
            } catch (InterruptedException e) {
            }
        }
        bUpdateNeeded = false;
        notify();
        /* Do the update */
    }
}
```

The Model-View-Controller Paradigm

Many GUI toolkits (aside from visual tools like Visual Basic or Powerbuilder) partition the classes into user interface and application data classes. (These are sometimes referred to as the presentation and logic layers.) Smalltalk-80 bestowed upon us the Model/View/Controller (MVC) architecture for presentation and logic layers. MVC refines the idea of presentation and logic layers by introducing another partition. An MVC triad consists of cooperating objects: the Model, the View, and the Controller. The Controller and View are typically user interface objects. The Controller allows a user to modify the Model. Once modified, the Model notifies the View that a change has occurred. The View queries the Model and displays the updated information. By separating the objects this way, the interactions are greatly simplified, the coupling is reduced, and the responsibilities of each object are very clear. The Model never has a user interface component. The View never changes the Model. The Controller never directly interacts with the View. Figure 23.9 shows the connections in an application with one Model, two Views, and two Controllers. You can see that the upper half of the figure looks just like the connections between an `Observable` and two `Observers`. Of course, that is hardly a coincidence. In many ways, you can consider MVC as one of the earliest occurrences of the **Observer** pattern.

FIGURE 23.9.

An example of a Model-View-Controller architecture.

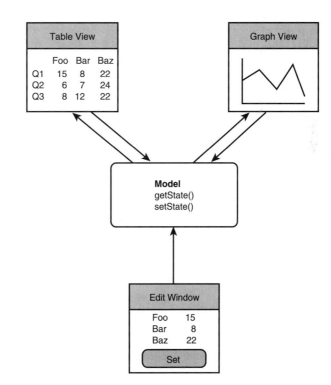

Although Java does not directly refer to MVC, the built-in **Observer** mechanism forms the foundation upon which you can build MVC applications. Java applications built with an MVC architecture evolve well over time. They can easily adopt new interfaces, new models, and new displays. Ideally, each component of MVC can be replaced or reused independently of the whole.

The Model (The `Observable`)

The first, and most pivotal, component of MVC is the Model—the aggregation of the application data and its internal rules. The model encapsulates all behavior that the data has *on its own*. It enforces consistency, handles persistence, and, most importantly, ensures that all accesses to its state variables go through accessor methods. The Model publishes notifications whenever its state changes. Many Views can subscribe to these notifications.

In Java, a Model inherits from `Observable`. It can contain other objects and implement whatever interfaces are helpful. The Model should not directly communicate with a View or a Controller. Likewise, the Model should not create network connections. (Odds are that the network connection would have been used for one of three purposes: to report the Model's status, to initiate some action on the remote side as a result of the Model's state, or to query an external system and change the Model's state accordingly. The first two should be done by `Observers` anyway, and the last one is a Controller's job.) The Model should always be able to stand alone, without the rest of the application around it. It should be completely independent. The Model always behaves in a reactive mode.

The View (The `Observer`)

The View is the visual display of the Model, or a relevant portion of the Model. A spreadsheet might have chart, graph, and tabular views into the underlying Model. The View does nothing more than display the Model; it never manipulates it. A View must always reflect the current state of its Model. Therefore, a View subscribes to its Model's notifications.

Of course, a Java View implements the `Observer` interface. It can be a subclassed `Component`, `Container`, or `Panel`. Although there can be `Observers` that are not Views (that is, have no user interface), all Views are `Observers`. Each View should be aware that there may be many other Views, and take care to be "friendly." Update is called synchronously. Therefore, if an update requires long calculations or extensive processing, it should spawn a new thread to do the work. That way, the Model can continue with its notifications.

The Controller

The Controller determines how the Model will react to the user interface. Most of the time, the Controller *is* the user interface. The Controller does not directly manipulate the View, but the View reflects its changes to the Model.

A Java controller can be any graphical component or group of components. Most of the time, the controller itself will be a Panel subclass, with a number of components within it.

The Advantages of MVC

The three advantages of using MVC are flexibility, flexibility, and flexibility. You can create new views for a model without modifying the model in the slightest. You can create new controllers without changing the model or the views. You can create and destroy any number of views at runtime. In short, MVC applications can grow and evolve, without turning into "code jungles."

The objects in an MVC application interact in a very well-defined way, which reduces bugs and enhances maintainability. The role of each object is clear. Because the number of interactions is kept to a minimum, the relationships are not fragile. Changes to one class frequently do not require changes to other classes. In an MVC application, the architecture is clear and obvious to even a casual observer.

An interesting point about MVC applications is that they are generally devoid of a mediator or controller object. One object does set up the relationships, and that object "owns" the others, in the sense that it is responsible for destroying them. But really, there is not a single overseer. This has good and bad consequences. On the plus side, by avoiding a single overseer, MVC objects interact quickly and simply. On the down side, it is sometimes unclear which object owns the MVC objects.

The `AppletCAD` Applet

Now, let's apply the full **Observer** pattern within the context of the Model/View/Controller architecture. This applet will use multiple views of a common data model, with a distinct controller. Figure 23.10 shows the applet in action. The main container uses a grid layout to hold four panels. Three of the panels are views that implement `Observer`. The fourth panel is the controller. Each view presents a two-dimensional projection of three-dimensional points, similar to the editing mode found in many CAD packages. The controller allows the user to add a new point at the specified coordinates.

FIGURE 23.10.

The `AppletCAD` *applet with several points added.*

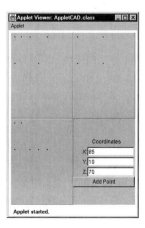

The Applet

Listing 23.9 shows the code for the applet itself. Event-handling code is conspicuous by its absence. The applet class constructs the model, views, and controller. It creates the relationships. Then, it gets out of the picture. After the MVC components are created, they handle all of the interaction. There is no further need for the applet to involve itself.

Listing 23.9. `AppletCAD` class.

```
/*
** AppletCAD.java
**
** Applet container for AppletCAD example
**
*/

import java.applet.*;
import java.awt.*;
import PointList;
import Point3D;

public class AppletCAD extends Applet {
    private XYView      xyView;
    private YZView      yzView;
    private XZView      xzView;
    private CoordControl coordControl;
    private PointList    pointList;

    public void init() {
        // Create the model
        pointList = new PointList();

        // Create the views
        xyView = new XYView();
        yzView = new YZView();
        xzView = new XZView();

        // Create the controller
        coordControl = new CoordControl(pointList);

        // Subscribe the views to the model.
        pointList.addObserver(xyView);
        pointList.addObserver(yzView);
        pointList.addObserver(xzView);

        // Add the views and controller,
        // using a layout manager
        setLayout(new GridLayout(2, 2));
        add(xyView);
        add(yzView);
        add(xzView);
        add(coordControl);
    }
```

```
        public Insets insets() {
            return new Insets(5, 5, 5, 5);
        }
}
```

The Observable

Point3D, shown in Listing 23.10, is used by the data model, the views, and the controller. It is simply a three-dimensional analogue to Point. It has public members x, y, and z, which are all integers.

Listing 23.10. The Point3D class used by the model, views, and controller.

```
/*
** Point3D.java
**
** An x, y, z coordinate
**
*/

public class Point3D {
    public int x, y, z;

    public Point3D(int ix, int iy, int iz) {
        x = ix;
        y = iy;
        z = iz;
    }

    public void move(int nx, int ny, int nz) {
        x = nx;
        y = ny;
        z = nz;
    }

    public void translate(int tx, int ty, int tz) {
        x += tx;
        y += ty;
        z += tz;
    }
}
```

The data model for this applet is shown in Listing 23.11. If Java supported multiple inheritance, PointList would inherit from Observable and from Vector. Instead, it inherits from Observable and aggregates a Vector. It would have been equally possible to inherit from Vector and aggregate an Observable with a reference back to Vector. Semantically, the two are equivalent. For this example, PointList does not define pass-through methods for all of the methods in Vector. In the addElement and setElementAt methods, you can see the update notifications being generated.

`PointList` does not have any intrinsic behavior other than storage. In another application, it might perform validation on the points, or provide persistent storage. Because the `Observers` and controller have no details about the inner workings of `PointList`, these features could be added without changing a single line of code in the other classes.

Listing 23.11. `PointList` class from the `AppletCAD` example.

```
/*
** PointList.java
**
** An Observable which includes a vector of Point3D.
**
*/

import java.util.*;
import Point3D;

public class PointList extends Observable {
    Vector _points;

    public PointList() {
        _points = new Vector(10);
    }

    public PointList(int capacity) {
        _points = new Vector(capacity);
    }

    public final Enumeration elements() {
        return _points.elements();
    }

    public final synchronized void addElement(Object obj) {
        setChanged();
        _points.addElement(obj);
        notifyObservers();
        clearChanged();
    }

    public final int indexOf(Object elem) {
        return _points.indexOf(elem);
    }

    public final synchronized void setElementAt(Object obj, int index) {
        setChanged();
        _points.setElementAt(obj, index);
        notifyObservers();
        clearChanged();
    }
}
```

The Observers

Although there are three Observers, each from their own class, they are sufficiently alike that we can examine just one. All three Observers are derived from a common base class. (This is not necessary in general; it happened to be convenient for this applet.) That base class, TwoDView, is shown in Listing 23.12, followed by the derived class XYView in Listing 23.13.

Listing 23.12. TwoDView, the base class for two-dimensional views in the AppletCAD example.

```
/*
** TwoDView.java
**
** Two dimensional view for AppletCAD example
**
*/

import java.awt.*;
import java.util.*;
import PointList;
import Point3D;

public abstract class TwoDView extends Panel implements Observer {
    protected PointList pl;
    private final int OVALWIDTH = 2;

    public void update(Observable item, Object arg) {
        if(item instanceof PointList) {
            pl = (PointList)item;

            repaint();
        }
        else
            System.out.println("Don't know how to observe that!");
    }

    public void paint(Graphics g) {
        Dimension d = size();

        super.paint(g);

        g.setColor(Color.darkGray);
        g.fill3DRect(0, 0, d.width, d.height, true);

        g.setColor(Color.white);
        drawPoints(g);
    }

    public Insets insets() {
        return new Insets(5, 5, 5, 5);
    }

    public final void drawPoints(Graphics g) {
        Point3D      vertex;
        Point        point;
```

continues

Listing 23.12. continued

```
            if(pl != null) {
                point = new Point(0, 0);

                for(Enumeration e = pl.elements(); e.hasMoreElements();) {
                    vertex = (Point3D)e.nextElement();
                    projectPoint(vertex, point);
                    drawPoint(g, point);
                }
            }
        }

        protected void drawPoint(Graphics g, Point p) {
            g.fillOval(p.x - OVALWIDTH/2,
                p.y - OVALWIDTH/2,
                OVALWIDTH, OVALWIDTH);
        }

        // Sub-classes must implement this.
        protected abstract void projectPoint(Point3D v, Point p);
}
```

TwoDView does maintain a reference to the model—PointList. It updates this reference each time update is called. Whenever a redisplay occurs, it obtains an enumerator from PointList (which in turn obtains it from its Vector). TwoDView walks the enumerator, drawing each point. In order to draw a three-dimensional point on a two-dimensional screen, TwoDView projects the point onto two dimensions. The details of the projection are deferred to a subclass by the abstract projectPoint method. The current three subclasses each select two dimensions of the three, performing an orthogonal projection. As an exercise, you could add a fourth view to perform a perspective or orthographic projection for realistic three-dimensional visualization, simply by inheriting from TwoDView and performing the calculations in projectPoint. A completely unrelated view might display each point as coordinates. By implementing Observer, you can add a new view without affecting any other class in the applet (except for AppletCAD, of course, which would need to construct the new view).

Listing 23.13. XYView class, a concrete subclass of TwoDView.

```
/*
** XYView.java
**
** Two dimensional view for AppletCAD example
**
*/

import java.awt.*;
import TwoDView;
import Point3D;
```

```
public class XYView extends TwoDView {
    protected void projectPoint(Point3D v, Point p) {
        p.x = v.x;
        p.y = v.y;
    }
}
```

The Controller

For this example, the controller is a simple derivative of Panel, shown in Listing 23.14. In response to the Add Point button, it constructs a new Point3D with the coordinates entered in the text fields. It then asks the PointList to add the new point. Notice that the views and the controller each have a reference to the model, but the model has no direct references to any other class. This is quite typical of a model/view/controller system. The model stands independently, whereas its manipulators must know how to find the model. The model simply knows that certain Observers have expressed an interest in its state.

Listing 23.14. CoordControl class.

```
/*
** CoordControl.java
**
** Coordinate entry controller for AppletCAD example.
**
*/

import java.awt.*;
import java.util.*;
import PointList;
import Point3D;

public class CoordControl extends Panel {
    private static String dimension[] = {"X:", "Y:", "Z:"};

    private PointList  _model;
    private Button     _addButton;
    private TextField  _field[];

    public CoordControl(PointList pl) {
        super();

        GridBagLayout       g;
        GridBagConstraints  c;
        TextField           textField;
        Label               label;
        int                 i;

        // Remember the model.
        _model = pl;
```

continues

Listing 23.14. continued

```java
        setBackground(Color.lightGray);
        setFont(new Font("Times", Font.PLAIN, 12));

        // Create the controls.  Use a GridBagLayout.
        g = new GridBagLayout();
        c = new GridBagConstraints();
        setLayout(g);
        c.fill = GridBagConstraints.HORIZONTAL;

        // Add a caption
        label = new Label("Coordinates", Label.CENTER);
        c.weightx = 0.0;
        c.gridwidth = GridBagConstraints.REMAINDER;
        g.setConstraints(label, c);
        add(label);

        // Add a label and text field for each dimension
        _field = new TextField[3];

        for(i = 0; i < 3; i++) {
            label = new Label(dimension[i], Label.RIGHT);
            c.weightx = .1;
            c.gridwidth = 1;
            g.setConstraints(label, c);
            add(label);

            _field[i] = new TextField();
            c.weightx = 1.0;
            c.gridwidth = GridBagConstraints.REMAINDER;
            g.setConstraints(_field[i], c);
            add(_field[i]);
        }

        // Add a button
        _addButton = new Button("Add Point");
        c.weightx = 0.0;
        c.gridwidth = GridBagConstraints.REMAINDER;
        g.setConstraints(_addButton, c);
        add(_addButton);
    }

    public boolean handleEvent(Event e) {
        Object target = e.target;

        if(e.id == Event.ACTION_EVENT) {
            if(target == _addButton) {
                createPoint();
            }
        }

        return super.handleEvent(e);
    }

    private final void createPoint() {
        Point3D p = new Point3D(0, 0, 0);
```

```
        p.x = Integer.parseInt(_field[0].getText());
        p.y = Integer.parseInt(_field[1].getText());
        p.z = Integer.parseInt(_field[2].getText());

        _model.addElement(p);
    }
}
```

HTML Container

The HTML container for this applet is shown in Listing 23.15. It just reserves some space for the applet and provides links to the applet code.

Listing 23.15. HTML container for the AppletCAD example.

```
<html>
<title>AppletCAD</title>
<body>
<h1>AppletCAD</h1>
<hr>
<applet code=AppletCAD.class width=300 height=400>
</applet>
<menu>
<li><a href="AppletCAD.java">AppletCAD.java</a><br>
<li><a href="PointList.java">PointList.java</a><br>
<li><a href="Point3D.java">Point3D.java</a><br>
<li><a href="CoordControl.java">CoordControl.java</a><br>
<li><a href="TwoDView.java">TwoDView.java</a><br>
<li><a href="XYView.java">XYView.java</a><br>
<li><a href="YZView.java">YZView.java</a><br>
<li><a href="XZView.java">XZView.java</a><br>
</menu>
<hr>
</html>
```

Interaction

The model, view, and controller classes in the AppletCAD example interact independently of the applet itself. The event diagram in Figure 23.11 should look familiar. AppletCAD is really nothing more than a concrete implementation of the MVC architecture, so the event diagram looks very similar. In this concrete example, as in the previous example, you can see that the Model, PointList, calls its own notifyObservers(). This yields adequate performance because the controller does not allow for rapid batches of updates. This class deals with the consistency problem by making all of its state-changing methods final. (This is one advantage of Java over C++ or Delphi.)

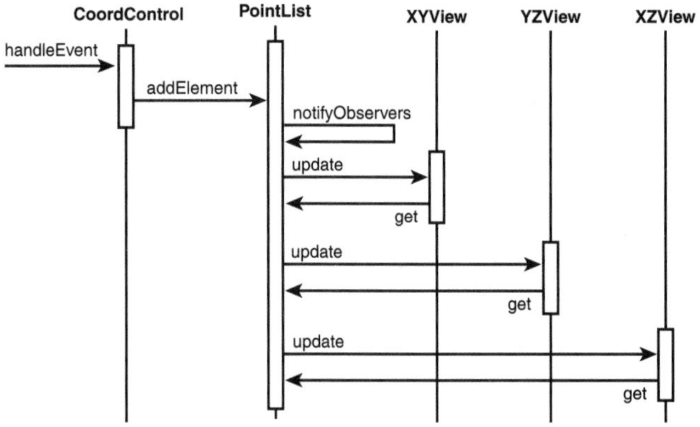

FIGURE 23.11.

Event interaction diagram for the `AppletCAD` *example.*

The chain of events begins when the user clicks the Add Point button on the controller panel. The controller knows the model, and it passes a new `Point3D` to the model. In response, the model notifies all interested `Observers` of the update. In this example, all three views derive from a common base class. They all share the implementation of `update()`. **Observer** does not require this. The `update()` method of a different view might store these points in an object store, or even send a message to another applet or server. Nothing limits `Observers` to graphical entities. The three views each query the model for its state, by enumerating the `Point3Ds` and drawing each point. Notice that the applet itself is missing from the event diagram.

Sometimes, instead of having the controller directly manipulate the model, you might want the controller to construct a "Command" object and pass it to a mediator. In that case, the mediator would have the reference to the model. Whether your controller directly manipulates the model or goes through an intermediary, the model has no knowledge of which controller sent a message. In fact, it has no knowledge of how many or what type of controllers exist. The model is decoupled from the controller(s), and it never needs to interact with the controller.

NOTE

You might ask, "What about a controller that adapts its interface according to the state of the model?" In that case, what you really have is a controller that is also a view! Remember the discussion earlier about mutually dependent classes? Clearly, it is also possible to have dependency trees or graphs! Be even more careful than usual with dependency graphs. They must be acyclic, or you risk "update storms."

Other Applications of Observer

Although most of this chapter has focused on **Observer** in the context of user interfaces, it has far more general applications. **Observer** applies whenever one object depends on another object's state. In other words, any time objects must remain consistent, think **Observer**. Here are a few examples outside of the GUI realm, which might spark some ideas.

For example, a simulation might require a `Clock` object to notify the actors on each second. By implementing the `Clock` as an `Observable`, the notification mechanism comes for free. By working at a higher, more abstract level, the simulation developers can focus on the important issues and not get bogged down in mechanics.

A point-of-sale system might use **Observer** to tally receipts. Whenever the cash register object rings up a sale, an inventory object needs to be notified. Call the cash register an `Observable` and call the inventory an `Observer`, and you've got it. Again, two objects need to remain synchronized. Here, the inventory object itself might also be an `Observable`, with an automatic ordering system object as the `Observer`.

Real-time data collection systems usually need some sort of data quality monitor. The monitor should raise an alert or flag data that falls outside of normal tolerances, due to bad inputs or malfunctioning hardware. The sensor input processing objects are `Observables`, and the monitor can be an `Observer`. In fact, the logging or post-processing objects can also be `Observers`.

The **Observable** pattern easily accomplishes these necessary tasks. By providing the `Observer/Observable` pair, Java assists you in creating extremely flexible object-oriented software. In the near future, Java will also run on cellular phones, television set-top boxes, and network computers. When that happens, the need to decouple dependent objects in Java applications will increase tenfold, as we try to support a mind-boggling variety of environments and interfaces.

Summary

Using the `java.util.Observer` interface and `java.util.Observable` class can greatly enhance your application's flexibility. By decoupling dependent classes, `Observables` establish a one-to-many publish-subscribe protocol. `Observers` are automatically notified of changes to the `Observables` state. `Observers` are often used as user interface components. The design pattern **Observer** captures this relationship as a "solution to a problem in a context." Design patterns provide a common vocabulary. The **Observer** pattern can be implemented with many variations for different situations. One such implementation is the Model-View-Controller architecture from Smalltalk-80. MVC separates the system into a Model, one or more Views, and one or more Controllers. The Model is an `Observable`, and the Views are `Observers`.

Observer has many applications beyond the GUI realm. Any time an object depends upon another object, **Observer** is applicable. Observers and Observables can be mutually dependent and layered. They can have dependency graphs, but cyclic graphs introduce special problems.

By using Observers in your applications, you gain several benefits, including flexibility, readability, maintainability, and robustness. Observers are more flexible because Observers can be extended, added, or replaced without changing the underlying Observable. Your code becomes more readable because the **Observer** pattern can easily be recognized and provides a well-known framework. Maintainability and robustness come directly from the fact that the classes are decoupled, reducing the ripple effect.

24

Using the Provided
Data Structures

by Michael Morrison

At the heart of even the most basic Java programs are data structures, which are responsible for modeling information within the context of a program. There are many varieties of data structures, ranging from primitive data types to arrays to more complex structures like hash tables. In this chapter, you learn about the data structures provided by the Java API. More specifically, you learn how to use the data structures in the Java utility package, also known as `java.util`. This package contains a wide range of data structures applicable to many different programming scenarios. The goal of this chapter is to familiarize you with these data structures and show you the basics of how to use them. If you want more complete details regarding the data structure classes, refer to Chapter 34, "Package `java.util`," which is a complete reference for the `java.util` package.

Overview of the Data Structures

The data structures provided by the Java utility package are very powerful and perform a wide range of functions. These data structures consist of an interface and five classes, which follow:

- Enumeration
- BitSet
- Vector
- Stack
- Dictionary
- Hashtable

The `Enumeration` interface isn't itself a data structure, but it is very important within the context of other data structures. The `Enumeration` interface defines a means to retrieve successive elements from a data structure. For example, `Enumeration` defines a method called `nextElement` that is used to get the next element in a data structure that contains multiple elements.

The `BitSet` class implements a group of bits, or flags, that can be set and cleared individually. This class is very useful in cases where you need to keep up with a set of Boolean values; you just assign a bit to each value and set it or clear it appropriately.

The `Vector` class is very similar to a traditional Java array, except that it can grow as necessary to accommodate new elements. Like an array, elements of a `Vector` object can be accessed through an index into the vector. The nice thing about using the `Vector` class is that you don't have to worry about setting it to a specific size upon creation.

The `Stack` class implements a last-in-first-out (LIFO) stack of elements. You can think of a stack as a vertical stack of objects; when you add a new element, it gets stacked on top of the others. When you pull an element off the stack, it comes off the top. In other words, the last element you added to the stack is the first one to come back off.

The Dictionary class is an abstract class that defines a data structure for mapping keys to values. This is useful in cases where you want to be able to access data through a particular key rather than on the value of the data itself. Because the Dictionary class is abstract, it only provides the framework for a key-mapped data structure, rather than a specific implementation.

An actual implementation of a key-mapped data structure is provided by the Hashtable class. The Hashtable class provides a means of organizing data based on some user-defined key structure. For example, in an address list hash table, you could store and sort data based on a key such as ZIP code rather than on a person's name. The specific meaning of keys in regard to hash tables is totally dependent on the usage of the hash table and the data it contains.

That sums up the data structures provided by the Java utility package. Now that you have a cursory understanding of them, let's dig into each in a little more detail and see how they work.

Enumeration

The Enumeration interface provides a standard means of iterating through a list of sequentially stored elements, which is a common task of many data structures. Since Enumeration is an interface, its role is limited to providing the method protocol for data structures that can be enumerated in a sequential manner. Even though you can't use the interface outside the context of a particular data structure, understanding how it works will put you well on your way to understanding other Java data structures. With that in mind, take a look at the only two methods defined by the Enumeration interface:

```
public abstract boolean hasMoreElements();
public abstract Object nextElement();
```

The hasMoreElements method is used to determine whether the enumeration contains any more elements. You will typically call this method to see if you can continue iterating through an enumeration. An example of this is calling hasMoreElements in the conditional clause of a while loop that is iterating through an enumeration.

The nextElement method is responsible for actually retrieving the next element in an enumeration. If no more elements are in the enumeration, nextElement will throw a NoSuchElementException exception. Because you want to avoid generating exceptions whenever possible, you should always use hasMoreElements in conjunction with nextElement to make sure there is another element to retrieve. Following is an example of a while loop that uses these two methods to iterate through a data structure object that implements the Enumeration interface:

```
// e is an object that implements the Enumeration interface
while (e.hasMoreElements()) {
  Object o = e.nextElement();
  System.out.println(o);
}
```

This example code prints out the contents of an enumeration using the `hasMoreElements` and `nextElement` methods. Pretty simple!

BitSet

The `BitSet` class is useful whenever you need to represent a group of Boolean flags. The nice thing about the `BitSet` class is that it alleviates the need for masking out the value of each bit; you simply refer to each bit using an index. Another nice feature about the `BitSet` class is that it automatically grows to represent the number of bits required by a program.

A good example of using a `BitSet` is an object that has a number of attributes that can easily be modeled by Boolean values. Because the individual bits in a bit set are accessed through an index, you can define each attribute as a constant index value:

```
class someBits {
  public static final int readable = 0;
  public static final int writeable = 1;
  public static final int streamable = 2;
  public static final int flexible = 3;
}
```

Notice that the attributes are assigned increasing values beginning with zero. You can use these values to get and set the appropriate bits in a bit set. But first, you need to create a `BitSet` object:

```
BitSet bits = new BitSet();
```

This constructor creates a bit set with no specified size. You can also create a bit set with a specific size:

```
BitSet bits = new BitSet(4);
```

This creates a bit set containing four Boolean bit fields. Regardless of the constructor used, all bits in new bit sets are initially set to `false`. Once you have a bit set created, you can easily set and clear the bits using the `set` and `clear` methods along with the bit constants you defined:

```
bits.set(someBits.writeable);
bits.set(someBits.streamable);
bits.set(someBits.flexible);
bits.clear(someBits.writeable);
```

In this code, the `writeable`, `streamable`, and `flexible` attributes are set, and then the `writeable` bit is cleared. Notice that the fully qualified name is used for each attribute because they are declared as static in the `someBits` class.

You can get the value of individual bits in a bit set using the `get` method:

```
boolean canIWrite = bits.get(someBits.writeable);
```

You can find out how many bits are being modeled by a bit set using the `size` method. An example of this follows:

```
int numBits = bits.size();
```

The `BitSet` class also provides other methods for performing comparisons and bitwise operations on bit sets such as `AND`, `OR`, and `XOR`. All of these methods take a `BitSet` object as their only parameter.

Vector

The `Vector` class implements a growable array of objects. Because the `Vector` class is responsible for growing itself as necessary to support more elements, it has to decide when and by how much to grow as new elements are added. You can easily control this aspect of vectors upon creation. Before getting into that, however, take a look at how to create a basic vector:

```
Vector v = new Vector();
```

That's about as simple as it gets! This constructor creates a default vector containing no elements. Actually, all vectors are empty upon creation. One of the attributes important to how a vector sizes itself is the initial capacity of a vector. The following code shows how to create a vector with a specified capacity:

```
Vector v = new Vector(25);
```

This vector is created to immediately support up to 25 elements. In other words, the vector will go ahead and allocate enough memory to support 25 elements. Once 25 elements have been added, however, the vector must decide how to grow itself to accept more elements. You can specify the value by which a vector grows using yet another `Vector` constructor:

```
Vector v = new Vector(25, 5);
```

This vector has an initial size of 25 elements, and it will grow in increments of 5 elements whenever its size grows to more than 25 elements. This means that the vector will first jump to 30 elements in size, then 35, and so on. A smaller grow value for a vector results in more efficient memory management, but at a cost of more execution overhead because more memory allocations are taking place. On the other hand, a larger grow value results in fewer memory allocations, but sometimes memory may be wasted if you don't use all the extra space created.

> **NOTE**
>
> The default grow value for a vector is 0, which actually results in the vector doubling its size whenever it needs to grow. In other words, a default grow value essentially acts like a grow value equal to the size of the vector.

Unlike arrays, you can't just use square brackets ([ ]) to access the elements in a vector; you have to use methods defined in the Vector class. To add an element to a vector, you use the addElement method:

```
v.addElement("carrots");
v.addElement("broccoli");
v.addElement("cauliflower");
```

This code shows how to add some vegetable strings to a vector. To get the last string added to the vector, you can use the lastElement method:

```
String s = (String)v.lastElement();
```

The lastElement method retrieves the last element added to the vector. Notice that you have to cast the return value of lastElement because the Vector class is designed to work with Objects. Although lastElement certainly has its usefulness, you will probably find more use with the elementAt method, which allows you to index into a vector to retrieve an element. Following is an example of using the elementAt method:

```
String s1 = (String)v.elementAt(0);
String s2 = (String)v.elementAt(2);
```

Because vectors are zero-based, the first call to elementAt retrieves the "carrots" string, and the second call retrieves the "cauliflower" string. Just as you can retrieve an element at a particular index, you can also add and remove elements at an index using the insertElementAt and removeElementAt methods:

```
v.insertElementAt("squash", 1);
v.insertElementAt("corn", 0);
v.removeElementAt(3);
```

The first call to insertElementAt inserts an element at index 1, in between the "carrots" and "broccoli" strings. The "broccoli" and "cauliflower" strings are moved up a space in the vector to accommodate the inserted "squash" string. The second call to insertElementAt inserts an element at index 0, which is the beginning of the vector. In this case, all existing elements are moved up a space in the vector to accommodate the inserted "corn" string. At this point, the contents of the vector look like this:

```
"corn"
"carrots"
"squash"
"broccoli"
"cauliflower"
```

The call to removeElementAt removes the element at index 3, which is the "broccoli" string. The resulting contents of the vector consist of the following strings:

```
"corn"
"carrots"
"squash"
"cauliflower"
```

You can use the `setElementAt` method to change a specific element:

```
v.setElementAt("peas", 1);
```

This method replaces the `"carrots"` string with the `"peas"` string, resulting in the following vector contents:

```
"corn"
"peas"
"squash"
"cauliflower"
```

If you want to clear out the vector completely, you can remove all the elements with the `removeAllElements` method:

```
v.removeAllElements();
```

The Vector class also provides some methods for working with elements without using indexes. These methods actually search through the vector for a particular element. The first of these methods is the `contains` method, which simply checks to see if an element is in the vector:

```
boolean isThere = v.contains("celery");
```

Another method that works in this manner is the `indexOf` method, which finds the index of an element based on the element itself:

```
int i = v.indexOf("squash");
```

The `indexOf` method returns the index of the element in question if it is in the vector, or -1 if not. The `removeElement` method works similarly in that it removes an element based on the element itself, rather than an index:

```
v.removeElement("cauliflower");
```

If you're interested in working with all the elements in a vector sequentially, you can use the `elements` method, which returns an enumeration of the elements:

```
Enumeration e = v.elements();
```

If you recall from earlier in this chapter, you can use an enumeration to step through elements sequentially.

You may find yourself wanting to work with the size of a vector. Fortunately, the Vector class provides a few methods for determining and manipulating the size of a vector. First, the `size` method determines the number of elements in the vector:

```
int size = v.size();
```

If you want to explicitly set the size of a vector, you can use the `setSize` method:

```
v.setSize(10);
```

The setSize method expands or truncates the vector to accommodate the new size specified. If the vector is expanded because of a larger size, null elements are inserted as the newly added elements. If the vector is truncated, any elements at indexes beyond the specified size are discarded.

If you recall, vectors have two different attributes relating to size: size and capacity. The size is the number of elements in the vector, and the capacity is the amount of memory allocated to hold new elements. The capacity is always greater than or equal to the size. You can force the capacity to exactly match the size using the trimToSize method:

```
v.trimToSize();
```

You can also check to see what the capacity is using the capacity method:

```
int capacity = v.capacity();
```

You'll find that the Vector class is one of the most useful data structures provided in the Java API. This tour of the class should give you an idea of how powerful and easy it is to use vectors.

Stack

Stacks are a classic data structure used to model information that is accessed in a specific order. The Stack class in Java is implemented as a last-in-first-out (LIFO) stack, which means that the last item added to the stack is the first one to come back off. The Stack class defines only one constructor, which is a default constructor that creates an empty stack. You use this constructor to create a stack like this:

```
Stack s = new Stack();
```

You add new elements to a stack using the push method, which pushes an element onto the top of the stack:

```
s.push("One");
s.push("Two");
s.push("Three");
s.push("Four");
s.push("Five");
s.push("Six");
```

This code pushes six strings onto the stack, with the last string ("Six") remaining on top. You pop elements back off the stack using the pop method:

```
String s1 = (String)s.pop();
String s2 = (String)s.pop();
```

This code pops the last two strings off the stack, leaving the first four strings remaining. This code results in the s1 variable containing the "Six" string and the s2 variable containing the "Five" string.

If you want to get the top element on the stack without actually popping it off the stack, you can use the peek method:

```
String s3 = (String)s.peek();
```

This call to peek returns the "Four" string, but it leaves the string on the stack. You can search for an element on the stack using the search method:

```
int i = s.search("Two");
```

The search method returns the distance from the top of the stack of the element if it is found, or -1 if not. In this case, the "Two" string is the third element from the top, so the search method returns 2 (zero-based).

The only other method defined in the Stack class is empty, which determines if a stack is empty:

```
boolean isEmpty = s.empty();
```

Although the Stack class may not be quite as useful as the Vector class, it provides the functionality for a very common and established data structure.

Dictionary

The Dictionary class defines a framework for implementing a basic key-mapped data structure. Although you can't actually create Dictionary objects because the Dictionary class is abstract, you can still learn a lot about key-mapped data modeling by learning how the Dictionary class works. You can put the key-mapped approach to work using the Hashtable class, which is derived from Dictionary, or by deriving your own class from Dictionary. You learn about the Hashtable class in the next section of this chapter.

The Dictionary class defines a means of storing information based on a key. This is similar in some ways to how the Vector class works, in that elements in a vector are accessed through an index, which is a type of key. However, keys in the Dictionary class can be just about anything. You can create your own class to use as the keys for accessing and manipulating data in a dictionary.

The Dictionary class defines a variety of methods for working with the data stored in a dictionary. All of these methods are defined as abstract, meaning that derived classes will have to implement all of them to actually be useful. The put and get methods are used to put objects in the dictionary and get them back. Assuming that dict is a Dictionary-derived class that implements these methods, the following code shows how to use the put method to add elements to a dictionary:

```
dict.put("small", new Rectangle(0, 0, 5, 5));
dict.put("medium", new Rectangle(0, 0, 15, 15));
dict.put("large", new Rectangle(0, 0, 25, 25));
```

This code adds three rectangles to the dictionary using strings as the keys. To get an element from the dictionary, you use the `get` method and specify the appropriate key:

```
Rectangle r = (Rectangle)dict.get("medium");
```

You can also remove an element from the dictionary with a key using the `remove` method:

```
dict.remove("large");
```

You can find out how many elements are in the dictionary using the `size` method, much as you did with the `Vector` class:

```
int size = dict.size();
```

You can also check to see if the dictionary is empty using the `isEmpty` method:

```
boolean isEmpty = dict.isEmpty();
```

Finally, the `Dictionary` class includes two methods for enumerating the keys and values contained within: `keys` and `elements`. The `keys` method returns an enumeration containing all the keys contained in a dictionary, and the `elements` method returns an enumeration of all the key-mapped values contained. Following is an example of retrieving both enumerations:

```
Enumeration keys = dict.keys();
Enumeration elements = dict.elements();
```

Note that because keys are mapped to elements on a one-to-one basis, these enumerations are of equal length.

Hashtable

The `Hashtable` class is derived from `Dictionary` and provides a complete implementation of a key-mapped data structure. Like dictionaries, hash tables allow you to store data based on some type of key. Unlike dictionaries, hash tables have an efficiency associated with them defined by the load factor of the table. The *load factor* of a hash table is a number between 0.0 and 1.0 that determines how and when the hash table allocates space for more elements. Like vectors, hash tables have a capacity, which is the amount of memory allocated for the table. Hash tables allocate more memory by comparing the current size of the table with the product of the capacity and load factor. If the size of the hash table exceeds this product, the table increases its capacity by rehashing itself.

Load factors closer to 1.0 result in a more efficient usage of memory at the expense of a longer look-up time for each element. Similarly, load factors closer to 0.0 result in more efficient look-ups but also tend to be more wasteful with memory. Determining the load factor for your own hash tables is really dependent on the usage of the hash table and whether your priority is on performance or memory efficiency.

You create hash tables using one of three methods. The first method creates a default hash table:

```
Hashtable hash = new Hashtable();
```

The second constructor creates a hash table with the specified initial capacity:

```
Hashtable hash = new Hashtable(20);
```

Finally, the third constructor creates a hash table with the specified initial capacity and load factor:

```
Hashtable hash = new Hashtable(20, 0.75);
```

All of the abstract methods defined in Dictionary are implemented in the Hashtable class. Because these methods perform the exact same function in Hashtable, there's no need to cover them again. However, they are listed here just so you'll have an idea of what support Hashtable provides:

- elements
- get
- isEmpty
- keys
- put
- remove
- size

In addition to these methods, the Hashtable class implements a few others that perform functions specific to supporting hash tables. One of these is the clear method, which clears a hash table of all its keys and elements:

```
hash.clear();
```

The contains method is used to see if an object is stored in the hash table. This method searches for an object value in the hash table rather than a key. The following code shows how to use the contains method:

```
boolean isThere = hash.contains(new Rectangle(0, 0, 5, 5));
```

Similar to contains, the containsKey method searches a hash table, but it searches based on a key rather than a value:

```
boolean isThere = hash.containsKey("Small");
```

As mentioned earlier, a hash table will rehash itself when it determines that it must increase its capacity. You can force a rehash yourself by calling the rehash method:

```
hash.rehash();
```

That sums up the important methods implemented by the Hashtable class. Even though you've seen all the methods, you still may be wondering exactly how the Hashtable class is useful. The practical usage of a hash table is actually in representing data that is too time-consuming to search or reference by value. In other words, it's much more efficient to access complex elements in a data structure using a key rather than by comparing the objects themselves. Furthermore, hash tables typically compute a key for elements, which is called a hash code. For example, an object such as a string can have an integer hash code computed for it that uniquely represents the string. When a bunch of strings are stored in a hash table, the table can access the strings by integer hash codes as opposed to the contents of the strings themselves.

This technique of computing and using hash codes for object storage and reference is exploited very heavily throughout the Java system. This is apparent in the fact that the parent of all classes, Object, defines a hashCode method that is overridden in most standard Java classes. Any class that defines a hashCode method can be efficiently stored and accessed in a hash table. A class that is to be hashed must also implement the equals method, which defines a way of telling whether two objects are equal. The equals method usually just performs a straight comparison of all the member variables defined in a class.

Hash tables are an extremely powerful data structure that you will probably want to integrate into some of your programs that manipulate large amounts of data. The fact that they are so widely supported in the Java API through the Object class should give you a clue as to their importance in Java programming.

Summary

In this chapter, you learned all about the data structures provided by the Java utility package (java.util). You learned exactly what each data structure provides in terms of modeling data in different ways. You then moved on to the details of each data structure and how to use it to actually model data. Although this chapter didn't go into great detail regarding practical scenarios that use the data structures in your own programs, it did cover the basics of how to use each of the data structures. The reality is that there are limitless uses of the data structures in your own programs, so the best approach is to learn how to use them in general terms and then apply them to your own code as you see fit.

25

Working with Databases

by Bryan Morgan

It can be argued that, due to the widespread use of computing technology throughout corporate America, no new tool or language can be considered "industrial strength" until support for relational databases is provided. In fact, during the first year of Java's growth, very few large-scale applications have been attempted using the language because of this shortcoming. Fortunately, Sun Microsystems and database tool makers such as Oracle, Sybase, and Microsoft realize the power of the Java environment, and they are currently rushing to fill the Java/database void.

This chapter will introduce the use of relational databases with Java to the reader. Following a preliminary section covering the basics of SQL (Structured Query Language) and relational databases, the remainder of the chapter will focus on three possible ways of building database-aware Java applications. Here are these three methods:

- Standard CGI scripts used to query databases and return information to the browser
- The JDBC (Java Database Connectivity) Applications Programming Interface that will be used to provide a Java interface to SQL-based relational databases
- Database-aware server code that allows all database code to reside and execute on a Web server for communication with a separate database server

A Brief Tutorial on SQL and Relational Databases

Before discussing how Java can be used to actually connect to relational databases, retrieve information, and return it to a Web browser, this section will briefly introduce the reader to the Structured Query Language and the world of relational databases.

What Is a Database Server?

Programmers who have never worked with relational databases may be somewhat confused by the term "database server." Fear not, however, because as a Web developer, you already have a great deal of experience with the client/server model of application development. A database server is simply a powerful piece of software running on a machine that is located on a network. This software monitors a port (just as a Web server typically monitors port 80 on a machine) and handles all incoming requests for the underlying database data. In the case of relational databases, this incoming request is presented to the server using SQL (Structured Query Language). The database server processes the SQL statement(s) and takes some action based on the contents of the SQL statement(s). This action could be a data retrieval operation, a data insertion or deletion, or even a security modification request sent by the database administrator (DBA).

Please take note here of what is meant by the word *database*. Many programmers accustomed to writing single-user file-based applications call these files *databases*, and this is fine. However, this chapter will focus on *relational databases,* which separate all data into related tables of information and are managed by a software product known as an RDBMS (relational database management system). Here are some of the most popular RDBMSs:

- Oracle
- Sybase SQL Server
- Microsoft SQL Server
- Informix
- IBM DB2

All of these database servers can run on a wide variety of platforms and can handle a great number of users simultaneously. Several features set these rather expensive systems apart from simple file-based databases such as Microsoft Access or dBASE. Among the valuable features are the following:

- Security. The database administrator (DBA) is allowed to completely control access to all tables, stored procedures, and triggers based on the user ID passed to the database when logging in.
- Data locking. With a large number of users running an application simultaneously, it is inevitable that at some point two users will try to modify the same data at the same time. Modern RDBMSs handle this using a wide variety of locking schemes that allow only one person at a time to modify a record within the database.
- Support for network protocols. Popular RDBMSs, such as Oracle7, support a wide variety of networking protocols for communications to and from the database server and client.
- Scalability. Many RDBMSs run on a wide variety of platforms and can be scaled to fit the user's needs.
- Replication. With the purchase of add-on products, many RDBMSs support real-time data replication among various sites. This allows corporate databases to copy data to remote sites as the data is updated.

As you can see, a huge amount of effort already has gone into the creation of extremely powerful database management systems. Many computing professionals make their living by administering large databases. Most professional developers within business environments today probably have worked on at least one relational database-aware application. No matter what language their application was written in (C, C++, Object Pascal, Visual Basic, and so on), at some point SQL commands had to be written and passed to the database in order to retrieve data. Because of its ubiquity, SQL will be the topic of the next section.

The Relational Database

Relational databases store all of their information in groups known as *tables*. Each database can contain one or more of these tables. (Keep in mind that an RDBMS can manage many individual underlying databases, with each one of these databases containing many tables.) These tables are *related* to each other using some type of common element. A table can be thought of as containing a number of rows and columns. Each individual element stored in the table is known as a *column*. Each set of data within the table is known as a *row*. The following example illustrates a simple database containing address information.

Using the Sybase SQL Server RDBMS, assume that we have created a database named ADDRESSES. Because this is a simple example, this database will contain only one table: ADDRESS. Here are the individual columns (and their datatypes) contained in the ADDRESS table:

```
STRUCTURE OF TABLE ADDRESS
LAST_NAME String(30)
FIRST_NAME String(30)
STREET STRING(50)
CITY STRING(50)
STATE STRING(2)
ZIP INTEGER
```

Therefore, it can be said that the ADDRESS table has six columns: LAST_NAME, FIRST_NAME, STREET, CITY, STATE, and ZIP. Note that these columns specify only the format of the table, not the actual information stored in the table. Some individual rows, or records as they are often called, could be the following:

LAST_NAME	FIRST_NAME	STREET	CITY	STATE	ZIP
BERRY	KATIE	123 Forest St.	Huntsville	AL	36507
LITTLE	PARKER	456 Wetwood Dr.	Pensacola	FL	32537
HOFFMAN	LINDA	709 Avenida	San Diego	CA	93426

This database works very well if this is all the designer intended it to do. However, a primary goal of the relational database architecture is to reduce redundant information. Looking at the previous example, you can quickly see how information could be repeated if one person has several addresses. Let's assume in the previous example that Linda Hoffman moves every few months to an entirely new part of the country. Because we want to keep track of her migrant lifestyle, we will design this table to store her address each time she moves without deleting the old one. As she continues to move, our table looks like the following:

LAST_NAME	FIRST_NAME	STREET	CITY	STATE	ZIP
BERRY	KATIE	123 Forest St.	Huntsville	AL	36507
LITTLE	PARKER	456 Wetwood Dr.	Pensacola	FL	32537
HOFFMAN	LINDA	709 Avenida	San Diego	CA	93426
HOFFMAN	LINDA	347 Rivers St.	Frankfort	KY	49682
HOFFMAN	LINDA	902 Woods Ave.	Alexandria	VA	23734
HOFFMAN	LINDA	920 Tiger Ln.	Clemson	SC	29632

Although the data is stored correctly, Linda Hoffman's name is stored repeatedly, resulting in the duplication of data stored in the table. Designers of relational databases often design using a process known as *normalization*. Although it is beyond the scope of this book, the normalization process essentially attempts to break data down into its smallest segments so that no data is duplicated throughout the database. Using the previous example, to reduce data duplication, the ADDRESS table would be broken up into two separate tables: NAME and ADDRESS.

```
STRUCTURE OF TABLE NAME
LAST_NAME String(30)
FIRST_NAME String(30)
ID INTEGER
STRUCTURE OF TABLE ADDRESS
ID INTEGER
STREET STRING(50)
CITY STRING(50)
STATE STRING(2)
ZIP INTEGER
```

Using this structure, or database *schema* as it is often called, the individuals' names will only be entered into the database one time. The ID field will be used to link, or relate, the two tables together. This linkage between tables is known as *referential integrity*. It is the responsibility of the database developer to strive to maintain the database's referential integrity so that data does not become corrupt. Corrupt data could occur in this example if a record was deleted from the NAME table without ever deleting the corresponding address information in the ADDRESS table. Because of this oversight, this information would remain unused in the ADDRESS table and could potentially result in problems if another user was assigned the deleted record's ID value.

This covers the basics of how relational databases are used to store information. The following topic examines SQL in more detail and explains how SQL is used to query relational databases to retrieve or modify the database contents.

Structured Query Language (SQL)

Structured Query Language (SQL) is an ANSI standard computer programming language used to query relational databases.

> **NOTE**
>
> SQL and the relational database were invented and introduced in 1970 by Dr. E. F. Codd of IBM. Dr. Codd's original paper titled "A Relational Model of Data for Large Shared Data Banks" was a revolutionary paper that has truly changed the face of modern computing.

The ANSI standard for SQL (the latest standard is commonly referred to as SQL-92 because it was voted on in 1992) specifies a core syntax for the language itself. The reader should be aware that many relational database management systems advertise themselves to be SQL-92 compliant, but that all of these RDBMSs have added vendor-specific extensions to the language to support advanced features such as security, stored procedures, and triggers. There is nothing wrong with these extensions as long as the vendor has at least standardized on the extensions across its own product line. Simply be aware that these extensions exist, and try to note the differences when porting from one RDBMS to another.

Basic SQL Syntax

SQL is most commonly used to retrieve or modify data in a relational database. The four most commonly used statements are SELECT, INSERT, DELETE, and UPDATE. This section will briefly discuss these statements, and then explain database programming constructs such as triggers and stored procedures.

The SELECT Statement

The SELECT statement is used to *select* data from a database. At its simplest, the SELECT statement retrieves data from a specified table using the FROM clause. To retrieve all of the addresses from the ADDRESSES database (see the previous section titled "The Relational Database"), the user would issue the following SQL statement to the RDBMS:

```
SELECT * FROM ADDRESS
```

Upon execution, the RDBMS would return all of the rows in the ADDRESS table to the user. This request also could have been worded using the following syntax in order to retrieve all of the data:

```
SELECT ID, STREET, CITY, STATE, ZIP FROM ADDRESS
```

This data retrieval also can be filtered using the WHERE clause. The WHERE clause is used to specify some condition that each row must meet in order to be returned to the user. The following statement returns all records to the user where the address is located in the state of Florida:

```
SELECT * FROM ADDRESS WHERE STATE = 'FL'
```

The ORDER BY clause can be used to order data in some default order (determined by the data type of the ordering field). To return all rows to the user ordered by the LAST_NAME field, execute the following statement:

```
SELECT * FROM ADDRESS ORDER BY LAST_NAME
```

The SELECT statement also can be used to *join* multiple tables together in order to retrieve a combination of each table's data. For example, to retrieve all records from the NAME and ADDRESS table that are related, issue the following join command:

```
SELECT * FROM NAME, ADDRESS where NAME.ID = ADDRESS.ID
```

NOTE

Many different types of joins can be used to return different subsets of data. For more information on joins, consult a bona fide book about SQL such as *Teach Yourself SQL In 14 Days*, by Sams Publishing.

In short, here is the basic syntax for the SELECT statement:

```
SELECT <FIELDNAME1, FIELDNAME2, … FIELDNAMEn ¦ *>
FROM <TABLE1, TABLE2, TABLE3,...>
WHERE <CONDITION>
```

The INSERT Statement

At this point, you may be wondering how data actually gets put into the tables in the first place. There are actually two methods:

■ Using the SQL INSERT statement
■ Using a vendor-supplied data import tool such as Oracle's SQL-Loader or Sybase's bcp

This discussion will focus on the use of the SQL INSERT statement to insert data into a table.

The INSERT statement syntax, at its simplest, looks like this:

```
INSERT INTO <TABLE_NAME>
(COLUMN1, COLUMN2, COLUMN3, ...)
VALUES (VALUE1, VALUE2, VALUE3, ...)
```

When inserting data, you must follow three rules:

■ The values used must be the exact same data type as the fields to which they are being added.

■ The data's size must be within the column's size. For instance, an 80-character string cannot be added to a 40-character column.

■ The data's location in the VALUES list must correspond to the location in the column list of the column it is being added to. (That is, the first value must be entered into the first column, the second value into the second column, and so on.)

As a quick example, the following statement inserts a record into the final ADDRESS table mentioned in the section titled "The Relational Database":

```
INSERT INTO ADDRESS(ID, STREET, CITY, STATE, ZIP)
VALUES (1, '123 Forest St.', 'Huntsville', 'AL', 36507)
```

The UPDATE Statement

The UPDATE statement is used to update existing information within a database table. For instance, to modify the zip code value of an existing ADDRESS row, the UPDATE statement would be used. Here's the format of the UPDATE statement:

```
UPDATE <TABLE_NAME>
SET <COLUMNNAME1 = VALUE1, COLUMNNAME2 = VALUE2, ...>
WHERE <CONDITION>
```

As you can see, the UPDATE statement makes use of the WHERE clause originally introduced in the previous SELECT statement discussion. As an example, the following statement could be used to correct an entry error where someone entered "Pensacola" instead of "Miami" for the CITY field in the ADDRESS table:

```
UPDATE ADDRESS
SET CITY = 'Miami'
WHERE CITY = 'Pensacola'
```

Take note here that if the WHERE clause is omitted from the UPDATE statement, all records in the specified table will be updated! Therefore, make sure that the records being updated are always specified.

The DELETE Statement

The DELETE statement is used to remove rows from a relational table. The DELETE statement makes use of the WHERE clause introduced in the previous SELECT statement discussion. Depending on how the WHERE clause is used, the DELETE statement can do the following:

■ Delete single rows
■ Delete multiple rows
■ Delete all rows

■ Delete no rows

When using the DELETE statement, you should remember several things:

■ The DELETE statement cannot be used to delete an individual field's (or column's) values (see UPDATE for this). The DELETE statement deletes entire records from a table.

■ Like INSERT and UPDATE, deleting records from one table can cause referential integrity problems within other tables. This should be kept in mind when modifying data within a database.

■ Using the DELETE statement deletes only records, not the table itself.

Here's the basic syntax of the DELETE statement:

```
DELETE FROM <TABLE_NAME> WHERE <CONDITION>
```

The following example statement shows the syntax used to delete all addresses located in the state of California:

```
DELETE FROM ADDRESS WHERE STATE = 'CA'
```

Using Java with Databases

The first portion of this chapter introduced Java programmers to the world of relational databases. By now, you should have a decent understanding of what a database server is, what SQL is, and some knowledge of how to query a set of tables within a database. Of course, all of the information presented up to this point has been focused on executing SQL statements directly. The remainder of this chapter will discuss different methods for passing queries to a database server from within a Java applet or application. Currently, there are three primary methodologies for Java database access:

■ CGI scripts called from Java.

■ The JDBC API that provides a structured interface to relational databases from Java.

■ Server-side code that can be written in Java and used to access a database. This method, in general, ties the developer to a specific software manufacturer's toolset.

The following sections examine each of these topics briefly so that the reader will have a basic understanding of what is required to do database operations using Java code. Each section will point the reader in the direction of much more detailed sources that can be used if more information is required.

Java and CGI Calls

Before the advent of powerful Java database connectivity tools, the Common Gateway Interface (CGI) was the database querying method used by the vast majority of Web developers.

This interface defines a methodology for HTTP-based Web servers to talk to programs. CGI programs provide a way for clients to issue a procedure call, have that procedure execute on the server, and then return data to the client. CGI applications were the first "dynamic" elements on the Web, and they continue to be extremely popular because of the momentum behind the technology. A beginning Web developer may wonder, "Why use Java then if CGI is dynamic and platform-independent?" The answer is that a CGI application is simply a program residing on a server that understands how to "speak" HTTP. CGI applications can only return data to the client using a format that the client understands. At the current time (and in the foreseeable future), this data consists of HTML code. Therefore, unlike Java, CGI can only return basic form elements (some of which could be Java applets!). In other words, CGI programs are used to *provide* information; they are not the actual information themselves.

Where does CGI fit in for Java developers? CGI's primary strength (for Java developers) is its support for scripts written in any language. At the current time, there are no open Java packages available that allow applets to connect directly to SQL databases without the addition of special software drivers on each client machine. Therefore, CGI is an excellent candidate for simple database access. A CGI script could be written in C++ to query an Oracle database based on a number of input parameters. The result set returned from the query could then be formatted in HTML and returned (through the Common Gateway Interface) to the client that requested the information. Of course, this information could be displayed on the client using a Java applet.

Passing Data from the Client to the Gateway Program

There are two primary ways for a client (an HTML page, or in the Java programmer's case, perhaps a Java applet) to pass input parameters to a CGI program residing on a Web server:

■ Use environment variables

■ Use standard input (stdin) to the CGI program

CGI-compliant Web servers use the QUERY_STRING and PATH_INFO environment variables to pass data to CGI scripts.

To pass information to the QUERY_STRING environment variable, include the arguments to be passed after a question mark (?) character on the command line. For instance, to call the query.pl script with the "address" argument using the QUERY_STRING variable, use the following syntax:

```
http://www.someserver.com/query.pl?address
```

To pass information to the PATH_INFO environment variable, include the arguments to be passed after a slash (/) followed by an equals sign and the parameters value. For instance, to call the query.pl script with the "address" argument using the PATH_INFO variable, use the following syntax:

```
http://www.someserver.com/query.pl/address=Miami
```

The query.pl CGI script then can extract this string from the environment variable, parse it, and do whatever needs to be done. Using environment variables to pass information is a risky undertaking, however, due to the memory or string size limitations of some environments.

Although somewhat out of the scope of this book, HTML forms also can be used to "post" data to the standard input (stdin) of CGI scripts. A brief example of this type of input will be supplied so that readers will have some idea how to call CGI scripts directly from Java. There are many online and textual sources that describe CGI and HTML in great detail. Consult these sources if you need in-depth information on developing CGI applications.

The following snippet of code (see Listing 25.1) can be used to post information to a CGI script. Note that this code monitors an input stream continuously in a loop. Therefore, if you do nothing else, make sure that this code is broken off and running in its own thread.

Listing 25.1. Sample Java code used to call the query.pl CGI script.

```
Socket theSocket = new Socket("http://www.someserver.com", 80);
DataOutputStream theOut = new DataOutputStream(theSocket.getOutputStream());
DataInputStream theIn = new DataInputStream(theSocket.getInputStream());

String theScript = "query.pl";
String theParameter = "Address";

theOut.writeBytes("POST " + theScript + " HTTP/1.0\r\n" + "Content-type:
➥ application/octet-stream\r\n"
  + "Content-length: " + theParameter.length() + "\r\n\r\n" + theParameter;

String theReturn;
String loopdeloop;
while ((theReturn = theIn.readLine()) != null)
  loopdeloop += theReturn + "\n";
theIn.close();
theOut.close;
```

The code in Listing 25.1 opens a connection to the Web server http://www.someserver.com on port 80. After this connection has been made, the code opens a new output and input stream for communication with the server. The script is called using the output stream and then the code reads the server's reply using the input stream. At this point, it is the Java code's responsibility to parse through the reply and do something with it (display to user, perform calculations, and so on).

CGI applications represented an important first step toward a truly dynamic World Wide Web, but CGI has definite shortcomings. Most notably, CGI programs return what looks like Romulan to unsuspecting clients, and therefore these programs can become difficult to maintain, particularly for anyone other than the original programmer. CGI programs also suffer from notoriously poor performance as servers become bogged down. Developers also are forced to segment their application into distinct pieces. One side of the application passes a query through a very thin pipe, and then the other side of the application retrieves the query information from the pipe and talks to the database. When the required information is retrieved, the information is parsed and sent back to the requesting side of the application through the thin pipe. The next section ("The JDBC API") discusses a way for developers to make database queries directly within Java code and retrieve the query results directly. This will result in much cleaner (and faster) application development, as well as provide a more generic database API for applications if database servers ever need to be switched.

The JDBC API

The Java Database Connectivity Application Programming Interface (API) is an API currently being designed by Sun Microsystems that provides a Java language interface to the X/Open SQL Call Level Interface standard. This standard provides a DBMS-independent interface to relational databases that defines a generic SQL database access framework. The most visible implementation of the X/Open SQL CLI is Microsoft's ODBC (Open Database Connectivity). This API defines a common SQL syntax and function calls that can be used by developers to send SQL commands to and retrieve data from SQL databases. ODBC-enabled applications make use of database drivers (similar in concept to other device drivers) installed on the system that allow applications to talk to a vendor's database. Using this methodology, all of the DBMS-specific code is placed inside the ODBC driver and the application developer is shielded from implementation-specific problems in theory. Practically speaking, it is sometimes difficult to completely remove vendor-specific syntax from all ODBC operations, but in most cases, it is a relatively simple task to port ODBC to run on a new database server.

For Java developers, ODBC's primary drawback is that it is written in C. Because of the limitations inherent in the use of native methods, the JDBC designers have designed the JDBC specification to most easily use ODBC in the short term, but they have provided the capability long-term for JDBC to be implemented in other ways.

> **NOTE**
>
> JDBC, like ODBC, is designed to be a call-level SQL interface. Because many of its low-level operations can be combined into a higher-level, object-oriented interface, expect to see Java class libraries released in the future that provide a mapping to the underlying JDBC calls. This happened with ODBC almost immediately, and the majority of ODBC developers currently use other interfaces rather than using the ODBC API directly.

The JDBC API is expressed as a series of abstract Java interfaces within the `java.sql` package that will be provided as part of the JDK 1.1 release. Here are the most commonly used interfaces:

- `java.sql.DriverManager`—Manages the loading and unloading of database drivers from the underlying system.
- `java.sql.Connection`—Handles the connection to a specific database.
- `java.sql.Statement`—Contains an SQL statement to be passed to the database; two subtypes in this interface are the `PreparedStatement` (for executing a precompiled SQL statement) and the `CallableStatement` (for executing a database stored procedure).
- `java.sql.ResultSet`—Contains the record result set from the SQL statement passed to the database.

JDBC-enabled applets and applications make use of database drivers to connect to remote databases. What sets JDBC apart from ODBC is that these drivers can actually be applets themselves that get uploaded to the client system at runtime. Therefore, the overall Java model of a "thin client" querying a powerful database remains.

There are several different configurations in which JDBC can be used to access a database. Among the possible configurations are the following:

- An untrusted applet uploaded over the Internet to a client. This applet will connect directly to a server database across the Internet. Because the client machine will have no configuration information installed on it, the applet will have to be aware of the database to connect to (unlike in ODBC, where database configuration information is stored in the Windows registry).
- A trusted applet (trusted either because of an encryption key or because the user has decided to trust the source of the applet) uploaded over the Internet to a client. Although this applet is trusted and can connect to machines other than the one that it was uploaded from, JDBC configuration information will still have to be loaded because it is not located on the client machine.
- An intranet Java application. As a stand-alone application, this instance will not be subject to the security restrictions placed upon Java applets. Typical methodologies for connecting to the database consist of traditional two-tier client/server applications and also three-tier applications that use Remote Procedure Calls (RPCs) or an Object Request Broker (ORB) to connect to objects on a middle tier. This provides a middle tier of services and allows the application to be partitioned for performance improvements.

Steps Required to Access a JDBC Database

For programmers familiar with ODBC or other call-level interfaces to databases, the steps required to access a JDBC database should be familiar. JDBC uses the concept of a "connection" handle to manage a program's connection to a database.

Acquiring a Connection

When a Java JDBC-enabled applet or application initially starts, it must first acquire a connection to the JDBC database. It does this by calling the `java.sql.DriverManager.getConnection()` method. The syntax for this method is

```
public static synchronized Connection getConnection(String url,
➥ java.util.Properties info) throws SQLException;
```

As you can see, the `getConnection()` method takes as arguments a URL (to determine the database server location) and a Properties list (usually containing at least a user name and password). The format for the JDBC URL is still being debated, but at the present time it appears that it will look something like this:

```
jdbc:<subprotocol>:<subname>
```

As an example, if the connection is to use an ODBC bridge to connect to the EMPLOYEES database, the URL would be

```
jdbc:odbc:EMPLOYEES.
```

If the Oracle SQLNet protocol was being used to connect to an Oracle listener on `www.someserver.com` at port 2025, the URL would be

```
jdbc:sqlnet://www.someserver.com:2025/EMPLOYEES
```

Like ODBC, JDBC needs to know which database drivers are available for use. It can load drivers using two methods:

- The JDBC Driver Manager can look for an `sql.drivers` system property and load all listed drivers.
- The Java programmer can load a driver class by calling the `Class.forName()` method.

Creating a Statement

Now that the connection has been required, a statement needs to be created so that it can be passed to the database for processing. This is done by calling the `connection` class's `createStatement()` method. Here's an example of this:

```
java.sql.Statement statement = connection.createStatement();
```

Executing a Query

Using the statement you created, an SQL query can be executed by using the statement's executeQuery() method. This method returns a ResultSet object so that the query's results can be examined. Here's a simple example:

```
ResultSet result = statement.executeQuery("select NAME, SALARY,
➡ EMPLOYEE_ID from EMPLOYEES");
```

Examining the Result Set

Use the ResultSet object returned from the executeQuery() method call to examine the returned data. The ResultSet class has member methods to scroll the ResultSet lists, such as first(), last(), next(), and prev(), as well as individual data member methods for examining returned data such as getInteger(), getVarChar(), getVarBinary(), and so on. To examine the returned data, methods such as getInteger() can be called in one of two ways:

- By passing in an integer index value that will return the column index value of the data returned (0 for the first item, 1 for the second item, ...). This method will result in better performance, but poor readability.

- By passing in a column name string identifying the column to be examined (for example, getInteger("SALARY")).

JDBC also can be used to modify data using common insert, delete, and update method calls.

Other JDBC Operations

JDBC supports a wide range of common database functions as well. Here are some examples:

- Transaction management
- Basic cursors
- Stored procedure execution
- Scalar functions such as numeric, string, system, and time/date functions

In short, JDBC promises to be a tremendous tool for Java programmers interested in connecting to remote SQL databases. At the current time, many major database manufacturers are preparing JDBC drivers so that application programmers will be able to access databases from Java applets. The biggest change for developers might be the performance change, particularly when using untrusted JDBC applets communicating with databases across the Internet. In the Intranet case, however, the appearance of native Java compilers should make high-performance, cross-platform JDBC application development a reality in the near future.

Server-Side Database Access

The final Java/database access method to be discussed has been termed Server-Side Database Access. This functionality is similar to that of Java applets/applications calling CGI scripts, except that in this case, the CGI scripts have been replaced by "intelligent" Web servers designed for database access such as the Oracle WebServer and the Microsoft Internet Information Server. Both of these products allow code to be executed on the server that connects directly to a database (possibly on yet another server). This code can be called directly or indirectly from a remote Java applet, but unlike CGI, it is loaded in the Web server's process.

Oracle WebServer 2.0

Currently, the Oracle WebServer 2.0 supports the creation of server code using a number of languages including Oracle PL/SQL, Java, and C/C++. The Oracle WebServer is built around the Oracle Web Request Broker. This process bypasses the CGI interface and uses a high-performance native connection to the Oracle7 server. Unfortunately (for non-Oracle developers) at the current time, only the Oracle7 database server can be connected to using this product. This server supports end-to-end encryption using SSL 2.0 (Secure Sockets Layer) and is available for a variety of operating platforms including Windows NT and SPARC Solaris. For situations in which the database to be used is definitely going to be an Oracle7 database, the Oracle WebServer allows developers to write more advanced, better performing server code that can be used by Java applets to query databases and return information.

Microsoft Internet Information Server

The Microsoft Internet Information Server (IIS) promises to be one of the more widely used Web servers in the near future due to Microsoft's decision to include it for free as part of its Windows NT 4.0 product. This product is currently freely downloadable from the Microsoft Web site (`http://www.microsoft.com`). IIS uses ODBC by default to connect to any database that has an available ODBC driver. (Although this makes IIS a more open product, there is a performance penalty to be paid for using ODBC in most cases.) For developers not wanting to use ODBC or who want a cleaner interface than the default `HTTPODBC.DLL` implementation, Microsoft's ISAPI (Internet Services API) can be used using the `OLEISAPI.DLL`. OLEISAPI allows the developer to start a server application, pass it some parameters, and retrieve its return values to return to the Web client. To do this, the server application must be an in-process OLE DLL, which can be created using Microsoft Visual C++ or Visual Basic. In the near future, IIS will be able to run code written in a number of other languages including VBScript, Microsoft's scripting language, which bears a syntactical resemblance to Visual Basic. Unlike Visual Basic, however, VBScript will be thread-scalable and should offer better performance.

Summary

This chapter was supplied to give Java developers some insight into Java's database access capabilities. During Java's first year of growth (1995–1996), much of the framework was laid to make the Java environment available on virtually every popular operating system. In addition to this, a great deal of effort has gone into producing new tools specifically tailored for Java developers. The second year of Java's growth should see the introduction of a host of database-access related products that will open the business enterprise up to Java applet and application developers. (Java will no longer be used only to scroll text across Web pages!) Following the widespread acceptance of Java as a full-fledged, industrial-strength programming language, the following year should see the introduction of component models such as Java Beans that will allow Java developers to access other object model objects (such as CORBA and COM).

The JDBC API appears to be a unifying API that many database tool manufacturers will standardize on, much as Microsoft's ODBC API helped standardize Windows-platform database access. As more and more products begin to emerge and the marketplace grows even more competitive, Java developers should make every effort possible to refrain from adding platform-specific extensions to their Java code, particularly in environments where users of other operating systems could access your code (such as the Internet).

26

Network-Aware Programming

by Dan Joshi

Network-aware programming with Java is not very hard to understand. Only a few classes and procedures need to be followed when you're dealing with the java.net package. The tricky part is understanding exactly how communication takes place. Once you have this understanding and you know what methods and procedures to use in the java.net package, you should be able to develop network-enabled Java programs with very little trouble. This chapter gives you a deeper understanding of how communication takes place in Java and on the Internet, and what you need to know to effectively design a Java program to connect to the Internet, a server, or even another applet.

Much of the material in this chapter is based on java.net. Note that Chapter 33, "Package java.net," gives a complete overview of the java.net package in the Java class library and you should refer to it periodically throughout this chapter. You can also use it if you want more details about the classes and methods used in this chapter.

The Server Discussion

As you know, a server's job is to facilitate and house information for clients in a network. In this section, you'll learn how to create a basic server in Java.

What makes up a server? The following attributes contribute to a Java program becoming a server:

■ Designates a port and listens for activity.

■ Responds to requests from clients on the designated port.

■ Interprets the incoming information and responds accordingly.

Typically, a server isn't designed to have a spiffy user interface; that's reserved for the client part of the application—the part usually seen by the application's user. Server applications are more function than form.

The first class to discuss in the java.net package is the java.net.ServerSocket class. ServerSocket is responsible for how TCP deals with retrieving a port, which is done when creating an instance of the ServerSocket class. The following shows an example using port 1234:

```
try {
    theServerSocket = new ServerSocket( 1055 );
} catch(IOException e) {}
```

> **NOTE**
>
> If the port you specified is already in use, then an IOException might be raised. If that happens, try using another port. The higher the port number you choose, the less likely it is to be in use.

Once you successfully get a port for a server, you need to have it continually listen for any activity by using the method `accept()` in the `ServerSocket` class:

```
try {
    Socket s = theServerSocket.accept();
} catch(IOException e) {}
```

This method cycles continually, listening to the designated port until a request comes through. If a request comes through and is successful, the method `accept()` returns a class `Socket` containing a connection to the client that initially requested a connection.

The returned class `java.net.Socket` represents an actual TCP connection. When a socket is created from the method `accept()`, a connection has been successfully opened between the client and the server. A `Socket` class can use an IP address or host name, a port, or both at the same time to establish a connection. You will see more of this class in subsequent sections about the client.

If everything goes smoothly, then you should be at the stage where you can begin receiving and sending information between the client and the server. The two methods in the `Socket` class responsible for that are the `getInputStream()` and the `getOutputStream()`. The `getInputStream()` returns an `InputStream` from the `java.io` package, and `getOutputStream` returns an `OutputStream` from the `java.io` package. You do your communicating between the client and the server in these returned classes. You have pretty much finished using networking tools in Java; now you need to implement streams.

The Server Workshop

Listing 26.1 is a server for the client/server example in this chapter. Go ahead and open a new file in your text editor, enter the code for Listing 26.1, and then save it as `myServer.java`. (The code for Listing 26.1 is available from this book's CD-ROM.)

Listing 26.1. The code for `myServer.java`.

```
 1:import java.io.*;
 2:import java.net.*;
 3:import java.awt.*;
 4:
 5:public class myServer extends Frame {
 6:
 7:        TextArea txtPane;
 8:
 9:        myServer() {
10:
11:            //Create the Interface
12:            super("The Server v 1.0");
13:            txtPane = new TextArea("Status Window:\n", 10, 30);
14:            add("Center", txtPane);
```

continues

Listing 26.1. continued

```
15:                  pack();
16:                  show();
17:
18:                  ServerSocket theSocketServer = null;
19:                  Socket socketReturn = null;
20:                  InputStream rawDataIn = null;
21:
22:     try {
23:
24:           theSocketServer = new ServerSocket( 1055 );
25:           txtPane.appendText( "Initializing the port... \n");
26:
27:           //Listen at the port 1055
28:           txtPane.appendText( "Listening... \n");
29:           socketReturn = theSocketServer.accept();
30:
31:           //Connection has been achieved with client
32:           txtPane.appendText( "Connected to a Client \n" );
33:
34:           //Get data from the Socket
35:           rawDataIn = socketReturn.getInputStream();
36:           DataInputStream DataIn = new DataInputStream(rawDataIn);
37:
38:           //Print Data our in the Statue Window
39:           String Value = DataIn.readLine();
40:           txtPane.appendText("Hello: " + Value + "!");
41:
42:           }
43:         catch( UnknownHostException e) {
44:             txtPane.appendText("Unable to find Server. Error" + e);
45:           }
46:         catch( IOException e ) {
47:             txtPane.appendText("IO Error has been raised. Error " + e);
48:           }
49:     }
50:
51:     public static void main(String argv[]) {
52:
53:                  new myServer();
54:     }
55:
56:     public boolean handleEvent(Event event) {
57:
58:           if(event.id == Event.WINDOW_DESTROY) {
59:
60:                  System.exit(0);
61:                  return true;
62:           }
63:           return super.handleEvent(event);
64:     }
65:}
```

In Listing 26.1, lines 12 to 16 should be nothing new to you; they are simply the code that builds the user interface (UI) for this application. Besides a frame, the only UI component created in this code is a TextArea because it has a method called appendText() that lets you attach text to the end of text already contained in a given TextArea. In effect, you're making a large status window where you can watch the application's progress.

Following the UI, Lines 18 to 20 are responsible for initializing all the network-related variables, including the streams that will accept and retrieve the input and output from a client. Notice that for simplicity's sake this server is only initializing an InputStream (Line 20) so it can just receive information from the client. In most real-world, and more complex, situations you want to have both streams to receive and send data across the line.

Line 24 initializes the server port, and Line 29 executes the accept() method to begin listening on that port. If a request comes in on the port, then Lines 35 and 36 are invoked to retrieve the InputStream from the connection, and on Line 39, the InputStream is placed into the String variable value. On the next line (Line 40), the information retrieved from the client is printed out in TextArea on the server.

The only other major piece of code that should be discussed are Lines 56 through 63, which shouldn't be anything new to you. These lines enable you to exit from the application without raising any exceptions.

Your next step is to compile the application; however, you shouldn't run it yet since the client hasn't been created. That will be the next step to accomplish before you can see your client/server application come to life.

The Client Discussion

The primary role of a client is to have a well-developed user interface. Usually, it is the client that users see whenever they execute your programs.

Once you have a user interface in place, your next step is to use the Socket class in the java.net package to request a connection with a port on the server. The following list describes a client's key features:

- The client should contain the front-end of your application.
- The client requests a connection with the server to send and receive data.
- The client application is a self-contained program from the server.

In Java, a client application uses the Socket class to connect to a particular port. The following code lines show an example of creating an instance of the Socket class on a client application; the first number is the IP address (or you can use the host name) and the port from which it should request a connection to.

```
try {
    Socket s = new Socket("123.123.123.123", 1234);
} catch(IOException e) {}
```

When a connection has been successfully established, you can use the same two methods—
`getOutputStream()`and `getInputStream()`—you used in the server example. By using these
streams, you can send information to the server and get information back.

In the next section, you actually write the client side of the sample application.

The Client Workshop

Open up your text editor and enter the code from Listing 26.2; when you're done, go ahead
and compile it. (Note that the code for Listing 26.2 is available from this book's CD-ROM.)

Listing 26.2. The code for `myClient.java`.

```
 1:import java.awt.*;
 2:import java.net.*;
 3:import java.io.*;
 4:
 5:public class myClient extends Frame {
 6:
 7:     //Variables for UI
 8:     Button btnServer;
 9:     TextField txtInput;
10:
11:     //Initialize Output Streams
12:     OutputStream rawDataOut = null;
13:     PrintStream DataOut = null;
14:
15:     //Initialize Socket
16:     Socket theClientSocket = null;
17:
18:     myClient() {
19:
20:         //Create the Interface
21:         super("The Client");
22:         setLayout(new FlowLayout());
23:         add(new Label("Enter Your Name: "));
24:         txtInput=new TextField(25);
25:         add(txtInput);
26:         btnServer=new Button("Send to Server");
27:         add(btnServer);
28:         pack();
29:         show();
30:         super.resize(400, 100);
31:
32:         try {
33:
34:             //Instantiate a new Socket
35:             theClientSocket = new Socket("127.0.0.1", 1055);
36:
37:             rawDataOut = theClientSocket.getOutputStream();
38:             DataOut = new PrintStream(rawDataOut);
39:
```

```
40:        } catch( UnknownHostException e) {
41:            System.out.println("Unable to find the Server. Error " + e);
42:
43:        } catch ( IOException e ) {
44:            System.out.println("An IO error has been raised. Error " + e);
45:        }
46:    }
47:
48:    public boolean handleEvent(Event event) {
49:
50:    if (event.id == Event.ACTION_EVENT && event.target == btnServer) {
51:        clickedBtnServer();
52:        return true;
53:    } else if (event.id == Event.WINDOW_DESTROY) {
54:        System.exit(0);
55:        return true;
56:    }
57:    return super.handleEvent(event);
58:    }
59:
60:    public static void main(String argv[]) {
61:
62:        new myClient();
63:    }
64:
65:    public void clickedBtnServer() {
66:
67:        // Send Data to Server
68:        try {
69:            DataOut.print(txtInput.getText());
70:            //Close the Socket
71:                theClientSocket.close();
72:        } catch(Exception e) {}
73:    }
74:}
```

Listing 26.2 is the sample client application. Starting at the top, notice that besides initializing two UI components (Lines 8 and 9), you are just initializing the output stream (Lines 12 and 13) for this application. That's because this is a simple model, so the client application will just be sending information to the server. In most cases, you use both input and output streams so you can get responses from the server. Finally, the Socket is initialized on Line 16.

Lines 21 through 30 build the interface for the application. Line 35 creates an instance of the Socket class that's sent to the server requesting a connection. Notice that you're using the local IP address because both the client and the server reside on your system locally.

In Lines 37 through 38, you see the code for retrieving the output stream from the Socket connection; this task is done by using the getOutputStream() method on Line 37.

The handleEvent() method on Line 48 checks for two actions: whether the button btnServer has been clicked (Line 50) or the Event.WINDOW_DESTROY has been invoked (Line 53). If the button btnServer is clicked, then the clickedBtnServer() method (Line 51) is called. This method, located on Lines 65 through 73, basically sends out the contents of the text box txtInput to the Socket so it can go to the server on Line 69. On Line 71, it closes the connection to the Socket.

The main() method (Lines 60 to 63) merely creates an instance of the class myClient using the myClient() constructor method.

Executing the Client/Server Application

When you execute the myServer and myClient applications, order is crucial if you want the demonstration to work properly. The myServer application should be loaded first so it can start listening at port 1055, then load the client application so that when it requests a connection on that port, it will get a response.

First, run the myServer application and watch the status pane in the server application as it initializes the port and starts to listen. When the myServer application looks like the one shown in Figure 26.1, then you are ready to execute the client application.

FIGURE 26.1.

The myServer *application listening at port 1055.*

Now run the myClient application while leaving the myServer application up. When you load the myClient application, it automatically requests a connection through that port to the server. Once a connection has been made, the server tells you it has connected to a client. (See Figure 26.2.)

FIGURE 26.2.

The myClient *application successfully connected to* myServer.

At this point, you have successfully initialized the port and created a socket between these two applications. To test your client/server application, enter your name in the myClient text field, then click the Send to Server button. You will see the server application respond, as shown in Figure 26.3.

FIGURE 26.3.

The myClient *application retrieving information from the server.*

Obviously, this is a very simple client/server application, but it does illustrate the material needed to develop more functional programs. You should now have a general understanding of how TCP/IP works and know how to work the methods in the java.net package to create client/server applications that can communicate with each other.

Inter-Applet Communication

Sockets aren't the only way to make your programs network aware. Another technique, known as *inter-applet communication*, is much easier to understand and fairly easy to do. Unlike the client/server model you used in the last section, inter-applet communication is based on a peer-to-peer networking environment in which there really is no designated server or client; each participant merely contributes resources and communicates.

When dealing with inter-applet communication, there are no complex procedures to follow. There are two key things you need to do to implement inter-applet communication:

- Use the getAppletContext()method to retrieve information about the other applet you want to connect with.

- Handle events so that when an event is passed to one applet, it can be "transported" to the other applet.

The method getAppletContext() is a member of the java.applet.Applet class. It returns an object known as AppletContext(). This class contains information about the applet's environment. The method getAppletContext() actually provides more information than just the existence of other applets in the environment; it's used in the next section when we discuss having an applet communicate with an Internet browser.

Since `getAppletContext()` actually returns the object `AppletContext`, which contains information about the applet's environment, the actual method that does the getting is a member of the `AppletContext` class called `getApplet()`. The `getApplet()` method takes a `String` that should contain the name of the applet you want to get information about.

> **NOTE**
>
> The `NAME` parameter is an optional part of the `APPLET` tag in HTML code. `NAME` is used to identify a name for a particular applet. For example, even though the class of this applet is `myApplet`, the name that it will be referred to by other applets is `theApplet`:
>
> `<APPLET CODE=myApplet.class NAME=theApplet WIDTH=100 HEIGHT=100> </APPLET>`
>
> When an applet is going to be referenced by another for communication purposes, you must give that applet a name.

The following is an example of using the `getAppletContext().getApplet()` method for an applet named `theApplet`:

```
Applet a = getAppletContext().getApplet("theApplet");
```

> **NOTE**
>
> Another method you can use is `getApplets()`, which returns a list of all the applets it found in the environment.

Now that you have a handle on the applet you want to communicate with, you need to see how to pass events from one applet to the other. For example, Applet A wants to communicate with Applet B, and it has created an `Applet` object referring to Applet B. Applet A gets an event from the user (such as a button click) in the `handleEvent()` method, so you want to pass that event off to Applet B:

```
public boolean handleEvent(Event event) {
    Applet a = getAppletContext().getApplet("theApplet");
    return a.handleEvent(event);
}
```

In the Applet B event handler, look for an event coming from Applet A and respond accordingly.

With event handling, it's a matter of having one applet pass an event to the other applet, which is the tricky part of inter-applet communication. Once you have mastered that, the rest is easy.

The First Applet

Begin by creating the applet First. Open a clean window in your text editor and enter the code for First.java, shown in Listing 26.3. (The code for Listing 26.3 is available from this book's CD-ROM.) The First applet will be the one receiving events from the applet.

Listing 26.3. The code for First.java.

```
 1:import java.awt.*;
 2:
 3:public class First extends java.applet.Applet {
 4:
 5:     //Variables for UI
 6:     Label lblOutput;
 7:
 8:     public void init() {
 9:
10:         //Create the UI
11:         add(new Label("The First applet."));
12:         lblOutput = new Label("Click on a button in the Second applet.");
13:         add(lblOutput);
14:     }
15:
16:     public boolean handleEvent(Event event) {
17:
18:         if ("One".equals(event.arg)) {
19:             lblOutput.setText("You clicked: One");
20:             return true;
21:         } else if ("Two".equals(event.arg)) {
22:             lblOutput.setText("You clicked: Two");
23:             return true;
24:         } else if ("Three".equals(event.arg)) {
25:             lblOutput.setText("You clicked: Three");
26:             return true;
27:         }
28:     return super.handleEvent(event);     }
29:
30:}
```

Lines 11 to 13 create the UI for the applet. The only other method in this applet is the handleEvent() method (starting on Line 16) in the applet. The handleEvent() method includes three if expressions (Lines 18, 21, and 24); each one checks to see whether the event being passed to it has an argument that's the label for the command button in the applet Second (the one created in the subsequent section). In response, it will change the label lblOutput to show the user that, indeed, a particular button from applet Second was clicked (Lines 19, 22, and 25).

The Second Applet

Here is the code for the second applet (see Listing 26.4). The applet Second is responsible for doing the sending to the applet First.

Listing 26.4. The code for Second.java.

```
1:import java.awt.*;
2:import java.applet.*;
3:public class Second extends java.applet.Applet {
4:
5:          //Declare the UI variables
6:          Button btnOne;
7:          Button btnTwo;
8:          Button btnThree;
9:
10:        public void init() {
11:
12:                  //Build the UI
13:                  btnOne = new Button("One");
14:                  add(btnOne);
15:                  btnTwo = new Button("Two");
16:                  add(btnTwo);
17:                  btnThree = new Button("Three");
18:                  add(btnThree);
19:
20:          }
21:
22:public boolean handleEvent(Event event) {
23:
24:      if (event.id == Event.ACTION_EVENT && event.target == btnOne) {
25:          Applet f = getAppletContext().getApplet("theFirst");
26:          return f.handleEvent(event);
27:          } else if (event.id == Event.ACTION_EVENT && event.target == btnTwo) {
28:          Applet f = getAppletContext().getApplet("theFirst");
29:          return f.handleEvent(event);
30:          } else if (event.id == Event.ACTION_EVENT && event.target == btnThree) {
31:          Applet f = getAppletContext().getApplet("theFirst");
32:          return f.handleEvent(event);
33:      }
34:
35:      return super.handleEvent(event);}
36:}
```

Starting with the life cycle method init(), Lines 13 to 18 build the interface. Notice, though, that the interface consists of three buttons labeled "One" (Line 13), "Two" (Line 15), and "Three" (Line 17). These labels help the applet First distinguish what to display in the output label.

The method handleEvent() (beginning on Line 22) has three if expressions (Lines 24, 27, and 30). Each of the if expressions looks for each of the three command buttons to see whether they were clicked. If one of the buttons was clicked, then each method uses the method getAppletContext()getApplet to retrieve the applet First and instance it to variable f, using the name theFirst (Lines 25, 28, and 31). Then, on the following line (Lines 26, 29, and 31), it sends the event to the applet First so that it can handle it. At that point, applet Second has done its job by finding out which button was clicked and sending the event with the appropriate attributes to the applet First. Now it waits until one of the buttons is clicked again.

Executing the Inter-Applet Communication Example

Now that you have created both files, it's time to compile and execute each one. You can compile both of them using the javac.exe command. Since these are applets, you can't use the java.exe interpreter; however, you can use the applet viewer that comes with the JDK. To use the applet viewer, though, you need to have an HTML file referring to both of these applets. Listing 26.5 shows the code for index.html. Go ahead and create index.html in your text editor and enter the HTML code from Listing 26.5.

Listing 26.5. The code for index.html.

```
1:<HTML>
2:<BODY>
3:<applet code=First.class name=theFirst width=250 height=100></applet>
4:<applet code=Second.class  width=200 height=100></applet>
5:</BODY>
6:</HTML>
```

Now you're ready to actually run the two applets through the applet viewer. Make sure both applets (First and Second) are in the same directory as the index.html and that the file applet viewer.exe that comes with the JDK is accessible from that directory. Finally, you can invoke the applet viewer by typing the following:

```
appletviewer index.html
```

You should then see two applets pop up on your desktop. (See Figure 26.4.)

Once the applets have finished loading, you're ready to begin by clicking any of the buttons on the Second applet pane. This creates an event inside the applet, which responds by kicking another message to the First applet. Next, the First applet displays what button was clicked on the Second applet. (See Figure 26.5.)

FIGURE 26.4.

Inter-applet example with both applets initialized.

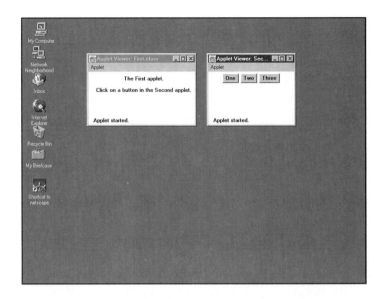

FIGURE 26.5.

Inter-applet example with the button Two clicked.

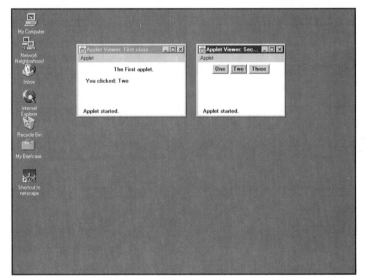

Applet Communication with the Browser

The `getAppletContext()` method can also be used to facilitate communicating to a browser from inside the applet itself. There are several ways to communicate to the browser externally (such as using HTML tags and attributes); however, applets are somewhat limited in what they can do internally. In this section, you'll learn about two methods directly related to browser communication—both deal with sending information from the applet to the host browser.

However, before you can deal with that you need to learn about another class in the `java.net` package called the URL class. *URL* stands for Uniform Resource Locator; you can use this class to house information on URLs from almost any location on the Internet. You can also use other Internet protocols besides HTTP, like FTP and gopher. Here's an example of creating a new URL for access to the Web site `http://café.symantec.com`:

```
try {
    URL myWebsite = new URL("http://café.symantec.com");
} catch(MalformedURLException e) {}
```

There are several other constructors for this class, including one for specifying the protocol and port for a given URL reference (see Chapter 33 for more information). Once you have a URL, you can pass it to your browser by using the `showDocument()` method from `getAppletContext()`.

The other method that comes from `getAppletContext()` is the `showStatus()` method, used for displaying messages in the browser's bottom status bar. This example shows how to display the line `Please wait for the applet to load...` in the user's browser status bar:

```
getAppletContext().showDocument("Please wait for the applet to load...");
```

Now you'll create a real-world example that sends requests to an Internet browser (in this case Internetscape, but it should work for any Java-capable browser) to either go to the Java home page (`http://www.javasoft.com`) or FTP to the directory where the JDK is located on the Java site (`ftp://ftp.javasoft.com/pub`).

In your text editor, create a new file and enter the code in Listing 26.6; save it as `BrowserLink.java`.

Listing 26.6. The code for `BrowserLink.java`.

```
1:import java.net.*;
2:import java.awt.*;
3:
4:public class BrowserLink extends java.applet.Applet {
5:
6:          //Declare variables
7:          URL urlJava;
8:          URL urlJDK;
9:          Button btnFirst;
10:          Button btnSecond;
11:
12:      public void init() {
13:
14:          //Build UI
15:          btnFirst = (new Button("Java Home Page"));
16:          add(btnFirst);
```

continues

Listing 26.6. continued

```
17:         btnSecond = (new Button("The JDK download Directory"));
18:         add(btnSecond);
19:     }
20:
21:     public void start() {
22:
23:         //Check to make sure the URL is accessible
24:         try {
25:             urlJava  = new URL("http://www.javasoft.com");
26:             urlJDK = new URL("ftp", "ftp.javasoft.com", "/pub");
27:         } catch (MalformedURLException e) {
28:             System.out.println("Unable to retieve URL. Error: " + e);
29:         }
30:     }
31:
32:     public boolean handleEvent(Event event) {
33:
34:     if (event.id == Event.ACTION_EVENT && event.target == btnFirst) {
35:             getAppletContext().showDocument(urlJava);
36:             return true;
37:         }else if (event.id == Event.ACTION_EVENT && event.target == btnSecond){
38:             getAppletContext().showDocument(urlJDK);
39:             return true;
40:         }
41:         return super.handleEvent(event);
42:     }
43:}
```

The UI is built in the init() life-cycle method in Lines 15 through 18. Inside the life cycle method start() (beginning with Line 21), the life cycle method is a try block, which is used to make sure that the two URLs, http://www.javasoft.com (Line 25) and ftp://ftp.javasoft.com (Line 26), are valid and accessible from the current environment (Lines 24 through 29).

The handleEvent() method (starting on Line 32) contains two if expressions: one to determine whether btnFirst is clicked (Line 34) and the other to determine whether btnSecond is clicked (Line 37).

If the first if expression (Line 34) returns true, meaning that btnFirst was indeed pressed, then the showDocument() method (Line 35) is invoked, going to the URL address http://www.javasoft.com. However, if the second if expression returns true, meaning that the button btnSecond is clicked, then on Line 38 the method showDocument() is used to take the user to the directory where the JDK is available for downloading on the JavaSoft site ftp://ftp.javasoft.com/pub.

Go ahead and compile Listing 26.7 in a file called BrowserLink.java. Your next step is to create an HTML file to run it out of, which is shown in Listing 26.7. In another clean text editor, create the file BrowserLink.html and enter the code in Listing 26.7.

Listing 26.7. The code for `BrowserLink.html`.

```
1:<HTML>
2:<HEAD>
3:</HEAD>
4:<BODY>
5:<APPLET CODE=BrowserLink.class WIDTH=200 HEIGHT=100> </APPLET>
6:</BODY>
7:</HTML>
```

Now you're ready to execute and run the program. With both files (`BrowserLink.java` and `BrowserLink.html`) in the same directory, load the HTML page `BrowserLink.html` in your Internet browser. This example uses Netscape Navigator, but any Internet browser will do.

You can see in Figure 26.6 that there are two command buttons available. The first one, "Java Home Page," is `btnFirst`, and the second, "The JDK Download Directory," is `btnSecond`. Click the Java Home Page button and watch as your browser automatically loads the URL `http://www.javasoft.com`. (See Figure 26.7.)

FIGURE 26.6.

The `BrowserLink` *applet loaded.*

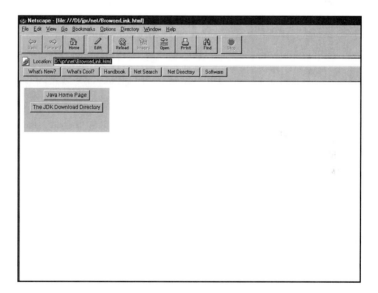

As you can see, the applet was replaced with the JavaSoft home page. Now, go back to the applet `BrowserLink` and click the JDK Download Directory button; this time, the applet will be replaced by the directory (including Sun's disclaimer) where you can download the JDK. (See Figure 26.8.)

FIGURE 26.7.

The JavaSoft home page.

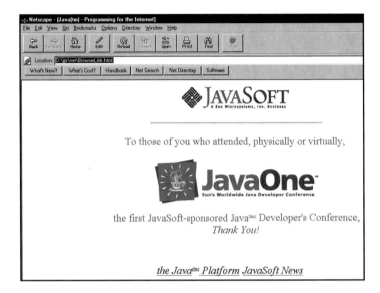

FIGURE 26.8.

The JavaSoft FTP archive in the /pub *directory.*

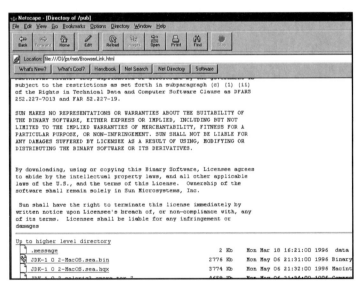

There are many ways for an applet to interact with the browser. However, always remember the trite security model for Java applets.

Java Communication with the Internet Using URLConnection

The final topic discussed in this chapter expands on the information in the previous section. Instead of retrieving information through the browser, you could retrieve information directly from the Internet to your applet. One way to do that is by using the class URLConnection, which represents a connection to a specified URL on the Internet. URLConnection is the class used to retrieve information from a URL passed to it. This is an example of how it's used:

```
try {
    URL myURL = "http://café.symantec.com";
    URLConnection myConnection = URLConnection.openConnection(myURL);
} catch(MalformedException e) {}
```

Once you have a valid connection, use getInputStream() and filter it through the DataInputStream, where you can successfully retrieve information directly to the applet.

Another method you can use is the openStream() method directly from the java.net.URL class.

The following example in Listing 26.8 is a Java application. When you click the command button, it will access the JavaSoft home page (http://www.javasoft.com) and retrieve the information, as a browser would.

Listing 26.8. The code for Retrieve.java.

```
1:import java.net.*;
2:import java.awt.*;
3:import java.io.*;
4:
5:public class Retrieve extends Frame {
6:
7:     //Declare variables
8:     Button btnRetrieve;
9:     TextArea txtPane;
10:    static URL urlJava;
11:    static URLConnection conJava;
12:    InputStream rawInput;
13:
14:    Retrieve() {
15:
16:        //Build the UI
17:        super("The Retrieve Application");
18:        setLayout(new FlowLayout());
19:        btnRetrieve = new Button("Retrieve the JavaSoft home page.");
20:        add(btnRetrieve);
21:        txtPane = new TextArea(30,70);
22:        add(txtPane);
23:        pack();
24:        show();
25:
```

continues

Listing 26.8. continued

```
26:    }
27:
28:    public static void main(String argv[]) {
29:
30:        new Retrieve();
31:    }
32:
33:    public boolean handleEvent(Event event) {
34:
35:        String Value;
36:
37:        if (event.id == Event.ACTION_EVENT && event.target == btnRerçâeve) {
38:            clickedbtnRetrieve();
39:            return true;
40:        } else if (event.id == Event.WINDOW_DESTROY) {
41:            System.exit(0);
42:            return true;
43:        }
44:        return super.handleEvent(event);
45:    }
46:
47:    public void clickedbtnRetrieve() {
48:
49:        //Check to make sure the URL is accessible
50:        try {
51:            urlJava  = new URL("http://www.javasoft.com");
52:        } catch(MalformedURLException e) {
53:            System.out.println("Unable to retieve URL. Error: " + e);
54:        }
54:
55:
56:        //Retrieve the information
57:        try {
58:            conJava = urlJava.openConnection();
59:            rawInput = conJava.getInputStream();
60:            DataInputStream DataIn = new DataInputStream(rawInput);
61:
62:            //Read and display data.
63:            for (int i = 1; i < 30; i++) {
64:
65:            String Value = DataIn.readLine();
66:            txtPane.appendText(Value + "\n");
67:            }
68:        } catch(IOException e) {
69:            System.out.println("an IO error has been raised. Error: " + e);
70:        }
71:    }
72:}
```

Starting on Lines 8 to 12, you declare variables for the UI, and Lines 17 to 24 build the UI. The main() method on Line 28 creates an instance of the class Retrieve when the application is executed.

The interesting part of this application is the `handleEvent()` method starting on Line 35. There are two if statements (Lines 37 and 40). The first if statement checks to see whether the button `btnRetrieve` is clicked. If this is true, then it will invoke the following:

- Check to see whether the URL is valid and accessible from this application's environment (Lines 50 to 55).
- Open a connection to the URL `http://www.javasoft.com` (Line 59).
- Invoke the method `getInputStream()` to retrieve the raw data from that server (Line 60).
- Pass the raw `InputStream` to the instance variable `In` from the `DataInputStream` (Line 61).
- Scroll through and read the data into `String` variable `Value` (Line 66), then display in the `TextArea` using the `appendText()` method (Line 67).

Compile and run the application `Retrieve`, and you should see something similar to Figure 26.9.

WARNING

Be sure you're connected to the Internet before running the `Retrieve` application in Listing 26.8.

FIGURE 26.9.

The `Retrieve` *application.*

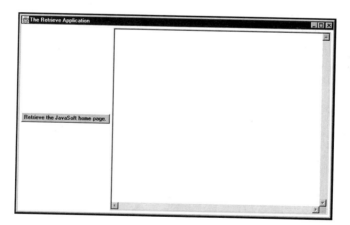

Next, click the button "Retrieve the JavaSoft home page," and you'll see the first 30 lines of HTML code from the site `http://www.javasoft.com`. (See Figure 26.10.)

FIGURE 26.10.

The Retrieve *application with the* http://www.javasoft.com *site downloaded.*

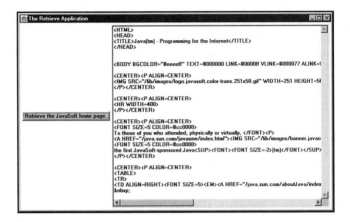

Summary

This chapter covered how the Internet communicates and included a high-level introduction to TCP/IP and client/server architecture. You also learned about inter-applet communication and how to bounce events off one applet to another on a single home page. Finally, you saw how to let Java applets and applications communicate with the Internet. This chapter concluded with a Java example you can actually run.

Network programming gives you several ways to do the same things. Although this chapter tried to show several of the most common techniques, for each potential solution in Java, there may be alternative methods. If you're interested in learning more, a good place to start is to become familiar with all the available classes in the java.net package, described in Chapter 33. No matter what people say (myself included), network programming can be a somewhat complex topic—but in the real world, it's a necessity that your Java programs have the capability to communicate with each other and the environment around them.

III

Package, Class, and Interface Reference

This part of the book adds efficiency to your day-to-day Java development by providing exhaustive, quick-reference entries to help you easily identify individual Java components. This section has strong visual cues and complete forward and backward references. Research has shown that judicious use of these cues provides much quicker comprehension than the written word. Though it's impossible to provide the same interactive capability in a printed document as in an online computer system, we've done the next best thing. Each entry has icons that are used to highlight the most important elements in the reference.

At the top of the hierarchy presented in this reference section are the packages. For convenience, classes and interfaces having similar purposes are grouped into a package. This same grouping has been used in the chapters. Each chapter corresponds to a package and its components. For easy identification, icons have been designed to represent each of these packages, as shown here:

lang	Package `java.lang`
io	Package `java.io`
util	Package `java.util`
net	Package `java.net`
awt	Package `java.awt`
awt.image	Package `java.awt.image`
awt.peer	Package `java.awt.peer`
applet	Package `java.applet`
tools	Package `sun.tools.debug`

Next in the hierarchy are the components of the Java packages—the classes and interfaces. The name of each of these is preceded by an icon representative of its type. On the right side of the title line is an icon showing the package of which it is a part. Here are these icons:

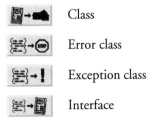

	Class
	Error class
	Exception class
	Interface

Delving deeper into the hierarchy, we arrive at the methods and constructors that are exposed by the classes and interfaces. The title line for each of these is preceded by an icon distinguishing its type. Then, on the far right of the title line, a backwards reference shows the class or interface of which it's a part. The following icons show these types of entries:

 **Constructor**. This is a special method that is called when an object is being instantiated.

 Method.

The lowest point on the hierarchy is a description and cross section of the element being described. In this description each important point is preceded by an icon showing its identity. Here are the icons:

Extends. This icon is applicable to a class or interface entry and is used to show its derivation from a superclass.

Implements. Applicable to a class, this icon points out an interface that is implemented in this class.

Overrides. This icon indicates a method that overrides a method from the superclass.

Parameter. This icon indicates a parameter into the method.

Returns. This icon indicates the return value from a method.

Throws. This icon indicates an exception that is thrown due to abnormal conditions.

Understanding the Reference

This section of the book deviates a little from the Sams Publishing norm. In order for a reference tome to succeed, there are two very important components. The first and certainly most important is the content of the information. Since books are similar to any other project in that different people bring different talents, we think that we have succeeded in this component by providing the expertise and viewpoint of more than one author.

The second vital component to a successful reference book is the presentation of the material. No matter how good and useful the information is, if it is not presented well, it becomes worthless. In the case of this part of *Java Developer's Reference*, we think we have succeeded because we have drawn on research findings in multimedia presentation.

Each element in this section has strong visual separation from other elements as well as strong visual cues in the presentation of its important facets. Each entry also has backward reference to its "parent" information. If you were to let this section fall open to any page, you could easily tell where the information falls in relation to the other information.

To help you understand how to read this section, here's an example from package `java.util`:

> **NOTE**
>
> The next line shows that the class `BitSet` (left in the title line) is defined in package `java.util` (right side of line).

 # BitSet

> **NOTE**
>
> The next line shows that the class `BitSet` is a subclass derived from superclass `Object`.

 Object

> **NOTE**
>
> The next line shows that the class `BitSet` implements the `Cloneable` interface.

 Cloneable

> **NOTE**
>
> The next part just talks about the class `BitSet`.

The class `java.util.BitSet` is derived directly from `Object` but also implements the `Cloneable` interface.

This class represents a dynamically sized set of bits. Two constructors are provided—one that creates an empty set of unspecified size and one that creates a set of a specified size.

The set method can be used to set an individual bit and clear can be used to clear an individual bit. The first bit in a BitSet is the zero bit; therefore, myBitset.set(0) is a valid statement.

The logical functions and, or, and xor are all supported and will combine the BitSet with another set. BitSets can be compared for equality using equals and can be converted to Strings using toString. For the purpose of converting a BitSet to a String, a set bit is represented by the value 1 and a clear bit is represented by 0.

> **NOTE**
>
> The next line shows that get is one of the methods (icon on left side of the line) for the class (icon on right side) BitSet, which is defined in package java.util.

 get  BitSet util

```
public boolean get(int bit)
```

Gets the value of a specified bit in the set.

> **NOTE**
>
> The next line shows that this method has a single parameter into it called bit.

▶ bit is the bit to get.

> **NOTE**
>
> The next line shows that this method returns either true or false:

↵ true if the bit is set; false if it is clear.

> **NOTE**
>
> The next line shows that this method throws an exception Ooops when the bit is both set and clear (<g>).

 Ooops if the bit is set and clear.

The Best Part

As an added value, the CD-ROM supplied with this book has the same information as this reference section. The best part is that this information is an HTML file that you can browse. Each of the visual elements in this file is a link to the other information.

27

Package
java.applet

by Bryan Morgan

The java.applet package contains the Applet class as well as three interfaces: AppletContext, AppletStub, and AudioClip. The java.applet package's class and interfaces are described in detail throughout this chapter.

Applet   applet

 Panel

The class hierarchy for the Applet class derives from class java.awt.Panel. This implies that every applet has some visual component. The basic visual component is a panel in an HTML page. Applet's overall derivation looks like Figure 27.1.

FIGURE 27.1.
Derivation of
java.applet.Applet.

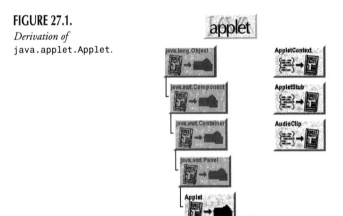

Listing 27.1 shows the declarations for all of the public methods included in the java.applet.Applet class.

Listing 27.1. Public members of java.applet.Applet.

```
public class Applet extends Panel {
    public final void setStub(AppletStub stub)
    public boolean isActive()
    public URL getDocumentBase()
    public URL getCodeBase()
    public String getParameter(String name)
    public AppletContext getAppletContext()
    public void resize(int width, int height)
    public void resize(Dimension d)
    public void showStatus(String msg)
    public Image getImage(URL url)
    public Image getImage(URL url, String name)
    public AudioClip getAudioClip(URL url)
```

```
        public AudioClip getAudioClip(URL url, String name)
        public String getAppletInfo()
        public String[][] getParameterInfo()
        public void play(URL url)
        public void play(URL url, String name)
        public void init()
        public void start()
        public void stop()
        public void destroy()
    }
```

Applet Applet applet

`public Applet()`

This is the default constructor for the `Applet` class. This function creates a new `Applet`. Each applet should implement at a minimum the `init()` or `start()` method to display itself on the screen and for initial setup.

setStub Applet applet

`public final void setStub(AppletStub stub)`

`setStub` sets the `AppletStub` to the stub passed in. This function is called automatically by the underlying system and usually is not called directly. The only time you need to implement `AppletStub` methods is if you are writing your own applet viewer or browser.

▶   `stub` is the underlying stub used to implement an applet viewer.

isActive Applet applet

`public boolean isActive()`

`isActive` is used to determine whether this applet is currently active. An applet is set `Active` just before the `Start` method is called (see `start()` later in this chapter).

getDocumentBase Applet applet

`public URL getDocumentBase()`

`getDocumentBase` returns the URL of the current page that this applet is embedded in.

   A URL object containing information about the current URL. (See the `java.net.URL` class documentation in Chapter 33, "Package `java.net`.")

getCodeBase   Applet

```
public URL getCodeBase()
```

getCodeBase returns the URL of the applet itself.

  A URL object (see the java.net.URL class documentation in Chapter 33) containing information about the applet's URL.

 getParameter   Applet

```
public String getParameter(String name)
```

getParameter returns the String value of the parameter passed in using the HTML <PARAM> tag (for more information on parameters, see Chapter 12, "HTML for Java Programmers").

Here's an HTML example:

```
<APPLET CODE="CoolApplet.class" WIDTH=150 HEIGHT=30>
<PARAM NAME=COLOR VALUE="WHITE">
</APPLET>
```

Here's a Java example:

```
tempString = getParameter("COLOR");
if (tempString.equals("WHITE"))
  tempColor = new Color(255, 255, 255);
```

▶ name is a case-sensitive string that matches (exactly!) the parameter name passed in using the HTML PARAM tag.

  A String value representing the PARAM tag's VALUE attribute.

 getAppletContext   Applet

```
public AppletContext getAppletContext()
```

getAppletContext returns an AppletContext object. This object can be used to determine information about the applet's runtime environment.

  An AppletContext object (see documentation on the AppletContext interface later in this chapter).

 resize   Applet

```
public void resize(int width, int height)
```

resize makes use of the Applet class's inheritance from the Panel class to resize the applet based on the input values.

  width is an integer value specifying the applet's new width.

  height is an integer value specifying the applet's new height.

resize   Applet applet

```
public void resize(Dimension d)
```

This `resize` function accepts a `Dimension` object as its argument. (For more information on the `Dimension` class, see the documentation on the `java.awt.Dimension` class in Chapter 28, "Package `java.awt`.")

▶ `d` is a `Dimension` object that specifies the new size of the applet.

showStatus   Applet applet

```
public void showStatus(String msg)
```

`showStatus` shows a status message using the applet's context.

▶ `msg` is a string containing the message to be displayed.

getImage   Applet applet

```
public Image getImage(URL url)
```

`getImage` retrieves image information based on the `URL` input parameter. Note that this function returns immediately and does not retrieve the entire image. This image will not be retrieved until the `Image` object is actually needed.

▶ `url` is a `URL` object containing location information for the image to be retrieved. For more information on the `URL` object, see the `java.net.URL` class documentation in Chapter 33.

↵ An `Image` object containing information about the URL passed in. For more information on the `Image` class, see the `java.awt.Image` documentation in Chapter 28.

getImage   Applet applet

```
public Image getImage(URL url, String name)
```

This `getImage` function accepts both the `URL` input parameter containing base location information as well as a `String` input parameter containing the filename. This function is useful if, for instance, the base URL of the applet is unknown. The applet could then call:

```
theImage = getImage(getDocumentBase(), "file.jpg");
```

Note that this function returns immediately and does not retrieve the entire image. This image will not be retrieved until the `Image` object is actually needed.

▶ `url` is a `URL` object containing base location information for the image to be retrieved (such as `http://www.javasoft.com`). For more information on the `URL` object, see the `java.net.URL` class documentation in Chapter 33.

▶ name is a `String` object containing a filename relative to the base URL passed using the `URL` argument.

↵ An `Image` object containing information about the URL passed in. For more information on the `Image` class, see the `java.awt.Image` documentation in Chapter 28.

getAudioClip   Applet   applet

```
public AudioClip getAudioClip(URL url)
```

`getAudioClip` retrieves an `AudioClip` based on the `URL` input parameter.

▶ url is a `URL` object containing location information for the clip to be retrieved. For more information on the `URL` object, see the `java.net.URL` class documentation in Chapter 33.

↵ An `AudioClip` object that can be played at a later time. For more information on the `AudioClip` interface, see the `java.applet.AudioClip` documentation later in this chapter.

getAudioClip   Applet   applet

```
public AudioClip getAudioClip(URL url, String name)
```

This `getAudioClip` function accepts both the `URL` input parameter containing base location information as well as a `String` input parameter containing the filename. This function is useful if, for instance, the base URL of the applet is unknown. The applet could then call:

```
RocknRoll = getAudioClip(getDocumentBase(), "paul_westerberg.au");
```

▶ url is a `URL` object containing base location information for the `AudioClip` to be retrieved (such as `http://www.sony.com`). For more information on the URL object, see the `java.net.URL` class documentation in Chapter 33.

▶ name is a `String` object containing a filename relative to the base URL passed using the `url` argument.

↵ An `AudioClip` object that can be played at a later time. For more information on the `AudioClip` interface, see the `java.applet.AudioClip` documentation later in this chapter.

getAppletInfo   Applet   applet

```
public String getAppletInfo()
```

`getAppletInfo` is provided for applet authors to return name, copyright, and version information for their applets. The default implementation returns null.

↵ A `String` containing author, version, and copyright information (or anything else) for the applet.

getParameterInfo Applet applet

```
public String[][] getParameterInfo()
```

`getParameterInfo` is provided for applet authors to provide information on any parameters that the applet may take as input. Conventional return values have the following information: *name*, *type*, and *comments*. The default implementation returns a null `String` array.

↵ A `String` array where each element contains, by Java conventions, three values: *name*, *type*, and *comments*. Each of these elements represents a parameter that the applet takes as input.

 ## play Applet applet

```
public void play(URL url)
```

`play` is used to play an `AudioClip` at the location given by the URL input parameter. For more information on the `AudioClip` interface, see the documentation on the `java.applet.AudioClip` interface later in this chapter.

▶ `url` is a URL object containing location information for the clip to be retrieved. For more information on the URL object, see the `java.net.URL` class documentation in Chapter 33.

 ## play Applet applet

```
public void play(URL url, String name)
```

This `play` method is used to play an `AudioClip` given a base URL and a filename for input parameters. For more information on the `AudioClip` interface, see the documentation on the `java.applet.AudioClip` interface later in this chapter.

▶ `url` is a URL object containing base location information for the `AudioClip` to be retrieved (such as `http://www.sony.com`). For more information on the URL object, see the `java.net.URL` class documentation in Chapter 33.

▶ `name` is a `String` object containing a filename relative to the base URL passed using the URL argument.

 ## init Applet applet

```
public void init()
```

The `init` method is called automatically after the applet is created. This function never needs to be called directly.

start   Applet

```
public void start()
```

The start method is called automatically to start the applet after it has been initialized. This function never needs to be called directly. Start is called when an applet is first displayed on a screen, or when a page is revisited within a Web browser.

 stop   Applet

```
public void stop()
```

The stop method is called automatically to stop an applet from running. This function never needs to be called directly unless the applet knows that it needs to stop executing. Stop is called when the Web page containing the applet is replaced by another Web page.

 destroy   Applet

```
public void destroy()
```

The destroy method is called automatically when the applet's system resources are being re-claimed. This function never needs to be called directly. Destroy is called after the Stop method has finished.

 # AppletContext

The AppletContext interface is provided to give information on an applet's environment. An AppletContext interface can be obtained by calling the Applet class's getAppletContext() method.

Listing 27.2 shows the declarations for all of the public methods included in the java.applet.AppletContext class.

Listing 27.2. Public members of java.applet.AppletContext.

```
public interface AppletContext {
    public abstract AudioClip getAudioClip(URL url)
    public abstract Image getImage(URL url)
    public abstract Applet getApplet(String name)
    public abstract Enumeration getApplets()
    public abstract void showDocument(URL url)
    public abstract void showDocument(URL url, String target)
    public abstract void showStatus(String status)
}
```

getAudioClip AppletContext applet

```
public abstract AudioClip getAudioClip(URL url)
```

getAudioClip retrieves an AudioClip based on the URL input parameter.

▶ url is a URL object containing location information for the clip to be retrieved. For more information on the URL object, see the `java.net.URL` class documentation in Chapter 33.

↵ An AudioClip object that can be played at a later time. For more information on the AudioClip interface, see the `java.applet.AudioClip` documentation later in this chapter.

getImage AppletContext applet

```
public abstract Image getImage(URL url)
```

getImage retrieves image information based on the URL input parameter. Note that this function returns immediately and does not retrieve the entire image. This image will not be retrieved until the Image object is actually needed.

▶ url is a URL object containing location information for the image to be retrieved. For more information on the URL object, see the `java.net.URL` class documentation in Chapter 33.

↵ An Image object containing information about the URL passed in. For more information on the Image class, see the `java.awt.Image` documentation in Chapter 28.

getApplet AppletContext applet

```
public abstract Applet getApplet(String name)
```

getApplet returns an applet from the current AppletContext based on the input name argument.

▶ name is a String object representing an applet's name. This name should correspond to the applet's HTML name attribute.

↵ An Applet object or null if no applet exists with the designated name.

getApplets AppletContext applet

```
public abstract Enumeration getApplets()
```

getApplets returns an Enumeration interface for all of the applets on the current AppletContext.

↵ An Enumeration interface that can be used to retrieve all of the applets on the current applet context. For more information on the Enumeration interface, see the documentation for `java.util.Enumeration` in Chapter 34, "Package `java.util`."

showDocument   `AppletContext`   `applet`

```
public abstract void showDocument(URL url)
```

`showDocument` loads the `URL` argument into the current `AppletContext` if it is a valid URL. This method may be ignored, depending on the applet context.

▶ `url` is a `URL` object containing location information for the image to be retrieved. For more information on the `URL` object, see the `java.net.URL class` documentation in Chapter 33.

showDocument   `AppletContext`   `applet`

```
public abstract void showDocument(URL url, String target)
```

This `showDocument` method loads the `URL` argument into a target window or frame depending on the target string. This method may be ignored, depending on the applet context.

▶ `url` is a `URL` object containing location information for the image to be retrieved. For more information on the `URL` object, see the `java.net.URL` class documentation in Chapter 33.

▶ `target`—The target string can be one of the following values:

- ■ `_self`—show in current frame
- ■ `_parent`—show in parent frame
- ■ `_top`—show in top-most frame
- ■ `_blank`—show in new unnamed top-level window
- ■ `<other>`—show in new top-level window named `<other>`

 showStatus   AppletContext   `applet`

```
public abstract void showStatus(String status)
```

`showStatus` shows a status message using the applet's context.

▶ `msg` is a string containing the message to be displayed.

 # AppletStub   `applet`

The `java.applet.AppletStub` interface is most often used to build applet viewers, browsers, or other tools that want to display applets within them. This interface is not normally implemented by Java applet developers.

Listing 27.3 shows the declarations for all of the public methods included in the `java.applet.AppletStub` class.

Listing 27.3. Public members of `java.applet.AppletStub`.

```
public interface AppletStub {
  public abstract boolean isActive()
  public abstract URL getDocumentBase()
  public abstract URL getCodeBase()
  public abstract String getParameter(String name)
  public abstract AppletContext getAppletContext()
  public abstract void appletResize(int width, int height)
}
```

 isActive AppletStub `applet`

```
public abstract boolean isActive()
```

isActive is used to determine whether this applet is currently active.

↵ isActive returns `true` if the applet is active; `false` if not.

 getDocumentBase AppletStub `applet`

```
public abstract URL getDocumentBase()
```

getDocumentBase returns the URL of the current page that this applet is embedded in.

↵ A URL object (see the `java.net.URL` class documentation in Chapter 33) containing information about the current URL.

 getCodeBase AppletStub `applet`

```
public abstract URL getCodeBase()
```

getCodeBase returns the URL of the applet itself.

↵ A URL object (see the `java.net.URL` class documentation in Chapter 33) containing information about the applet's URL.

 getParameter AppletStub `applet`

```
public abstract String getParameter(String name)
```

getParameter returns the `String` value of the parameter passed in using the HTML `<PARAM>` tag. (For more information on parameters, see Chapter 12.)

getAppletContext AppletStub **applet**

```
public abstract AppletContext getAppletContext()
```

getAppletContext returns an AppletContext object. This object can be used to determine information about the applet's runtime environment.

↵   An AppletContext object (see documentation on the AppletContext interface earlier in this chapter).

 appletResize AppletStub **applet**

```
public abstract void appletResize(int width, int height)
```

appletResize is called when the applet wants to be resized.

▶   width is an integer value specifying the applet's new width.

▶   height is an integer value specifying the applet's new height.

AudioClip   **applet**

The AudioClip interface is used to provide high-level access to sound playback capabilities. This interface, like AppletContext and AppletStub, is usually only implemented by applet viewers.

Listing 27.4 shows the declarations for all of the public methods included in the java.applet.AudioClip class.

Listing 27.4. Public members of java.applet.AudioClip.

```
public interface AudioClip {
  public abstract void play()
  public abstract void loop()
  public abstract void stop()
}
```

 play AudioClip **applet**

```
public abstract void play()
```

The play method plays audio files from the beginning until the end or stop method is called.

 loop AudioClip **applet**

```
public abstract void loop()
```

The loop method plays audio files in a loop continuously.

stop

AudioClip applet

```
public abstract void stop()
```

The stop method stops the playing of an audio file.

28

Package java.awt

by Bryan Morgan

The java.awt package contains what is known as the Java Abstract Windowing Toolkit. The classes within this package make up the pre-built graphical user interface components that are available to Java developers through the Java Developer's Kit. Classes defined within this package include such useful components as colors, fonts, and widgets, such as buttons and scrollbars. This package also defines two interfaces, LayoutManager and MenuContainer, as well as the exception AWTException and the error AWTError. The java.awt package also contains two subpackages: java.awt.image and java.awt.peer. This chapter documents all public instance variables and methods of each subpackage, class, interface, exception, and error in the java.awt package. Because the java.awt package is so large, Table 28.1 shows a complete list of its contents, and Figure 28.1 shows the hierarchy of the contents of that package.

Table 28.1. Contents of package java.awt.

Class Index		*Interface Index*
BorderLayout	GridBagLayout	LayoutManager
Button	GridLayout	MenuContainer
Canvas	Image	
CardLayout	Insets	
Checkbox	Label	
CheckboxGroup	List	
CheckboxMenuItem	MediaTracker	
Choice	Menu	
Color	MenuBar	
Component	MenuComponent	
Container	MenuItem	
Dialog	Panel	
Dimension	Point	
Event	Polygon	
FileDialog	Rectangle	
FlowLayout	Scrollbar	
Font	TextArea	
FontMetrics	TextComponent	
Frame	TextField	
Graphics	Toolkit	
GridBagConstraints	Window	

Exception Index	Error Index
AWTException	AWTError

FIGURE 28.1.

Contents of package java.awt.

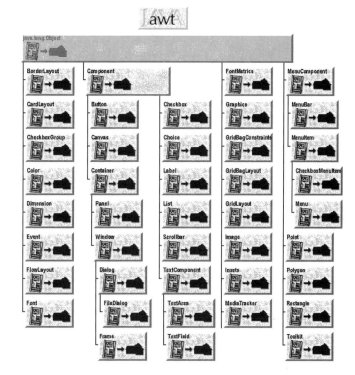

FIGURE 28.1.

Continued.

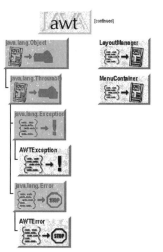

BorderLayout awt

 Object

 LayoutManager

The class hierarchy for the `BorderLayout` class derives from the class `java.lang.Object`. (See Listing 28.1.) A `BorderLayout` lays out components on a panel by implementing the `LayoutManager` interface. Components are laid out using members named `North`, `South`, `East`, `West`, and `Center`. `BorderLayout`'s overall derivation is shown in Figure 28.1.

Listing 28.1. Public members of `java.awt.BorderLayout`.

```
public class BorderLayout implements LayoutManager {
  public BorderLayout()
  public BorderLayout(int hgap, int vgap)
  public void addLayoutComponent(String name, Component comp)
  public void removeLayoutComponent(Component comp)
  public Dimension minimumLayoutSize(Container target)
  public Dimension preferredLayoutSize(Container target)
  public void layoutContainer(Container target)
  public String toString()
}
```

 BorderLayout BorderLayout awt

```
public BorderLayout()
```

This `BorderLayout` constructor constructs a `BorderLayout` layout manager.

 BorderLayout BorderLayout awt

```
public BorderLayout(int hgap, int vgap)
```

This `BorderLayout` constructor constructs a `BorderLayout` layout manager using the *hgap* and *vgap* values to set the horizontal and vertical gap sizes.

▶   *hgap* is an integer value used to set the horizontal gap size.

▶   *vgap* is an integer value used to set the vertical gap size.

 addLayoutComponent BorderLayout awt

```
public void addLayoutComponent(String name, Component comp)
```

addLayoutComponent adds a component to the `BorderLayout` according to that component's name (`North`, `South`, `East`, `West`, or `Center`). The component's preferred size is used for all layout types except `Center`.

▶ *name* is a string value that must correspond to one of the following names: North, South, East, West, or Center.

▶ *comp* is a component object to be added to this layout manager.

---

removeLayoutComponent BorderLayout awt

```
public void removeLayoutComponent(Component comp)
```

removeLayoutComponent removes the specified component from the layout manager.

▶ *comp* is the component object to be removed.

---

minimumLayoutSize BorderLayout awt

```
public Dimension minimumLayoutSize(Container target)
```

minimumLayoutSize returns the minimum Dimension needed to lay out the components contained in the *target* parameter. Note that this function only determines the required size based on visible components.

▶ *target* is a Container class containing components to be laid out. This class could be a Frame, Window, or any other class derived from the Container class.

---

preferredLayoutSize BorderLayout awt

```
public Dimension preferredLayoutSize(Container target)
```

preferredLayoutSize returns the preferred Dimension needed to lay out the components contained in the *target* parameter. This Dimension is based on the individual component's preferred sizes. Note that this function only determines the required size based on visible components.

▶ *target* is a Container class containing components to be laid out. This class could be a Frame, Window, or any other class derived from the Container class.

---

layoutContainer BorderLayout awt

```
public void layoutContainer(Container target)
```

layoutContainer lays out the components contained in the *target* Container parameter. This method reshapes the components in the Container based on the requirements of the BorderLayout itself.

▶ *target* is a Container class containing components to be laid out. This class could be a Frame, Window, or any other class derived from the Container class.

toString   **BorderLayout** awt

```
public String toString()
```

toString returns a string representation of the BorderLayout class.

 A String value containing the BorderLayout class's name plus its *hgap* and *vgap* values (see the BorderLayout() constructor).

⃠ toString() in class Object.

 # Button   awt

 Component

The class hierarchy for the Button class derives from the class java.awt.Component. (See Listing 28.2.) A Button can be placed on any type of layout because it derives directly from Component. Button's overall derivation is shown in Figure 28.1.

Listing 28.2. Public members of java.awt.Button.

```
public class Button extends Component {
  public Button()
  public Button(String label)
  public synchronized void addNotify()
  public String getLabel()
  public void setLabel(String label)
}
```

 Button   Button awt

```
public Button()
```

This Button constructor constructs a simple button with no text label.

 Button   Button awt

```
public Button(String label)
```

This Button constructor constructs a simple button with a text label.

▶ *label* is a String value used to set the button's label.

 addNotify   Button awt

```
public synchronized void addNotify()
```

addNotify sets the peer of the button using the function getToolkit().createButton(). Using peer interfaces allows you to change the user interface of the button without changing its functionality.

 addNotify() in class Component.

---

 getLabel   **Button** awt

```
public String getLabel()
```

getLabel returns the button's label string.

 A String value representing the button's label string.

---

 setLabel   **Button** awt

```
public void setLabel(String label)
```

setLabel modifies the button's label string.

▶ label is a String value representing the button's new label string.

Canvas awt

 Component

The class hierarchy for the Canvas class derives from the class java.awt.Component. (See Listing 28.3.) A Canvas is used as a drawing surface for GUI applications. Canvas's overall derivation is shown in Figure 28.1.

> **Listing 28.3. Public members of java.awt.Canvas.**
> ```
> public class Canvas extends Component {
>   public synchronized void addNotify()
>   public void paint(Graphics g)
> }
> ```

---

 addNotify   **Canvas** awt

```
public synchronized void addNotify()
```

addNotify sets the peer of the Canvas using the function getToolkit().createCanvas(). Using peer interfaces allows you to change the user interface of the canvas without changing its functionality.

 addNotify() in class Component.

paint Canvas awt

```
public void paint(Graphics g)
```

The paint() method paints the Graphics canvas (specified by the g parameter) using the default background color, which is determined by calling getBackground().

 paint() in class Component.

 CardLayout awt

 Object

 LayoutManager

The class hierarchy for the CardLayout class derives from the class java.lang.Object. (See Listing 28.4.) The CardLayout class is a LayoutManager that allows the addition of cards, only one of which can be visible at any given time. The user is allowed to flip through the cards. CardLayout's overall derivation is shown in Figure 28.1.

Listing 28.4. Public members of java.awt.CardLayout.

```
public class CardLayout implements LayoutManager {
    public CardLayout()
    public CardLayout(int hgap, int vgap)
    public void addLayoutComponent(String name, Component comp)
    public void removeLayoutComponent(Component comp)
    public Dimension preferredLayoutSize(Container target)
    public Dimension minimumLayoutSize(Container target)
    public void layoutContainer(Container parent)
    public void first(Container parent)
    public void next(Container parent)
    public void previous(Container parent)
    public void last(Container parent)
    public void show(Container parent, String name)
    public String toString()
}
```

 CardLayout CardLayout awt

```
public CardLayout()
```

This CardLayout constructor creates a new CardLayout layout manager.

 CardLayout CardLayout awt

```
public CardLayout(int hgap, int vgap)
```

This CardLayout constructor constructs a CardLayout layout manager using the *hgap* and *vgap* values to set the horizontal and vertical gap sizes.

▶ *hgap* is an integer value used to set the horizontal gap size.

▶ *vgap* is an integer value used to set the vertical gap size.

addLayoutComponent CardLayout awt

```
public void addLayoutComponent(String name, Component comp)
```

▶ *name* is a string value that corresponds to the component's name.

▶ *comp* is a component object to be added to this layout manager.

removeLayoutComponent CardLayout awt

```
public void removeLayoutComponent(Component comp)
```

removeLayoutComponent removes the specified component from the layout manager.

▶ *comp* is the component object to be removed.

minimumLayoutSize CardLayout awt

```
public Dimension minimumLayoutSize(Container target)
```

minimumLayoutSize returns the minimum Dimension needed to lay out the components contained in the *target* parameter. Note that this function only determines the required size based on visible components.

▶ *target* is a Container class containing components to be laid out. This class could be a Frame, Window, or any other class derived from the Container class.

preferredLayoutSize CardLayout awt

```
public Dimension preferredLayoutSize(Container target)
```

preferredLayoutSize returns the preferred Dimension needed to lay out the components contained in the *target* parameter. This Dimension is based on the individual component's preferred sizes. Note that this function only determines the required size based on visible components.

▶ *target* is a Container class containing components to be laid out. This class could be a Frame, Window, or any other class derived from the Container class.

layoutContainer CardLayout awt

```
public void layoutContainer(Container parent)
```

layoutContainer lays out the components contained in the *parent* Container parameter. This method reshapes the components in the Container based on the requirements of the BorderLayout itself.

▶ *parent* is a Container class containing components to be laid out. This class could be a Frame, Window, or any other class derived from the Container class.

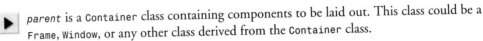

first   CardLayout   awt

```
public void first(Container parent)
```

The first() method shows the first component in CardLayout (the first card).

▶ *parent* is the parent Container class containing the components to be flipped through.

next   CardLayout   awt

```
public void next(Container parent)
```

The next() method shows the next component in CardLayout (the next card).

▶ *parent* is the parent Container class containing the components to be flipped through.

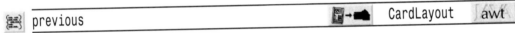

previous   CardLayout   awt

```
public void previous(Container parent)
```

The previous() method shows the previous component in CardLayout (the previous card).

▶ *parent* is the parent Container class containing the components to be flipped through.

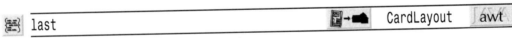

last   CardLayout   awt

```
public void last(Container parent)
```

The last() method shows the last component in CardLayout (the last card).

▶ *parent* is the parent Container class containing the components to be flipped through.

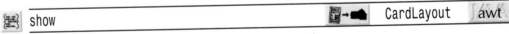

show   CardLayout   awt

```
public void show(Container parent, String name)
```

The show() method flips to the component specified in the *name* parameter.

▶ *parent* is the parent Container class containing the components to be flipped through.

▶ *name* is a string value representing the name of the component to be displayed.

toString CardLayout awt

```
public String toString()
```

toString returns a string representation of the CardLayout class.

 A String value containing the CardLayout class's name plus its *hgap* and *vgap* values (see the CardLayout() constructor).

Ø toString() in class Object.

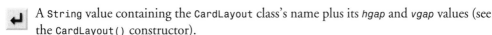 # Checkbox awt

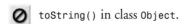 Component

The class hierarchy for the Checkbox class derives from the class java.awt.Component. (See Listing 28.5.) A Checkbox is a user interface component that represents a true/false (or on/off) value. Checkbox's overall derivation is shown in Figure 28.1.

Listing 28.5. Public members of `java.awt.Checkbox`.

```
public class Checkbox extends Component {
  public Checkbox()
  public Checkbox(String label)
  public Checkbox(String label, CheckboxGroup group, boolean state)
  public synchronized void addNotify()
  public String getLabel()
  public void setLabel(String label)
  public boolean getState()
  public void setState(boolean state)
  public CheckboxGroup getCheckboxGroup()
  public void setCheckboxGroup(CheckboxGroup g)
}
```

 Checkbox Checkbox awt

```
public Checkbox()
```

This Checkbox constructor constructs the simplest of all checkboxes: one with no label, no group, and a false state value.

 Checkbox Checkbox awt

```
public Checkbox(String label)
```

This Checkbox constructor constructs a checkbox using the *label* parameter to set the checkbox's label. This checkbox belongs to no group and is set to a false state value.

label is a string value representing the Checkbox's label.

 Checkbox Checkbox awt

```
public Checkbox(String label, CheckboxGroup group, boolean state)
```

This Checkbox constructor constructs a checkbox including the label, group, and initial value.

 label is a string value representing the Checkbox's label.

 group is a CheckboxGroup object that this Checkbox is a member of. (For more information on CheckboxGroups, see the documentation for the CheckboxGroup class later in this chapter.)

 state is the initial state value for this Checkbox.

---

 addNotify Checkbox awt

```
public synchronized void addNotify()
```

addNotify sets the peer of the Checkbox using the function getToolkit().createCheckbox(). Using peer interfaces allows you to change the user interface of the Checkbox without changing its functionality.

 addNotify() in class Component.

---

 getLabel Checkbox awt

```
public String getLabel()
```

getLabel returns the Checkbox's label string.

 A String value representing the Checkbox's label string.

---

 setLabel Checkbox awt

```
public void setLabel(String label)
```

setLabel modifies the Checkbox's label string.

 label is a String value representing the Checkbox's new label string.

---

 getState Checkbox awt

```
public boolean getState()
```

getState returns the Checkbox's current state value.

 A Boolean value representing the Checkbox's current state.

setState Checkbox

```
public void setState(boolean state)
```

setState sets the Checkbox to the value represented by the *state* parameter.

 state is a Boolean value containing the new value of the Checkbox's state.

 getCheckboxGroup Checkbox

```
public CheckboxGroup getCheckboxGroup()
```

The getCheckboxGroup() method returns the CheckboxGroup that this Checkbox is a member of.

 A CheckboxGroup class that this Checkbox is a member of. (For more information on CheckboxGroups, see the documentation for the CheckboxGroup class later in this chapter.)

 setCheckboxGroup Checkbox

```
public void setCheckboxGroup(CheckboxGroup g)
```

The setCheckboxGroup() method adds this Checkbox to a CheckboxGroup.

▶ *g* is a CheckboxGroup class that this Checkbox is to be added to. (For more information on CheckboxGroups, see the documentation for the CheckboxGroup class later in this chapter.)

CheckboxGroup   awt

➕ Object

The class hierarchy for the CheckboxGroup class derives from the class java.lang.Object. (See Listing 28.6.) A CheckboxGroup groups a set of Checkbox classes. When Checkboxes are created within a CheckboxGroup, only one Checkbox can be selected at one time. CheckboxGroup's overall derivation is shown in Figure 28.1.

Listing 28.6. Public members of java.awt.CheckboxGroup.

```
public class CheckboxGroup {
  public CheckboxGroup()
  public Checkbox getCurrent()
  public synchronized void setCurrent(Checkbox box)
  public String toString()
}
```

CheckboxGroup   CheckboxGroup   awt

```
public CheckboxGroup()
```

This CheckboxGroup constructor constructs a CheckboxGroup instance with no checkbox members.

 getCurrent   CheckboxGroup   awt

```
public Checkbox getCurrent()
```

The getCurrent() method returns the current Checkbox.

 A Checkbox object representing the currently selected Checkbox.

 setCurrent   CheckboxGroup   awt

```
public synchronized void setCurrent(Checkbox box)
```

The setCurrent() method sets the current Checkbox in this CheckboxGroup.

 box is the Checkbox object that is to be made current.

 toString   CheckboxGroup   awt

```
public String toString()
```

toString() returns a string containing CheckboxGroup information.

 A String value containing the CheckboxGroup's name as well as the name of the currently selected Checkbox.

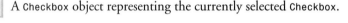 toString() in class Object.

 # CheckboxMenuItem   awt

+ MenuItem

The class hierarchy for the CheckboxMenuItem class derives from the class java.awt.MenuItem. (See Listing 28.7.) A CheckboxMenuItem is a user interface component that can be added to a menu to represent a Boolean value selection. CheckboxMenuItem's overall derivation is shown in Figure 28.1.

Listing 28.7. Public members of `java.awt.CheckboxMenuItem`.

```
public class CheckboxMenuItem extends MenuItem {
    public CheckboxMenuItem(String label)
    public synchronized void addNotify()
    public boolean getState()
    public void setState(boolean t)
    public String paramString()
}
```

 CheckboxMenuItem CheckboxMenuItem awt

`public CheckboxMenuItem(String label)`

This `CheckboxMenuItem` constructor creates a `CheckboxMenuItem` with a text label containing the string passed in.

▶ `label` is a string value representing the label of the `CheckboxMenuItem` to be displayed.

 addNotify CheckboxMenuItem awt

`public synchronized void addNotify()`

`addNotify` sets the peer of the `CheckboxMenuItem` using the function `getToolkit()`. `createCheckboxMenuItem()`. Using peer interfaces allows you to change the user interface of the `CheckboxMenuItem` without changing its functionality.

⊘ `addNotify()` in class `Component`.

 getState CheckboxMenuItem awt

`public boolean getState()`

`getState()` returns the state value of the `CheckboxMenuItem`'s checkbox.

↵ A Boolean value representing the `CheckboxMenuItem`'s checkbox state value.

 setState CheckboxMenuItem awt

`public void setState(boolean t)`

`setState()` sets the `CheckboxMenuItem`'s checkbox state value.

▶ `t` is a Boolean value representing the `CheckboxMenuItem`'s checkbox state value.

 paramString CheckboxMenuItem awt

`public String paramString()`

`paramString()` returns a string containing `CheckboxMenuItem` information.

A string value containing the `CheckboxMenuItem`'s label as well as the state value of the `CheckboxMenuItem`'s checkbox.

`paramString()` in class `MenuItem`.

 # Choice   `awt`

Component

The class hierarchy for the `Choice` class derives from the class `java.awt.Component`. (See Listing 28.8.) A `Choice` is a user interface component that displays a pop-up menu. The current selection is displayed as the pop-up menu's title. `Choice`'s overall derivation is shown in Figure 28.1.

Listing 28.8. Public members of `java.awt.Choice`.

```
public class Choice extends Component {
    public Choice()
    public synchronized void addNotify()
    public int countItems()
    public String getItem(int index)
    public synchronized void addItem(String item)
    public String getSelectedItem()
    public int getSelectedIndex()
    public synchronized void select(int pos)
    public void select(String str)
}
```

 Choice   Choice `awt`

```
public Choice()
```

This `Choice` constructor creates a default `Choice` object that contains no information.

 addNotify   Choice `awt`

```
public synchronized void addNotify()
```

`addNotify` sets the peer of the `Choice` using the function `getToolkit().createChoice()`. Using peer interfaces allows you to change the user interface of the `Choice` without changing its functionality.

`addNotify()` in class `Component`.

countItems   Choice   awt

```
public int countItems()
```

countItems() returns the number of items (or choices) that are available in this Choice object. See the addItem() method later in this section for information on Choice items.

↵ An integer value containing the number of items stored in this Choice object.

getItem   Choice   awt

```
public String getItem(int index)
```

The getItem() method returns the choice string at the index represented by the index value passed in.

▶ *index* is an integer value representing the index of the string item to be returned.

↵ A String value representing the string at the index passed into this method. See the addItem() method for information on Choice items.

addItem   Choice   awt

```
public synchronized void addItem(String item)
```

addItem() adds a String to a Choice object's internal list. The currently selected item in that list is displayed in the Choice object's pop-up menu.

▶ *item* is a String object containing a string to be added to the choice list.

☞ A NullPointerException if the string item to be added is null.

getSelectedItem   Choice   awt

```
public String getSelectedItem()
```

getSelectedItem() returns the string value of the currently selected item. See the select() method later in this section for information on selecting Choice items.

↵ A String value containing the currently selected item's string.

getSelectedIndex   Choice   awt

```
public int getSelectedIndex()
```

getSelectedIndex() returns the index of the currently selected item. See the select() method for information on selecting Choice items.

↵ An integer value containing the index of the currently selected item.

select   Choice

```
public synchronized void select(int pos)
```

This `select()` method selects the item at the position represented by the *pos* parameter.

▶   *pos* is an integer value representing the position of the item to be selected.

    An `IllegalArgumentException` if the position value passed in is invalid.

 select   Choice

```
public void select(String str)
```

This `select()` method selects the item represented by the *str* parameter.

▶   *str* is a `String` value representing the string value of the choice to be selected.

Color   awt

    Object

The class hierarchy for the `Color` class derives from the class `java.awt.Object`. (See Listing 28.9.) The `Color` 1 class is provided to encapsulate RGB (Red-Green-Blue) color values. `Color`'s overall derivation is shown in Figure 28.1.

Listing 28.9. Public members of `java.awt.Color`.
```
public final class Color {
  public final static Color white
  public final static Color lightGray
  public final static Color gray
  public final static Color darkGray
  public final static Color black
  public final static Color red
  public final static Color pink
  public final static Color orange
  public final static Color yellow
  public final static Color green
  public final static Color magenta
  public final static Color cyan
  public final static Color blue
  public Color(int r, int g, int b)
  public Color(int rgb)
  public Color(float r, float g, float b)
  public int getRed()
  public int getGreen()
  public int getBlue()
  public int getRGB()
  public Color brighter()
  public Color darker()
```

```
    public int hashCode()
    public boolean equals(Object obj)
    public String toString()
    public static Color getColor(String nm)
    public static Color getColor(String nm, Color v)
    public static Color getColor(String nm, int v)
    public static int HSBtoRGB(float hue, float saturation, float brightness)
    public static float[] RGBtoHSB(int r, int g, int b, float[] hsbvals)
    public static Color getHSBColor(float h, float s, float b)
}
```

Public Static Values

public final static Color white

Static value representing the color white.

public final static Color lightGray

Static value representing the color light gray.

public final static Color gray

Static value representing the color gray.

public final static Color darkGray

Static value representing the color dark gray.

public final static Color black

Static value representing the color black.

public final static Color red

Static value representing the color red.

public final static Color pink

Static value representing the color pink.

public final static Color orange

Static value representing the color orange.

public final static Color yellow

Static value representing the color yellow.

public final static Color green

Static value representing the color green.

```
public final static Color magenta
```

Static value representing the color magenta.

```
public final static Color cyan
```

Static value representing the color cyan.

```
public final static Color blue
```

Static value representing the color blue.

 Color   Color   awt

```
public Color(int r, int g, int b)
```

This `Color` constructor accepts as arguments individual red, green, and blue color values. These values must be in the range 0-255 and are used to build a 24-bit color value using the following method:

> The red value represents bits 16–23.
> The green value represents bits 8–15.
> The blue value represents bits 0–7.

This `Color` constructor determines the closest color to the value supported by the current output device.

▶   *r* is the red color value.

▶   *g* is the green color value.

▶   *b* is the blue color value.

 Color   Color   awt

```
public Color(int rgb)
```

This `Color` constructor creates a `Color` object based on the RGB color value passed in.

▶   *rgb* is an integer value containing the red, green, and blue color values that are used to create this `Color` object.

 Color   Color   awt

```
public Color(float r, float g, float b)
```

This `Color` constructor creates a `Color` object based on the color values passed in. This constructor is similar to the `Color` constructor that accepts integer red, green, and blue inputs except that this `Color` constructor accepts `float` values. These values must be in the range 0–1.0 and are used to build a 24-bit color value using the following method:

The red value * 255 represents bits 16–23.
The green value * 255 represents bits 8–15.
The blue value * 255 represents bits 0–7.

This `Color` constructor determines the closest color to the value supported by the current output device.

▶ *r* is the red color value.

▶ *g* is the green color value.

▶ *b* is the blue color value.

 getRed 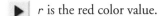 Color awt

```
public int getRed()
```

The `getRed()` method returns the red component of this `Color`.

↵ An integer value representing this `Color`'s red component.

 getGreen  Color awt

```
public int getGreen()
```

The `getGreen()` method returns the green component of this `Color`.

↵ An integer value representing this `Color`'s green component.

getBlue  Color awt

```
public int getBlue()
```

The `getBlue()` method returns the blue component of this `Color`.

↵ An integer value representing this `Color`'s blue component.

 getRGB Color awt

```
public int getRGB()
```

The `getRGB()` method returns the RGB value of this `Color`.

↵ An integer value representing this `Color`'s RGB value in the default RGB color model.

brighter  Color awt

```
public Color brighter()
```

The `brighter()` method brightens this `Color` by modifying the RGB color value. This method increases the individual red, green, and blue color components by a factor of approximately 1.4.

↵   A `Color` object representing a brighter version of the current color.

darker  Color awt

```
public Color darker()
```

The `darker()` method darkens this `Color` by modifying the RGB color value. This method decreases the individual red, green, and blue color components by a factor of approximately 1.4.

↵   A `Color` object representing a darker version of the current color.

hashCode  Color awt

```
public int hashCode()
```

`hashCode()` returns this `Color`'s hash code. This is useful when storing `Colors` in a hash table.

↵   An integer value representing this `Color`'s hash code.

⊘   `hashCode()` in class `Object`.

equals  Color awt

```
public boolean equals(Object obj)
```

The `equals()` method compares the `Object` parameter with this `Color` object. It returns a Boolean value representing the result of this comparison.

▶   `obj` is an `Object` object to be compared with this `Color`.

↵   A Boolean value representing the result of the comparison of the `Object` parameter to this `Color`.

⊘   `equals()` in class `Object`.

toString  Color awt

```
public String toString()
```

`toString()` returns a string representation of the `Color` class.

A String value containing the Color class's name plus its red, green, and blue values (see the Color() constructors).

⊘ toString() in class Object.

getColor   Color   awt

```
public static Color getColor(String nm)
```

getColor() returns the specified color property based on the name that is passed in.

▶ *nm* is the name of the color property.

↵ A Color value representing the desired color property.

getColor   Color   awt

```
public static Color getColor(String nm, Color v)
```

getColor() returns the specified Color property of the specified color.

▶ *nm* is the name of the color property.

▶ *v* is the specified color to be examined.

↵ A Color value representing the desired color property.

getColor   Color   awt

```
public static Color getColor(String nm, int v)
```

getColor() returns the specified Color property of the color value that is passed in.

▶ *nm* is the name of the color property.

▶ *v* is the color value.

↵ A Color value representing the desired color property.

HSBtoRGB   Color   awt

```
public static int HSBtoRGB(float hue, float saturation, float brightness)
```

HSB stands for hue, saturation, and brightness. To convert from an HSB value to an RGB value, simply call this function with the appropriate arguments.

▶ *hue* is the color's hue component.

▶ *saturation* is the color's saturation component.

▶ *brightness* is the color's brightness component.

↵ An RGB value that corresponds to the HSB inputs.

RGBtoHSB   Color   awt

```
public static float[] RGBtoHSB(int r, int g, int b, float[] hsbvals)
```

HSB stands for hue, saturation, and brightness. To convert from an RGB value to an HSB value, simply call this function with the appropriate arguments.

▶   *r* is the color's red component.

▶   *g* is the color's green component.

▶   *b* is the color's blue component.

hsbvals is an array that stores the HSB result values.

↵   An array containing the resultant HSB values.

getHSBColor   Color   awt

```
public static Color getHSBColor(float h, float s, float b)
```

The getHSBColor() method returns a Color object representing the RGB value of the input HSB parameters.

▶   *h* is the color's hue component.

▶   *s* is the color's saturation component.

▶   *b* is the color's brightness component.

↵   A Color object representing the RGB value of the input hue, saturation, and brightness.

Component   awt

   Object

   ImageObserver

The class hierarchy for the Component class derives from the class java.lang.Object. (See Listing 28.10.) The Component class represents a generic user interface component. All AWT UI components derive from the Component class. Component's overall derivation is shown in Figure 28.1.

Listing 28.10. Public members of java.awt.Component.

```
public abstract class Component implements ImageObserver {
    public Container getParent()
    public ComponentPeer getPeer()
    public Toolkit getToolkit()
    public boolean isValid()
    public boolean isVisible()
    public boolean isShowing()
    public boolean isEnabled()
    public Point location()
    public Dimension size()
    public Rectangle bounds()
    public synchronized void enable()
    public void enable(boolean cond)
    public synchronized void disable()
    public synchronized void show()
    public void show(boolean cond)
    public synchronized void hide()
    public Color getForeground()
    public synchronized void setForeground(Color c)
    public Color getBackground()
    public synchronized void setBackground(Color c)
    public Font getFont()
    public synchronized void setFont(Font f)
    public synchronized ColorModel getColorModel()
    public void move(int x, int y)
    public void resize(int width, int height)
    public void resize(Dimension d)
    public synchronized void reshape(int x, int y, int width, int height)
    public Dimension preferredSize()
    public Dimension minimumSize()
    public void layout()
    public void validate()
    public void invalidate()
    public Graphics getGraphics()
    public FontMetrics getFontMetrics(Font font)
    public void paint(Graphics g)
    public void update(Graphics g)
    public void paintAll(Graphics g)
    public void repaint()
    public void repaint(long tm)
    public void repaint(int x, int y, int width, int height)
    public void repaint(long tm, int x, int y, int width, int height)
    public void print(Graphics g)
    public void printAll(Graphics g)
    public boolean imageUpdate(Image img, int flags,
                              int x, int y, int w, int h)
    public Image createImage(ImageProducer producer)
    public Image createImage(int width, int height)
    public boolean prepareImage(Image image, ImageObserver observer)
    public boolean prepareImage(Image image, int width, int height,
                               ImageObserver observer)
    public int checkImage(Image image, ImageObserver observer)
```

continues

Listing 28.10. continued

```
public int checkImage(Image image, int width, int height,
                      ImageObserver observer)
public synchronized boolean inside(int x, int y)
public Component locate(int x, int y)
public void deliverEvent(Event e)
public boolean postEvent(Event e)
public boolean handleEvent(Event evt)
public boolean mouseDown(Event evt, int x, int y)
public boolean mouseDrag(Event evt, int x, int y)
public boolean mouseUp(Event evt, int x, int y)
public boolean mouseMove(Event evt, int x, int y)
public boolean mouseEnter(Event evt, int x, int y)
public boolean mouseExit(Event evt, int x, int y)
public boolean keyDown(Event evt, int key)
public boolean keyUp(Event evt, int key)
public boolean action(Event evt, Object what)
public void addNotify()
public synchronized void removeNotify()
public boolean gotFocus(Event evt, Object what)
public boolean lostFocus(Event evt, Object what)
public void requestFocus()
public void nextFocus()
public String toString()
public void list()
public void list(PrintStream out)
public void list(PrintStream out, int indent)
}
```

---

 getParent   Component awt

```
public Container getParent()
```

getParent() returns this component's parent (a Container class).

  A Container class representing the component's parent. For more information on Containers, see the documentation for the Container class later in this chapter.

---

 getPeer   Component awt

```
public ComponentPeer getPeer()
```

getPeer() returns this component's peer (a ComponentPeer interface).

A ComponentPeer interface representing the component's peer. For more information on ComponentPeers, see the documentation for the ComponentPeer interface later in this chapter.

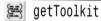 **getToolkit** **Component** awt

```
public Toolkit getToolkit()
```

`getToolkit()` returns the toolkit of this component. The toolkit creates the peer for the component.

↵ A `Toolkit` class. A toolkit is required to bind the abstract AWT classes to a native toolkit implementation. For more information on the `Toolkit` class, see the documentation for the `Toolkit` class later in this chapter.

isValid **Component** awt

```
public boolean isValid()
```

`isValid()` determines whether this component is valid. A `Component` is considered to be invalid when it is first shown on the screen.

↵ A Boolean value representing the valid state of this component.

isVisible **Component** awt

```
public boolean isVisible()
```

`isVisible()` determines whether this component is visible. A `Component` is by default visible until told otherwise. A `Component` can be visible yet not show on the screen if the component's container is invisible.

↵ A Boolean value representing the visible state of this component.

isShowing **Component** awt

```
public boolean isShowing()
```

`isShowing()` determines whether this component is shown on the screen. A `Component` can be visible yet not show on the screen if the component's container is invisible.

↵ A Boolean value representing the show state of this component.

isEnabled **Component** awt

```
public boolean isEnabled()
```

`isEnabled()` determines whether this component is currently enabled. By default, components are enabled until told otherwise.

↵ A Boolean value representing the enabled state of this component.

location 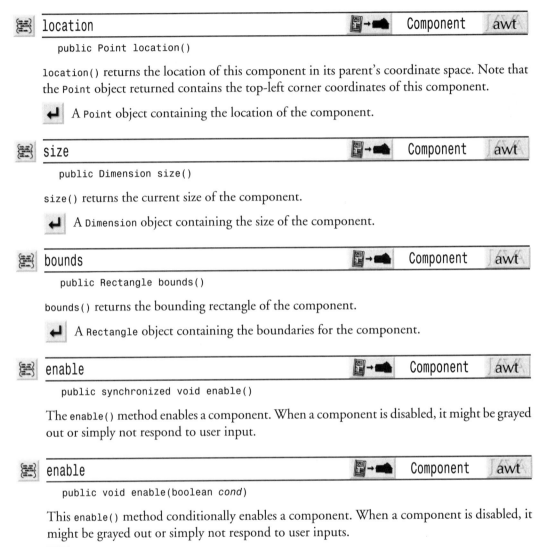 Component awt

```
public Point location()
```

`location()` returns the location of this component in its parent's coordinate space. Note that the `Point` object returned contains the top-left corner coordinates of this component.

↵ A `Point` object containing the location of the component.

size Component awt

```
public Dimension size()
```

`size()` returns the current size of the component.

↵ A `Dimension` object containing the size of the component.

bounds Component awt

```
public Rectangle bounds()
```

`bounds()` returns the bounding rectangle of the component.

↵ A `Rectangle` object containing the boundaries for the component.

enable Component awt

```
public synchronized void enable()
```

The `enable()` method enables a component. When a component is disabled, it might be grayed out or simply not respond to user input.

enable Component awt

```
public void enable(boolean cond)
```

This `enable()` method conditionally enables a component. When a component is disabled, it might be grayed out or simply not respond to user inputs.

▶ *cond* is a Boolean value representing the new enabled state of the component.

disable Component awt

```
public synchronized void disable()
```

The `disable()` method disables a component. When a component is disabled, it might be grayed out or simply not respond to user inputs.

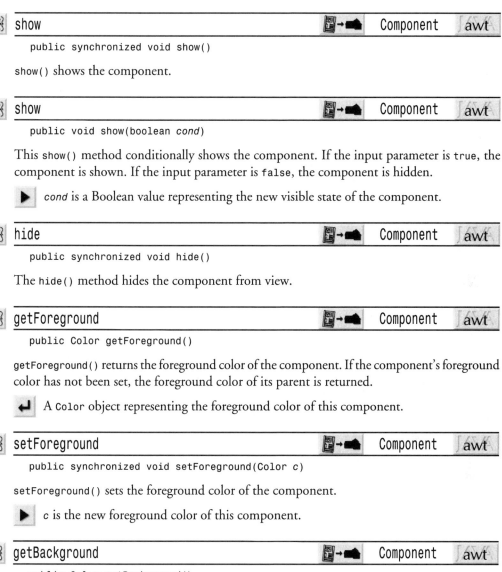

show   Component   awt

```
public synchronized void show()
```

show() shows the component.

show   Component   awt

```
public void show(boolean cond)
```

This show() method conditionally shows the component. If the input parameter is true, the component is shown. If the input parameter is false, the component is hidden.

▶ *cond* is a Boolean value representing the new visible state of the component.

hide   Component   awt

```
public synchronized void hide()
```

The hide() method hides the component from view.

getForeground   Component   awt

```
public Color getForeground()
```

getForeground() returns the foreground color of the component. If the component's foreground color has not been set, the foreground color of its parent is returned.

↵ A Color object representing the foreground color of this component.

setForeground   Component   awt

```
public synchronized void setForeground(Color c)
```

setForeground() sets the foreground color of the component.

▶ *c* is the new foreground color of this component.

getBackground   Component   awt

```
public Color getBackground()
```

getBackground() returns the background color of the component. If the component's background color has not been set, the background color of its parent is returned.

↵ A Color object representing the background color of this component.

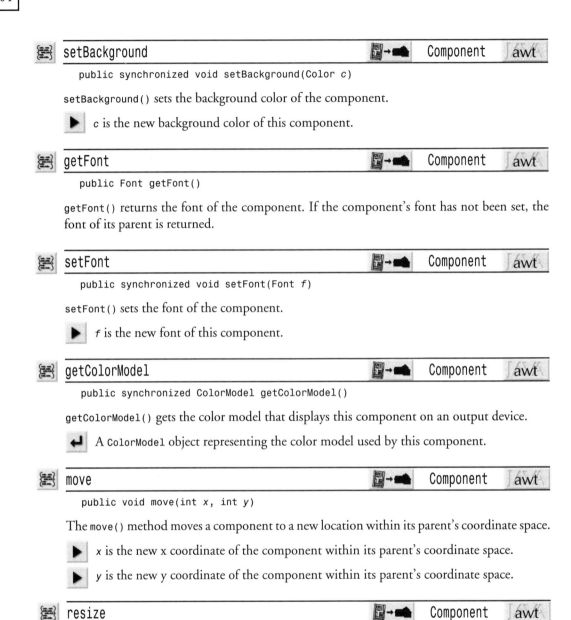

setBackground   Component   awt

```
public synchronized void setBackground(Color c)
```

setBackground() sets the background color of the component.

▶ *c* is the new background color of this component.

getFont   Component   awt

```
public Font getFont()
```

getFont() returns the font of the component. If the component's font has not been set, the font of its parent is returned.

setFont   Component   awt

```
public synchronized void setFont(Font f)
```

setFont() sets the font of the component.

▶ *f* is the new font of this component.

getColorModel   Component   awt

```
public synchronized ColorModel getColorModel()
```

getColorModel() gets the color model that displays this component on an output device.

↩ A ColorModel object representing the color model used by this component.

move   Component   awt

```
public void move(int x, int y)
```

The move() method moves a component to a new location within its parent's coordinate space.

▶ *x* is the new x coordinate of the component within its parent's coordinate space.

▶ *y* is the new y coordinate of the component within its parent's coordinate space.

resize   Component   awt

```
public void resize(int width, int height)
```

resize() resizes the component to the specified width and height.

▶ *width* is the new width size of the component.

▶ *height* is the new height size of the component.

resize 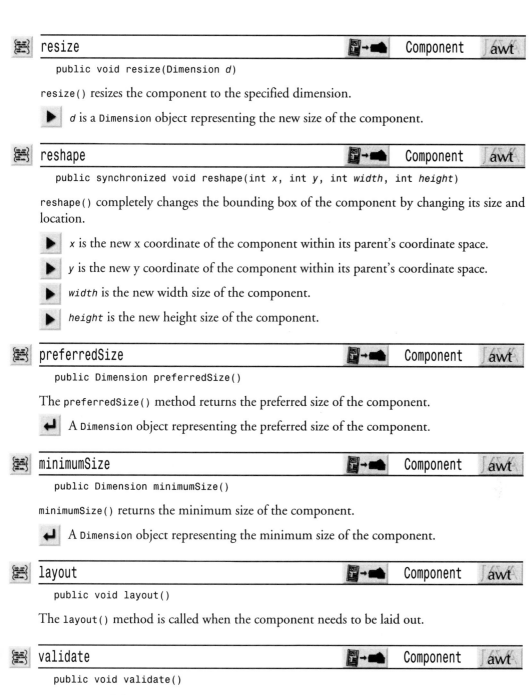 Component awt

```
public void resize(Dimension d)
```

resize() resizes the component to the specified dimension.

▶ *d* is a Dimension object representing the new size of the component.

reshape Component awt

```
public synchronized void reshape(int x, int y, int width, int height)
```

reshape() completely changes the bounding box of the component by changing its size and location.

▶ *x* is the new x coordinate of the component within its parent's coordinate space.

▶ *y* is the new y coordinate of the component within its parent's coordinate space.

▶ *width* is the new width size of the component.

▶ *height* is the new height size of the component.

preferredSize Component awt

```
public Dimension preferredSize()
```

The preferredSize() method returns the preferred size of the component.

↵ A Dimension object representing the preferred size of the component.

minimumSize Component awt

```
public Dimension minimumSize()
```

minimumSize() returns the minimum size of the component.

↵ A Dimension object representing the minimum size of the component.

layout Component awt

```
public void layout()
```

The layout() method is called when the component needs to be laid out.

validate Component awt

```
public void validate()
```

validate() validates a component by calling its layout() method.

invalidate Component awt

```
public void invalidate()
```

invalidate() invalidates a component, forcing the component and all parents above it to be laid out.

 ## getGraphics Component awt

```
public Graphics getGraphics()
```

getGraphics() returns a Graphics context for the component. If the component is not currently on the screen, this function returns null.

A Graphics object representing the component's graphics context.

getFontMetrics Component awt

```
public FontMetrics getFontMetrics(Font font)
```

getFontMetrics() returns the current FontMetrics for a specified font. If the component is not currently on the screen, this function returns null.

font is a Font object to be examined.

A FontMetrics object representing the component's FontMetrics.

paint Component awt

```
public void paint(Graphics g)
```

The paint() method paints the component on the screen using the Graphics context parameter.

g is the Graphics context that the component paints itself onto.

update Component awt

```
public void update(Graphics g)
```

The update() method repaints the component in response to a call to the repaint() method. For more information on the repaint() method, see the documentation later in this chapter.

g is the Graphics context that the component paints itself onto.

paintAll Component awt

```
public void paintAll(Graphics g)
```

The `paintAll()` method paints the component along with all its subcomponents.

▶ *g* is the `Graphics` context that the component paints itself onto.

repaint Component awt

```
public void repaint()
```

`repaint()` forces a component to repaint itself. Calling this function results in a call to `update()`. For more information on the `update()` method, see the documentation earlier in this chapter.

repaint Component awt

```
public void repaint(long tm)
```

This `repaint()` method forces a component to repaint itself in *tm* milliseconds.

▶ *tm* is the time, in milliseconds, that the component has to repaint itself from the time this method is called.

repaint Component awt

```
public void repaint(int x, int y, int width, int height)
```

This `repaint()` method forces the component to repaint part of its surface area based on the input coordinates.

▶ *x* is the x coordinate marking the surface area to be repainted.

▶ *y* is the y coordinate marking the surface area to be repainted.

▶ *width* is the width of the surface area to be repainted.

▶ *height* is the height of the surface area to be repainted.

repaint Component awt

```
public void repaint(long tm, int x, int y, int width, int height)
```

This `repaint()` method forces the component to repaint part of its surface area based on the input coordinates at a specified time in the future.

▶ *tm* is the time, in milliseconds, from the time this method is called that the component has to repaint itself.

▶ *x* is the x coordinate marking the surface area to be repainted.

▶ *y* is the y coordinate marking the surface area to be repainted.

▶ `width` is the width of the surface area to be repainted.

▶ `height` is the height of the surface area to be repainted.

print   Component   awt

```
public void print(Graphics g)
```

`print()` prints the component using the `Graphics` context. The default implementation of this method calls `paint()`.

▶ *g* is the `Graphics` context to be printed on.

printAll   Component   awt

```
public void printAll(Graphics g)
```

`printAll()` prints the component and all of its subcomponents using the `Graphics` context.

▶ *g* is the `Graphics` context to be printed on.

imageUpdate   Component   awt

```
public boolean imageUpdate(Image img, int flags, int x, int y, int w, int h)
```

`imageUpdate()` repaints the component when the specified image has changed.

▶ *img* is an `Image` object to be examined for changes.

▶ *flags* contains imaging flags such as `FRAMEBITS`, `ALLBITS`, and `SOMEBITS` (see documentation for the `ImageObserver` interface later in this chapter).

▶ *x* is the x coordinate marking the surface area to be repainted.

▶ *y* is the y coordinate marking the surface area to be repainted.

▶ `width` is the width of the surface area to be repainted.

▶ `height` is the height of the surface area to be repainted.

↵ A Boolean value that is true if the image has changed, false if it hasn't.

createImage   Component   awt

```
public Image createImage(ImageProducer producer)
```

`createImage()` creates an `Image` using the specified `ImageProducer`.

▶ *producer* is an `ImageProducer` interface that produces a new image.

↵ An `Image` object.

---

createImage Component awt

```
public Image createImage(int width, int height)
```

This `createImage()` creates an off-screen image object using the specified width and height. This image object can be used for things like double-buffering.

▶ *width* is the width of the `Image` object to be created.

▶ *height* is the height of the `Image` object to be created.

↵ An `Image` object.

---

prepareImage Component awt

```
public boolean prepareImage(Image image, ImageObserver observer)
```

`prepareImage()` prepares an `Image` for rendering on this component. Because the `Image` is downloaded using a separate thread, the `ImageObserver` interface is notified when the `Image` is ready to be rendered.

▶ *image* is an `Image` object that is rendered on this component.

▶ *observer* is an `Observer` interface that is notified when the `Image` is ready to be rendered.

↵ A Boolean value that is true if the `Image` has been prepared, false if it hasn't.

---

prepareImage Component awt

```
public boolean prepareImage(Image image, int width, int height, ImageObserver
observer)
```

This `prepareImage()` method is similar to the `prepareImage()` method documented previously except that this method scales the `Image` based on the width and height parameters.

▶ *image* is an `Image` object that is rendered on this component.

▶ *width* is the width of the image to be rendered.

▶ *height* is the height of the image to be rendered.

▶ *observer* is an `Observer` interface that is notified when the `Image` is ready to be rendered.

↵ A Boolean value that is true if the `Image` has been prepared, false if it hasn't.

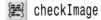 checkImage   Component   awt

```
public int checkImage(Image image, ImageObserver observer)
```

checkImage() checks the status of the construction of the Image to be rendered.

▶   *image* is an Image object that is rendered on this component.

▶   *observer* is an Observer interface that is notified when the Image is ready to be rendered.

↵   An integer value that is the Boolean OR of the ImageObserver flags for the data that is currently available (see the documentation for the ImageObserver interface later in this chapter).

 checkImage   Component   awt

```
public int checkImage(Image image, int width, int height, ImageObserver
➥observer)
```

This checkImage() method checks the status of the construction of a scaled representation of this image.

▶   *image* is an Image object that is rendered on this component.

▶   *width* is the width of the image to be checked.

▶   *height* is the height of the image to be checked.

▶   *observer* is an Observer interface that is notified when the Image is ready to be rendered.

↵   An integer value that is the Boolean OR of the ImageObserver flags for the data that is currently available (see the documentation for the ImageObserver interface later in this chapter).

 inside   Component   awt

```
public synchronized boolean inside(int x, int y)
```

The inside() method determines whether the x and y coordinates are within the bounding rectangle of the component.

▶   *x* is the x coordinate to be examined.

▶   *y* is the y coordinate to be examined.

↵   A Boolean value representing the result of the coordinates check.

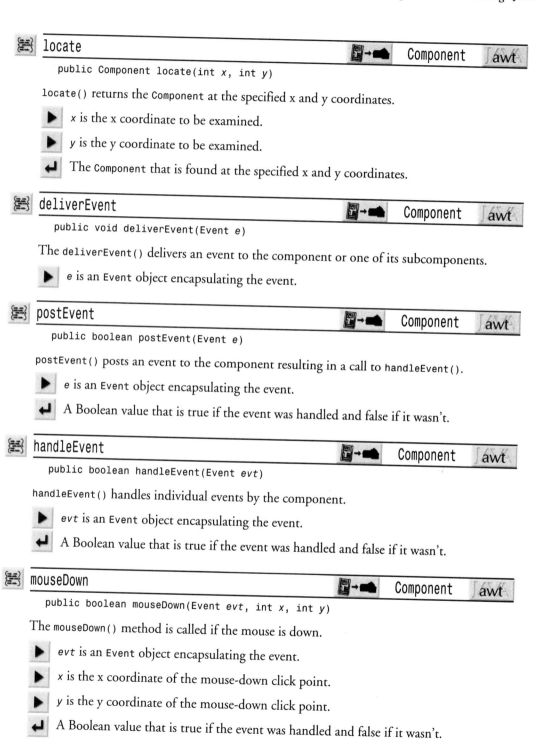

locate   Component — awt

```
public Component locate(int x, int y)
```

`locate()` returns the `Component` at the specified x and y coordinates.

▶ *x* is the x coordinate to be examined.

▶ *y* is the y coordinate to be examined.

↵ The `Component` that is found at the specified x and y coordinates.

deliverEvent   Component — awt

```
public void deliverEvent(Event e)
```

The `deliverEvent()` delivers an event to the component or one of its subcomponents.

▶ *e* is an `Event` object encapsulating the event.

postEvent   Component — awt

```
public boolean postEvent(Event e)
```

`postEvent()` posts an event to the component resulting in a call to `handleEvent()`.

▶ *e* is an `Event` object encapsulating the event.

↵ A Boolean value that is true if the event was handled and false if it wasn't.

handleEvent   Component — awt

```
public boolean handleEvent(Event evt)
```

`handleEvent()` handles individual events by the component.

▶ *evt* is an `Event` object encapsulating the event.

↵ A Boolean value that is true if the event was handled and false if it wasn't.

mouseDown   Component — awt

```
public boolean mouseDown(Event evt, int x, int y)
```

The `mouseDown()` method is called if the mouse is down.

▶ *evt* is an `Event` object encapsulating the event.

▶ *x* is the x coordinate of the mouse-down click point.

▶ *y* is the y coordinate of the mouse-down click point.

↵ A Boolean value that is true if the event was handled and false if it wasn't.

mouseDrag  Component   awt

```
public boolean mouseDrag(Event evt, int x, int y)
```

The mouseDrag() method is called if the mouse is dragged.

▶ *evt* is an Event object encapsulating the event.

▶ *x* is the x coordinate of the current mouse point coordinate.

▶ *y* is the y coordinate of the current mouse point coordinate.

↵ A Boolean value that is true if the event was handled and false if it wasn't.

mouseUp   Component   awt

```
public boolean mouseUp(Event evt, int x, int y)
```

The mouseUp() method is called when the mouse button is released.

▶ *evt* is an Event object encapsulating the event.

▶ *x* is the x coordinate of the mouse up point.

▶ *y* is the y coordinate of the mouse up point.

↵ A Boolean value that is true if the event was handled and false if it wasn't.

mouseMove   Component   awt

```
public boolean mouseMove(Event evt, int x, int y)
```

The mouseMove() method is called if the mouse is moved.

▶ *evt* is an Event object encapsulating the event.

▶ *x* is the x coordinate of the current mouse point coordinate.

▶ *y* is the y coordinate of the current mouse point coordinate.

↵ A Boolean value that is true if the event was handled and false if it wasn't.

mouseEnter   Component   awt

```
public boolean mouseEnter(Event evt, int x, int y)
```

The mouseEnter() method is called if the mouse enters the component.

▶ *evt* is an Event object encapsulating the event.

▶ *x* is the x coordinate of the current mouse point coordinate.

▶ *y* is the y coordinate of the current mouse point coordinate.

↵ A Boolean value that is true if the event was handled and false if it wasn't.

mouseExit

Component | awt

```
public boolean mouseExit(Event evt, int x, int y)
```

The mouseExit() method is called if the mouse exits the component.

▶ *evt* is an Event object encapsulating the event.

▶ *x* is the x coordinate of the mouse exit point.

▶ *y* is the y coordinate of the mouse exit point.

↵ A Boolean value that is true if the event was handled and false if it wasn't.

keyDown

Component | awt

```
public boolean keyDown(Event evt, int key)
```

The keyDown() method is called when a key is pressed.

▶ *evt* is an Event object encapsulating the event.

▶ *key* is an integer value representing the code of the key that was pressed.

↵ A Boolean value that is true if the event was handled and false if it wasn't.

keyUp

Component | awt

```
public boolean keyUp(Event evt, int key)
```

The keyUp() method is called when a key is released.

▶ *evt* is an Event object encapsulating the event.

▶ *key* is an integer value representing the code of the key that was pressed.

↵ A Boolean value that is true if the event was handled and false if it wasn't.

action

Component | awt

```
public boolean action(Event evt, Object what)
```

The action() method is called if an action occurs within the component. For more information on handling actions, see the handleEvent() method.

▶ *evt* is an Event object encapsulating the event.

▶ *what* is an object representing the action that is occurring.

↵ A Boolean value that is true if the event was handled and false if it wasn't.

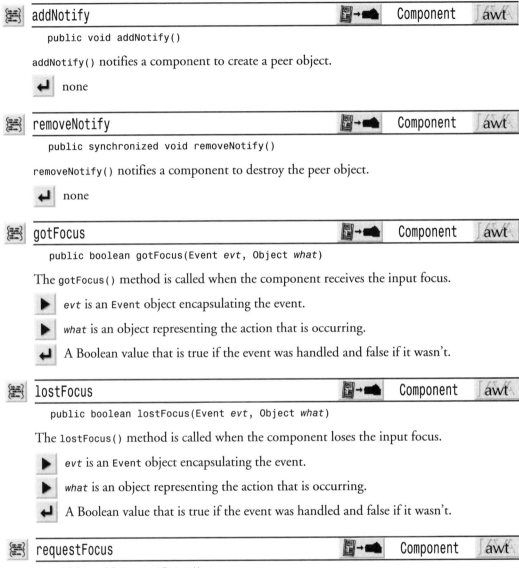

addNotify — Component — awt

```
public void addNotify()
```

addNotify() notifies a component to create a peer object.

↵ none

removeNotify — Component — awt

```
public synchronized void removeNotify()
```

removeNotify() notifies a component to destroy the peer object.

↵ none

gotFocus — Component — awt

```
public boolean gotFocus(Event evt, Object what)
```

The gotFocus() method is called when the component receives the input focus.

▶ *evt* is an Event object encapsulating the event.

▶ *what* is an object representing the action that is occurring.

↵ A Boolean value that is true if the event was handled and false if it wasn't.

lostFocus — Component — awt

```
public boolean lostFocus(Event evt, Object what)
```

The lostFocus() method is called when the component loses the input focus.

▶ *evt* is an Event object encapsulating the event.

▶ *what* is an object representing the action that is occurring.

↵ A Boolean value that is true if the event was handled and false if it wasn't.

requestFocus — Component — awt

```
public void requestFocus()
```

The requestFocus() method requests the current input focus. If this method is successful, gotFocus() is then called.

↵ none

nextFocus   Component   awt

```
public void nextFocus()
```

The nextFocus() method switches the focus to the next component. The next component can be determined by examining the tab order of the components on a form.

↵ none

toString   Component   awt

```
public String toString()
```

toString returns a string representation of the Component class.

↵ A String value containing the Component class's name plus its x, y, height, and width values (see the Component() constructors).

⊘ toString() in class Object.

list   Component   awt

```
public void list()
```

The list() method prints a listing of the component to the print stream.

↵ none

list   Component   awt

```
public void list(PrintStream out)
```

This list() method prints a listing of the component to the specified output stream.

▶ out is a PrintStream object.

list   Component   awt

```
public void list(PrintStream out, int indent)
```

This list() method prints a listing of the component to the specified output stream at the specified indention.

▶ out is a PrintStream object.

▶ indent is an integer value representing the amount to be indented.

Container

awt

 Component

The class hierarchy for the Container class derives from the class java.awt.Component. (See Listing 28.11.) A Container class is defined as a class that can contain other components. Container's overall derivation is shown in Figure 28.1.

Listing 28.11. Public members of java.awt.Container.

```
public abstract class Container extends Component {
  public int countComponents()
  public synchronized Component getComponent(int n)
  ➥throws ArrayIndexOutOfBoundsException
  public synchronized Component[] getComponents()
  public Insets insets()
  public Component add(Component comp)
  public synchronized Component add(Component comp, int pos)
  public synchronized Component add(String name, Component comp)
  public synchronized void remove(Component comp)
  public synchronized void removeAll()
  public LayoutManager getLayout()
  public void setLayout(LayoutManager mgr)
  public synchronized void layout()
  public synchronized void validate()
  public synchronized Dimension preferredSize()
  public synchronized Dimension minimumSize()
  public void paintComponents(Graphics g)
  public void printComponents(Graphics g)
  public void deliverEvent(Event e)
  public Component locate(int x, int y)
  public synchronized void addNotify()
  public synchronized void removeNotify()
  public void list(PrintStream out, int indent)
}
```

 countComponents   Container   awt

```
public int countComponents()
```

countComponents() returns the number of components contained within the container.

 An integer value representing the number of components within the container.

getComponent  Container awt

```
public synchronized Component getComponent(int n)
```

The getComponent() method returns the component at the specified index.

▶ *n* is an integer value representing the index of where to retrieve a component.

↵ A Component object within the Container.

☛ An ArrayIndexOutOfBoundsException if the component does not exist.

getComponents  Container awt

```
public synchronized Component[] getComponents()
```

getComponents() returns an array of Component objects contained within the Container.

↵ An array of Components contained within the container.

insets Container awt

```
public Insets insets()
```

The insets() method returns the borders of this container.

↵ An Insets object representing the insets of the container. For more information, see the documentation for the Insets class later in this chapter.

add Container awt

```
public Component add(Component comp)
```

The add() method adds a Component to the container at the end of the container's array of components.

▶ *comp* is the component to be added.

↵ The Component object that was added to the container's list.

add  Container awt

```
public synchronized Component add(Component comp, int pos)
```

This add() method adds a Component to the container at the specified index in the container's array of components.

▶ *comp* is the component to be added.

▶ *pos* is the position where the component is to be added.

↵ The Component object that was added to the container's list.

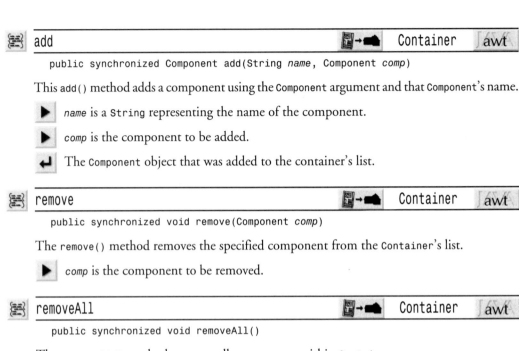

add   Container   awt

```
public synchronized Component add(String name, Component comp)
```

This add() method adds a component using the Component argument and that Component's name.

▶ *name* is a String representing the name of the component.

▶ *comp* is the component to be added.

↵ The Component object that was added to the container's list.

remove   Container   awt

```
public synchronized void remove(Component comp)
```

The remove() method removes the specified component from the Container's list.

▶ *comp* is the component to be removed.

removeAll   Container   awt

```
public synchronized void removeAll()
```

The removeAll() method removes all components within Container.

↵ none

getLayout   Container   awt

```
public LayoutManager getLayout()
```

getLayout() returns this Container's LayoutManager. For more information on the LayoutManager interface, see the LayoutManager documentation later in this chapter.

↵ A LayoutManager interface representing the Container's LayoutManager.

setLayout   Container   awt

```
public void setLayout(LayoutManager mgr)
```

setLayout() sets the current LayoutManager of the Container. For more information on the LayoutManager interface, see the LayoutManager documentation later in this chapter.

▶ *mgr* is the LayoutManager that controls the layouts of this Container's components.

layout 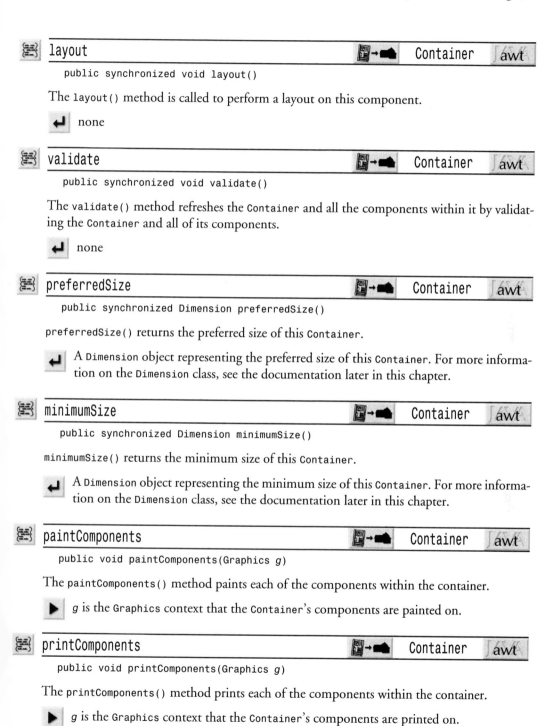 Container awt

```
public synchronized void layout()
```

The layout() method is called to perform a layout on this component.

↵ none

validate Container awt

```
public synchronized void validate()
```

The validate() method refreshes the Container and all the components within it by validating the Container and all of its components.

↵ none

preferredSize Container awt

```
public synchronized Dimension preferredSize()
```

preferredSize() returns the preferred size of this Container.

↵ A Dimension object representing the preferred size of this Container. For more information on the Dimension class, see the documentation later in this chapter.

minimumSize Container awt

```
public synchronized Dimension minimumSize()
```

minimumSize() returns the minimum size of this Container.

↵ A Dimension object representing the minimum size of this Container. For more information on the Dimension class, see the documentation later in this chapter.

paintComponents Container awt

```
public void paintComponents(Graphics g)
```

The paintComponents() method paints each of the components within the container.

▶ g is the Graphics context that the Container's components are painted on.

printComponents Container awt

```
public void printComponents(Graphics g)
```

The printComponents() method prints each of the components within the container.

▶ g is the Graphics context that the Container's components are printed on.

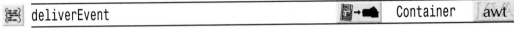

deliverEvent   Container   awt

```
public void deliverEvent(Event e)
```

`deliverEvent()` locates the appropriate component within the container that the event applies to and delivers the event to that component.

▶ *e* is the event to be delivered.

locate   Container   awt

```
public Component locate(int x, int y)
```

The `locate()` method locates and returns the component that lies at the specified x and y co-ordinates within the container.

▶ *x* is the x coordinate of the component to be located.

▶ *y* is the y coordinate of the component to be located.

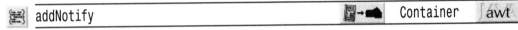

addNotify   Container   awt

```
public synchronized void addNotify()
```

`addNotify()` notifies the container to create a peer interface. This method also notifies each of the container's components to do likewise.

↵ none

removeNotify   Container   awt

```
public synchronized void removeNotify()
```

`removeNotify()` notifies the container to remove its peer. This method also notifies each of the container's components to do likewise.

↵ none

list   Container   awt

```
public void list(PrintStream out, int indent)
```

The `list()` method prints a list for each component within the container to the specified output stream at the specified indentation.

▶ *out* is a `PrintStream` object.

▶ *indent* is an integer amount representing the value to indent the list.

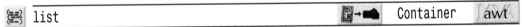

 # Dialog awt

 Window

The class hierarchy for the `Dialog` class derives from the class `java.awt.Window`. (See Listing 28.12.) The `Dialog` class creates a window that can be closed by the user. Dialogs are usually temporary windows that are used for entering information. `Dialog`'s overall derivation is shown in Figure 28.1.

Listing 28.12. Public members of java.awt.Dialog.

```
public class Dialog extends Window {
    public Dialog(Frame parent, boolean modal)
    public Dialog(Frame parent, String title, boolean modal)
    public synchronized void addNotify()
    public boolean isModal()
    public String getTitle()
    public void setTitle(String title)
    public boolean isResizable()
    public void setResizable(boolean resizable)
}
```

Dialog   Dialog awt

`public Dialog(Frame parent, boolean modal)`

This `Dialog()` constructor constructs a `Dialog` object from a parent `Frame` object. This `Dialog` is initially invisible.

▶ *parent* is the parent frame of the `Dialog`.

▶ *modal* is a Boolean value designating this dialog to be either modal or nonmodal. If a dialog is modal, it blocks out all user input to other objects and retains the sole focus on the screen.

Dialog   Dialog awt

`public Dialog(Frame parent, String title, boolean modal)`

This `Dialog()` constructor constructs a `Dialog` object with a title from a parent `Frame` object. This `Dialog` is initially invisible.

▶ *parent* is the parent frame of the `Dialog`.

▶ *title* is a `String` value representing the title to be displayed for this `Dialog`.

▶ *modal* is a Boolean value designating this dialog to be either modal or nonmodal. If a dialog is modal, it blocks out all user input to other objects and retains the sole focus on the screen.

addNotify 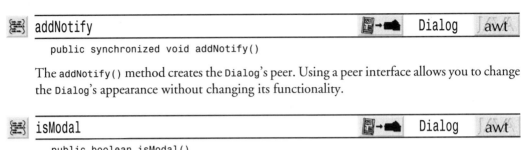 Dialog   awt

```
public synchronized void addNotify()
```

The addNotify() method creates the Dialog's peer. Using a peer interface allows you to change the Dialog's appearance without changing its functionality.

isModal  Dialog   awt

```
public boolean isModal()
```

isModal() returns the modal status of the dialog.

A Boolean value representing the Dialog's modal status. If this is true, the dialog is modal. If false, the dialog is nonmodal.

getTitle  Dialog   awt

```
public String getTitle()
```

getTitle() returns the dialog's title string.

A String value representing the title string of the dialog.

setTitle   Dialog   awt

```
public void setTitle(String title)
```

The setTitle() method sets the Dialog's title string.

▶   *title* is a String value representing the Dialog's new title.

isResizable   Dialog   awt

```
public boolean isResizable()
```

The isResizable() method is called to determine whether this dialog can be resized.

A Boolean value that is true if the dialog is resizable and false if it is not.

setResizable   Dialog   awt

```
public void setResizable(boolean resizable)
```

The setResizable() method changes whether a dialog can be resized.

▶   *resizable* is a Boolean value that is true if the dialog is to be resizable and false if not.

Dimension awt

 Object

The class hierarchy for the Dimension class derives from the class java.lang.Object. (See Listing 28.13.) A Dimension class encapsulates an object's height and width. Dimension's overall derivation is shown in Figure 28.1.

Listing 28.13. Public members of java.awt.Dimension.

```
public class Dimension {
  public int width;
  public int height;
  public Dimension()
  public Dimension(Dimension d)
  public Dimension(int width, int height)
  public String toString()
}
```

Public Instance Variables

public int width

The *width* instance variable contains the integer value representing the Dimension's width value.

public int height

The *height* instance variable contains the integer value representing the Dimension's height value.

 Dimension   Dimension   awt

public Dimension()

This Dimension() constructor constructs an empty Dimension object (zero width and zero height, by default).

 Dimension   Dimension   awt

public Dimension(Dimension d)

This Dimension() constructor constructs a Dimension object from an existing Dimension object.

 d is a Dimension object whose values are used to create the new Dimension.

Dimension Dimension | awt

```
public Dimension(int width, int height)
```

This `Dimension()` constructor constructs a `Dimension` object based on the width and height input parameters.

    width is an integer value representing the width of the new `Dimension`.

▶   *height* is an integer value representing the height of the new `Dimension`.

 toString Dimension | awt

```
public String toString()
```

The `toString()` method returns a `String` representation of this `Dimension` object.

    A `String` containing this `Dimension`'s height and width values.

 # Event   awt

╋   Object

The class hierarchy for the `Event` class derives from the class `java.lang.Object`. (See Listing 28.14.) The `Event` class encapsulates GUI events in a platform-independent manner. `Event`'s overall derivation is shown in Figure 28.1.

Listing 28.14. Public members of `java.awt.Event`.

```
public class Event {
    public static final int SHIFT_MASK
    public static final int CTRL_MASK
    public static final int META_MASK
    public static final int ALT_MASK
    public static final int HOME
    public static final int END
    public static final int PGUP
    public static final int PGDN
    public static final int UP
    public static final int DOWN
    public static final int LEFT
    public static final int RIGHT
    public static final int F1
    public static final int F2
    public static final int F3
    public static final int F4
    public static final int F5
    public static final int F6
    public static final int F7
    public static final int F8
    public static final int F9
```

```
    public static final int F10
    public static final int F11
    public static final int F12
    public static final int WINDOW_DESTROY
    public static final int WINDOW_EXPOSE
    public static final int WINDOW_ICONIFY
    public static final int WINDOW_DEICONIFY
    public static final int WINDOW_MOVED
    public static final int KEY_PRESS
    public static final int KEY_RELEASE
    public static final int KEY_ACTION
    public static final int KEY_ACTION_RELEASE
    public static final int MOUSE_DOWN
    public static final int MOUSE_UP
    public static final int MOUSE_MOVE
    public static final int MOUSE_ENTER
    public static final int MOUSE_EXIT
    public static final int MOUSE_DRAG
    public static final int SCROLL_LINE_UP
    public static final int SCROLL_LINE_DOWN
    public static final int SCROLL_PAGE_UP
    public static final int SCROLL_PAGE_DOWN
    public static final int SCROLL_ABSOLUTE
    public static final int LIST_SELECT
    public static final int LIST_DESELECT
    public static final int ACTION_EVENT
    public static final int LOAD_FILE
    public static final int SAVE_FILE
    public static final int GOT_FOCUS
    public static final int LOST_FOCUS
    public Object target;
    public long when;
    public int id;
    public int x;
    public int y;
    public int key;
    public int modifiers;
    public int clickCount;
    public Object arg;
    public Event evt;
    public Event(Object target, long when, int id, int x, int y, int key,
                 int modifiers, Object arg)
    public Event(Object target, long when, int id, int x, int y, int key, int
    ↪modifiers)
    public Event(Object target, int id, Object arg)
    public void translate(int x, int y)
    public boolean shiftDown()
    public boolean controlDown()
    public boolean metaDown()
    public String toString()
}
```

Public Static Values

`public static final int SHIFT_MASK`

The SHIFT_MASK value represents the Shift Modifier constant.

`public static final int CTRL_MASK`

The CTRL_MASK value represents the Control Modifier constant.

`public static final int META_MASK`

The META_MASK value represents the Meta Modifier constant.

`public static final int ALT_MASK`

The ALT_MASK value represents the Alt Modifier constant.

`public static final int HOME`

The HOME value represents the Home key.

`public static final int END`

The END value represents the End key.

`public static final int PGUP`

The PGUP value represents the Page Up key.

`public static final int PGDN`

The PGDN value represents the Page Down key.

`public static final int UP`

The UP value represents the Up Arrow key.

`public static final int DOWN`

The DOWN value represents the Down Arrow key.

`public static final int LEFT`

The LEFT value represents the Left Arrow key.

`public static final int RIGHT`

The RIGHT value represents the Right Arrow key.

`public static final int F1`

The F1 value represents the F1 key.

`public static final int F2`

The F2 value represents the F2 key.

`public static final int F3`

The F3 value represents the F3 key.

`public static final int F4`

The F4 value represents the F4 key.

`public static final int F5`

The F5 value represents the F5 key.

`public static final int F6`

The F6 value represents the F6 key.

`public static final int F7`

The F7 value represents the F7 key.

`public static final int F8`

The F8 value represents the F8 key.

`public static final int F9`

The F9 value represents the F9 key.

`public static final int F10`

The F10 value represents the F10 key.

`public static final int F11`

The F11 value represents the F11 key.

`public static final int F12`

The F12 value represents the F12 key.

`public static final int WINDOW_DESTROY`

The WINDOW_DESTROY value represents the destroy window event.

`public static final int WINDOW_EXPOSE`

The WINDOW_EXPOSE value represents the expose window event.

`public static final int WINDOW_ICONIFY`

The WINDOW_ICONIFY value represents the iconify window event.

`public static final int WINDOW_DEICONIFY`

The DEICONIFY_WINDOW value represents the deiconify window event.

```
public static final int WINDOW_MOVED
```

The WINDOW_MOVED value represents the window moved event.

```
public static final int KEY_PRESS
```

The KEY_PRESS value represents the key press event.

```
public static final int KEY_RELEASE
```

The KEY_RELEASE value represents the key release event.

```
public static final int KEY_ACTION
```

The KEY_ACTION value represents the key action keyboard event.

```
public static final int KEY_ACTION_RELEASE
```

The KEY_ACTION_RELEASE value represents the key action release keyboard event.

```
public static final int MOUSE_DOWN
```

The MOUSE_DOWN value represents the mouse down event.

```
public static final int MOUSE_UP
```

The MOUSE_UP value represents the mouse up event.

```
public static final int MOUSE_MOVE
```

The MOUSE_MOVE value represents the mouse move event.

```
public static final int MOUSE_ENTER
```

The MOUSE_ENTER value represents the mouse enter event.

```
public static final int MOUSE_EXIT
```

The MOUSE_EXIT value represents the mouse exit event.

```
public static final int MOUSE_DRAG
```

The MOUSE_DRAG value represents the mouse drag event.

```
public static final int SCROLL_LINE_UP
```

The SCROLL_LINE_UP value represents the line up scroll event.

```
public static final int SCROLL_LINE_DOWN
```

The SCROLL_LINE_DOWN value represents the line down scroll event.

```
public static final int SCROLL_PAGE_UP
```

The SCROLL_PAGE_UP value represents the page up scroll event.

```
public static final int SCROLL_PAGE_DOWN
```

The SCROLL_PAGE_DOWN value represents the page down scroll event.

```
public static final int SCROLL_ABSOLUTE
```

The SCROLL_ABSOLUTE value represents the absolute scroll event.

```
public static final int LIST_SELECT
```

The LIST_SELECT value represents the select list event.

```
public static final int LIST_DESELECT
```

The LIST_DESELECT value represents the deselect list event.

```
public static final int ACTION_EVENT
```

The ACTION_EVENT value represents an action event.

```
public static final int LOAD_FILE
```

The LOAD_FILE value represents a file load event.

```
public static final int SAVE_FILE
```

The SAVE_FILE value represents a file save event.

```
public static final int GOT_FOCUS
```

The GOT_FOCUS value represents a got focus event.

```
public static final int LOST_FOCUS
```

The LOST_FOCUS value represents a lost focus event.

Public Instance Variables

```
public Object target
```

The *target* instance variable represents the object that is the target of the event.

```
public long when
```

The *when* instance variable represents the timestamp of the event.

```
public int id
```

The *id* instance variable represents the type of the event.

```
public int x
```

The *x* instance variable represents the x coordinate of the event.

```
public int y
```

The *y* instance variable represents the y coordinate of the event.

```
public int key
```

The *key* instance variable represents the key that was pressed to trigger the keyboard event (see the key values listed previously).

```
public int modifiers
```

The *modifiers* instance variable represents the state of the modifier keys.

```
public int clickCount
```

The *clickCount* instance variable represents the number of clicks during the mouse down event. If this event wasn't triggered by a mouse down action, this value is 0. It is 1 for a single click and 2 for a double click.

```
public Object arg
```

The *arg* instance variable represents an arbitrary argument.

```
public Event evt
```

The *evt* instance variable represents the next event. This is useful when multiple events are stored in an array or linked list.

 ## Event   📖→📦   Event   awt

```
public Event(Object target, long when, int id, int x, int y, int key,
➥ int modifiers, Object arg)
```

This Event() constructor constructs an event using the target, current time, event ID, location, key pressed, modifiers, and some argument.

▶ *target* is the target object for the event.

▶ *when* is the timestamp for the event.

▶ *id* is the event type.

▶ *x* is the x coordinate of the event.

▶ *y* is the y coordinate of the event.

▶ *key* is the key pressed that triggered a keyboard event.

▶ *modifiers* is the state of the modifier keys.

▶ *arg* is an arbitrary argument.

Event   Event   awt

```
public Event(Object target, long when, int id, int x, int y,
➥ int key, int modifiers)
```

This Event() constructor constructs an event using the target, current time, event ID, location, key pressed, and modifiers.

▶ *target* is the target object for the event.

▶ *when* is the timestamp for the event.

▶ *id* is the event type.

▶ *x* is the x coordinate of the event.

▶ *y* is the y coordinate of the event.

▶ *key* is the key pressed that triggered a keyboard event.

▶ *modifiers* contains the state of the modifier keys.

 Event   Event   awt

```
public Event(Object target, int id, Object arg)
```

This Event() constructor constructs an event using the target, event ID, and some argument.

▶ *target* is the target object for the event.

▶ *id* is the event type.

▶ *arg* is an arbitrary argument.

translate   Event   awt

```
public void translate(int x, int y)
```

The translate() method translates coordinates for a given component. If the object sending this event has targeted a certain component, this method translates the coordinates to make sense for that particular component.

▶ *x* is the x coordinate.

▶ *y* is the y coordinate.

shiftDown   Event   awt

```
public boolean shiftDown()
```

The shiftDown() method returns the current state of the Shift key.

↵ A Boolean value that is true if the Shift key is down and false if it is up.

controlDown Event awt

```
public boolean controlDown()
```

The controlDown() method returns the current state of the Control key.

 A Boolean value that is true if the Control key is down and false if it is up.

 metaDown Event awt

```
public boolean metaDown()
```

The metaDown() method returns the current state of the Meta key.

A Boolean value that is true if the Meta key is down and false if it is up.

toString Event

```
public String toString()
```

The toString() method returns the string representation of the current event.

A String value containing information on the event, including the *id*, *x*, *y*, *key*, *shiftDown*, *controlDown*, and *metaDown* values.

 # FileDialog awt

 Dialog

The class hierarchy for the FileDialog class derives from the class java.awt.Dialog. (See Listing 28.15.) A FileDialog is presented for a user to select a file. This dialog is a modal dialog; therefore, the calling thread is blocked until this dialog exits. FileDialog's overall derivation is shown in Figure 28.1.

Listing 28.15. Public members of java.awt.FileDialog.

```
public class FileDialog extends Dialog {
  public static final int LOAD
  public static final int SAVE
  public FileDialog(Frame parent, String title)
  public FileDialog(Frame parent, String title, int mode)
  public synchronized void addNotify()
  public int getMode()
  public String getDirectory()
  public void setDirectory(String dir)
  public String getFile()
  public void setFile(String file)
  public void setFilenameFilter(FilenameFilter filter)
  public FilenameFilter getFilenameFilter()
}
```

Public Static Values

`public static final int LOAD`

The LOAD static value represents the file load variable.

`public static final int SAVE`

The SAVE static value represents the file save variable.

 FileDialog   FileDialog   awt

`public FileDialog(Frame parent, String title)`

This `FileDialog()` constructor constructs a file dialog using a parent frame and a title string.

▶   *parent* is the parent frame of the `FileDialog`.

▶   *title* is a `String` containing the dialog's title.

 FileDialog   FileDialog   awt

`public FileDialog(Frame parent, String title, int mode)`

This `FileDialog()` constructor constructs a file dialog using a parent frame, a title string, and a mode value representing either a LOAD or SAVE dialog.

▶   *parent* is the parent frame of the `FileDialog`.

▶   *title* is a `String` containing the dialog's title.

▶   mode is an integer value representing the dialog mode (LOAD or SAVE).

addNotify   FileDialog   awt

`public synchronized void addNotify()`

addNotify() notifies the `FileDialog` to create a peer. Using a peer interface allows you to change the user interface of the `FileDialog` without changing its functionality.

↵   none

 getMode   FileDialog   awt

`public int getMode()`

getMode() returns the current mode of the `FileDialog`.

↵   An integer value representing the current mode (LOAD or SAVE) of the `FileDialog`.

getDirectory FileDialog awt

```
public String getDirectory()
```

The getDirectory() method returns the current directory of the FileDialog.

↵ A String value representing the FileDialog's current directory.

setDirectory FileDialog awt

```
public void setDirectory(String dir)
```

The setDirectory() method sets the current directory of the FileDialog.

▶ *dir* is a String value representing the directory to be set.

getFile FileDialog awt

```
public String getFile()
```

The getFile() method returns the currently selected file within the FileDialog.

↵ A String value representing the FileDialog's current file.

setFile FileDialog awt

```
public void setFile(String file)
```

The setFile() method sets the current file of the FileDialog.

▶ *file* is a String value representing the file to be set.

setFilenameFilter FileDialog awt

```
public void setFilenameFilter(FilenameFilter filter)
```

The setFilenameFilter() method sets the file filter for the FileDialog to the specified FilenameFilter.

▶ *filter* is a FilenameFilter representing the filter to be set. For more information on the FilenameFilter class, see the documentation in Chapter 31, "Package java.io."

getFilenameFilter FileDialog awt

```
public FilenameFilter getFilenameFilter()
```

The getFilenameFilter() method returns the current FilenameFilter being used by the FileDialog.

↵ A FilenameFilter object containing the file filter displayed by the FileDialog. For more information on the FilenameFilter class, see the documentation in Chapter 31.

FlowLayout

 Object

 LayoutManager

The class hierarchy for the FlowLayout class derives from the class java.lang.Object. (See Listing 28.16.) A FlowLayout implements the LayoutManager interface. This class lays out buttons from left to right until no more buttons fit on the Panel. FlowLayout's overall derivation is shown in Figure 28.1.

Listing 28.16. Public members of java.awt.FlowLayout.

```
public class FlowLayout implements LayoutManager {
  public static final int LEFT
  public static final int CENTER
  public static final int RIGHT
  public FlowLayout()
  public FlowLayout(int align)
  public FlowLayout(int align, int hgap, int vgap)
  public void addLayoutComponent(String name, Component comp)
  public void removeLayoutComponent(Component comp)
  public Dimension preferredLayoutSize(Container target)
  public Dimension minimumLayoutSize(Container target)
  public void layoutContainer(Container target)
  public String toString()
}
```

Public Static Values

public static final int LEFT

The LEFT static value represents the left alignment variable.

public static final int CENTER

The CENTER static value represents the center alignment variable.

public static final int RIGHT

The RIGHT static value represents the right alignment variable.

 FlowLayout FlowLayout awt

public FlowLayout()

This FlowLayout() constructor constructs a default FlowLayout class with a centered alignment.

 none

FlowLayout

```
public FlowLayout(int align)
```

This FlowLayout() constructor constructs a FlowLayout class using the specified alignment.

▶ align is the alignment value (LEFT, CENTER, or RIGHT).

FlowLayout

```
public FlowLayout(int align, int hgap, int vgap)
```

This FlowLayout() constructor constructs a FlowLayout class using the specified alignment and gap values.

▶ align is the alignment value (LEFT, CENTER, or RIGHT).

▶ hgap is the horizontal gap value.

▶ vgap is the vertical gap value.

addLayoutComponent

```
public void addLayoutComponent(String name, Component comp)
```

The addLayoutComponent() method adds a component to the FlowLayout class.

▶ name is a String value representing the name of the component to be added.

▶ comp is the component object to be added to the FlowLayout.

removeLayoutComponent

```
public void removeLayoutComponent(Component comp)
```

removeLayoutComponent() removes a component from the FlowLayout class.

▶ comp is a component object to be removed from the FlowLayout.

preferredLayoutSize

```
public Dimension preferredLayoutSize(Container target)
```

The preferredLayoutSize() method returns the preferred size for this FlowLayout given the components in the specified container.

▶ target is a Container object that is examined to determine the preferred layout size for this FlowLayout.

↵ A Dimension class containing the preferred size of the FlowLayout.

minimumLayoutSize   FlowLayout   awt

```
public Dimension minimumLayoutSize(Container target)
```

The `minimumLayoutSize()` method returns the minimum size for this `FlowLayout` given the components in the specified container.

▶ *target* is a `Container` object that is examined to determine the minimum layout size for this `FlowLayout`.

↵ A `Dimension` class containing the minimum size of the `FlowLayout`.

 layoutContainer   FlowLayout   awt

```
public void layoutContainer(Container target)
```

The `layoutContainer()` method lays out the components within the specified container.

▶ *target* is a `Container` class containing a set of components that are laid out according to the `FlowLayout` rules.

 toString   ▦→▲   awt

```
public String toString()
```

The `toString()` method returns a string representation of the `FlowLayout` class.

↵ A `String` containing information about the `FlowLayout`, including the `FlowLayout`'s name, alignment, *hgap*, and *vgap* values.

 # Font   awt

 Object

The class hierarchy for the `Font` class derives from the class `java.lang.Object`. (See Listing 28.17.) This class encapsulates a font. `Font`'s overall derivation is shown in Figure 28.1.

Listing 28.17. Public members of java.awt.Font.

```
public class Font {
    public static final int PLAIN
    public static final int BOLD
    public static final int ITALIC
    public Font(String name, int style, int size)
    public String getFamily()
    public String getName()
    public int getStyle()
    public int getSize()
```

continues

Listing 28.17. continued

```
  public boolean isPlain()
  public boolean isBold()
  public boolean isItalic()
  public static Font getFont(String nm)
  public static Font getFont(String nm, Font font)
  public int hashCode()
  public boolean equals(Object obj)
  public String toString()
}
```

Public Static Values

`public static final int PLAIN`

The PLAIN static value represents the plain style constant.

`public static final int BOLD`

The BOLD static value represents the bold style constant.

`public static final int ITALIC`

The ITALIC static value represents the italic style constant.

 Font Font awt

`public Font(String name, int style, int size)`

The Font() constructor constructs a Font of the specified name, style, and size.

▶ *name* is the name of the font to be created. The possible fonts that can be created can be determined by calling the Toolkit class's getFontList() method.

▶ *style* is the style (PLAIN, BOLD, and ITALIC) of the font to be created.

▶ *size* is the size of the font to be created.

 getFamily Font awt

`public String getFamily()`

getFamily() returns the font family that this font belongs to.

↵ A String value representing the Font's family name.

getName 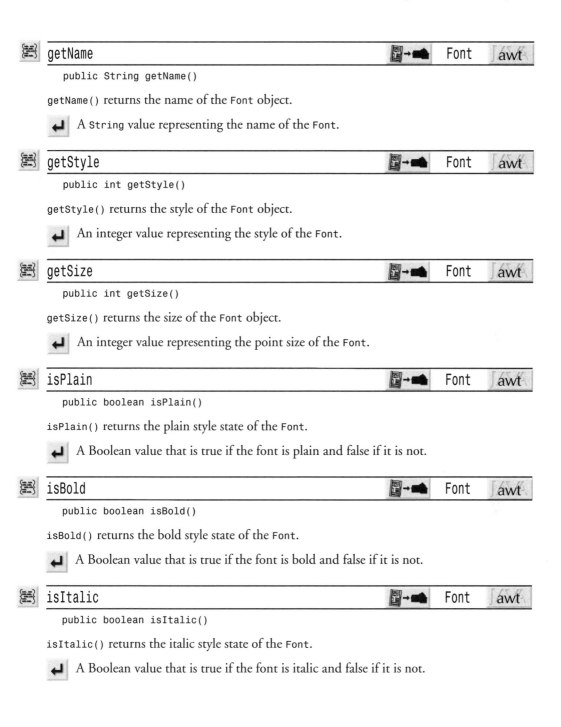 Font   awt

```
public String getName()
```

getName() returns the name of the Font object.

↵ A String value representing the name of the Font.

getStyle Font   awt

```
public int getStyle()
```

getStyle() returns the style of the Font object.

↵ An integer value representing the style of the Font.

getSize Font   awt

```
public int getSize()
```

getSize() returns the size of the Font object.

↵ An integer value representing the point size of the Font.

isPlain Font   awt

```
public boolean isPlain()
```

isPlain() returns the plain style state of the Font.

↵ A Boolean value that is true if the font is plain and false if it is not.

isBold Font   awt

```
public boolean isBold()
```

isBold() returns the bold style state of the Font.

↵ A Boolean value that is true if the font is bold and false if it is not.

isItalic Font   awt

```
public boolean isItalic()
```

isItalic() returns the italic style state of the Font.

↵ A Boolean value that is true if the font is italic and false if it is not.

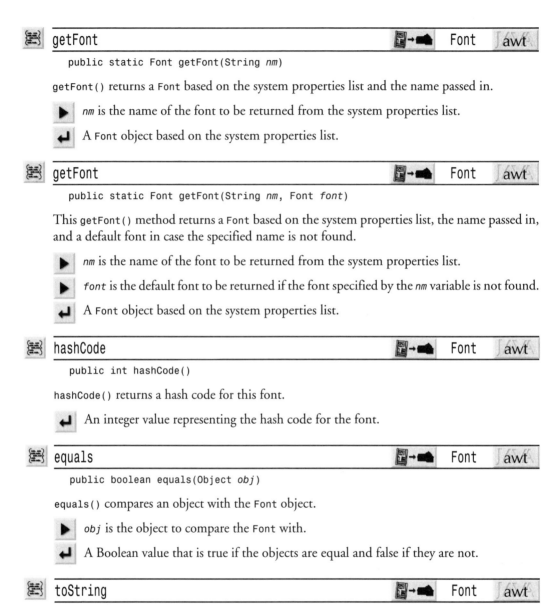

getFont   Font   awt

```
public static Font getFont(String nm)
```

getFont() returns a Font based on the system properties list and the name passed in.

▶ *nm* is the name of the font to be returned from the system properties list.

↵ A Font object based on the system properties list.

getFont   Font   awt

```
public static Font getFont(String nm, Font font)
```

This getFont() method returns a Font based on the system properties list, the name passed in, and a default font in case the specified name is not found.

▶ *nm* is the name of the font to be returned from the system properties list.

▶ *font* is the default font to be returned if the font specified by the *nm* variable is not found.

↵ A Font object based on the system properties list.

hashCode   Font   awt

```
public int hashCode()
```

hashCode() returns a hash code for this font.

↵ An integer value representing the hash code for the font.

equals   Font   awt

```
public boolean equals(Object obj)
```

equals() compares an object with the Font object.

▶ *obj* is the object to compare the Font with.

↵ A Boolean value that is true if the objects are equal and false if they are not.

toString   Font   awt

```
public String toString()
```

The toString() method returns a string representation of the Font.

↵ A String value containing the Font family, name, style, and size values.

FontMetrics

 Object

The class hierarchy for the FontMetrics class derives from the class java.lang.Object. (See Listing 28.18.) The FontMetrics class encapsulates a font metrics object containing font information. FontMetrics' overall derivation is shown in Figure 28.1.

Listing 28.18. Public members of java.awt.FontMetrics.

```
public abstract class FontMetrics {
  public Font getFont()
  public int getLeading()
  public int getAscent()
  public int getDescent()
  public int getHeight()
  public int getMaxAscent()
  public int getMaxDescent()
  public int getMaxDecent()
  public int getMaxAdvance()
  public int charWidth(int ch)
  public int charWidth(char ch)
  public int stringWidth(String str)
  public int charsWidth(char data[], int off, int len)
  public int bytesWidth(byte data[], int off, int len)
  public int[] getWidths()
  public String toString()
}
```

 getFont FontMetrics awt

```
public Font getFont()
```

The getFont() method returns the font that FontMetrics refers to.

 A Font class.

 getLeading FontMetrics awt

```
public int getLeading()
```

The getLeading() method gets the line spacing of the font.

 An integer value containing the standard leading, or line spacing, of the font. The line spacing of a font is the space reserved between the descent of a text character and the ascent of a text character below it.

getAscent   FontMetrics   awt

```
public int getAscent()
```

The getAscent() method gets the ascent value for a Font.

An integer value containing the ascent value for a Font. This value is the distance from the bottom of a character to its top.

getDescent   FontMetrics   awt

```
public int getDescent()
```

The getDescent() method gets the descent value for a Font.

An integer value containing the descent value for a Font. This value is the bottom coordinate of a character.

getHeight   FontMetrics   awt

```
public int getHeight()
```

The getHeight() method gets the height of a line of text using the current Font.

An integer value containing the height of a line of text. This value is calculated by adding the ascent, descent, and leading values.

getMaxAscent   FontMetrics   awt

```
public int getMaxAscent()
```

getMaxAscent() returns the maximum value of a font's ascent.

An integer value containing the maximum value of a font's ascent for all of that font's characters.

getMaxDescent   FontMetrics   awt

```
public int getMaxDescent()
```

getMaxDescent() returns the maximum value of a font's descent.

An integer value containing the maximum value of a font's descent for all of that font's characters.

getMaxDecent FontMetrics   awt

```
public int getMaxDecent()
```

The getMaxDecent() method is provided only for backward compatibility. It simply calls the getMaxDescent() method.

 An integer value containing the maximum value of a font's descent for all of that font's characters.

 getMaxAdvance FontMetric   awt

```
public int getMaxAdvance()
```

The getMaxAdvance() method gets the maximum amount for a character's advance value. The advance is the amount that is advanced from the beginning of one character to the next character.

 charWidth FontMetrics   awt

```
public int charWidth(int ch)
```

charWidth() returns the width of a particular character for the current font.

▶ *ch* is an integer value representing the character to be checked.

 An integer value representing the width of the specified character.

 charWidth FontMetrics   awt

```
public int charWidth(char ch)
```

This charWidth() method returns the width of a particular character for the current font.

▶ *ch* is a char value representing the character to be checked.

◀ An integer value representing the width of the specified character.

 stringWidth FontMetrics   awt

```
public int stringWidth(String str)
```

The stringWidth() method returns the width of a specified string using the current font.

▶ *str* is a string representing the characters to be checked.

◀ An integer value representing the advance width of the specified string.

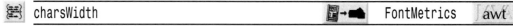

charsWidth — FontMetrics — awt

```
public int charsWidth(char data[], int off, int len)
```

The charsWidth() method returns the width of a specified string of characters using the current font.

▶ *data* is an array of characters to be checked.

▶ *off* is an integer value representing the offset into the array where the string starts.

▶ *len* is the number of characters to be measured.

↵ An integer value representing the advance width of the specified string.

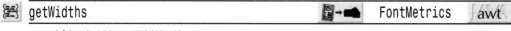

bytesWidth — FontMetrics — awt

```
public int bytesWidth(byte data[], int off, int len)
```

The bytesWidth() method returns the width of a specified array of bytes.

▶ *data* is an array of bytes to be checked.

▶ *off* is an integer value representing the offset into the array where the string starts.

▶ *len* is the number of bytes to be measured.

↵ An integer value representing the advance width of the specified string.

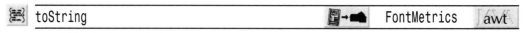

getWidths — FontMetrics — awt

```
public int[] getWidths()
```

The getWidths() method gets the advance widths of the first 256 characters of the font.

↵ An integer array containing the advance widths of the first 256 characters of the font.

toString — FontMetrics — awt

```
public String toString()
```

The toString() method returns a string representation of the FontMetrics class.

↵ A String value containing the FontMetrics' name, font, ascent, descent, and height.

 # Frame awt

 Window

MenuContainer

The class hierarchy for the `Frame` class derives from the class `java.awt.Window`. (See Listing 28.19.) A `Frame` class represents a basic window. `Frame`'s overall derivation is shown in Figure 28.1.

Listing 28.19. Public members of `java.awt.Frame`.

```
public class Frame extends Window implements MenuContainer {
    public static final int     DEFAULT_CURSOR
    public static final int     CROSSHAIR_CURSOR
    public static final int     TEXT_CURSOR
    public static final int     WAIT_CURSOR
    public static final int     SW_RESIZE_CURSOR
    public static final int     SE_RESIZE_CURSOR
    public static final int     NW_RESIZE_CURSOR
    public static final int     NE_RESIZE_CURSOR
    public static final int     N_RESIZE_CURSOR
    public static final int     S_RESIZE_CURSOR
    public static final int     W_RESIZE_CURSOR
    public static final int     E_RESIZE_CURSOR
    public static final int     HAND_CURSOR
    public static final int     MOVE_CURSOR
    public Frame()
    public Frame(String title)
    public synchronized void addNotify()
    public String getTitle()
    public void setTitle(String title)
    public Image getIconImage()
    public void setIconImage(Image image)
    public MenuBar getMenuBar()
    public synchronized void setMenuBar(MenuBar mb)
    public synchronized void remove(MenuComponent m)
    public synchronized void dispose()
    public boolean isResizable()
    public void setResizable(boolean resizable)
    public void setCursor(int cursorType)
    public int getCursorType()
}
```

Public Static Values

```
public static final int     DEFAULT_CURSOR
```

The DEFAULT_CURSOR static value represents the default cursor.

```
public static final int     CROSSHAIR_CURSOR
```

The CROSSHAIR_CURSOR static value represents the crosshair cursor.

```
public static final int     TEXT_CURSOR
```

The TEXT_CURSOR static value represents the text cursor.

```
public static final int     WAIT_CURSOR
```

The WAIT_CURSOR static value represents the wait cursor.

```
public static final int     SW_RESIZE_CURSOR
```

The SW_RESIZE_CURSOR static value represents the southwest resize cursor.

```
public static final int     SE_RESIZE_CURSOR
```

The SE_RESIZE_CURSOR static value represents the southeast resize cursor.

```
public static final int     NW_RESIZE_CURSOR
```

The NW_RESIZE_CURSOR static value represents the northwest resize cursor.

```
public static final int     NE_RESIZE_CURSOR
```

The NE_RESIZE_CURSOR static value represents the northeast resize cursor.

```
public static final int     N_RESIZE_CURSOR
```

The N_RESIZE_CURSOR static value represents the north resize cursor.

```
public static final int     S_RESIZE_CURSOR
```

The S_RESIZE_CURSOR static value represents the south resize cursor.

```
public static final int     W_RESIZE_CURSOR
```

The W_RESIZE_CURSOR static value represents the west resize cursor.

```
public static final int     E_RESIZE_CURSOR
```

The E_RESIZE_CURSOR static value represents the east resize cursor.

```
public static final int     HAND_CURSOR
```

The HAND_CURSOR static value represents the hand cursor.

```
public static final int     MOVE_CURSOR
```

The MOVE_CURSOR static value represents the move cursor.

 Frame   ⊞→◼   Frame   awt

```
public Frame()
```

The Frame() constructor constructs a default frame that is invisible and that uses the BorderLayout layout manager.

Frame Frame   awt

```
public Frame(String title)
```

This `Frame()` constructor constructs a default frame using the specified title that is invisible and that uses the `BorderLayout` layout manager.

▶ *title* is a `String` value containing the `Frame`'s title string.

addNotify   Frame   awt

```
public synchronized void addNotify()
```

The `addNotify()` method creates a peer interface for the `Frame`. Peer interfaces allow you to change the user interface of the frame without changing its functionality.

↵ none

getTitle   Frame   awt

```
public String getTitle()
```

`getTitle()` returns the frame's title.

↵ A `String` value representing the title of the `Frame`.

setTitle   Frame   awt

```
public void setTitle(String title)
```

`setTitle()` sets the frame's title.

▶ *title* is a `String` value representing the title of the `Frame`.

getIconImage   Frame   awt

```
public Image getIconImage()
```

The `getIconImage()` method returns an `Image` representing the iconized image of the `Frame`.

↵ An `Image` class representing the iconized image of the frame.

setIconImage   Frame   awt

```
public void setIconImage(Image image)
```

`setIconImage()` sets the image that is used when the frame is iconized.

▶ *image* is an `Image` class that is displayed when the frame is iconized.

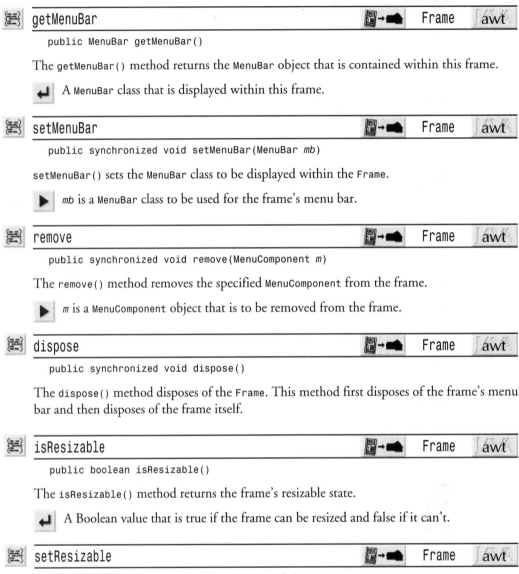

getMenuBar   Frame   awt

`public MenuBar getMenuBar()`

The `getMenuBar()` method returns the `MenuBar` object that is contained within this frame.

A `MenuBar` class that is displayed within this frame.

setMenuBar   Frame   awt

`public synchronized void setMenuBar(MenuBar mb)`

`setMenuBar()` sets the `MenuBar` class to be displayed within the `Frame`.

mb is a `MenuBar` class to be used for the frame's menu bar.

remove   Frame   awt

`public synchronized void remove(MenuComponent m)`

The `remove()` method removes the specified `MenuComponent` from the frame.

m is a `MenuComponent` object that is to be removed from the frame.

dispose   Frame   awt

`public synchronized void dispose()`

The `dispose()` method disposes of the `Frame`. This method first disposes of the frame's menu bar and then disposes of the frame itself.

isResizable   Frame   awt

`public boolean isResizable()`

The `isResizable()` method returns the frame's resizable state.

A Boolean value that is true if the frame can be resized and false if it can't.

setResizable   Frame   awt

`public void setResizable(boolean resizable)`

The `setResizable()` method sets the frame's resizable state.

A Boolean value that is true if the frame can be resized and false if it can't.

setCursor   Frame   awt

```
public void setCursor(int cursorType)
```

The setCursor() method sets the cursor to be displayed within the frame.

▶ *cursorType* is an integer value representing the cursor to be displayed. This can be any of the frame's static values such as WAIT_CURSOR, MOVE_CURSOR, and so on.

 getCursorType   Frame   awt

```
public int getCursorType()
```

The getCursorType() method returns the frame's current cursor type.

↵ An integer value representing the current cursor type for the frame.

 # Graphics   Java

 Object

The class hierarchy for the Graphics class derives from the class java.lang.Object. (See Listing 28.20.) The Graphics class represents the base class for all types of graphics contexts. Graphics's overall derivation is shown in Figure 28.1.

Listing 28.20. Public members of java.awt.Graphics.

```
public abstract class Graphics {
  public abstract Graphics create()
  public Graphics create(int x, int y, int width, int height)
  public abstract void translate(int x, int y)
  public abstract Color getColor()
  public abstract void setColor(Color c)
  public abstract void setPaintMode()
  public abstract void setXORMode(Color c1)
  public abstract Font getFont()
  public abstract void setFont(Font font)
  public FontMetrics getFontMetrics()
  public abstract FontMetrics getFontMetrics(Font f)
  public abstract Rectangle getClipRect()
  public abstract void clipRect(int x, int y, int width, int height)
  public abstract void copyArea(int x, int y, int width, int height, int dx,
      int dy)
  public abstract void drawLine(int x1, int y1, int x2, int y2)
  public abstract void fillRect(int x, int y, int width, int height)
  public void drawRect(int x, int y, int width, int height)
  public abstract void clearRect(int x, int y, int width, int height)
  public abstract void drawRoundRect(int x, int y, int width, int height,
      int arcWidth, int arcHeight)
```

continues

Listing 28.20. continued

```
public abstract void fillRoundRect(int x, int y, int width, int height,
     int arcWidth, int arcHeight)
public void draw3DRect(int x, int y, int width, int height, boolean raised)
public void fill3DRect(int x, int y, int width, int height, boolean raised)
public abstract void drawOval(int x, int y, int width, int height)
public abstract void fillOval(int x, int y, int width, int height)
public abstract void drawArc(int x, int y, int width, int height,
     int startAngle, int arcAngle)
public abstract void fillArc(int x, int y, int width, int height,
     int startAngle, int arcAngle)
public abstract void drawPolygon(int xPoints[], int yPoints[], int nPoints)
public void drawPolygon(Polygon p)
public abstract void fillPolygon(int xPoints[], int yPoints[], int nPoints)
public void fillPolygon(Polygon p)
public abstract void drawString(String str, int x, int y)
public void drawChars(char data[], int offset, int length, int x, int y)
public void drawBytes(byte data[], int offset, int length, int x, int y)
public abstract boolean drawImage(Image img, int x, int y,
                                  ImageObserver observer)
public abstract boolean drawImage(Image img, int x, int y,
                                  int width, int height,
                                  ImageObserver observer)
public abstract boolean drawImage(Image img, int x, int y,
                                  Color bgcolor,
                                  ImageObserver observer)
public abstract boolean drawImage(Image img, int x, int y,
                                  int width, int height,
                                  Color bgcolor,
                                  ImageObserver observer)
public abstract void dispose()
public void finalize()
public String toString()
}
```

---

 create Graphics `awt`

```
public abstract Graphics create()
```

This abstract function creates a new graphics object.

---

 create Graphics `awt`

```
public Graphics create(int x, int y, int width, int height)
```

The create() method creates a new Graphics object using the specified parameters.

▶   *x* is the x coordinate of the graphics context.

▶   *y* is the y coordinate of the graphics context.

▶   *width* is the width of the graphics context.

▶ *height* is the height of the graphics context.

↵ A `Graphics` class corresponding to the `create()` method's specifications.

translate  Graphics awt

```
public abstract void translate(int x, int y)
```

The `translate()` method translates the `Graphics` object to the new x and y origin coordinates.

▶ *x* is the new x origin coordinate.

▶ *y* is the new y origin coordinate.

getColor  Graphics awt

```
public abstract Color getColor()
```

The `getColor()` method returns the current color.

↵ A `Color` object representing the current color used for drawing operations. For more information on the `Color` class, see the documentation earlier in this chapter.

setColor Graphics awt

```
public abstract void setColor(Color c)
```

The `setColor()` method sets the current color.

▶ *c* is a `Color` object to be used for graphics drawing operations. For more information on the `Color` class, see the documentation earlier in this chapter.

setPaintMode Graphics awt

```
public abstract void setPaintMode()
```

The `setPaintMode()` method sets the paint mode to overwrite the destination with the current color.

setXORMode Graphics awt

```
public abstract void setXORMode(Color c1)
```

The `setXORMode()` method sets the paint mode to XOR the current colors with the specified color. This means that when redrawing over an existing area, colors that match the current color are changed to the specified color *c1* and vice versa.

▶ *c1* is the `Color` object specified to be XORed with the current color. For more information on the `Color` class, see the documentation earlier in this chapter.

getFont Graphics   awt

```
public abstract Font getFont()
```

The getFont() method returns the current font used for the graphics context.

A Font object representing the graphics context's current Font. For more information on the Font class, see the documentation earlier in this chapter.

setFont Graphics   awt

```
public abstract void setFont(Font font)
```

The setFont() method sets the graphics context's font.

font is a Font object that is used as the current font. For more information on the Font class, see the documentation earlier in this chapter.

getFontMetrics Graphics   awt

```
public FontMetrics getFontMetrics()
```

The getFontMetrics() method returns the font metrics for the current font.

A FontMetrics object representing the font metrics for the current font. For more information on the FontMetrics class, see the documentation earlier in this chapter.

getFontMetrics Graphics   awt

```
public abstract FontMetrics getFontMetrics(Font f)
```

This getFontMetrics() method returns the font metrics for the specified font.

A FontMetrics object representing the font metrics for the specified font. For more information on the FontMetrics class, see the documentation earlier in this chapter.

getClipRect Graphics   awt

```
public abstract Rectangle getClipRect()
```

The getClipRect() method returns the current clipping rectangle for the Graphics class.

A Rectangle object representing the current clipping rectangle. For more information on the Rectangle class, see the documentation later in this chapter.

clipRect

Graphics awt

```
public abstract void clipRect(int x, int y, int width, int height)
```

The clipRect() method sets the current clipping rectangle for the Graphics class.

▶ *x* is the x coordinate of the clipping rectangle.

▶ *y* is the y coordinate of the clipping rectangle.

▶ *width* is the width of the clipping rectangle.

▶ *height* is the height of the clipping rectangle.

copyArea

Graphics awt

```
public abstract void copyArea(int x, int y, int width, int height, int dx, int dy)
```

The copyArea() method copies a specified section of the screen to another location.

▶ *x* is the x coordinate of the region to be copied.

▶ *y* is the y coordinate of the region to be copied.

▶ *width* is the width of the region to be copied.

▶ *height* is the height of the region to be copied.

▶ *dx* is the horizontal distance of the region to be copied to.

▶ *dy* is the vertical distance of the region to be copied to.

drawLine

Graphics awt

```
public abstract void drawLine(int x1, int y1, int x2, int y2)
```

The drawLine() method draws a line on the graphics context from one point to another point specified by the input parameters.

▶ *x1* is the x coordinate of the line's starting point.

▶ *y1* is the y coordinate of the line's starting point.

▶ *x2* is the x coordinate of the line's ending point.

▶ *y2* is the y coordinate of the line's ending point.

fillRect 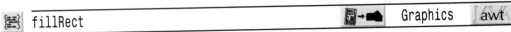 Graphics awt

```
public abstract void fillRect(int x, int y, int width, int height)
```

The fillRect() method fills the specified rectangular region with the current Color.

▶ *x* is the x coordinate of the rectangle to be filled.

▶ *y* is the y coordinate of the rectangle to be filled.

▶ *width* is the width of the rectangle to be filled.

▶ *height* is the height of the rectangle to be filled.

drawRect Graphics awt

```
public void drawRect(int x, int y, int width, int height)
```

The drawRect() method draws the outline of a rectangle using the current color and the specified dimensions.

▶ *x* is the x coordinate of the rectangle to be drawn.

▶ *y* is the y coordinate of the rectangle to be drawn.

▶ *width* is the width of the rectangle to be drawn.

▶ *height* is the height of the rectangle to be drawn.

clearRect Graphics awt

```
public abstract void clearRect(int x, int y, int width, int height)
```

The clearRect() method clears a rectangle by filling it with the current background color of the current drawing surface.

▶ *x* is the x coordinate of the rectangle to be cleared.

▶ *y* is the y coordinate of the rectangle to be cleared.

▶ *width* is the width of the rectangle to be cleared.

▶ *height* is the height of the rectangle to be cleared.

drawRoundRect Graphics | awt

```
public abstract void drawRoundRect(int x, int y, int width, int height,
   ➥ int arcWidth, int arcHeight)
```

The drawRoundRect() method draws the outline of a rectangle with rounded edges using the current color and the specified coordinates.

▶ *x* is the x coordinate of the rectangle to be drawn.

▶ *y* is the y coordinate of the rectangle to be drawn

▶ *width* is the width of the rectangle to be drawn.

▶ *height* is the height of the rectangle to be drawn.

▶ *arcWidth* is the horizontal diameter of the arc at the four corners.

▶ *arcHeight* is the vertical diameter of the arc at the four corners.

 fillRoundRect Graphics | awt

```
public abstract void fillRoundRect(int x, int y, int width, int height,
   ➥ int arcWidth, int arcHeight)
```

The fillRoundRect() method fills a rectangle with rounded edges using the current color and the specified coordinates.

▶ *x* is the x coordinate of the rectangle to be filled.

▶ *y* is the y coordinate of the rectangle to be filled.

▶ *width* is the width of the rectangle to be filled.

▶ *height* is the height of the rectangle to be filled.

▶ *arcWidth* is the horizontal diameter of the arc at the four corners.

▶ *arcHeight* is the vertical diameter of the arc at the four corners.

 draw3DRect Graphics | awt

```
public void draw3DRect(int x, int y, int width, int height, boolean raised)
```

The draw3DRect() method draws a highlighted 3D rectangle at a default viewing angle.

▶ *x* is the x coordinate of the rectangle to be drawn.

▶ *y* is the y coordinate of the rectangle to be drawn.

▶ *width* is the width of the rectangle to be drawn.

▶ *height* is the height of the rectangle to be drawn.

▶ *raised* is a Boolean value determining whether the rectangle is raised or not.

fill3DRect Graphics awt

```
public void fill3DRect(int x, int y, int width, int height, boolean raised)
```

The fill3DRect() method fills a highlighted 3D rectangle using the current color and specified coordinates at a default viewing angle.

 x is the x coordinate of the rectangle to be filled.

▶ *y* is the y coordinate of the rectangle to be filled.

▶ *width* is the width of the rectangle to be filled.

▶ *height* is the height of the rectangle to be filled.

▶ *raised* is a Boolean value determining whether the rectangle is raised or not.

 drawOval Graphics awt

```
public abstract void drawOval(int x, int y, int width, int height)
```

The drawOval() method draws the outline of an oval shape using the current color and the specified coordinates. The oval is drawn inside the rectangle represented by the input coordinates.

▶ *x* is the x coordinate of the rectangle to draw the oval within.

▶ *y* is the y coordinate of the rectangle to draw the oval within.

▶ *width* is the width of the rectangle to draw the oval within.

▶ *height* is the height of the rectangle to draw the oval within.

 fillOval Graphics awt

```
public abstract void fillOval(int x, int y, int width, int height)
```

The fillOval() method fills an oval using the current color and the specified coordinates. The oval is drawn inside the rectangle represented by the input coordinates.

▶ *x* is the x coordinate of the rectangle to draw the oval within.

▶ *y* is the y coordinate of the rectangle to draw the oval within.

▶ *width* is the width of the rectangle to draw the oval within.

▶ *height* is the height of the rectangle to draw the oval within.

drawArc   Graphics   awt

```
public abstract void drawArc(int x, int y, int width, int height,
➥ int startAngle, int arcAngle)
```

The drawArc() method draws an arc outline using the current color that is bounded by the specified input coordinates. Note that 0 degrees represents the 3 o'clock position and that positive angles are measured in a counterclockwise direction.

▶ *x* is the x coordinate of the rectangle to draw the arc within.

▶ *y* is the y coordinate of the rectangle to draw the arc within.

▶ *width* is the width of the rectangle to draw the arc within.

▶ *height* is the height of the rectangle to draw the arc within.

▶ *startAngle* is the starting angle of the arc to be drawn.

▶ *arcAngle* is the angle of the arc relative to the start angle.

 fillArc   Graphics   awt

```
public abstract void fillArc(int x, int y, int width, int height,
➥ int startAngle, int arcAngle)
```

The fillArc() method fills an arc using the current color that is bounded by the specified input coordinates. Note that 0 degrees represents the 3 o'clock position and that positive angles are measured in a counterclockwise direction.

▶ *x* is the x coordinate of the rectangle to draw the arc within.

▶ *y* is the y coordinate of the rectangle to draw the arc within.

▶ *width* is the width of the rectangle to draw the arc within.

▶ *height* is the height of the rectangle to draw the arc within.

▶ *startAngle* is the starting angle of the arc to be drawn.

▶ *arcAngle* is the angle of the arc relative to the start angle.

drawPolygon   Graphics   awt

```
public abstract void drawPolygon(int xPoints[], int yPoints[], int nPoints)
```

The drawPolygon() method draws a polygon using the current color and the specified coordinates.

▶ *xPoints* is an array of integers containing the starting x coordinates for each edge of the polygon.

▶ *yPoints* is an array of integers containing the starting y coordinates for each edge of the polygon.

▶ *nPoints* is an integer value representing the number of edges of the polygon.

drawPolygon   Graphics   awt

```
public void drawPolygon(Polygon p)
```

This drawPolygon() method draws a polygon using the specified Polygon class.

▶ *p* is a Polygon class containing the coordinates for the polygon to be drawn. For more information on the Polygon class, see the documentation later in this chapter.

fillPolygon   Graphics   awt

```
public abstract void fillPolygon(int xPoints[], int yPoints[], int nPoints)
```

The fillPolygon() method fills a polygon using the current color and the specified coordinates.

▶ *xPoints* is an array of integers containing the starting x coordinates for each edge of the polygon.

▶ *yPoints* is an array of integers containing the starting y coordinates for each edge of the polygon.

▶ *nPoints* is an integer value representing the number of edges of the polygon.

fillPolygon   Graphics   awt

```
public void fillPolygon(Polygon p)
```

This fillPolygon() method fills a polygon using the specified Polygon class and the current color.

▶ *p* is a Polygon class containing the coordinates for the polygon to be drawn. For more information on the Polygon class, see the documentation later in this chapter.

drawString   Graphics   awt

```
public abstract void drawString(String str, int x, int y)
```

The drawString() method draws a string using the current font at the specified coordinates.

► *str* is the string to be displayed.

► *x* is the x coordinate of where the string is drawn.

► *y* is the y coordinate of where the string is drawn.

drawChars   Graphics   awt

```
public void drawChars(char data[], int offset, int length, int x, int y)
```

The drawChars() method draws a string using the current font at the specified coordinates.

► *data* is an array of characters.

► *offset* is the offset within the array of characters where the displayed string starts.

► *length* is the number of characters to draw.

► *x* is the x coordinate of where the string is drawn.

► *y* is the y coordinate of where the string is drawn.

drawBytes   Graphics   awt

```
public void drawBytes(byte data[], int offset, int length, int x, int y)
```

The drawChars() method draws a string using the current font at the specified coordinates.

► *data* is an array of bytes.

► *offset* is the offset within the array of bytes where the displayed string starts.

► *length* is the number of bytes to draw.

► *x* is the x coordinate of where the string is drawn.

► *y* is the y coordinate of where the string is drawn.

drawImage   Graphics   awt

```
public abstract boolean drawImage(Image img, int x, int y,
➥ ImageObserver observer)
```

The drawImage() method draws an image at a specified location.

► *img* is an Image class to be drawn using the graphics context.

► *x* is the x coordinate of where the image is drawn.

▶ *y* is the y coordinate of where the image is drawn.

▶ *observer* is an `ImageObserver` interface that notifies when the drawing is done.

↵ A Boolean value indicating the success or failure of the draw operation.

---

drawImage Graphics   awt

```
public abstract boolean drawImage(Image img, int x, int y, int width,
➡ int height, ImageObserver observer)
```

This `drawImage()` method draws an image at a specified location within the specified bounding rectangle.

▶ *img* is an `Image` class to be drawn using the graphics context.

▶ *x* is the x coordinate of where the image is drawn.

▶ *y* is the y coordinate of where the image is drawn.

▶ *width* is the width of the rectangle to draw the image within.

▶ *height* is the height of the rectangle to draw the image within.

▶ *observer* is an `ImageObserver` interface that notifies when the drawing is done.

↵ A Boolean value indicating the success or failure of the draw operation.

---

drawImage   Graphics   awt

```
public abstract boolean drawImage(Image img, int x, int y, Color bgcolor,
➡ ImageObserver observer)
```

This `drawImage()` method draws an image at a specified location using the specified background color.

▶ *img* is an `Image` class to be drawn using the graphics context.

▶ *x* is the x coordinate of where the image is drawn.

▶ *y* is the y coordinate of where the image is drawn.

▶ *bgcolor* is the background color to be used.

▶ *observer* is an `ImageObserver` interface that notifies when the drawing is done.

↵ A Boolean value indicating the success or failure of the draw operation.

drawImage  Graphics awt

```
public abstract boolean drawImage(Image img, int x, int y, int width,
➡ int height, Color bgcolor, ImageObserver observer)
```

The drawImage() method draws an image at a specified location within a specified bounding rectangle using a specified background color.

▶ *img* is an Image class to be drawn using the graphics context.

▶ *x* is the x coordinate of where the image is drawn.

▶ *y* is the y coordinate of where the image is drawn.

▶ *width* is the width of the bounding rectangle.

▶ *height* is the height of the bounding rectangle.

▶ *bgcolor* is the background color to be used.

▶ *observer* is an ImageObserver interface that notifies when the drawing is done.

↵ A Boolean value indicating the success or failure of the draw operation.

dispose  Graphics awt

```
public abstract void dispose()
```

The dispose() method disposes of the Graphics object.

↵ none

finalize Graphics awt

```
public void finalize()
```

The finalize() method disposes of the Graphics object once it is no longer referenced.

↵ none

toString Graphics awt

```
public String toString()
```

The toString() method returns a string representation of the Graphics object.

↵ A String containing the Graphics class name, current color, and current font.

GridBagConstraints

➕ Object

⚡ Cloneable

The class hierarchy for the GridBagConstraints class derives from the class java.lang.Object. (See Listing 28.21.) A GridBagConstraints class is used in conjunction with a GridBagLayout in order to specify the constraints of the objects being laid out. GridBagConstraints' overall derivation is shown in Figure 28.1.

Listing 28.21. Public members of java.awt.GridBagConstraints.

```
public class GridBagConstraints implements Cloneable {
  public static final int RELATIVE
  public static final int REMAINDER
  public static final int NONE
  public static final int BOTH
  public static final int HORIZONTAL
  public static final int VERTICAL
  public static final int CENTER
  public static final int NORTH
  public static final int NORTHEAST
  public static final int EAST
  public static final int SOUTHEAST
  public static final int SOUTH
  public static final int SOUTHWEST
  public static final int WEST
  public static final int NORTHWEST
  public int gridx, gridy, gridwidth, gridheight
  public double weightx, weighty
  public int anchor, fill
  public Insets insets
  public int ipadx, ipady
  public GridBagConstraints()
  public Object clone()
}
```

Public Static Values

public static final int RELATIVE

A public static value representing the relative constraint.

public static final int REMAINDER

A public static value representing the remainder constraint.

public static final int NONE

A public static value representing the none constraint.

```
public static final int BOTH
```

A public static value representing the both constraint.

```
public static final int HORIZONTAL
```

A public static value representing the horizontal constraint.

```
public static final int VERTICAL
```

A public static value representing the vertical constraint.

```
public static final int CENTER
```

A public static value representing the center constraint.

```
public static final int NORTH
```

A public static value representing the north constraint.

```
public static final int NORTHEAST
```

A public static value representing the northeast constraint.

```
public static final int EAST
```

A public static value representing the east constraint.

```
public static final int SOUTHEAST
```

A public static value representing the southeast constraint.

```
public static final int SOUTH
```

A public static value representing the south constraint.

```
public static final int SOUTHWEST
```

A public static value representing the southwest constraint.

```
public static final int WEST
```

A public static value representing the west constraint.

```
public static final int NORTHWEST
```

A public static value representing the northwest constraint.

Public Instance Variables

```
public int gridx
```

The *gridx* variable stores the grid x coordinate.

`public int gridy`

The `gridy` variable stores the grid y coordinate.

`public int gridwidth`

The `gridwidth` variable stores the grid bounding rectangle width.

`public int gridheight`

The `gridheight` variable stores the grid bounding rectangle height.

`public double weightx`

The `weightx` variable stores the horizontal space for a component to reserve for itself. If this is set to zero (the default), all components within a row are bunched together in the center of the row.

`public double weighty`

The `weighty` variable stores the vertical space for a component to reserve for itself. If this is set to zero (the default), all components within a column are bunched together in the center of the column.

`public int anchor`

The `anchor` variable determines how to display a component when it is smaller than its display area. Valid values for this variable are CENTER (the default), NORTH, NORTHEAST, EAST, SOUTHEAST, SOUTH, SOUTHWEST, WEST, and NORTHWEST.

`public int fill`

The `fill` variable determines how to display a component when it is larger than its display area. Valid values for this variable are NONE, HORIZONTAL, VERTICAL, and BOTH.

`public Insets insets`

The `insets` variable determines the space between the component and its bounding area. For more information on the Insets class, see the documentation later in this chapter.

`public int ipadx`

The `ipadx` variable determines the amount of padding to always add to the component on its left and right sides.

`public int ipady`

The `ipady` variable determines the amount of padding to always add to the component on its top and bottom sides.

GridBagConstraints   GridBagConstraints   awt

```
public GridBagConstraints()
```

The GridBagConstraints() constructor creates a GridBagConstraints class containing default values. The default values are

```
gridx = RELATIVE;
gridy = RELATIVE
gridwidth = 1
gridheight = 1

weightx = 0
weighty = 0
anchor = CENTER
fill = NONE

insets = new Insets(0, 0, 0, 0)
ipadx = 0
ipady = 0
```

 clone   GridBagConstraints   awt

```
public Object clone()
```

The clone() method creates a clone of this GridBagConstraints object.

 An Object object representing a clone of this GridBagConstraints object.

 # GridBagLayout   awt

 Object

 LayoutManager

The class hierarchy for the GridBagLayout class derives from the class java.lang.Object. (See Listing 28.22.) The GridBagLayout implements the LayoutManager interface. This class uses a rectangular grid of cells to lay out components within the cells. Each component is associated with a GridBagConstraints object that controls how the component is actually laid out within the grid. GridBagLayout's overall derivation is shown in Figure 28.1.

Listing 28.22. Public members of java.awt.GridBagLayout.

```
public class GridBagLayout implements LayoutManager {
    public int columnWidths[]
    public int rowHeights[]
    public double columnWeights[]
    public double rowWeights[]
    public GridBagLayout()
```

continues

Listing 28.22. continued

```
public void setConstraints(Component comp, GridBagConstraints constraints)
public GridBagConstraints getConstraints(Component comp)
public Point getLayoutOrigin()
public int [][] getLayoutDimensions()
public double [][] getLayoutWeights()
public Point location(int x, int y)
public void addLayoutComponent(String name, Component comp)
public void removeLayoutComponent(Component comp)
public Dimension preferredLayoutSize(Container parent)
public Dimension minimumLayoutSize(Container parent)
public void layoutContainer(Container parent)
public String toString()
}
```

Public Instance Variables

public int *columnWidths*[ ]

The *columnWidths* variable is an array of integers representing the widths of each column used by the GridBagLayout.

public int *rowHeights*[ ]

The *rowHeights* variable is an array of integers representing the heights of each row used by the GridBagLayout.

public double *columnWeights*[ ]

The *columnWeights* variable is an array of doubles representing the space to be distributed for each column.

public double *rowWeights*[ ]

The *rowWeights* variable is an array of doubles representing the space to be distributed for each row.

 GridBagLayout   GridBagLayout   awt

public GridBagLayout()

The GridBagLayout() constructor constructs a GridBagLayout class for use in laying out components on a form.

setConstraints GridBagLayout awt

`public void setConstraints(Component comp, GridBagConstraints constraints)`

The `setConstraints()` method sets the `GridBagConstraints` for the specified component.

▶ `comp` is a `Component` to be modified within the `GridBagLayout`.

▶ `constraints` is the `GridBagConstraints` that is applied to the component.

getConstraints GridBagLayout awt

`public GridBagConstraints getConstraints(Component comp)`

The `getConstraints()` method returns the constraints currently applied to the specified component.

▶ `comp` is a `Component` managed by the `GridBagLayout`.

↵ A `GridBagConstraints` class representing the constraints placed upon the specified component.

getLayoutOrigin GridBagLayout awt

`public Point getLayoutOrigin()`

The `getLayoutOrigin()` method returns the origin of the layout manager.

↵ A `Point` class representing the origin of the `GridBagLayout`. For more information on the `Point` class, see the documentation later in this chapter.

getLayoutDimensions GridBagLayout awt

`public int [][] getLayoutDimensions()`

The `getLayoutDimensions()` method returns an array of dimensions with an element for each component.

↵ An array containing layout dimensions for components managed by the `GridBagLayout`.

getLayoutWeights GridBagLayout awt

`public double [][] getLayoutWeights()`

The `getLayoutWeights()` method returns an array of weights with an element for each component.

↵ An array containing layout weights for components managed by the `GridBagLayout`.

location   GridBagLayout   awt

```
public Point location(int x, int y)
```

The `location()` method returns a `Point` object representing the point within the layout manager corresponding to the specified coordinates.

▶ *x* is the x coordinate.

▶ *y* is the y coordinate.

↵ A `Point` object. For more information on the `Point` class, see the documentation later in this chapter.

addLayoutComponent   GridBagLayout   awt

```
public void addLayoutComponent(String name, Component comp)
```

The `addLayoutComponent()` method adds a component to the `GridBagLayout`.

▶ *name* is the name of the component to be added.

▶ *comp* is the `Component` to be added.

removeLayoutComponent   GridBagLayout   awt

```
public void removeLayoutComponent(Component comp)
```

The `removeLayoutComponent()` method removes a component from the `GridBagLayout`.

▶ *comp* is the `Component` to be removed.

preferredLayoutSize   GridBagLayout   awt

```
public Dimension preferredLayoutSize(Container parent)
```

The `preferredLayoutSize()` method returns the preferred size for the layout manager given the specified container and the components within it.

▶ *parent* is a `Container` object containing components. For more information on the `Container` class, see the documentation earlier in this chapter.

↵ A `Dimension` object specifying the preferred size of the layout manager. For more information on the `Dimension` class, see the documentation earlier in this chapter.

minimumLayoutSize   GridBagLayout   awt

```
public Dimension minimumLayoutSize(Container parent)
```

The `minimumLayoutSize()` method returns the minimum size for the layout manager given the specified container and the components within it.

▶ *parent* is a `Container` object containing components. For more information on the `Container` class, see the documentation earlier in this chapter.

↵ A `Dimension` object specifying the minimum size of the layout manager. For more information on the `Dimension` class, see the documentation earlier in this chapter.

---

 layoutContainer GridBagLayout awt

```
public void layoutContainer(Container parent)
```

The `layoutContainer()` method lays out the specified container within the layout manager.

▶ *parent* is a `Container` object containing components. For more information on the `Container` class, see the documentation earlier in this chapter.

---

 toString GridBagLayout awt

```
public String toString()
```

The `toString()` method returns a string containing information about the `GridBagLayout`.

↵ A `String` containing the name of the `GridBagLayout`.

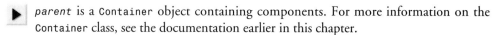 # GridLayout awt

 Object

 LayoutManager

The class hierarchy for the `GridLayout` class derives from the class `java.lang.Object`. (See Listing 28.23.) The `GridLayout` class implements the `LayoutManager` interface. It lays out grid objects. `GridLayout`'s overall derivation is shown in Figure 28.1.

Listing 28.23. Public members of `java.awt.GridLayout`.

```
public class GridLayout implements LayoutManager {
    public GridLayout(int rows, int cols)
    public GridLayout(int rows, int cols, int hgap, int vgap)
    public void addLayoutComponent(String name, Component comp)
    public void removeLayoutComponent(Component comp)
    public Dimension preferredLayoutSize(Container parent)
    public Dimension minimumLayoutSize(Container parent)
    public void layoutContainer(Container parent)
    public String toString()
}
```

GridLayout GridLayout `awt`

```
public GridLayout(int rows, int cols)
```

The `GridLayout()` constructor constructs a grid layout manager using the specified number of rows and columns.

▶ *rows* is the number of rows to be laid out. Either *rows* or *cols* can be set to zero in order to set either the rows or columns to 'any number.'

▶ *cols* is the number of columns to be laid out. Either *rows* or *cols* can be set to zero in order to set either the rows or columns to 'any number.'

 GridLayout GridLayout `awt`

```
public GridLayout(int rows, int cols, int hgap, int vgap)
```

This `GridLayout()` constructor constructs a grid layout manager using the specified number of rows and columns as well as the horizontal and vertical gaps to be used.

▶ *rows* is the number of rows to be laid out.

▶ *cols* is the number of columns to be laid out.

▶ *hgap* is the horizontal gap value.

▶ *vgap* is the vertical gap value.

addLayoutComponent GridLayout `awt`

```
public void addLayoutComponent(String name, Component comp)
```

The `addLayoutComponent()` method adds a component to the `GridLayout`.

▶ *name* is the name of the component to be added.

▶ *comp* is the component to be added.

removeLayoutComponent GridLayout `awt`

```
public void removeLayoutComponent(Component comp)
```

The `removeLayoutComponent()` method removes a component from the `GridBagLayout`.

▶ *comp* is the component to be removed.

preferredLayoutSize GridLayout `awt`

```
public Dimension preferredLayoutSize(Container parent)
```

The `preferredLayoutSize()` method returns the preferred size for the layout manager given the specified container and the components within it.

▶ *parent* is a Container object containing components. For more information on the Container class, see the documentation earlier in this chapter.

↵ A Dimension object specifying the preferred size of the layout manager. For more information on the Dimension class, see the documentation earlier in this chapter.

minimumLayoutSize 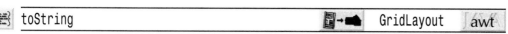 GridLayout ⟨awt⟩

`public Dimension minimumLayoutSize(Container parent)`

The `minimumLayoutSize()` method returns the minimum size for the layout manager given the specified container and the components within it.

▶ *parent* is a Container object containing components. For more information on the Container class, see the documentation earlier in this chapter.

↵ A Dimension object specifying the minimum size of the layout manager. For more information on the Dimension class, see the documentation earlier in this chapter.

layoutContainer GridLayout ⟨awt⟩

`public void layoutContainer(Container parent)`

The `layoutContainer()` method lays out the specified container within the layout manager.

▶ *parent* is a Container object containing components. For more information on the Container class, see the documentation earlier in this chapter.

toString GridLayout ⟨awt⟩

`public String toString()`

The `toString()` method returns a string containing information about the GridLayout.

↵ A String containing the GridLayout's name, *hgap*, *vgap*, *rows*, and *cols* values.

 Image ⟨awt⟩

✚ Object

The class hierarchy for the Image class derives from the class `java.lang.Object`. (See Listing 28.24.) An Image class is actually an abstract class. You must provide a platform-specific implementation to use it. Image's overall derivation is shown in Figure 28.1.

Listing 28.24. Public members of `java.awt.Image`.

```
public abstract class Image {
    public abstract int getWidth(ImageObserver observer)
    public abstract int getHeight(ImageObserver observer)
    public abstract ImageProducer getSource()
    public abstract Graphics getGraphics()
    public abstract Object getProperty(String name, ImageObserver observer)
    public static final Object UndefinedProperty
    public abstract void flush()
}
```

---

getWidth Image │ awt

```
public abstract int getWidth(ImageObserver observer)
```

The getWidth() method returns the width of the Image. If the width of the image is not yet known, the ImageObserver is notified at a later time and -1 is returned.

▶ *observer* is an ImageObserver interface that is notified if the image is not yet available.

↵ An integer value representing the width of the image (-1 if the image is not yet available).

---

getHeight Image │ awt

```
public abstract int getHeight(ImageObserver observer)
```

The getWidth() method returns the height of the Image. If the height of the image is not yet known, the ImageObserver is notified at a later time and -1 is returned.

▶ *observer* is an ImageObserver interface that is notified if the image is not yet available.

↵ An integer value representing the height of the image (-1 if the image is not yet available).

---

getSource Image │ awt

```
public abstract ImageProducer getSource()
```

The getSource() method returns the ImageProducer interface responsible for producing the Image's pixels.

↵ An ImageProducer interface used by the image filtering classes in package java.awt.Image (see documentation later in this chapter).

getGraphics 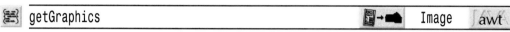 Image | awt

```
public abstract Graphics getGraphics()
```

The getGraphics() method returns a graphics context for drawing. This function is used for off-screen image operations such as double-buffering an image.

↵ A Graphics object used for image drawing purposes.

getProperty  Image | awt

```
public abstract Object getProperty(String name, ImageObserver observer)
```

The getProperty() method returns image property information (each image type has its own set of properties).

▶ *name* is the image property name to be returned.

▶ *observer* is an ImageObserver interface that is notified if the image is not yet ready.

↵ The Property object that corresponds with the property requested. If the image is not yet available, this method returns null. If the property was undefined, an UndefinedProperty object is returned.

Undefined Property awt

```
public static final Object UndefinedProperty
```

The UndefinedProperty object is returned when a property is requested that does not exist within the image.

flush  Image | awt

```
public abstract void flush()
```

The flush() method flushes all image data. Calling this method returns the image to its initial empty state; as a result, you must re-create the image after calling this method.

↵ none

Insets   awt

✚ Object

 Cloneable

The class hierarchy for the Insets class derives from the class java.lang.Object. (See Listing 28.25.) The Insets class encapsulates the insets of a container. Insets's overall derivation is shown in Figure 28.1.

Listing 28.25. Public members of `java.awt.Insets`.

```
public class Insets implements Cloneable {
    public int top
    public int left
    public int bottom
    public int right
    public Insets(int top, int left, int bottom, int right)
    public String toString()
    public Object clone()
}
```

Public Instance Variables

`public int top`

An integer value representing the inset from the top.

`public int left`

An integer value representing the inset from the left.

`public int bottom`

An integer value representing the inset from the bottom.

`public int right`

An integer value representing the inset from the right.

 Insets   Insets   awt

`public Insets(int top, int left, int bottom, int right)`

This `Insets()` constructor creates an `Insets` object from the specified values.

▶ *top* is an integer value representing the inset from the top.

▶ *left* is an integer value representing the inset from the left.

▶ *bottom* is an integer value representing the inset from the bottom.

▶ *right* is an integer value representing the inset from the right.

 toString   Insets   awt

`public String toString()`

The `toString()` method provides a string representation of the `Insets` class.

↵ A `String` value containing the `Insets`' name, top, left, bottom, and right values.

clone   Insets   awt

```
public Object clone()
```

The clone() method creates and returns a clone of the Insets object.

 An Object class representing a clone of the current Insets.

 # Label   awt

 Component

The class hierarchy for the Label class derives from the class java.awt.Component. (See Listing 28.26.) A Label is a component used to display a single line of text on the screen. Label's overall derivation is shown in Figure 28.1.

Listing 28.26. Public members of java.awt.Label.

```
public class Label extends Component {
  public static final int LEFT
  public static final int CENTER
  public static final int RIGHT
  public Label()
  public Label(String label)
  public Label(String label, int alignment)
  public synchronized void addNotify()
  public int getAlignment()
  public void setAlignment(int alignment)
  public String getText()
  public void setText(String label)
}
```

Public Static Values

public static final int LEFT

A static integer value representing left alignment.

public static final int CENTER

A static integer value representing center alignment.

public static final int RIGHT

A static integer value representing right alignment.

 Label   Label   awt

```
public Label()
```

The Label() constructor constructs a label with no string.

Label — Label (awt)

```
public Label(String label)
```

This Label() constructor constructs a label using the specified string.

▶ *label* is a String that is displayed as the label.

Label — Label (awt)

```
public Label(String label, int alignment)
```

This Label() constructor constructs a label using the specified string and alignment.

▶ *label* is a String that is displayed as the label.

▶ *alignment* is an alignment value (CENTER, LEFT, or RIGHT).

addNotify — Label (awt)

```
public synchronized void addNotify()
```

The addNotify() method creates the peer interface for the label. Using a peer interface allows you to modify the user interface of the label without changing the functionality.

↵ none

getAlignment — Label (awt)

```
public int getAlignment()
```

The getAlignment() method returns the label's current alignment.

↵ An integer value representing the label's current alignment (LEFT, RIGHT, or CENTER).

setAlignment — Label (awt)

```
public void setAlignment(int alignment)
```

The setAlignment() method sets the label's current alignment.

▶ *alignment* is an integer value representing the label's new alignment (LEFT, RIGHT, or CENTER).

getText — Label (awt)

```
public String getText()
```

The getText() method returns the label's current text string.

↵ A String value representing the label's current text.

setText Label awt

```
public void setText(String label)
```

The setText() method sets the label's current text string.

▶ *label* is a String value representing the label's new text.

 # List awt

 Component

The class hierarchy for the List class derives from the class java.awt.Component. (See Listing 28.27.) A List component is a scrolling list of text items. Lists can allow multiple selection and visible lines. List's overall derivation is shown in Figure 28.1.

Listing 28.27. Public members of java.awt.List.

```
public class List extends Component {
  public List()
  public List(int rows, boolean multipleSelections)
  public synchronized void addNotify()
  public synchronized void removeNotify()
  public int countItems()
  public String getItem(int index)
  public synchronized void addItem(String item)
  public synchronized void addItem(String item, int index)
  public synchronized void replaceItem(String newValue, int index)
  public synchronized void clear()
  public synchronized void delItem(int position)
  public synchronized void delItems(int start, int end)
  public synchronized int getSelectedIndex()
  public synchronized int[] getSelectedIndexes()
  public synchronized String getSelectedItem()
  public synchronized String[] getSelectedItems()
  public synchronized void select(int index)
  public synchronized void deselect(int index)
  public synchronized boolean isSelected(int index)
  public int getRows()
  public boolean allowsMultipleSelections()
  public void setMultipleSelections(boolean v)
  public int getVisibleIndex()
  public void makeVisible(int index)
  public Dimension preferredSize(int rows)
  public Dimension preferredSize()
  public Dimension minimumSize(int rows)
  public Dimension minimumSize()
}
```

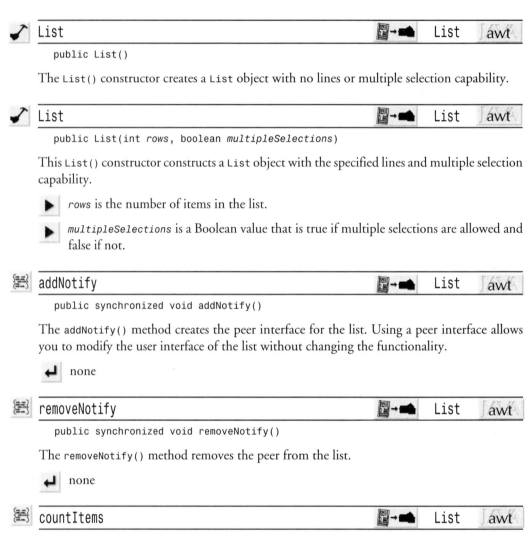

List   List   awt

```
public List()
```

The List() constructor creates a List object with no lines or multiple selection capability.

List   List   awt

```
public List(int rows, boolean multipleSelections)
```

This List() constructor constructs a List object with the specified lines and multiple selection capability.

► *rows* is the number of items in the list.

► *multipleSelections* is a Boolean value that is true if multiple selections are allowed and false if not.

addNotify   List   awt

```
public synchronized void addNotify()
```

The addNotify() method creates the peer interface for the list. Using a peer interface allows you to modify the user interface of the list without changing the functionality.

↵ none

removeNotify   List   awt

```
public synchronized void removeNotify()
```

The removeNotify() method removes the peer from the list.

↵ none

countItems   List   awt

```
public int countItems()
```

The countItems() method returns the number of items in the list.

↵ An integer value representing the number of items in the list.

getItem List awt

`public String getItem(int index)`

The `getItem()` method returns the item at the specified list index.

▶ *index* is an integer value representing the index into the list's string elements.

↵ The `String` value stored at the specified list index.

addItem List awt

`public synchronized void addItem(String item)`

The `addItem()` method adds a `String` item to the end of the list.

▶ *item* is a `String` item to be added to the end of the list.

addItem List awt

`public synchronized void addItem(String item, int index)`

This `addItem()` method adds a `String` item at the specified index within the list.

▶ *item* is a `String` item to be added to the list.

▶ *index* is an integer value representing the index within the list to add the `String` to. If this value is -1 or greater than the number of items within the list, the string item is added to the end of the list.

replaceItem List awt

`public synchronized void replaceItem(String newValue, int index)`

The `replaceItems()` method replaces the current item at the specified index with the new `String` item.

▶ *newValue* is a `String` value representing the new `String` to be used to modify the list.

▶ *index* is an integer value representing the index within the list to be replaced with the new string. If this value is -1 or greater than the number of items within the list, the string item is added to the end of the list.

clear List awt

`public synchronized void clear()`

The `clear()` method clears the list's string of items.

↵ none

delItem List   awt

```
public synchronized void delItem(int position)
```

The delItem() method deletes the string item stored at the specified position within the list.

▶   *position* is an integer value representing the position of the string to be deleted.

delItems List   awt

```
public synchronized void delItems(int start, int end)
```

The delItems() method deletes a sequence of string items stored at the specified positions within the list.

▶   *start* is an integer value representing the first position containing a string to be deleted.

▶   *end* is an integer value representing the last position containing a string to be deleted.

getSelectedIndex List   awt

```
public synchronized int getSelectedIndex()
```

The getSelectedIndex() method returns the index of the currently selected position within the list.

↵   An integer value representing the currently selected position within the list.

getSelectedIndexes List   awt

```
public synchronized int[] getSelectedIndexes()
```

The getSelectedIndexes() method returns an array containing all the currently selected positions within the list.

↵   An array of integers containing the currently selected positions within the list.

getSelectedItem List   awt

```
public synchronized String getSelectedItem()
```

The getSelectedItem() method returns the string at the currently selected position within the list.

↵   The String value at the currently selected position within the list.

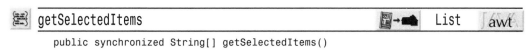

getSelectedItems   List   awt

```
public synchronized String[] getSelectedItems()
```

The getSelectedItems() method returns an array of Strings at the currently selected positions within the list.

↵ An array of strings at the currently selected positions within the list.

select   List   awt

```
public synchronized void select(int index)
```

The select() method selects the item in the list at the specified index position.

▶ index is an integer value representing the position to be selected within the list.

deselect   List   awt

```
public synchronized void deselect(int index)
```

The deselect() method deselects the item in the list at the specified index position.

▶ index is an integer value representing the position to be deselected within the list.

isSelected   List   awt

```
public synchronized boolean isSelected(int index)
```

The isSelected() method checks the specified index position to see if it is currently selected.

▶ index is an integer value representing the position to be checked within the list.

↵ A Boolean value that is true if the specified index position is selected and false if it isn't.

getRows   List   awt

```
public int getRows()
```

The getRows() method returns the number of rows within the list.

↵ An integer value representing the number of rows currently in the list.

allowsMultipleSelections   List   awt

```
public boolean allowsMultipleSelections()
```

The `allowsMultipleSelections()` method returns the multiple selection state of the `List` object.

A Boolean value that is true if multiple selections are allowed and false if they aren't.

setMultipleSelections   List   awt

```
public void setMultipleSelections(boolean v)
```

The `setMultipleSelections()` method sets the multiple selection state of the `List` object.

v is a Boolean value that is true if multiple selections are allowed and false if they aren't.

getVisibleIndex   List   awt

```
public int getVisibleIndex()
```

The `getVisibleIndex()` method returns the index of the item that was last made visible by the `makeVisible()` method.

An integer value representing the index of the item that was just made visible by the `makeVisible()` method.

makeVisible   List   awt

```
public void makeVisible(int index)
```

The `makeVisible()` method forces the list item at the specified index position to be visible.

index is the index position of the item that is to be made visible.

preferredSize   List   awt

```
public Dimension preferredSize(int rows)
```

The `preferredSize()` method returns the preferred size of the `List` object based on the specified number of rows.

rows is the number of rows used to determine the list's preferred size.

A `Dimension` object representing the preferred size of the list. For more information on the `Dimension` class, see the documentation earlier in this chapter.

preferredSize List awt

```
public Dimension preferredSize()
```

This `preferredSize()` method returns the preferred size of the `List` object based on its current number of rows.

↵ A `Dimension` object representing the preferred size of the list. For more information on the `Dimension` class, see the documentation earlier in this chapter.

 minimumSize List awt

```
public Dimension minimumSize(int rows)
```

The `minimumSize()` method returns the minimum size of the `List` object based on the specified number of rows.

▶ *rows* is the number of rows used to determine the list's minimum size.

↵ A `Dimension` object representing the minimum size of the list. For more information on the `Dimension` class, see the documentation earlier in this chapter.

 minimumSize List awt

```
public Dimension minimumSize()
```

This `minimumSize()` method returns the minimum size of the `List` object based on its current number of rows.

↵ A `Dimension` object representing the minimum size of the list. For more information on the `Dimension` class, see the documentation earlier in this chapter.

  # MediaTracker awt

✛ Object

The class hierarchy for the `MediaTracker` class derives from the class `java.lang.Object`. (See Listing 28.28.) The `MediaTracker` class is provided to track the status of media objects. At the current time, only images are supported, but this functionality could be extended to support audio and video as well. `MediaTracker`'s overall derivation is shown in Figure 28.1.

Listing 28.28. Public members of `java.awt.MediaTracker`.

```
public class MediaTracker {
  public MediaTracker(Component comp)
  public void addImage(Image image, int id)
  public synchronized void addImage(Image image, int id, int w, int h)
  public static final int LOADING
  public static final int ABORTED
  public static final int ERRORED
  public static final int COMPLETE
  public boolean checkAll()
  public synchronized boolean checkAll(boolean load)
  public synchronized boolean isErrorAny()
  public synchronized Object[] getErrorsAny()
  public void waitForAll() throws InterruptedException
  public synchronized boolean waitForAll(long ms)
        throws InterruptedException
  public int statusAll(boolean load)
  public boolean checkID(int id)
  public synchronized boolean checkID(int id, boolean load)
  public synchronized boolean isErrorID(int id)
  public synchronized Object[] getErrorsID(int id)
  public void waitForID(int id) throws InterruptedException
  public synchronized boolean waitForID(int id, long ms)
        throws InterruptedException
  public int statusID(int id, boolean load)
}
```

Public Static Values

`public static final int LOADING`

A static integer value representing the LOADING status.

`public static final int ABORTED`

A static integer value representing the ABORTED status.

`public static final int ERRORED`

A static integer value representing the ERRORED status.

`public static final int COMPLETE`

A static integer value representing the COMPLETE status.

MediaTracker MediaTracker ｜awt

```
public MediaTracker(Component comp)
```

The MediaTracker() constructor creates a MediaTracker object to track images for the specified component.

▶   comp is a component that uses a MediaTracker class to track images.

 ## addImage MediaTracker ｜awt

```
public void addImage(Image image, int id)
```

The addImage() method adds the specified Image to the list of images being tracked by the MediaTracker. The Image is rendered at its default size.

▶   image is the Image object to be added to the list.

▶   id is an identification used to reference the Image object.

addImage  MediaTracker ｜awt

```
public synchronized void addImage(Image image, int id, int w, int h)
```

This addImage() method adds the specified Image to the list of images being tracked by the MediaTracker. The Image is rendered at its specified size.

▶   image is the Image object to be added to the list.

▶   id is an ID used to reference the Image object.

▶   w is the width the Image is rendered.

▶   h is the height the Image is rendered.

checkAll MediaTracker ｜awt

```
public boolean checkAll()
```

The checkAll() method checks whether all the images have been loaded.

↵   A Boolean value that is true if all the images have been loaded and false if they haven't.

 ## checkAll MediaTracker ｜awt

```
public synchronized boolean checkAll(boolean load)
```

This checkAll() method checks whether all the images have been loaded. The load parameter forces the MediaTracker to load any images that are not currently loaded.

▶ *load* is a Boolean value that, if true, forces the MediaTracker to load any images that are not currently loaded.

↵ A Boolean value that is true if all the images have been loaded and false if they haven't.

isErrorAny  MediaTracker awt

```
public synchronized boolean isErrorAny()
```

The isErrorAny() method checks the status of all images that are tracked by the MediaTracker.

↵ A Boolean value that is true if any image loaded has an error value and false if not.

getErrorsAny  MediaTracker awt

```
public synchronized Object[] getErrorsAny()
```

The getErrorsAny() method checks the status of all images that are tracked by the MediaTracker and returns an array of all media objects that have generated an error.

↵ An array of media objects that have encountered an error. This array is null if no objects have encountered an error.

waitForAll  MediaTracker awt

```
public void waitForAll() throws InterruptedException
```

The waitForAll() method begins to load all Images without being interrupted. If there is an error, the InterruptedException is thrown.

↗ InterruptedException is the exception that is thrown if another thread interrupts this thread.

waitForAll MediaTracker awt

```
public synchronized boolean waitForAll(long ms) throws InterruptedException
```

This waitForAll() method begins to load all Images without being interrupted. This method continues to load Images until there is an error or until the specified time-out has elapsed. If there is an error, the InterruptedException is thrown.

▶ *ms* is a long integer value representing the time-out value (in milliseconds) to wait before halting the image loading.

↵ A Boolean value that returns true if all the images were successfully loaded before timing out and false if they weren't.

↗ InterruptedException is the exception that is thrown if another thread interrupts this thread.

statusAll MediaTracker awt

```
public int statusAll(boolean load)
```

The `statusAll()` method returns the Boolean OR of all the media objects being tracked.

▶ *load* is a Boolean value that specifies whether to start the image loading.

↵ The Boolean OR of all the media objects being tracked. This value can be LOADED, ABORTED, ERRORED, or COMPLETE.

checkID MediaTracker awt

```
public boolean checkID(int id)
```

The `checkID()` method checks to see whether all images tagged with the specified *id* have been loaded.

▶ *id* is an integer tag used to identify a media object or objects.

↵ A Boolean value that is true if all objects with the specified *id* have been loaded and false if they haven't.

checkID MediaTracker awt

```
public synchronized boolean checkID(int id, boolean load)
```

The `checkID()` method checks to see whether all images tagged with the specified *id* have been loaded. These images are loaded based on the value of the *load* parameter.

▶ *id* is an integer tag used to identify a media object or objects.

▶ *load* is a Boolean value that is true if the images with the specified *id* should be loaded and false if they shouldn't.

↵ A Boolean value that is true if all objects with the specified *id* have been loaded and false if not.

isErrorID MediaTracker awt

```
public synchronized boolean isErrorID(int id)
```

The `isErrorID()` method checks the error status of all media objects with the specified *id*.

▶ *id* is an integer tag used to identify a media object or objects.

↵ A Boolean value that is true if all objects were loaded without error and false if they weren't.

getErrorsID **MediaTracker** awt

```
public synchronized Object[] getErrorsID(int id)
```

The getErrorsAny() method checks the status of all images that are tracked by the MediaTracker whose *id* match the specified *id*. It returns an array of all media objects that have generated an error.

 id is an integer tag used to identify a media object or objects.

 An array of media objects that have encountered an error. This array is null if no objects have encountered an error.

 waitForID 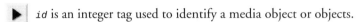 **MediaTracker** awt

```
public void waitForID(int id) throws InterruptedException
```

The waitForID() method begins to load all Images with the specified *id* without being interrupted. If there is an error, the InterruptedException is thrown.

 id is an integer tag used to identify a media object or objects.

InterruptedException is the exception that is thrown if another thread interrupts this thread.

 waitForID **MediaTracker** awt

```
public synchronized boolean waitForID(int id, long ms) throws
➡ InterruptedException
```

This waitForID() method begins to load all Images with the specified *id* without being interrupted. This method continues to load Images until there is an error or until the specified time-out has elapsed. If there is an error, the InterruptedException is thrown.

 id is an integer tag used to identify a media object or objects.

ms is a long integer value representing the time-out value (in milliseconds) to wait before halting the image loading.

A Boolean value that returns true if all the images were successfully loaded before timing out and false if they weren't.

InterruptedException is the exception that is thrown if another thread interrupts this thread.

statusID   MediaTracker   awt

```
public int statusID(int id, boolean load)
```

The statusID() method returns the Boolean OR of all the media objects that are tracked with the specified *id*.

▶ *id* is an integer tag used to identify a media object or objects.

▶ *load* is a Boolean value that specifies whether to start the image loading.

↵ The Boolean OR of all the media objects being tracked. This value can be LOADED, ABORTED, ERRORED, or COMPLETE.

 # Menu   awt

 MenuItem

 MenuContainer

The class hierarchy for the Menu class derives from the class java.awt.MenuItem. (See Listing 28.29.) A Menu is a component of a menu bar. Menu's overall derivation is shown in Figure 28.1.

Listing 28.29. Public members of java.awt.Menu.

```
public class Menu extends MenuItem implements MenuContainer {
  public Menu(String label)
  public Menu(String label, boolean tearOff)
  public synchronized void addNotify()
  public synchronized void removeNotify()
  public boolean isTearOff()
  public int countItems()
  public MenuItem getItem(int index)
  public synchronized MenuItem add(MenuItem mi)
  public void add(String label)
  public void addSeparator()
  public synchronized void remove(int index)
  public synchronized void remove(MenuComponent item)
}
```

 Menu   Menu   awt

```
public Menu(String label)
```

The Menu() constructor constructs a menu using the specified label string.

▶ *label* is a String value that is displayed as the menu's label.

Menu   Menu   awt

```
public Menu(String label, boolean tearOff)
```

This `Menu()` constructor constructs a menu using the specified label string and tear-off option.

▶ *label* is a `String` value that is displayed as the menu's label.

▶ *tearOff* is a Boolean value that is true if this menu is to be a tear-off menu and false if it isn't. A tear-off menu is still displayed on-screen after the mouse button is released.

addNotify   Menu   awt

```
public synchronized void addNotify()
```

The `addNotify()` method creates the peer interface for the menu. Using a peer interface allows you to modify the user interface of the menu without changing the functionality.

↵ none

removeNotify   Menu   awt

```
public synchronized void removeNotify()
```

The `removeNotify()` method removes the peer for the menu.

↵ none

isTearOff   Menu   awt

```
public boolean isTearOff()
```

The `isTearOff()` method returns the tear-off status of the `Menu`.

↵ A Boolean value that is true if the menu is a tear-off menu and false if it isn't.

countItems   Menu   awt

```
public int countItems()
```

The `countItems()` method returns the number of items in this menu.

↵ An integer value representing the number of items that have been added to this menu.

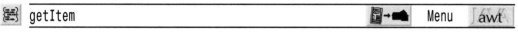

getItem

```
public MenuItem getItem(int index)
```

The getItem() method returns the MenuItem object at the specified index in the menu list.

▶ *index* is an integer value representing the position of the MenuItem to be returned.

↵ A MenuItem object at the specified position. For more information on the MenuItem class, see the documentation later in this chapter.

add

```
public synchronized MenuItem add(MenuItem mi)
```

The add() method adds the specified MenuItem to the Menu's list.

▶ *mi* is the MenuItem to be added to the list.

↵ A MenuItem object that is added to the list. For more information on the MenuItem class, see the documentation later in this chapter.

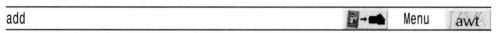

add

```
public void add(String label)
```

This add() method adds a MenuItem with the specified label to the Menu.

▶ *label* is a String value representing the label to be added to the Menu's list.

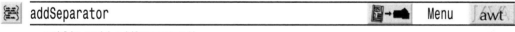

addSeparator

```
public void addSeparator()
```

The addSeparator() method adds a Separator menu item to the Menu.

↵ none

remove

```
public synchronized void remove(int index)
```

The remove() method removes the menu item at the specified index.

▶ *index* is the position within the menu's item list to be removed from the list.

remove Menu

```
public synchronized void remove(MenuComponent item)
```

This remove() method removes the menu item specified in the *item* parameter.

▶   *item* is the MenuComponent to be removed from the menu's item list. For more information on the MenuComponent class, see the documentation later in this chapter.

 # MenuBar   *awt*

 MenuComponent

MenuContainer

The class hierarchy for the MenuBar class derives from the class java.awt.MenuComponent. (See Listing 28.30.) A MenuBar represents a menu bar on a Frame. A MenuBar attaches to a Frame object using the method Frame.setMenuBar(). MenuBar's overall derivation is shown in Figure 28.1.

Listing 28.30. Public members of java.awt.MenuBar.

```
public class MenuBar extends MenuComponent implements MenuContainer {
    public MenuBar()
    public synchronized void addNotify()
    public void removeNotify()
    public Menu getHelpMenu()
    public synchronized void setHelpMenu(Menu m)
    public synchronized Menu add(Menu m)
    public synchronized void remove(int index)
    public synchronized void remove(MenuComponent m)
    public int countMenus()
    public Menu getMenu(int i)
}
```

 MenuBar MenuBar

```
public MenuBar()
```

The MenuBar() constructor constructs an empty MenuBar object.

 addNotify MenuBar *awt*

```
public synchronized void addNotify()
```

The addNotify() method creates the peer interface for the MenuBar. Using a peer interface allows you to modify the user interface of the MenuBar without changing the functionality.

↵   none

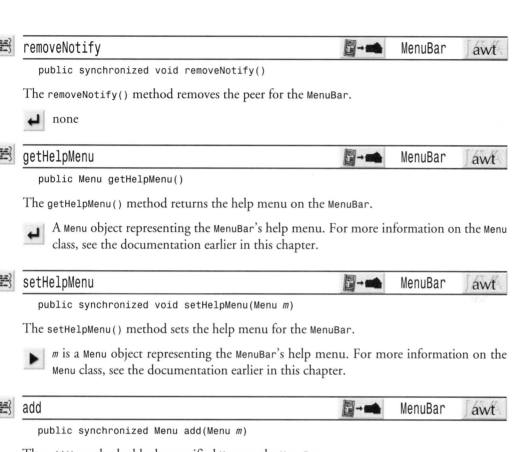

removeNotify   MenuBar   awt

```
public synchronized void removeNotify()
```

The removeNotify() method removes the peer for the MenuBar.

↵ none

getHelpMenu   MenuBar   awt

```
public Menu getHelpMenu()
```

The getHelpMenu() method returns the help menu on the MenuBar.

↵ A Menu object representing the MenuBar's help menu. For more information on the Menu class, see the documentation earlier in this chapter.

setHelpMenu   MenuBar   awt

```
public synchronized void setHelpMenu(Menu m)
```

The setHelpMenu() method sets the help menu for the MenuBar.

▶ *m* is a Menu object representing the MenuBar's help menu. For more information on the Menu class, see the documentation earlier in this chapter.

add   MenuBar   awt

```
public synchronized Menu add(Menu m)
```

The add() method adds the specified Menu to the MenuBar.

▶ *m* is a Menu object to be added to the MenuBar. For more information on the Menu class, see the documentation earlier in this chapter.

↵ The Menu object that was added to the MenuBar.

remove   MenuBar   awt

```
public synchronized void remove(int index)
```

The remove() method removes the menu located at the specified index on the MenuBar.

▶ *index* is the position of the Menu to be removed within the MenuBar's list of menus.

remove MenuBar awt

```
public synchronized void remove(MenuComponent m)
```

This remove() method removes the specified MenuComponent from the MenuBar.

► *m* is a MenuComponent object to be removed from the MenuBar. For more information on the MenuComponent class, see the documentation later in this chapter.

 countMenus MenuBar awt

```
public int countMenus()
```

The countMenus() method returns the number of menus located on this MenuBar.

↵ An integer value representing the number of menus located on this MenuBar.

 getMenu MenuBar awt

```
public Menu getMenu(int i)
```

The getMenu() method returns the Menu object at the specified location within the MenuBar's list of menus.

► *i* is an integer value representing the position of the menu to be retrieved from the MenuBar's list.

↵ A Menu object returned from the MenuBar's list. For more information on the Menu class, see the documentation earlier in this chapter.

 # MenuComponent awt

 Object

The class hierarchy for the MenuComponent class derives from the class java.lang.Object. (See Listing 28.31.) The MenuComponent class serves as the base class for all menu-type components such as Menu, MenuBar, and MenuItem. MenuComponent's overall derivation is shown in Figure 28.1.

Listing 28.31. Public members of java.awt.MenuComponent.
```
public abstract class MenuComponent {
    public MenuContainer getParent()
    public MenuComponentPeer getPeer()
    public Font getFont()
    public void setFont(Font f)
    public void removeNotify()
    public boolean postEvent(Event evt)
    public String toString()
}
```

getParent   MenuComponent   awt

```
public MenuContainer getParent()
```

The getParent() method returns the parent MenuContainer of the MenuComponent.

A MenuContainer object that is the parent of the MenuComponent.

getPeer   MenuComponent   awt

```
public MenuComponentPeer getPeer()
```

The getPeer() method returns the MenuComponentPeer interface for the MenuComponent object. The MenuComponentPeer interface allows you to change the user interface of a MenuComponent without changing its functionality.

A MenuComponentPeer interface.

getFont   MenuComponent   awt

```
public Font getFont()
```

The getFont() method returns the current default font for the MenuComponent.

A Font object. For more information on the Font class, see the documentation earlier in this chapter.

setFont   MenuComponent   awt

```
public void setFont(Font f)
```

The setFont() method sets the display font for the MenuComponent.

f is the Font object representing the MenuComponent's new font. For more information on the Font class, see the documentation earlier in this chapter.

removeNotify   MenuComponent   awt

```
public void removeNotify()
```

The removeNotify() removes the peer for this MenuComponent.

postEvent   MenuComponent   awt

```
public boolean postEvent(Event evt)
```

The postEvent() method posts the specified event to the MenuComponent.

▶   *evt* is the Event object containing the current event that applies to the MenuComponent. For more information on the Event class, see the documentation earlier in this chapter.

 toString   MenuComponent   awt

```
public String toString()
```

The toString() method returns a string representation of the MenuComponent object.

↵   A String containing the MenuComponent's name.

 # MenuItem   awt

 MenuComponent

The class hierarchy for the MenuItem class derives from the class java.awt.MenuComponent. (See Listing 28.32.) A MenuItem represents a choice in a menu. MenuItem's overall derivation is shown in Figure 28.1.

Listing 28.32. Public members of java.awt.MenuItem.

```
public class MenuItem extends MenuComponent {
    public MenuItem(String label)
    public synchronized void addNotify()
    public String getLabel()
    public void setLabel(String label)
    public boolean isEnabled()
    public void enable()
    public void enable(boolean cond)
    public void disable()
    public String paramString()
}
```

 MenuItem   MenuItem   awt

```
public MenuItem(String label)
```

The MenuItem() constructor constructs a MenuItem using the specified label string.

▶   *label* is the String that is displayed as the MenuItem's label.

addNotify MenuItem awt

```
public synchronized void addNotify()
```

The `addNotify()` method creates the peer interface for the `MenuItem`. Using a peer interface allows you to modify the user interface of the `MenuItem` without changing the functionality.

↵   none

getLabel MenuItem awt

```
public String getLabel()
```

The `getLabel()` method returns the label string for the `MenuItem`.

↵   A `String` value representing the `MenuItem`'s displayed label.

setLabel MenuItem awt

```
public void setLabel(String label)
```

The `setLabel()` method changes the `String` label of the `MenuItem`.

▶   *label* is a `String` value representing the `MenuItem`'s displayed label.

isEnabled MenuItem awt

```
public boolean isEnabled()
```

The `isEnabled()` method determines whether the `MenuItem` is enabled.

↵   A Boolean value that is true if the `MenuItem` is enabled and false if it isn't.

enable MenuItem awt

```
public void enable()
```

The `enable()` method enables the `MenuItem`.

↵   none

enable MenuItem awt

```
public void enable(boolean cond)
```

This `enable()` method enables the `MenuItem` based on the specified condition.

▶   *cond* is a Boolean value that conditionally enables the `MenuItem`. If it is true, the `MenuItem` is enabled; if it is false, the `MenuItem` is disabled.

disable MenuItem   awt

```
public void disable()
```

The `disable()` method disables the `MenuItem`, making it unselectable by the user.

 none

 ## paramString MenuItem   awt

```
public String paramString()
```

The `paramString()` method returns a string representation of the `MenuItem`.

 A `String` value containing the `MenuItem`'s label string.

 # Panel   awt

╋ Container

The class hierarchy for the `Panel` class derives from the class `java.awt.Container`. (See Listing 28.33.) A `Panel` represents a generic container class. `Panel`'s overall derivation is shown in Figure 28.1.

> **Listing 28.33. Public members of `java.awt.Panel`.**
>
> ```
> public class Panel extends Container {
>   public Panel()
>   public synchronized void addNotify()
> }
> ```

Panel Panel   awt

```
public Panel()
```

The `Panel()` constructor constructs a default `Panel` object that uses the `FlowLayout` layout manager as the default layout manager.

 ## addNotify Panel   awt

```
public synchronized void addNotify()
```

The `addNotify()` method creates the peer interface for the `Panel`. Using a peer interface allows you to modify the user interface of the `Panel` without changing the functionality.

 none

 Point awt

+ `Object`

The class hierarchy for the `Point` class derives from the class `java.lang.Object`. (See Listing 28.34.) A `Point` class encapsulates an x, y coordinate. `Point`'s overall derivation is shown in Figure 28.1.

Listing 28.34. Public members of `java.awt.Point`.

```
public class Point {
    public int x
    public int y
    public Point(int x, int y)
    public void move(int x, int y)
    public void translate(int x, int y)
    public int hashCode()
    public boolean equals(Object obj)
    public String toString()
}
```

Public Instance Variables

`public int x`

The *x* variable represents the x coordinate of the `Point`.

`public int y`

The *y* variable represents the y coordinate of the `Point`.

 Point Point awt

`public Point(int x, int y)`

The `Point()` constructor constructs a `Point` object using the specified coordinates.

▶ *x* is the x coordinate of the `Point`.

▶ *y* is the y coordinate of the `Point`.

 move  Point awt

`public void move(int x, int y)`

The `move()` method moves the `Point` to the new specified coordinates.

▶ *x* is the new x coordinate of the `Point`.

▶ *y* is the new y coordinate of the `Point`.

translate Point awt

```
public void translate(int x, int y)
```

The `translate()` method translates the `Point` by the specified coordinates.

▶ *x* is the x amount to transfer the `Point`.

▶ *y* is the y amount to transfer the `Point`.

hashCode Point awt

```
public int hashCode()
```

The `hashCode()` method returns a hash code for the `Point`.

↵ An integer value that represents the `Point`'s hash code.

equals Point awt

```
public boolean equals(Object obj)
```

The `equals()` method compares the `Point` object to the specified object.

▶ *obj* is the `Object` to compare the `Point` to.

↵ A Boolean value representing the result of the comparison (`true` or `false`).

toString Point awt

```
public String toString()
```

The `toString()` method returns a string representation of the `Point` object.

↵ A `String` containing the `Point`'s name, x, and y values.

Polygon awt

✚ Object

The class hierarchy for the `Polygon` class derives from the class `java.lang.Object`. (See Listing 28.35.) A `Polygon` contains a list of x, y coordinates, unlike a `Point` class, which only contains one coordinate set. `Polygon`'s overall derivation is shown in Figure 28.1.

Listing 28.35. Public members of `java.awt.Polygon`.

```
public class Polygon {
  public int npoints
  public int xpoints[]
```

```
      public int ypoints[]
      public Polygon()
      public Polygon(int xpoints[], int ypoints[], int npoints)
      public void addPoint(int x, int y)
      public Rectangle getBoundingBox()
      public boolean inside(int x, int y)
  }
```

Public Instance Variables

public int npoints

The *npoint* variable represents the total number of points within the Polygon.

public int xpoints[]

The *xpoints* variable is an integer array of all the x coordinate points.

public int ypoints[]

The *ypoints* variable is an integer array of all the y coordinate points.

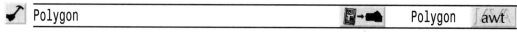

Polygon   Polygon   awt

public Polygon()

The Polygon() constructor constructs an empty Polygon object.

Polygon   Polygon   awt

public Polygon(int xpoints[], int ypoints[], int npoints)

This Polygon() constructor constructs a Polygon object using the specified coordinates.

► *xpoints* is an array of integers representing the x coordinate points of the Polygon.

► *ypoints* is an array of integers representing the y coordinate points of the Polygon.

► *npoints* is an integer value representing the number of points in the Polygon.

addPoint   Polygon   awt

public void addPoint(int x, int y)

The addPoint() method adds a point to the Polygon.

► *x* is the x coordinate of the point to be added.

► *y* is the y coordinate of the point to be added.

getBoundingBox Polygon │awt│

```
public Rectangle getBoundingBox()
```

The getBoundingBox() returns the rectangular bounding box for the Polygon.

 A Rectangle object representing the bounding box for the Polygon. For more information on the Rectangle class, see the documentation later in this chapter.

 inside Polygon │awt│

```
public boolean inside(int x, int y)
```

The inside() method determines whether the specified coordinates are inside the Polygon's bounding rectangle.

▶ *x* is the x coordinate to check.

▶ *y* is the y coordinate to check.

 A Boolean value that is true if the coordinates are inside the Polygon's bounding rectangle and false if they aren't.

Rectangle │awt│

 Object

The class hierarchy for the Rectangle class derives from the class java.lang.Object. (See Listing 28.36.) A Rectangle class specifies the dimensions of a rectangle using x, y, height, and width values. Rectangle's overall derivation is shown in Figure 28.1.

Listing 28.36. Public members of java.awt.Rectangle.

```
public class Rectangle {
  public int x
  public int y
  public int width
  public int height
  public Rectangle()
  public Rectangle(int x, int y, int width, int height)
  public Rectangle(int width, int height)
  public Rectangle(Point p, Dimension d)
  public Rectangle(Point p)
  public Rectangle(Dimension d)
  public void reshape(int x, int y, int width, int height)
  public void move(int x, int y)
  public void translate(int x, int y)
  public void resize(int width, int height)
  public boolean inside(int x, int y)
  public boolean intersects(Rectangle r)
```

```
    public Rectangle intersection(Rectangle r)
    public Rectangle union(Rectangle r)
    public void add(int newx, int newy)
    public void add(Point pt)
    public void add(Rectangle r)
    public void grow(int h, int v)
    public boolean isEmpty()
    public int hashCode()
    public boolean equals(Object obj)
    public String toString()
}
```

Public Instance Variables

public int x

The *x* variable stores the Rectangle's x coordinate.

public int y

The *y* variable stores the Rectangle's y coordinate.

public int width

The *width* variable stores the Rectangle's width.

public int height

The *height* variable stores the Rectangle's height.

 Rectangle Rectangle awt

```
    public Rectangle()
```

The Rectangle() constructor constructs a Rectangle of zero size.

 Rectangle Rectangle awt

```
    public Rectangle(int x, int y, int width, int height)
```

This Rectangle() constructor constructs a Rectangle using the specified coordinates.

▶ *x* is the x coordinate of the Rectangle.

▶ *y* is the y coordinate of the Rectangle.

▶ *width* is the width of the Rectangle.

▶ *height* is the height of the Rectangle.

Rectangle Rectangle awt

```
public Rectangle(int width, int height)
```

This `Rectangle()` constructor constructs a `Rectangle` using the specified width and height.

► *width* is the width of the `Rectangle`.

► *height* is the height of the `Rectangle`.

 Rectangle Rectangle awt

```
public Rectangle(Point p, Dimension d)
```

This `Rectangle()` constructor constructs a `Rectangle` using the specified coordinates and size.

► *p* is a `Point` object containing the `Rectangle`'s x and y coordinates. For more information on the `Point` class, see the documentation earlier in this chapter.

► *d* is a `Dimension` object containing the `Rectangle`'s size. For more information on the `Dimension` class, see the documentation earlier in this chapter.

 Rectangle Rectangle awt

```
public Rectangle(Point p)
```

This `Rectangle()` constructor constructs a `Rectangle` using the specified `Point`.

► *p* is a `Point` object containing the `Rectangle`'s x and y coordinates. For more information on the `Point` class, see the documentation earlier in this chapter.

 Rectangle Rectangle awt

```
public Rectangle(Dimension d)
```

This `Rectangle()` constructor constructs a `Rectangle` using the specified `Dimension`.

► *d* is a `Dimension` object containing the `Rectangle`'s size. For more information on the `Dimension` class, see the documentation earlier in this chapter.

reshape Rectangle awt

```
public void reshape(int x, int y, int width, int height)
```

The `reshape()` method resizes the `Rectangle`'s coordinates and size.

► *x* is the x coordinate of the `Rectangle`.

► *y* is the y coordinate of the `Rectangle`.

▶ *width* is the width of the `Rectangle`.

▶ *height* is the height of the `Rectangle`.

 move Rectangle awt

```
public void move(int x, int y)
```

The `move()` method moves the `Rectangle` to the specified coordinates.

▶ *x* is the x coordinate of the `Rectangle`.

▶ *y* is the y coordinate of the `Rectangle`.

 translate Rectangle awt

```
public void translate(int x, int y)
```

The `translate()` method translates the `Rectangle` by the specified coordinates.

▶ *x* is the x translation amount of the `Rectangle`'s coordinates.

▶ *y* is the y translation amount of the `Rectangle`'s coordinates.

 resize Rectangle awt

```
public void resize(int width, int height)
```

The `resize()` method changes the `Rectangle`'s size to the specified parameters.

▶ *width* is the width of the `Rectangle`.

▶ *height* is the height of the `Rectangle`.

 inside Rectangle awt

```
public boolean inside(int x, int y)
```

The `inside()` method determines if the specified coordinates are inside the `Rectangle`'s bounding rectangle.

▶ *x* is the x coordinate to be checked.

▶ *y* is the y coordinate to be checked.

↵ A Boolean value that is true if the coordinates are within the bounding rectangle and false if they aren't.

intersects

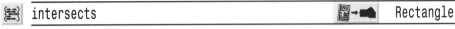

```
public boolean intersects(Rectangle r)
```

The `intersects()` method determines if the specified `Rectangle` intersects the `Rectangle`'s bounding rectangle.

▶ *r* is a `Rectangle` object to be checked for intersection with the `Rectangle`'s bounding rectangle.

↵ A Boolean value that is true if the objects intersect and false if they don't.

intersection

```
public Rectangle intersection(Rectangle r)
```

The `intersection()` computes the intersection rectangle (if any) of the two `Rectangles`.

▶ *r* is a `Rectangle` object to be combined with the current `Rectangle` to determine their intersection `Rectangle`.

↵ A `Rectangle` object that is the intersection of the two `Rectangle` objects.

union

```
public Rectangle union(Rectangle r)
```

The `union()` method returns the union of the two `Rectangles`.

▶ *r* is a `Rectangle` object that determines the union rectangle.

↵ A `Rectangle` object representing the union of the two `Rectangles`.

add

```
public void add(int newx, int newy)
```

The `add()` method adds a new point to the `Rectangle` using the specified coordinates. This results in the smallest possible `Rectangle` that contains the current `Rectangle` and the coordinates.

▶ *newx* is an integer value representing the x coordinate of the point.

▶ *newy* is an integer value representing the y coordinate of the point.

add Rectangle `awt`

```
public void add(Point pt)
```

This add() method adds a new point to the Rectangle using the specified Point object. This results in the smallest possible Rectangle that contains the current Rectangle and the Point's coordinates.

▶ *pt* is a Point object representing the point's coordinates. For more information on the Point class, see the documentation earlier in this chapter.

 add Rectangle `awt`

```
public void add(Rectangle r)
```

This add() method adds a new rectangle to the existing Rectangle. This results in the union of the two rectangles (current and new).

▶ *r* is a Rectangle object that performs a union with the current Rectangle object.

 grow 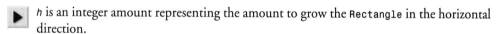 Rectangle `awt`

```
public void grow(int h, int v)
```

The grow() method grows the Rectangle object by the specified horizontal and vertical amounts. The x and y coordinates are shifted by the specified amounts, and the height and width sizes are also increased by the specified amounts.

▶ *h* is an integer amount representing the amount to grow the Rectangle in the horizontal direction.

▶ *v* is an integer amount representing the amount to grow the Rectangle in the vertical direction.

 isEmpty 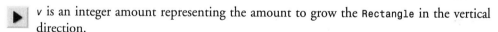 Rectangle `awt`

```
public boolean isEmpty()
```

The isEmpty() method determines if the Rectangle's width and height are less than or equal to zero.

 A Boolean value that is true if the Rectangle is empty and false if it isn't.

hashCode Rectangle awt

```
public int hashCode()
```

The hashCode() method returns the hash code for the Rectangle.

▶ An integer value representing the Rectangle's hash code.

 equals Rectangle awt

```
public boolean equals(Object obj)
```

The equals() method compares the specified Object with the Rectangle.

▶ obj is an Object to be compared with the Rectangle.

↵ A Boolean value that is true if the two objects are equal and false if they are not.

 toString Rectangle awt

```
public String toString()
```

The toString() method returns a String representation of the Rectangle's contents.

↵ A String containing the Rectangle's name, x, y, height, and width values.

 # Scrollbar awt

 Component

The class hierarchy for the Scrollbar class derives from the class java.awt.Component. (See Listing 28.37.) You can add a Scrollbar component to a frame or other object to provide scrolling capabilities. Scrollbar's overall derivation is shown in Figure 28.1.

Listing 28.37. Public members of java.awt.Scrollbar.

```
public class Scrollbar extends Component {
    public static final int    HORIZONTAL
    public static final int    VERTICAL
    public Scrollbar()
    public Scrollbar(int orientation)
    public Scrollbar(int orientation, int value, int visible, int minimum,
        int maximum)
    public synchronized void addNotify()
    public int getOrientation()
    public int getValue()
    public void setValue(int value)
    public int getMinimum()
    public int getMaximum()
    public int getVisible()
```

```
    public void setLineIncrement(int l)
    public int getLineIncrement()
    public void setPageIncrement(int l)
    public int getPageIncrement()
    public void setValues(int value, int visible, int minimum, int maximum)
}
```

Public Static Values

public static final int HORIZONTAL

The HORIZONTAL static int value represents the horizontal scrollbar orientation variable.

public static final int VERTICAL

The VERTICAL static int value represents the vertical scrollbar orientation variable.

 Scrollbar  Scrollbar   awt

public Scrollbar()

The Scrollbar() constructor constructs a default Scrollbar.

 Scrollbar Scrollbar   awt

public Scrollbar(int orientation)

This Scrollbar() constructor constructs a Scrollbar with the specified orientation.

▶ *orientation* is an integer value that can be either HORIZONTAL or VERTICAL.

 Scrollbar  Scrollbar   awt

public Scrollbar(int orientation, int value, int visible, int minimum,
➥ int maximum)

This Scrollbar() constructor constructs a complete Scrollbar using the specified orientation and properties.

▶ *orientation* is an integer value that can be either HORIZONTAL or VERTICAL.

▶ *value* is an integer value representing the Scrollbar's value.

▶ *visible* is an integer value representing the size of the Scrollbar's visible portion.

▶ *minimum* is an integer value representing the Scrollbar's minimum value.

▶ *maximum* is an integer value representing the Scrollbar's maximum value.

addNotify   Scrollbar   awt

```
public synchronized void addNotify()
```

The addNotify() method creates the peer interface for the Scrollbar. Using a peer interface allows you to modify the user interface of the Scrollbar without changing the functionality.

↵ none

getOrientation   Scrollbar   awt

```
public int getOrientation()
```

The getOrientation() method returns the orientation value of the Scrollbar.

↵ An integer value that can be either HORIZONTAL or VERTICAL.

getValue   Scrollbar   awt

```
public int getValue()
```

The getValue() method returns the current value of the Scrollbar.

↵ An integer value representing the value of the Scrollbar.

setValue   Scrollbar   awt

```
public void setValue(int value)
```

The setValue() method sets the value of the Scrollbar to the specified value.

▶ value is an integer value representing the new value of the Scrollbar.

getMinimum   Scrollbar   awt

```
public int getMinimum()
```

The getMinimum() method returns the minimum value of the Scrollbar.

↵ An integer value representing the Scrollbar's minimum value.

getMaximum   Scrollbar   awt

```
public int getMaximum()
```

The getMaximum() method returns the maximum value of the Scrollbar.

↵ An integer value representing the Scrollbar's maximum value.

getVisible Scrollbar awt

`public int getVisible()`

The getVisible() portion returns the visible amount of the Scrollbar.

↵ An integer value representing the Scrollbar's visible amount.

setLineIncrement Scrollbar awt

`public void setLineIncrement(int l)`

The setLineIncrement() method sets the line increment for the Scrollbar.

▶ *l* is the line increment for the scrollbar. This is the amount that the scrollbar's position increases or decreases when the user clicks a scrollbar's up or down widgets.

getLineIncrement Scrollbar awt

`public int getLineIncrement()`

The getLineIncrement() method returns the line increment for the Scrollbar.

↵ An integer value representing the line increment for the scrollbar. This is the amount that the scrollbar's position increases or decreases when the user clicks a scrollbar's up or down widgets.

setPageIncrement Scrollbar awt

`public void setPageIncrement(int l)`

The setPageIncrement() method sets the page increment for the Scrollbar.

▶ *l* is an integer value representing the page increment for the scrollbar. This is the amount that the scrollbar's position increases or decreases when the user clicks the scrollbar's page down or up widgets.

getPageIncrement Scrollbar awt

`public int getPageIncrement()`

The getPageIncrement() method returns the page increment for the Scrollbar.

↵ An integer value representing the page increment for the scrollbar. This is the amount that the scrollbar's position increases or decreases when the user clicks the scrollbar's page down or up widgets.

setValues   Scrollbar   awt

```
public void setValues(int value, int visible, int minimum, int maximum)
```

The setValues() method sets the Scrollbar's properties based on the specified values.

▶   *value* is an integer value representing the current value of the Scrollbar.

▶   *visible* is an integer value representing the visible amount of the Scrollbar.

▶   *minimum* is an integer value representing the Scrollbar's minimum value.

▶   *maximum* is an integer value representing the Scrollbar's maximum value.

 # TextArea   awt

╂ TextComponent

The class hierarchy for the TextArea class derives from the class java.awt.TextComponent. (See Listing 28.38.) A TextArea class represents a multiline component that can be used for text display or editing. TextArea's overall derivation is shown in Figure 28.1.

Listing 28.38. Public members of java.awt.TextArea.

```
public class TextArea extends TextComponent {
  public TextArea()
  public TextArea(int rows, int cols)
  public TextArea(String text)
  public TextArea(String text, int rows, int cols)
  public synchronized void addNotify()
  public void insertText(String str, int pos)
  public void appendText(String str)
  public void replaceText(String str, int start, int end)
  public int getRows()
  public int getColumns()
  public Dimension preferredSize(int rows, int cols)
  public Dimension preferredSize()
  public Dimension minimumSize(int rows, int cols)
  public Dimension minimumSize()
}
```

 TextArea   TextArea   awt

```
public TextArea()
```

The TextArea() constructor constructs a TextArea object.

TextArea

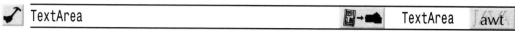

```
public TextArea(int rows, int cols)
```

This TextArea() constructor constructs a TextArea object using the specified row and column values.

▶ *rows* is an integer value specifying the number of rows to use.

▶ *cols* is an integer value specifying the number of columns to use.

TextArea

```
public TextArea(String text)
```

This TextArea() constructor constructs a TextArea object using the specified Text.

▶ *text* is a String value containing the text to be displayed in the TextArea.

TextArea

```
public TextArea(String text, int rows, int cols)
```

This TextArea() constructor constructs a TextArea object using the specified row, column, and text values.

▶ *text* is a String value containing the text to be displayed in the TextArea.

▶ *rows* is an integer value specifying the number of rows to use.

▶ *cols* is an integer value specifying the number of columns to use.

addNotify

```
public synchronized void addNotify()
```

The addNotify() method creates the peer interface for the TextArea. Using a peer interface allows you to modify the user interface of the TextArea without changing the functionality.

↵ none

insertText

```
public void insertText(String str, int pos)
```

The insertText() method inserts a text string into the TextArea's text at the specified position.

▶ *str* is a String value containing the text to be inserted in the TextArea.

▶ *pos* is an integer value specifying the location to insert the text string.

appendText   TextArea   awt

```
public void appendText(String str)
```

The appendText() method appends a text string onto the TextArea's text.

▶ *str* is a String value containing the text to be appended in the TextArea.

replaceText   TextArea   awt

```
public void replaceText(String str, int start, int end)
```

The replaceText() method replaces a section of the TextArea's text at the specified positions with the specified text string.

▶ *str* is a String value containing the text that replaces the TextArea's current text.

▶ *start* is the starting position of the text to be replaced within the TextArea.

▶ *end* is the ending position of the text to be replaced within the TextArea.

getRows   TextArea   awt

```
public int getRows()
```

The getRows() method returns the number of rows within the TextArea.

↵ An integer value representing the number of rows within the TextArea.

getColumns   TextArea   awt

```
public int getColumns()
```

The getColumns() method returns the number of columns within the TextArea.

↵ An integer value representing the number of rows within the TextArea.

preferredSize   TextAre   awt

```
public Dimension preferredSize(int rows, int cols)
```

The preferredSize() method returns the preferred size of a TextArea comprised of the specified rows and columns.

▶ *rows* is the number of rows in the TextArea.

▶ *cols* is the number of columns in the TextArea.

↵ A Dimension object representing the preferred size of the specified TextArea. For more information on the Dimension class, see the documentation earlier in this chapter.

preferredSize TextArea awt

```
public Dimension preferredSize()
```

This `preferredSize()` method returns the preferred size `Dimension` of a `TextArea` object.

 A `Dimension` object representing the preferred size of a `TextArea`. For more information on the `Dimension` class, see the documentation earlier in this chapter.

 minimumSize TextArea awt

```
public Dimension minimumSize(int rows, int cols)
```

The `minimumSize()` method returns the minimum size of a `TextArea` comprised of the specified rows and columns.

▶ *rows* is the number of rows in the `TextArea`.

▶ *cols* is the number of columns in the `TextArea`.

 A `Dimension` object representing the minimum size of the specified `TextArea`. For more information on the `Dimension` class, see the documentation earlier in this chapter.

 minimumSize TextArea awt

```
public Dimension minimumSize()
```

This `minimumSize()` method returns the minimum size `Dimension` of a `TextArea` object.

 A `Dimension` object representing the minimum size of a `TextArea`. For more information on the `Dimension` class, see the documentation earlier in this chapter.

 # TextComponent

➕ Component

The class hierarchy for the `TextComponent` class derives from the class `java.awt.Component`. (See Listing 28.39.) The `TextComponent` class is a component that provides some text for display or editing. It serves as the base class for the `TextArea` and `TextField` classes. `TextComponent`'s overall derivation is shown in Figure 28.1.

Listing 28.39. Public members of `java.awt.TextComponent`.

```
public class TextComponent extends Component {
    public synchronized void removeNotify()
    public void setText(String t)
    public String getText()
    public String getSelectedText()
```

```
public boolean isEditable()
public void setEditable(boolean t)
public int getSelectionStart()
public int getSelectionEnd()
public void select(int selStart, int selEnd)
public void selectAll()
}
```

 removeNotify 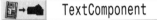 TextComponent   awt

```
public synchronized void removeNotify()
```

The removeNotify() method removes the TextComponent's peer interface. You can use a peer interface to modify the TextComponent's user interface without changing its functionality.

 none

 setText  TextComponent   awt

```
public void setText(String t)
```

The setText() method sets the TextComponent's displayed text to the specified String value.

 t is a String value representing the string to be stored in the TextComponent's text value.

 getText  TextComponent   awt

```
public String getText()
```

The getText() method returns the TextComponent's text value.

 A String value representing the TextComponent's text value.

 getSelectedText TextComponent   awt

```
public String getSelectedText()
```

The getSelectedText() method returns the selected text contained in this TextComponent.

 A String value representing the TextComponent's text value.

 isEditable TextComponent   awt

```
public boolean isEditable()
```

The isEditable() method determines whether the TextComponent's text can be edited.

 A Boolean value that is true if the text can be edited and false if it can't.

setEditable TextComponent `awt`

```
public void setEditable(boolean t)
```

The `setEditable()` method sets the `TextComponent`'s edit property.

▶ *t* is a Boolean value that is true if the text can be edited and false if it can't.

getSelectionStart TextComponent `awt`

```
public int getSelectionStart()
```

The `getSelectionStart()` method returns the starting position of the selected text in the `TextComponent`.

↵ An integer value representing the position of the first selected character in the `TextComponent`.

getSelectionEnd TextComponent `awt`

```
public int getSelectionEnd()
```

The `getSelectionEnd()` method returns the ending position of the selected text in the `TextComponent`.

↵ An integer value representing the position of the last selected character in the `TextComponent`.

select TextComponent `awt`

```
public void select(int selStart, int selEnd)
```

The `select()` method selects a portion of the `TextComponent`'s text based on the specified position.

▶ *selStart* is an integer value representing the position of the first character to be selected in the `TextComponent`.

▶ *selEnd* is an integer value representing the position of the last character to be selected in the `TextComponent`.

selectAll TextComponent `awt`

```
public void selectAll()
```

The `selectAll()` method selects all the `TextComponent`'s text.

 none

 # TextField   awt

 TextComponent

The class hierarchy for the TextField class derives from the class java.awt.TextComponent. (See Listing 28.40.) The TextField class provides a single line of text for displaying or editing. TextField's overall derivation is shown in Figure 28.1.

Listing 28.40. Public members of java.awt.TextField.

```
public class TextField extends TextComponent {
  public TextField()
  public TextField(int cols)
  public TextField(String text)
  public TextField(String text, int cols)
  public synchronized void addNotify()
  public char getEchoChar()
  public boolean echoCharIsSet()
  public int getColumns()
  public void setEchoCharacter(char c)
  public Dimension preferredSize(int cols)
  public Dimension preferredSize()
  public Dimension minimumSize(int cols)
  public Dimension minimumSize()
}
```

 TextField   TextField   awt

```
public TextField()
```

The TextField() constructor constructs a TextField of default size.

 TextField   TextField   awt

```
public TextField(int cols)
```

This TextField() constructor constructs a TextField using the specified column size.

▶ *cols* represents the number of characters that can be entered into the component because the TextField object represents a single-line text control.

 TextField   TextField   awt

```
public TextField(String text)
```

This TextField() constructor constructs a TextField using the specified input string.

▶ *text* is the default text to be displayed within the TextField object.

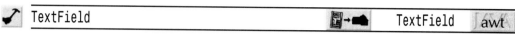

TextField   TextField   awt

```
public TextField(String text, int cols)
```

This `TextField()` constructor constructs a `TextField` using the specified input string and column values.

▶ *text* is the default text to be displayed within the `TextField` object. The display of this text is truncated if the number of columns is less than the number of characters in this text string.

▶ *cols* is the number of columns to display.

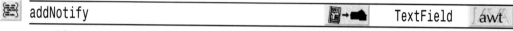

addNotify   TextField   awt

```
public synchronized void addNotify()
```

The `addNotify()` method creates the peer interface for the `TextField`. Using a peer interface allows you to modify the user interface of the `TextField` without changing the functionality.

↵ none

getEchoChar   TextField   awt

```
public char getEchoChar()
```

The `getEchoChar()` method retrieves the character that is used for echoing.

↵ A character value that represents the character that is used for echoing.

echoCharIsSet   TextField   awt

```
public boolean echoCharIsSet()
```

The `echoCharIsSet()` method determines whether the echo character has been set.

↵ A Boolean value that is true if the echo character has been set and false if it hasn't.

getColumns   TextField   awt

```
public int getColumns()
```

The `getColumns()` method returns the number of columns used in the display area of this `TextField`.

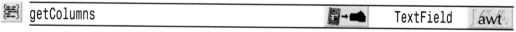

↵ An integer value representing the number of columns (characters) that is displayed by the `TextField`.

setEchoCharacter   TextField   awt

```
public void setEchoCharacter(char c)
```

The setEchoCharacter() method sets the character that is used for echoing. Echoing is often used on password fields so that the actual characters entered won't be echoed to the screen.

▶ *c* is a character value representing the character to be echoed to the screen.

preferredSize   TextField   awt

```
public Dimension preferredSize(int cols)
```

This preferredSize() method returns the preferred size Dimension of a TextField object.

▶ *cols* is an integer value used to specify a number of columns used by the TextField. This column count is used to calculate the preferred size of the TextField.

 A Dimension object representing the preferred size of a TextField. For more information on the Dimension class, see the documentation earlier in this chapter.

minimumSize   TextField   awt

```
public Dimension minimumSize(int cols)
```

The minimumSize() method returns the minimum size of a TextField comprised of the specified number of columns.

▶ *cols* is the number of columns in the TextField.

 A Dimension object representing the minimum size of the specified TextField. For more information on the Dimension class, see the documentation earlier in this chapter.

minimumSize   TextField   awt

```
public Dimension minimumSize()
```

This minimumSize() method returns the minimum size Dimension of a TextField object.

 A Dimension object representing the minimum size of a TextField. For more information on the Dimension class, see the documentation earlier in this chapter.

Toolkit   awt

 Object

The class hierarchy for the Toolkit class derives from the class java.lang.Object. (See Listing 28.41.) The Toolkit class binds a native toolkit to the abstract AWT classes. Toolkit's overall derivation is shown in Figure 28.1.

Listing 28.41. Public members of java.awt.Toolkit.

```
public abstract class  Toolkit {
  public abstract Dimension getScreenSize()
  public abstract int getScreenResolution()
  public abstract ColorModel getColorModel()
  public abstract String[] getFontList()
  public abstract FontMetrics getFontMetrics(Font font)
  public abstract void sync()
  public static synchronized Toolkit getDefaultToolkit()
  public abstract Image getImage(String filename)
  public abstract Image getImage(URL url)
  public abstract boolean prepareImage(Image image, int width, int height,
                                       ImageObserver observer)
  public abstract int checkImage(Image image, int width, int height,
                                 ImageObserver observer)
  public abstract Image createImage(ImageProducer producer)
}
```

---

getScreenSize Toolkit awt

```
public abstract Dimension getScreenSize()
```

The getScreenSize() method returns the size of the screen.

 A Dimension object containing the size of the screen. For more information on the Dimension class, see the documentation earlier in this chapter.

getScreenResolution Toolkit awt

```
public abstract int getScreenResolution()
```

The getScreenResolution() method returns the current screen resolution in units of dots-per-inch.

 An integer value representing the current screen resolution in dots-per-inch.

getColorModel Toolkit awt

```
public abstract ColorModel getColorModel()
```

The getColorModel() returns the current ColorModel being used.

 A ColorModel class representing the current ColorModel. For more information on the ColorModel class, see the documentation on the java.awt.Image.ColorModel class in Chapter 29, "Package java.awt.image."

getFontList   Toolkit   awt

```
public abstract String[] getFontList()
```

The getFontList() method returns a list of the fonts available.

An array of strings containing the names of all fonts available to the system. For more information on the Font class, see the documentation earlier in this chapter.

getFontMetrics   Toolkit   awt

```
public abstract FontMetrics getFontMetrics(Font font)
```

The getFontMetrics() method returns the FontMetrics for a specified font.

font is a Font object. For more information on the Font class, see the documentation earlier in this chapter.

A FontMetrics object containing information on the specified font. For more information on the FontMetrics class, see the documentation earlier in this chapter.

sync   Toolkit   awt

```
public abstract void sync()
```

The sync() method syncs the graphics state, which is useful with animation.

getDefaultToolkit   Toolkit   awt

```
public static synchronized Toolkit getDefaultToolkit()
```

The getDefaultToolkit() method returns a Toolkit object that is used as the default toolkit.

A Toolkit object representing the default system toolkit.

getImage   Toolkit   awt

```
public abstract Image getImage(String filename)
```

The getImage() method returns an Image object that corresponds with the specified Image filename.

filename is a String value containing the filename of the Image to be loaded.

An Image object. For more information on the Image class, see the documentation earlier in this chapter.

getImage Toolkit awt

```
public abstract Image getImage(URL url)
```

The getImage() method retrieves an Image object that corresponds with the specified URL.

▶ *url* is the Uniform Resource Locator (URL) of the specified Image object. For more information on the URL class, see the java.net package documentation in Chapter 33, "Package java.net."

↵ An Image object. For more information on the Image class, see the documentation earlier in this chapter.

 prepareImage Toolkit awt

```
public abstract boolean prepareImage(Image image, int width, int height,
➡ ImageObserver observer)
```

The prepareImage() method prepares an Image for rendering on the screen based on the specified Image sizes.

▶ *image* is an Image object. For more information on the Image class, see the documentation earlier in this chapter.

▶ *width* is an integer value representing the width of the Image when displayed.

▶ *height* is an integer value representing the height of the Image when displayed.

▶ *observer* is an ImageObserver object that is notified when the Image is prepared. For more information on the ImageObserver interface, see the documentation in Chapter 29.

↵ A Boolean value that is true if the image was prepared successfully and false if it wasn't.

 checkImage Toolkit awt

```
public abstract int checkImage(Image image, int width, int height,
➡ ImageObserver observer)
```

The checkImage() method checks the status of the Image construction.

▶ *image* is an Image object. For more information on the Image class, see the documentation earlier in this chapter.

▶ *width* is an integer value representing the width of the Image when displayed.

▶ *height* is an integer value representing the height of the Image when displayed.

▶ *observer* is an ImageObserver object that is notified when the Image is prepared. For more information on the ImageObserver interface, see the documentation in Chapter 29.

↵ An integer value representing the status of the Image construction.

createImage Toolkit awt

```
public abstract Image createImage(ImageProducer producer)
```

The `createImage()` method creates an image using the `ImageProducer` interface.

 producer is an `ImageProducer` object that is notified when the `Image` is prepared. For more information on the `ImageProducer` interface, see the documentation in Chapter 29.

 An `Image` object. For more information on the `Image` class, see the documentation earlier in this chapter.

 # Window awt

 Container

The class hierarchy for the `Window` class derives from the class `java.awt.Container`. (See Listing 28.42.) The `Window` class is defined as a top-level window with no borders and no menu bar. `Window`'s overall derivation is shown in Figure 28.1.

Listing 28.42. Public members of `java.awt.Window`.

```
public class Window extends Container {
    public Window(Frame parent)
    public synchronized void addNotify()
    public synchronized void pack()
    public void show()
    public synchronized void dispose()
    public void toFront()
    public void toBack()
    public Toolkit getToolkit()
    public final String getWarningString()
}
```

 Window Window

```
public Window(Frame parent)
```

The `Window()` constructor constructs a window whose parent is specified by the *parent* parameter. This window is invisible after creation and acts as a modal dialog when initially shown.

 parent is a `Frame` object that is the parent of this `Window`. For more information on the `Frame` class, see the documentation earlier in this chapter.

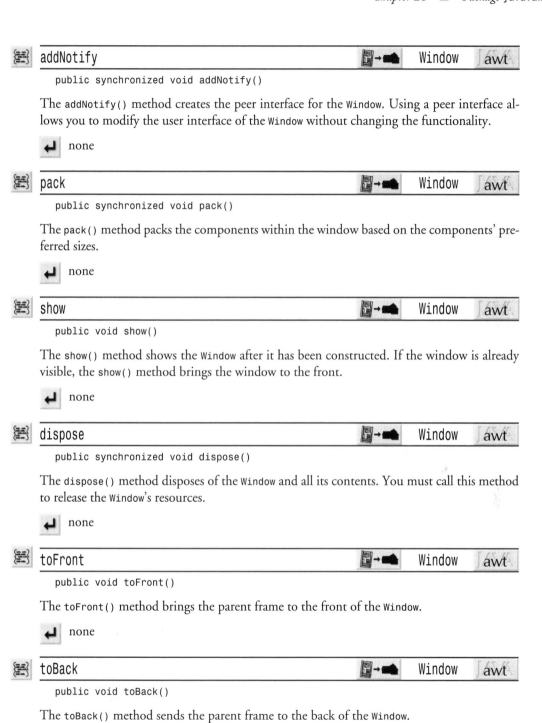

addNotify   Window   awt

```
public synchronized void addNotify()
```

The addNotify() method creates the peer interface for the Window. Using a peer interface allows you to modify the user interface of the Window without changing the functionality.

↵ none

pack   Window   awt

```
public synchronized void pack()
```

The pack() method packs the components within the window based on the components' preferred sizes.

↵ none

show   Window   awt

```
public void show()
```

The show() method shows the Window after it has been constructed. If the window is already visible, the show() method brings the window to the front.

↵ none

dispose   Window   awt

```
public synchronized void dispose()
```

The dispose() method disposes of the Window and all its contents. You must call this method to release the Window's resources.

↵ none

toFront   Window   awt

```
public void toFront()
```

The toFront() method brings the parent frame to the front of the Window.

↵ none

toBack   Window   awt

```
public void toBack()
```

The toBack() method sends the parent frame to the back of the Window.

↵ none

getToolkit   Window awt

```
public Toolkit getToolkit()
```

The getToolkit() method returns the current Toolkit for the Window.

 A Toolkit object. For more information on the Toolkit class, see the documentation earlier in this chapter.

  getWarningString   Window awt

```
public final String getWarningString()
```

The getWarningString() method returns a string that warns users. This string typically displays a security warning and is displayed in an area of the window visible to users.

 A String value containing a warning string for users.

 # AWTException awt

 Exception

The class hierarchy for the AWTException class derives from the class java.lang.Exception. (See Listing 28.43.) The AWTException signals that an Abstract Window Toolkit exception has occurred. AWTException's overall derivation is shown in Figure 28.1.

Listing 28.43. Public members of java.awt.AWTException.

```
public class AWTException extends Exception {
    public AWTException(String msg)
}
```

 AWTException   AWTException awt

```
public AWTException(String msg)
```

The AWTException() constructor constructs an AWTException object using the specified detail message.

▶ *msg* is a String value that contains a detail message that describes the AWTException.

 # AWTError awt

 Error

The class hierarchy for the AWTError class derives from the class java.lang.Error. (See Listing 28.44.) The AWTError encapsulates an Abstract Windowing Toolkit error. AWTError's overall derivation is shown in Figure 28.1.

Listing 28.44. Public members of java.awt.AWTError.

```
public class AWTError extends Error {
    public AWTError(String msg)
}
```

AWTError   AWTError   awt

```
public AWTError(String msg)
```

The AWTError() constructor constructs an AWTError object using the specified detail message.

▶ *msg* is a String value that contains a detail message that describes the AWTError.

LayoutManager   awt

The LayoutManager interface is implemented by objects that know how to lay out containers. (See Listing 28.45.)

Listing 28.45. Members of java.awt.LayoutManager.

```
public interface LayoutManager {
    void addLayoutComponent(String name, Component comp)
    void removeLayoutComponent(Component comp)
    Dimension preferredLayoutSize(Container parent)
    Dimension minimumLayoutSize(Container parent)
    void layoutContainer(Container parent)
}
```

addLayoutComponent   LayoutManager   awt

```
void addLayoutComponent(String name, Component comp)
```

The addLayoutComponent() method lays out the specified component within the layout manager.

▶ *name* is the name of the component to be laid out.

▶ *comp* is the Component object to be laid out within the layout manager.

removeLayoutComponent   LayoutManager   awt

```
void removeLayoutComponent(Component comp)
```

The removeLayoutComponent() method removes a specified component from the layout manager.

▶ *comp* is the Component object to be removed from the layout manager.

preferredLayoutSize   LayoutManager   awt

```
Dimension preferredLayoutSize(Container parent)
```

The preferredLayoutSize() method determines the preferred layout size for a specified Container.

▶ *parent* is a Container object to be laid out using the layout manager. For more information on the Container class, see the documentation earlier in this chapter.

↵ A Dimension object containing the preferred size of the Container parameter. For more information on the Dimension class, see the documentation earlier in this chapter.

minimumLayoutSize   LayoutManager   awt

```
Dimension minimumLayoutSize(Container parent)
```

The minimumLayoutSize() method determines the minimum layout size for a specified Container.

▶ *parent* is a Container object to be laid out using the layout manager. For more information on the Container class, see the documentation earlier in this chapter.

↵ A Dimension object containing the minimum size of the Container parameter. For more information on the Dimension class, see the documentation earlier in this chapter.

layoutContainer LayoutManager awt

```
void layoutContainer(Container parent)
```

The layoutContainer() method lays out the specified Container object within the layout manager.

 parent is a Container object to be laid out using the layout manager. For more information on the Container class, see the documentation earlier in this chapter.

MenuContainer awt

The MenuContainer is an interface that is implemented by all menu-related containers. (See Listing 28.46.)

Listing 28.46. Members of java.awt.MenuContainer.

```
public interface MenuContainer {
    Font getFont()
    boolean postEvent(Event evt)
    void remove(MenuComponent comp)
}
```

 getFont MenuContainer awt

```
Font getFont()
```

The getFont() method returns the current Font of the menu container.

 The current Font object. For more information on the Font class, see the documentation earlier in the chapter.

postEvent MenuContainer awt

```
boolean postEvent(Event evt)
```

The postEvent() method posts the specified event to the MenuContainer.

evt is the Event object to be posted to the menu container. For more information on the Event class, see the documentation earlier in this chapter.

A Boolean value containing true if the event was handled and false if it wasn't.

remove   MenuContainer   awt

```
void remove(MenuComponent comp)
```

The remove() method removes the specified MenuComponent object from the MenuContainer.

▶   *comp* is the MenuComponent class to be removed from the MenuContainer. For more information on the MenuComponent class, see the documentation earlier in this chapter.

29

Package
java.awt.image

by Bryan Morgan

Although nearly all of the java.awt package consisted of graphical user interface components to be used for screen layout, the java.awt.image package contains classes that provide functionality for various image transformations and operations. The key interfaces within this package are the ImageConsumer and ImageProducer interfaces because they define the behavior for consumers and producers of images. Table 29.1 shows the contents of the java.awt.image package and Figure 29.1 shows its contents graphically.

Table 29.1. Contents of package java.awt.image.

Class Index	*Interface Index*
ColorModel	ImageConsumer
CropImageFilter	ImageObserver
DirectColorModel	ImageProducer
FilteredImageSource	
ImageFilter	
IndexColorModel	
MemoryImageSource	
PixelGrabber	
RGBImageFilter	

FIGURE 29.1.

The contents of package java.awt.image.

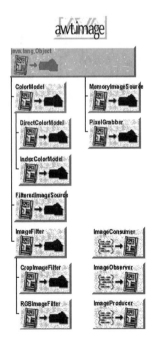

ColorModel

 `Object`

The class hierarchy for the `ColorModel` class derives from class `java.lang.Object`. The `ColorModel` class is an abstract class that provides functions for translating pixel values into RGB color values. `ColorModel`'s overall derivation can be seen in Figure 29.1.

Listing 29.1 shows the declarations for all of the public methods included in the `java.awt.image.ColorModel` class.

Listing 29.1. Public members of `java.awt.image.ColorModel`.

```
public abstract class ColorModel {
  public static ColorModel getRGBdefault()
  public ColorModel(int bits)
  public int getPixelSize()
  public abstract int getRed(int pixel)
  public abstract int getGreen(int pixel)
  public abstract int getBlue(int pixel)
  public abstract int getAlpha(int pixel)
  public int getRGB(int pixel)
  public void finalize()
}
```

 ## ColorModel   ColorModel awt.image

`    public ColorModel(int bits)`

The `ColorModel()` constructor constructs a color model that describes a pixel of the specified number of bits.

▶ `bits` is an integer value containing the number of bits that will describe a pixel using this `ColorModel`.

 ## getRGBdefault   ColorModel awt.image

`    public static ColorModel getRGBdefault()`

The `getRGBdefault()` method returns the default `ColorModel` that is used throughout all AWT image interfaces. This default `ColorModel` uses a pixel format that encapsulates alpha, red, green, and blue color values (eight bits each), using the following methodology: `0xAARRGGBB`.

↵ A `ColorModel` object representing the default color model for all AWT image interfaces.

getPixelSize   ColorModel   awt.image

```
public int getPixelSize()
```

The getPixelSize() method returns the size of the ColorModel's pixel.

↵ An integer value representing the number of bits that make up a pixel in this ColorModel.

getRed   ColorModel   awt.image

```
public abstract int getRed(int pixel)
```

The getRed() method returns the red component of the specified pixel.

▶ pixel is an integer containing the pixel representation for this color model.

↵ An integer value representing the red component of the pixel.

getGreen   ColorModel   awt.image

```
public abstract int getGreen(int pixel)
```

The getGreen() method returns the green component of the specified pixel.

▶ pixel is an integer containing the pixel representation for this color model.

↵ An integer value representing the green component of the pixel.

getBlue   ColorModel   awt.image

```
public abstract int getBlue(int pixel)
```

The getBlue() method returns the blue component of the specified pixel.

▶ pixel is an integer containing the pixel representation for this color model.

↵ An integer value representing the blue component of the pixel.

getAlpha   ColorModel   awt.image

```
public abstract int getAlpha(int pixel)
```

The getAlpha() method returns the alpha component of the specified pixel.

▶ pixel is an integer containing the pixel representation for this color model.

↵ An integer value representing the alpha component of the pixel.

getRGB ColorModel awt.image

```
public int getRGB(int pixel)
```

The `getRGB()` method returns the RGB value of the pixel using the default color model.

▶ `pixel` is an integer containing the pixel representation for this color model.

↵ An integer value representing the RGB value of the pixel using the default color model.

 ## finalize ColorModel awt.image

```
public void finalize()
```

The `finalize()` method is used to clean up internal data allocated by the `ColorModel`.

↵ The `finalize()` method does not return a value.

CropImageFilter awt.image

 `ImageFilter`

The class hierarchy for the `CropImageFilter` class derives from class `java.awt.image.ImageFilter`. The `CropImageFilter` class provides the ability to extract a rectangular subset of a given image (cropping it). This class is used in conjunction with a `FilteredImageSource` class to provide a source for the cropped image. `CropImageFilter`'s overall derivation can be seen in Figure 29.1.

Listing 29.2 shows the declarations for all of the public methods included in the `java.awt.image.CropImageFilter` class.

Listing 29.2. Public members of `java.awt.image.CropImageFilter`.
```
public class CropImageFilter extends ImageFilter {
  public CropImageFilter(int x, int y, int w, int h)
  public void setProperties(Hashtable props)
  public void setDimensions(int w, int h)
  public void setPixels(int x, int y, int w, int h,
                        ColorModel model, byte pixels[], int off,
                        int scansize)
  public void setPixels(int x, int y, int w, int h,
                        ColorModel model, int pixels[], int off,
                        int scansize)
}
```

CropImageFilter  CropImageFilter awt.image

```
public CropImageFilter(int x, int y, int w, int h)
```

The CropImageFilter() constructor constructs a CropImageFilter to crop an image using a cropping rectangle. The dimensions of this rectangle are specified using the following parameters.

▶ x is the top x coordinate of the cropping rectangle containing the image.

▶ y is the top y coordinate of the cropping rectangle containing the image.

▶ w is the width of the rectangular cropping area.

▶ h is the height of the rectangular cropping area.

setProperties CropImageFilter awt.image

```
public void setProperties(Hashtable props)
```

The setProperties() method takes the props parameter from a source object and adds the croprect property to it to identify the region being cropped.

▶ props is a Hashtable object containing properties from the source object.

⊘ setProperties() in class ImageFilter.

setDimensions CropImageFilter awt.image

```
public void setDimensions(int w, int h)
```

The setDimensions() method overrides the source's dimensions and passes the dimensions of the cropped region to the ImageConsumer interface.

▶ w is the width value in pixels.

▶ h is the height value in pixels.

⊘ setDimensions() in class ImageFilter.

setPixels CropImageFilter awt.image

```
public void setPixels(int x, int y, int w, int h, ColorModel model,
➥ byte pixels[], int off, int scansize)
```

The setPixels() method filters the pixels array by determining which pixels lie in the cropped region. Those that do are passed on to the Consumer interface.

▶ x is the x coordinate of the image.

▶ y is the y coordinate of the image.

▶ `w` is the width of the image.

▶ `h` is the height of the image.

▶ `model` is the `ColorModel` that the `pixels` array conforms to.

▶ `pixels` is a byte array containing pixels to be examined.

▶ `off` is a variable that is passed on to the `ImageConsumer`'s `setPixels()` method. For more information, see the `ImageConsumer` interface documentation later in this chapter.

▶ `scansize` is an integer value representing the scansize of the operation.

⊘ `setPixels()` in class `ImageFilter`.

---

 setPixels    CropImageFilter   awt.image

```
public void setPixels(int x, int y, int w, int h, ColorModel model,
➡ int pixels[], int off, int scansize)
```

The `setPixels()` method filters the `pixels` array by determining which pixels lie in the cropped region. Those that do are passed on to the `Consumer` interface.

▶ `x` is the x coordinate of the image.

▶ `y` is the y coordinate of the image.

▶ `w` is the width of the image.

▶ `h` is the height of the image.

▶ `model` is the `ColorModel` that the `pixels` array conforms to.

▶ `pixels` is an array of integers containing pixels to be examined.

▶ `off` is a variable that is passed on to the `ImageConsumer`'s `setPixels()` method. For more information, see the `ImageConsumer` interface documentation later in this chapter.

▶ `scansize` is an integer value representing the scansize of the operation.

⊘ `setPixels()` in class `ImageFilter`.

DirectColorModel   awt.image

✛ `ColorModel`

The class hierarchy for the `DirectColorModel` class derives from class `java.awt.image.ColorModel`. The `DirectColorModel` class specifies translations from pixel values to RGB color values for pixels that have the colors embedded directly in the pixel bits. The `DirectColorModel`'s overall derivation can be seen in Figure 29.1.

Listing 29.3 shows the declarations for all of the public methods included in the `java.awt.image.DirectColorModel` class.

Listing 29.3. Public members of `java.awt.image.DirectColorModel`.

```
public class DirectColorModel extends ColorModel {
    public DirectColorModel(int bits, int rmask, int gmask, int bmask)
    public DirectColorModel(int bits, int rmask, int gmask, int bmask, int amask)
    final public int getRedMask()
    final public int getGreenMask()
    final public int getBlueMask()
    final public int getAlphaMask()
    final public int getRed(int pixel)
    final public int getGreen(int pixel)
    final public int getBlue(int pixel)
    final public int getAlpha(int pixel)
    final public int getRGB(int pixel)
}
```

 DirectColorModel   DirectColorModel

```
public DirectColorModel(int bits, int rmask, int gmask, int bmask)
```

The `DirectColorModel()` constructor constructs a `DirectColorModel` using the specified parameters. `DirectColorModel`s built using this constructor have a default alpha mask value of 255. An alpha mask is a value used to interpolate between the each color value when two figures are overlaid.

▶ `bits` is the number of bits used to represent a pixel.

▶ `rmask` is the number of bits required to represent the red component.

▶ `gmask` is the number of bits required to represent the green component.

▶ `bmask` is the number of bits required to represent the blue component.

DirectColorModel   DirectColorModel

```
public DirectColorModel(int bits, int rmask, int gmask, int bmask, int amask)
```

The `DirectColorModel()` constructor constructs a `DirectColorModel` using the specified parameters.

▶ `bits` is the number of bits used to represent a pixel.

▶ `rmask` is the number of bits required to represent the red component.

▶ `gmask` is the number of bits required to represent the green component.

▶ `bmask` is the number of bits required to represent the blue component.

▶ `amask` is the number of bits required to represent the alpha component.

getRedMask DirectColorModel *awt.image*

```
final public int getRedMask()
```

The `getRedMask()` method returns the current red mask value.

↵ An integer value representing the red mask value.

getGreenMask DirectColorModel *awt.image*

```
final public int getGreenMask()
```

The `getGreenMask()` method returns the current green mask value.

↵ An integer value representing the green mask value.

getBlueMask DirectColorModel *awt.image*

```
final public int getBlueMask()
```

The `getBlueMask()` method returns the current blue mask value.

↵ An integer value representing the blue mask value.

getAlphaMask DirectColorModel *awt.image*

```
final public int getAlphaMask()
```

The `getAlphaMask()` method returns the current alpha mask value.

↵ An integer value representing the alpha mask value.

getRed DirectColorModel *awt.image*

```
final public int getRed(int pixel)
```

The `getRed()` method returns the red component for the specified pixel in the range 0–255.

▶ `pixel` is an integer value representing a pixel under the `DirectColorModel`.

↵ An integer value representing the red component of the pixel.

getGreen DirectColorModel *awt.image*

```
final public int getGreen(int pixel)
```

The `getGreen()` method returns the green component for the specified pixel in the range 0–255.

▶ `pixel` is an integer value representing a pixel under the `DirectColorModel`.

↵ An integer value representing the green component of the pixel.

getBlue   DirectColorModel   awt.image

```
final public int getBlue(int pixel)
```

The getBlue() method returns the blue component for the specified pixel in the range 0–255.

▶ pixel is an integer value representing a pixel under the DirectColorModel.

↵ An integer value representing the blue component of the pixel.

getAlpha   DirectColorModel   awt.image

```
final public int getAlpha(int pixel)
```

The getAlpha() method returns the alpha component for the specified pixel in the range 0–255.

▶ pixel is an integer value representing a pixel under the DirectColorModel.

↵ An integer value representing the alpha component of the pixel.

getRGB   DirectColorModel   awt.image

```
final public int getRGB(int pixel)
```

The getRGB() method returns the RGB color value for the specified pixel in the range 0–255.

▶ pixel is an integer value representing a pixel under the DirectColorModel.

↵ An integer value representing the RGB color value of the pixel using the default RGB color model.

FilteredImageSource   awt.image

 Object

 ImageProducer

The class hierarchy for the FilteredImageSource class derives from class java.lang.Object. The FilteredImageSource takes as input an existing image and a filter object. It applies the filter to the image to produce a new version of the original image. The FilteredImageSource class implements the ImageProducer interface. FilteredImageSource's overall derivation can be seen in Figure 29.1.

Listing 29.4 shows the declarations for all of the public methods included in the java.awt.image.FilteredImageSource class.

Listing 29.4. Public members of `java.awt.image.FilteredImageSource`.

```
public class FilteredImageSource implements ImageProducer {
  public FilteredImageSource(ImageProducer orig, ImageFilter imgf)
  public synchronized void addConsumer(ImageConsumer ic)
  public synchronized boolean isConsumer(ImageConsumer ic)
  public synchronized void removeConsumer(ImageConsumer ic)
  public void startProduction(ImageConsumer ic)
  public void requestTopDownLeftRightResend(ImageConsumer ic)
}
```

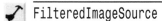 FilteredImageSource FilteredImageSource awt.image

```
public FilteredImageSource(ImageProducer orig, ImageFilter imgf)
```

The `FilteredImageSource()` constructor constructs a `FilteredImageSource` object, which takes a producer source and an `ImageFilter` to produce a filtered version of the image.

▶ `orig` is an `ImageProducer` interface that supplies the image source.

▶ `imgf` is an `ImageFilter` that filters the image to produce a new image.

 addConsumer FilteredImageSource awt.image

```
public synchronized void addConsumer(ImageConsumer ic)
```

The `addConsumer()` method adds an `ImageConsumer` interface to a list of consumers interested in image data.

▶ `ic` is an `ImageConsumer` interface to be added to a list of `ImageConsumers`.

---

 isConsumer FilteredImageSource awt.image

```
public synchronized boolean isConsumer(ImageConsumer ic)
```

The `isConsumer()` method determines whether the specified `ImageConsumer` is currently on the list of `ImageConsumers` for the image data.

▶ `ic` is an `ImageConsumer` interface to be used for the check.

↵ A Boolean value that is `true` if the specified `ImageConsumer` is on the list, `false` if not.

---

 removeConsumer FilteredImageSource awt.image

```
public synchronized void removeConsumer(ImageConsumer ic)
```

The `removeConsumer()` method removes the specified `ImageConsumer` from the list of `ImageConsumers`.

▶ `ic` is the `ImageConsumer` interface to be removed from the list.

startProduction FilteredImageSource `awt.image`

```
public void startProduction(ImageConsumer ic)
```

The `startProduction()` method adds the specified `ImageConsumer` to the list of `ImageConsumers` and immediately starts delivery of the image data to the interface.

▶ `ic` is the `ImageConsumer` that will be used to produce new image data.

 requestTopDownLeftRightResend FilteredImageSource `awt.image`

```
public void requestTopDownLeftRightResend(ImageConsumer ic)
```

The `requestTopDownLeftRightResend()` method is used to deliver the image data to the specified `ImageConsumer` in top-down, left-right order.

▶ `ic` is the `ImageConsumer` that will be the recipient of the image data when it is present.

ImageFilter `awt.image`

 Object

 ImageConsumer, Cloneable

The class hierarchy for the `ImageFilter` class derives from class `java.lang.Object`. The `ImageFilter` class acts as a base class for all image filtering classes. It implements the `ImageConsumer` and `Cloneable` interfaces. `ImageFilter`'s overall derivation can be seen in Figure 29.1.

Listing 29.5 shows the declarations for all of the public methods included in the `java.awt.image.ImageFilter` class.

Listing 29.5. Public members of `java.awt.image.ImageFilter`.

```
public class ImageFilter implements ImageConsumer, Cloneable {
  public ImageFilter getFilterInstance(ImageConsumer ic)
  public void setDimensions(int width, int height}
  public void setProperties(Hashtable props)
  public void setColorModel(ColorModel model)
  public void setHints(int hints)
  public void setPixels(int x, int y, int w, int h, ColorModel model,
  ➥byte pixels[], int off, int scansize)
  public void setPixels(int x, int y, int w, int h, ColorModel model,
  ➥int pixels[], int off,  int scansize)
public void imageComplete(int status)
  public void resendTopDownLeftRight(ImageProducer ip)
  public Object clone()
}
```

getFilterInstance ImageFilter awt.image

```
public ImageFilter getFilterInstance(ImageConsumer ic)
```

The `getFilterInstance()` method returns an `ImageFilter` object that will be used to perform the filtering for the specified `ImageConsumer`.

▶ `ic` is the `ImageConsumer` that requires the image filtering.

↵ An `ImageFilter` object to be used to perform the image filtering.

 ## setDimensions ImageFilter awt.image

```
public void setDimensions(int width, int height}
```

The `setDimensions()` method filters the information provided in the `setDimensions()` method of the `ImageConsumer` interface.

▶ `width` is the filter width.

▶ `height` is the filter height.

 ## setProperties ImageFilter awt.image

```
public void setProperties(Hashtable props)
```

The `setProperties()` method passes the `props` value along after a property is added that identifies which filters have been applied to the image.

▶ `props` is a `Hashtable` object containing a set of properties. For more information on the `Hashtable` object, see the `java.util` package documentation in Chapter 34, "Package `java.util`."

 ## setColorModel ImageFilter awt.image

```
public void setColorModel(ColorModel model)
```

The `setColorModel()` method filters the information provided in the `setColorModel()` method of the `ImageConsumer` interface. For more information on the `ImageConsumer` interface, see the documentation later in this chapter.

▶ `model` is a `ColorModel` object.

 ## setHints ImageFilter awt.image

```
public void setHints(int hints)
```

The `setHints()` method filters the information provided in the `setHints()` method of the `ImageConsumer` interface. For more information on the `ImageConsumer` interface, see the documentation later in this chapter.

 ▶ `hints` is an integer value containing hints.

setPixels ImageFilter awt.image

```
public void setPixels(int x, int y, int w, int h, ColorModel model,
➥ byte pixels[], int off, int scansize)
```

The setPixels() method filters the pixels array. The pixels that pass through the filter are passed onto the ImageConsumer interface.

▶ x is the x coordinate of the image.

▶ y is the y coordinate of the image.

▶ w is the width of the image.

▶ h is the height of the image.

▶ model is the ColorModel that the pixels array conforms to.

▶ pixels is a byte array containing pixels to be examined.

▶ off is a variable that is passed on to the ImageConsumer's setPixels() method. For more information, see the ImageConsumer interface documentation later in this chapter.

▶ scansize is an integer value representing the scansize of the operation.

setPixels ImageFilter awt.image

```
public void setPixels(int x, int y, int w, int h, ColorModel model,
➥ int pixels[], int off, int scansize)
```

The setPixels() method filters the pixels array. The pixels that pass through the filter are passed onto the ImageConsumer interface.

▶ x is the x coordinate of the image.

▶ y is the y coordinate of the image.

▶ w is the width of the image.

▶ h is the height of the image.

▶ model is the ColorModel that the pixels array conforms to.

▶ pixels is an integer array containing pixels to be examined.

▶ off is a variable that is passed onto the ImageConsumer's setPixels() method. For more information, see the ImageConsumer interface documentation later in this chapter.

▶ scansize is an integer value representing the scansize of the operation.

imageComplete **ImageFilter** awt.image

```
public void imageComplete(int status)
```

The `imageComplete()` method filters the information provided by the `imageComplete()` method in the `ImageConsumer` interface. For more information on the `ImageConsumer` interface, see the documentation later in this chapter.

▶ status is an integer value representing the status of the filter operation.

 resendTopDownLeftRight **ImageFilter** awt.image

```
public void resendTopDownLeftRight(ImageProducer ip)
```

The `resendTopDownLeftRight()` method is used to deliver the image data to the specified `ImageConsumer` in top-down, left-right order.

▶ ip is the `ImageProducer` that is responsible for production of the image data.

 clone **ImageFilter** awt.image

```
public Object clone()
```

The `clone()` method returns a clone of the `ImageFilter`.

↵ An object that is identical to the `ImageFilter`.

 # IndexColorModel

 ColorModel

The class hierarchy for the `IndexColorModel` class derives from class `java.awt.image.ColorModel`. This class translates from pixel values to RGB color values for pixels that represent indexes into a color map. The `IndexColorModel` class's overall derivation can be seen in Figure 29.1.

Listing 29.6 shows the declarations for all of the public methods included in the `java.awt.image.IndexColorModel` class.

Listing 29.6. Public members of `java.awt.image.IndexColorModel`.

```
public class IndexColorModel extends ColorModel {
  public IndexColorModel(int bits, int size, byte r[], byte g[], byte b[])
  public IndexColorModel(int bits, int size, byte r[], byte g[],
  ➥ byte b[], int trans)
public IndexColorModel(int bits, int size, byte r[], byte g[],
➥ byte b[], byte a[])
public IndexColorModel(int bits, int size, byte cmap[],
➥ int start, boolean hasalpha)
```

continues

Listing 29.6. continued

```
public IndexColorModel(int bits, int size, byte cmap[],
➥ int start, boolean hasalpha, int trans)
final public int getMapSize()
  final public int getTransparentPixel()
  final public void getReds(byte r[])
  final public void getGreens(byte g[])
  final public void getBlues(byte b[])
  final public void getAlphas(byte a[])
  final public int getRed(int pixel)
  final public int getGreen(int pixel)
  final public int getBlue(int pixel)
  final public int getAlpha(int pixel)
  final public int getRGB(int pixel)
}
```

 IndexColorModel   IndexColorModel   awt.image

```
public IndexColorModel(int bits, int size, byte r[], byte g[], byte b[])
```

The IndexColorModel() constructor constructs a color model from the specified information.

▶   bits is the number of bits required to represent a pixel.

▶   size is the size of the color arrays.

▶   r is the red color array.

▶   g is the green color array.

▶   b is the blue color array.

 IndexColorModel   IndexColorModel   awt.image

```
public IndexColorModel(int bits, int size, byte r[], byte g[],
➥ byte b[], int trans)
```

The IndexColorModel() constructor constructs a color model from the specified information.

▶   bits is the number of bits required to represent a pixel.

▶   size is the size of the color arrays.

▶   r is the red color array.

▶   g is the green color array.

▶   b is the blue color array.

▶   trans is an integer value representing the index that identifies the transparent pixel.

IndexColorModel IndexColorModel awt.image

```
public IndexColorModel(int bits, int size, byte r[], byte g[],
➡ byte b[], byte a[])
```

The `IndexColorModel()` constructor constructs a color model from the specified information.

▶ `bits` is the number of bits required to represent a pixel.

▶ `size` is the size of the color arrays.

▶ `r` is the red color array.

▶ `g` is the green color array.

▶ `b` is the blue color array.

▶ `a` is the alpha color array.

 IndexColorModel IndexColorModel awt.image

```
public IndexColorModel(int bits, int size, byte cmap[],
➡ int start, boolean hasalpha)
```

The `IndexColorModel()` constructor constructs a color model from the specified information.

▶ `bits` is the number of bits required to represent a pixel.

▶ `size` is the size of the color arrays.

▶ `cmap` is a byte array representing the color map array.

▶ `start` is the index representing the first color component within the color array.

▶ `hasalpha` is a Boolean value indicating whether alpha values are contained within the color map. This Boolean value will be `true` if alpha values are contained.

 IndexColorModel IndexColorModel awt.image

```
public IndexColorModel(int bits, int size, byte cmap[],
➡ int start, boolean hasalpha, int trans)
```

The `IndexColorModel()` constructor constructs a color model from the specified information.

▶ `bits` is the number of bits required to represent a pixel.

▶ `size` is the size of the color arrays.

▶ `cmap` is a byte array representing the color map array.

▶ `start` is the index representing the first color component within the color array.

▶ `hasalpha` is a Boolean value indicating whether alpha values are contained within the color map. This Boolean value will be `true` if alpha values are contained.

▶ `trans` is an integer value representing the index of the transparent pixel.

getMapSize IndexColorModel awt.image

```
final public int getMapSize()
```

The getMapSize() method returns the size of the color map used by the IndexColorModel.

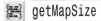 An integer value representing the size of the color map used by the IndexColorModel.

getTransparentPixel IndexColorModel awt.image

```
final public int getTransparentPixel()
```

The getTransparentPixel() method returns the index into the color map of the transparent pixel.

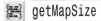 An integer value representing the index into the color map of the transparent pixel. If there is no transparent pixel, this method returns -1.

getReds IndexColorModel awt.image

```
final public void getReds(byte r[])
```

The getReds() method fills the byte array with the red color components.

▶ r is a byte array that is filled by the getReds() method with the red color components.

getGreens IndexColorModel awt.image

```
final public void getGreens(byte g[])
```

The getGreens() method fills the byte array with the green color components.

▶ r is a byte array that is filled by the getGreens() method with the green color components.

getBlues IndexColorModel awt.image

```
final public void getBlues(byte b[])
```

The getBlues() method fills the byte array with the blue color components.

▶ r is a byte array that is filled by the getBlues() method with the blue color components.

getAlphas IndexColorModel awt.image

```
final public void getAlphas(byte a[])
```

The getAlphas() method fills the byte array with the alpha components.

▶ r is a byte array that is filled by the getAlphas() method with the alpha components.

getRed IndexColorModel awt.image

```
final public int getRed(int pixel)
```

The `getRed()` method returns the red color component for the specified pixel using the `IndexColorModel`.

▶ `pixel` is an integer value representing a pixel.

↵ An integer value in the range 0–255 representing the red component for the specified pixel.

getGreen IndexColorModel awt.image

```
final public int getGreen(int pixel)
```

The `getGreen()` method returns the green color component for the specified pixel using the `IndexColorModel`.

▶ `pixel` is an integer value representing a pixel.

↵ An integer value in the range 0–255 representing the green component for the specified pixel.

getBlue IndexColorModel awt.image

```
final public int getBlue(int pixel)
```

The `getBlue()` method returns the blue color component for the specified pixel using the `IndexColorModel`.

▶ `pixel` is an integer value representing a pixel.

↵ An integer value in the range 0–255 representing the blue component for the specified pixel.

getAlpha IndexColorModel awt.image

```
final public int getAlpha(int pixel)
```

The `getAlpha()` method returns the alpha color component for the specified pixel using the `IndexColorModel`.

▶ `pixel` is an integer value representing a pixel.

↵ An integer value in the range 0–255 representing the alpha component for the specified pixel.

getRGB IndexColorModel

```
final public int getRGB(int pixel)
```

The getRGB() method returns the RGB color value for the specified pixel using the default RGB color model.

 pixel is an integer value representing a pixel.

 An integer value in the range 0–255 representing the RGB color value for the specified pixel.

 MemoryImageSource

 Object

 ImageProducer

The class hierarchy for the MemoryImageSource class derives from class java.lang.Object. This class uses an array to produce image pixel values. MemoryImageSource's overall derivation can be seen in Figure 29.1.

Listing 29.7 shows the declarations for all of the public methods included in the java.awt.image.MemoryImageSource class.

Listing 29.7. Public members of java.awt.image.MemoryImageSource.

```
public class MemoryImageSource implements ImageProducer {
  public MemoryImageSource(int w, int h, ColorModel cm, byte[] pix,
➥ int off, int scan)
  public MemoryImageSource(int w, int h, ColorModel cm, byte[] pix,
➥ int off, int scan, Hashtable props)
  public MemoryImageSource(int w, int h, ColorModel cm, int[] pix,
➥ int off, int scan)
  public MemoryImageSource(int w, int h, ColorModel cm, int[] pix,
➥ int off, int scan, Hashtable props)
  public MemoryImageSource(int w, int h, int pix[], int off, int scan)
  public MemoryImageSource(int w, int h, int pix[], int off,
➥ int scan, Hashtable props)
public synchronized void addConsumer(ImageConsumer ic)
  public synchronized boolean isConsumer(ImageConsumer ic)
  public synchronized void removeConsumer(ImageConsumer ic)
  public void startProduction(ImageConsumer ic)
  public void requestTopDownLeftRightResend(ImageConsumer ic)
}
```

MemoryImageSource MemoryImageSource awt.image

```
public MemoryImageSource(int w, int h, ColorModel cm, byte[] pix,
➡ int off, int scan)
```

The `MemoryImageSource()` constructor uses an array of bytes to produce image data for an image object.

 w is the width of the image to be created in pixels.

▶ h is the height of the image to be created in pixels.

▶ cm is the color model used to translate the pixel values.

▶ pix is a byte array containing the image data.

▶ off is the offset into the array to begin reading.

▶ scan is the scan value.

MemoryImageSource MemoryImageSource awt.image

```
public MemoryImageSource(int w, int h, ColorModel cm, byte[] pix,
➡ int off, int scan, Hashtable props)
```

The `MemoryImageSource()` constructor uses an array of bytes to produce image data for an image object.

▶ w is the width of the image to be created in pixels.

▶ h is the height of the image to be created in pixels.

▶ cm is the color model used to translate the pixel values.

▶ pix is a byte array containing the image data.

▶ off is the offset into the array to begin reading.

▶ scan is the scan value.

▶ props is a `Hashtable` object containing properties to be used by the `ImageProducer`. For more information on the `Hashtable` class, see the `java.util` package documentation in Chapter 34.

 MemoryImageSource MemoryImageSource awt.image

```
public MemoryImageSource(int w, int h, ColorModel cm, int[] pix,
➡ int off, int scan)
```

The `MemoryImageSource()` constructor uses an array of bytes to produce image data for an image object.

▶ w is the width of the image to be created in pixels.

▶ h is the height of the image to be created in pixels.

▶ cm is the color model used to translate the pixel values.

▶ pix is an integer array containing the image data.

▶ off is the offset into the array to begin reading.

▶ scan is the scan value.

MemoryImageSource MemoryImageSource   awt.image

```
public MemoryImageSource(int w, int h, ColorModel cm, int[] pix,
➥ int off, int scan, Hashtable props)
```

The MemoryImageSource() constructor uses an array of bytes to produce image data for an image object.

▶ w is the width of the image to be created in pixels.

▶ h is the height of the image to be created in pixels.

▶ cm is the color model used to translate the pixel values.

▶ pix is an integer array containing the image data.

▶ off is the offset into the array to begin reading.

▶ scan is the scan value.

▶ props is a Hashtable object containing properties to be used by the ImageProducer. For more information on the Hashtable class, see the java.util package documentation in Chapter 34.

 MemoryImageSource MemoryImageSource   awt.image

```
public MemoryImageSource(int w, int h, int pix[], int off, int scan)
```

The MemoryImageSource() constructor uses an array of bytes to produce image data for an image object.

▶ w is the width of the image to be created in pixels.

▶ h is the height of the image to be created in pixels.

▶ pix is an integer array containing the image data.

▶ off is the offset into the array to begin reading.

▶ scan is the scan value.

MemoryImageSource   MemoryImageSource   awt.image

```
public MemoryImageSource(int w, int h, int pix[],
➥ int off, int scan, Hashtable props)
```

The MemoryImageSource() constructor uses an array of bytes to produce image data for an image object.

▶ w is the width of the image to be created in pixels.

▶ h is the height of the image to be created in pixels.

▶ pix is an integer array containing the image data.

▶ off is the offset into the array to begin reading.

▶ scan is the scan value.

▶ props is a Hashtable object containing properties to be used by the ImageProducer. For more information on the Hashtable class, see the java.util package documentation in Chapter 34.

 addConsumer   MemoryImageSource   awt.image

```
public synchronized void addConsumer(ImageConsumer ic)
```

The addConsumer() method adds an ImageConsumer interface to a list of image consumers who are interested in data for the image.

▶ ic is an ImageConsumer interface. For more information on the ImageConsumer interface, see the documentation later in this chapter.

isConsumer   MemoryImageSource   awt.image

```
public synchronized boolean isConsumer(ImageConsumer ic)
```

The isConsumer() method determines if the specified ImageConsumer is currently in the list.

▶ ic is an ImageConsumer interface. For more information on the ImageConsumer interface, see the documentation later in this chapter.

↵ A Boolean value that is true if the ImageConsumer is already in the list, false if not.

 removeConsumer   MemoryImageSource   awt.image

```
public synchronized void removeConsumer(ImageConsumer ic)
```

The removeConsumer() method removes the specified ImageConsumer from the list of image consumers interested in receiving image data.

▶ ic is an ImageConsumer interface. For more information on the ImageConsumer interface, see the documentation later in this chapter.

startProduction MemoryImageSource   awt.image

```
public void startProduction(ImageConsumer ic)
```

The `startProduction()` method adds the specified `ImageConsumer` to a list of image consumers interested in receiving image data. This method also immediately starts production of image data to be sent to the `ImageConsumer` interfaces.

► ic is an `ImageConsumer` interface. For more information on the `ImageConsumer` interface, see the documentation later in this chapter.

 requestTopDownLeftRightResend MemoryImageSource   awt.image

```
public void requestTopDownLeftRightResend(ImageConsumer ic)
```

The `requestTopDownLeftRightResend()` method is used to deliver the image data to the specified `ImageConsumer` in top-down, left-right order.

► ic is an `ImageConsumer` interface. For more information on the `ImageConsumer` interface, see the documentation later in this chapter.

PixelGrabber

 Object

 ImageConsumer

The class hierarchy for the `PixelGrabber` class derives from class `java.lang.Object`. The `PixelGrabber` class implements the `ImageConsumer` interface to retrieve a subset of pixels from an `Image`. `PixelGrabber`'s overall derivation can be seen in Figure 29.1.

Listing 29.8 shows the declarations for all of the public methods included in the `java.awt.image.PixelGrabber` class.

Listing 29.8. Public members of `java.awt.image.PixelGrabber`.

```
public class PixelGrabber implements ImageConsumer {
  public PixelGrabber(Image img, int x, int y, int w, int h, int[] pix,
  ➥ int off, int scansize)
  public PixelGrabber(ImageProducer ip, int x, int y, int w, int h, int[] pix,
  ➥ int off, int scansize)
  public boolean grabPixels() throws InterruptedException
    public synchronized boolean grabPixels(long ms) throws InterruptedException
    public synchronized int status()
    public void setDimensions(int width, int height)
    public void setHints(int hints)
    public void setProperties(Hashtable props)
    public void setColorModel(ColorModel model)
    public void setPixels(int srcX, int srcY, int srcW, int srcH,
    ➥ ColorModel model, byte pixels[], int srcOff, int srcScan)
```

```
public void setPixels(int srcX, int srcY, int srcW, int srcH,
➡ ColorModel model, int pixels[], int srcOff, int srcScan)
public synchronized void imageComplete(int status)
}
```

 ## PixelGrabber 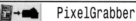 PixelGrabber *awt.image*

```
public PixelGrabber(Image img, int x, int y, int w, int h, int[] pix,
➡ int off, int scansize)
```

The `PixelGrabber()` constructor constructs a `PixelGrabber` object to retrieve a subset of pixels from the `Image`. In this case, the `PixelGrabber` will grab a rectangular section of pixels.

▶ `img` is an `Image` object to be "grabbed." For more information on the `Image` class, see the documentation earlier in this chapter.

▶ `x` is the x coordinate at which to begin grabbing pixels.

▶ `y` is the y coordinate at which to begin grabbing pixels.

▶ `w` is the width of the `PixelGrabber` bounding rectangle.

▶ `h` is the height of the `PixelGrabber` bounding rectangle.

▶ `pix` is an array of integers used to store the grabbed pixels.

▶ `off` is the offset into the `Image` to begin calculations.

▶ `scan` is an integer value used to represent the scan size.

 ## PixelGrabber PixelGrabber *awt.image*

```
public PixelGrabber(ImageProducer ip, int x, int y, int w, int h, int[] pix,
➡ int off, int scansize)
```

The `PixelGrabber()` constructor constructs a `PixelGrabber` object to retrieve a subset of pixels from the `Image`. In this case, the `PixelGrabber` will grab a rectangular section of pixels.

▶ `ip` is an `ImageProducer` object to be "grabbed." For more information on the `ImageProducer` interface, see the documentation later in this chapter.

▶ `x` is the x coordinate at which to begin grabbing pixels.

▶ `y` is the y coordinate at which to begin grabbing pixels.

▶ `w` is the width of the `PixelGrabber` bounding rectangle.

▶ `h` is the height of the `PixelGrabber` bounding rectangle.

▶ `pix` is an array of integers used to store the grabbed pixels.

▶   off is the offset into the Image to begin calculations.

▶   scan is an integer value used to represent the scan size.

grabPixels   PixelGrabber   awt.image

```
public boolean grabPixels() throws InterruptedException
```

The grabPixels() method notifies the PixelGrabber to begin grabbing pixels and wait until all of the pixels to be grabbed have been delivered.

↵   A Boolean value that is true if the operation was successful, false if not.

☛   An InterruptedException if the process was interrupted.

grabPixels   PixelGrabber   awt.image

```
public synchronized boolean grabPixels(long ms) throws InterruptedException
```

This grabPixels() method notifies the PixelGrabber to begin grabbing pixels at some specified time in the future and wait until all of the pixels to be grabbed have been delivered.

▶   ms is a long integer value representing the start time in milliseconds.

↵   A Boolean value that is true if the operation was successful, false if not.

☛   An InterruptedException if the process was interrupted.

status   PixelGrabber   awt.image

```
public synchronized int status()
```

The status() method returns a value representing the status of the grab operation.

↵   An integer value representing the operation's status. This value will be a bitwise OR of all relevant ImageObserver flags.

setDimensions   PixelGrabber   awt.image

```
public void setDimensions(int width, int height)
```

The setDimensions() method must be implemented by this class to fulfill its interface with the ImageConsumer interface. For more information on the ImageConsumer interface, see the documentation later in this chapter.

▶   width is the width parameter.

▶   height is the height parameter.

setHints PixelGrabber awt.image

```
public void setHints(int hints)
```

The setHints() method must be implemented by this class to fulfill its interface with the ImageConsumer interface. For more information on the ImageConsumer interface, see the documentation later in this chapter.

 hints is the hints parameter.

 setProperties PixelGrabber awt.image

```
public void setProperties(Hashtable props)
```

The setProperties() method must be implemented by this class to fulfill its interface with the ImageConsumer interface. For more information on the ImageConsumer interface, see the documentation later in this chapter.

 props is a Hashtable object. For more information on the Hashtable class, see the java.util package documentation in Chapter 34.

 setColorModel PixelGrabber awt.image

```
public void setColorModel(ColorModel model)
```

The setColorModel() method must be implemented by this class to fulfill the ImageConsumer interface. This interface is implemented by the PixelGrabber class to retrieve pixels. For more information on the ImageConsumer interface, see the documentation later in this chapter.

 model is a ColorModel object. For more information on the ColorModel class, see the documentation earlier in this chapter.

 setPixels PixelGrabber awt.image

```
public void setPixels(int srcX, int srcY, int srcW, int srcH,
  ⮕ ColorModel model, byte pixels[], int srcOff, int srcScan)
```

The setPixels() method must be implemented by this class to fulfill the ImageConsumer interface. This interface must be implemented by the PixelGrabber class to retrieve its pixels. For more information on the ImageConsumer interface, see the documentation later in this chapter.

▶ srcX is an integer value representing the source x coordinate.

▶ srcY is an integer value representing the source y coordinate.

▶ srcW is an integer value representing the source width.

▶ srcH is an integer value representing the source height.

▶ model is the ColorModel to be used.

▶ `pixels` is a byte array of pixel values.

▶ `srcOff` is the offset into the source array.

▶ `srcScan` is the source scan value.

 `setPixels` **PixelGrabber** awt.image

```
public void setPixels(int srcX, int srcY, int srcW, int srcH,
➥ ColorModel model, int pixels[], int srcOff, int srcScan)
```

The `setPixels()` method must be implemented by this class to fulfill `ImageConsumer` interface. This interface must be implemented by the `PixelGrabber` class to retrieve its pixels. For more information on the `ImageConsumer` interface, see the documentation later in this chapter.

▶ `srcX` is an integer value representing the source x coordinate.

▶ `srcY` is an integer value representing the source y coordinate.

▶ `srcW` is an integer value representing the source width.

▶ `srcH` is an integer value representing the source height.

▶ `model` is the `ColorModel` to be used.

▶ `pixels` is an integer array of pixel values.

▶ `srcOff` is the offset into the source array.

▶ `srcScan` is the source scan value.

 `imageComplete` **PixelGrabber** awt.image

```
public synchronized void imageComplete(int status)
```

The `imageComplete()` method must be implemented by this class to fulfill its interface with the `ImageConsumer` interface. For more information on the `ImageConsumer` interface, see the documentation later in this chapter.

▶ `status` is an integer value representing the status of the pixel grab operation.

 # RGBImageFilter   awt.image

 `ImageFilter`

The class hierarchy for the `RGBImageFilter` class derives from class `java.awt.image.ImageFilter`. The `RGBImageFilter` abstract class provides the functionality to process image data within a single method that converts pixels in the default RGB `ColorModel`. `RGBImageFilter`'s overall derivation can be seen in Figure 29.1.

Listing 29.9 shows the declarations for all of the public methods included in the `java.awt.image.RGBImageFilter` class.

Listing 29.9. Public members of java.awt.image.RGBImageFilter.

```
public abstract class RGBImageFilter extends ImageFilter {
  public void setColorModel(ColorModel model)
  public void substituteColorModel(ColorModel oldcm, ColorModel newcm)
  public IndexColorModel filterIndexColorModel(IndexColorModel icm)
  public void filterRGBPixels(int x, int y, int w, int h, int pixels[],
  ➥ int off, int scansize)
  public void setPixels(int x, int y, int w, int h, ColorModel model,
  ➥ byte pixels[], int off, int scansize)
  public void setPixels(int x, int y, int w, int h, ColorModel model,
  ➥ int pixels[], int off, int scansize)
  public abstract int filterRGB(int x, int y, int rgb)
}
```

---

setColorModel RGBImageFilter awt.image

```
public void setColorModel(ColorModel model)
```

The setColorModel() method checks the type of the specified ColorModel. If it is an IndexColorModel and the protected canFilterIndexColorModel variable is true, then the color model will be set to the IndexColorModel. Otherwise, the default RGB color model will be used for all filtering operations.

▶ Model is the color model to be used for filtering.

substituteColorModel RGBImageFilter awt.image

```
public void substituteColorModel(ColorModel oldcm, ColorModel newcm)
```

The substituteColorModel() method allows color models to be interchanged on-the-fly. If the old color model is encountered during a setPixels() method call, then the new color model will be used instead.

▶ oldcm is the old color model to be replaced.

▶ newcm is the new color model.

filterIndexColorModel RGBImageFilter awt.image

```
public IndexColorModel filterIndexColorModel(IndexColorModel icm)
```

The filterIndexColorModel() method runs each entry in the specified IndexColorModel through the filterRGB() method and returns a new color model.

▶ icm is the IndexColorModel to be filtered.

↵ An IndexColorModel that has been filtered by the RGBImageFilter class.

filterRGBPixels **RGBImageFilter** awt.image

```
public void filterRGBPixels(int x, int y, int w, int h, int pixels[],
➡ int off, int scansize)
```

The `filterRGBPixels()` method filters an array of pixels through the `filterRGB()` method.

▶ x is the x coordinate at which to start the filtering.

▶ y is the y coordinate at which to start the filtering.

▶ w is the width of the image to be filtered.

▶ h is the height of the image to be filtered.

▶ `pixels` is an array of integers representing pixel values.

▶ `off` is the offset used.

▶ `scansize` is the scan size used.

 setPixels **RGBImageFilter** awt.image

```
public void setPixels(int x, int y, int w, int h, ColorModel model,
➡ byte pixels[], int off, int scansize)
```

The `setPixels()` method converts the pixels and color model before passing them on. If the `ColorModel` has already been converted, the pixels are passed through with the converted `ColorModel`. If not, then the pixel array is converted to the default RGB color model using the `filterRGBPixels()` method.

▶ x is the x coordinate at which to start the filtering.

▶ y is the y coordinate at which to start the filtering.

▶ w is the width of the image to be filtered.

▶ h is the height of the image to be filtered.

▶ `model` is the `ColorModel` with which the pixels comply.

▶ `pixels` is an array of bytes representing pixel values.

▶ `off` is the offset used.

▶ `scansize` is the scan size used.

setPixels **RGBImageFilter** awt.image

```
public void setPixels(int x, int y, int w, int h, ColorModel model,
➡ int pixels[], int off, int scansize)
```

The `setPixels()` method converts the pixels and color model before passing them on. If the `ColorModel` has already been converted, the pixels are passed through with the converted

Listing 29.9. Public members of `java.awt.image.RGBImageFilter`.

```
public abstract class RGBImageFilter extends ImageFilter {
    public void setColorModel(ColorModel model)
    public void substituteColorModel(ColorModel oldcm, ColorModel newcm)
    public IndexColorModel filterIndexColorModel(IndexColorModel icm)
    public void filterRGBPixels(int x, int y, int w, int h, int pixels[],
    ➡ int off, int scansize)
    public void setPixels(int x, int y, int w, int h, ColorModel model,
    ➡ byte pixels[], int off, int scansize)
    public void setPixels(int x, int y, int w, int h, ColorModel model,
    ➡ int pixels[], int off, int scansize)
    public abstract int filterRGB(int x, int y, int rgb)
}
```

 **setColorModel** RGBImageFilter awt.image

```
public void setColorModel(ColorModel model)
```

The `setColorModel()` method checks the type of the specified `ColorModel`. If it is an `IndexColorModel` and the protected `canFilterIndexColorModel` variable is true, then the color model will be set to the `IndexColorModel`. Otherwise, the default RGB color model will be used for all filtering operations.

▶ `Model` is the color model to be used for filtering.

 substituteColorModel RGBImageFilter awt.image

```
public void substituteColorModel(ColorModel oldcm, ColorModel newcm)
```

The `substituteColorModel()` method allows color models to be interchanged on-the-fly. If the old color model is encountered during a `setPixels()` method call, then the new color model will be used instead.

▶ `oldcm` is the old color model to be replaced.

▶ `newcm` is the new color model.

 filterIndexColorModel RGBImageFilter awt.image

```
public IndexColorModel filterIndexColorModel(IndexColorModel icm)
```

The `filterIndexColorModel()` method runs each entry in the specified `IndexColorModel` through the `filterRGB()` method and returns a new color model.

▶ `icm` is the `IndexColorModel` to be filtered.

 An `IndexColorModel` that has been filtered by the `RGBImageFilter` class.

filterRGBPixels   RGBImageFilter awt.image

```
public void filterRGBPixels(int x, int y, int w, int h, int pixels[],
➡ int off, int scansize)
```

The `filterRGBPixels()` method filters an array of pixels through the `filterRGB()` method.

▶ x is the x coordinate at which to start the filtering.

▶ y is the y coordinate at which to start the filtering.

▶ w is the width of the image to be filtered.

▶ h is the height of the image to be filtered.

▶ pixels is an array of integers representing pixel values.

▶ off is the offset used.

▶ scansize is the scan size used.

setPixels   RGBImageFilter   awt.image

```
public void setPixels(int x, int y, int w, int h, ColorModel model,
➡ byte pixels[], int off, int scansize)
```

The `setPixels()` method converts the pixels and color model before passing them on. If the `ColorModel` has already been converted, the pixels are passed through with the converted `ColorModel`. If not, then the pixel array is converted to the default RGB color model using the `filterRGBPixels()` method.

▶ x is the x coordinate at which to start the filtering.

▶ y is the y coordinate at which to start the filtering.

▶ w is the width of the image to be filtered.

▶ h is the height of the image to be filtered.

▶ model is the `ColorModel` with which the pixels comply.

▶ pixels is an array of bytes representing pixel values.

▶ off is the offset used.

▶ scansize is the scan size used.

setPixels   RGBImageFilter awt.image

```
public void setPixels(int x, int y, int w, int h, ColorModel model,
➡ int pixels[], int off, int scansize)
```

The `setPixels()` method converts the pixels and color model before passing them on. If the `ColorModel` has already been converted, the pixels are passed through with the converted

`ColorModel`. If not, then the pixel array is converted to the default RGB color model using the `filterRGBPixels()` method.

▶ x is the x coordinate to start the filtering at.

▶ y is the y coordinate to start the filtering at.

▶ w is the width of the image to be filtered.

▶ h is the height of the image to be filtered.

▶ model is the `ColorModel` that the pixels comply with.

▶ pixels is an array of integers representing pixel values.

▶ off is the offset used.

▶ scansize is the scan size used.

filterRGB  RGBImageFilter *awt.image*

```
public abstract int filterRGB(int x, int y, int rgb)
```

The `filterRGB()` method allows subclasses to specify a method that converts an input pixel using the default RGB color model to an output pixel.

▶ x is the x coordinate of the pixel.

▶ y is the y coordinate of the pixel.

▶ rgb is the pixel value using the default RGB color model.

▶ An integer value representing the filtered pixel value.

ImageConsumer *awt.image*

╋ Object

The class hierarchy for the `ImageConsumer` interface extends from class `java.lang.Object`. This interface is implemented by objects that are responsible for acquiring data provided by the `ImageProducer` interface. `ImageConsumer`'s overall derivation can be seen in Figure 29.1.

Listing 29.10 shows the declarations for all of the public methods and variables included in the `java.awt.image.ImageConsumer` interface.

Listing 29.10. Members of `java.awt.image.ImageConsumer`.

```
public interface ImageConsumer {
  void setDimensions(int width, int height)
  void setProperties(Hashtable props)
  void setColorModel(ColorModel model)
  void setHints(int hintflags)
  int RANDOMPIXELORDER
  int TOPDOWNLEFTRIGHT
  int COMPLETESCANLINES
  int SINGLEPASS
  int SINGLEFRAME
  int IMAGEERROR
  int SINGLEFRAMEDONE
  int STATICIMAGEDONE
  int IMAGEABORTED
  void setPixels(int x, int y, int w, int h, ColorModel model,
  ➥ byte pixels[], int off, int scansize)
  void setPixels(int x, int y, int w, int h, ColorModel model,
  ➥ int pixels[], int off, int scansize)
  void imageComplete(int status)
}
```

Instance Variables

The following instance variables are all declared as public static variables within the `ImageConsumer` interface. These variables are used to specify options to the `ImageConsumer` methods:

int RANDOMPIXELORDER

The pixels will be delivered in a random order.

int TOPDOWNLEFTRIGHT

The pixels will be delivered in top-down, left-right order.

int COMPLETESCANLINES

The pixels will be delivered in complete scan lines.

int SINGLEPASS

The pixels will be delivered in a single pass.

int SINGLEFRAME

The pixels will be delivered in a single frame.

int IMAGEERROR

An error occurred during image processing.

int SINGLEFRAMEDONE

A single frame is complete, but the overall operation has not been completed.

`int STATICIMAGEDONE`

The image construction is complete.

`int IMAGEABORTED`

The image creation was aborted.

 ## setDimensions

 ImageConsumer awt.image

`void setDimensions(int width, int height)`

The `setDimensions()` method is used to report the dimensions of the source image to the `ImageConsumer`.

▶ `width` is the width of the source image.

▶ `height` is the height of the source image.

 ## setProperties

ImageConsumer awt.image

`void setProperties(Hashtable props)`

The `setProperties()` method is used to report the properties of the source image to the `ImageConsumer`.

▶ `props` is a `Hashtable` object containing the image properties. For more information on the `Hashtable` class, see the `java.util` package documentation in Chapter 34.

setColorModel

 ImageConsumer awt.image

`void setColorModel(ColorModel model)`

The `setColorModel()` method is used to report the color model of the source image to the `ImageConsumer`.

▶ `model` is the color model used by the source image. For more information on the `ColorModel` class, see the documentation earlier in this chapter.

 ## setHints

ImageConsumer awt.image

`void setHints(int hintflags)`

The `setHints()` method is used to report hints to the `ImageConsumer`. These hints are usually a bitmask of the `ImageConsumer` variables that are used to give information about the manner in which the pixels will be delivered.

▶ `hintflags` is an integer value containing hints about the manner in which the pixels will be delivered.

setPixels   **ImageConsumer**   awt.image

```
void setPixels(int x, int y, int w, int h, ColorModel model,
➥ byte pixels[], int off, int scansize)
```

The setPixels() method is used to deliver the pixels to the ImageConsumer. Note: Pixel (m,n) is stored in the pixels array at index (n * scansize + m + off).

▶ x is the x coordinate.

▶ y is the y coordinate.

▶ w is the width of the image.

▶ h is the height of the image.

▶ model is the ColorModel used.

▶ pixels is an array of bytes containing pixel information.

▶ off is the offset value.

▶ scansize is the scan size value.

setPixels   **ImageConsumer**   awt.image

```
void setPixels(int x, int y, int w, int h, ColorModel model,
➥ int pixels[], int off, int scansize)
```

The setPixels() method is used to deliver the pixels to the ImageConsumer. Note: Pixel (m,n) is stored in the pixels array at index (n * scansize + m + off).

▶ x is the x coordinate.

▶ y is the y coordinate.

▶ w is the width of the image.

▶ h is the height of the image.

▶ model is the ColorModel used.

▶ pixels is an array of integers containing pixel information.

▶ off is the offset value.

▶ scansize is the scan size value.

imageComplete   **ImageConsumer**

```
void imageComplete(int status)
```

The `imageComplete()` method is called when the `ImageProducer` is finished delivering an image frame. The `ImageConsumer` should remove itself from the `ImageProducer`'s list at this time.

 # ImageObserver

➕ `Object`

The class hierarchy for the `ImageObserver` interface extends from class `java.lang.Object`. This interface is implemented by objects that are responsible for receiving information about an image as it is being constructed. `ImageObserver`'s overall derivation can be seen in Figure 29.1.

Listing 29.11 shows the declarations for all of the public methods included in the `java.awt.image.ImageObserver` interface.

Listing 29.11. Members of `java.awt.image.ImageObserver`.

```
public interface ImageObserver {
  public boolean imageUpdate(Image img, int infoflags, int x, int y,
  ➥ int width, int height)
public static final int WIDTH
  public static final int HEIGHT
  public static final int PROPERTIES
  public static final int SOMEBITS
  public static final int FRAMEBITS
  public static final int ALLBITS
  public static final int ERROR
  public static final int ABORT
}
```

Static Instance Variables

The following instance variables are all declared as public static variables within the `ImageObserver` interface. These variables are used to specify options to the `ImageObserver` methods:

`public static final int WIDTH`

The width of the base image is now available.

`public static final int HEIGHT`

The height of the base image is now available.

`public static final int PROPERTIES`

The properties of the base image are now available.

```
public static final int SOMEBITS
```

Some bits of the image for drawing are now available.

```
public static final int FRAMEBITS
```

Another complete frame of a multiframe image is now available.

```
public static final int ALLBITS
```

A static image that was previously drawn is now complete and can be drawn again.

```
public static final int ERROR
```

An image that was being tracked asynchronously has encountered an error.

```
public static final int ABORT
```

An image that was being tracked was aborted before production completed.

---

imageUpdate ImageObserver awt.image

```
public boolean imageUpdate(Image img, int infoflags, int x, int y,
    ➡ int width, int height)
```

The `imageUpdate()` method is called every time image information becomes available. The recipient of the update messages is an `ImageObserver` object that has requested information about an image.

▶ `img` is the image of interest.

▶ `infoflags` are status flags indicating the progress of the image process.

▶ `x` is the x coordinate that applies (if necessary).

▶ `y` is the y coordinate that applies (if necessary).

▶ `width` is the width of the image (if necessary).

▶ `height` is the height of the image (if necessary).

ImageProducer awt.image

➕ Object

The class hierarchy for the `ImageProducer` interface extends from class `java.lang.Object`. The `ImageProducer` interface is implemented by objects that produce images. Each image contains an `ImageProducer`. `ImageProducer`'s overall derivation can be seen in Figure 29.1.

Listing 29.12 shows the declarations for all of the public methods included in the `java.awt.image.ImageProducer` interface.

Listing 29.12. Members of `java.awt.image.ImageProducer`.

```
public interface ImageProducer {
    public void addConsumer(ImageConsumer ic)
    public boolean isConsumer(ImageConsumer ic)
    public void removeConsumer(ImageConsumer ic)
    public void startProduction(ImageConsumer ic)
    public void requestTopDownLeftRightResend(ImageConsumer ic)
}
```

 addConsumer ImageProducer awt.image

`public void addConsumer(ImageConsumer ic)`

The `addConsumer()` method adds the `ImageConsumer` to a list to receive image data during reconstruction of the image.

 `ic` is an `ImageConsumer` interface. For more information on the `ImageConsumer` interface, see the documentation earlier in this chapter.

 isConsumer ImageProducer awt.image

`public boolean isConsumer(ImageConsumer ic)`

The `isConsumer()` method determines if the specified `ImageConsumer` is currently on the `ImageProducer`'s list of recipients.

 `ic` is an `ImageConsumer` interface. For more information on the `ImageConsumer` interface, see the documentation earlier in this chapter.

 A Boolean value that is `true` if the `ImageConsumer` is registered, `false` if not.

 removeConsumer ImageProducer awt.image

`public void removeConsumer(ImageConsumer ic)`

The `removeConsumer()` method removes the specified `ImageConsumer` from the internal list.

 `ic` is an `ImageConsumer` interface. For more information on the `ImageConsumer` interface, see the documentation earlier in this chapter.

 startProduction ImageProducer awt.image

`public void startProduction(ImageConsumer ic)`

The `startProduction()` method adds the specified `ImageConsumer` to the list of image data recipients and immediately begins production of the image data.

▶ ic is an `ImageConsumer` interface. For more information on the `ImageConsumer` interface, see the documentation earlier in this chapter.

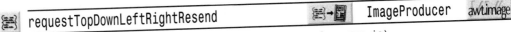

requestTopDownLeftRightResend   ImageProducer   awt.image

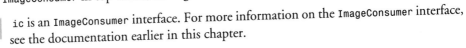

```
public void requestTopDownLeftRightResend(ImageConsumer ic)
```

The `requestTopDownLeftRightResend()` method is used to deliver the image data to the specified `ImageConsumer` in top-down, left-right order.

▶ ic is an `ImageConsumer` interface. For more information on the `ImageConsumer` interface, see the documentation earlier in this chapter.

30

Package
java.awt.peer

by Bryan Morgan

The java.awt.peer package is interesting in that it contains no classes. Every object defined within the java.awt.peer package is an interface. By examining the contents of the classes in the java.awt package, you will find that all of the GUI components in that package implement the interfaces found in the java.awt.peer package. The remainder of this chapter lists the interfaces found within the java.awt.peer package and these interfaces' methods. Table 30.1 shows the contents of the java.awt.peer package, and Figure 30.1 shows the hierarchy of the contents of the package.

NOTE

Nearly all of the methods defined in the java.awt.peer interfaces are *friendly* methods. This means that they can only be accessed from within java.awt package classes. Therefore, if you are developing a class for a package outside of java.awt (which you probably are), these interfaces are not accessible. They are only provided to give some insight into java.awt class functionality.

Table 30.1. Contents of package java.awt.peer.

Interface index

ButtonPeer	FileDialogPeer	MenuPeer
CanvasPeer	FramePeer	PanelPeer
CheckboxMenuItemPeer	LabelPeer	ScrollbarPeer
CheckboxPeer	ListPeer	TextAreaPeer
ChoicePeer	MenuBarPeer	TextComponentPeer
ComponentPeer	MenuComponentPeer	TextFieldPeer
ContainerPeer	MenuItemPeer	WindowPeer
DialogPeer		

FIGURE 30.1.

Contents of package `java.awt.peer`.

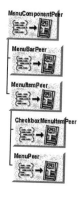
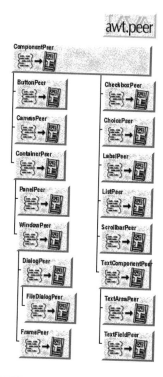

 # ButtonPeer

■ ComponentPeer

The `ButtonPeer` interface extends interface `java.awt.peer.ComponentPeer`. The `ButtonPeer` interface provides the basic structure required for button component functionality.

Listing 30.1 shows the declarations for all of the public methods included in the `java.awt.peer.ButtonPeer` interface.

Listing 30.1. Members of `java.awt.peer.ButtonPeer`.

```
public interface ButtonPeer extends ComponentPeer {
    void setLabel(String label)
}
```

setLabel ButtonPeer awt.peer

```
void setLabel(String label)
```

The setLabel() method should set the displayed label for the Button using the specified label string.

▶ label is a String that will be displayed as the button's label.

 # CanvasPeer awt.peer

 ComponentPeer

The CanvasPeer interface extends interface java.awt.peer.ComponentPeer. The CanvasPeer interface provides the basic structure required for canvas component functionality.

Listing 30.2 shows the declarations for all of the public methods included in the java.awt.peer.ComponentPeer interface.

Listing 30.2. Members of java.awt.peer.CanvasPeer.

```
public interface CanvasPeer extends ComponentPeer {
}
```

CheckboxMenuItemPeer awt.peer

 MenuItemPeer

The CheckboxMenuItemPeer interface extends interface java.awt.peer.MenuItemPeer. The CheckboxMenuItemPeer interface provides the basic structure required for CheckboxMenuItem component functionality.

Listing 30.3 shows the declarations for all of the public methods included in the java.awt.peer.CheckboxMenuItemPeer interface.

Listing 30.3. Members of java.awt.peer.CheckboxMenuItemPeer.

```
public interface CheckboxMenuItemPeer extends MenuItemPeer {
  void setState(boolean t)
}
```

setState CheckboxMenuItemPeer  awt.peer

```
void setState(boolean t)
```

The `setState()` method sets the checked state of a `CheckboxMenuItem`.

 t is a Boolean value that will be `true` if the `Checkbox` is to be checked, `false` if not.

 # CheckboxPeer awt.peer

✚ ComponentPeer

The `CheckboxPeer` interface extends interface `java.awt.peer.ComponentPeer`. The `CheckboxPeer` interface provides the basic structure required for checkbox component functionality.

Listing 30.4 shows the declarations for all of the public methods included in the `java.awt.peer.CheckboxPeer` interface.

Listing 30.4. Members of `java.awt.peer.CheckboxPeer`.
```
public interface CheckboxPeer extends ComponentPeer {
  void setState(boolean state)
  void setCheckboxGroup(CheckboxGroup g)
  void setLabel(String label)
}
```

 setState CheckboxPeer awt.peer

```
void setState(boolean state)
```

The `setState()` method sets the checked state of a `Checkbox`.

▶ t is a Boolean value that should be set to `true` if the `Checkbox` is to be checked, `false` if not.

 setCheckboxGroup CheckboxPeer awt.peer

```
void setCheckboxGroup(CheckboxGroup g)
```

The `setCheckboxGroup()` method should set which checkbox group the checkbox belongs to using the specified `CheckboxGroup`.

▶ g is a `CheckboxGroup` object of which this `Checkbox` will be a member.

 setLabel CheckboxPeer awt.peer

```
void setLabel(String label)
```

The `setLabel()` method should set the displayed label for the `Checkbox` using the specified label string.

 `label` is a `String` that will be displayed as the checkbox's label.

 # ChoicePeer   awt.peer

✚ ComponentPeer

The `ChoicePeer` interface extends interface `java.awt.peer.ComponentPeer`. The `ChoicePeer` interface provides the basic structure required for `Choice` component functionality.

Listing 30.5 shows the declarations for all of the public methods included in the `java.awt.peer.ChoicePeer` interface.

Listing 30.5. Members of `java.awt.peer.ChoicePeer`.
```
public interface ChoicePeer extends ComponentPeer {
  void addItem(String item, int index)
  void select(int index)
}
```

 addItem   ChoicePeer   awt.peer

```
void addItem(String item, int index)
```
The `addItem()` method adds the specified item to the `Choice` list at the specified list index.

▶ `item` is a `String` value representing the item to be added to the `Choice` list.

▶ `index` is the integer index into the `Choice` list where the item parameter is to be added.

 select   ChoicePeer   awt.peer

```
void select(int index)
```
The `select()` method selects the `Choice` list item at the specified index.

▶ `index` is the index into the `Choice` list to be selected.

 # ComponentPeer   awt.peer

✚ Object

The `ComponentPeer` interface extends class `java.lang.Object`. The `ComponentPeer` interface provides the basic structure required for component functionality.

Listing 30.6 shows the declarations for all of the public methods included in the `java.awt.peer.ComponentPeer` interface.

Listing 30.6. Members of `java.awt.peer.ComponentPeer`.

```
public interface ComponentPeer {
    void            show()
    void            hide()
    void            enable()
    void            disable()
    void            paint(Graphics g)
    void            repaint(long tm, int x, int y, int width, int height)
    void            print(Graphics g)
    void            reshape(int x, int y, int width, int height)
    boolean         handleEvent(Event e)
    Dimension       minimumSize()
    Dimension       preferredSize()
    ColorModel      getColorModel()
    java.awt.Toolkit getToolkit()
    Graphics        getGraphics()
    FontMetrics     getFontMetrics(Font font)
    void            dispose()
    void            setForeground(Color c)
    void            setBackground(Color c)
    void            setFont(Font f)
    void            requestFocus()
    void            nextFocus()
    Image           createImage(ImageProducer producer)
    Image           createImage(int width, int height)
    boolean         prepareImage(Image img, int w, int h, ImageObserver o)
    int             checkImage(Image img, int w, int h, ImageObserver o)
}
```

 show  ComponentPeer awt.peer

```
void show()
```

The `show()` method should be implemented to make the `Component` object visible.

 none

 hide ComponentPeer awt.peer

```
void hide()
```

The `hide()` method should hide the component so that is not visible.

 none

---

enable  ComponentPeer   awt.peer

```
void enable()
```

The `enable()` method should enable the component so that it can be selected by the user.

 none

---

disable ComponentPeer   awt.peer

```
void disable()
```

The `disable()` method should disable the component (gray it out, etc.) so that it cannot be selected by the user.

---

paint ComponentPeer   awt.peer

```
void paint(Graphics g)
```

The `paint()` method should display the component using the specified `Graphics` context.

▶ g is a `Graphics` object used for drawing purposes. For more information on the `Graphics` class, see the documentation in Chapter 28, "Package `java.awt`."

---

repaint ComponentPeer   awt.peer

```
void repaint(long tm, int x, int y, int width, int height)
```

The `repaint()` method repaints a part of the component at some specified time in the future.

▶ tm sets the maximum time in milliseconds before the update.

▶ x is the x coordinate of the component's bounding rectangle to repaint.

▶ y is the y coordinate of the component's bounding rectangle to repaint.

▶ width is the width of the component's bounding rectangle to repaint.

▶ height is the height of the component's bounding rectangle to repaint.

---

print  ComponentPeer   awt.peer

```
void print(Graphics g)
```

The `print()` method should print the component using the specified `Graphics` object.

▶ g is a `Graphics` object used for drawing purposes. For more information on the `Graphics` class, see the documentation in Chapter 28.

reshape ComponentPeer awt.peer

```
void reshape(int x, int y, int width, int height)
```

The `reshape()` method reshapes the component to the specified bounding rectangle.

▶ x is the x coordinate of the component's new bounding rectangle.

▶ y is the y coordinate of the component's new bounding rectangle.

▶ width is the width of the component's new bounding rectangle.

▶ height is the height of the component's new bounding rectangle.

handleEvent ComponentPeer awt.peer

```
boolean handleEvent(Event e)
```

The `handleEvent()` method should handle the specified event for the component.

▶ e is an Event object encapsulating some system event. For more information on the Event class, see the documentation in Chapter 28.

↩ A Boolean value that should be true if the event was handled.

minimumSize ComponentPeer awt.peer

```
Dimension minimumSize()
```

The `minimumSize()` method returns the minimum size allowable for the component.

↩ A Dimension object containing the component's minimum size. For more information on the Dimension class, see the documentation in Chapter 28.

preferredSize ComponentPeer awt.peer

```
Dimension preferredSize()
```

The `preferredSize()` method returns the preferred size allowable for the component.

↩ A Dimension object containing the component's preferred size. For more information on the Dimension class, see the documentation in Chapter 28.

getColorModel ComponentPeer awt.peer

```
ColorModel getColorModel()
```

The `getColorModel()` method returns the ColorModel used for this component.

↩ A ColorModel object that contains the component's ColorModel information. For more information on the ColorModel class, see the documentation in Chapter 29, "Package java.awt.image."

getToolkit   ComponentPeer   awt.peer

```
Toolkit getToolkit()
```

The getToolkit() method returns the component's managing Toolkit.

A Toolkit object. For more information on the Toolkit class, see the documentation in Chapter 28.

getGraphics   ComponentPeer   awt.peer

```
Graphics getGraphics()
```

The getGraphics() method returns a Graphics context for the component.

A Graphics class used for drawing purposes. For more information on the Graphics class, see the documentation in Chapter 28.

getFontMetrics   ComponentPeer   awt.peer

```
FontMetrics getFontMetrics(Font font)
```

The getFontMetrics() method returns the FontMetrics information for the specified Font.

font is a Font object. For more information on the Font class, see the documentation in Chapter 28.

A FontMetrics object containing metrics information on the specified font. For more information on the FontMetrics class, see the documentation in Chapter 28.

dispose   ComponentPeer   awt.peer

```
void dispose()
```

The dispose() method disposes of a component's resources and the component itself.

setForeground   ComponentPeer   awt.peer

```
void setForeground(Color c)
```

The setForeground() method sets the foreground color for the component using the specified color.

c is a Color object specifying which color to use for the foreground color. For more information on the Color class, see the documentation in Chapter 28.

setBackground ComponentPeer awt.peer

```
void setBackground(Color c)
```

The `setBackground()` method sets the background color for the component using the specified color.

 c is a `Color` object specifying which color to use for the background color. For more information on the `Color` class, see the documentation in Chapter 28.

 ## setFont ComponentPeer awt.peer

```
void setFont(Font f)
```

The `setFont()` method sets the font to use for this component using the specified font.

f is a `Font` object specifying which font to use for the component. For more information on the `Font` class, see the documentation in Chapter 28.

 ## requestFocus ComponentPeer awt.peer

```
void requestFocus()
```

The `requestFocus()` method requests the input focus for the component.

 none

nextFocus ComponentPeer awt.peer

```
void nextFocus()
```

The `nextFocus()` method shifts the focus to the next component on the screen.

 ## createImage ▦→▤ ComponentPeer awt.peer

```
Image createImage(ImageProducer producer)
```

The `createImage()` method creates an `Image` object using the specified `ImageProducer` interface.

producer is an `ImageProducer` interface used to produce an image. For more information on the `ImageProducer` interface, see the documentation in Chapter 29.

An `Image` object. For more information on the `Image` class, see the documentation in Chapter 28.

createImage   ComponentPeer   awt.peer

```
Image createImage(int width, int height)
```

This `createImage()` method creates an image for off-screen use using the specified sizes.

▶ `width` is the width of the image to be created.

▶ `height` is the height of the image to be created.

↵ An `Image` object. For more information on the `Image` class, see the documentation in Chapter 28.

 prepareImage   ComponentPeer   awt.peer

```
boolean prepareImage(Image img, int w, int h, ImageObserver o)
```

The `prepareImage()` method prepares the image for rendering on this component using the specified parameters.

▶ `img` is an `Image` object to be rendered. For more information on the `Image` class, see the documentation in Chapter 28.

▶ `w` is the width of the rectangle in which to render the image.

▶ `h` is the height of the rectangle in which to render the image.

▶ `o` is the `ImageObserver` interface used to monitor the `Image` rendering. For more information on the `ImageObserver` interface, see the documentation in Chapter 29.

↵ A Boolean value that is `true` if the image was rendered successfully, `false` if not.

checkImage   ComponentPeer   awt.peer

```
int checkImage(Image img, int w, int h, ImageObserver o)
```

The `checkImage()` method returns the status of a scaled rendering of a specified `Image`.

▶ `img` is an `Image` object to be rendered. For more information on the `Image` class, see the documentation in Chapter 28.

▶ `w` is the width of the rectangle in which to render the image.

▶ `h` is the height of the rectangle in which to render the image.

▶ `o` is the `ImageObserver` interface used to monitor the `Image` rendering. For more information on the `ImageObserver` interface, see the documentation in Chapter 29.

↵ An integer value containing the Boolean `OR` of the `ImageObserver` status flags. For more information on the `ImageObserver` class, see the documentation in Chapter 29.

ContainerPeer

awt.peer

➕ ComponentPeer

The `ContainerPeer` interface extends interface `java.awt.peer.ComponentPeer`. The `ContainerPeer` interface provides the basic structure required for container component functionality.

Listing 30.7 shows the declarations for all of the public methods included in the `java.awt.peer.ContainerPeer` interface.

Listing 30.7. Members of `java.awt.peer.ContainerPeer`.

```
public interface ContainerPeer extends ComponentPeer {
    Insets insets()
}
```

 insets   ContainerPeer   awt.peer

```
Insets insets()
```

The `insets()` method returns an `Insets` object representing the `Insets` of the container.

↵ An `Insets` object. For more information on the `Insets` class, see the documentation in Chapter 28.

 # DialogPeer

awt.peer

➕ WindowPeer

The `DialogPeer` interface extends the `java.awt.peer.WindowPeer` interface. The `DialogPeer` interface provides the basic structure required for dialog box component functionality.

Listing 30.8 shows the declarations for all of the public methods included in the `java.awt.peer.WindowPeer` interface.

Listing 30.8. Members of `java.awt.peer.DialogPeer`.

```
public interface DialogPeer extends WindowPeer {
    void setTitle(String title)
    void setResizable(boolean resizeable)
}
```

setTitle   DialogPeer awt.peer

```
void setTitle(String title)
```

The setTitle() method sets the title to be displayed on the dialog's title bar.

▶ title is a String value that will be used as the dialog's title.

 setResizable   DialogPeer awt.peer

```
void setResizable(boolean resizeable)
```

The setResizable() method determines the dialog's resize state.

▶ resizeable is a Boolean value that is true if the dialog can be resized, false if not.

 FileDialogPeer   awt.peer

 DialogPeer

The FileDialogPeer interface extends interface java.awt.peer.DialogPeer. The FileDialogPeer interface provides the basic structure required for file selection dialog component functionality.

Listing 30.9 shows the declarations for all of the public methods included in the java.awt.peer.FileDialogPeer interface.

Listing 30.9. Members of java.awt.peer.FileDialogPeer.

```
public interface FileDialogPeer extends DialogPeer {
    void setFile(String file)
    void setDirectory(String dir)
    void setFilenameFilter(FilenameFilter filter)
}
```

 setFile   FileDialogPeer awt.peer

```
void setFile(String file)
```

The setFile() method sets the filename to be displayed in the FileDialog.

  file is a String value representing a filename.

setDirectory   FileDialogPeer   awt.peer

void setDirectory(String dir)

The setDirectory() method sets the directory to be selected in the FileDialog.

▶ dir is a String value representing the directory name.

 setFilenameFilter   FileDialogPeer   awt.peer

void setFilenameFilter(FilenameFilter filter)

The setFilenameFilter() sets the filter to be used in the FileDialog.

▶ filter is a FilenameFilter object used to filter filenames. For more information on the FilenameFilter interface, see the documentation for the java.io package in Chapter 31, "Package java.io."

 FramePeer   awt.peer

 WindowPeer

The FramePeer interface extends interface java.awt.peer.WindowPeer. The FramePeer interface provides the basic structure required for frame component functionality.

Listing 30.10 shows the declarations for all of the public methods included in the java.awt.peer.FramePeer interface.

Listing 30.10. Members of java.awt.peer.FramePeer.

```
public interface FramePeer extends WindowPeer {
    void setTitle(String title)
    void setIconImage(Image im)
    void setMenuBar(MenuBar mb)
    void setResizable(boolean resizeable)
    void setCursor(int cursorType)
}
```

 setTitle   FramePeer   awt.peer

void setTitle(String title)

The setTitle() method sets the title of the frame to the specified title string.

▶ title is a String value representing the frame's title.

setIconImage

 FramePeer   awt.peer

```
void setIconImage(Image im)
```

The `setIconImage()` method sets the image to be used when the frame is iconized.

▶ `im` is an `Image` object. For more information on the `Image` class, see the documentation in Chapter 28.

setMenuBar

 FramePeer   awt.peer

```
void setMenuBar(MenuBar mb)
```

The `setMenuBar()` method sets the menu bar to be used for the frame.

▶ `mb` is a `MenuBar` object. For more information on the `MenuBar` class, see the documentation in Chapter 28.

setResizable

 FramePeer   awt.peer

```
void setResizable(boolean resizeable)
```

The `setResizable()` method determines the resize state of the frame.

▶ `resizeable` is a Boolean value that is `true` if the frame can be resized, `false` if not.

setCursor

FramePeer   awt.peer

```
void setCursor(int cursorType)
```

The `setCursor()` method sets the cursor type for the frame.

▶ `cursorType` is an integer value representing the cursor type. For more information on the `Frame` class, see the documentation in Chapter 28.

LabelPeer

awt.peer

 `ComponentPeer`

The `LabelPeer` interface extends interface `java.awt.peer.ComponentPeer`. The `LabelPeer` interface provides the basic structure required for label component functionality.

Listing 30.11 shows the declarations for all of the public methods included in the `java.awt.peer.LabelPeer` interface.

```
public interface LabelPeer extends ComponentPeer {
  void setText(String label)
  void setAlignment(int alignment)
}
```

 ## setText LabelPeer awt.peer

```
void setText(String label)
```

The setText() method sets the text to be displayed on the label.

 label is a String value that will be used as the label string.

setAlignment LabelPeer awt.peer

```
void setAlignment(int alignment)
```

The setAlignment() method sets the alignment type of the label.

▶ alignment is an integer value that determines the alignment of the label (LEFT, RIGHT, or CENTER).

 # ListPeer awt.peer

➕ ComponentPeer

The ListPeer interface extends interface java.awt.peer.ComponentPeer. The ListPeer interface provides the basic structure required for list component functionality.

Listing 30.12 shows the declarations for all of the public methods included in the java.awt.peer.ListPeer interface.

```
public interface ListPeer extends ComponentPeer {
  int[] getSelectedIndexes()
  void addItem(String item, int index)
  void delItems(int start, int end)
  void clear()
  void select(int index)
  void deselect(int index)
```

continues

Listing 30.12. continued
```
    void makeVisible(int index)
    void setMultipleSelections(boolean v)
    Dimension preferredSize(int v)
    Dimension minimumSize(int v)
}
```

getSelectedIndexes   ▨→▧   ListPeer   awt.peer

```
int[] getSelectedIndexes()
```

The getSelectedIndexes() method returns an array containing the selected indexes in the list.

▶ An integer array containing the indexes that are currently selected in the list.

addItem   ▨→▧   ListPeer   awt.peer

```
void addItem(String item, int index)
```

The addItem() method adds a String item at the specified index.

▶ item is a String value to be added to the list.

▶ index is an integer value representing the index into the list.

delItems   ▨→▧   ListPeer   awt.peer

```
void delItems(int start, int end)
```

The delItems() method deletes a range of values from the list using the specified range values.

▶ start is an integer value marking the start of the deletion range.

▶ end is an integer value marking the end of the deletion range.

clear   ▨→▧   ListPeer   awt.peer

```
void clear()
```

The clear() method clears all elements from the list.

↵ none

select   ▨→▧   ListPeer   awt.peer

```
void select(int index)
```

This select() method selects the specified index.

▶ index is an integer value specifying the item in the list to be selected.

deselect ListPeer awt.peer

```
void deselect(int index)
```

The `deselect()` method deselects an item within the list.

▶ `index` is an integer value specifying the item in the list to be deselected.

makeVisible ListPeer awt.peer

```
void makeVisible(int index)
```

The `makeVisible()` method forces the list to scroll, if necessary, so that the specified index will be made visible to the user.

▶ `index` is an integer value representing the index to be made visible.

setMultipleSelections ListPeer awt.peer

```
void setMultipleSelections(boolean v)
```

The `setMultipleSelections()` method specifies whether the list should allow multiple selections or not.

▶ `v` is a Boolean value that is `true` if multiple selections are to be allowed, `false` if not.

preferredSize ListPeer awt.peer

```
Dimension preferredSize(int v)
```

The `preferredSize()` method sets the preferred size for a list of the specified number of items.

▶ `v` is an integer value specifying the number of items within the list.

↵ A `Dimension` object containing the preferred size of the list. For more information on the `Dimension` class, see the documentation in Chapter 28.

minimumSize ListPeer awt.peer

```
Dimension minimumSize(int v)
```

The `minimumSize()` method sets the minimum size for a list of the specified number of items.

▶ `v` is an integer value specifying the number of items within the list.

↵ A `Dimension` object containing the minimum size of the list. For more information on the `Dimension` class, see the documentation in Chapter 28.

MenuBarPeer awt.peer

 MenuComponentPeer

The MenuBarPeer interface extends interface java.awt.peer.MenuComponentPeer. The MenuBarPeer interface provides the basic structure required for menu bar component functionality.

Listing 30.13 shows the declarations for all of the public methods included in the java.awt.peer.MenuBarPeer interface.

Listing 30.13. Members of java.awt.peer.MenuBarPeer.

```
public interface MenuBarPeer extends MenuComponentPeer {
  void addMenu(Menu m)
  void delMenu(int index)
  void addHelpMenu(Menu m)
}
```

addMenu MenuBarPeer awt.peer

```
void addMenu(Menu m)
```

The addMenu() method adds the specified Menu to the MenuBar.

▶ m is the Menu object to be added to the MenuBar. For more information on the Menu class, see the documentation in Chapter 28.

delMenu MenuBarPeer awt.peer

```
void delMenu(int index)
```

The delMenu() method deletes the menu at the specified index from the MenuBar.

▶ index is an integer value representing the index to be deleted from the MenuBar.

addHelpMenu MenuBarPeer awt.peer

```
void addHelpMenu(Menu m)
```

The addHelpMenu adds a help menu to the MenuBar.

▶ m is the Menu object to be added to the MenuBar. For more information on the Menu class, see the documentation in Chapter 28.

MenuComponentPeer   awt.peer

 Object

The MenuComponentPeer interface extends the class java.lang.Object. The MenuComponentPeer interface provides the basic structure required for menu component functionality.

Listing 30.14 shows the declarations for all of the public methods included in the java.awt.peer.MenuComponentPeer interface.

Listing 30.14. Members of java.awt.peer.MenuComponentPeer.

```
public interface MenuComponentPeer {
  void dispose()
}
```

 dispose   MenuComponentPeer   awt.peer

```
void dispose()
```

The dispose() method disposes of a MenuComponent's allocated resources.

 # MenuItemPeer   awt.peer

 MenuComponentPeer

The MenuItemPeer interface extends interface java.awt.peer.MenuComponentPeer. The MenuItemPeer interface provides the basic structure required for menu item component functionality.

Listing 30.15 shows the declarations for all of the public methods included in the java.awt.peer.MenuItemPeer interface.

Listing 30.15. Members of java.awt.peer.MenuItemPeer.

```
public interface MenuItemPeer extends MenuComponentPeer {
  void setLabel(String label)
  void enable()
  void disable()
}
```

setLabel MenuItemPeer   awt.peer

```
void setLabel(String label)
```

The `setLabel()` method sets the label string that will be displayed on the `MenuItem`.

▶ `label` is a `String` value that will be displayed as the `MenuItem`'s label.

 ## enable MenuItemPeer   awt.peer

```
void enable()
```

The `enable()` method enables the `MenuItem` for user selection.

 ## disable MenuItemPeer   awt.peer

```
void disable()
```

The `disable()` method disables the `MenuItem` for user selection.

 # MenuPeer   awt.peer

✚   MenuItemPeer

The `MenuPeer` interface extends interface `java.awt.peer.MenuItemPeer`. The `MenuPeer` interface provides the basic structure required for menu component functionality.

Listing 30.16 shows the declarations for all of the public methods included in the `java.awt.peer.MenuPeer` interface.

Listing 30.16. Members of `java.awt.peer.MenuPeer`.

```
public interface MenuPeer extends MenuItemPeer {
  void addSeparator()
  void addItem(MenuItem item)
  void delItem(int index)
}
```

 ## addSeparator MenuPeer   awt.peer

```
void addSeparator()
```

The `addSeparator()` method adds a separator element to the `Menu`. A separator is an item, such as a line, which cannot be selected by the user and will not trigger a menu selection event.

addItem   MenuPeer   awt.peer

```
void addItem(MenuItem item)
```

The addItem() method adds a MenuItem to the Menu.

▶ item is a MenuItem object. For more information on the MenuItem class, see the documentation in Chapter 28.

 delItem   MenuPeer   awt.peer

```
void delItem(int index)
```

The delItem() method deletes the menu item at the specified index.

▶ index is an integer value representing the index on the menu to be deleted.

 # PanelPeer   awt.peer

 ContainerPeer

The PanelPeer interface extends interface java.awt.peer.ContainerPeer. The PanelPeer interface provides the basic structure required for panel component functionality.

Listing 30.17 shows the declarations for all of the public methods included in the java.awt.peer.PanelPeer interface.

Listing 30.17. Members of java.awt.peer.PanelPeer.

```
public interface PanelPeer extends ContainerPeer {
}
```

 # ScrollbarPeer   awt.peer

 ComponentPeer

The ScrollbarPeer interface extends interface java.awt.peer.ComponentPeer. The ScrollbarPeer interface provides the basic structure required for scrollbar component functionality.

Listing 30.18 shows the declarations for all of the public methods included in the java.awt.peer.ScrollbarPeer interface.

Listing 30.18. Members of `java.awt.peer.ScrollbarPeer`.

```
public interface ScrollbarPeer extends ComponentPeer {
    void setValue(int value)
    void setValues(int value, int visible, int minimum, int maximum)
    void setLineIncrement(int l)
    void setPageIncrement(int l)
}
```

 setValue   ScrollbarPeer   awt.peer

```
void setValue(int value)
```

The setValue() method sets the value of the Scrollbar.

▶   value is an integer value representing the value (position) of the Scrollbar.

setValues   ScrollbarPeer   awt.peer

```
void setValues(int value, int visible, int minimum, int maximum)
```

The setValues() method sets the specified properties of the scrollbar.

▶   value is the new value of the scrollbar.

▶   visible is the number of units to be displayed by the scrollbar.

▶   minimum is the minimum value of the scrollbar.

▶   maximum is the maximum value of the scrollbar.

setLineIncrement   ScrollbarPeer   awt.peer

```
void setLineIncrement(int l)
```

The setLineIncrement() method sets the increment value represented by a user clicking on a scrollbar line up/down widget.

▶   l is an integer value representing the line increment value.

setPageIncrement   ScrollbarPeer   awt.peer

```
void setPageIncrement(int l)
```

The setPageIncrement() method sets the increment value represented by a user clicking on a scrollbar page up/down widget.

▶   l is an integer value representing the page increment value.

TextAreaPeer awt.peer

 TextComponentPeer

The TextAreaPeer interface extends interface java.awt.peer.TextComponentPeer. The TextAreaPeer interface provides the basic structure required for text area component functionality.

Listing 30.19 shows the declarations for all of the public methods included in the java.awt.peer.TextAreaPeer interface.

Listing 30.19. Members of java.awt.peer.TextAreaPeer.

```
public interface TextAreaPeer extends TextComponentPeer {
  void insertText(String txt, int pos)
  void replaceText(String txt, int start, int end)
  Dimension preferredSize(int rows, int cols)
  Dimension minimumSize(int rows, int cols)
}
```

insertText TextAreaPeer awt.peer

```
void insertText(String txt, int pos)
```

The insertText() method inserts the specified text at the specified position within the TextArea.

▶ txt is a String value representing the text to be inserted.

▶ pos is an integer value representing the position within the TextArea at which to insert the text.

replaceText TextAreaPeer awt.peer

```
void replaceText(String txt, int start, int end)
```

The replaceText() method replaces text at the specified positions with the new text.

▶ txt is a String value representing the text to be inserted into the TextArea.

▶ start is an integer value containing the start position of the text to be replaced.

▶ end is an integer value containing the end position of the text to be replaced.

preferredSize TextAreaPeer awt.peer

```
Dimension preferredSize(int rows, int cols)
```

The preferredSize() method returns the preferred size of a TextArea of the specified dimensions.

▶ rows is the number of rows in the TextArea.

▶ cols is the number of columns in the TextArea.

↵ A Dimension object containing the preferred size of the TextArea. For more information on the Dimension class, see the documentation earlier in the chapter.

---

minimumSize   TextAreaPeer awt.peer

```
Dimension minimumSize(int rows, int cols)
```

The minimumSize() method returns the minimum size of a TextArea of the specified dimensions.

▶ rows is the number of rows in the TextArea.

▶ cols is the number of columns in the TextArea.

↵ A Dimension object containing the minimum size of the TextArea. For more information on the Dimension class, see the documentation in Chapter 28.

TextComponentPeer   awt.peer

✚ ComponentPeer

The TextComponentPeer interface extends interface java.awt.peer.ComponentPeer. The TextComponentPeer interface provides the basic structure required for text component functionality.

Listing 30.20 shows the declarations for all of the public methods included in the java.awt.peer.TextComponentPeer interface.

Listing 30.20. Members of java.awt.peer.TextComponentPeer.

```
public interface TextComponentPeer extends ComponentPeer {
   void setEditable(boolean editable)
   String getText()
   void setText(String l)
   int getSelectionStart()
   int getSelectionEnd()
   void select(int selStart, int selEnd)
}
```

setEditable   TextComponentPeer   awt.peer

```
void setEditable(boolean editable)
```

The setEditable() method is used to the set the TextComponent's editable state.

↵ A Boolean value that is true if the text can be edited, false if not.

getText   TextComponentPeer   awt.peer

```
String getText()
```

The getText() method returns the TextComponent's displayed text.

↵ A String value representing the text contained in the TextComponent.

setText   TextComponentPeer   awt.peer

```
void setText(String 1)
```

The setText() method sets the text to be displayed in the TextComponent.

▶ 1 is a String value to be displayed by the TextComponent.

getSelectionStart   TextComponentPeer   awt.peer

```
int getSelectionStart()
```

The getSelectionStart() method returns the position of the first selected character in the TextComponent.

↵ An integer value specifying the position of the first selected character in the TextComponent.

getSelectionEnd   TextComponentPeer   awt.peer

```
int getSelectionEnd()
```

The getSelectionEnd() method returns the position of the last selected character in the TextComponent.

↵ An integer value specifying the position of the last selected character in the TextComponent.

select   TextComponentPeer   awt.peer

```
void select(int selStart, int selEnd)
```

The select() method selects the specified text within the TextComponent.

▶ selStart is an integer value representing the starting character to be selected.

▶ selEnd is an integer value representing the ending character to be selected.

TextFieldPeer

 TextComponentPeer

The `TextFieldPeer` interface extends interface `java.awt.peer.TextComponentPeer`. The `TextFieldPeer` interface provides the basic structure required for text field component functionality.

Listing 30.21 shows the declarations for all of the public methods included in the `java.awt.peer.TextFieldPeer` interface.

Listing 30.21. Members of `java.awt.peer.TextFieldPeer`.

```
public interface TextFieldPeer extends TextComponentPeer {
    void setEchoCharacter(char c)
    Dimension preferredSize(int cols)
    Dimension minimumSize(int cols)
}
```

---

setEchoCharacter

 TextFieldPeer awt.peer

```
void setEchoCharacter(char c)
```

The `setEchoCharacter()` method sets the Echo character to be echoed to the screen as the user types.

▶ c is a character value to be displayed no matter what character the user types.

preferredSize

 TextFieldPeer awt.peer

```
Dimension preferredSize(int cols)
```

The `preferredSize()` method returns the preferred size of the `TextField` based on the specified number of characters.

▶ cols is an integer value containing the number of characters in the text field.

  A `Dimension` object containing the preferred size of the `TextField`. For more information on the `Dimension` class, see the documentation in Chapter 28.

minimumSize

 TextFieldPeer awt.peer

```
Dimension minimumSize(int cols)
```

The `minimumSize()` method returns the minimum size of the `TextField` based on the specified number of characters.

▶ `cols` is an integer value containing the number of characters in the text field.

↵ A `Dimension` object containing the minimum size of the `TextField`. For more information on the `Dimension` class, see the documentation in Chapter 28.

WindowPeer awt.peer

➕ `ContainerPeer`

The `WindowPeer` interface extends interface `java.awt.peer.ContainerPeer`. The `WindowPeer` interface provides the basic structure required for window component functionality.

Listing 30.22 shows the declarations for all of the public methods included in the `java.awt.peer.ContainerPeer` interface.

Listing 30.22. Members of `java.awt.peer.WindowPeer`.

```
public interface WindowPeer extends ContainerPeer {
    void toFront()
    void toBack()
}
```

 toFront   WindowPeer   awt.peer

`void toFront()`

The `toFront()` method moves the `Window` to the front of the display.

 toBack   WindowPeer   awt.peer

`void toBack()`

The `toBack()` method moves the `Window` to the back of the display.

31

Package java.io

by Michael Morrison

The Java I/O package, also known as `java.io`, gives classes support for reading and writing data to and from different input and output devices, including files, strings, and other data sources. The I/O package includes classes for inputting streams of data, outputting streams of data, working with files, and tokenizing streams of data. Table 31.1 shows the contents of the `java.io` package, and Figure 31.1 illustrates the contents' hierarchy.

Table 31.1. Contents of the `java.io` package.

Class index	Exception index	Interface index
BufferedInputStream	EOFException	DataInput
BufferedOutputStream	FileNotFoundException	DataOutput
ByteArrayInputStream	InterruptedIOException	FilenameFilter
ByteArrayOutputStream	IOException	
DataInputStream	UTFDataFormatException	
DataOutputStream		
File		
FileDescriptor		
FileInputStream		
FileOutputStream		
FilterInputStream		
FilterOutputStream		
InputStream		
LineNumberInputStream		
OutputStream		
PipedInputStream		
PipedOutputStream		
PrintStream		
PushbackInputStream		
RandomAccessFile		
SequenceInputStream		
StreamTokenizer		
StringBufferInputStream		

FIGURE 31.1.

Contents of the java.io *package.*

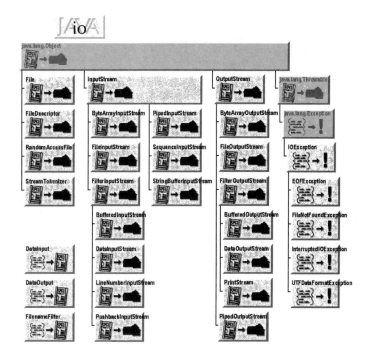

  # DataInput

➕ Object

See also: DataInputStream, DataOutput.

The DataInput interface describes an input stream that can read input data in a platform-independent manner; here is its definition:

```
public interface java.io.DataInput {
    // Methods
    public abstract boolean readBoolean();
    public abstract byte readByte();
    public abstract char readChar();
    public abstract double readDouble();
    public abstract float readFloat();
    public abstract void readFully(byte b[]);
    public abstract void readFully(byte b[], int off, int len);
    public abstract int readInt();
    public abstract String readLine();
    public abstract long readLong();
    public abstract short readShort();
    public abstract int readUnsignedByte();
    public abstract int readUnsignedShort();
    public abstract String readUTF();
    public abstract int skipBytes(int n);
}
```

readBoolean DataInput io

```
public abstract boolean readBoolean() throws IOException
```

This method reads a Boolean value (byte) from the input stream. A value of 0 is interpreted as false, but all other values are interpreted as true.

↵ the Boolean value read.

⟋• EOFException if the end of the stream is reached before reading the value.

⟋• IOException if an I/O error occurs.

 readByte DataInput io

```
public abstract byte readByte() throws IOException
```

This method reads a signed byte (8-bit) value from the input stream.

↵ the byte value read.

⟋• EOFException if the end of the stream is reached before reading the value.

⟋• IOException if an I/O error occurs.

readChar DataInput io

```
public abstract char readChar() throws IOException
```

This method reads a Unicode character (16-bit) value from the input stream.

↵ the Unicode character value read.

⟋• EOFException if the end of the stream is reached before reading the value.

⟋• IOException if an I/O error occurs.

readDouble DataInput io

```
public abstract double readDouble() throws IOException
```

This method reads a double (64-bit) value from the input stream.

↵ the double value read.

⟋• EOFException if the end of the stream is reached before reading the value.

⟋• IOException if an I/O error occurs.

readFloat

```
public abstract float readFloat() throws IOException
```

This method reads a float (32-bit) value from the input stream.

↵ the float value read.

☛ EOFException if the end of the stream is reached before reading the value.

☛ IOException if an I/O error occurs.

readFully

DataInput

```
public abstract void readFully(byte b[]) throws IOException
```

This method reads up to b.length bytes from the input stream into the byte array b, blocking until all bytes are read.

▶ b is the byte array into which the data is read.

☛ EOFException if the end of the stream is reached before reading the specified number of bytes.

☛ IOException if an I/O error occurs.

readFully

DataInput

```
public abstract void readFully(byte b[], int off, int len) throws IOException
```

This method reads up to len bytes from the input stream into the byte array b beginning off bytes into the array, blocking until all bytes are read.

▶ b is the byte array into which the data is read.

▶ off is the starting offset into the array for the data to be written to.

▶ len is the maximum number of bytes to read.

☛ EOFException if the end of the stream is reached before reading the specified number of bytes.

☛ IOException if an I/O error occurs.

readInt

DataInput

```
public abstract int readInt() throws IOException
```

This method reads an integer (32-bit) value from the input stream.

↵ the integer value read.

EOFException if the end of the stream is reached before reading the value.

IOException if an I/O error occurs.

readLine   DataInput   io

```
public abstract String readLine() throws IOException
```

This method reads a line of text from the input stream.

a string containing the line of text read.

EOFException if the end of the stream is reached before reading the line of text.

IOException if an I/O error occurs.

readLong   DataInput   io

```
public abstract long readLong() throws IOException
```

This method reads a long (64-bit) value from the input stream.

the long value read.

EOFException if the end of the stream is reached before reading the value.

IOException if an I/O error occurs.

readShort   DataInput   io

```
public abstract short readShort() throws IOException
```

This method reads a short (16-bit) value from the input stream.

the short value read.

EOFException if the end of the stream is reached before reading the value.

IOException if an I/O error occurs.

readUnsignedByte   DataInput   io

```
public abstract int readUnsignedByte() throws IOException
```

This method reads an unsigned byte (8-bit) value from the input stream.

the unsigned byte value read.

EOFException if the end of the stream is reached before reading the value.

IOException if an I/O error occurs.

readUnsignedShort   DataInput   io

```
public abstract int readUnsignedShort() throws IOException
```

This method reads an unsigned short (16-bit) value from the input stream.

↵   the short value read.

☛   EOFException if the end of the stream is reached before reading the value.

☛   IOException if an I/O error occurs.

readUTF   DataInput   io

```
public abstract String readUTF() throws IOException
```

This method reads a string encoded by using a modified UTF-8 format from the input stream.

↵   the string read.

☛   EOFException if the end of the stream is reached before reading the string.

☛   UTFDataFormatException if the bytes read do not represent a valid UTF-8 encoding of a string.

☛   IOException if an I/O error occurs.

skipBytes   DataInput   io

```
public abstract int skipBytes(int n) throws IOException
```

This method skips n bytes of data in the input stream, blocking until all bytes are skipped.

▶   n is the number of bytes to skip.

↵   the actual number of bytes skipped.

☛   EOFException if the end of the stream is reached before skipping the specified number of bytes.

☛   IOException if an I/O error occurs.

DataOutput   io

╋   Object

See also: DataOutputStream, DataInput.

The DataOutput interface describes an output stream that can write output data in a platform-independent manner; this is its definition:

```
public interface java.io.DataOutput {
   // Methods
   public abstract void write(byte b[]);
   public abstract void write(byte b[], int off, int len)
   public abstract void write(int b);
   public abstract void writeBoolean(boolean v);
   public abstract void writeByte(int v);
   public abstract void writeBytes(String s);
   public abstract void writeChar(int v);
   public abstract void writeChars(String s);
   public abstract void writeDouble(double v);
   public abstract void writeFloat(float v);
   public abstract void writeInt(int v);
   public abstract void writeLong(long v);
   public abstract void writeShort(int v);
   public abstract void writeUTF(String str);
}
```

 write   DataOutput   io

`public abstract void write(byte b[]) throws IOException`

This method writes b.length bytes to the output stream from the byte array b, blocking until all bytes are written.

    b is the byte array from which the data is written.

IOException if an I/O error occurs.

 write   DataOutput   io

`public abstract void write(byte b[], int off, int len) throws IOException`

This method writes len bytes to the output stream from the byte array b beginning off bytes into the array, blocking until all bytes are written.

    b is the byte array from which the data is written.

off is the starting offset into the array for the data to be read from.

len is the number of bytes to write.

IOException if an I/O error occurs.

 write   DataOutput   io

`public abstract void write(int b) throws IOException`

This method writes a byte value to the output stream, blocking until the byte is written.

b is the byte value to be written.

IOException if an I/O error occurs.

writeBoolean — DataOutput — io

```
public abstract void writeBoolean(boolean v) throws IOException
```

This method writes a Boolean value to the output stream. The Boolean value `true` is written as the byte value `1`, and `false` is written as the byte value `0`.

▶ v is the Boolean value to be written.

☞ `IOException` if an I/O error occurs.

writeByte — DataOutput — io

```
public abstract void writeByte(int v) throws IOException
```

This method writes a byte (8-bit) value to the output stream.

▶ v is the byte value to be written.

☞ `IOException` if an I/O error occurs.

writeBytes — DataOutput — io

```
public abstract void writeBytes(String s) throws IOException
```

This method writes a string to the output stream as a sequence of bytes.

▶ s is the string to be written as bytes.

☞ `IOException` if an I/O error occurs.

writeChar — DataOutput — io

```
public abstract void writeChar(int v) throws IOException
```

This method writes a character (16-bit) value to the output stream.

▶ v is the character value to be written.

☞ `IOException` if an I/O error occurs.

writeChars — DataOutput — io

```
public abstract void writeChars(String s) throws IOException
```

This method writes a string to the output stream as a sequence of characters.

▶ s is the string to be written as characters.

☞ `IOException` if an I/O error occurs.

writeDouble DataOutput */io/*

```
public abstract void writeDouble(double v) throws IOException
```

This method writes a double (64-bit) value to the output stream.

▶ v is the double value to be written.

🐾 IOException if an I/O error occurs.

writeFloat DataOutput */io/*

```
public abstract void writeFloat(float v) throws IOException
```

This method writes a float (32-bit) value to the output stream.

▶ v is the float value to be written.

🐾 IOException if an I/O error occurs.

writeInt DataOutput */io/*

```
public abstract void writeInt(int v) throws IOException
```

This method writes an integer (32-bit) value to the output stream.

▶ v is the integer value to be written.

🐾 IOException if an I/O error occurs.

writeLong DataOutput */io/*

```
public abstract void writeLong(long v) throws IOException
```

This method writes a long (64-bit) value to the output stream.

▶ v is the long value to be written.

🐾 IOException if an I/O error occurs.

writeShort DataOutput */io/*

```
public abstract void writeShort(int v) throws IOException
```

This method writes a short (16-bit) value to the output stream.

▶ v is the short value to be written.

🐾 IOException if an I/O error occurs.

writeUTF   DataOutput io

```
public abstract void writeUTF(String str) throws IOException
```

This method encodes a string using a modified UTF-8 format and writes it to the output stream.

► str is the string to be written.

↝ IOException if an I/O error occurs.

FilenameFilter io

 Object

See also: File

The FilenameFilter interface describes a filename filter used to filter directory listings. Filename filters are used by the list method defined in the File class, as well as the AWT's FileDialog component; here is the definition for the interface:

```
public interface java.io.FilenameFilter {
    // Methods
    public abstract boolean accept(File dir, String name);
}
```

 accept FilenameFilter io

```
public abstract boolean accept(File dir, String name)
```

This method determines whether a file should be included in a directory listing.

► dir is the directory in which the file is located.

► name is the filename.

↵ true if the file should be included in the directory list; false otherwise.

BufferedInputStream io

 FilterInputStream

See also: BufferedOutputStream.

This class implements a buffered input stream, which allows you to read data from a stream without causing a call to the underlying system for each byte read. This is done by reading blocks of data into a buffer, where the data is readily accessible, independent of the underlying stream. Subsequent reads are much faster since they read from the buffer rather than the underlying input stream. Here is the definition for the BufferedInputStream class:

```
public class java.io.BufferedInputStream extends java.io.FilterInputStream
{
    // Member Variables
    protected byte buf[];
    protected int count;
    protected int marklimit;
    protected int markpos;
    protected int pos;

    // Constructors
    public BufferedInputStream(InputStream in);
    public BufferedInputStream(InputStream in, int size);

    // Methods
    public int available();
    public void mark(int readlimit);
    public boolean markSupported();
    public int read();
    public int read(byte b[], int off, int len);
    public void reset();
    public long skip(long n);
}
```

Member Variables

Following are the member variables defined in BufferedInputStream:

protected byte buf[]

This is the buffer where data is stored.

protected int count

This is the number of bytes of data currently in the buffer.

protected int marklimit

This is the maximum number of bytes that can be read before the marked position (markpos) is invalidated.

protected int markpos

This is the position in the buffer of the current mark, used to return to a particular location in the buffer with the mark and reset methods. The mark position is set to -1 if there is no current mark.

protected int pos

This is the current read position in the buffer.

BufferedInputStream BufferedInputStream io

```
public BufferedInputStream(InputStream in)
```

This constructor creates a new buffered input stream, with a default buffer size of 512 bytes, to read data from the `in` input stream.

▶ `in` is the input stream to read data from.

 BufferedInputStream BufferedInputStream io

```
public BufferedInputStream(InputStream in, int size)
```

This constructor creates a new buffered input stream, with a buffer size of `size` bytes, to read data from the `in` input stream.

▶ `in` is the input stream to read data from.

▶ `size` is the buffer size.

 available BufferedInputStream io

```
public int available() throws IOException
```

This method determines the number of bytes that can be read from the input stream without blocking. That number is calculated by adding the number of free bytes in the buffer and the number of bytes available in the input stream.

↵ the number of available bytes.

✎ `IOException` if an I/O error occurs.

⊘ `available` in class `FilterInputStream`.

 mark BufferedInputStream io

```
public void mark(int readlimit)
```

This method marks the current read position in the input stream. The `reset` method can be used to reset the read position to this mark; subsequent reads will read data beginning at the mark position. The mark position is invalidated after `readlimit` bytes have been read.

▶ `readlimit` is the maximum number of bytes that can be read before the mark position becomes invalid.

⊘ `mark` in class `FilterInputStream`.

markSupported · BufferedInputStream · io

```
public boolean markSupported()
```

This method determines whether the input stream supports the mark and reset methods.

↵   true if the mark and reset methods are supported; false otherwise.

⊘   markSupported in class FilterInputStream.

read · BufferedInputStream · io

```
public int read() throws IOException
```

This method reads a byte value from the buffered input stream, blocking until the byte is read.

↵   an integer representing the byte value read, or -1 if the end of the stream is reached.

↱   IOException if an I/O error occurs.

⊘   read in class FilterInputStream.

read · BufferedInputStream · io

```
public int read(byte b[], int off, int len) throws IOException
```

This method reads up to len bytes from the buffered input stream into the byte array b beginning off bytes into the array, blocking until all bytes are read.

▶   b is the byte array into which the data is read.

▶   off is the starting offset into the array for the data to be written to.

▶   len is the maximum number of bytes to read.

↵   the actual number of bytes read, or -1 if the end of the stream is reached.

↱   IOException if an I/O error occurs.

⊘   read in class FilterInputStream.

reset · BufferedInputStream · io

```
public void reset() throws IOException
```

This method resets the read position in the input stream to the current mark position, as set by the mark method.

↱   IOException if the stream has not been marked or if the mark is invalid.

⊘   reset in class FilterInputStream.

skip BufferedInputStream io

```
public long skip(long n) throws IOException
```

This method skips n bytes of data in the input stream.

▶ n is the number of bytes to skip.

↵ the actual number of bytes skipped.

➤ IOException if an I/O error occurs.

⊘ skip in class FilterInputStream.

BufferedOutputStream   io

✚ FilterOutputStream

See also: BufferedInputStream.

This class implements a buffered output stream, which enables you to write data to a stream without causing a call to the underlying system for each byte written. This is done by writing blocks of data into a buffer rather than directly to the underlying output stream. The buffer is then written to the underlying output stream when the buffer fills up or is flushed or when the stream is closed. This is the definition for the BufferedOutputStream class:

```
public class java.io.BufferedOutputStream extends java.io.FilterOutputStream {
    // Member Variables
    protected byte buf[];
    protected int count;

    // Constructors
    public BufferedOutputStream(OutputStream out);
    public BufferedOutputStream(OutputStream out, int size);

    // Methods
    public void flush();
    public void write(byte b[], int off, int len);
    public void write(int b);
}
```

Member Variables

Following are the member variables defined in BufferedOutputStream:

protected byte buf[]

This is the buffer where data is stored.

protected int count

This is the number of bytes of data currently in the buffer.

BufferedOutputStream **BufferedOutputStream** io

```
public BufferedOutputStream(OutputStream out)
```

This constructor creates a new buffered output stream, with a default buffer size of 512 bytes, to write data to the out output stream.

▶ out is the output stream to write data to.

 BufferedOutputStream **BufferedOutputStream** io

```
public BufferedOutputStream(OutputStream out, int size)
```

This constructor creates a new buffered output stream, with a buffer size of size bytes, to write data to the out output stream.

▶ out is the output stream to write data to.

▶ size is the buffer size.

 flush **BufferedOutputStream** io

```
public void flush() throws IOException
```

This method flushes the output stream, resulting in any buffered data being written to the underlying output stream.

🖐 IOException if an I/O error occurs.

🚫 flush in class FilterOutputStream.

 write **BufferedOutputStream** io

```
public void write(byte b[], int off, int len) throws IOException
```

This method writes len bytes to the buffered output stream from the byte array b beginning off bytes into the array.

▶ b is the byte array from which the data is written.

▶ off is the starting offset into the array for the data to be read from.

▶ len is the number of bytes to write.

🖐 IOException if an I/O error occurs.

🚫 write in class FilterOutputStream.

write BufferedOutputStream /io/

```
public void write(int b) throws IOException
```

This method writes a byte value to the buffered output stream.

▶ b is the byte value to be written.

☞ IOException if an I/O error occurs.

⊘ write in class FilterOutputStream.

  # ByteArrayInputStream /io/

✚ InputStream

See also: ByteArrayOutputStream.

The ByteArrayInputStream class implements an input stream whose data is read from an array of bytes; here is the definition for the class:

```
public class java.io.ByteArrayInputStream extends java.io.InputStream {
    // Member Variables
    protected byte buf[];
    protected int count;
    protected int pos;

    // Constructors
    public ByteArrayInputStream(byte b[]);
    public ByteArrayInputStream(byte b[], int off, int len);

    // Methods
    public int available();
    public int read();
    public int read(byte b[], int off, int len);
    public void reset();
    public long skip(long n);
}
```

Member Variables

Following are the member variables defined in ByteArrayInputStream:

protected byte buf[]

This is the buffer where data is stored.

protected int count

This is the number of bytes of data currently in the buffer.

protected int pos

This is the current read position in the buffer.

ByteArrayInputStream ByteArrayInputStream io

```
public ByteArrayInputStream(byte b[])
```

This constructor creates a new input stream from the byte array b. Note that the byte array is not copied to create the stream.

▶ b is the byte array from which the data is read.

 ByteArrayInputStream ByteArrayInputStream io

```
public ByteArrayInputStream(byte b[], int off, int len)
```

This constructor creates a new input stream of size len from the byte array b beginning off bytes into the array. Note that the byte array is not copied to create the stream.

▶ b is the byte array from which the data is read.

▶ off is the starting offset into the array for the data to be read from.

▶ len is the maximum number of bytes to read.

 available ByteArrayInputStream io

```
public int available()
```

This method determines the number of bytes that can be read from the input stream.

↵ the number of available bytes.

Ø available in class InputStream.

 read ByteArrayInputStream io

```
public int read()
```

This method reads a byte value from the input stream.

↵ an integer representing the byte value read, or -1 if the end of the stream is reached.

Ø read in class InputStream.

read ByteArrayInputStream io

```
public int read(byte b[], int off, int len)
```

This method reads up to len bytes from the input stream into the byte array b beginning off bytes into the array.

▶ b is the byte array into which the data is read.

▶ off is the starting offset into the array for the data to be written to.

▶ len is the maximum number of bytes to read.

↵ the actual number of bytes read, or -1 if the end of the stream is reached.

⊘ read in class InputStream.

reset — ByteArrayInputStream /io/

```
public void reset()
```

This method resets the read position to the beginning of the input stream.

⊘ reset in class InputStream.

skip — ByteArrayInputStream /io/

```
public long skip(long n)
```

This method skips n bytes of data in the input stream.

▶ n is the number of bytes to skip.

↵ the actual number of bytes skipped.

⊘ skip in class InputStream.

ByteArrayOutputStream /io/

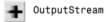
➕ OutputStream

See also: ByteArrayInputStream.

The ByteArrayOutputStream class implements an output stream whose data is written to an array of bytes. The byte array automatically grows as data is written to it. Here is the definition for the class:

```
public class java.io.ByteArrayOutputStream extends java.io.OutputStream {
  // Member Variables
  protected byte buf[];
  protected int count;

  // Constructors
  public ByteArrayOutputStream();
  public ByteArrayOutputStream(int size);

  // Methods
  public void reset();
  public int size();
  public byte[] toByteArray();
  public String toString();
  public String toString(int hibyte);
  public void write(byte b[], int off, int len);
```

```
    public void write(int b);
    public void writeTo(OutputStream out);
}
```

Member Variables

Following are the member variables defined in `ByteArrayOutputStream`:

protected byte buf[]

This is the buffer where data is stored.

protected int count

This is the number of bytes of data currently in the buffer.

ByteArrayOutputStream

```
    public ByteArrayOutputStream()
```

This constructor creates a new output stream with a default buffer size of 32 bytes. The size of the buffer automatically grows as data is written to it.

ByteArrayOutputStream

```
    public ByteArrayOutputStream(int size)
```

This constructor creates a new output stream with an initial size of `size` bytes. The size of the buffer automatically grows as data is written to it.

▶   `size` is the initial size of the buffer.

reset

```
    public void reset()
```

This method resets the contents of the underlying byte array by setting the `count` member variable to zero, resulting in the accumulated data being discarded.

size

```
    public int size()
```

This method returns the current size of the buffer, which is stored in the `count` member variable.

↵   the current size of the buffer.

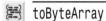 **toByteArray** 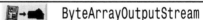 **ByteArrayOutputStream** io

```
public byte[] toByteArray()
```

This method creates a new byte array containing the data currently stored in the underlying byte array associated with the output stream.

 a byte array containing the current data stored in the output stream.

 toString 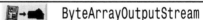 **ByteArrayOutputStream** io

```
public String toString()
```

This method creates a new string containing the data currently stored in the underlying byte array associated with the output stream.

↵ a string containing the current data stored in the output stream.

⊘ toString in class `Object`.

toString 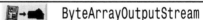 **ByteArrayOutputStream** io

```
public String toString(int hibyte)
```

This method creates a new string containing the data currently stored in the underlying byte array associated with the output stream, with the top 8 bits of each string character set to `hibyte`.

▶ hibyte is the high byte value for each character.

↵ a string containing the current data stored in the output stream, with the high byte of each character set to `hibyte`.

write 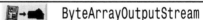 **ByteArrayOutputStream** io

```
public void write(byte b[], int off, int len)
```

This method writes `len` bytes to the output stream from the byte array `b` beginning `off` bytes into the array.

▶ b is the byte array from which the data is written.

▶ off is the starting offset into the array for the data to be read from.

▶ len is the number of bytes to write.

⊘ write in class `OutputStream`.

write ByteArrayOutputStream

```
public void write(int b)
```

This method writes a byte value to the output stream.

▶ b is the byte value to be written.

⊘ write in class OutputStream.

 writeTo ByteArrayOutputStream

```
public void writeTo(OutputStream out) throws IOException
```

This method writes the contents of the underlying byte array to another output stream.

▶ out is the output stream to write to.

🖝 IOException if an I/O error occurs.

 # DataInputStream

 FilterInputStream

 DataInput

See also: DataOutputStream.

The DataInputStream class implements an input stream that can read Java primitive data types in a platform-independent manner. Here is the definition for the class:

```
public class java.io.DataInputStream extends java.io.FilterInputStream
    implements java.io.DataInput {
    // Constructors
    public DataInputStream(InputStream in);

    // Methods
    public final int read(byte b[]);
    public final int read(byte b[], int off, int len);
    public final boolean readBoolean();
    public final byte readByte();
    public final char readChar();
    public final double readDouble();
    public final float readFloat();
    public final void readFully(byte b[]);
    public final void readFully(byte b[], int off, int len);
    public final int readInt();
    public final String readLine();
    public final long readLong();
    public final short readShort();
    public final int readUnsignedByte();
    public final int readUnsignedShort();
    public final String readUTF();
```

```
public final static String readUTF(DataInput in);
public final int skipBytes(int n);
}
```

 DataInputStream DataInputStream

`public DataInputStream(InputStream in)`

This method creates a new data input stream to read data from the `in` input stream.

▶   `in` is the input stream to read data from.

 read DataInputStream

`public final int read(byte b[]) throws IOException`

This method reads up to `b.length` bytes from the data input stream into the byte array `b`, blocking until all bytes are read.

▶   `b` is the byte array into which the data is read.

↵   the actual number of bytes read, or `-1` if the end of the stream is reached.

🖋   `IOException` if an I/O error occurs.

⊘   read in class `FilterInputStream`.

 read DataInputStream

`public final int read(byte b[], int off, int len) throws IOException`

This method reads up to `len` bytes from the data input stream into the byte array `b` beginning `off` bytes into the array, blocking until all bytes are read.

▶   `b` is the byte array into which the data is read.

▶   `off` is the starting offset into the array for the data to be written to.

▶   `len` is the maximum number of bytes to read.

↵   the actual number of bytes read, or `-1` if the end of the stream is reached.

🖋   `IOException` if an I/O error occurs.

⊘   read in class `FilterInputStream`.

 readBoolean DataInputStream

`public final boolean readBoolean() throws IOException`

This method reads a Boolean value (byte) from the data input stream, blocking until the byte is read. A value of `0` is interpreted as `false`, and all other values are interpreted as `true`.

the Boolean value read.

EOFException if the end of the stream is reached before reading the value.

IOException if an I/O error occurs.

readByte DataInputStream /io/

```
public final byte readByte() throws IOException
```

This method reads a signed byte (8-bit) value from the data input stream, blocking until the byte is read.

the byte value read.

EOFException if the end of the stream is reached before reading the value.

IOException if an I/O error occurs.

readChar DataInputStream /io/

```
public final char readChar() throws IOException
```

This method reads a character (16-bit) value from the data input stream, blocking until both bytes are read.

the character value read.

EOFException if the end of the stream is reached before reading the value.

IOException if an I/O error occurs.

readDouble DataInputStream /io/

```
public final double readDouble() throws IOException
```

This method reads a double (64-bit) value from the data input stream, blocking until all eight bytes are read.

the double value read.

EOFException if the end of the stream is reached before reading the value.

IOException if an I/O error occurs.

readFloat DataInputStream /io/

```
public final float readFloat() throws IOException
```

This method reads a float (32-bit) value from the data input stream, blocking until all four bytes are read.

the float value read.

EOFException if the end of the stream is reached before reading the value.

IOException if an I/O error occurs.

readFully  DataInputStream io

```
public final void readFully(byte b[]) throws IOException
```

This method reads up to b.length bytes from the data input stream into the byte array b, blocking until all bytes are read.

b is the byte array into which the data is read.

EOFException if the end of the stream is reached before reading the specified number of bytes.

IOException if an I/O error occurs.

readFully DataInputStream io

```
public final void readFully(byte b[], int off, int len) throws IOException
```

This method reads up to len bytes from the data input stream into the byte array b beginning off bytes into the array, blocking until all bytes are read.

b is the byte array into which the data is read.

off is the starting offset into the array for the data to be written to.

len is the maximum number of bytes to read.

EOFException if the end of the stream is reached before reading the specified number of bytes.

IOException if an I/O error occurs.

readInt DataInputStream io

```
public final int readInt() throws IOException
```

This method reads an integer (32-bit) value from the data input stream, blocking until all four bytes are read.

the integer value read.

EOFException if the end of the stream is reached before reading the value.

IOException if an I/O error occurs.

readLine   DataInputStream   io

```
public final String readLine() throws IOException
```

This method reads a line of text from the data input stream, blocking until either a newline character (\n) or a carriage return character (\r) is read.

↵   a string containing the line of text read.

↱   EOFException if the end of the stream is reached before reading the line of text.

↱   IOException if an I/O error occurs.

readLong   DataInputStream   io

```
public final long readLong() throws IOException
```

This method reads a long (64-bit) value from the data input stream, blocking until all eight bytes are read.

↵   the long value read.

↱   EOFException if the end of the stream is reached before reading the value.

↱   IOException if an I/O error occurs.

readShort   DataInputStream   io

```
public final short readShort() throws IOException
```

This method reads a signed short (16-bit) value from the data input stream, blocking until both bytes are read.

↵   the short value read.

↱   EOFException if the end of the stream is reached before reading the value.

↱   IOException if an I/O error occurs.

readUnsignedByte   DataInputStream   io

```
public final int readUnsignedByte() throws IOException
```

This method reads an unsigned byte (8-bit) value from the data input stream, blocking until the byte is read.

↵   the unsigned byte value read.

↱   EOFException if the end of the stream is reached before reading the value.

↱   IOException if an I/O error occurs.

readUnsignedShort **DataInputStream** /io/

```
public final int readUnsignedShort() throws IOException
```

This method reads an unsigned short (16-bit) value from the data input stream, blocking until both bytes are read.

↵ the unsigned short value read.

➤ EOFException if the end of the stream is reached before reading the value.

➤ IOException if an I/O error occurs.

 readUTF **DataInputStream** /io/

```
public final String readUTF() throws IOException
```

This method reads a string that has been encoded using a modified UTF-8 format from the data input stream, blocking until all bytes are read.

↵ the string read.

➤ EOFException if the end of the stream is reached before reading the string.

➤ UTFDataFormatException if the bytes read do not represent a valid UTF-8 encoding of a string.

➤ IOException if an I/O error occurs.

 readUTF ■→■ **DataInputStream** /io/

```
public final static String readUTF(DataInput in) throws IOException
```

This method reads a string from the in data input stream that has been encoded using a modified UTF-8 format, blocking until all bytes are read.

▶ in is the data input stream to read the string from.

↵ the string read.

➤ EOFException if the end of the stream is reached before reading the string.

➤ UTFDataFormatException if the bytes read do not represent a valid UTF-8 encoding of a string.

➤ IOException if an I/O error occurs.

skipBytes **DataInputStream** io

```
public final int skipBytes(int n) throws IOException
```

This method skips n bytes of data in the data input stream, blocking until all bytes are skipped.

 n is the number of bytes to skip.

 the actual number of bytes skipped.

EOFException if the end of the stream is reached before skipping the specified number of bytes.

IOException if an I/O error occurs.

DataOutputStream

➕ FilterOutputStream

DataOutput

See also: DataInputStream.

The DataOutputStream class implements an output stream that can write Java primitive data types in a platform-independent manner; this is the definition for the class:

```java
public class java.io.DataOutputStream extends java.io.FilterOutputStream
    implements java.io.DataOutput {
    // Member Variables
    protected int written;

    // Constructors
    public DataOutputStream(OutputStream out);

    // Methods
    public void flush();
    public final int size();
    public void write(byte b[], int off, int len);
    public void write(int b);
    public final void writeBoolean(boolean v);
    public final void writeByte(int v);
    public final void writeBytes(String s);
    public final void writeChar(int v);
    public final void writeChars(String s);
    public final void writeDouble(double v);
    public final void writeFloat(float v);
    public final void writeInt(int v);
    public final void writeLong(long v);
    public final void writeShort(int v);
    public final void writeUTF(String str);
}
```

Member Variables

Following are the member variables defined in `DataOutputStream`:

protected int written

This is the number of bytes written to the output stream so far.

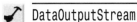 DataOutputStream   DataOutputStream   *io*

```
public DataOutputStream(OutputStream out)
```

This method creates a new data output stream to write data to the out output stream.

▶ out is the output stream to write data to.

 flush   DataOutputStream   *io*

```
public void flush() throws IOException
```

This method flushes the data output stream, resulting in any buffered data being written to the underlying output stream.

☞ IOException if an I/O error occurs.

⊘ flush in class FilterOutputStream.

 size   DataOutputStream   *io*

```
public final int size()
```

This method returns the number of bytes written to the data output stream thus far, which is stored in the `written` member variable.

↵ the number of bytes written to the data output stream so far.

write   DataOutputStream   *io*

```
public void write(byte b[], int off, int len) throws IOException
```

This method writes `len` bytes to the data output stream from the byte array `b` beginning off bytes into the array.

▶ b is the byte array from which the data is written.

▶ off is the starting offset into the array for the data to be read from.

▶ len is the number of bytes to write.

☞ IOException if an I/O error occurs.

⊘ write in class FilterOutputStream.

write DataOutputStream io

```
public void write(int b) throws IOException
```

This method writes a byte value to the data output stream.

▶ b is the byte value to be written.

▶ IOException if an I/O error occurs.

⊘ write in class FilterOutputStream.

 writeBoolean DataOutputStream io

```
public final void writeBoolean(boolean v) throws IOException
```

This method writes a Boolean value to the data output stream. The Boolean value true is written as the byte value 1, and false is written as the byte value 0.

▶ v is the Boolean value to be written.

IOException if an I/O error occurs.

writeByte DataOutputStream io

```
public final void writeByte(int v) throws IOException
```

This method writes a byte (8-bit) value to the data output stream.

▶ v is the byte value to be written.

IOException if an I/O error occurs.

writeBytes DataOutputStream io

```
public final void writeBytes(String s) throws IOException
```

This method writes a string to the data output stream as a sequence of bytes.

▶ s is the string to be written as bytes.

IOException if an I/O error occurs.

 writeChar DataOutputStream io

```
public final void writeChar(int v) throws IOException
```

This method writes a character (16-bit) value to the data output stream.

▶ v is the character value to be written.

IOException if an I/O error occurs.

writeChars 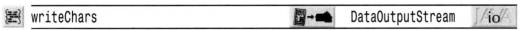 DataOutputStream io

```
public final void writeChars(String s) throws IOException
```

This method writes a string to the data output stream as a sequence of characters.

▶ s is the string to be written as characters.

☛ IOException if an I/O error occurs.

writeDouble 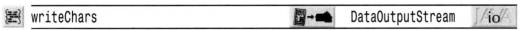 DataOutputStream io

```
public final void writeDouble(double v) throws IOException
```

This method writes a double (64-bit) value to the data output stream.

▶ v is the double value to be written.

☛ IOException if an I/O error occurs.

writeFloat 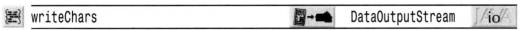 DataOutputStream io

```
public final void writeFloat(float v) throws IOException
```

This method writes a float (32-bit) value to the data output stream.

▶ v is the float value to be written.

☛ IOException if an I/O error occurs.

writeInt 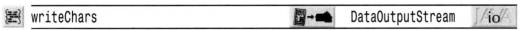 DataOutputStream io

```
public final void writeInt(int v) throws IOException
```

This method writes an integer (32-bit) value to the data output stream.

▶ v is the integer value to be written.

☛ IOException if an I/O error occurs.

writeLong 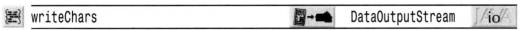 DataOutputStream io

```
public final void writeLong(long v) throws IOException
```

This method writes a long (64-bit) value to the data output stream.

▶ v is the long value to be written.

☛ IOException if an I/O error occurs.

writeShort DataOutputStream

```
public final void writeShort(int v) throws IOException
```

This method writes a short (16-bit) value to the data output stream.

 v is the short value to be written.

 IOException if an I/O error occurs.

 writeUTF DataOutputStream

```
public final void writeUTF(String str) throws IOException
```

This method encodes a string using a modified UTF-8 format and writes it to the data output stream.

 str is the string to be written.

 IOException if an I/O error occurs.

 # File

 Object

See also: FileDescriptor.

The File class implements a filename in a platform-independent manner; it gives you the functionality needed to work with filenames and directories without having to deal with the complexities associated with filenames on a particular platform. Here is the class definition:

```java
public class java.io.File extends java.lang.Object {
    // Member Variables
    public final static String pathSeparator;
    public final static char pathSeparatorChar;
    public final static String separator;
    public final static char separatorChar;

    // Constructors
    public File(File dir, String name);
    public File(String path);
    public File(String path, String name);

    // Methods
    public boolean canRead();
    public boolean canWrite();
    public boolean delete();
    public boolean equals(Object obj);
    public boolean exists();
    public String getAbsolutePath();
    public String getName();
    public String getParent();
    public String getPath();
```

```
    public int hashCode();
    public boolean isAbsolute();
    public boolean isDirectory();
    public boolean isFile();
    public long lastModified();
    public long length();
    public String[] list();
    public String[] list(FilenameFilter filter);
    public boolean mkdir();
    public boolean mkdirs();
    public boolean renameTo(File dest);
    public String toString();
}
```

Member Variables

Following are the member variables defined in `File`:

public final static String pathSeparator

This is the platform-specific path separator string.

public final static char pathSeparatorChar

This is the platform-specific path separator character, which separates filenames in a path list.

public final static String separator

This is the platform-specific file separator string.

public final static char separatorChar

This is the platform-specific file separator character, which separates the file and directory components in a filename.

 ## File

```
    public File(File dir, String name)
```

This constructor creates the filename of an underlying file based on the specified directory and filename. If no directory is specified in the `dir` argument, the constructor assumes the file is in the current directory.

▶ `dir` is the directory where the file is located.

▶ `name` is the filename.

File File io

```
public File(String path)
```

This constructor creates the filename of an underlying file based on the specified file path.

▶ `path` is the file path.

`NullPointerException` if the file path is null.

 File File io

```
public File(String path, String name)
```

This constructor creates the filename of an underlying file based on the specified path and filename.

▶ `path` is the path where the file is located.

▶ `name` is the filename.

canRead File io

```
public boolean canRead()
```

This method determines whether the underlying file can be read from. In other words, if the file is readable, `canRead` determines whether the file exists.

▶ `true` if the file can be read from; `false` otherwise.

`SecurityException` if the application doesn't have read access to the file.

canWrite File io

```
public boolean canWrite()
```

This method determines whether the underlying file can be written to. In other words, if the file is writeable, `canWrite` determines whether the file exists.

▶ `true` if the file can be written to; `false` otherwise.

`SecurityException` if the application doesn't have write access to the file.

delete File io

```
public boolean delete()
```

This method deletes the underlying file.

 `true` if the file is deleted; `false` otherwise.

`SecurityException` if the application doesn't have access to delete the file.

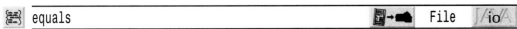

equals

```
public boolean equals(Object obj)
```

This method compares the path name of the obj File object to the path name of the underlying file.

▶ obj is the object to compare with.

↵ true if the path names are equal; false otherwise.

⊘ equals in class Object.

exists

```
public boolean exists()
```

This method determines whether the underlying file exists by opening it for reading and then closing it.

▶ true if the file exists; false otherwise.

↗ SecurityException if the application doesn't have read access to the file.

getAbsolutePath

```
public String getAbsolutePath()
```

This method determines the platform-specific absolute path name of the underlying file.

↵ the absolute path name of the file.

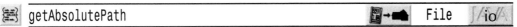

getName

```
public String getName()
```

This method determines the filename of the underlying file, which doesn't include any path information.

↵ the filename of the file.

getParent

```
public String getParent()
```

This method determines the parent directory of the underlying file, which is the immediate directory where the file is located.

↵ the parent directory of the file, or null if the file is located in the root directory.

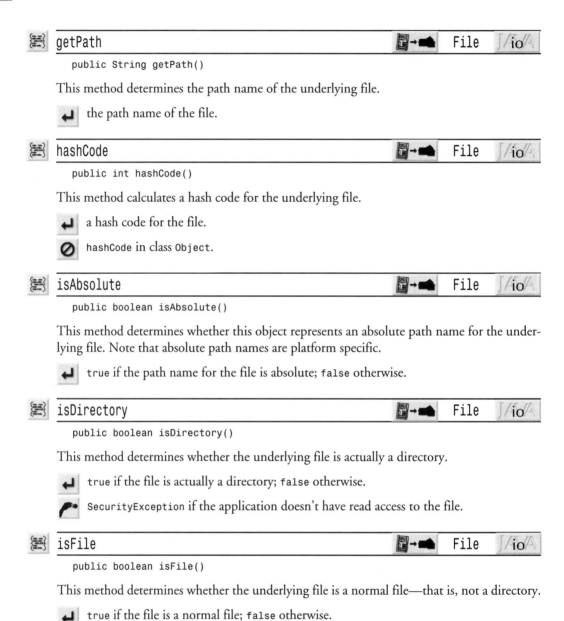

getPath   File   io

```
public String getPath()
```

This method determines the path name of the underlying file.

↵   the path name of the file.

hashCode   File   io

```
public int hashCode()
```

This method calculates a hash code for the underlying file.

↵   a hash code for the file.

⊘   hashCode in class Object.

isAbsolute   File   io

```
public boolean isAbsolute()
```

This method determines whether this object represents an absolute path name for the under-lying file. Note that absolute path names are platform specific.

↵   true if the path name for the file is absolute; false otherwise.

isDirectory   File   io

```
public boolean isDirectory()
```

This method determines whether the underlying file is actually a directory.

↵   true if the file is actually a directory; false otherwise.

☞   SecurityException if the application doesn't have read access to the file.

isFile   File   io

```
public boolean isFile()
```

This method determines whether the underlying file is a normal file—that is, not a directory.

↵   true if the file is a normal file; false otherwise.

☞   SecurityException if the application doesn't have read access to the file.

lastModified   File /io/

```
public long lastModified()
```

This method determines the last modification time of the underlying file. Note that this time is system specific and is not absolute; in other words, use the time only to compare against other times retrieved by using this method.

↵ the last modification time of the file, or 0 if the file doesn't exist.

☞ SecurityException if the application doesn't have read access to the file.

length   File /io/

```
public long length()
```

This method determines the length in bytes of the underlying file.

↵ the length of the file in bytes.

☞ SecurityException if the application doesn't have read access to the file.

list   File /io/

```
public String[] list()
```

This method builds a list of the filenames in the directory represented by this object. Note that the underlying file must actually be a directory for this method to work.

↵ an array containing the filenames located in the directory.

☞ SecurityException if the application doesn't have read access to the file.

list   File /io/

```
public String[] list(FilenameFilter filter)
```

This method builds a list, using the specified filename filter, of the filenames in the directory represented by this object. Note that the underlying file must actually be a directory for this method to work.

▶ filter is the filename filter used to select the filenames.

↵ an array containing the filtered filenames in the directory.

☞ SecurityException if the application doesn't have read access to the file.

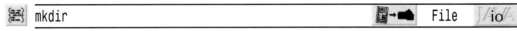

mkdir

```
public boolean mkdir()
```

This method creates a directory based on the path name specified by this object.

↵   true if the directory is created; `false` otherwise.

↱   `SecurityException` if the application doesn't have write access to the file.

mkdirs

```
public boolean mkdirs()
```

This method creates a directory based on the path name specified by this object, including all necessary parent directories.

↵   true if the directory (or directories) is created; `false` otherwise.

↱   `SecurityException` if the application doesn't have write access to the file.

renameTo

```
public boolean renameTo(File dest)
```

This method renames the underlying file to the filename specified by the `dest` file object.

▶   `dest` is the new filename.

↵   true if the file is renamed; `false` otherwise.

↱   `SecurityException` if the application doesn't have write access to both the underlying file and the file represented by the `dest` file object.

toString

```
public String toString()
```

This method determines a string representation of the path name for the underlying file.

↵   a string representing the path name of the file.

⊘   toString in class `Object`.

 FileDescriptor

 Object

See also: File.

The FileDescriptor class implements a handle to a platform-specific file or socket structure. FileDescriptor objects are primarily used internally by the Java system and are never created by an application directly. Here is the class definition:

```
public final class java.io.FileDescriptor extends java.lang.Object {
  // Member Variables
  public final static FileDescriptor err;
  public final static FileDescriptor in;
  public final static FileDescriptor out;

  // Constructors
  public FileDescriptor();

  // Methods
  public boolean valid();
}
```

Member Variables

Following are the member variables defined in FileDescriptor:

public final static FileDescriptor err

This is a handle to the standard error stream.

public final static FileDescriptor in

This is a handle to the standard input stream.

public final static FileDescriptor out

This is a handle to the standard output stream.

 FileDescriptor   FileDescriptor /io/

```
public FileDescriptor()
```

This constructor creates a default FileDescriptor object.

 valid   FileDescriptor /io/

```
public boolean valid()
```

This method determines whether this object represents a valid open file or socket.

 true if the underlying file or socket is valid; false otherwise.

 # FileInputStream

 InputStream

See also: FileOutputStream.

The FileInputStream class implements an input stream for reading data from a file or file descriptor; this is the class definition:

```
public class java.io.FileInputStream extends java.io.InputStream
{
  // Constructors
  public FileInputStream(File file);
  public FileInputStream(FileDescriptor fdObj);
  public FileInputStream(String name);

  // Methods
  public int available();
  public void close();
  protected void finalize();
  public final FileDescriptor getFD();
  public int read();
  public int read(byte b[]);
  public int read(byte b[], int off, int len);
  public long skip(long n);
}
```

 FileInputStream   FileInputStream   io

public FileInputStream(File file) throws FileNotFoundException

This constructor creates a file input stream to read data from the specified file.

▶   file is the file to be opened for reading.

☛   FileNotFoundException if the file is not found.

☛   SecurityException if the application doesn't have read access to the file.

 FileInputStream   FileInputStream   io

public FileInputStream(FileDescriptor fdObj)

This constructor creates a file input stream to read data from the file represented by the specified file descriptor.

▶   fdObj is the file descriptor representing the file to be opened for reading.

☛   SecurityException if the application doesn't have read access to the file.

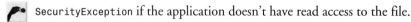

 FileInputStream FileInputStream io

```
public FileInputStream(String name) throws FileNotFoundException
```

This constructor creates a file input stream to read data from the file with the specified filename.

▶ name is the filename of the file to be opened for reading.

☞ FileNotFoundException if the file is not found.

☞ SecurityException if the application doesn't have read access to the file.

available FileInputStream io

```
public int available() throws IOException
```

This method determines the number of bytes that can be read from the file input stream without blocking.

↵ the number of available bytes.

☞ IOException if an I/O error occurs.

⊘ available in class InputStream.

close FileInputStream io

```
public void close() throws IOException
```

This method closes the file input stream, releasing any resources associated with the stream.

☞ IOException if an I/O error occurs.

⊘ close in class InputStream.

finalize FileInputStream io

```
protected void finalize() throws IOException
```

This method makes sure the close method is called when the file input stream is cleaned up by the Java garbage collector.

☞ IOException if an I/O error occurs.

⊘ finalize in class Object.

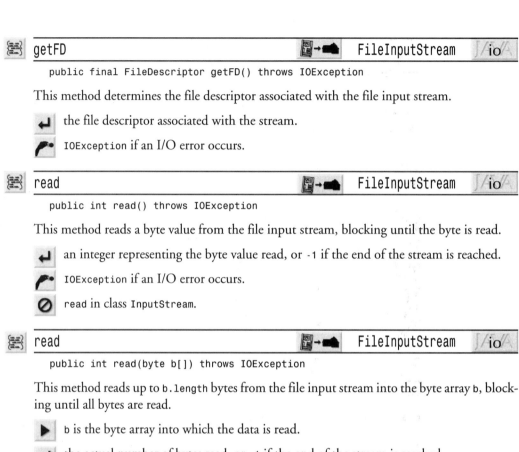

getFD   FileInputStream   io

```
public final FileDescriptor getFD() throws IOException
```

This method determines the file descriptor associated with the file input stream.

↵   the file descriptor associated with the stream.

↰   IOException if an I/O error occurs.

read   FileInputStream   io

```
public int read() throws IOException
```

This method reads a byte value from the file input stream, blocking until the byte is read.

↵   an integer representing the byte value read, or -1 if the end of the stream is reached.

↰   IOException if an I/O error occurs.

⊘   read in class InputStream.

read   FileInputStream   io

```
public int read(byte b[]) throws IOException
```

This method reads up to b.length bytes from the file input stream into the byte array b, blocking until all bytes are read.

▶   b is the byte array into which the data is read.

↵   the actual number of bytes read, or -1 if the end of the stream is reached.

↰   IOException if an I/O error occurs.

⊘   read in class InputStream.

read   FileInputStream   io

```
public int read(byte b[], int off, int len) throws IOException
```

This method reads up to len bytes from the file input stream into the byte array b beginning off bytes into the array, blocking until all bytes are read.

▶   b is the byte array into which the data is read.

▶   off is the starting offset into the array for the data to be written to.

▶   len is the maximum number of bytes to read.

↵   the actual number of bytes read, or -1 if the end of the stream is reached.

IOException if an I/O error occurs.

read in class InputStream.

---

 skip   FileInputStream   io

```
public long skip(long n) throws IOException
```

This method skips n bytes of data in the file input stream.

► n is the number of bytes to skip.

↵ the actual number of bytes skipped.

IOException if an I/O error occurs.

skip in class InputStream.

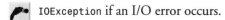 FileOutputStream   io

✛ OutputStream

See also: FileInputStream.

The FileOutputStream class implements an output stream for writing data to a file or file descriptor; this is the class definition:

```java
public class java.io.FileOutputStream extends java.io.OutputStream
{
  // Constructors
  public FileOutputStream(File file);
  public FileOutputStream(FileDescriptor fdObj);
  public FileOutputStream(String name);

  // Methods
  public void close();
  protected void finalize();
  public final FileDescriptor getFD();
  public void write(byte b[]);
  public void write(byte b[], int off, int len);
  public void write(int b);
}
```

 FileOutputStream   FileOutputStream   io

```
public FileOutputStream(File file) throws IOException
```

This constructor creates a file output stream to write data to the specified file.

► file is the file to be opened for writing.

FileNotFoundException if the file could not be opened for writing.

SecurityException if the application doesn't have write access to the file.

FileOutputStream FileOutputStream io

```
public FileOutputStream(FileDescriptor fdObj)
```

This constructor creates a file output stream to write data to the file represented by the specified file descriptor.

▶ fdObj is the file descriptor representing the file to be opened for writing.

☞ SecurityException if the application doesn't have write access to the file.

 FileOutputStream FileOutputStream io

```
public FileOutputStream(String name) throws IOException
```

This constructor creates a file output stream to write data to the file with the specified filename.

▶ name is the filename of the file to be opened for writing.

☞ FileNotFoundException if the file is not found.

☞ SecurityException if the application doesn't have read access to the file.

 close FileOutputStream io

```
public void close() throws IOException
```

This method closes the file output stream, releasing any resources associated with it.

☞ IOException if an I/O error occurs.

⊘ close in class OutputStream.

 finalize FileOutputStream io

```
protected void finalize() throws IOException
```

This method makes sure the close method is called when the file output stream is cleaned up by the Java garbage collector.

☞ IOException if an I/O error occurs.

⊘ finalize in class Object.

 getFD FileOutputStream io

```
public final FileDescriptor getFD() throws IOException
```

This method determines the file descriptor associated with the file output stream.

↵ the file descriptor associated with the stream.

☞ IOException if an I/O error occurs.

write   FileOutputStream `io`

```
public void write(byte b[]) throws IOException
```

This method writes `b.length` bytes to the file output stream from the byte array `b`.

▶ `b` is the byte array from which the data is written.

⌇ `IOException` if an I/O error occurs.

⊘ `write` in class `OutputStream`.

write   FileOutputStream `io`

```
public void write(byte b[], int off, int len) throws IOException
```

This method writes `len` bytes to the file output stream from the byte array `b` beginning `off` bytes into the array.

▶ `b` is the byte array from which the data is written.

▶ `off` is the starting offset into the array for the data to be read from.

▶ `len` is the number of bytes to write.

⌇ `IOException` if an I/O error occurs.

⊘ `write` in class `OutputStream`.

write   FileOutputStream `io`

```
public void write(int b) throws IOException
```

This method writes a byte value to the file output stream.

▶ `b` is the byte value to be written.

⌇ `IOException` if an I/O error occurs.

⊘ `write` in class `OutputStream`.

FilterInputStream `io`

 InputStream

See also: `FilterOutputStream`.

The `FilterInputStream` class defines an input stream filter used to filter data on an underlying input stream. Most of the methods defined in this class merely call corresponding methods in the underlying input stream, and you simply override appropriate methods to supply the filtering functionality. `FilterInputStream` is the basis for all other input stream filter imple-mentations. Derived filtered input streams can be linked for complex filtering operations; here is the class definition:

```
public class java.io.FilterInputStream extends java.io.InputStream {
    // Member Variables
    protected InputStream in;

    // Constructors
    protected FilterInputStream(InputStream in);

    // Methods
    public int available();
    public void close();
    public void mark(int readlimit);
    public boolean markSupported();
    public int read();
    public int read(byte b[]);
    public int read(byte b[], int off, int len);
    public void reset();
    public long skip(long n);
}
```

Member Variables

Following are the member variables defined in `FilterInputStream`:

protected InputStream in

This is the underlying input stream being filtered.

 FilterInputStream   FilterInputStream io

protected FilterInputStream(InputStream in)

This constructor creates a filtered input stream based on the specified underlying input stream.

    in is the input stream to be filtered.

 available   FilterInputStream io

public int available() throws IOException

This method determines the number of bytes that can be read from the filtered input stream without blocking.

    the number of available bytes.

    `IOException` if an I/O error occurs.

    available in class `InputStream`.

close FilterInputStream /io/

```
public void close() throws IOException
```

This method closes the filtered input stream, releasing any resources associated with it.

IOException if an I/O error occurs.

close in class InputStream.

 mark FilterInputStream /io/

```
public void mark(int readlimit)
```

This method marks the current read position in the filtered input stream. The reset method can be used to reset the read position to this mark; subsequent reads will read data beginning at the mark position. The mark position is invalidated after readlimit bytes have been read.

readlimit is the maximum number of bytes that can be read before the mark position becomes invalid.

mark in class InputStream.

 markSupported  FilterInputStream /io/

```
public boolean markSupported()
```

This method determines whether the filtered input stream supports the mark and reset methods.

true if the mark and reset methods are supported; false otherwise.

markSupported in class InputStream.

 read FilterInputStream /io/

```
public int read() throws IOException
```

This method reads a byte value from the filtered input stream, blocking until the byte is read.

an integer representing the byte value read, or -1 if the end of the stream is reached.

IOException if an I/O error occurs.

read in class InputStream.

read FilterInputStream /io/

```
public int read(byte b[]) throws IOException
```

This method reads up to b.length bytes from the filtered input stream into the byte array b, blocking until all bytes are read.

▶   b is the byte array into which the data is read.

↵   the actual number of bytes read, or -1 if the end of the stream is reached.

☛   IOException if an I/O error occurs.

⊘   read in class InputStream.

 read FilterInputStream /io/

```
public int read(byte b[], int off, int len) throws IOException
```

This method reads up to len bytes from the filtered input stream into the byte array b beginning off bytes into the array, blocking until all bytes are read.

▶   b is the byte array into which the data is read.

▶   off is the starting offset into the array for the data to be written to.

▶   len is the maximum number of bytes to read.

↵   the actual number of bytes read, or -1 if the end of the stream is reached.

☛   IOException if an I/O error occurs.

⊘   read in class InputStream.

 reset FilterInputStream /io/

```
public void reset() throws IOException
```

This method resets the read position in the input stream to the current mark position, as set by the mark method.

☛   IOException if the stream has not been marked or if the mark is invalid.

⊘   reset in class InputStream.

skip FilterInputStream /io/

```
public long skip(long n) throws IOException
```

This method skips n bytes of data in the input stream.

▶ n is the number of bytes to skip.

↵ the actual number of bytes skipped.

⌐ IOException if an I/O error occurs.

⊘ skip in class InputStream.

 # FilterOutputStream /io/

✚ OutputStream

See also: FilterOutputStream.

The FilterOutputStream class defines an output stream filter used to filter data on an underlying output stream. Most of the methods defined in this class merely call corresponding methods in the underlying output stream, and you simply override appropriate methods to supply the filtering functionality. FilterOutputStream is the basis for all other output stream filter implementations. Derived filtered output streams can be linked for complex filtering operations; this is the class definition:

```
public class java.io.FilterOutputStream extends java.io.OutputStream {
  // Member Variables
  protected OutputStream out;

  // Constructors
  public FilterOutputStream(OutputStream  out);

  // Methods
  public void close();
  public void flush();
  public void write(byte b[]);
  public void write(byte b[], int off, int len);
  public void write(int b);
}
```

Member Variables

Following are the member variables defined in FilterOutputStream:

protected OutputStream out

This is the underlying output stream being filtered.

FilterOutputStream FilterOutputStream io

```
public FilterOutputStream(OutputStream out)
```

This constructor creates a filtered output stream based on the specified underlying output stream.

▶ out is the output stream to be filtered.

 close FilterOutputStream io

```
public void close() throws IOException
```

This method closes the filtered output stream, releasing any resources associated with it.

IOException if an I/O error occurs.

⊘ close in class OutputStream.

 flush FilterOutputStream io

```
public void flush() throws IOException
```

This method flushes the filtered output stream, resulting in any buffered data being written to the underlying output stream.

IOException if an I/O error occurs.

⊘ flush in class OutputStream.

 write FilterOutputStream io

```
public void write(byte b[]) throws IOException
```

This method writes b.length bytes to the filtered output stream from the byte array b.

▶ b is the byte array from which the data is written.

IOException if an I/O error occurs.

⊘ write in class OutputStream.

 write FilterOutputStream io

```
public void write(byte b[], int off, int len) throws IOException
```

This method writes len bytes to the filtered output stream from the byte array b beginning off bytes into the array, blocking until all bytes are written.

▶ b is the byte array from which the data is written.

▶ off is the starting offset into the array for the data to be read from.

len is the number of bytes to write.

IOException if an I/O error occurs.

write in class OutputStream.

write FilterOutputStream /io/

```
public void write(int b) throws IOException
```

This method writes a byte value to the buffered output stream.

▶ b is the byte value to be written.

IOException if an I/O error occurs.

write in class OutputStream.

InputStream /io/

➕ Object

See also: OutputStream.

The InputStream class is an abstract class representing an input stream of bytes; all input streams are based on this class. Here is the InputStream definition:

```
public abstract class java.io.InputStream extends java.lang.Object {
  // Constructors
  public InputStream();

  // Methods
  public int available();
  public void close();
  public void mark(int readlimit);
  public boolean markSupported();
  public abstract int read();
  public int read(byte b[]);
  public int read(byte b[], int off, int len);
  public void reset();
  public long skip(long n);
}
```

InputStream InputStream /io/

```
public InputStream()
```

This constructor creates a default input stream.

available   InputStream   io

```
public int available() throws IOException
```

This method determines the number of bytes that can be read from the input stream without blocking. This method should be overridden in all subclasses because it returns 0 in InputStream.

↵ the number of available bytes.

⤷ IOException if an I/O error occurs.

close   InputStream   io

```
public void close() throws IOException
```

This method closes the input stream, releasing any resources associated with it. This method should usually be overridden in subclasses, since it does nothing in InputStream.

⤷ IOException if an I/O error occurs.

mark   InputStream   io

```
public void mark(int readlimit)
```

This method marks the current read position in the input stream. The reset method can be used to reset the read position to this mark; subsequent reads will read data beginning at the mark position. The mark position is invalidated after readlimit bytes have been read. This method should usually be overridden in subclasses because it does nothing in InputStream.

▶ readlimit is the maximum number of bytes that can be read before the mark position becomes invalid.

markSupported   InputStream   io

```
public boolean markSupported()
```

This method determines whether the input stream supports the mark and reset methods. This method should usually be overridden in subclasses, since it always returns false in InputStream.

↵ true if the mark and reset methods are supported; false otherwise.

read   InputStream   io

```
public abstract int read() throws IOException
```

This method reads a byte value from the input stream, blocking until the byte is read. This method must be overridden in all subclasses because it's defined as abstract in InputStream.

↵ an integer representing the byte value read, or -1 if the end of the stream is reached.

⤷ IOException if an I/O error occurs.

read InputStream `io`

```
public int read(byte b[]) throws IOException
```

This method reads up to b.length bytes from the input stream into the byte array b, blocking until all bytes are read. This method actually calls the three-parameter version of read, passing b, 0, and b.length as the parameters.

▶ b is the byte array into which the data is read.

↵ the actual number of bytes read, or -1 if the end of the stream is reached.

↗ IOException if an I/O error occurs.

 read InputStream `io`

```
public int read(byte b[], int off, int len) throws IOException
```

This method reads up to len bytes from the input stream into the byte array b beginning off bytes into the array, blocking until all bytes are read. This method actually reads each byte by calling the read method that takes no parameters. Subclasses should offer a more efficient implementation of this method, one that doesn't rely on the other read method, if possible.

▶ b is the byte array into which the data is read.

▶ off is the starting offset into the array for the data to be written to.

▶ len is the maximum number of bytes to read.

↵ the actual number of bytes read, or -1 if the end of the stream is reached.

↗ IOException if an I/O error occurs.

 reset InputStream `io`

```
public void reset() throws IOException
```

This method resets the read position in the input stream to the current mark position, as set by the mark method. This method should be overridden in subclasses requiring mark/reset functionality, since it always throws an IOException in InputStream; this happens because input streams don't support, by default, mark/reset functionality.

↗ IOException if the stream has not been marked or if the mark is invalid.

 skip InputStream `io`

```
public long skip(long n) throws IOException
```

This method skips n bytes of data in the input stream. This method should usually be overridden with a more efficient version in subclasses because it reads skipped data into a temporary byte array in InputStream.

▶ n is the number of bytes to skip.

↵ the actual number of bytes skipped.

➤ IOException if an I/O error occurs.

LineNumberInputStream

➕ FilterInputStream

The LineNumberInputStream class implements an input stream that keeps track of how many lines have passed through the stream. A line is defined as a sequence of bytes followed by either a carriage return character (\r), a newline character (\n), or a carriage return character immediately followed by a newline character. In all three cases, the newline is interpreted as a single character. Here is the class definition:

```
public class java.io.LineNumberInputStream extends java.io.FilterInputStream {
    // Constructors
    public LineNumberInputStream(InputStream  in);

    // Methods
    public int available();
    public int getLineNumber();
    public void mark(int readlimit);
    public int read();
    public int read(byte b[], int off, int len);
    public void reset();
    public void setLineNumber(int lineNumber);
    public long skip(long n);
}
```

 LineNumberInputStream   LineNumberInputStream

```
public LineNumberInputStream(InputStream in)
```

This constructor creates a line number input stream that counts lines based on the specified input stream.

▶ in is the input stream to count lines from.

 available   LineNumberInputStream

```
public int available() throws IOException
```

This method determines the number of bytes that can be read from the input stream without blocking. Note that this number could be as small as half that of the underlying stream, since LineNumberInputStream combines carriage return/newline character pairs into a single newline byte.

↵ the number of available bytes.

⊘ available in class `FilterInputStream`.

---

getLineNumber   🖥→📦   LineNumberInputStream   /io/

```
public int getLineNumber()
```

This method determines the current line number for the input stream, which is the count of how many lines the stream has processed.

↵ the current line number.

---

mark   🖥→📦   LineNumberInputStream   /io/

```
public void mark(int readlimit)
```

This method marks the current read position in the input stream. The `reset` method can be used to reset the read position to this mark; subsequent reads will read data beginning at the mark position. The mark position is invalidated after `readlimit` bytes have been read. The `mark` method ensures that the current line number is stored so it isn't invalidated by a subsequent call to `reset`.

▶ `readlimit` is the maximum number of bytes that can be read before the mark position becomes invalid.

⊘ mark in class `FilterInputStream`.

---

read   🖥→📦   LineNumberInputStream   /io/

```
public int read() throws IOException
```

This method reads a byte value from the input stream, blocking until the byte is read.

↵ an integer representing the byte value read, or -1 if the end of the stream is reached.

➤ `IOException` if an I/O error occurs.

⊘ read in class `FilterInputStream`.

---

read   🖥→📦   LineNumberInputStream   /io/

```
public int read(byte b[], int off, int len) throws IOException
```

This method reads up to `len` bytes from the input stream into the byte array `b` beginning `off` bytes into the array, blocking until all bytes are read.

▶ `b` is the byte array into which the data is read.

▶ `off` is the starting offset into the array for the data to be written to.

▶ `len` is the maximum number of bytes to read.

↵ the actual number of bytes read, or -1 if the end of the stream is reached.

➤ `IOException` if an I/O error occurs.

⊘ `read` in class `FilterInputStream`.

---

 reset LineNumberInputStream /io/

```
public void reset() throws IOException
```

This method resets the read position in the input stream to the current mark position, as set by the `mark` method. The current line number is reset to the value it held when the `mark` method was called.

⊘ `reset` in class `FilterInputStream`.

---

setLineNumber LineNumberInputStream /io/

```
public void setLineNumber(int lineNumber)
```

This method sets the current line number to the specified line number.

▶ `lineNumber` is the new line number to be set.

---

skip LineNumberInputStream /io/

```
public long skip(long n) throws IOException
```

This method skips n bytes of data in the input stream.

▶ n is the number of bytes to skip.

↵ the actual number of bytes skipped.

➤ `IOException` if an I/O error occurs.

⊘ `skip` in class `FilterInputStream`.

 # OutputStream

✛ `Object`

See also: `InputStream`.

`OutputStream` is an abstract class representing an output stream of bytes. All output streams are based on `OutputStream`; here is its class definition:

```
public abstract class java.io.OutputStream extends java.lang.Object {
    // Constructors
    public OutputStream();

    // Methods
    public void close();
    public void flush();
    public void write(byte b[]);
    public void write(byte b[], int off, int len);
    public abstract void write(int b);
}
```

 OutputStream   OutputStream

```
public OutputStream()
```

This constructor creates a default output stream.

 close   OutputStream io

```
public void close() throws IOException
```

This method closes the output stream, releasing any resources associated with it. This method should usually be overridden in subclasses, since it does nothing in `OutputStream`.

 `IOException` if an I/O error occurs.

 flush OutputStream io

```
public void flush() throws IOException
```

This method flushes the output stream, resulting in any buffered data being written to the underlying output stream. It should usually be overridden in subclasses because it does nothing in `OutputStream`.

 `IOException` if an I/O error occurs.

 write OutputStream io

```
public void write(byte b[]) throws IOException
```

This method writes `b.length` bytes to the output stream from the byte array `b`. This method actually calls the three-parameter version of `write`, passing `b`, `0`, and `b.length` as the parameters.

 `b` is the byte array from which the data is written.

`IOException` if an I/O error occurs.

write   OutputStream   /io/

```
public void write(byte b[], int off, int len) throws IOException
```

This method writes `len` bytes to the output stream from the byte array `b` beginning `off` bytes into the array. It actually writes each byte by calling the `write` method that takes one parameter. Subclasses should offer a more efficient way for this method to work that doesn't rely on the other `write` method, if possible.

▶ `b` is the byte array from which the data is written.

▶ `off` is the starting offset into the array for the data to be read from.

▶ `len` is the number of bytes to write.

➤ `IOException` if an I/O error occurs.

 write   OutputStream   /io/

```
public abstract void write(int b) throws IOException
```

This method writes a byte value to the output stream. This method must be overridden in all subclasses because it's defined as abstract in `OutputStream`.

▶ `b` is the byte value to be written.

➤ `IOException` if an I/O error occurs.

PipedInputStream   /io/

 InputStream

See also: `PipedOutputStream`.

This class implements a piped input stream, which acts as the receiving end of a communications pipe. Piped input streams must be connected to a piped output stream to receive data. In other words, a piped output stream must be used to send the data received by a piped input stream. Here is the definition for the `PipedInputStream` class:

```
public class java.io.PipedInputStream extends java.io.InputStream {
    // Constructors
    public PipedInputStream();
    public PipedInputStream(PipedOutputStream src);

    // Methods
    public void close();
    public void connect(PipedOutputStream src);
    public int read();
    public int read(byte b[], int off, int len);
}
```

PipedInputStream

```
public PipedInputStream()
```

This constructor creates a piped input stream that isn't connected to anything. The stream must be connected to a piped output stream with the connect method before it can be used.

PipedInputStream

```
public PipedInputStream(PipedOutputStream src) throws IOException
```

This constructor creates a piped input stream connected to the specified piped output stream.

▶ src is the piped output stream to connect to.

🐾 IOException if an I/O error occurs.

close

```
public void close() throws IOException
```

This method closes the piped input stream, releasing any resources associated with it.

🐾 IOException if an I/O error occurs.

⊘ close in class InputStream.

connect

```
public void connect(PipedOutputStream src) throws IOException
```

This method connects the input stream to the specified piped output stream.

▶ src is the piped output stream to connect to.

🐾 IOException if an I/O error occurs.

read

```
public int read() throws IOException
```

This method reads a byte value from the piped input stream, blocking until the byte is read.

↵ an integer representing the byte value read, or -1 if the end of the stream is reached.

🐾 IOException if an I/O error occurs.

⊘ read in class InputStream.

read   **PipedInputStream**   io

```
public int read(byte b[], int off, int len) throws IOException
```

This method reads up to `len` bytes from the piped input stream into the byte array `b` beginning `off` bytes into the array, blocking until all bytes are read.

▶ `b` is the byte array into which the data is read.

▶ `off` is the starting offset into the array for the data to be written to.

▶ `len` is the maximum number of bytes to read.

↵ the actual number of bytes read, or `-1` if the end of the stream is reached.

➦ `IOException` if an I/O error occurs.

⊘ `read` in class `InputStream`.

 # PipedOutputStream   io

➕ `OutputStream`

See also: `PipedInputStream`.

The `PipedOutputStream` class implements a piped output stream, which acts as the sending end of a communications pipe. Piped output streams must be connected to a piped input stream to send data. In other words, a piped input stream must be used to receive the data sent by a piped output stream. This is the definition for the class:

```
public class java.io.PipedOutputStream extends java.io.OutputStream {
    // Constructors
    public PipedOutputStream();
    public PipedOutputStream(PipedInputStream snk);

    // Methods
    public void close();
    public void connect(PipedInputStream snk);
    public void write(byte b[], int off, int len);
    public void write(int b);
}
```

 PipedOutputStream   **PipedOutputStream**   io

```
public PipedOutputStream()
```

This constructor creates a piped output stream that isn't connected to anything. The stream must be connected to a piped input stream with the `connect` method before it can be used.

PipedOutputStream

```
public PipedOutputStream(PipedInputStream snk) throws IOException
```

This constructor creates a piped output stream connected to the specified piped input stream.

▶ snk is the piped input stream to connect to.

IOException if an I/O error occurs.

close

```
public void close() throws IOException
```

This method closes the piped output stream, releasing any resources associated with it.

IOException if an I/O error occurs.

⊘ close in class OutputStream.

connect

```
public void connect(PipedInputStream snk) throws IOException
```

This method connects the output stream to the specified piped input stream.

▶ snk is the piped input stream to connect to.

IOException if an I/O error occurs.

write

```
public void write(byte b[], int off, int len) throws IOException
```

This method writes len bytes to the piped output stream from the byte array b beginning off bytes into the array.

▶ b is the byte array from which the data is written.

▶ off is the starting offset into the array for the data to be read from.

▶ len is the number of bytes to write.

IOException if an I/O error occurs.

⊘ write in class OutputStream.

write

```
public void write(int b) throws IOException
```

This method writes a byte value to the piped output stream.

▶ b is the byte value to be written.

↗ IOException if an I/O error occurs.

⊘ write in class OutputStream.

PrintStream

╋ FilterOutputStream

This class implements an output stream that has additional methods for printing basic types of data. You can set up the stream so that it's flushed every time a newline character (\n) is written. Note that only the lower 8 bits of any 16-bit value are printed to the stream. Here is the definition for the PrintStream class:

```
public class java.io.PrintStream extends java.io.FilterOutputStream {
    // Constructors
    public PrintStream(OutputStream out);
    public PrintStream(OutputStream out, boolean autoflush);

    // Methods
    public boolean checkError();
    public void close();
    public void flush();
    public void print(boolean b);
    public void print(char c);
    public void print(char s[]);
    public void print(double d);
    public void print(float f);
    public void print(int i);
    public void print(long l);
    public void print(Object obj);
    public void print(String s);
    public void println();
    public void println(boolean b);
    public void println(char c);
    public void println(char s[]);
    public void println(double d);
    public void println(float f);
    public void println(int i);
    public void println(long l);
    public void println(Object obj);
    public void println(String s);
    public void write(byte b[], int off, int len);
    public void write(int b);
}
```

↗ PrintStream   PrintStream   /io\

public PrintStream(OutputStream out)

This constructor creates a print stream that writes data to the specified underlying output stream.

  out is the output stream to be written to.

PrintStream   PrintStream io

```
public PrintStream(OutputStream out, boolean autoflush)
```

This constructor creates a print stream that writes data to the specified underlying output stream, with an option of flushing its output each time a newline character (\n) is encountered.

▶ out is the output stream to be written to.

▶ autoflush is a Boolean value specifying whether the stream is flushed when a newline character is encountered.

 ## checkError 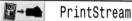 PrintStream io

```
public boolean checkError()
```

This method flushes the underlying output stream and determines whether an error has occurred on the stream. Note that errors are cumulative, meaning that once an error is encountered, checkError will continue to return true on all successive calls.

 true if the print stream has ever encountered an error on the underlying output stream; false otherwise.

 ## close PrintStream io

```
public void close()
```

This method closes the print stream, releasing any resources associated with the underlying output stream.

⊘ close in class FilterOutputStream.

 ## flush PrintStream io

```
public void flush()
```

This method flushes the print stream, resulting in any buffered data being written to the underlying output stream.

⊘ flush in class FilterOutputStream.

 ## print   PrintStream io

```
public void print(boolean b)
```

This method prints the string representation of a Boolean value to the underlying output stream. If the Boolean value is true, the string "true" is printed; otherwise, the string "false" is printed.

▶ b is the Boolean value to be printed.

print

```
public void print(char c)
```

This method prints the lower 8 bits of a character value to the underlying output stream.

▶ c is the character value to be printed.

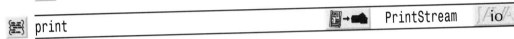

print

```
public void print(char s[])
```

This method prints the lower 8 bits of each character value in an array of characters to the underlying output stream.

▶ s is the array of characters to be printed.

print

```
public void print(double d)
```

This method prints the string representation of a double value to the underlying output stream. Note that the string representation is the same as that returned by the toString method of the Double class.

▶ d is the double value to be printed.

print

```
public void print(float f)
```

This method prints the string representation of a float value to the underlying output stream. Note that the string representation is the same as that returned by the toString method of the Float class.

▶ f is the float value to be printed.

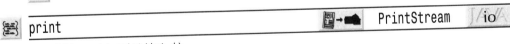

print

```
public void print(int i)
```

This method prints the string representation of an integer value to the underlying output stream. Note that the string representation is the same as that returned by the toString method of the Integer class.

▶ i is the integer value to be printed.

print   PrintStream   io

```
public void print(long l)
```

This method prints the string representation of a long value to the underlying output stream. Note that the string representation is the same as that returned by the toString method of the Long class.

▶ l is the long value to be printed.

 print   PrintStream   io

```
public void print(Object obj)
```

This method prints the string representation of an object to the underlying output stream. Note that the string representation is the same as that returned by the toString method of the object.

▶ obj is the object to be printed.

 print   PrintStream   io

```
public void print(String s)
```

This method prints the lower 8 bits of each character in a string to the underlying output stream. If the string is null, the string "null" is printed.

▶ s is the string to be printed.

 println   PrintStream   io

```
public void println()
```

This method prints the newline character (\n) to the underlying output stream.

 println   PrintStream   io

```
public void println(boolean b)
```

This method prints the string representation of a Boolean value to the underlying output stream, followed by a newline character (\n). If the Boolean value is true, the string "true" is printed; otherwise, the string "false" is printed.

▶ b is the Boolean value to be printed.

println PrintStream io

```
public void println(char c)
```

This method prints the lower 8 bits of a character value to the underlying output stream, followed by a newline character.

▶ c is the character value to be printed.

 println PrintStream io

```
public void println(char s[])
```

This method prints the lower 8 bits of each character value in an array of characters to the underlying output stream, followed by a newline character.

▶ s is the array of characters to be printed.

 println PrintStream io

```
public void println(double d)
```

This method prints the string representation of a double value to the underlying output stream, followed by a newline character. Note that the string representation is the same as that returned by the toString method of the Double class.

▶ d is the double value to be printed.

 println PrintStream io

```
public void println(float f)
```

This method prints the string representation of a float value to the underlying output stream, followed by a newline character. Note that the string representation is the same as that returned by the toString method of the Float class.

▶ f is the float value to be printed.

 println PrintStream io

```
public void println(int i)
```

This method prints the string representation of an integer value to the underlying output stream, followed by a newline character. Note that the string representation is the same as that returned by the toString method of the Integer class.

 i is the integer value to be printed.

println   PrintStream /io/

```
public void println(long l)
```

This method prints the string representation of a long value to the underlying output stream, followed by a newline character. Note that the string representation is the same as that returned by the `toString` method of the `Long` class.

▶   `l` is the long value to be printed.

 println   PrintStream /io/

```
public void println(Object obj)
```

This method prints the string representation of an object to the underlying output stream, followed by a newline character. Note that the string representation is the same as that returned by the `toString` method of the object.

▶   `obj` is the object to be printed.

println   PrintStream /io/

```
public void println(String s)
```

This method prints the lower 8 bits of each character in a string to the underlying output stream, followed by a newline character. If the string is null, the string `"null"` is printed.

▶   `s` is the string to be printed.

 write   PrintStream /io/

```
public void write(byte b[], int off, int len)
```

This method writes `len` bytes to the underlying output stream from the byte array `b` beginning `off` bytes into the array.

▶   `b` is the byte array from which the data is written.

▶   `off` is the starting offset into the array for the data to be read from.

▶   `len` is the number of bytes to write.

⊘   `write` in class `FilterOutputStream`.

 write   PrintStream /io/

```
public void write(int b)
```

This method writes a byte value to the underlying output stream. The `write` method of the underlying output stream is actually called to write the byte value. Additionally, if the byte represents the newline character (`\n`), and autoflush is turned on, the `flush` method is called.

If an IOException is thrown while writing the byte, the exception is caught and an internal error flag is set; this flag can be checked by calling the checkError method. This technique alleviates having to use a try-catch clause every time you want to print something.

 b is the byte value to be written.

IOException if an I/O error occurs.

write in class FilterOutputStream.

 # PushbackInputStream

FilterInputStream

The PushbackInputStream class implements a input stream filter that provides a one-byte pushback buffer. Using the PushbackInputStream class, an application can push the last byte read back into the stream so it's re-read the next time the read method is called. This function is useful when byte-delimited data is being read; the delimited bytes can be pushed back into the stream so the next read operation will read them. Here is the class definition:

```
public class java.io.PushbackInputStream extends java.io.FilterInputStream {
    // Member Variables
    protected int pushBack;

    // Constructors
    public PushbackInputStream(InputStream in);

    // Methods
    public int available();
    public boolean markSupported();
    public int read();
    public int read(byte bytes[], int off, int len);
    public void unread(int ch);
}
```

Member Variables

protected int pushBack

This is the pushback buffer containing the character that was pushed back. A value of -1 indicates that the pushback buffer is empty.

 PushbackInputStream   PushbackInputStream /io/

public PushbackInputStream(InputStream in)

This constructor creates a pushback input stream using the specified underlying input stream.

 in is the input stream to use the pushback filter on.

available   PushbackInputStream   io

```
public int available() throws IOException
```

This method determines the number of bytes that can be read from the pushback input stream without blocking.

↵   the number of available bytes.

✆   `IOException` if an I/O error occurs.

⊘   `available` in class `FilterInputStream`.

markSupported   PushbackInputStream   io

```
public boolean markSupported()
```

This method determines whether the pushback input stream supports the `mark` and `reset` methods.

↵   `true` if the `mark` and `reset` methods are supported; `false` otherwise.

⊘   `markSupported` in class `FilterInputStream`.

read   PushbackInputStream   io

```
public int read() throws IOException
```

This method reads a byte value from the pushback input stream, blocking until the byte is read. The `read` method actually returns the pushback character, if there is one, and calls the underlying input stream's `read` method, if not.

↵   an integer representing the byte value read, or `-1` if the end of the stream is reached.

✆   `IOException` if an I/O error occurs.

⊘   `read` in class `FilterInputStream`.

read   PushbackInputStream   io

```
public int read(byte bytes[], int off, int len) throws IOException
```

This method reads up to `len` bytes from the buffered input stream into the byte array `bytes` beginning `off` bytes into the array, blocking until all bytes are read.

▶   `bytes` is the byte array into which the data is read.

▶   `off` is the starting offset into the array for the data to be written to.

▶   `len` is the maximum number of bytes to read.

↵ the actual number of bytes read, or -1 if the end of the stream is reached.

🖰 IOException if an I/O error occurs.

⊘ read in class FilterInputStream.

---

unread  PushbackInputStream io

```
public void unread(int ch) throws IOException
```

This method pushes a character back into the stream so that it's read the next time the read method is called. Note that there can be only one pushback character, meaning that multiple calls to unread without matching calls to read result in an IOException being thrown.

▶ ch is the character to push back into the stream.

🖰 IOException if an attempt is made to push back more than one character.

RandomAccessFile 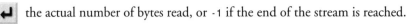 io

✚ Object

 DataOutput, DataInput

The RandomAccessFile class implements a random access file stream, enabling you to both read from and write to random access files. Here is the class definition:

```
public class java.io.RandomAccessFile extends java.lang.Object
   implements java.io.DataOutput java.io.DataInput {
   // Constructors
   public RandomAccessFile(File file, String mode);
   public RandomAccessFile(String name, String mode);

   // Methods
   public void close();
   public final FileDescriptor getFD();
   public long getFilePointer();
   public long length();
   public int read();
   public int read(byte b[]);
   public int read(byte b[], int off, int len);
   public final boolean readBoolean();
   public final byte readByte();
   public final char readChar();
   public final double readDouble();
   public final float readFloat();
   public final void readFully(byte b[]);
   public final void readFully(byte b[], int off, int len);
   public final int readInt();
   public final String readLine();
   public final long readLong();
   public final short readShort();
   public final int readUnsignedByte();
```

```
      public final int readUnsignedShort();
      public final String readUTF();
      public void seek(long pos);
      public int skipBytes(int n);
      public void write(byte b[]);
      public void write(byte b[], int off, int len);
      public void write(int b);
      public final void writeBoolean(boolean v);
      public final void writeByte(int v);
      public final void writeBytes(String s);
      public final void writeChar(int v);
      public final void writeChars(String s);
      public final void writeDouble(double v);
      public final void writeFloat(float v);
      public final void writeInt(int v);
      public final void writeLong(long v);
      public final void writeShort(int v);
      public final void writeUTF(String str);
    }
```

 RandomAccessFile RandomAccessFile io

```
      public RandomAccessFile(String name, String mode) throws IOException
```

This constructor creates a random access file stream based on the file with the specified filename and access mode. There are two supported access modes: mode "r" is for read-only files, and mode "rw" is for read/write files.

▶ name is the filename of the file to access.

▶ mode is the access mode.

🏃 IOException if an I/O error occurs.

🏃 IllegalArgumentException if the access mode is not equal to "r" or "rw".

🏃 SecurityException if the access mode is "r" and the application doesn't have read access to the file, or if the access mode is "rw" and the application doesn't have both read and write access to the file.

 RandomAccessFile RandomAccessFile io

```
      public RandomAccessFile(File file, String mode) throws IOException
```

This constructor creates a random access file stream based on the specified file and access mode. There are two supported access modes: mode "r" is for read-only files, and mode "rw" is for read/write files.

▶ file is the file to access.

▶ mode is the access mode.

🏃 IOException if an I/O error occurs.

IllegalArgumentException if the access mode is not equal to "r" or "rw".

SecurityException if the access mode is "r" and the application doesn't have read access to the file, or if the access mode is "rw" and the application doesn't have both read and write access to the file.

close   RandomAccessFile   io

```
public void close() throws IOException
```

This method closes the random access file stream, releasing any resources associated with it.

IOException if an I/O error occurs.

getFD   RandomAccessFile   io

```
public final FileDescriptor getFD() throws IOException
```

This method determines the file descriptor associated with the random access file stream.

the file descriptor associated with the stream.

IOException if an I/O error occurs.

getFilePointer   RandomAccessFile   io

```
public long getFilePointer() throws IOException
```

This method determines the current read/write position in bytes of the random access file stream, which is the offset of the read/write position from the beginning of the stream.

the current read/write position of the stream.

IOException if an I/O error occurs.

length   RandomAccessFile   io

```
public long length() throws IOException
```

This method determines the length in bytes of the underlying file.

the length of the underlying file.

IOException if an I/O error occurs.

read   RandomAccessFile   io

```
public int read() throws IOException
```

This method reads a byte value from the random access file stream, blocking until the byte is read.

↵ an integer representing the byte value read, or -1 if the end of the stream is reached.

👣 IOException if an I/O error occurs.

read   RandomAccessFile   io

```
public int read(byte b[]) throws IOException
```

This method reads up to `b.length` bytes from the random access file stream into the byte array b, blocking until at least one byte is available.

▶ b is the byte array into which the data is read.

↵ the total number of bytes read, or -1 if the end of the stream is reached.

👣 IOException if an I/O error occurs.

read   RandomAccessFile   io

```
public int read(byte b[], int off, int len) throws IOException
```

This method reads up to `len` bytes from the random access file stream into the byte array b beginning `off` bytes into the array, blocking until at least one byte is available.

▶ b is the byte array into which the data is read.

▶ off is the starting offset into the array for the data to be written to.

▶ len is the maximum number of bytes to read.

↵ the total number of bytes read, or -1 if the end of the stream is reached.

👣 IOException if an I/O error occurs.

readBoolean   RandomAccessFile   io

```
public final boolean readBoolean() throws IOException
```

This method reads a Boolean value (byte) from the random access file stream. A value of 0 is interpreted as `false`; all other values are interpreted as `true`.

↵ the Boolean value read.

👣 EOFException if the end of the stream is reached before reading the value.

👣 IOException if an I/O error occurs.

readByte   RandomAccessFile   io

```
public final byte readByte() throws IOException
```

This method reads a signed byte (8-bit) value from the random access file stream, blocking until the byte is read.

↵ the byte value read.

🔴 EOFException if the end of the stream is reached before reading the value.

🔴 IOException if an I/O error occurs.

readChar · RandomAccessFile · io

```
public final char readChar() throws IOException
```

This method reads a character (16-bit) value from the random access file stream, blocking until both bytes are read.

↵ the character value read.

🔴 EOFException if the end of the stream is reached before reading the value.

🔴 IOException if an I/O error occurs.

readDouble · RandomAccessFile · io

```
public final double readDouble() throws IOException
```

This method reads a double (64-bit) value from the random access file stream, blocking until all eight bytes are read.

↵ the double value read.

🔴 EOFException if the end of the stream is reached before reading the value.

🔴 IOException if an I/O error occurs.

readFloat · RandomAccessFile · io

```
public final float readFloat() throws IOException
```

This method reads a float (32-bit) value from the random access file stream, blocking until all four bytes are read.

↵ the float value read.

🔴 EOFException if the end of the stream is reached before reading the value.

🔴 IOException if an I/O error occurs.

readFully · RandomAccessFile · io

```
public final void readFully(byte b[]) throws IOException
```

This method reads up to b.length bytes from the random access file stream into the byte array b, blocking until all bytes are read.

► b is the byte array into which the data is read.

✦ EOFException if the end of the stream is reached before reading the value.

✦ IOException if an I/O error occurs.

readFully ▮→◀ RandomAccessFile io

```
public final void readFully(byte b[], int off, int len) throws IOException
```

This method reads up to len bytes from the random access file stream into the byte array b beginning off bytes into the array, blocking until all bytes are read.

► b is the byte array into which the data is read.

► off is the starting offset into the array for the data to be written to.

► len is the maximum number of bytes to read.

✦ EOFException if the end of the stream is reached before reading the value.

✦ IOException if an I/O error occurs.

readInt ▮→◀ RandomAccessFile io

```
public final int readInt() throws IOException
```

This method reads an integer (32-bit) value from the random access file stream, blocking until all four bytes are read.

↵ the integer value read.

✦ EOFException if the end of the stream is reached before reading the value.

✦ IOException if an I/O error occurs.

readLine ▮→◀ RandomAccessFile io

```
public final String readLine() throws IOException
```

This method reads a line of text from the random access file stream, blocking until either a newline character (\n) or a carriage return character (\r) is read.

↵ a string containing the line of text read.

✦ IOException if an I/O error occurs.

readLong ▮→◀ RandomAccessFile io

```
public final long readLong() throws IOException
```

This method reads a long (64-bit) value from the random access file stream, blocking until all eight bytes are read.

↵ the long value read.

↰ EOFException if the end of the stream is reached before reading the value.

↰ IOException if an I/O error occurs.

readShort RandomAccessFile /io/

```
public final short readShort() throws IOException
```

This method reads a short (16-bit) value from the random access file stream, blocking until both bytes are read.

↵ the short value read.

↰ EOFException if the end of the stream is reached before reading the value.

↰ IOException if an I/O error occurs.

readUnsignedByte RandomAccessFile /io/

```
public final int readUnsignedByte() throws IOException
```

This method reads an unsigned byte (8-bit) value from the random access file stream, blocking until the byte is read.

↵ the unsigned byte value read.

↰ EOFException if the end of the stream is reached before reading the value.

↰ IOException if an I/O error occurs.

readUnsignedShort RandomAccessFile /io/

```
public final int readUnsignedShort() throws IOException
```

This method reads an unsigned short (16-bit) value from the random access file stream, blocking until both bytes are read.

↵ the unsigned short value read.

↰ EOFException if the end of the stream is reached before reading the value.

↰ IOException if an I/O error occurs.

readUTF RandomAccessFile /io/

```
public final String readUTF() throws IOException
```

This method reads a string that has been encoded using a modified UTF-8 format from the random access file stream, blocking until all bytes are read.

↵ the string read.

✏ `EOFException` if the end of the stream is reached before reading the string.

✏ `UTFDataFormatException` if the bytes read don't represent a valid UTF-8 encoding of a string.

✏ `IOException` if an I/O error occurs.

---

 seek RandomAccessFile io

```
public void seek(long pos) throws IOException
```

This method sets the current stream position to the specified absolute position; the position is absolute because it's always determined in relation to the beginning of the stream.

▶ pos is the absolute position to seek to.

✏ `IOException` if an I/O error occurs.

---

skipBytes RandomAccessFile io

```
public int skipBytes(int n) throws IOException
```

This method skips n bytes of data in the random access file stream, blocking until all bytes are skipped.

▶ n is the number of bytes to skip.

↵ the actual number of bytes skipped.

✏ `EOFException` if the end of the stream is reached before skipping the specified number of bytes.

✏ `IOException` if an I/O error occurs.

---

write RandomAccessFile io

```
public void write(byte b[]) throws IOException
```

This method writes `b.length` bytes to the random access file stream from the byte array `b`.

▶ b is the byte array from which the data is written.

✏ `IOException` if an I/O error occurs.

---

write RandomAccessFile io

```
public void write(byte b[], int off, int len) throws IOException
```

This method writes `len` bytes to the random access file stream from the byte array `b` beginning `off` bytes into the array.

▶ b is the byte array from which the data is written.

▶ off is the starting offset into the array for the data to be read from.

▶ len is the number of bytes to write.

☞ IOException if an I/O error occurs.

write — RandomAccessFile — io

```
public void write(int b) throws IOException
```

This method writes a byte value to the random access file stream.

▶ b is the byte value to be written.

☞ IOException if an I/O error occurs.

writeBoolean — RandomAccessFile — io

```
public final void writeBoolean(boolean v) throws IOException
```

This method writes a Boolean value to the random access file stream. The Boolean value true is written as the byte value 1, and false is written as the byte value 0.

▶ v is the Boolean value to be written.

☞ IOException if an I/O error occurs.

writeByte — RandomAccessFile — io

```
public final void writeByte(int v) throws IOException
```

This method writes a byte (8-bit) value to the random access file stream.

▶ v is the byte value to be written.

☞ IOException if an I/O error occurs.

writeBytes — RandomAccessFile — io

```
public final void writeBytes(String s) throws IOException
```

This method writes a string to the random access file stream as a sequence of bytes.

▶ s is the string to be written as bytes.

☞ IOException if an I/O error occurs.

writeChar  RandomAccessFile

```
public final void writeChar(int v) throws IOException
```

This method writes a character (16-bit) value to the random access file stream.

▶ v is the character value to be written.

🖝 IOException if an I/O error occurs.

writeChars  RandomAccessFile

```
public final void writeChars(String s) throws IOException
```

This method writes a string to the random access file stream as a sequence of characters.

▶ s is the string to be written as characters.

🖝 IOException if an I/O error occurs.

writeDouble  RandomAccessFile

```
public final void writeDouble(double v) throws IOException
```

This method writes a double (64-bit) value to the random access file stream.

▶ v is the double value to be written.

🖝 IOException if an I/O error occurs.

writeFloat  RandomAccessFile

```
public final void writeFloat(float v) throws IOException
```

This method writes a float (32-bit) value to the random access file stream.

▶ v is the float value to be written.

🖝 IOException if an I/O error occurs.

writeInt  RandomAccessFile

```
public final void writeInt(int v) throws IOException
```

This method writes an integer (32-bit) value to the random access file stream.

▶ v is the integer value to be written.

🖝 IOException if an I/O error occurs.

writeLong RandomAccessFile

```
public final void writeLong(long v) throws IOException
```

This method writes a long (64-bit) value to the random access file stream.

 v is the long value to be written.

IOException if an I/O error occurs.

 writeShort RandomAccessFile io

```
public final void writeShort(int v) throws IOException
```

This method writes a short (16-bit) value to the random access file stream.

 v is the short value to be written.

IOException if an I/O error occurs.

writeUTF RandomAccessFile io

```
public final void writeUTF(String str) throws IOException
```

This method encodes a string using a modified UTF-8 format and writes it to the random access file stream.

 str is the string to be written.

IOException if an I/O error occurs.

 # SequenceInputStream

InputStream

The SequenceInputStream class implements an input stream that can combine several input streams serially so that they function together as a single input stream. Each input stream forming the sequence is read from in turn; the sequence input stream handles closing streams as they finish and switching to the next one. This is the class definition:

```
public class java.io.SequenceInputStream extends java.io.InputStream {
    // Constructors
    public SequenceInputStream(Enumeration e);
    public SequenceInputStream(InputStream s1, InputStream s2);

    // Methods
    public void close();
    public int read();
    public int read(byte buf[], int pos, int len);
}
```

SequenceInputStream SequenceInputStream /io/

```
public SequenceInputStream(Enumeration e)
```

This constructor creates a sequence input stream containing the specified enumerated list of input streams.

▶ e is the list of input streams for the sequence.

 SequenceInputStream SequenceInputStream /io/

```
public SequenceInputStream(InputStream s1, InputStream s2)
```

This constructor creates a sequence input stream containing the two specified input streams.

▶ s1 is the first input stream in the sequence.

▶ s2 is the second input stream in the sequence.

 close SequenceInputStream /io/

```
public void close() throws IOException
```

This method closes the sequence input stream, releasing any resources associated with it. Additionally, this `close` method calls the `close` method for the substream currently being read from as well as the substreams that have yet to be read from.

🖎 IOException if an I/O error occurs.

⊘ close in class InputStream.

 read SequenceInputStream /io/

```
public int read() throws IOException
```

This method reads a byte value from the currently active substream in the sequence input stream, blocking until the byte is read. If the end of the substream is reached, the `close` method is called on the substream and `read` begins reading from the next substream.

↵ an integer representing the byte value read, or -1 if the end of the stream is reached.

⊘ read in class InputStream.

 read SequenceInputStream /io/

```
public int read(byte b[], int pos, int len) throws IOException
```

This method reads up to `len` bytes from the currently active substream in the sequence input stream into the byte array `b` beginning `off` bytes into the array, blocking until all bytes are read. If the end of the substream is reached, the `close` method is called on the substream and `read` begins reading from the next substream.

▶   b is the byte array into which the data is read.

▶   off is the starting offset into the array for the data to be written to.

▶   len is the maximum number of bytes to read.

↵   the actual number of bytes read, or -1 if the end of the stream is reached.

➔   IOException if an I/O error occurs.

⊘   read in class InputStream.

StreamTokenizer

✛   Object

The StreamTokenizer class implements a string tokenizer stream, which parses an input stream into a stream of tokens. The StreamTokenizer class gives you different methods for establishing how the tokens are parsed. Each character read from the stream is evaluated as having zero or more of the following attributes: whitespace, alphabetic, numeric, string quote, or comment. Here is the definition for the class:

```
public class java.io.StreamTokenizer extends java.lang.Object {
    // Member Variables
    public double nval;
    public String sval;
    public int ttype;

    // possible values for the ttype member variable
    public final static int TT_EOF;
    public final static int TT_EOL;
    public final static int TT_NUMBER;
    public final static int TT_WORD;

    // Constructors
    public StreamTokenizer(InputStream I);

    // Methods
    public void commentChar(int ch);
    public void eolIsSignificant(boolean flag);
    public int lineno();
    public void lowerCaseMode(boolean fl);
    public int nextToken();
    public void ordinaryChar(int ch);
    public void ordinaryChars(int low, int hi);
    public void parseNumbers();
    public void pushBack();
    public void quoteChar(int ch);
    public void resetSyntax();
    public void whitespaceChars(int low, int hi);
    public void slashStarComments(boolean flag);
    public String toString();
    public void whitespaceChars(int low, int hi);
    public void wordChars(int low, int hi);
}
```

Member Variables

public double nval

This member variable holds a numeric token value whenever the `ttype` member variable is set to `TT_NUMBER`.

public String sval

This member variable holds a string representation of a word token whenever the `ttype` member variable is set to `TT_WORD`, or it holds the body of a quoted string token when `ttype` is set to a quote character.

public int ttype

This is the type of the current token, which can be one of the following:

- an integer representation of a character for single-character tokens
- the quote character for quoted string tokens
- `TT_WORD` for word tokens
- `TT_NUMERIC` for numeric tokens
- `TT_EOL` if the end of a line has been reached on the input stream
- `TT_EOF` if the end of the stream has been reached

public final static int TT_EOF

This is a constant token type representing the end-of-file token.

public final static int TT_EOL

This is a constant token type representing the end-of-line token.

public final static int TT_NUMBER

This is a constant token type identifying a numeric token; the actual numeric value is stored in `nval`.

public final static int TT_WORD

This is a constant token type identifying a word token; the actual word value is stored in `sval`.

 StreamTokenizer  StreamTokenizer io

public StreamTokenizer(InputStream I)

This constructor creates a string tokenizer stream that parses the specified input stream. By default, the string tokenizer stream recognizes numbers, strings quoted with single and double quotes, all alphabetic characters, and comments preceded by a / character.

▶ I is the input stream to be parsed.

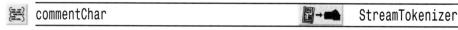

commentChar   StreamTokenizer   io

```
public void commentChar(int ch)
```

This method specifies what character starts single-line comments.

▶ ch is the new single-line comment character.

eolIsSignificant   StreamTokenizer   io

```
public void eolIsSignificant(boolean flag)
```

This method establishes whether end-of-line characters are recognized as tokens.

  flag is a Boolean value specifying whether end-of-line characters are treated as tokens; a value of true means end-of-line characters are treated as tokens, but a value of false means they are treated as whitespace.

lineno   StreamTokenizer   io

```
public int lineno()
```

This method determines the current line number of the string tokenizer stream.

  the current line number of the stream.

lowerCaseMode   StreamTokenizer   io

```
public void lowerCaseMode(boolean flag)
```

This method establishes whether word tokens (TT_WORD) are forced to lowercase letters when they are parsed.

  flag is a Boolean value specifying whether word tokens are forced to lowercase letters; a value of true means they are, but a value of false means they are left unmodified.

nextToken   StreamTokenizer   io

```
public int nextToken() throws IOException
```

This method parses the next token from the underlying input stream. After the token is parsed, the ttype member variable is set to the type of the token, but the value of some tokens is contained in either the nval or sval member variables, depending on the token type.

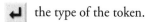 the type of the token.

  IOException if an I/O error occurs.

ordinaryChar StreamTokenizer io

```
public void ordinaryChar(int ch)
```

This method establishes that the specified character is handled as an ordinary character by the tokenizer, meaning that the character is not interpreted as a comment character, word component, string delimiter, whitespace, or numeric character. Ordinary characters are parsed as single-character tokens.

▶ ch is the character to be set as ordinary.

 ordinaryChars StreamTokenizer io

```
public void ordinaryChars(int low, int hi)
```

This method establishes that the characters in the specified range are handled as ordinary characters by the tokenizer, meaning that the characters are not interpreted as comment characters, word components, string delimiters, whitespace, or numeric characters. Ordinary characters are parsed as single-character tokens.

▶ low is the low end of the ordinary character range.

▶ hi is the high end of the ordinary character range.

 parseNumbers StreamTokenizer io

```
public void parseNumbers()
```

This method establishes that numbers should be parsed. When a number is parsed, the `ttype` member variable is set to `TT_NUMBER`, with the corresponding numeric value stored in `nval`.

 pushBack StreamTokenizer io

```
public void pushBack()
```

This method pushes the current token back into the string tokenizer stream, meaning that the next call to `nextToken` results in this token being handled.

 quoteChar StreamTokenizer io

```
public void quoteChar(int ch)
```

This method establishes that matching pairs of the specified character are used to delimit string constants. When a string constant is parsed, the `ttype` member variable is set to the delimiting character, with the corresponding string body stored in `sval`.

▶ ch is the new string delimiter character.

resetSyntax StreamTokenizer

```
public void resetSyntax()
```

This method resets the syntax table so that all characters are considered ordinary. An ordinary character is a character that isn't interpreted as a comment character, word component, string delimiter, whitespace, or numeric character. Ordinary characters are parsed as single-character tokens.

 slashSlashComments StreamTokenizer

```
public void slashSlashComments(boolean flag)
```

This method establishes whether C++ style comments (//) are recognized by the parser. A C++ style comment is defined by two consecutive forward slash characters, which start a comment that extends to the end of the line.

 flag is a Boolean value specifying whether C++ style comments are recognized; a value of true means C++ style comments are recognized, but a value of false means they aren't treated specially.

 slashStarComments StreamTokenizer

```
public void slashStarComments(boolean flag)
```

This method establishes whether C style comments (/*...*/) are recognized by the parser. A C style comment is defined by a forward slash character followed by an asterisk to start a comment. The comment continues until a corresponding asterisk followed by a forward slash character is reached.

 flag is a Boolean value specifying whether C style comments are recognized; a value of true means C style comments are recognized, but a value of false means they aren't treated specially.

 toString StreamTokenizer

```
public String toString()
```

This method determines the string representation of the current token in the string tokenizer stream.

↵ the string representation of the current token.

⊘ toString in class Object.

whitespaceChars StreamTokenizer

```
public void whitespaceChars(int low, int hi)
```

This method establishes that the characters in the specified range are handled as whitespace by the tokenizer, meaning that the characters serve only to separate tokens.

▶ low is the low end of the whitespace character range.

▶ hi is the high end of the whitespace character range.

 wordChars StreamTokenizer

```
public void wordChars(int low, int hi)
```

This method establishes that the characters in the specified range are handled as words by the tokenizer.

▶ low is the low end of the word character range.

▶ hi is the high end of the word character range.

 # StringBufferInputStream

➕ InputStream

This class implements an input stream whose data is fed by a string. Note that only the lower 8 bits of each character in the string are used by this class. This is the definition for the StringBufferInputStream class:

```java
public class java.io.StringBufferInputStream extends java.io.InputStream {
    // Member Variables
    protected String buffer;
    protected int count;
    protected int pos;

    // Constructors
    public StringBufferInputStream(String s);

    // Methods
    public int available();
    public int read();
    public int read(byte b[], int off, int len);
    public void reset();
    public long skip(long n);
}
```

Member Variables

`protected String buffer`

This is the string buffer from which the data is read.

`protected int count`

This is the number of characters currently in the buffer.

`protected int pos`

This is the current read position in the buffer.

 StringBufferInputStream   StringBufferInputStream   io

`public StringBufferInputStream(String s)`

This constructor creates a string buffer input stream based on the specified string. Note that the string buffer is not copied to create the input stream.

▶   s is the input string buffer.

 available   StringBufferInputStream   io

`public int available()`

This method determines the number of bytes that can be read from the string buffer input stream without blocking.

↵   the number of available bytes.

⊘   available in class `InputStream`.

read   StringBufferInputStream   io

`public int read()`

This method reads a byte value from the string buffer input stream, which is the lower 8 bits of the next character in the underlying string buffer.

↵   an integer representing the byte value read, or -1 if the end of the stream is reached.

⊘   read in class `InputStream`.

 read   StringBufferInputStream   io

`public int read(byte b[], int off, int len)`

This method reads up to `len` bytes from the string buffer input stream into the byte array `b` beginning `off` bytes into the array. Note that each byte is actually the lower 8 bits of the corresponding character in the underlying string buffer.

▶ b is the byte array into which the data is read.

▶ off is the starting offset into the array for the data to be written to.

▶ len is the maximum number of bytes to read.

↵ the actual number of bytes read, or -1 if the end of the stream is reached.

⊘ read in class InputStream.

🖩 **reset**   📭➔📪   **StringBufferInputStream**   J/io/A

```
public void reset()
```

This method resets the read position to the beginning of the string buffer input stream.

⊘ reset in class InputStream.

🖩 **skip**   📭➔📪   **StringBufferInputStream**   J/io/A

```
public long skip(long n)
```

This method skips n bytes of data in the string buffer input stream.

▶ n is the number of bytes to skip.

↵ the actual number of bytes skipped.

⊘ skip in class InputStream.

 # EOFException   J/io/A

➕ IOException

This exception class signals that an end-of-file (EOF) has been reached unexpectedly during an input operation. This exception is primarily used by data input streams, which typically expect a binary file in a specific format, in which case an end-of-file is an unusual condition. Here is the definition for the EOFException class:

```
public class java.io.EOFException extends java.io.IOException {
  // Constructors
  public EOFException();
  public EOFException(String s);
}
```

 EOFException   🖩➔! **EOFException**   J/io/A

```
public EOFException()
```

This constructor creates a default EOF exception with no detail message.

EOFException EOFException io

```
public EOFException(String s)
```

This constructor creates an EOF exception with the specified detail message containing information specific to this particular exception.

▶ s is the detail message.

FileNotFoundException io

 IOException

This exception class signals that a file could not be found; here is the definition for the FileNotFoundException class:

```
public class java.io.FileNotFoundException extends java.io.IOException {
  // Constructors
  public FileNotFoundException();
  public FileNotFoundException(String s);
}
```

 FileNotFoundException FileNotFoundException io

```
public FileNotFoundException()
```

This constructor creates a default file-not-found exception with no detail message.

 FileNotFoundException FileNotFoundException io

```
public FileNotFoundException(String s)
```

This constructor creates a file-not-found exception with the specified detail message containing information specific to this particular exception.

▶ s is the detail message.

IOException io

 Exception

This exception class signals that some kind of input/output (I/O) exception has occurred; this is the definition for the IOException class:

```
public class java.io.IOException extends java.lang.Exception {
  // Constructors
  public IOException();
  public IOException(String s);
}
```

IOException   IOException io

```
public IOException()
```

This constructor creates a default I/O exception with no detail message.

 IOException   IOException io

```
public IOException(String s)
```

This constructor creates an I/O exception with the specified detail message containing information specific to this particular exception.

▶   s is the detail message.

InterruptedIOException   io

✚ IOException

See also: InputStream, OutputStream, Thread.

This exception class signals that an input/output (I/O) operation has been interrupted; this is the definition for the InterruptedIOException class:

```
public class java.io.InterruptedIOException extends java.io.IOException {
  // Member Variables
  public int bytesTransferred;

  // Constructors
  public InterruptedIOException();
  public InterruptedIOException(String s);
}
```

Member Variables

public int bytesTransferred

This is the number of bytes that had been transferred during the I/O operation before it was interrupted.

 InterruptedIOException   InterruptedIOException io

```
public InterruptedIOException()
```

This constructor creates a default interrupted I/O exception with no detail message.

InterruptedIOException   InterruptedIOException   *io*

```
public InterruptedIOException(String s)
```

This constructor creates an interrupted I/O exception with the specified detail message containing information specific to this particular exception.

  s is the detail message.

UTFDataFormatException   *io*

  IOException

This exception class signals that a malformed UTF-8 string has been read in a data input stream. This is the definition for the UTFDataFormatException class:

```
public class java.io.UTFDataFormatException extends java.io.IOException {
    // Constructors
    public UTFDataFormatException();
    public UTFDataFormatException(String s);
}
```

 UTFDataFormatException   UTFDataFormatException   *io*

```
public UTFDataFormatException()
```

This constructor creates a default UTF data format exception with no detail message.

 UTFDataFormatException   UTFDataFormatException   *io*

```
public UTFDataFormatException(String s)
```

This constructor creates a UTF data format exception with the specified detail message containing information specific to this particular exception.

  s is the detail message.

32

Package java.lang

by Michael Morrison

The Java language package, also known as java.lang, provides the core classes that make up the Java programming environment. The language package includes classes representing numbers, strings, and objects, as well as classes for handling compilation, the runtime environment, security, and threaded programming. The java.lang package is imported automatically into every Java program. Table 32.1 shows the contents of the java.lang package, and Figure 32.1 presents the hierarchy graphically.

Table 32.1. Contents of the java.lang package.

Class Index	Exception Index	Error Index	Interface Index
Boolean	ArithmeticException	AbstractMethodError	Cloneable
Character	ArrayIndexOutOfBoundsException	ClassCircularityError	Runnable
Class	ArrayStoreException	ClassFormatError	
ClassLoader	ClassCastException	Error	
Compiler	ClassNotFoundException	IllegalAccessError	
Double	CloneNotSupportedException	IncompatibleClassChangeError	
Float	Exception	InstantiationError	
Integer	IllegalAccessException	InternalError	
Long	IllegalArgumentException	LinkageError	
Math	IllegalMonitorStateException	NoClassDefFoundError	
Number	IllegalThreadStateException	NoSuchFieldError	
Object	IndexOutOfBoundsException	NoSuchMethodError	
Process	InstantiationException	OutOfMemoryError	
Runtime	InterruptedException	StackOverflowError	
SecurityManager	NegativeArraySizeException	ThreadDeath	
String	NoSuchMethodException	UnknownError	
StringBuffer	NullPointerException	UnsatisfiedLinkError	
System	NumberFormatException	VerifyError	
Thread	RuntimeException	VirtualMachineError	
ThreadGroup	SecurityException		
Throwable	StringIndexOutOfBoundsException		

FIGURE 32.1.
Contents of package
`java.lang`.

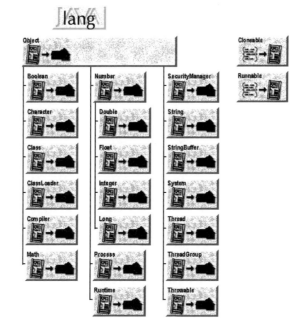

FIGURE 32.1.
Continued.

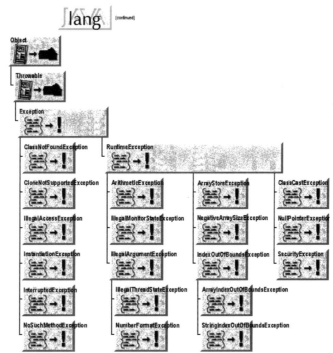

FIGURE 32.1.
Continued.

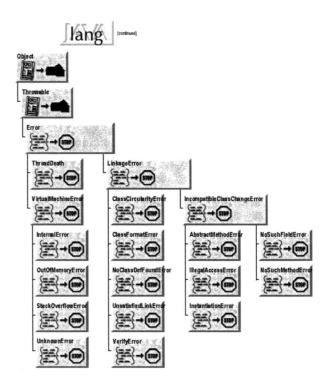

 # Cloneable   lang

 Object

This interface indicates that an object can be cloned using the clone method defined in Object. The clone method clones an object by copying each of its member variables. Attempts to clone an object that doesn't implement the Cloneable interface results in a CloneNotSupportedException being thrown. The definition for the Cloneable interface follows:

```
public interface java.lang.Cloneable {
}
```

 # Runnable   lang

 Object

See also: Thread

This interface provides a means for an object to be executed within a thread without having to be derived from the Thread class. Classes implementing the Runnable interface supply a run method that defines the threaded execution for the class. The definition for the Runnable interface follows:

```
public interface java.lang.Runnable {
  // Methods
  public abstract void run();
}
```

 run Runnable lang

`public abstract void run()`

This method is executed when a thread associated with an object implementing the `Runnable` interface is started. All of the threaded execution for the object takes place in the `run` method, which means that you should place all threaded code in this method.

Boolean lang

 Object

This class implements an object type wrapper for Boolean values. Object type wrappers are useful because many Java classes operate on objects rather than primitive data types. In addition, the `Boolean` class provides support constants and methods for working with Boolean values. The definition for the `Boolean` class follows:

```
public final class java.lang.Boolean extends java.lang.Object {
  // Member Constants
  public final static Boolean FALSE;
  public final static Boolean TRUE;

  // Constructors
  public Boolean(boolean value);
  public Boolean(String s);

  // Methods
  public boolean booleanValue();
  public boolean equals(Object obj);
  public static boolean getBoolean(String name);
  public int hashCode();
  public String toString();
  public static Boolean valueOf(String s);
}
```

Member Constants

`public final static Boolean FALSE`

This is a constant `Boolean` object representing the primitive Boolean value `FALSE`.

`public final static Boolean TRUE`

This is a constant `Boolean` object representing the primitive Boolean value `TRUE`.

Boolean Boolean lang

```
public Boolean(boolean value)
```

This constructor creates a Boolean wrapper object representing the specified primitive Boolean value.

▶ value is the Boolean value to be wrapped.

 Boolean Boolean lang

```
public Boolean(String s)
```

This constructor creates a Boolean wrapper object representing the specified string. If the string is set to "true", the wrapper represents the primitive Boolean value TRUE; otherwise, the wrapper represents FALSE.

▶ s is the string representation of a Boolean value to be wrapped.

 booleanValue Boolean lang

```
public boolean booleanValue()
```

This method determines the primitive Boolean value represented by this object.

↵ The Boolean value represented.

equals Boolean lang

```
public boolean equals(Object obj)
```

This method compares the Boolean value of the specified object to the Boolean value of this object. The equals method only returns TRUE if the specified object is a Boolean object representing the same primitive Boolean value as this object.

▶ obj is the object to compare.

↵ TRUE if the specified object is a Boolean object representing the same primitive Boolean value as this object; FALSE otherwise.

⊘ equals in class Object.

 getBoolean Boolean lang

```
public static boolean getBoolean(String name)
```

This method determines the Boolean value of the system property with the specified name.

▶ name is the system property name for which to check the Boolean value.

↵ The Boolean value of the specified system property.

hashCode Boolean lang

```
public int hashCode()
```

This method calculates a hash code for this object.

↵ A hash code for this object.

⊘ hashCode in class Object.

 toString Boolean lang

```
public String toString()
```

This method determines a string representation of the primitive Boolean value for this object. If the Boolean value is TRUE, the string "true" is returned; otherwise, the string "false" is returned.

↵ A string representing the Boolean value of this object.

⊘ toString in class Object.

 valueOf Boolean lang

```
public static Boolean valueOf(String s)
```

This method creates a new Boolean wrapper object based on the Boolean value represented by the specified string. If the string is set to "true", the wrapper represents the primitive Boolean value TRUE; otherwise, the wrapper represents FALSE.

▶ s is the string representation of a Boolean value to be wrapped.

↵ A Boolean wrapper object representing the specified string.

Character lang

✚ Object

This class implements an object type wrapper for character values. Object type wrappers are useful because many Java classes operate on objects rather than primitive data types. In addition, the Character class provides support constants and methods for working with character values. The definition for the Character class follows:

```
public final class java.lang.Character extends java.lang.Object {
    // Member Constants
    public final static int MAX_RADIX;
    public final static char MAX_VALUE;
    public final static int MIN_RADIX;
    public final static char MIN_VALUE;
```

```
// Constructors
public Character(char value);

// Methods
public char charValue();
public static int digit(char ch, int radix);
public boolean equals(Object obj);
public static char forDigit(int digit, int radix);
public int hashCode();
public static boolean isDefined(char ch);
public static boolean isDigit(char ch);
public static boolean isJavaLetter(char ch);
public static boolean isJavaLetterOrDigit(char ch);
public static boolean isLetter(char ch);
public static boolean isLetterOrDigit(char ch);
public static boolean isLowerCase(char ch);
public static boolean isSpace(char ch);
public static boolean isTitleCase(char ch);
public static boolean isUpperCase(char ch);
public static char toLowerCase(char ch);
public String toString();
public static char toTitleCase(char ch);
public static char toUpperCase(char ch);
}
```

Member Constants

public final static int MAX_RADIX

This is a constant representing the maximum radix value allowed for conversion between numbers and strings. This constant is set to 36.

public final static int MAX_VALUE

This is a constant representing the largest character value supported. This constant is set to \uffff.

public final static int MIN_RADIX

This is a constant representing the minimum radix value allowed for conversion between numbers and strings. This constant is set to 2.

public final static int MIN_VALUE

This is a constant representing the smallest character value supported. This constant is set to \u0000.

 Character   Character   lang

public Character(char value)

This constructor creates a character wrapper object representing the specified primitive character value.

▶   value is the character value to be wrapped.

charValue   Character   lang

```
public char charValue()
```

This method determines the primitive character value represented by this object.

↵ The character value represented.

digit   Character   lang

```
public static int digit(char ch, int radix)
```

This method determines the numeric value of the specified character digit using the specified radix.

▶ ch is the character to be converted to a number.

▶ radix is the radix to use in the conversion.

↵ The numeric value of the specified character digit using the specified radix, or -1 if the character isn't a valid numeric digit.

equals   Character   lang

```
public boolean equals(Object obj)
```

This method compares the character value of the specified object to the character value of this object. The equals method only returns TRUE if the specified object is a Character object representing the same primitive character value as this object.

▶ obj is the object to compare.

↵ TRUE if the specified object is a Character object representing the same primitive character value as this object; otherwise, returns FALSE.

⊘ equals in class Object.

forDigit   Character   lang

```
public static char forDigit(int digit, int radix)
```

This method determines the character value of the specified numeric digit using the specified radix.

▶ digit is the numeric digit to be converted to a character.

▶ radix is the radix to use in the conversion.

↵ The character value of the specified numeric digit using the specified radix, or 0 if the number isn't a valid character.

hashCode Character lang

```
public int hashCode()
```

This method calculates a hash code for this object.

 A hash code for this object.

⊘ hashCode in class Object.

 ## isDefined Character lang

```
public static boolean isDefined(char ch)
```

This method determines whether the specified character has a defined Unicode meaning. A character is defined if it has an entry in the Unicode attribute table.

▶ ch is the character to be checked.

↵ TRUE if the character has a defined Unicode meaning; otherwise, returns FALSE.

 ## isDigit Character lang

```
public static boolean isDigit(char ch)
```

This method determines whether the specified character is a numeric digit. A character is a numeric digit if its Unicode name contains the word DIGIT.

▶ ch is the character to be checked.

↵ TRUE if the character is a numeric digit; otherwise, returns FALSE.

 ## isJavaLetter Character lang

```
public static boolean isJavaLetter(char ch)
```

This method determines whether the specified character is permissible as the leading character in a Java identifier. A character is considered a Java letter if it is a letter, the ASCII dollar sign character ($), or the underscore character (_).

▶ ch is the character to be checked.

↵ TRUE if the character is a Java letter; otherwise, returns FALSE.

isJavaLetterOrDigit Character lang

```
public static boolean isJavaLetterOrDigit(char ch)
```

This method determines whether the specified character is permissible as a nonleading character in a Java identifier. A character is considered a Java letter or digit if it is a letter, a digit, the ASCII dollar sign character ($), or the underscore character (_).

▶ ch is the character to be checked.

↵ TRUE if the character is a Java letter or digit; otherwise, returns FALSE.

isLetter Character lang

```
public static boolean isLetter(char ch)
```

This method determines whether the specified character is a letter.

▶ ch is the character to be checked.

↵ TRUE if the character is a letter; otherwise, returns FALSE.

isLetterOrDigit Character lang

```
public static boolean isLetterOrDigit(char ch)
```

This method determines whether the specified character is a letter or digit.

▶ ch is the character to be checked.

↵ TRUE if the character is a letter or digit; otherwise, returns FALSE.

isLowerCase Character lang

```
public static boolean isLowerCase(char ch)
```

This method determines whether the specified character is a lowercase character.

▶ ch is the character to be checked.

↵ TRUE if the character is a lowercase character; otherwise, returns FALSE.

  isSpace Character lang

```
public static boolean isSpace(char ch)
```

This method determines whether the specified character is a whitespace character.

▶ ch is the character to be checked.

↵ TRUE if the character is a whitespace character; otherwise, returns FALSE.

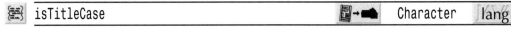

isTitleCase   Character   lang

```
public static boolean isTitleCase(char ch)
```

This method determines whether the specified character is a titlecase character. Titlecase characters are those for which the printed representations look like pairs of Latin letters.

▶   ch is the character to be checked.

↵   TRUE if the character is a titlecase character; otherwise, returns FALSE.

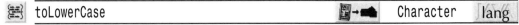

isUpperCase   Character   lang

```
public static boolean isUpperCase(char ch)
```

This method determines whether the specified character is an uppercase character.

▶   ch is the character to be checked.

↵   TRUE if the character is an uppercase character; otherwise, returns FALSE.

toLowerCase   Character   lang

```
public static char toLowerCase(char ch)
```

This method converts the specified character to a lowercase character if the character isn't already lowercase and a lowercase equivalent exists.

▶   ch is the character to be converted.

↵   The lowercase equivalent of the specified character, if one exists; otherwise, returns the original character.

toString   Character   lang

```
public String toString()
```

This method determines a string representation of the primitive character value for this object; the resulting string is one character in length.

↵   A string representing the character value of this object.

⊘   toString in class Object.

---

 toTitleCase Character lang

```
public static char toTitleCase(char ch)
```

This method converts the specified character to a titlecase character if the character isn't already a titlecase character and a titlecase equivalent exists. Titlecase characters are characters for which the printed representations look like pairs of Latin letters.

▶ ch is the character to be converted.

↵ The titlecase equivalent of the specified character, if one exists; otherwise, returns the original character.

---

 toUpperCase Character lang

```
public static char toUpperCase(char ch)
```

This method converts the specified character to an uppercase character if the character isn't already uppercase and an uppercase equivalent exists.

▶ ch is the character to be converted.

↵ The uppercase equivalent of the specified character, if one exists; otherwise, returns the original character.

Class lang

 Object

This class implements a runtime descriptor for classes and interfaces in a running Java program. Instances of `Class` are constructed automatically by the Java virtual machine when classes are loaded, which explains why there are no public constructors for the class. The definition for the `Class` class follows:

```
public final class java.lang.Class extends java.lang.Object {
    // Methods
    public static Class forName(String className);
    public ClassLoader getClassLoader();
    public Class[] getInterfaces();
    public String getName();
    public Class getSuperclass();
    public boolean isInterface();
    public Object newInstance();
    public String toString();
}
```

forName Class   lang

```
public static Class forName(String className) throws ClassNotFoundException
```

This method determines the runtime class descriptor for the class with the specified name.

▶   `className` is the fully qualified name of the desired class.

↵   The runtime class descriptor for the class with the specified name.

↬   `ClassNotFoundException` if the class could not be found.

 getClassLoader Class   lang

```
public ClassLoader getClassLoader()
```

This method determines the class loader for this object.

↵   The class loader for this object, or NULL if the class wasn't created by a class loader.

 getInterfaces Class   lang

```
public Class[] getInterfaces()
```

This method determines the interfaces implemented by the class or interface represented by this object.

↵   An array of interfaces implemented by the class or interface represented by this object, or an array of length 0 if no interfaces are implemented.

 getName Class   lang

```
public String getName()
```

This method determines the fully qualified name of the class or interface represented by this object.

↵   The fully qualified name of the class or interface represented by this object.

 getSuperclass Class   lang

```
public Class getSuperclass()
```

This method determines the superclass of the class represented by this object.

↵   The superclass of the class represented by this object, or NULL if this object represents the `Object` class.

isInterface Class lang

```
public boolean isInterface()
```

This method determines whether the class represented by this object is actually an interface.

↵ TRUE if the class is an interface; otherwise, returns FALSE.

 newInstance Class lang

```
public Object newInstance() throws InstantiationException,
➥IllegalAccessException
```

This method creates a new default instance of the class represented by this object.

↵ A new default instance of the class represented by this object.

➤ InstantiationException if you try to instantiate an abstract class or an interface, or if the instantiation fails for some other reason.

➤ IllegalAccessException if the class is not accessible.

 toString Class lang

```
public String toString()
```

This method determines the name of the class or interface represented by this object, with the string "class" or the string "interface" prepended appropriately.

↵ The name of the class or interface represented by this object, with a descriptive string prepended indicating whether the object represents a class or interface.

⊘ toString in class Object.

 # ClassLoader lang

✚ Object

This class is an abstract class that defines a mechanism for dynamically loading classes into the Java runtime system. By default, the runtime system loads classes from files in the directory defined in the CLASSPATH environment variable. This is a platform-dependent process and doesn't involve ClassLoader objects. The ClassLoader class comes into play when you want to define other techniques of loading classes, such as across a network connection. The definition for the ClassLoader class follows:

```
public abstract class java.lang.ClassLoader extends java.lang.Object {
    // Constructors
    protected ClassLoader();
```

```
// Methods
protected final Class defineClass(byte data[], int off, int len);
protected final Class findSystemClass(String name);
protected abstract Class loadClass(String name, boolean resolve);
protected final void resolveClass(Class c);
}
```

 ## ClassLoader ClassLoader lang

protected ClassLoader()

This constructor creates a default class loader. If a security manager is present, it is checked to see whether the current thread has permission to create the class loader. If not, a SecurityException is thrown.

 SecurityException if the current thread doesn't have permission to create the class loader.

 ## defineClass ClassLoader lang

protected final Class defineClass(byte b[], int off, int len)

This method converts an array of bytes into an instance of class Class by reading len bytes from the array b beginning off bytes into the array.

▶ b is the byte array containing the class data.

▶ off is the starting offset into the array for the data.

▶ len is the length in bytes of the class data.

↵ A Class object created from the class data.

● ClassFormatError if the class data does not define a valid class.

 ## findSystemClass ClassLoader lang

protected final Class findSystemClass(String name) throws ClassNotFoundException

This method finds the system class with the specified name, loading it if necessary. A system class is a class loaded from the local file system with no class loader in a platform-specific manner.

▶ name is the name of the system class to find.

↵ A Class object representing the system class.

● ClassNotFoundException if the class is not found.

● NoClassDefFoundError if a definition for the class is not found.

loadClass **ClassLoader** lang

```
protected abstract Class loadClass(String name, boolean resolve) throws
➥ClassNotFoundException
```

This method loads the class with the specified name, resolving it if the `resolve` parameter is set to TRUE. This method must be implemented in all derived class loaders, because it is defined as abstract.

▶ name is the name of the desired class.

▶ `resolve` is a Boolean value specifying whether the class is to be resolved. A value of TRUE means the class is resolved, whereas a value of FALSE means that the class isn't resolved.

↵ The loaded `Class` object, or NULL if the class isn't found.

✦ `ClassNotFoundException` if the class is not found.

 resolveClass **ClassLoader** lang

```
protected final void resolveClass(Class c)
```

This method resolves the specified class so that instances of it can be created or so that its methods can be called.

▶ c is the class to be resolved.

 # Compiler lang

 Object

This class provides the framework for native Java code compilers and related services. The Java runtime system looks for a native code compiler on startup, in which case the compiler is called to compile Java bytecode classes into native code. The default implementation for the `Compiler` class does nothing. The definition for the `Compiler` class follows:

```java
public final class java.lang.Compiler extends java.lang.Object {
  // Methods
  public static Object command(Object any);
  public static boolean compileClass(Class clazz);
  public static boolean compileClasses(String string);
  public static void disable();
  public static void enable();
}
```

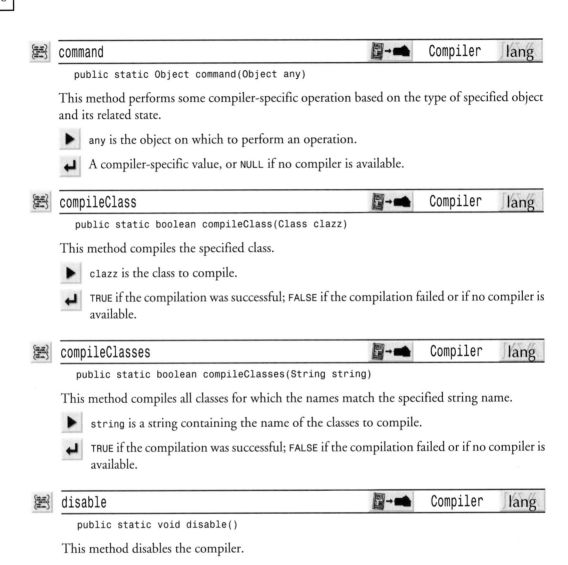

command   Compiler   lang

```
public static Object command(Object any)
```

This method performs some compiler-specific operation based on the type of specified object and its related state.

▶ any is the object on which to perform an operation.

↵ A compiler-specific value, or NULL if no compiler is available.

compileClass   Compiler   lang

```
public static boolean compileClass(Class clazz)
```

This method compiles the specified class.

▶ clazz is the class to compile.

↵ TRUE if the compilation was successful; FALSE if the compilation failed or if no compiler is available.

compileClasses   Compiler   lang

```
public static boolean compileClasses(String string)
```

This method compiles all classes for which the names match the specified string name.

▶ string is a string containing the name of the classes to compile.

↵ TRUE if the compilation was successful; FALSE if the compilation failed or if no compiler is available.

disable   Compiler   lang

```
public static void disable()
```

This method disables the compiler.

enable   Compiler   lang

```
public static void enable()
```

This method enables the compiler.

 ## Double lang

 Number

This class implements an object type wrapper for double values. Object type wrappers are useful because many Java classes operate on objects rather than primitive data types. In addition, the Double class provides support constants and methods for working with double values. The definition for the Double class follows:

```
public final class java.lang.Double extends java.lang.Number {
   // Member Constants
   public final static double MAX_VALUE;
   public final static double MIN_VALUE;
   public final static double NaN;
   public final static double NEGATIVE_INFINITY;
   public final static double POSITIVE_INFINITY;

   // Constructors
   public Double(double value);
   public Double(String s);

   // Methods
   public static long doubleToLongBits(double value);
   public double doubleValue();
   public boolean equals(Object obj);
   public float floatValue();
   public int hashCode();
   public int intValue();
   public boolean isInfinite();
   public static boolean isInfinite(double v);
   public boolean isNaN();
   public static boolean isNaN(double v);
   public static double longBitsToDouble(long bits);
   public long longValue();
   public String toString();
   public static String toString(double d);
   public static Double valueOf(String s);
}
```

Member Constants

`public final static double MAX_VALUE`

This is a constant representing the maximum value allowed for a double. This constant is set to `1.79769313486231570e+308d`.

`public final static double MIN_VALUE`

This is a constant representing the minimum value allowed for a double. This constant is set to `4.94065645841246544e-324d`.

`public final static double NaN`

This is a constant representing the not-a-number value for double types, which is not equal to anything, including itself.

```
public final static double NEGATIVE_INFINITY
```

This is a constant representing negative infinity for double types.

```
public final static double POSITIVE_INFINITY
```

This is a constant representing positive infinity for double types.

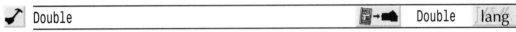

Double   Double   lang

```
public Double(double value)
```

This constructor creates a double wrapper object representing the specified primitive double value.

▶   `value` is the double value to be wrapped.

Double   Double   lang

```
public Double(String s) throws NumberFormatException
```

This constructor creates a double wrapper object representing the specified string. The string is converted to a double using a similar technique as the `valueOf` method.

▶   `s` is the string representation of a double value to be wrapped.

☇   `NumberFormatException` if the string does not contain a parsable double.

doubleToLongBits   Double   lang

```
public static long doubleToLongBits(double value)
```

This method determines the IEEE 754 floating-point double precision representation of the specified double value. The IEEE 754 floating-point double precision format specifies the following bit layout:

■   Bit 63 represents the sign of the number.

■   Bits 62–52 represent the exponent of the number.

■   Bits 51–0 represent the mantissa of the number.

▶   `value` is the double value to convert to the IEEE 754 format.

↵   The IEEE 754 floating-point representation of the specified double value.

doubleValue — Double lang

```
public double doubleValue()
```

This method determines the primitive double value represented by this object.

↵ The double value represented.

⊘ doubleValue in class Number.

equals — Double lang

```
public boolean equals(Object obj)
```

This method compares the double value of the specified object to the double value of this object. The equals method returns TRUE only if the specified object is a Double object representing the same primitive double value as this object. Note that in order to be useful in hash tables, this method considers two NaN double values to be equal, even though NaN technically is not equal to itself.

▶ obj is the object to compare.

↵ TRUE if the specified object is a Double object representing the same primitive double value as this object; otherwise, returns FALSE.

⊘ equals in class Object.

floatValue — Double lang

```
public float floatValue()
```

This method converts the primitive double value represented by this object to a float.

↵ A float conversion of the double value represented.

⊘ floatValue in class Number.

hashCode — Double lang

```
public int hashCode()
```

This method calculates a hash code for this object.

↵ A hash code for this object.

⊘ hashCode in class Object.

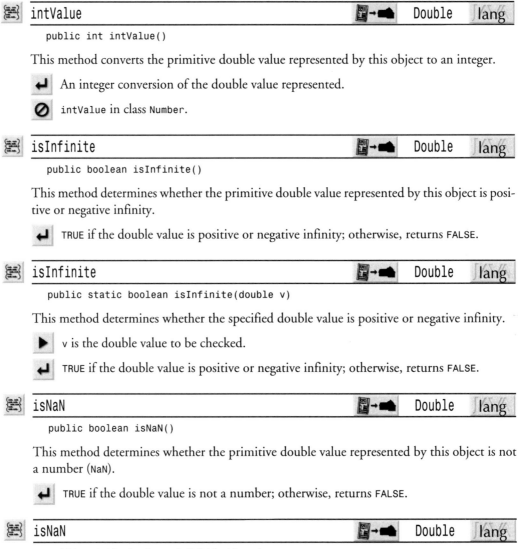

intValue   Double   lang

```
public int intValue()
```

This method converts the primitive double value represented by this object to an integer.

An integer conversion of the double value represented.

intValue in class `Number`.

isInfinite   Double   lang

```
public boolean isInfinite()
```

This method determines whether the primitive double value represented by this object is positive or negative infinity.

TRUE if the double value is positive or negative infinity; otherwise, returns FALSE.

isInfinite   Double   lang

```
public static boolean isInfinite(double v)
```

This method determines whether the specified double value is positive or negative infinity.

v is the double value to be checked.

TRUE if the double value is positive or negative infinity; otherwise, returns FALSE.

isNaN   Double   lang

```
public boolean isNaN()
```

This method determines whether the primitive double value represented by this object is not a number (NaN).

TRUE if the double value is not a number; otherwise, returns FALSE.

isNaN   Double   lang

```
public static boolean isNaN(double v)
```

This method determines whether the specified double value is not a number (NaN).

v is the double value to be checked.

TRUE if the double value is not a number; otherwise, returns FALSE.

longBitsToDouble  Double lang

```
public static double longBitsToDouble(long bits)
```

This method determines the double representation of the specified IEEE 754 floating-point double precision value. The IEEE 754 floating-point double precision format specifies the following bit layout:

- Bit 63 represents the sign of the number.
- Bits 62–52 represent the exponent of the number.
- Bits 51–0 represent the mantissa of the number.

▶ `bits` is the IEEE 754 floating-point value to convert to a double.

↵ The double representation of the specified IEEE 754 floating-point value.

longValue Double lang

```
public long longValue()
```

This method converts the primitive double value represented by this object to a long.

↵ A long conversion of the double value represented.

⊘ `longValue` in class `Number`.

toString Double lang

```
public String toString()
```

This method determines a string representation of the primitive double value for this object.

↵ A string representing the double value of this object.

⊘ `toString` in class `Object`.

toString Double lang

```
public static String toString(double d)
```

This method determines a string representation of the specified double value.

▶ `d` is the double value to be converted.

↵ A string representing the specified double value.

valueOf  Double lang

```
public static Double valueOf(String s) throws NumberFormatException
```

This method creates a new double wrapper object based on the double value represented by the specified string.

 s is the string representation of a double value to be wrapped.

A double wrapper object representing the specified string.

NumberFormatException if the string does not contain a parsable double.

Float lang

Number

This class implements an object type wrapper for float values. Object type wrappers are useful because many Java classes operate on objects rather than primitive data types. In addition, the Float class provides support constants and methods for working with float values. The definition for the Float class follows:

```
public final class java.lang.Float extends java.lang.Number {
    // Member Constants
    public final static float MAX_VALUE;
    public final static float MIN_VALUE;
    public final static float NaN;
    public final static float NEGATIVE_INFINITY;
    public final static float POSITIVE_INFINITY;

    // Constructors
    public Float(double value);
    public Float(float value);
    public Float(String s);

    // Methods
    public double doubleValue();
    public boolean equals(Object obj);
    public static int floatToIntBits(float value);
    public float floatValue();
    public int hashCode();
    public static float intBitsToFloat(int bits);
    public int intValue();
    public boolean isInfinite();
    public static boolean isInfinite(float v);
    public boolean isNaN();
    public static boolean isNaN(float v);
    public long longValue();
    public String toString();
    public static String toString(float f);
    public static Float valueOf(String s);
}
```

Member Constants

`public final static float MAX_VALUE`

This is a constant representing the maximum value allowed for a float. This constant is set to `3.40282346638528860e+38`.

`public final static float MIN_VALUE`

This is a constant representing the minimum value allowed for a float. This constant is set to `1.40129846432481707e-45`.

`public final static float NaN`

This is a constant representing the not-a-number value for float types, which is not equal to anything, including itself.

`public final static float NEGATIVE_INFINITY`

This is a constant representing negative infinity for float types.

`public final static float POSITIVE_INFINITY`

This is a constant representing positive infinity for float types.

Float Float lang

`public Float(double value)`

This constructor creates a float wrapper object representing the specified primitive double value.

▶ value is the double value to be wrapped.

Float Float lang

`public Float(float value)`

This constructor creates a float wrapper object representing the specified primitive float value.

▶ value is the float value to be wrapped.

Float Float lang

`public Float(String s) throws NumberFormatException`

This constructor creates a float wrapper object representing the specified string. The string is converted to a float using a technique similar to the `valueOf` method.

▶ s is the string representation of a float value to be wrapped.

☞ `NumberFormatException` if the string does not contain a parsable float.

doubleValue — Float lang

```
public double doubleValue()
```

This method converts the primitive float value represented by this object to a double.

↵ A double conversion of the float value represented.

⊘ doubleValue in class Number.

equals — Float lang

```
public boolean equals(Object obj)
```

This method compares the float value of the specified object to the float value of this object. The equals method returns TRUE only if the specified object is a Float object representing the same primitive float value as this object. Note that in order to be useful in hash tables, this method considers two NaN float values to be equal, even though NaN technically is not equal to itself.

▶ obj is the object to compare.

↵ TRUE if the specified object is a Float object representing the same primitive float value as this object; otherwise, returns FALSE.

⊘ equals in class Object.

floatToIntBits — Float lang

```
public static int floatToIntBits(float value)
```

This method determines the IEEE 754 floating-point single precision representation of the specified float value. The IEEE 754 floating-point single precision format specifies the following bit layout:

■ Bit 31 represents the sign of the number.

■ Bits 30–23 represent the exponent of the number.

■ Bits 22–0 represent the mantissa of the number.

▶ value is the float value to convert to the IEEE 754 format.

↵ The IEEE 754 floating-point representation of the specified float value.

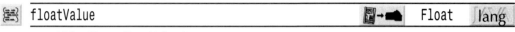

floatValue — Float lang

```
public float floatValue()
```

This method determines the primitive float value represented by this object.

↵ The float value represented.

⊘ `floatValue` in class `Number`.

hashCode — Float lang

```
public int hashCode()
```

This method calculates a hash code for this object.

↵ A hash code for this object.

⊘ `hashCode` in class `Object`.

intBitsToFloat — Float lang

```
public static float intBitsToFloat(int bits)
```

This method determines the float representation of the specified IEEE 754 floating-point single precision value. The IEEE 754 floating-point single precision format specifies the following bit layout:

- Bit 31 represents the sign of the number.
- Bits 30–23 represent the exponent of the number.
- Bits 22–0 represent the mantissa of the number.

▶ `bits` is the IEEE 754 floating-point value to convert to a float.

↵ The float representation of the specified IEEE 754 floating-point value.

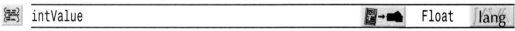

intValue — Float lang

```
public int intValue()
```

This method converts the primitive float value represented by this object to an integer.

↵ An integer conversion of the float value represented.

⊘ `intValue` in class `Number`.

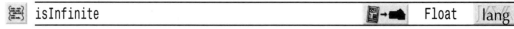

isInfinite

```
public boolean isInfinite()
```

This method determines whether the primitive float value represented by this object is positive or negative infinity.

↵ TRUE if the float value is positive or negative infinity; otherwise, returns FALSE.

isInfinite

```
public static boolean isInfinite(float v)
```

This method determines whether the specified float value is positive or negative infinity.

▶ v is the float value to be checked.

↵ TRUE if the float value is positive or negative infinity; otherwise, returns FALSE.

isNaN

```
public boolean isNaN()
```

This method determines whether the primitive float value represented by this object is not a number (NaN).

↵ TRUE if the float value is not a number; otherwise, returns FALSE.

isNaN

```
public static boolean isNaN(float v)
```

This method determines whether the specified float value is not a number (NaN).

▶ v is the float value to be checked.

↵ TRUE if the float value is not a number; otherwise, returns FALSE.

longValue

```
public long longValue()
```

This method converts the primitive float value represented by this object to a long.

↵ A long conversion of the float value represented.

⊘ longValue in class Number.

toString Float lang

```
public String toString()
```

This method determines a string representation of the primitive float value for this object.

 A string representing the float value of this object.

⊘ toString in class `Object`.

 ## toString Float lang

```
public static String toString(float f)
```

This method determines a string representation of the specified float value.

▶ f is the float value to be converted.

◀ A string representing the specified float value.

 ## valueOf Float lang

```
public static Float valueOf(String s) throws NumberFormatException
```

This method creates a new float wrapper object based on the float value represented by the specified string.

▶ s is the string representation of a float value to be wrapped.

◀ A float wrapper object representing the specified string.

↱ NumberFormatException if the string does not contain a parsable float.

 # Integer lang

 Number

This class implements an object type wrapper for integer values. Object type wrappers are useful because many Java classes operate on objects rather than primitive data types. In addition, the Integer class provides support constants and methods for working with integer values. The definition for the Integer class follows:

```
public final class java.lang.Integer extends java.lang.Number {
    // Member Constants
    public final static int MAX_VALUE;
    public final static int MIN_VALUE;

    // Constructors
    public Integer(int value);
    public Integer(String s);
```

```
// Methods
public double doubleValue();
public boolean equals(Object obj);
public float floatValue();
public static Integer getInteger(String nm);
public static Integer getInteger(String nm, int val);
public static Integer getInteger(String nm, Integer val);
public int hashCode();
public int intValue();
public long longValue();
public static int parseInt(String s);
public static int parseInt(String s, int radix);
public static String toBinaryString(int i);
public static String toHexString(int i);
public static String toOctalString(int i);
public String toString();
public static String toString(int i);
public static String  toString(int i, int radix);
public static Integer valueOf(String s);
public static Integer valueOf(String s, int radix);
}
```

Member Constants

public final static int MAX_VALUE

This is a constant representing the maximum value allowed for an integer. This constant is set to `0x7fffffff`.

public final static int MIN_VALUE

This is a constant representing the minimum value allowed for an integer. This constant is set to `0x80000000`.

 Integer Integer lang

```
public Integer(int value)
```

This constructor creates an integer wrapper object representing the specified primitive integer value.

▶ `value` is the integer value to be wrapped.

 Integer Integer lang

```
public Integer(String s) throws NumberFormatException
```

This constructor creates an integer wrapper object representing the specified string. The string is converted to an integer using a technique similar to the `valueOf` method.

▶ `s` is the string representation of an integer value to be wrapped.

 `NumberFormatException` if the string does not contain a parsable integer.

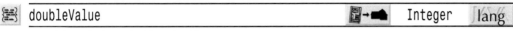

doubleValue

```
public double doubleValue()
```

This method converts the primitive integer value represented by this object to a double.

↵ A double conversion of the integer value represented.

⊘ doubleValue in class Number.

equals

```
public boolean equals(Object obj)
```

This method compares the integer value of the specified object to the integer value of this object. The equals method returns TRUE only if the specified object is an integer object representing the same primitive integer value as this object.

▶ obj is the object to compare.

↵ TRUE if the specified object is an integer object representing the same primitive integer value as this object; otherwise, returns FALSE.

⊘ equals in class Object.

floatValue

```
public float floatValue()
```

This method converts the primitive integer value represented by this object to a float.

↵ A float conversion of the integer value represented.

⊘ floatValue in class Number.

getInteger

```
public static Integer getInteger(String nm)
```

This method determines an integer object representing the value of the system property with the specified name. If the system property doesn't exist, NULL is returned.

▶ nm is the system property name for which to check the integer value.

↵ An integer object representing the value of the specified system property, or NULL if the property doesn't exist.

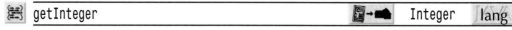

getInteger   Integer   lang

```
public static Integer getInteger(String nm, int val)
```

This method determines an integer object representing the value of the system property with the specified name. If the system property doesn't exist, an integer object representing the specified default property value is returned.

▶ nm is the system property name for which to check the integer value.

▶ val is the default integer property value.

↵ An integer object representing the value of the specified system property, or an integer object representing val if the property doesn't exist.

getInteger   Integer   lang

```
public static Integer getInteger(String nm, Integer val)
```

This method determines an integer object representing the value of the system property with the specified name. In addition, this version of getInteger includes support for reading hexadecimal and octal property values. If the system property doesn't exist, the specified default property value is returned.

▶ nm is the system property name for which to check the integer value.

▶ val is the default integer property value object.

↵ An integer object representing the value of the specified system property, or val if the property doesn't exist.

hashCode   Integer   lang

```
public int hashCode()
```

This method calculates a hash code for this object.

↵ A hash code for this object.

⊘ hashCode in class Object.

intValue   Integer   lang

```
public int intValue()
```

This method determines the primitive integer value represented by this object.

↵ The integer value represented.

⊘ intValue in class Number.

longValue   Integer   lang

```
public long longValue()
```

This method converts the primitive integer value represented by this object to a long.

↵ A long conversion of the integer value represented.

⊘ longValue in class Number.

parseInt   Integer   lang

```
public static int parseInt(String s) throws NumberFormatException
```

This method parses a signed decimal integer value from the specified string. Note that all the characters in the string must be decimal digits, with the exception that the first character can be a minus character (–) to denote a negative number.

▶ s is the string representation of an integer value.

↵ The integer value represented by the specified string.

☛ NumberFormatException if the string does not contain a parsable integer.

parseInt   Integer   lang

```
public static int parseInt(String s, int radix) throws NumberFormatException
```

This method parses a signed integer value in the specified radix from the specified string. Note that all the characters in the string must be digits in the specified radix, with the exception that the first character can be a minus character (–) to denote a negative number.

▶ s is the string representation of an integer value.

▶ radix is the radix to use for the integer.

↵ The integer value represented by the specified string.

☛ NumberFormatException if the string does not contain a parsable integer.

toBinaryString   Integer   lang

```
public static String toBinaryString(int i)
```

This method determines a string representation of the specified unsigned base 2 integer value.

▶ i is the unsigned base 2 integer value to be converted.

↵ A string representing the specified unsigned base 2 integer value.

toHexString

Integer   lang

```
public static String toHexString(int i)
```

This method determines a string representation of the specified unsigned base 16 integer value.

▶ i is the unsigned base 16 integer value to be converted.

↵ A string representing the specified unsigned base 16 integer value.

toOctalString

Integer   lang

```
public static String toOctalString(int i)
```

This method determines a string representation of the specified unsigned base 8 integer value.

▶ i is the unsigned base 8 integer value to be converted.

↵ A string representing the specified unsigned base 8 integer value.

toString

Integer   lang

```
public String toString()
```

This method determines a string representation of the primitive decimal integer value for this object.

↵ A string representing the decimal integer value of this object.

⊘ toString in class Object.

toString

Integer   lang

```
public static String toString(int i)
```

This method determines a string representation of the specified decimal integer value.

▶ i is the decimal integer value to be converted.

↵ A string representing the specified decimal integer value.

toString

Integer   lang

```
public static String toString(int i, int radix)
```

This method determines a string representation of the specified integer value in the specified radix.

▶ i is the integer value to be converted.

▶ radix is the radix to use for the conversion.

↵ A string representing the specified integer value in the specified radix.

valueOf Integer lang

```
public static Integer valueOf(String s) throws NumberFormatException
```

This method creates a new integer wrapper object based on the decimal integer value represented by the specified string.

▶ s is the string representation of a decimal integer value to be wrapped.

↵ An integer wrapper object representing the specified string.

↰ NumberFormatException if the string does not contain a parsable integer.

 valueOf Integer lang

```
public static Integer valueOf(String s, int radix) throws NumberFormatException
```

This method creates a new integer wrapper object based on the integer value in the specified radix represented by the specified string.

▶ s is the string representation of an integer value to be wrapped.

▶ radix is the radix to use for the integer.

↵ An integer wrapper object in the specified radix representing the specified string.

↰ NumberFormatException if the string does not contain a parsable integer.

Long lang

 Number

This class implements an object type wrapper for long values. Object type wrappers are useful because many Java classes operate on objects rather than primitive data types. In addition, the Long class provides support constants and methods for working with long values. The definition for the Long class follows:

```
public final class java.lang.Long extends java.lang.Number {
    // Member Constants
    public final static long MAX_VALUE;
    public final static long MIN_VALUE;

    // Constructors
    public Long(long value);
    public Long(String s);

    // Methods
    public double doubleValue();
    public boolean equals(Object obj);
    public float floatValue();
    public static Long getLong(String nm);
```

```
    public static Long getLong(String nm, long val);
    public static Long getLong(String nm, Long val);
    public int hashCode();
    public int intValue();
    public long longValue();
    public static long parseLong(String s);
    public static long parseLong(String s, int radix);
    public static String toBinaryString(long i);
    public static String toHexString(long i);
    public static String toOctalString(long i);
    public String toString();
    public static String toString(long i);
    public static String toString(long i, int radix);
    public static Long valueOf(String s);
    public static Long valueOf(String s, int radix);
}
```

Member Constants

public final static int MAX_VALUE

This is a constant representing the maximum value allowed for a long. This constant is set to `0x7fffffffffffffff`.

public final static int MIN_VALUE

This is a constant representing the minimum value allowed for a long. This constant is set to `0x8000000000000000`.

 Long   Long   lang

public Long(long value)

This constructor creates a long wrapper object representing the specified primitive long value.

▶ value is the long value to be wrapped.

 Long   Long   lang

public Long(String s) throws NumberFormatException

This constructor creates a long wrapper object representing the specified string. The string is converted to a long using a technique similar to the valueOf method.

▶ s is the string representation of a long value to be wrapped.

 NumberFormatException if the string does not contain a parsable long.

doubleValue  Long lang

```
public double doubleValue()
```

This method converts the primitive long value represented by this object to a double.

↵ A double conversion of the long value represented.

⊘ doubleValue in class Number.

equals  Long lang

```
public boolean equals(Object obj)
```

This method compares the long value of the specified object to the long value of this object. The equals method returns TRUE only if the specified object is a long object representing the same primitive long value as this object.

▶ obj is the object to compare.

↵ TRUE if the specified object is a Long object representing the same primitive long value as this object; otherwise, FALSE.

⊘ equals in class Object.

floatValue  Long lang

```
public float floatValue()
```

This method converts the primitive long value represented by this object to a float.

↵ A float conversion of the long value represented.

⊘ floatValue in class Number.

getLong  Long lang

```
public static Long getLong(String nm)
```

This method determines a long object representing the value of the system property with the specified name. If the system property doesn't exist, NULL is returned.

▶ nm is the system property name for which to check the long value.

↵ A long object representing the value of the specified system property, or NULL if the property doesn't exist.

getLong   Long   lang

```
public static Long getLong(String nm, long val)
```

This method determines a long object representing the value of the system property with the specified name. If the system property doesn't exist, a long object representing the specified default property value is returned.

▶ nm is the system property name for which to check the long value.

▶ val is the default long property value.

↵ A long object representing the value of the specified system property, or a long object representing val if the property doesn't exist.

 getLong   Long   lang

```
public static Long getLong(String nm, Long val)
```

This method determines a long object representing the value of the system property with the specified name. In addition, this version of getLong includes support for reading hexadecimal and octal property values. If the system property doesn't exist, the specified default property value is returned.

▶ nm is the system property name for which to check the long value.

▶ val is the default long property value object.

↵ A long object representing the value of the specified system property, or val if the property doesn't exist.

 hashCode   Long   lang

```
public int hashCode()
```

This method calculates a hash code for this object.

↵ A hash code for this object.

⊘ hashCode in class Object.

 intValue   Long   lang

```
public int intValue()
```

This method converts the primitive long value represented by this object to an integer.

↵ An integer conversion of the long value represented.

⊘ intValue in class Number.

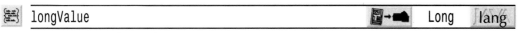

longValue   Long   lang

```
public long longValue()
```

This method determines the primitive long value represented by this object.

The long value represented.

longValue in class Number.

parseLong   Long   lang

```
public static long parseLong(String s) throws NumberFormatException
```

This method parses a signed decimal long value from the specified string. Note that all the characters in the string must be decimal digits, with the exception that the first character can be a minus character (–) to denote a negative number.

▶ s is the string representation of a long value.

The long value represented by the specified string.

NumberFormatException if the string does not contain a parsable long.

parseLong   Long   lang

```
public static long parseLong(String s, int radix) throws NumberFormatException
```

This method parses a signed long value in the specified radix from the specified string. Note that all the characters in the string must be digits in the specified radix, with the exception that the first character can be a minus character (–) to denote a negative number.

▶ s is the string representation of a long value.

▶ radix is the radix to use for the long.

The long value represented by the specified string.

NumberFormatException if the string does not contain a parsable long.

toBinaryString   Long   lang

```
public static String toBinaryString(long l)
```

This method determines a string representation of the specified unsigned base 2 long value.

▶ l is the unsigned base 2 long value to be converted.

A string representing the specified unsigned base 2 long value.

toHexString Long lang

```
public static String toHexString(long l)
```

This method determines a string representation of the specified unsigned base 16 long value.

▶ l is the unsigned base 16 long value to be converted.

↵ A string representing the specified unsigned base 16 long value.

 toOctalString Long lang

```
public static String toOctalString(long l)
```

This method determines a string representation of the specified unsigned base 8 long value.

▶ l is the unsigned base 8 long value to be converted.

↵ A string representing the specified unsigned base 8 long value.

 toString Long lang

```
public String toString()
```

This method determines a string representation of the primitive decimal long value for this object.

↵ A string representing the decimal long value of this object.

⊘ toString in class Object.

toString Long lang

```
public static String toString(long l)
```

This method determines a string representation of the specified decimal long value.

▶ l is the decimal long value to be converted.

↵ A string representing the specified decimal long value.

toString Long lang

```
public static String toString(long l, int radix)
```

This method determines a string representation of the specified long value in the specified radix.

▶ i is the long value to be converted.

▶ radix is the radix to use for the conversion.

↵ A string representing the specified long value in the specified radix.

valueOf Long lang

```
public static Long valueOf(String s) throws NumberFormatException
```

This method creates a new long wrapper object based on the decimal long value represented by the specified string.

► s is the string representation of a decimal long value to be wrapped.

↵ A long wrapper object representing the specified string.

↗ NumberFormatException if the string does not contain a parsable long.

 ## valueOf Long lang

```
public static Long valueOf(String s, int radix) throws NumberFormatException
```

This method creates a new long wrapper object based on the long value in the specified radix represented by the specified string.

► s is the string representation of a long value to be wrapped.

► radix is the radix to use for the long.

↵ A long wrapper object in the specified radix representing the specified string.

↗ NumberFormatException if the string does not contain a parsable long.

 # Math lang

 Object

This class implements a library of common math functions, including methods for performing basic numerical operations such as elementary exponential, logarithm, square root, and trigonometric functions. The definition for the Math class follows:

```
public final class java.lang.Math extends java.lang.Object {
    // Member Constants
    public final static double E;
    public final static double PI;

    // Methods
    public static double abs(double a);
    public static float abs(float a);
    public static int abs(int a);
    public static long abs(long a);
    public static double acos(double a);
    public static double asin(double a);
    public static double atan(double a);
    public static double atan2(double a, double b);
    public static double ceil(double a);
```

```
        public static double cos(double a);
        public static double exp(double a);
        public static double floor(double a);
        public static double IEEEremainder(double f1, double f2);
        public static double log(double a);
        public static double max(double a, double b);
        public static float max(float a, float b);
        public static int max(int a, int b);
        public static long max(long a, long b);
        public static double min(double a, double b);
        public static float min(float a, float b);
        public static int min(int a, int b);
        public static long min(long a, long b);
        public static double pow(double a, double b);
        public static double random();
        public static double rint(double a);
        public static long round(double a);
        public static int round(float a);
        public static double sin(double a);
        public static double sqrt(double a);
        public static double tan(double a);
    }
```

Member Constants

public final static double E

This is a constant representing the double value of E, which is the base of the natural logarithms. This constant is set to 2.7182818284590452354.

public final static double PI

This is a constant representing the double value of PI, which is the ratio of the circumference of a circle to its diameter. This constant is set to 3.14159265358979323846.

 abs Math lang

```
        public static double abs(double a)
```

This method calculates the absolute value of the specified double value.

▶ a is the double value for which to calculate the absolute value.

↵ The absolute value of the double value.

abs Math lang

```
        public static float abs(float a)
```

This method calculates the absolute value of the specified float value.

▶ a is the float value for which to calculate the absolute value.

↵ The absolute value of the float value.

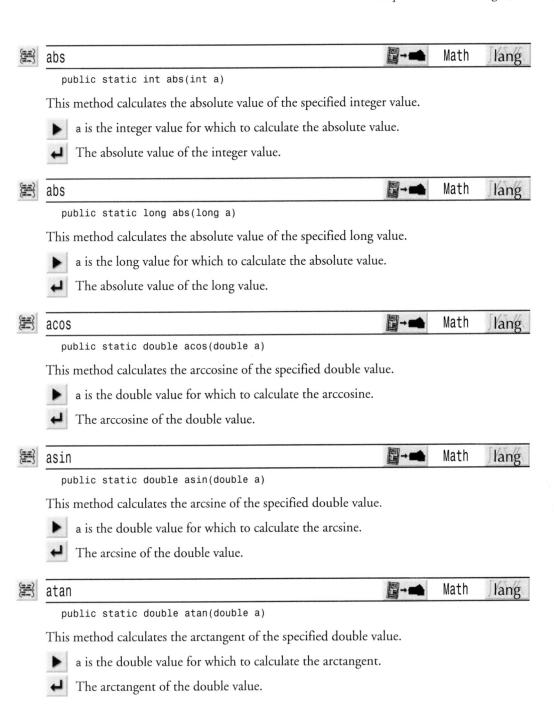

abs Math lang

```
public static int abs(int a)
```

This method calculates the absolute value of the specified integer value.

▶ a is the integer value for which to calculate the absolute value.

↵ The absolute value of the integer value.

abs Math lang

```
public static long abs(long a)
```

This method calculates the absolute value of the specified long value.

▶ a is the long value for which to calculate the absolute value.

↵ The absolute value of the long value.

acos Math lang

```
public static double acos(double a)
```

This method calculates the arccosine of the specified double value.

▶ a is the double value for which to calculate the arccosine.

↵ The arccosine of the double value.

asin Math lang

```
public static double asin(double a)
```

This method calculates the arcsine of the specified double value.

▶ a is the double value for which to calculate the arcsine.

↵ The arcsine of the double value.

atan Math lang

```
public static double atan(double a)
```

This method calculates the arctangent of the specified double value.

▶ a is the double value for which to calculate the arctangent.

↵ The arctangent of the double value.

atan2   Math   lang

```
public static double atan2(double a, double b)
```

This method calculates the theta component of the polar coordinate (r, theta) corresponding to the rectangular coordinate (x, y) specified by the double values.

▶   a is the x component value of the rectangular coordinate.

▶   b is the y component value of the rectangular coordinate.

↵   The theta component of the polar coordinate corresponding to the rectangular coordinate specified by the double values.

ceil   Math   lang

```
public static double ceil(double a)
```

This method determines the smallest double whole number that is greater than or equal to the specified double value.

▶   a is the double value for which to calculate the ceiling.

↵   The smallest double whole number that is greater than or equal to the specified double value.

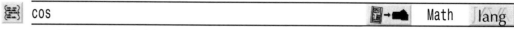

cos   Math   lang

```
public static double cos(double a)
```

This method calculates the cosine of the specified double value, which is specified in radians.

▶   a is the double value for which to calculate the cosine, in radians.

↵   The cosine of the double value.

exp   Math   lang

```
public static double exp(double a)
```

This method calculates the exponential value of the specified double value, which is E raised to the power of a.

▶   a is the double value for which to calculate the exponential value.

↵   The exponential value of the specified double value.

floor 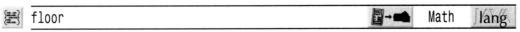 Math lang

```
public static double floor(double a)
```

This method determines the largest double whole number that is less than or equal to the specified double value.

▶ a is the double value for which to calculate the floor.

↵ The largest double whole number that is less than or equal to the specified double value.

IEEEremainder  Math lang

```
public static double IEEEremainder(double f1, double f2)
```

This method calculates the remainder of f1 divided by f2, as defined by the IEEE 754 standard.

▶ f1 is the dividend for the division operation.

▶ f2 is the divisor for the division operation.

↵ The remainder of f1 divided by f2, as defined by the IEEE 754 standard.

log Math lang

```
public static double log(double a) throws ArithmeticException
```

This method calculates the natural logarithm (base E) of the specified double value.

▶ a is the double value, which is greater than 0.0, for which to calculate the natural logarithm.

↵ The natural logarithm of the specified double value.

↝ ArithmeticException if the specified double value is less than 0.0.

max  Math lang

```
public static double max(double a, double b)
```

This method determines the larger of the two specified double values.

▶ a is the first double value to be compared.

▶ b is the second double value to be compared.

↵ The larger of the two specified double values.

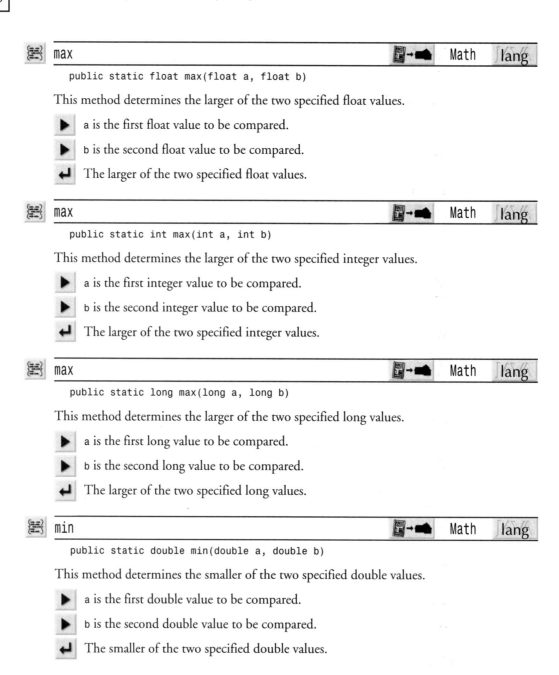

max   Math   lang

```
public static float max(float a, float b)
```

This method determines the larger of the two specified float values.

▶ a is the first float value to be compared.

▶ b is the second float value to be compared.

↵ The larger of the two specified float values.

max   Math   lang

```
public static int max(int a, int b)
```

This method determines the larger of the two specified integer values.

▶ a is the first integer value to be compared.

▶ b is the second integer value to be compared.

↵ The larger of the two specified integer values.

max   Math   lang

```
public static long max(long a, long b)
```

This method determines the larger of the two specified long values.

▶ a is the first long value to be compared.

▶ b is the second long value to be compared.

↵ The larger of the two specified long values.

min   Math   lang

```
public static double min(double a, double b)
```

This method determines the smaller of the two specified double values.

▶ a is the first double value to be compared.

▶ b is the second double value to be compared.

↵ The smaller of the two specified double values.

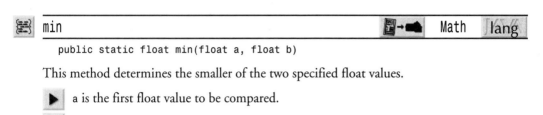

min — Math lang

```
public static float min(float a, float b)
```

This method determines the smaller of the two specified float values.

▶ a is the first float value to be compared.

▶ b is the second float value to be compared.

↵ The smaller of the two specified float values.

min — Math lang

```
public static int min(int a, int b)
```

This method determines the smaller of the two specified integer values.

▶ a is the first integer value to be compared.

▶ b is the second integer value to be compared.

↵ The smaller of the two specified integer values.

min — Math lang

```
public static long min(long a, long b)
```

This method determines the smaller of the two specified long values.

▶ a is the first long value to be compared.

▶ b is the second long value to be compared.

↵ The smaller of the two specified long values.

pow — Math lang

```
public static double pow(double a, double b) throws ArithmeticException
```

This method calculates the double value a raised to the power of b. Note that if a equals 0.0, b must be greater than 0.0; otherwise, an `ArithmeticException` is thrown. Also, if a is less than or equal to 0.0 and b is not a whole number, an `ArithmeticException` is thrown.

▶ a is a double value to be raised to a power specified by b.

▶ b is the power by which to raise a.

↵ The double value a raised to the power of b.

☛ `ArithmeticException` if a equals 0.0 and b is less than or equal to 0.0, or if a is less than or equal to 0.0 and b is not a whole number.

random   Math   lang

```
public static double random()
```

This method generates a pseudo-random double between 0.0 and 1.0.

A pseudo-random double between 0.0 and 1.0.

rint   Math   lang

```
public static double rint(double a)
```

This method determines the closest whole number to the specified double value. If the double value is equally spaced between two whole numbers, rint returns the even number.

a is the double value used to determine the closest whole number.

The closest whole number to the specified double value.

round   Math   lang

```
public static long round(double a)
```

This method rounds off the specified double value by determining the closest long value.

a is the double value to round off.

The closest long value to the specified double value.

round   Math   lang

```
public static int round(float a)
```

This method rounds off the specified float value by determining the closest integer value.

a is the float value to round off.

The closest integer value to the specified float value.

sin   Math   lang

```
public static double sin(double a)
```

This method calculates the sine of the specified double value, which is specified in radians.

a is the double value of which to calculate the sine, in radians.

The sine of the double value.

sqrt Math lang

```
public static double sqrt(double a) throws ArithmeticException
```

This method calculates the square root of the specified double value.

▶ a is the double value, which is greater than 0.0, for which to calculate the square root.

↵ The square root of the double value.

☛ `ArithmeticException` if the specified double value is less than 0.0.

 tan Math lang

```
public static double tan(double a)
```

This method calculates the tangent of the specified double value, which is specified in radians.

▶ a is the double value of which to calculate the tangent, in radians.

↵ The tangent of the double value.

 # Number lang

✚ Object

See also: `Double`, `Float`, `Integer`, `Long`

This class is an abstract class that provides the basic functionality required of a numeric object. All specific numeric objects are derived from `Number`. The definition for the `Number` class follows:

```
public abstract class java.lang.Number extends java.lang.Object {
    // Methods
    public abstract double doubleValue();
    public abstract float floatValue();
    public abstract int intValue();
    public abstract long longValue();
}
```

 doubleValue Number lang

```
public abstract double doubleValue()
```

This method determines the primitive double value represented by this object. Note that this may involve rounding if the number is not already a double.

↵ The double value represented.

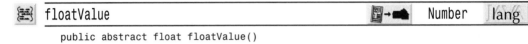

floatValue   Number   lang

```
public abstract float floatValue()
```

This method determines the primitive float value represented by this object. Note that this may involve rounding if the number is not already a float.

↵ The float value represented.

intValue   Number   lang

```
public abstract int intValue()
```

This method determines the primitive integer value represented by this object.

↵ The integer value represented.

longValue   Number   lang

```
public abstract long longValue()
```

This method determines the primitive long value represented by this object.

↵ The long value represented.

Object   lang

This class is the root of the Java class hierarchy, providing the core functionality required of all objects. All classes have `Object` as a superclass, and all classes implement the methods defined in `Object`. The definition for the `Object` class follows:

```
public class java.lang.Object {
    // Constructors
    public Object();

    // Methods
    protected Object clone();
    public boolean equals(Object obj);
    protected void finalize();
    public final Class getClass();
    public int hashCode();
    public final void notify();
    public final void notifyAll();
    public String toString();
    public final void wait();
    public final void wait(long timeout);
    public final void wait(long timeout, int nanos);
}
```

Object

Object | lang

```
public Object()
```

This constructor creates a default object.

clone

Object | lang

```
protected Object clone() throws CloneNotSupportedException
```

This method creates a clone of this object by creating a new instance of the class and copying each of the member variables of this object to the new object. To be cloneable, derived classes must implement the `Cloneable` interface.

↵ A clone of this object.

↝ `OutOfMemoryError` if there is not enough memory.

↝ `CloneNotSupportedException` if the object doesn't support the `Cloneable` interface or if it explicitly doesn't want to be cloned.

equals

Object | lang

```
public boolean equals(Object obj)
```

This method compares this object with the specified object for equality. The `equals` method is used by the `Hashtable` class to compare objects stored in the hash table.

▶ `obj` is the object to compare.

↵ `TRUE` if this object is equivalent to the specified object; otherwise, returns `FALSE`.

finalize

Object | lang

```
protected void finalize() throws Throwable
```

This method is called by the Java garbage collector when an object is being destroyed. The default behavior of `finalize` is to do nothing. Derived classes can override `finalize` to include cleanup code that is to be executed when the object is destroyed. Note that any exception thrown by the `finalize` method causes the finalization to halt.

getClass

Object | lang

```
public final Class getClass()
```

This method determines the runtime class descriptor for this object.

↵ The runtime class descriptor for this object.

hashCode Object lang

```
public int hashCode()
```

This method calculates a hash code for this object, which is a unique integer identifying the object. Hash codes are used by the Hashtable class.

 A hash code for this object.

 ### notify Object lang

```
public final void notify()
```

This method wakes up a single thread that is waiting on this object's monitor. A thread is set to wait on an object's monitor when the wait method is called. The notify method should be called only by a thread that is the owner of this object's monitor. Note that the notify method can be called only from within a synchronized method.

 IllegalMonitorStateException if the current thread is not the owner of this object's monitor.

 ### notifyAll Object lang

```
public final void notifyAll()
```

This method wakes up all threads that are waiting on this object's monitor. A thread is set to wait on an object's monitor when the wait method is called. The notifyAll method should be called only by a thread that is the owner of this object's monitor. Note that the notifyAll method can be called only from within a synchronized method.

 IllegalMonitorStateException if the current thread is not the owner of this object's monitor.

 ### toString Object lang

```
public String toString()
```

This method determines a string representation of this object. It is recommended that all derived classes override toString.

 A string representing this object.

wait ▦→◣ Object lang

```
public final void wait() throws InterruptedException
```

This method causes the current thread to wait forever until it is notified via a call to the `notify` or `notifyAll` method. The `wait` method should be called only by a thread that is the owner of this object's monitor. Note that the `wait` method can be called only from within a synchronized method.

🖝 `IllegalMonitorStateException` if the current thread is not the owner of this object's monitor.

🖝 `InterruptedException` if another thread has interrupted this thread.

 wait ▦→◣ Object lang

```
public final void wait(long timeout) throws InterruptedException
```

This method causes the current thread to wait until it is notified via a call to the `notify` or `notifyAll` method, or until the specified timeout period has elapsed. The `wait` method should be called only by a thread that is the owner of this object's monitor. Note that the `wait` method can be called only from within a synchronized method.

▶ `timeout` is the maximum timeout period to wait, in milliseconds.

🖝 `IllegalMonitorStateException` if the current thread is not the owner of this object's monitor.

🖝 `InterruptedException` if another thread has interrupted this thread.

 wait ▦→◣ Object lang

```
public final void wait(long timeout, int nanos) throws InterruptedException
```

This method causes the current thread to wait until it is notified via a call to the `notify` or `notifyAll` method, or until the specified timeout period has elapsed. The timeout period, in this case, is the addition of the `timeout` and `nanos` parameters, which provide finer control over the timeout period. The `wait` method should be called only by a thread that is the owner of this object's monitor. Note that the `wait` method can be called only from within a synchronized method.

▶ `timeout` is the maximum timeout period to wait, in milliseconds.

▶ `nanos` is the additional time for the timeout period, in nanoseconds.

🖝 `IllegalMonitorStateException` if the current thread is not the owner of this object's monitor.

🖝 `InterruptedException` if another thread has interrupted this thread.

 # Process lang

 Object

See also: Runtime

This class is an abstract class that provides the basic functionality required of a system process. Derived Process objects (subprocesses) are returned from the exec methods defined in the Runtime class. The definition for the Process class follows:

```
public abstract class java.lang.Process extends java.lang.Object {
  // Constructors
  public Process();

  // Methods
  public abstract void destroy();
  public abstract int exitValue();
  public abstract InputStream getErrorStream();
  public abstract InputStream getInputStream();
  public abstract OutputStream getOutputStream();
  public abstract int waitFor();
}
```

 ## Process Process   lang

```
public Process()
```

This constructor creates a default process.

 ## destroy Process   lang

```
public abstract void destroy()
```

This method kills the subprocess.

 ## exitValue Process   lang

```
public abstract int exitValue()
```

This method determines the exit value of the subprocess.

  The integer exit value for the subprocess.

  IllegalThreadStateException if the subprocess has not yet terminated.

 ## getErrorStream Process   lang

```
public abstract InputStream getErrorStream()
```

This method determines the error stream associated with the subprocess.

  The error stream associated with the subprocess.

getInputStream 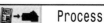 Process lang

```
public abstract InputStream getInputStream()
```

This method determines the input stream associated with the subprocess.

 The input stream associated with the subprocess.

getOutputStream Process lang

```
public abstract OutputStream getOutputStream()
```

This method determines the output stream associated with the subprocess.

The output stream associated with the subprocess.

waitFor Process lang

```
public abstract int waitFor() throws InterruptedException
```

This method waits for the subprocess to finish executing. When the subprocess finishes executing, the integer exit value is returned.

The integer exit value for the subprocess.

`InterruptedException` if another thread has interrupted this thread.

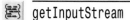 Runtime 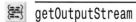 lang

 Object

See also: `System`, `Process`

This class provides a mechanism for interacting with the Java runtime environment. Each running Java application has access to a single instance of the `Runtime` class, which it can use to query and modify the runtime environment. Note that `Runtime` objects cannot be created directly by a Java program. The definition for the `Runtime` class follows:

```
public class java.lang.Runtime extends java.lang.Object {
    // Methods
    public Process exec(String command);
    public Process exec(String command, String envp[]);
    public Process exec(String cmdarray[]);
    public Process exec(String cmdarray[], String envp[]);
    public void exit(int status);
    public long freeMemory();
    public void gc();
    public InputStream getLocalizedInputStream(InputStream in);
    public OutputStream getLocalizedOutputStream(OutputStream out);
    public static Runtime getRuntime();
    public void load(String filename);
```

```
    public void loadLibrary(String libname);
    public void runFinalization();
    public long totalMemory();
    public void traceInstructions(boolean on);
    public void traceMethodCalls(boolean on);
}
```

 exec Runtime lang

```
    public Process exec(String command) throws IOException
```

This method executes the system command represented by the specified string in a separate subprocess.

▶ command is a string representing the system command to execute.

↵ The subprocess that is executing the system command.

🐾 SecurityException if the current thread cannot create the subprocess.

 exec Runtime lang

```
    public Process exec(String command, String envp[]) throws IOException
```

This method executes the system command represented by the specified string in a separate subprocess with the specified environment.

▶ command is a string representing the system command to execute.

▶ envp is an array of strings representing the environment.

↵ The subprocess that is executing the system command.

🐾 SecurityException if the current thread cannot create the subprocess.

 exec Runtime lang

```
    public Process exec(String cmdarray[]) throws IOException
```

This method executes the system command with arguments represented by the specified string array in a separate subprocess.

▶ cmdarray is an array of strings representing the system command to execute along with its arguments.

↵ The subprocess that is executing the system command.

🐾 SecurityException if the current thread cannot create the subprocess.

exec   Runtime   lang

```
public Process exec(String cmdarray[], String envp[]) throws IOException
```

This method executes the system command with arguments represented by the specified string array in a separate subprocess with the specified environment.

▶ `cmdarray` is an array of strings representing the system command to execute along with its arguments.

▶ `envp` is an array of strings representing the environment.

↵ The subprocess that is executing the system command.

☞ `SecurityException` if the current thread cannot create the subprocess.

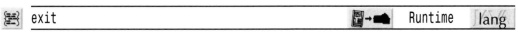

exit   Runtime   lang

```
public void exit(int status)
```

This method exits the Java runtime system (virtual machine) with the specified integer exit status. Note that because `exit` kills the runtime system, it never returns.

▶ `status` is the integer exit status; this should be set to nonzero if this is an abnormal exit.

☞ `SecurityException` if the current thread cannot exit with the specified exit status.

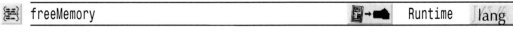

freeMemory   Runtime   lang

```
public long freeMemory()
```

This method determines the approximate amount of free memory available in the runtime system, in bytes. Note that calling the `gc` method may free up more memory.

↵ Approximate amount of free memory available, in bytes.

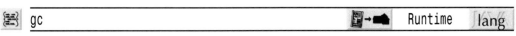

gc   Runtime   lang

```
public void gc()
```

This method invokes the Java garbage collector to clean up any objects that no longer are needed, usually resulting in more free memory.

getLocalizedInputStream   Runtime   lang

```
public InputStream getLocalizedInputStream(InputStream in)
```

This method creates a localized input stream based on the specified input stream. A localized input stream is a stream in which the local characters are mapped to Unicode characters as they are read.

▶   in is the input stream to localize.

↵   A localized input stream based on the specified input stream.

getLocalizedOutputStream   Runtime   lang

```
public OutputStream getLocalizedOutputStream(OutputStream out)
```

This method creates a localized output stream based on the specified output stream. A localized output stream is a stream in which Unicode characters are mapped to local characters as they are written.

▶   out is the output stream to localize.

↵   A localized output stream based on the specified output stream.

getRuntime   Runtime   lang

```
public static Runtime getRuntime()
```

This method gets the runtime environment object associated with the current Java program.

↵   The runtime environment object associated with the current Java program.

load   Runtime   lang

```
public void load(String pathname)
```

This method loads the dynamic library with the specified complete path name.

▶   pathname is the path name of the library to load.

↝   UnsatisfiedLinkError if the library doesn't exist.

↝   SecurityException if the current thread can't load the library.

loadLibrary   Runtime   lang

```
public void loadLibrary(String libname)
```

This method loads the dynamic library with the specified library name. Note that the mapping from library name to a specific filename is performed in a platform-specific manner.

▶ `libname` is the name of the library to load.

🪝 `UnsatisfiedLinkError` if the library doesn't exist.

🪝 `SecurityException` if the current thread can't load the library.

runFinalization · Runtime · lang

```
public void runFinalization()
```

This method explicitly causes the `finalize` methods of any discarded objects to be called. Typically, the `finalize` methods of discarded objects are automatically called asynchronously when the garbage collector cleans up the objects. You can use `runFinalization` to have the `finalize` methods called synchronously.

totalMemory · Runtime · lang

```
public long totalMemory()
```

This method determines the total amount of memory in the runtime system, in bytes.

↵ The total amount of memory, in bytes.

traceInstructions · Runtime · lang

```
public void traceInstructions(boolean on)
```

This method is used to determine whether the Java virtual machine prints out a detailed trace of each instruction executed.

▶ `on` is a Boolean value specifying whether the Java virtual machine prints a detailed trace of each instruction executed. A value of TRUE means that the instruction trace is printed, whereas a value of FALSE means that the instruction trace isn't printed.

traceMethodCalls · Runtime · lang

```
public void traceMethodCalls(boolean on)
```

This method is used to determine whether the Java virtual machine prints a detailed trace of each method that is called.

▶ `on` is a Boolean value specifying whether the Java virtual machine prints a detailed trace of each method that is called. A value of TRUE means that the method call trace is printed, whereas a value of FALSE means that the method call trace isn't printed.

SecurityManager lang

 Object

This class is an abstract class that defines a security policy that can be used by Java programs to check for potentially unsafe operations. The definition for the SecurityManager class follows:

```
public abstract class java.lang.SecurityManager extends java.lang.Object {
    // Member Variables
    protected boolean inCheck;

    // Constructors
    protected SecurityManager();

    // Methods
    public void  checkAccept(String host, int port);
    public void checkAccess(Thread g);
    public void checkAccess(ThreadGroup g);
    public void checkConnect(String host, int port);
    public void checkConnect(String host, int port, Object context);
    public void checkCreateClassLoader();
    public void checkDelete(String file);
    public void checkExec(String cmd);
    public void checkExit(int status);
    public void checkLink(String lib);
    public void checkListen(int port);
    public void checkPackageAccess(String pkg);
    public void checkPackageDefinition(String pkg);
    public void checkPropertiesAccess();
    public void checkPropertyAccess(String key);
    public void checkRead(FileDescriptor fd);
    public void checkRead(String file);
    public void checkRead(String file, Object context);
    public void checkSetFactory();
    public boolean checkTopLevelWindow(Object window);
    public void checkWrite(FileDescriptor fd);
    public void checkWrite(String file);
    protected int classDepth(String name);
    protected int classLoaderDepth();
    protected ClassLoader currentClassLoader();
    protected Class[] getClassContext();
    public boolean getInCheck();
    public Object getSecurityContext();
    protected boolean inClass(String name);
    protected boolean inClassLoader();
}
```

Member Variables

protected boolean inCheck

This member variable specifies whether a security check is in progress. A value of TRUE indicates that a security check is in progress, whereas a value of FALSE means that no check is taking place.

SecurityManager SecurityManager lang

```
protected SecurityManager()
```

This constructor creates a default security manager. Note that only one security manager is allowed for each Java program.

 SecurityException if the security manager cannot be created.

 checkAccept SecurityManager lang

```
public void checkAccept(String host, int port)
```

This method checks to see whether the calling thread is allowed to establish a socket connection to the specified port on the specified host.

▶ host is the host name to which the socket will be connected.

▶ port is the number of the port to which the socket will be connected.

 SecurityException if the calling thread doesn't have permission to establish the socket connection.

 checkAccess SecurityManager lang

```
public void checkAccess(Thread g)
```

This method checks to see whether the calling thread is allowed access to the specified thread.

▶ g is the thread to check for access.

 SecurityException if the calling thread doesn't have access to the specified thread.

 checkAccess SecurityManager lang

```
public void checkAccess(ThreadGroup g)
```

This method checks to see whether the calling thread is allowed access to the specified thread group.

▶ g is the thread group to check for access.

 SecurityException if the calling thread doesn't have access to the specified thread group.

 checkConnect SecurityManager lang

```
public void checkConnect(String host, int port)
```

This method checks to see whether the calling thread has established a socket connection to the specified port on the specified host.

▶ host is the host name for which to check the connection.

▶ sort is the number of the port for which to check the connection.

✦ SecurityException if the calling thread doesn't have permission to establish the socket connection.

---

checkConnect   SecurityManager   lang

```
public void checkConnect(String host, int port, Object context)
```

This method checks to see whether the specified security context has established a socket connection to the specified port on the specified host.

▶ host is the host name for which to check the connection.

▶ port is the number of the port for which to check the connection.

▶ context is the security context for the check.

✦ SecurityException if the specified security context doesn't have permission to establish the socket connection.

---

checkCreateClassLoader   SecurityManager   lang

```
public void checkCreateClassLoader()
```

This method checks to see whether the calling thread is allowed access to create a new class loader.

✦ SecurityException if the calling thread doesn't have permission to create a new class loader.

---

checkDelete   SecurityManager   lang

```
public void checkDelete(String file)
```

This method checks to see whether the calling thread is allowed access to delete the file with the specified platform-specific filename.

▶ file is the platform-specific filename for the file to be checked.

✦ SecurityException if the calling thread doesn't have permission to delete the file.

checkExec — SecurityManager — lang

```
public void checkExec(String cmd)
```

This method checks to see whether the calling thread is allowed access to create a subprocess to execute the specified system command.

 cmd is a string representing the system command to be checked.

 SecurityException if the calling thread doesn't have permission to create a subprocess to execute the system command.

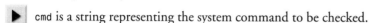

checkExit — SecurityManager — lang

```
public void checkExit(int status)
```

This method checks to see whether the calling thread is allowed access to exit the Java runtime system with the specified exit status.

 status is the integer exit status to be checked.

 SecurityException if the calling thread doesn't have permission to exit with the specified exit status.

checkLink — SecurityManager — lang

```
public void checkLink(String lib)
```

This method checks to see whether the calling thread is allowed access to dynamically link the library with the specified name.

 lib is the name of the library to be checked.

 SecurityException if the calling thread doesn't have permission to dynamically link the library.

checkListen — SecurityManager — lang

```
public void checkListen(int port)
```

This method checks to see whether the calling thread is allowed to wait for a connection request on the specified port.

 port is the number of the port for which to check the connection.

 SecurityException if the calling thread doesn't have permission to wait for a connection request on the specified port.

checkPackageAccess 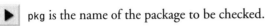 SecurityManager lang

```
public void checkPackageAccess(String pkg)
```

This method checks to see whether the calling thread is allowed access to the package with the specified name.

 pkg is the name of the package to be checked.

SecurityException if the calling thread doesn't have permission to access the package.

 checkPackageDefinition SecurityManager lang

```
public void checkPackageDefinition(String pkg)
```

This method checks to see whether the calling thread is allowed to define classes in the package with the specified name.

pkg is the name of the package to be checked.

SecurityException if the calling thread doesn't have permission to define classes in the package.

 checkPropertiesAccess SecurityManager lang

```
public void checkPropertiesAccess()
```

This method checks to see whether the calling thread is allowed access to the system properties.

SecurityException if the calling thread doesn't have permission to access the system properties.

 checkPropertyAccess SecurityManager lang

```
public void checkPropertyAccess(String key)
```

This method checks to see whether the calling thread is allowed access to the system property with the specified key name.

 key is the key name for the system property to check.

SecurityException if the calling thread doesn't have permission to access the system property with the specified key name.

checkRead SecurityManager lang

```
public void checkRead(FileDescriptor fd)
```

This method checks to see whether the calling thread is allowed access to read from the file with the specified file descriptor.

▶ fd is the file descriptor for the file to be checked.

🐾 SecurityException if the calling thread doesn't have permission to read from the file.

 checkRead SecurityManager lang

```
public void checkRead(String file)
```

This method checks to see whether the calling thread is allowed access to read from the file with the specified platform-specific filename.

▶ file is the platform-specific filename for the file to be checked.

🐾 SecurityException if the calling thread doesn't have permission to read from the file.

checkRead SecurityManager lang

```
public void checkRead(String file, Object context)
```

This method checks to see whether the specified security context is allowed access to read from the file with the specified platform-specific filename.

▶ file is the platform-specific filename for the file to be checked.

▶ context is the security context for the check.

🐾 SecurityException if the specified security context doesn't have permission to read from the file.

 checkSetFactory SecurityManager lang

```
public void checkSetFactory()
```

This method checks to see whether the calling thread is allowed access to set the socket or stream handler factory used by the URL class.

🐾 SecurityException if the calling thread doesn't have permission to set the socket or stream handler factory.

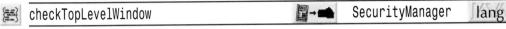

checkTopLevelWindow — SecurityManager — lang

```
public boolean checkTopLevelWindow(Object window)
```

This method checks to see whether the calling thread is trusted to show the specified top-level window. Note that even if the calling thread isn't trusted to show the window, the window still can be shown with some sort of visual warning.

▶ window is the top-level window to be checked.

↵ TRUE if the calling thread is trusted to show the top-level window; otherwise, returns FALSE.

checkWrite — SecurityManager — lang

```
public void checkWrite(FileDescriptor fd)
```

This method checks to see whether the calling thread is allowed access to write to the file with the specified file descriptor.

▶ fd is the file descriptor for the file to be checked.

☞ SecurityException if the calling thread doesn't have permission to write to the file.

checkWrite — SecurityManager — lang

```
public void checkWrite(String file)
```

This method checks to see whether the calling thread is allowed access to write to the file with the specified platform-specific filename.

▶ file is the platform-specific filename for the file to be checked.

☞ SecurityException if the calling thread doesn't have permission to write to the file.

classDepth — SecurityManager — lang

```
protected int classDepth(String name)
```

This method determines the stack depth of the class with the specified name.

▶ name is the fully qualified name of the class for which to determine the stack depth.

↵ The stack depth of the class, or –1 if the class can't be found in any stack frame.

classLoaderDepth · SecurityManager · lang

```
protected int classLoaderDepth()
```

This method determines the stack depth of the most recently executing method of a class defined using a class loader.

↵ The stack depth of the most recently executing method of a class defined using a class loader, or -1 if no method is executing within a class defined by a class loader.

currentClassLoader · SecurityManager · lang

```
protected ClassLoader currentClassLoader()
```

This method determines the current class loader on the stack.

↵ The current class loader on the stack, or NULL if no class loader exists on the stack.

getClassContext · SecurityManager · lang

```
protected Class[] getClassContext()
```

This method determines the current execution stack, which is an array of classes corresponding to each method call on the stack.

↵ An array of classes corresponding to each method call on the stack.

getInCheck · SecurityManager · lang

```
public boolean getInCheck()
```

This method determines whether there is a security check in progress.

↵ TRUE if a security check is in progress; otherwise, returns FALSE.

getSecurityContext · SecurityManager · lang

```
public Object getSecurityContext()
```

This method creates a platform-specific security context based on the current runtime environment.

↵ A platform-specific security context based on the current runtime environment.

inClass SecurityManager   lang

```
protected boolean inClass(String name)
```

This method determines whether a method in the class with the specified name is on the execution stack.

▶ name is the name of the class to check.

↵ TRUE if a method in the class is on the execution stack; otherwise, returns FALSE.

 inClassLoader SecurityManager   lang

```
protected boolean inClassLoader()
```

This method determines whether a method in a class defined using a class loader is on the execution stack.

↵ TRUE if a method in a class defined using a class loader is on the execution stack; otherwise, returns FALSE.

 String lang

 Object

See also: StringBuffer

This class implements a constant string of characters. The String class provides a wide range of support for working with strings of characters. Note that literal string constants are converted automatically to String objects by the Java compiler. The definition for the String class follows:

```
public final class java.lang.String extends java.lang.Object {
    // Constructors
    public String();
    public String(byte ascii[], int hibyte);
    public String(byte ascii[], int hibyte, int off, int count);
    public String(char value[]);
    public String(char value[], int off, int count);
    public String(String value);
    public String(StringBuffer buffer);

    // Methods
    public char charAt(int index);
    public int compareTo(String anotherString);
    public String concat(String str);
    public static String copyValueOf(char data[]);
    public static String copyValueOf(char data[], int off, int count);
    public boolean endsWith(String suffix);
    public boolean equals(Object anObject);
    public boolean equalsIgnoreCase(String anotherString);
```

```
    public void getBytes(int srcBegin, int srcEnd, byte dst[], int dstBegin);
    public void getChars(int srcBegin, int srcEnd, char dst[], int dstBegin);
    public int hashCode();
    public int indexOf(int ch);
    public int indexOf(int ch, int fromIndex);
    public int indexOf(String str);
    public int indexOf(String str, int fromIndex);
    public String intern();
    public int lastIndexOf(int ch);
    public int lastIndexOf(int ch, int fromIndex);
    public int lastIndexOf(String str);
    public int lastIndexOf(String str, int fromIndex);
    public int length();
    public boolean regionMatches(boolean ignoreCase, int toffset, String other,
      int ooffset, int len);
    public boolean regionMatches(int toffset, String other, int ooffset,
      int len);
    public String replace(char oldChar, char newChar);
    public boolean startsWith(String prefix);
    public boolean startsWith(String prefix, int toffset);
    public String substring(int beginIndex);
    public String substring(int beginIndex, int endIndex);
    public char[] toCharArray();
    public String toLowerCase();
    public String toString();
    public String toUpperCase();
    public String trim();
    public static String valueOf(boolean b);
    public static String valueOf(char c);
    public static String valueOf(char data[]);
    public static String valueOf(char data[], int off, int count);
    public static String valueOf(double d);
    public static String valueOf(float f);
    public static String valueOf(int i);
    public static String valueOf(long l);
    public static String valueOf(Object obj);
}
```

String — String lang

```
    public String()
```

This constructor creates a default string containing no characters.

String — String lang

```
    public String(byte ascii[], int hibyte)
```

This constructor creates a string from the specified array of bytes, with the top 8 bits of each string character set to hibyte.

 ascii is the byte array that is to be converted to string characters.

 hibyte is the high byte value for each character.

String String lang

```
public String(byte ascii[], int hibyte, int off, int count)
```

This constructor creates a string of length count from the specified array of bytes beginning off bytes into the array, with the top 8 bits of each string character set to hibyte.

▶ ascii is the byte array that is to be converted to string characters.

▶ hibyte is the high byte value for each character.

▶ off is the starting offset into the array of bytes.

▶ count is the number of bytes from the array to convert.

🐾 StringIndexOutOfBoundsException if the offset or count for the byte array is invalid.

String String lang

```
public String(char value[])
```

This constructor creates a string from the specified array of characters.

▶ value is the character array used to initialize the string.

String String lang

```
public String(char value[], int off, int count)
```

This constructor creates a string of length count from the specified array of characters beginning off bytes into the array.

▶ value is the character array used to initialize the string.

▶ off is the starting offset into the array of characters.

▶ count is the number of characters from the array to use in initializing the string.

🐾 StringIndexOutOfBoundsException if the offset or count for the character array is invalid.

String String lang

```
public String(String value)
```

This constructor creates a new string that is a copy of the specified string.

▶ value is the string by which to initialize this string.

String String lang

```
public String(StringBuffer buffer)
```

This constructor creates a new string that is a copy of the contents of the specified string buffer.

▶ `buffer` is the string buffer used to initialize this string.

charAt String lang

```
public char charAt(int index)
```

This method determines the character at the specified index. Note that string indexes are zero-based, meaning that the first character is located at index 0.

▶ `index` is the index of the desired character.

↵ The character at the specified index.

☞ `StringIndexOutOfBoundsException` if the index is out of range.

compareTo String lang

```
public int compareTo(String anotherString)
```

This method compares this string with the specified string lexicographically.

▶ `anotherString` is the string to which the comparison is made.

↵ `0` if this string is equal to the specified string, a value less than 0 if this string is lexicographically less than the specified string, or a value greater than 0 if this string is lexicographically greater than the specified string.

concat String lang

```
public String concat(String str)
```

This method concatenates the specified string onto the end of this string.

▶ `str` is the string to concatenate.

↵ This string, with the specified string concatenated onto the end.

copyValueOf 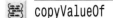 String lang

```
public static String copyValueOf(char data[])
```

This method converts a character array to an equivalent string by creating a new string and copying the characters into it.

▶ data is the character array to convert to a string.

↵ A string representation of the specified character array.

copyValueOf 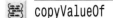 String lang

```
public static String copyValueOf(char data[], int off, int count)
```

This method converts a character array to an equivalent string by creating a new string and copying count characters into it beginning at off.

▶ data is the character array to convert to a string.

▶ off is the starting offset into the character array.

▶ count is the number of characters from the array to use in initializing the string.

↵ A string representation of the specified character array beginning at off and of length count.

endsWith 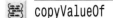 String lang

```
public boolean endsWith(String suffix)
```

This method determines whether this string ends with the specified suffix.

▶ suffix is the suffix to check.

↵ TRUE if this string ends with the specified suffix; otherwise, returns FALSE.

equals 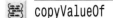 String lang

```
public boolean equals(Object anObject)
```

This method compares the specified object to this string. The equals method returns TRUE only if the specified object is a String object of the same length and contains the same characters as this string.

▶ anObject is the object to compare.

↵ TRUE if the specified object is a String object of the same length and contains the same characters as this string; otherwise, returns FALSE.

⊘ equals in class Object.

equalsIgnoreCase String lang

```
public boolean equalsIgnoreCase(String anotherString)
```

This method compares the specified string to this string, ignoring case.

▶ `anotherString` is the string to compare.

↵ `TRUE` if the specified string is of the same length and contains the same characters as this string, ignoring case; otherwise, returns `FALSE`.

getBytes String lang

```
public void getBytes(int srcBegin, int srcEnd, byte dst[], int dstBegin)
```

This method copies the lower 8 bits of each character in this string, beginning at `srcBegin` and ending at `srcEnd`, into the byte array `dst` beginning at `dstBegin`.

▶ `srcBegin` is the index of the first character in the string to copy.

▶ `srcEnd` is the index of the last character in the string to copy.

▶ `dst` is the destination byte array.

▶ `dstBegin` is the starting offset into the byte array.

getChars String lang

```
public void getChars(int srcBegin, int srcEnd, char dst[], int dstBegin)
```

This method copies each character in this string, beginning at `srcBegin` and ending at `srcEnd`, into the character array `dst` beginning at `dstBegin`.

▶ `srcBegin` is the index of the first character in the string to copy.

▶ `srcEnd` is the index of the last character in the string to copy.

▶ `dst` is the destination character array.

▶ `dstBegin` is the starting offset into the character array.

☛ `StringIndexOutOfBoundsException` if there is an invalid index in the buffer.

hashCode String lang

```
public int hashCode()
```

This method calculates a hash code for this object.

↵ A hash code for this object.

⊘ `hashCode` in class `Object`.

indexOf String lang

```
public int indexOf(int ch)
```

This method determines the index of the first occurrence of the specified character in this string.

▶ ch is the character for which to search.

↵ The index of the first occurrence of the specified character, or –1 if the character doesn't occur.

 indexOf String lang

```
public int indexOf(int ch, int fromIndex)
```

This method determines the index of the first occurrence of the specified character in this string, beginning at fromIndex.

▶ ch is the character for which to search.

▶ fromIndex is the index from which to start the search.

↵ The index of the first occurrence of the specified character beginning at fromIndex, or –1 if the character doesn't occur.

 indexOf String lang

```
public int indexOf(String str)
```

This method determines the index of the first occurrence of the specified substring in this string.

▶ str is the substring for which to search.

↵ The index of the first occurrence of the specified substring, or –1 if the substring doesn't occur.

 indexOf String lang

```
public int indexOf(String str, int fromIndex)
```

This method determines the index of the first occurrence of the specified substring in this string, beginning at fromIndex.

▶ str is the substring for which to search.

▶ fromIndex is the index from which to start the search.

↵ The index of the first occurrence of the specified substring beginning at fromIndex, or –1 if the substring doesn't occur.

intern String lang

```
public String intern()
```

This method determines a string that is equal to this string but is guaranteed to be from a pool of unique strings.

↵ A string that is equal to this string but is guaranteed to be from a pool of unique strings.

lastIndexOf String lang

```
public int lastIndexOf(int ch)
```

This method determines the index of the last occurrence of the specified character in this string.

▶ ch is the character for which to search.

↵ The index of the last occurrence of the specified character, or -1 if the character doesn't occur.

lastIndexOf String lang

```
public int lastIndexOf(int ch, int fromIndex)
```

This method determines the index of the last occurrence of the specified character in this string, beginning at fromIndex.

▶ ch is the character for which to search.

▶ fromIndex is the index from which to start the search.

↵ The index of the last occurrence of the specified character beginning at fromIndex, or -1 if the character doesn't occur.

lastIndexOf String lang

```
public int lastIndexOf(String str)
```

This method determines the index of the last occurrence of the specified substring in this string.

▶ str is the substring for which to search.

↵ The index of the last occurrence of the specified substring, or -1 if the substring doesn't occur.

lastIndexOf String lang

```
public int lastIndexOf(String str, int fromIndex)
```

This method determines the index of the last occurrence of the specified substring in this string, beginning at fromIndex.

▶ str is the substring for which to search.

▶ fromIndex is the index from which to start the search.

↵ The index of the last occurrence of the specified substring beginning at fromIndex, or -1 if the substring doesn't occur.

length String lang

```
public int length()
```

This method determines the length of this string, which is the number of Unicode characters in the string.

↵ The length of this string.

regionMatches 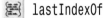 String lang

```
public boolean regionMatches(boolean ignoreCase, int toffset, String other, int
 ooffset, int len)
```

This method determines whether a substring of this string matches a substring of the specified string, with an option for ignoring case.

▶ ignoreCase is a Boolean value specifying whether case is ignored; a value of TRUE means that case is ignored, whereas a value of FALSE means that case isn't ignored.

▶ toffset is the index from which to start the substring for this string.

▶ other is the other string to compare.

▶ ooffset is the index from which to start the substring for the string to compare.

▶ len is the number of characters to compare.

↵ TRUE if the substring of this string matches the substring of the specified string; otherwise, returns FALSE.

regionMatches — String lang

```
public boolean regionMatches(int toffset, String other, int ooffset, int len)
```

This method determines whether a substring of this string matches a substring of the specified string.

▶ `toffset` is the index from which to start the substring for this string.

▶ `other` is the other string to compare.

▶ `ooffset` is the index from which to start the substring for the string to compare.

▶ `len` is the number of characters to compare.

↵ TRUE if the substring of this string matches the substring of the specified string; otherwise, returns FALSE.

replace — String lang

```
public String replace(char oldChar, char newChar)
```

This method replaces all occurrences of `oldChar` in this string with `newChar`.

▶ `oldChar` is the old character to replace.

▶ `newChar` is the new character to take its place.

↵ This string, with all occurrences of `oldChar` replaced with `newChar`.

startsWith — String lang

```
public boolean startsWith(String prefix)
```

This method determines whether this string starts with the specified prefix.

▶ `prefix` is the prefix to check.

↵ TRUE if this string starts with the specified prefix; otherwise, returns FALSE.

startsWith — String lang

```
public boolean startsWith(String prefix, int toffset)
```

This method determines whether this string starts with the specified prefix, beginning at `toffset`.

▶ `prefix` is the prefix to check.

▶ `toffset` is the index from which to start the search.

↵ TRUE if this string starts with the specified prefix beginning at `toffset`; otherwise, returns FALSE.

substring 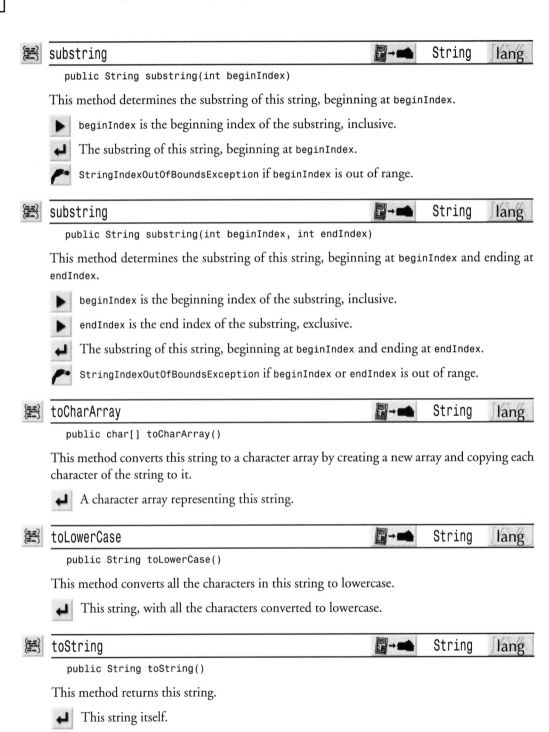 String lang

```
public String substring(int beginIndex)
```

This method determines the substring of this string, beginning at beginIndex.

▶ beginIndex is the beginning index of the substring, inclusive.

↵ The substring of this string, beginning at beginIndex.

☞ StringIndexOutOfBoundsException if beginIndex is out of range.

substring String lang

```
public String substring(int beginIndex, int endIndex)
```

This method determines the substring of this string, beginning at beginIndex and ending at endIndex.

▶ beginIndex is the beginning index of the substring, inclusive.

▶ endIndex is the end index of the substring, exclusive.

↵ The substring of this string, beginning at beginIndex and ending at endIndex.

☞ StringIndexOutOfBoundsException if beginIndex or endIndex is out of range.

toCharArray String lang

```
public char[] toCharArray()
```

This method converts this string to a character array by creating a new array and copying each character of the string to it.

↵ A character array representing this string.

toLowerCase String lang

```
public String toLowerCase()
```

This method converts all the characters in this string to lowercase.

↵ This string, with all the characters converted to lowercase.

toString String lang

```
public String toString()
```

This method returns this string.

↵ This string itself.

⊘ toString in class Object.

toUpperCase — String lang

```
public String toUpperCase()
```

This method converts all the characters in this string to uppercase.

↵ This string, with all the characters converted to uppercase.

trim — String lang

```
public String trim()
```

This method trims leading and trailing whitespace from this string.

↵ This string, with leading and trailing whitespace removed.

valueOf — String lang

```
public static String valueOf(boolean b)
```

This method creates a string representation of the specified Boolean value. If the Boolean value is TRUE, the string `"true"` is returned; otherwise, the string `"false"` is returned.

▶ b is the Boolean value from which to get the string representation.

↵ A string representation of the specified Boolean value.

valueOf — String lang

```
public static String valueOf(char c)
```

This method creates a string representation of the specified character value.

▶ c is the character value from which to get the string representation.

↵ A string representation of the specified character value.

valueOf — String lang

```
public static String valueOf(char data[])
```

This method creates a string representation of the specified character array.

▶ data is the character array from which to get the string representation.

↵ A string representation of the specified character array.

valueOf String lang

```
public static String valueOf(char data[], int off, int count)
```

This method creates a string representation of length count from the specified array of characters, beginning off bytes into the array.

▶ data is the character array from which to get the string representation.

▶ off is the starting offset into the array of characters.

▶ count is the number of characters from the array to use in initializing the string.

↵ A string representation of the specified character array.

valueOf String lang

```
public static String valueOf(double d)
```

This method creates a string representation of the specified double value.

▶ d is the double value from which to get the string representation.

↵ A string representation of the specified double value.

valueOf String lang

```
public static String valueOf(float f)
```

This method creates a string representation of the specified float value.

▶ f is the float value from which to get the string representation.

↵ A string representation of the specified float value.

valueOf String lang

```
public static String valueOf(int i)
```

This method creates a string representation of the specified integer value.

▶ i is the integer value from which to get the string representation.

↵ A string representation of the specified integer value.

valueOf String lang

```
public static String valueOf(long l)
```

This method creates a string representation of the specified long value.

▶ `l` is the long value from which to get the string representation.

↵ A string representation of the specified long value.

 valueOf String lang

```
public static String valueOf(Object obj)
```

This method creates a string representation of the specified object. Note that the string representation is the same as that returned by the `toString` method of the object.

▶ `obj` is the object from which to get the string representation.

↵ A string representation of the specified object value, or the string `"null"` if the object is null.

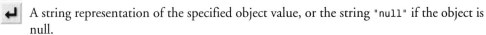 # StringBuffer lang

 Object

See also: `String`

This class implements a variable string of characters. The `StringBuffer` class provides a wide range of append and insert methods, along with some other support methods for getting information about the string buffer. Note that the `StringBuffer` class is synchronized appropriately so that it can be used by multiple threads. The definition for the `StringBuffer` class follows:

```
public class java.lang.StringBuffer extends java.lang.Object {
    // Constructors
    public StringBuffer();
    public StringBuffer(int length);
    public StringBuffer(String str);

    // Methods
    public StringBuffer append(boolean b);
    public StringBuffer append(char c);
    public StringBuffer append(char str[]);
    public StringBuffer append(char str[], int off, int len);
    public StringBuffer append(double d);
    public StringBuffer append(float f);
    public StringBuffer append(int i);
    public StringBuffer append(long l);
    public StringBuffer append(Object obj);
    public StringBuffer append(String str);
```

```
        public int capacity();
        public char charAt(int index);
        public void ensureCapacity(int minimumCapacity);
        public void getChars(int srcBegin, int srcEnd, char dst[], int dstBegin);
        public StringBuffer insert(int off, boolean b);
        public StringBuffer insert(int off, char c);
        public StringBuffer insert(int off, char str[]);
        public StringBuffer insert(int off, double d);
        public StringBuffer insert(int off, float f);
        public StringBuffer insert(int off, int i);
        public StringBuffer insert(int off, long l);
        public StringBuffer insert(int off, Object obj);
        public StringBuffer insert(int off, String str);
        public int length();
        public StringBuffer reverse();
        public void setCharAt(int index, char ch);
        public void setLength(int newLength);
        public String toString();
}
```

 StringBuffer    **StringBuffer**   lang

```
        public StringBuffer()
```

This constructor creates a default string buffer with no characters.

 StringBuffer    **StringBuffer**   lang

```
        public StringBuffer(int length)
```

This constructor creates a string buffer with the specified length.

▶   length is the initial length of the string buffer.

 StringBuffer    **StringBuffer**   lang

```
        public StringBuffer(String str)
```

This constructor creates a string buffer with the specified initial string value.

▶   str is the initial string value of the string buffer.

 append    **StringBuffer**   lang

```
        public StringBuffer append(boolean b)
```

This method appends the string representation of the specified Boolean value to the end of this string buffer.

▶   b is the Boolean value to be appended.

↵   This string buffer, with the Boolean appended.

append   StringBuffer   lang

```
public StringBuffer append(char c)
```

This method appends the string representation of the specified character value to the end of this string buffer.

▶ c is the character value to be appended.

↵ This string buffer, with the character appended.

append   StringBuffer   lang

```
public StringBuffer append(char str[])
```

This method appends the string representation of the specified character array to the end of this string buffer.

▶ str is the character array to be appended.

↵ This string buffer, with the character array appended.

append   StringBuffer   lang

```
public StringBuffer append(char str[], int off, int len)
```

This method appends the string representation of the specified character subarray to the end of this string buffer.

▶ str is the character array to be appended.

▶ off is the starting offset into the character array to append.

▶ len is the number of characters to append.

↵ This string buffer, with the character subarray appended.

append   StringBuffer   lang

```
public StringBuffer append(double d)
```

This method appends the string representation of the specified double value to the end of this string buffer.

▶ d is the double value to be appended.

↵ This string buffer, with the double appended.

append   StringBuffer   lang

```
public StringBuffer append(float f)
```

This method appends the string representation of the specified float value to the end of this string buffer.

▶   `f` is the float value to be appended.

↵   This string buffer, with the float appended.

append   StringBuffer   lang

```
public StringBuffer append(int i)
```

This method appends the string representation of the specified integer value to the end of this string buffer.

▶   `i` is the integer value to be appended.

↵   This string buffer, with the integer appended.

append   StringBuffer   lang

```
public StringBuffer append(long l)
```

This method appends the string representation of the specified long value to the end of this string buffer.

▶   `l` is the long value to be appended.

↵   This string buffer, with the long appended.

append   StringBuffer   lang

```
public StringBuffer append(Object obj)
```

This method appends the string representation of the specified object to the end of this string buffer. Note that the string representation is the same as that returned by the `toString` method of the object.

▶   `obj` is the object to be appended.

↵   This string buffer, with the object appended.

append   StringBuffer   lang

```
public StringBuffer append(String str)
```

This method appends the specified string to the end of this string buffer.

▶ `str` is the string to be appended.

↵ This string buffer, with the string appended.

capacity StringBuffer lang

```
public int capacity()
```

This method determines the capacity of this string buffer, which is the amount of character storage currently allocated in the string buffer.

↵ The capacity of this string buffer.

charAt StringBuffer lang

```
public char charAt(int index)
```

This method determines the character at the specified index. Note that string buffer indexes are zero-based, meaning that the first character is located at index 0.

▶ `index` is the index of the desired character.

↵ The character at the specified index.

➤ `StringIndexOutOfBoundsException` if the index is out of range.

ensureCapacity StringBuffer lang

```
public void ensureCapacity(int minimumCapacity)
```

This method ensures that the capacity of this string buffer is at least equal to the specified minimum.

▶ `minimumCapacity` is the minimum desired capacity.

getChars StringBuffer lang

```
public void getChars(int srcBegin, int srcEnd, char dst[], int dstBegin)
```

This method copies each character in this string buffer, beginning at `srcBegin` and ending at `srcEnd`, into the character array `dst` beginning at `dstBegin`.

▶ `srcBegin` is the index of the first character in the string buffer to copy.

▶ `srcEnd` is the index of the last character in the string buffer to copy.

▶ `dst` is the destination character array.

▶ `dstBegin` is the starting offset into the character array.

➤ `StringIndexOutOfBoundsException` if there is an invalid index in the buffer.

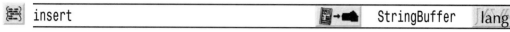

insert   StringBuffer   lang

```
public StringBuffer insert(int off, boolean b)
```

This method inserts the string representation of the specified Boolean value at the specified offset of this string buffer.

▶ `off` is the offset at which to insert the Boolean.

▶ `b` is the Boolean value to be inserted.

↵ This string buffer, with the Boolean inserted.

⤷ `StringIndexOutOfBoundsException` if the offset is invalid.

insert   StringBuffer   lang

```
public StringBuffer insert(int off, char c)
```

This method inserts the string representation of the specified character value at the specified offset of this string buffer.

▶ `off` is the offset at which to insert the character.

▶ `c` is the character value to be inserted.

↵ This string buffer, with the character inserted.

⤷ `StringIndexOutOfBoundsException` if the offset is invalid.

insert   StringBuffer   lang

```
public StringBuffer insert(int off, char str[])
```

This method inserts the string representation of the specified character array at the specified offset of this string buffer.

▶ `off` is the offset at which to insert the character array.

▶ `str` is the character array to be inserted.

↵ This string buffer, with the character array inserted.

⤷ `StringIndexOutOfBoundsException` if the offset is invalid.

insert   StringBuffer   lang

```
public StringBuffer insert(int off, double d)
```

This method inserts the string representation of the specified double value at the specified offset of this string buffer.

▶ `off` is the offset at which to insert the double.

▶ `d` is the double value to be inserted.

↵ This string buffer, with the double inserted.

⟋• `StringIndexOutOfBoundsException` if the offset is invalid.

---

 insert   ▣→◣   **StringBuffer**   lang

```
public StringBuffer insert(int off, float f)
```

This method inserts the string representation of the specified float value at the specified offset of this string buffer.

▶ `off` is the offset at which to insert the float.

▶ `f` is the float value to be inserted.

↵ This string buffer, with the float inserted.

⟋• `StringIndexOutOfBoundsException` if the offset is invalid.

---

insert   ▣→◣   **StringBuffer**   lang

```
public StringBuffer insert(int off, int i)
```

This method inserts the string representation of the specified integer value at the specified offset of this string buffer.

▶ `off` is the offset at which to insert the integer.

▶ `i` is the integer value to be inserted.

↵ This string buffer, with the integer inserted.

⟋• `StringIndexOutOfBoundsException` if the offset is invalid.

---

insert   ▣→◣   **StringBuffer**   lang

```
public StringBuffer insert(int off, long l)
```

This method inserts the string representation of the specified long value at the specified offset of this string buffer.

▶ `off` is the offset at which to insert the long.

▶ `l` is the long value to be inserted.

↵ This string buffer, with the long inserted.

⟋• `StringIndexOutOfBoundsException` if the offset is invalid.

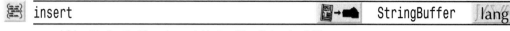

insert   StringBuffer   lang

```
public StringBuffer insert(int off, Object obj)
```

This method inserts the string representation of the specified object at the specified offset of this string buffer. Note that the string representation is the same as that returned by the `toString` method of the object.

▶   off is the offset at which to insert the object.

▶   obj is the object to be inserted.

↵   This string buffer, with the object inserted.

↝   StringIndexOutOfBoundsException if the offset is invalid.

insert   StringBuffer   lang

```
public StringBuffer insert(int off, String str)
```

This method inserts the specified string at the specified offset of this string buffer.

▶   off is the offset at which to insert the string.

▶   str is the string to be inserted.

↵   This string buffer, with the string inserted.

↝   StringIndexOutOfBoundsException if the offset is invalid.

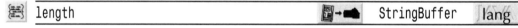

length   StringBuffer   lang

```
public int length()
```

This method determines the length of this string buffer, which is the actual number of characters stored in the buffer.

↵   The length of this string buffer.

reverse   StringBuffer   lang

```
public StringBuffer reverse()
```

This method reverses the character sequence in this string buffer.

↵   This string buffer, with the characters reversed.

setCharAt StringBuffer lang

```
public void setCharAt(int index, char ch)
```

This method changes the character at the specified index in this string to the specified character.

▶ index is the index of the character to change.

▶ ch is the new character.

☞ StringIndexOutOfBoundsException if the index is invalid.

 setLength StringBuffer lang

```
public void setLength(int newLength)
```

This method explicitly sets the length of this string buffer. If the length is reduced, characters are lost; if the length is increased, new characters are set to 0 (NULL). The new length must be greater than or equal to 0.

▶ newLength is the new length of the string buffer.

☞ StringIndexOutOfBoundsException if the length is invalid.

toString StringBuffer lang

```
public String toString()
```

This method determines a constant string representation of this string buffer.

↵ The constant string representation of this string buffer.

⊘ toString in class Object.

 # System lang

╋ Object

This class provides a platform-independent means of interacting with the Java runtime system. The System class provides support for standard input, standard output, and standard error streams, along with providing access to system properties, among other things. Note that the System class cannot be instantiated or subclassed because all its methods and variables are static. The definition for the System class follows:

```
public final class java.lang.System extends java.lang.Object {
    // Member Variables
    public static PrintStream err;
    public static InputStream in;
    public static PrintStream out;
```

```
// Methods
public static void arraycopy(Object src, int src_position, Object dst,
  int dst_position, int length);
public static long currentTimeMillis();
public static void exit(int status);
public static void gc();
public static Properties getProperties();
public static String getProperty(String key);
public static String getProperty(String key, String def);
public static SecurityManager getSecurityManager();
public static void load(String pathname);
public static void loadLibrary(String libname);
public static void runFinalization();
public static void setProperties(Properties props);
public static void setSecurityManager(SecurityManager s);
}
```

Member Variables

`public static PrintStream err`

This is the standard error stream, which is used for printing error information. Typically, this stream corresponds to display output, because it is important that the user see the error information.

`public static InputStream in`

This is the standard input stream, which is used for reading character data. Typically, this stream corresponds to keyboard input or another input source specified by the host environment or user.

`public static PrintStream out`

This is the standard output stream, which is used for printing character data. Typically, this stream corresponds to display output or another output destination specified by the host environment or user.

 arraycopy 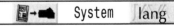 System lang

```
public static void arraycopy(Object src, int src_position, Object dst, int
  ►dst_position, int length)
```

This method copies `len` array elements from the `src` array, beginning at `src_position`, to the dst array, beginning at `dst_position`. Both src and dst must be array objects. Note that arraycopy does not allocate memory for the destination array; the memory already must be allocated.

▶ src is the source array from which to copy data.

▶ src_position is the start position in the source array.

▶ dst is the destination array to which data is copied.

▶ `dst_position` is the start position in the destination array.

▶ `length` is the number of array elements to be copied.

↝ `ArrayIndexOutOfBoundsException` if the copy would cause data to be accessed outside of array bounds.

↝ `ArrayStoreException` if an element in the source array could not be stored in the destination array due to a type mismatch.

currentTimeMillis   System lang

```
public static long currentTimeMillis()
```

This method determines the current UTC time relative to midnight, January 1, 1970 UTC, in milliseconds.

↵ The current UTC time relative to midnight, January 1, 1970 UTC, in milliseconds.

exit   System lang

```
public static void exit(int status)
```

This method exits the Java runtime system (virtual machine) with the specified integer exit status. Note that because `exit` kills the runtime system, it never returns. This method simply calls the `exit` method in the `Runtime` class.

▶ `status` is the integer exit status; this should be set to nonzero if this is an abnormal exit.

↝ `SecurityException` if the current thread cannot exit with the specified exit status.

gc   System lang

```
public static void gc()
```

This method invokes the Java garbage collector to clean up any objects that no longer are needed, usually resulting in more free memory. This method simply calls the `gc` method in the `Runtime` class.

getProperties   System lang

```
public static Properties getProperties()
```

This method determines the current system properties. Table 32.2 lists all the system properties guaranteed to be supported.

Table 32.2. Supported `getProperties` system properties.

Property	Description
java.version	Java version number
java.vendor	Java vendor-specific string
java.vendor.url	Java vendor URL
java.home	Java installation directory
java.class.version	Java class format version number
java.class.path	Java CLASSPATH environment variable
os.name	Operating system name
os.arch	Operating system architecture
os.version	Operating system version
file.separator	File separator
path.separator	Path separator
line.separator	Line separator
user.name	User's account name
user.home	User's home directory
user.dir	User's current working directory

The current system properties.

`SecurityException` if the current thread cannot access the system properties.

getProperty  System   lang

```
public static String getProperty(String key)
```

This method determines the system property with the specified key name.

▶ `key` is the key name of the system property.

↵ The system property with the specified key name.

`SecurityException` if the current thread cannot access the system property.

getProperty   System   lang

```
public static String getProperty(String key, String def)
```

This method determines the system property with the specified key name; it returns the specified default property value if the key isn't found.

► `key` is the key name of the system property.

► `def` is the default property value to use if the key isn't found.

↵ The system property with the specified key name, or the specified default property value if the key isn't found.

✦ `SecurityException` if the current thread cannot access the system property.

getSecurityManager System lang

```
public static SecurityManager getSecurityManager()
```

This method gets the security manager for the Java program, or `NULL` if none exists.

↵ The security manager for the Java program, or `NULL` if none exists.

load System lang

```
public static void load(String pathname)
```

This method loads the dynamic library with the specified complete path name. This method simply calls the `load` method in the `Runtime` class.

► `pathname` is the path name of the library to load.

✦ `UnsatisfiedLinkError` if the library doesn't exist.

✦ `SecurityException` if the current thread can't load the library.

loadLibrary System lang

```
public static void loadLibrary(String libname)
```

This method loads the dynamic library with the specified library name. Note that the mapping from library name to a specific filename is performed in a platform-specific manner. This method simply calls the `loadLibrary` method in the `Runtime` class.

► `libname` is the name of the library to load.

✦ `UnsatisfiedLinkError` if the library doesn't exist.

✦ `SecurityException` if the current thread can't load the library.

runFinalization System lang

```
public static void runFinalization()
```

This method explicitly causes the `finalize` methods of any discarded objects to be called. Typically, the `finalize` methods of discarded objects are automatically called asynchronously when the garbage collector cleans up the objects. You can use `runFinalization` to have the `finalize` methods called synchronously. This method simply calls the `runFinalization` method in the `Runtime` class.

 setProperties System lang

```
public static void setProperties(Properties props)
```

This method sets the system properties to the specified properties.

 props specifies the new properties to be set.

 setSecurityManager System lang

```
public static void setSecurityManager(SecurityManager s)
```

This method sets the security manager to the specified security manager. Note that the security manager can be set only once for a Java program.

 s is the new security manager to be set.

SecurityException if the security manager already has been set.

Thread lang

 Object

 Runnable

See also: ThreadGroup

This class provides the overhead necessary to manage a single thread of execution within a process. The `Thread` class is the basis for multithreaded programming in Java. The definition for the `Thread` class follows:

```
public class java.lang.Thread extends java.lang.Object
  implements java.lang.Runnable {
  // Member Constants
  public final static int MAX_PRIORITY;
  public final static int MIN_PRIORITY;
  public final static int NORM_PRIORITY;
```

```
// Constructors
public Thread();
public Thread(Runnable target);
public Thread(Runnable target, String name);
public Thread(String name);
public Thread(ThreadGroup group, Runnable target);
public Thread(ThreadGroup group, Runnable target, String name);
public Thread(ThreadGroup group, String name);

// Methods
public static int activeCount();
public void checkAccess();
public int countStackFrames();
public static Thread currentThread();
public void destroy();
public static void dumpStack();
public static int enumerate(Thread list[]);
public final String getName();
public final int getPriority();
public final ThreadGroup getThreadGroup();
public void interrupt();
public static boolean interrupted();
public final boolean isAlive();
public final boolean isDaemon();
public boolean isInterrupted();
public final void join();
public final void  join(long timeout);
public final void join(long timeout, int nanos);
public final void resume();
public void run();
public final void setDaemon(boolean daemon);
public final void setName(String name);
public final void setPriority(int newPriority);
public static void sleep(long millis);
public static void sleep(long millis, int nanos);
public void start();
public final void stop();
public final void  stop(Throwable obj);
public final void suspend();
public String toString();
public static void yield();
}
```

Member Constants

public final static int MAX_PRIORITY

This is a constant representing the maximum priority a thread can have, which is set to 10.

public final static int MIN_PRIORITY

This is a constant representing the minimum priority a thread can have, which is set to 1.

public final static int NORM_PRIORITY

This is a constant representing the normal (default) priority for a thread, which is set to 5.

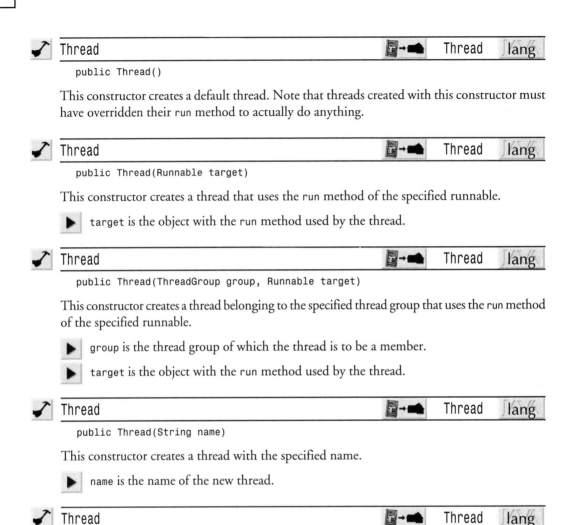

Thread   Thread   lang

```
public Thread()
```

This constructor creates a default thread. Note that threads created with this constructor must have overridden their run method to actually do anything.

Thread   Thread   lang

```
public Thread(Runnable target)
```

This constructor creates a thread that uses the run method of the specified runnable.

▶ target is the object with the run method used by the thread.

Thread   Thread   lang

```
public Thread(ThreadGroup group, Runnable target)
```

This constructor creates a thread belonging to the specified thread group that uses the run method of the specified runnable.

▶ group is the thread group of which the thread is to be a member.

▶ target is the object with the run method used by the thread.

Thread   Thread   lang

```
public Thread(String name)
```

This constructor creates a thread with the specified name.

▶ name is the name of the new thread.

Thread   Thread   lang

```
public Thread(ThreadGroup group, String name)
```

This constructor creates a thread belonging to the specified thread group with the specified name.

▶ group is the thread group of which the thread is to be a member.

▶ name is the name of the new thread.

Thread   Thread   lang

```
public Thread(Runnable target, String name)
```

This constructor creates a thread with the specified name that uses the run method of the specified runnable.

▶   target is the object with the run method used by the thread.

▶   name is the name of the new thread.

 Thread   Thread   lang

```
public Thread(ThreadGroup group, Runnable target, String name)
```

This constructor creates a thread belonging to the specified thread group with the specified name that uses the run method of the specified runnable.

▶   group is the thread group of which the thread is to be a member.

▶   target is the object with the run method used by the thread.

▶   name is the name of the new thread.

 activeCount   Thread   lang

```
public static int activeCount()
```

This method determines the number of active threads in this thread's thread group.

↵   The number of active threads in this thread's thread group.

 checkAccess   Thread   lang

```
public void checkAccess()
```

This method checks to see whether the currently running thread is allowed access to this thread.

   SecurityException if the calling thread doesn't have access to this thread.

 countStackFrames   Thread   lang

```
public int countStackFrames()
```

This method determines the number of stack frames in this thread. Note that the thread must be suspended in order to use this method.

↵   The number of stack frames in this thread.

   IllegalThreadStateException if the thread is not suspended.

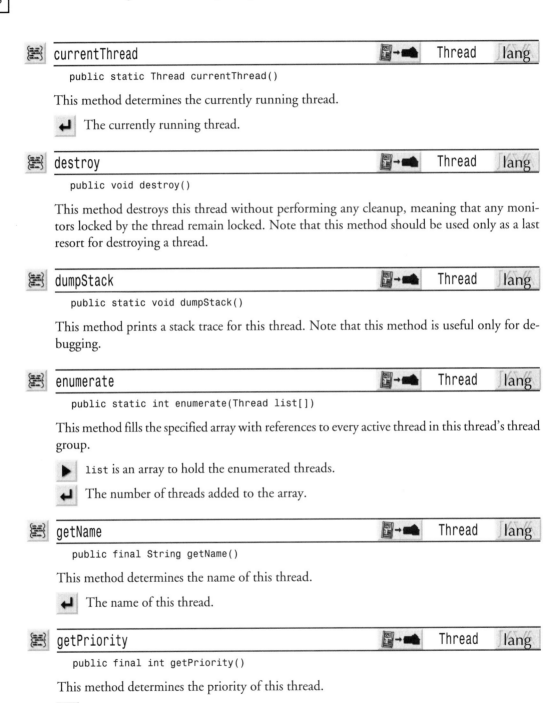

currentThread   Thread   lang

```
public static Thread currentThread()
```

This method determines the currently running thread.

↵ The currently running thread.

destroy   Thread   lang

```
public void destroy()
```

This method destroys this thread without performing any cleanup, meaning that any monitors locked by the thread remain locked. Note that this method should be used only as a last resort for destroying a thread.

dumpStack   Thread   lang

```
public static void dumpStack()
```

This method prints a stack trace for this thread. Note that this method is useful only for debugging.

enumerate   Thread   lang

```
public static int enumerate(Thread list[])
```

This method fills the specified array with references to every active thread in this thread's thread group.

▶ list is an array to hold the enumerated threads.

↵ The number of threads added to the array.

getName   Thread   lang

```
public final String getName()
```

This method determines the name of this thread.

↵ The name of this thread.

getPriority   Thread   lang

```
public final int getPriority()
```

This method determines the priority of this thread.

↵ The priority of this thread.

getThreadGroup 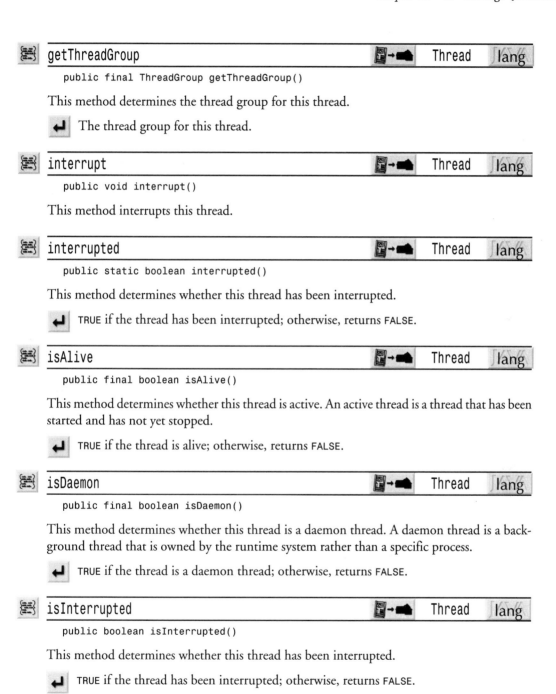 Thread lang

```
public final ThreadGroup getThreadGroup()
```

This method determines the thread group for this thread.

↵ The thread group for this thread.

interrupt Thread lang

```
public void interrupt()
```

This method interrupts this thread.

interrupted Thread lang

```
public static boolean interrupted()
```

This method determines whether this thread has been interrupted.

↵ TRUE if the thread has been interrupted; otherwise, returns FALSE.

isAlive Thread lang

```
public final boolean isAlive()
```

This method determines whether this thread is active. An active thread is a thread that has been started and has not yet stopped.

↵ TRUE if the thread is alive; otherwise, returns FALSE.

isDaemon Thread lang

```
public final boolean isDaemon()
```

This method determines whether this thread is a daemon thread. A daemon thread is a background thread that is owned by the runtime system rather than a specific process.

↵ TRUE if the thread is a daemon thread; otherwise, returns FALSE.

isInterrupted Thread lang

```
public boolean isInterrupted()
```

This method determines whether this thread has been interrupted.

↵ TRUE if the thread has been interrupted; otherwise, returns FALSE.

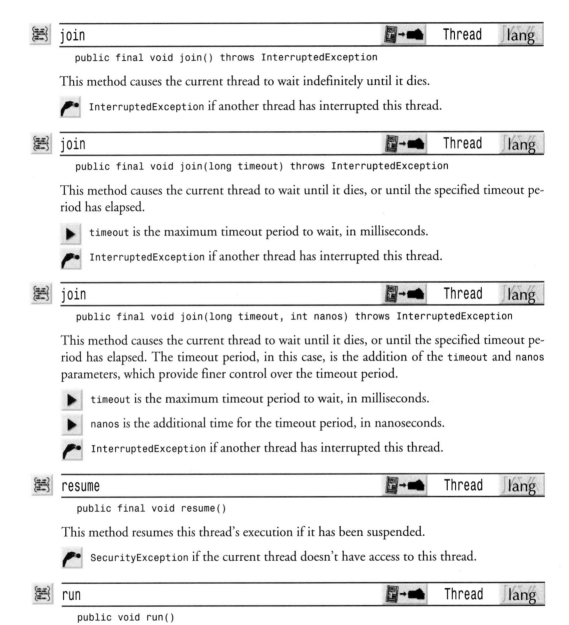

join   Thread   lang

`public final void join() throws InterruptedException`

This method causes the current thread to wait indefinitely until it dies.

▸ InterruptedException if another thread has interrupted this thread.

join   Thread   lang

`public final void join(long timeout) throws InterruptedException`

This method causes the current thread to wait until it dies, or until the specified timeout period has elapsed.

▸ timeout is the maximum timeout period to wait, in milliseconds.

▸ InterruptedException if another thread has interrupted this thread.

join   Thread   lang

`public final void join(long timeout, int nanos) throws InterruptedException`

This method causes the current thread to wait until it dies, or until the specified timeout period has elapsed. The timeout period, in this case, is the addition of the timeout and nanos parameters, which provide finer control over the timeout period.

▸ timeout is the maximum timeout period to wait, in milliseconds.

▸ nanos is the additional time for the timeout period, in nanoseconds.

▸ InterruptedException if another thread has interrupted this thread.

resume   Thread   lang

`public final void resume()`

This method resumes this thread's execution if it has been suspended.

▸ SecurityException if the current thread doesn't have access to this thread.

run   Thread   lang

`public void run()`

This method is the body of the thread, which performs the actual work of the thread. The run method is called when the thread is started. The run method is overridden in a derived Thread class or implemented in a class implementing the Runnable interface.

setDaemon  Thread lang

```
public final void setDaemon(boolean daemon)
```

This method sets this thread as a daemon thread or a user thread based on the specified Boolean value. Note that the thread must be inactive in order to use this method.

▶ daemon is a Boolean value that determines whether the thread is a daemon thread.

✎ IllegalThreadStateException if the thread is active.

setName  Thread lang

```
public final void setName(String name)
```

This method sets the name of this thread.

▶ name is the new name of the thread.

✎ SecurityException if the current thread doesn't have access to this thread.

setPriority Thread lang

```
public final void setPriority(int newPriority)
```

This method sets the priority of this thread.

▶ newPriority is the new priority of the thread.

✎ IllegalArgumentException if the priority is not within the range MIN_PRIORITY to MAX_PRIORITY.

✎ SecurityException if the current thread doesn't have access to this thread.

sleep Thread lang

```
public static void sleep(long millis) throws InterruptedException
```

This method causes the current thread to sleep for the specified length of time, in milliseconds.

▶ millis is the length of time to sleep, in milliseconds.

✎ InterruptedException if another thread has interrupted this thread.

sleep Thread lang

```
public static void sleep(long millis, int nanos) throws InterruptedException
```

This method causes the current thread to sleep for the specified length of time. The length of time, in this case, is the addition of the millis and nanos parameters, which provide finer control over the sleep time.

▶ `millis` is the length of time to sleep, in milliseconds.

▶ `nanos` is the additional time for the sleep time, in nanoseconds.

☞ `InterruptedException` if another thread has interrupted this thread.

start 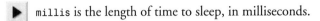 Thread   lang

```
public void start()
```

This method starts this thread, causing the `run` method to be executed.

☞ `IllegalThreadStateException` if the thread already was running.

stop Thread   lang

```
public final void stop()
```

This method abnormally stops this thread, causing it to throw a `ThreadDeath` object. You can catch the `ThreadDeath` object to perform cleanup, but there is rarely a need to do so.

☞ `SecurityException` if the current thread doesn't have access to this thread.

stop Thread   lang

```
public final synchronized void stop(Throwable obj)
```

This method abnormally stops this thread, causing it to throw the specified object. Note that this version of `stop` should be used only in very rare situations.

▶ `obj` is the object to be thrown.

☞ `SecurityException` if the current thread doesn't have access to this thread.

suspend Thread   lang

```
public final void suspend()
```

This method suspends the execution of this thread.

☞ `SecurityException` if the current thread doesn't have access to this thread.

toString Thread   lang

```
public String toString()
```

This method determines a string representation of this thread, which includes the thread's name, priority, and thread group.

↵ A string representation of this thread.

⊘ `toString` in class `Object`.

yield   Thread   lang

```
public static void yield()
```

This method causes the currently executing thread to yield so that other threads can execute.

ThreadGroup   lang

➕ Object

See also: Thread

This class implements a thread group, which is a set of threads that can be manipulated as one. Thread groups also can contain other thread groups, resulting in a thread hierarchy. The definition for the ThreadGroup class follows:

```
public class java.lang.ThreadGroup extends java.lang.Object {
    // Constructors
    public ThreadGroup(String name);
    public ThreadGroup(ThreadGroup parent, String name);

    // Methods
    public int activeCount();
    public int activeGroupCount();
    public final void checkAccess();
    public final void destroy();
    public int enumerate(Thread list[]);
    public int enumerate(Thread list[], boolean recurse);
    public int enumerate(ThreadGroup list[]);
    public int enumerate(ThreadGroup list[], boolean recurse);
    public final int getMaxPriority();
    public final String getName();
    public final ThreadGroup getParent();
    public final boolean isDaemon();
    public void list();
    public final boolean parentOf(ThreadGroup g);
    public final void resume();
    public final void setDaemon(boolean daemon);
    public final void  setMaxPriority(int pri);
    public final synchronized void stop();
    public final synchronized void suspend();
    public String toString();
    public void uncaughtException(Thread t, Throwable e);
}
```

 ThreadGroup   ThreadGroup   lang

```
public ThreadGroup(String name)
```

This constructor creates a thread group with the specified name. The newly created thread group belongs to the thread group of the current thread.

▶ name is the name of the new thread group.

ThreadGroup ThreadGroup lang

```
public ThreadGroup(ThreadGroup parent, String name)
```

This constructor creates a thread group with the specified name that belongs to the specified parent thread group.

▶ parent is the parent thread group.

▶ name is the name of the new thread group.

NullPointerException if the specified thread group is NULL.

SecurityException if the current thread cannot create a thread in the specified thread group.

activeCount ThreadGroup lang

```
public int activeCount()
```

This method determines the number of active threads in this thread group or in any other thread group that has this thread group as an ancestor.

↵ The number of active threads in this thread group or in any other thread group that has this thread group as an ancestor.

activeGroupCount ThreadGroup lang

```
public int activeGroupCount()
```

This method determines the number of active thread groups that have this thread group as an ancestor.

↵ The number of active thread groups that have this thread group as an ancestor.

checkAccess ThreadGroup lang

```
public final void checkAccess()
```

This method checks to see whether the currently running thread is allowed access to this thread group.

SecurityException if the calling thread doesn't have access to this thread group.

destroy ThreadGroup lang

```
public final void destroy()
```

This method destroys this thread group and all its subgroups. Note that the thread group must be empty, meaning that all threads that belonged to the group have since stopped.

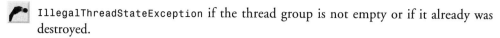 `IllegalThreadStateException` if the thread group is not empty or if it already was destroyed.

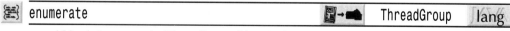 `SecurityException` if the calling thread doesn't have access to this thread group.

enumerate  ThreadGroup lang

```
public int enumerate(Thread list[])
```

This method fills the specified array with references to every active thread in this thread group.

▶ `list` is an array to hold the enumerated threads.

↵ The number of threads added to the array.

enumerate ThreadGroup lang

```
public int enumerate(Thread list[], boolean recurse)
```

This method fills the specified array with references to every active thread in this thread group. If the `recurse` parameter is set to TRUE, all the active threads belonging to subgroups of this thread also are added to the array.

▶ `list` is an array to hold the enumerated threads.

▶ `recurse` is a Boolean value specifying whether to recursively enumerate active threads in subgroups.

↵ The number of threads added to the array.

enumerate ThreadGroup lang

```
public int enumerate(ThreadGroup list[])
```

This method fills the specified array with references to every active subgroup in this thread group.

▶ `list` is an array to hold the enumerated thread groups.

↵ The number of thread groups added to the array.

enumerate ThreadGroup lang

```
public int enumerate(ThreadGroup list[], boolean recurse)
```

This method fills the specified array with references to every active subgroup in this thread group. If the `recurse` parameter is set to TRUE, all the active thread groups belonging to subgroups of this thread also are added to the array.

▶ `list` is an array to hold the enumerated thread groups.

▶ `recurse` is a Boolean value specifying whether to recursively enumerate active thread groups in subgroups.

↵ The number of thread groups added to the array.

getMaxPriority 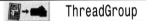 ThreadGroup lang

```
public final int getMaxPriority()
```

This method determines the maximum priority of this thread group. Note that threads in this thread group cannot have a higher priority than the maximum priority.

↵ The maximum priority of this thread group.

getName ThreadGroup lang

```
public final String getName()
```

This method determines the name of this thread group.

↵ The name of this thread group.

getParent ThreadGroup lang

```
public final ThreadGroup getParent()
```

This method determines the parent of this thread group.

↵ The parent of this thread group.

isDaemon ThreadGroup lang

```
public final boolean isDaemon()
```

This method determines whether this thread group is a daemon thread group. A daemon thread group is destroyed automatically when all its threads finish executing.

↵ TRUE if the thread group is a daemon thread group; otherwise, returns FALSE.

list ThreadGroup lang

```
public void list()
```

This method prints information about this thread group to standard output, including the active threads in the group. Note that this method is useful only for debugging.

parentOf ThreadGroup lang

```
public final boolean parentOf(ThreadGroup g)
```

This method checks to see whether this thread group is a parent or ancestor of the specified thread group.

▶ g is the thread group to be checked.

↵ TRUE if this thread group is the parent or ancestor of the specified thread group; otherwise, returns FALSE.

resume ThreadGroup lang

```
public final void resume()
```

This method resumes execution of all the threads in this thread group that have been suspended.

🐾 SecurityException if the current thread doesn't have access to this thread group or any of its threads.

setDaemon ThreadGroup lang

```
public final void setDaemon(boolean daemon)
```

This method sets this thread group as a daemon thread group or a user thread group based on the specified Boolean value. A daemon thread group is destroyed automatically when all its threads finish executing.

▶ daemon is a Boolean value that determines whether the thread group is a daemon thread group.

🐾 SecurityException if the current thread doesn't have access to this thread group.

setMaxPriority ThreadGroup lang

```
public final void setMaxPriority(int pri)
```

This method sets the maximum priority of this thread group.

▶ pri is the new maximum priority of the thread group.

🐾 SecurityException if the current thread doesn't have access to this thread group.

stop   ThreadGroup lang

```
public final synchronized void stop()
```

This method stops all the threads in this thread group and in all its subgroups.

> `SecurityException` if the current thread doesn't have access to this thread group, any of its threads, or threads in subgroups.

 suspend   ThreadGroup lang

```
public final synchronized void suspend()
```

This method suspends all the threads in this thread group and in all its subgroups.

> `SecurityException` if the current thread doesn't have access to this thread group, any of its threads, or threads in subgroups.

 toString   ThreadGroup lang

```
public String toString()
```

This method determines a string representation of this thread group.

> A string representation of this thread group.

> `toString` in class `Object`.

 uncaughtException   ThreadGroup lang

```
public void uncaughtException(Thread t, Throwable e)
```

This method is called when a thread in this thread group exits because of an uncaught exception. You can override this method to provide specific handling of uncaught exceptions.

> ▶ t is the thread that is exiting.

> ▶ e is the uncaught exception.

Throwable   lang

➕ Object

This class provides the core functionality for signaling when exceptional conditions occur. All errors and exceptions in the Java system are derived from `Throwable`. The `Throwable` class contains a snapshot of the execution stack for helping to track down why exceptional conditions occur. The definition for the `Throwable` class follows:

```
public class java.lang.Throwable extends java.lang.Object {
    // Constructors
    public Throwable();
    public Throwable(String message);

    // Methods
    public Throwable fillInStackTrace();
    public String getMessage();
    public void printStackTrace();
    public void printStackTrace(PrintStream s);
    public String toString();
}
```

 Throwable Throwable lang

public Throwable()

This constructor creates a default throwable with no detail message; the stack trace is filled in automatically.

 Throwable Throwable lang

public Throwable(String message)

This constructor creates a throwable with the specified detail message; the stack trace is filled in automatically.

▶ message is the detail message.

 fillInStackTrace Throwable lang

public Throwable fillInStackTrace()

This method fills in the execution stack trace. Note that this method is useful only when rethrowing this throwable.

↵ This throwable.

 getMessage Throwable lang

public String getMessage()

This method determines the detail message of this throwable.

↵ The detail message of this throwable.

printStackTrace Throwable lang

public void printStackTrace()

This method prints this throwable and its stack trace to the standard error stream.

printStackTrace   Throwable | lang

```
public void printStackTrace(PrintStream s)
```

This method prints this throwable and its stack trace to the specified print stream.

▶   s is the print stream to which the stack will be printed.

 toString   Throwable | lang

```
public String toString()
```

This method determines a string representation of this throwable.

↵   A string representation of this throwable.

⊘   toString in class Object.

ArithmeticException   lang

✚   RuntimeException

This exception class signals that an exceptional arithmetic condition has occurred, such as a division by zero. The definition for the ArithmeticException class follows:

```
public class java.lang.ArithmeticException
  extends java.lang.RuntimeException {
  // Constructors
  public ArithmeticException();
  public ArithmeticException(String s);
}
```

 ArithmeticException   ArithmeticException | lang

```
public ArithmeticException()
```

This constructor creates a default arithmetic exception with no detail message.

 ArithmeticException   ArithmeticException | lang

```
public ArithmeticException(String s)
```

This constructor creates an arithmetic exception with the specified detail message, which contains information specific to this particular exception.

▶   s is the detail message.

ArrayIndexOutOfBoundsException `lang`

 `IndexOutOfBoundsException`

This exception class signals that an invalid array index has been used. The definition for the `ArrayIndexOutOfBoundsException` class follows:

```
public class java.lang.ArrayIndexOutOfBoundsException
  extends java.lang.IndexOutOfBoundsException {
  // Constructors
  public ArrayIndexOutOfBoundsException();
  public ArrayIndexOutOfBoundsException(int index);
  public ArrayIndexOutOfBoundsException(String s);
}
```

 ArrayIndexOutOfBoundsException ArrayIndexOutOfBoundsException `lang`

```
public ArrayIndexOutOfBoundsException()
```

This constructor creates a default array-index-out-of-bounds exception with no detail message.

 ArrayIndexOutOfBoundsException ArrayIndexOutOfBoundsException `lang`

```
public ArrayIndexOutOfBoundsException(int index)
```

This constructor creates an array-index-out-of-bounds exception with the specified invalid index.

▶ `index` is the invalid index that caused the error.

 ArrayIndexOutOfBoundsException ArrayIndexOutOfBoundsException `lang`

```
public ArrayIndexOutOfBoundsException(String s)
```

This constructor creates an array-index-out-of-bounds exception with the specified detail message, which contains information specific to this particular exception.

▶ `s` is the detail message.

 # ArrayStoreException `lang`

 `RuntimeException`

This exception class signals that an attempt has been made to store the wrong type of object in an array of objects. The definition for the `ArrayStoreException` class follows:

```
public class java.lang.ArrayStoreException
  extends java.lang.RuntimeException {
  // Constructors
  public ArrayStoreException();
  public ArrayStoreException(String s);
}
```

ArrayStoreException   →! ArrayStoreException   lang

```
public ArrayStoreException()
```

This constructor creates a default array-store exception with no detail message.

 ArrayStoreException   →! ArrayStoreException   lang

```
public ArrayStoreException(String s)
```

This constructor creates an array-store exception with the specified detail message, which contains information specific to this particular exception.

▶ s is the detail message.

→! ClassCastException   lang

 RuntimeException

This exception class signals that an invalid cast has occurred. The definition for the ClassCastException class follows:

```
public class java.lang.ClassCastException
  extends java.lang.RuntimeException {
  // Constructors
  public ClassCastException();
  public ClassCastException(String s);
}
```

 ClassCastException   →! ClassCastException   lang

```
public ClassCastException()
```

This constructor creates a default class-cast exception with no detail message.

 ClassCastException   →! ClassCastException   lang

```
public ClassCastException(String s)
```

This constructor creates a class-cast exception with the specified detail message, which contains information specific to this particular exception.

▶ s is the detail message.

ClassNotFoundException lang

+ Exception

This exception class signals that a class could not be found. The definition for the `ClassNotFoundException` class follows:

```
public class java.lang.ClassNotFoundException extends java.lang.Exception {
  // Constructors
  public ClassNotFoundException();
  public ClassNotFoundException(String s);
}
```

 ClassNotFoundException ClassNotFoundException lang

```
public ClassNotFoundException()
```

This constructor creates a default class-not-found exception with no detail message.

 ClassNotFoundException ClassNotFoundException lang

```
public ClassNotFoundException(String s)
```

This constructor creates a class-not-found exception with the specified detail message, which contains information specific to this particular exception.

▶ s is the detail message.

 # CloneNotSupportedException lang

+ Exception

This exception class signals that an attempt has been made to clone an object that doesn't support the `Cloneable` interface. The definition for the `CloneNotSupportedException` class follows:

```
public class java.lang.CloneNotSupportedException
  extends java.lang.Exception {
  // Constructors
  public CloneNotSupportedException();
  public CloneNotSupportedException(String s);
}
```

 CloneNotSupportedException CloneNotSupportedException lang

```
public CloneNotSupportedException()
```

This constructor creates a default clone-not-supported exception with no detail message.

CloneNotSupportedException   CloneNotSupportedException   lang

```
public CloneNotSupportedException(String s)
```

This constructor creates a clone-not-supported exception with the specified detail message, which contains information specific to this particular exception.

  s is the detail message.

 # Exception   lang

 Throwable

This throwable class indicates exceptional conditions that a Java program might want to know about. The definition for the Exception class follows:

```
public class java.lang.Exception extends java.lang.Throwable {
    // Constructors
    public Exception();
    public Exception(String s);
}
```

 Exception   Exception   lang

```
public Exception()
```

This constructor creates a default exception with no detail message.

 Exception   Exception   lang

```
public Exception(String s)
```

This constructor creates an exception with the specified detail message, which contains information specific to the exception.

  s is the detail message.

 # IllegalAccessException   lang

 Exception

This exception class signals that the current thread doesn't have access to a class. The definition for the IllegalAccessException class follows:

```
public class java.lang.IllegalAccessException extends java.lang.Exception {
    // Constructors
    public IllegalAccessException();
    public IllegalAccessException(String s);
}
```

IllegalAccessException IllegalAccessException lang

```
public IllegalAccessException()
```

This constructor creates a default illegal-access exception with no detail message.

 IllegalAccessException IllegalAccessException lang

```
public IllegalAccessException(String s)
```

This constructor creates an illegal-access exception with the specified detail message, which contains information specific to this particular exception.

▶ s is the detail message.

IllegalArgumentException lang

✚ RuntimeException

This exception class signals that a method has been passed an illegal argument. The definition for the `IllegalArgumentException` class follows:

```
public class java.lang.IllegalArgumentException
    extends java.lang.RuntimeException {
    // Constructors
    public IllegalArgumentException();
    public IllegalArgumentException(String s);
}
```

 IllegalArgumentException IllegalArgumentException lang

```
public IllegalArgumentException()
```

This constructor creates a default illegal-argument exception with no detail message.

 IllegalArgumentException IllegalArgumentException lang

```
public IllegalArgumentException(String s)
```

This constructor creates an illegal-argument exception with the specified detail message, which contains information specific to this particular exception.

 s is the detail message.

IllegalMonitorStateException   lang

 RuntimeException

This exception class signals that a thread has attempted to access an object's monitor without owning the monitor. The definition for the `IllegalMonitorStateException` class follows:

```
public class java.lang.IllegalMonitorStateException
  extends java.lang.RuntimeException {
  // Constructors
  public IllegalMonitorStateException();
  public IllegalMonitorStateException(String s);
}
```

 IllegalMonitorStateException   IllegalMonitorStateException   lang

```
public IllegalMonitorStateException()
```

This constructor creates a default illegal-monitor-state exception with no detail message.

 IllegalMonitorStateException   IllegalMonitorStateException   lang

```
public IllegalMonitorStateException(String s)
```

This constructor creates an illegal-monitor-state exception with the specified detail message, which contains information specific to this particular exception.

▶   s is the detail message.

 # IllegalThreadStateException   lang

✚ IllegalArgumentException

This exception class signals that a thread is not in the proper state for the requested operation. The definition for the `IllegalThreadStateException` class follows:

```
public class java.lang.IllegalThreadStateException
  extends java.lang.IllegalArgumentException {
  // Constructors
  public IllegalThreadStateException();
  public IllegalThreadStateException(String s);
}
```

 IllegalThreadStateException   IllegalThreadStateException   lang

```
public IllegalThreadStateException()
```

This constructor creates a default illegal-thread-state exception with no detail message.

IllegalThreadStateException   IllegalThreadStateException   lang

```
public IllegalThreadStateException(String s)
```

This constructor creates an illegal-thread-state exception with the specified detail message, which contains information specific to this particular exception.

▶ s is the detail message.

IndexOutOfBoundsException   lang

 RuntimeException

This exception class signals that an index of some sort is out of bounds. The definition for the `IndexOutOfBoundsException` class follows:

```
public class java.lang.IndexOutOfBoundsException
  extends java.lang.RuntimeException {
  // Constructors
  public IndexOutOfBoundsException();
  public IndexOutOfBoundsException(String s);
}
```

 IndexOutOfBoundsException   IndexOutOfBoundsException   lang

```
public IndexOutOfBoundsException()
```

This constructor creates a default index-out-of-bounds exception with no detail message.

 IndexOutOfBoundsException   IndexOutOfBoundsException   lang

```
public IndexOutOfBoundsException(String s)
```

This constructor creates an index-out-of-bounds exception with the specified detail message, which contains information specific to this particular exception.

▶ s is the detail message.

InstantiationException   lang

 Exception

This exception class signals that an attempt has been made to instantiate an abstract class or an interface. The definition for the `InstantiationException` class follows:

```
public class java.lang.InstantiationException extends java.lang.Exception {
  // Constructors
  public InstantiationException();
  public InstantiationException(String s);
}
```

InstantiationException InstantiationException `lang`

```
public InstantiationException()
```

This constructor creates a default instantiation exception with no detail message.

 InstantiationException InstantiationException `lang`

```
public InstantiationException(String s)
```

This constructor creates an instantiation exception with the specified detail message, which contains information specific to this particular exception.

 s is the detail message.

InterruptedException `lang`

 Exception

This exception class signals that a thread has been interrupted that already is waiting or sleeping. The definition for the InterruptedException class follows:

```
public class java.lang.InterruptedException extends java.lang.Exception {
  // Constructors
  public InterruptedException();
  public InterruptedException(String s);
}
```

 InterruptedException InterruptedException `lang`

```
public InterruptedException()
```

This constructor creates a default interrupted exception with no detail message.

 InterruptedException InterruptedException `lang`

```
public InterruptedException(String s)
```

This constructor creates an interrupted exception with the specified detail message, which contains information specific to this particular exception.

 s is the detail message.

NegativeArraySizeException lang

 RuntimeException

This exception class signals that an attempt has been made to create an array with a negative size. The definition for the `NegativeArraySizeException` class follows:

```
public class java.lang.NegativeArraySizeException
  extends java.lang.RuntimeException {
  // Constructors
  public NegativeArraySizeException();
  public NegativeArraySizeException(String s);
}
```

 NegativeArraySizeException NegativeArraySizeException lang

```
public NegativeArraySizeException()
```

This constructor creates a default negative-array-size exception with no detail message.

 NegativeArraySizeException NegativeArraySizeException lang

```
public NegativeArraySizeException(String s)
```

This constructor creates a negative-array-size exception with the specified detail message, which contains information specific to this particular exception.

▶ s is the detail message.

 NullPointerException lang

RuntimeException

This exception class signals an attempt to access a null pointer as an object. The definition for the `NullPointerException` class follows:

```
public class java.lang.NullPointerException extends java.lang.RuntimeException {
  // Constructors
  public NullPointerException();
  public NullPointerException(String s);
}
```

 NullPointerException NullPointerException lang

```
public NullPointerException()
```

This constructor creates a default null-pointer exception with no detail message.

NullPointerException   NullPointerException lang

```
public NullPointerException(String s)
```

This constructor creates a null-pointer exception with the specified detail message, which contains information specific to this particular exception.

▶ s is the detail message.

NumberFormatException   lang

 IllegalArgumentException

This exception class signals an attempt to convert a string to an invalid number format. The definition for the NumberFormatException class follows:

```
public class java.lang.NumberFormatException extends
  java.lang.IllegalArgumentException {
  // Constructors
  public NumberFormatException();
  public NumberFormatException(String s);
}
```

 NumberFormatException   NumberFormatException lang

```
public NumberFormatException()
```

This constructor creates a default number-format exception with no detail message.

 NumberFormatException   NumberFormatException lang

```
public NumberFormatException(String s)
```

This constructor creates a number-format exception with the specified detail message, which contains information specific to this particular exception.

▶ s is the detail message.

RuntimeException   lang

 Exception

This exception class signals an exceptional condition that can reasonably occur in the Java runtime system. The definition for the RuntimeException class follows:

```
public class java.lang.RuntimeException extends java.lang.Exception {
  // Constructors
  public RuntimeException();
  public RuntimeException(String s);
}
```

RuntimeException RuntimeException lang

```
public RuntimeException()
```

This constructor creates a default runtime exception with no detail message.

 RuntimeException RuntimeException lang

```
public RuntimeException(String s)
```

This constructor creates a runtime exception with the specified detail message, which contains information specific to this particular exception.

▶ s is the detail message.

SecurityException lang

 RuntimeException

This exception class signals that a security violation has occurred. The definition for the SecurityException class follows:

```
public class java.lang.SecurityException
  extends java.lang.RuntimeException {
  // Constructors
  public SecurityException();
  public SecurityException(String s);
}
```

 SecurityException SecurityException lang

```
public SecurityException()
```

This constructor creates a default security exception with no detail message.

 SecurityException SecurityException lang

```
public SecurityException(String s)
```

This constructor creates a security exception with the specified detail message, which contains information specific to this particular exception.

▶ s is the detail message.

StringIndexOutOfBoundsException lang

IndexOutOfBoundsException

This exception class signals that an invalid string index has been used. The definition for the StringIndexOutOfBoundsException class follows:

```
public class java.lang.StringIndexOutOfBoundsException
  extends java.lang.IndexOutOfBoundsException {
  // Constructors
  public StringIndexOutOfBoundsException();
  public StringIndexOutOfBoundsException(int index);
  public StringIndexOutOfBoundsException(String s);
}
```

 StringIndexOutOfBoundsException StringIndexOutOfBoundsException lang

```
public StringIndexOutOfBoundsException()
```

This constructor creates a default string-index-out-of-bounds exception with no detail message.

 StringIndexOutOfBoundsException StringIndexOutOfBoundsException lang

```
public StringIndexOutOfBoundsException(int index)
```

This constructor creates a string-index-out-of-bounds exception with the specified invalid index.

▶ index is the invalid index that caused the error.

 StringIndexOutOfBoundsException StringIndexOutOfBoundsException lang

```
public StringIndexOutOfBoundsException(String s)
```

This constructor creates a string-index-out-of-bounds exception with the specified detail message, which contains information specific to this particular exception.

▶ s is the detail message.

 # AbstractMethodError lang

IncompatibleClassChangeError

This error class signals an attempt to call an abstract method. The definition for the AbstractMethodError class follows:

```
public class java.lang.AbstractMethodError
  extends java.lang.IncompatibleClassChangeError {
  // Constructors
  public AbstractMethodError();
  public AbstractMethodError(String s);
}
```

AbstractMethodError AbstractMethodError lang

```
public AbstractMethodError()
```

This constructor creates a default abstract-method error with no detail message.

 AbstractMethodError AbstractMethodError lang

```
public AbstractMethodError(String s)
```

This constructor creates an abstract-method error with the specified detail message, which contains information specific to this particular error.

▶ s is the detail message.

   # ClassFormatError lang

✛ LinkageError

This error class signals an attempt to read a file in an invalid format. The definition for the `ClassFormatError` class follows:

```
public class java.lang.ClassFormatError extends java.lang.LinkageError {
  // Constructors
  public ClassFormatError();
  public ClassFormatError(String s);
}
```

 ClassFormatError ClassFormatError lang

```
public ClassFormatError()
```

This constructor creates a default class-format error with no detail message.

 ClassFormatError ClassFormatError lang

```
public ClassFormatError(String s)
```

This constructor creates a class-format error with the specified detail message, which contains information specific to this particular error.

▶ s is the detail message.

 # Error lang

 Throwable

This throwable class indicates a serious problem beyond the scope of what a Java program can fix. The definition for the Error class follows:

```
public class java.lang.Error extends java.lang.Throwable {
  // Constructors
  public Error();
  public Error(String s);
}
```

 Error   Error   lang

```
public Error()
```

This constructor creates a default error with no detail message.

 Error   Error   lang

```
public Error(String s)
```

This constructor creates an error with the specified detail message, which contains information specific to this particular error.

   s is the detail message.

 # IllegalAccessError   lang

 IncompatibleClassChangeError

This error class signals an attempt to access a member variable or call a method without proper access. The definition for the IllegalAccessError class follows:

```
public class java.lang.IllegalAccessError
  extends java.lang.IncompatibleClassChangeError {
  // Constructors
  public IllegalAccessError();
  public IllegalAccessError(String s);
}
```

 IllegalAccessError   IllegalAccessError   lang

```
public IllegalAccessError()
```

This constructor creates a default illegal-access error with no detail message.

IllegalAccessError IllegalAccessError lang

```
public IllegalAccessError(String s)
```

This constructor creates an illegal-access error with the specified detail message, which contains information specific to this particular error.

▶ s is the detail message.

 ## IncompatibleClassChangeError lang

➕ LinkageError

This error class signals that an incompatible change has been made to some class definition. The definition for the IncompatibleClassChangeError class follows:

```
public class java.lang.IncompatibleClassChangeError
  extends java.lang.LinkageError {
  // Constructors
  public IncompatibleClassChangeError();
  public IncompatibleClassChangeError(String s);
}
```

 IncompatibleClassChangeError IncompatibleClassChangeError lang

```
public IncompatibleClassChangeError()
```

This constructor creates a default incompatible-class-change error with no detail message.

 IncompatibleClassChangeError IncompatibleClassChangeError lang

```
public IncompatibleClassChangeError(String s)
```

This constructor creates an incompatible-class-change error with the specified detail message, which contains information specific to this particular error.

▶ s is the detail message.

 ## InstantiationError lang

 IncompatibleClassChangeError

This error class signals an attempt to instantiate an abstract class or an interface. The definition for the InstantiationError class follows:

```
public class java.lang.InstantiationError
  extends java.lang.IncompatibleClassChangeError {
  // Constructors
  public InstantiationError();
  public InstantiationError(String s);
}
```

InstantiationError   InstantiationError   lang

```
public InstantiationError()
```

This constructor creates a default instantiation error with no detail message.

 InstantiationError   InstantiationError   lang

```
public InstantiationError(String s)
```

This constructor creates an instantiation error with the specified detail message, which contains information specific to this particular error.

    s is the detail message.

 # InternalError   lang

    VirtualMachineError

This error class signals that some unexpected internal error has occurred. The definition for the InternalError class follows:

```
public class java.lang.InternalError
  extends java.lang.VirtualMachineError {
  // Constructors
  public InternalError();
  public InternalError(String s);
}
```

 InternalError   InternalError   lang

```
public InternalError()
```

This constructor creates a default internal error with no detail message.

 InternalError   InternalError   lang

```
public InternalError(String s)
```

This constructor creates an internal error with the specified detail message, which contains information specific to this particular error.

    s is the detail message.

LinkageError lang

 Error

This error class signals that a class has some dependency on another class, but that the latter class has incompatibly changed after the compilation of the former class. The definition for the `LinkageError` class follows:

```
public class java.lang.LinkageError extends java.lang.Error {
    // Constructors
    public LinkageError();
    public LinkageError(String s);
}
```

 ### LinkageError LinkageError lang

```
public LinkageError()
```

This constructor creates a default linkage error with no detail message.

 ### LinkageError LinkageError lang

```
public LinkageError(String s)
```

This constructor creates a linkage error with the specified detail message, which contains information specific to this particular error.

▶ s is the detail message.

 # NoClassDefFoundError lang

 LinkageError

This error class signals that a class definition could not be found. The definition for the `NoClassDefFoundError` class follows:

```
public class java.lang.NoClassDefFoundError
    extends java.lang.LinkageError {
    // Constructors
    public NoClassDefFoundError();
    public NoClassDefFoundError(String s);
}
```

NoClassDefFoundError NoClassDefFoundError lang

```
public NoClassDefFoundError()
```

This constructor creates a default no-class-definition-found error with no detail message.

NoClassDefFoundError   NoClassDefFoundError   lang

```
public NoClassDefFoundError(String s)
```

This constructor creates a no-class-definition-found error with the specified detail message, which contains information specific to this particular error.

► s is the detail message.

  # NoSuchFieldError   lang

 IncompatibleClassChangeError

This error class signals an attempt to access a member variable that doesn't exist. The definition for the NoSuchFieldError class follows:

```
public class java.lang.NoSuchFieldError
  extends java.lang.IncompatibleClassChangeError {
  // Constructors
  public NoSuchFieldError();
  public NoSuchFieldError(String s);
}
```

 NoSuchFieldError   NoSuchFieldError   lang

```
public NoSuchFieldError()
```

This constructor creates a default no-such-field error with no detail message.

 NoSuchFieldError   NoSuchFieldError   lang

```
public NoSuchFieldError(String s)
```

This constructor creates a no-such-field error with the specified detail message, which contains information specific to this particular error.

► s is the detail message.

  # NoSuchMethodError   lang

 IncompatibleClassChangeError

This error class signals an attempt to call a method that doesn't exist. The definition for the NoSuchMethodError class follows:

```
public class java.lang.NoSuchMethodError
  extends java.lang.IncompatibleClassChangeError {
  // Constructors
  public NoSuchMethodError();
  public NoSuchMethodError(String s);
}
```

NoSuchMethodError NoSuchMethodError lang

```
public NoSuchMethodError()
```

This constructor creates a default no-such-method error with no detail message.

 NoSuchMethodError NoSuchMethodError lang

```
public NoSuchMethodError(String s)
```

This constructor creates a no-such-method error with the specified detail message, which contains information specific to this particular error.

▶ s is the detail message.

 # OutOfMemoryError lang

✚ VirtualMachineError

This error class signals that the Java runtime system is out of memory. The definition for the `OutOfMemoryError` class follows:

```
public class java.lang.OutOfMemoryError
  extends java.lang.VirtualMachineError {
  // Constructors
  public OutOfMemoryError();
  public OutOfMemoryError(String s);
}
```

 OutOfMemoryError OutOfMemoryError lang

```
public OutOfMemoryError()
```

This constructor creates a default out-of-memory error with no detail message.

 OutOfMemoryError OutOfMemoryError lang

```
public OutOfMemoryError(String s)
```

This constructor creates an out-of-memory error with the specified detail message, which contains information specific to this particular error.

▶ s is the detail message.

StackOverflowError

 VirtualMachineError

This error class signals that a stack overflow has occurred. The definition for the StackOverflowError class follows:

```
public class java.lang.StackOverflowError
  extends java.lang.VirtualMachineError {
  // Constructors
  public StackOverflowError();
  public StackOverflowError(String s);
}
```

StackOverflowError StackOverflowError lang

```
public StackOverflowError()
```

This constructor creates a default stack-overflow error with no detail message.

StackOverflowError StackOverflowError lang

```
public StackOverflowError(String s)
```

This constructor creates a stack-overflow error with the specified detail message, which contains information specific to this particular error.

 s is the detail message.

 # ThreadDeath

 Error

This error class signals that a thread is being stopped abnormally via the stop method. The definition for the ThreadDeath class follows:

```
public class java.lang.ThreadDeath extends java.lang.Error {
  public ThreadDeath();
}
```

ThreadDeath ThreadDeath lang

```
public ThreadDeath()
```

This constructor creates a default thread death object.

UnknownError lang

 VirtualMachineError

This error class signals that an unknown but serious error has occurred. The definition for the UnknownError class follows:

```
public class java.lang.UnknownError extends java.lang.VirtualMachineError {
    // Constructors
    public UnknownError();
    public UnknownError(String s);
}
```

 UnknownError UnknownError lang

```
public UnknownError()
```

This constructor creates a default unknown error with no detail message.

 UnknownError UnknownError lang

```
public UnknownError(String s)
```

This constructor creates an unknown error with the specified detail message, which contains information specific to this particular error.

 s is the detail message.

 # UnsatisfiedLinkError lang

 LinkageError

This error class signals that a native implementation of a method declared native cannot be found. The definition for the UnsatisfiedLinkError class follows:

```
public class java.lang.UnsatisfiedLinkError extends java.lang.LinkageError {
    // Constructors
    public UnsatisfiedLinkError();
    public UnsatisfiedLinkError(String s);
}
```

 UnsatisfiedLinkError UnsatisfiedLinkError lang

```
public UnsatisfiedLinkError()
```

This constructor creates a default unsatisfied-link error with no detail message.

UnsatisfiedLinkError   UnsatisfiedLinkError   lang

```
public UnsatisfiedLinkError(String s)
```

This constructor creates an unsatisfied-link error with the specified detail message, which contains information specific to this particular error.

▶ s is the detail message.

 # VerifyError   lang

 LinkageError

This error class signals that a class has failed the runtime verification test. The definition for the VerifyError class follows:

```
public class java.lang.VerifyError extends java.lang.LinkageError {
  // Constructors
  public VerifyError();
  public VerifyError(String s);
}
```

 VerifyError   VerifyError   lang

```
public VerifyError()
```

This constructor creates a default verify error with no detail message.

 VerifyError   VerifyError   lang

```
public VerifyError(String s)
```

This constructor creates a verify error with the specified detail message, which contains information specific to this particular error.

▶ s is the detail message.

VirtualMachineError   lang

 Error

This error class signals that the Java virtual machine is broken or has run out of resources necessary for it to continue operating. The definition for the VirtualMachineError class follows:

```
public class java.lang.VirtualMachineError extends java.lang.Error {
  // Constructors
  public VirtualMachineError();
  public VirtualMachineError(String s);
}
```

VirtualMachineError

```
public VirtualMachineError()
```

This constructor creates a default virtual-machine error with no detail message.

VirtualMachineError

```
public VirtualMachineError(String s)
```

This constructor creates a virtual-machine error with the specified detail message, which contains information specific to this particular error.

▶ s is the detail message.

33

Package java.net

by Bryan Morgan

The `java.net` package contains the most common classes used for networking. This includes classes to create and store sockets, data packets, and URLs as well as a set of interfaces. The `java.net` package's classes and interfaces are described in detail throughout the remainder of this chapter. Table 33.1 lists all classes, interfaces, and exceptions that have public members. Figure 33.1 shows a graphic representation of the hierarchy of the package.

FIGURE 33.1.

Contents of package `java.net`.

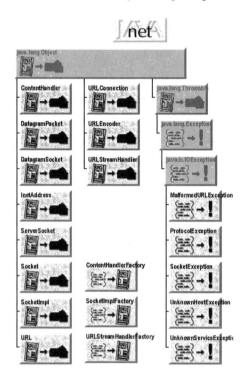

Table 33.1. Contents of package `java.net`.

Class Index	Interface Index	Exception Index
ContentHandler	ContentHandlerFactory	MalformedURLException
DatagramPacket	SocketImplFactory	ProtocolException
DatagramSocket	URLStreamHandlerFactory	SocketException
InetAddress		UnknownHostException
ServerSocket		UnknownServiceException
Socket		
SocketImpl		
URL		
URLConnection		

ContentHandler

 Object

The class hierarchy for the `ContentHandler` class derives from class `java.lang.Object`. (See Listing 33.1.) The `ContentHandler` class is used as a base class for classes that will handle specific MIME content types. The `ContentHandlerFactory` interface is used to select the appropriate `ContentHandler` for a given content type. `ContentHandler`'s overall derivation can be seen in Figure 33.1.

> **Listing 33.1. Public members of `java.net.ContentHandler`.**
> ```
> abstract public class ContentHandler {
>   abstract public Object getContent(URLConnection urlc) throws IOException
> }
> ```

 getContent ContentHandler net

```
abstract public Object getContent(URLConnection urlc)
```

The `getContent()` method accepts a `URLConnection` argument positioned at the beginning of an input stream and constructs an object from the input stream.

▶ `urlc` is a `URLConnection` object representing the input stream to be read in by the `ContentHandler`.

↵ An `Object` object that was constructed from the specified `URLConnection`.

↪ An `IOException` if the input stream could not be read.

DatagramPacket net

 Object

The class hierarchy for the `DatagramPacket` class derives from class `java.lang.Object`. (See Listing 33.2.) The `DatagramPacket` class is used to store packet data such as data, length, Internet address, and port. `DatagramPacket`'s overall derivation can be seen in Figure 33.1.

Listing 33.2. Public members of `java.net.DatagramPacket`.

```
public final class DatagramPacket {
  public DatagramPacket(byte ibuf[], int ilength)
  public DatagramPacket(byte ibuf[], int ilength, InetAddress iaddr, int iport)
  public InetAddress getAddress()
  public int getPort()
  public byte[] getData()
  public int getLength()
}
```

 DatagramPacket DatagramPacket net

```
public DatagramPacket(byte ibuf[], int ilength)
```

This `DatagramPacket` constructor constructs a `DatagramPacket` object to be used for receiving datagrams.

▶ ibuf is an array of bytes that will be used to store the `DatagramPacket`.

▶ ilength is an integer value specifying the size of the `DatagramPacket`.

 DatagramPacket DatagramPacket net

```
public DatagramPacket(byte ibuf[], int ilength, InetAddress iaddr, int iport)
```

This `DatagramPacket` constructor constructs a `DatagramPacket` object to be sent.

▶ ibuf is an array of bytes that will be used to store the `DatagramPacket`.

▶ ilength is an integer value specifying the size of the `DatagramPacket`.

▶ iaddr is the destination IP address.

▶ iport is the destination port.

---

 getAddress DatagramPacket net

```
public InetAddress getAddress()
```

The `getAddress()` method returns the IP address value of the `DatagramPacket`.

↵ An InetAddress object containing the IP address of the `DatagramPacket`.

---

 getPort DatagramPacket net

```
public int getPort()
```

The `getPort()` method returns the port value of the `DatagramPacket`.

↵ An integer value containing the port address of the `DatagramPacket`.

getData DatagramPacket `net`

```
public byte[] getData()
```

The `getData()` method returns the array of `DatagramPacket` values.

An array of bytes containing the contents of the `DatagramPacket`.

 getLength DatagramPacket `net`

```
public int getLength()
```

The `getLength()` method returns the length of the `DatagramPacket`.

An integer value containing the length of the `DatagramPacket`.

 # DatagramSocket `net`

 Object

The class hierarchy for the `DatagramSocket` class derives from class `java.lang.Object`. (See Listing 33.3.) The `DatagramSocket` class is used to designate a dedicated socket for implementing unreliable datagrams. These packages are unreliable because there is no verification scheme for ensuring that the packets were not corrupted during transmission. `DatagramSocket`'s overall derivation can be seen in Figure 33.1.

Listing 33.3. Public members of `java.net.DatagramSocket`.

```
public class DatagramSocket {
  public DatagramSocket() throws SocketException
  public DatagramSocket(int port) throws SocketException
  public void send(DatagramPacket p) throws IOException
  public synchronized void receive(DatagramPacket p) throws IOException
  public int getLocalPort()
  public synchronized void close()
}
```

 DatagramSocket DatagramSocket `net`

```
public DatagramSocket() throws SocketException
```

The `DatagramSocket` constructor is used to implement an unreliable `Datagram` connection.

 none

 This constructor throws a `SocketException` if the socket could not be created.

DatagramSocket **DatagramSocket** net

```
public DatagramSocket(int port) throws SocketException
```

This `DatagramSocket` constructor implements an unreliable `Datagram` connection using the specified port value.

▶ `port` is an integer value specifying the port to be used for the socket.

 This constructor throws a `SocketException` if the socket could not be created.

 send **DatagramSocket** net

```
public void send(DatagramPacket p) throws IOException
```

The `send()` method sends a `DatagramPacket` to the destination address specified in the `DatagramPacket`'s address value. For more information on the `DatagramPacket` class, see the documentation earlier in this chapter.

▶ `p` is a `DatagramPacket` object containing data to be sent through the socket.

 This method throws an `IOException` if an I/O exception has occurred.

 receive **DatagramSocket** net

```
public synchronized void receive(DatagramPacket p) throws IOException
```

The `receive()` method receives a `DatagramPacket`. This method will block until the `DatagramPacket` has been received. For more information on the `DatagramPacket` class, see the documentation earlier in this chapter.

▶ `p` is the `DatagramPacket` to be received.

This method throws an `IOException` if an I/O exception has occurred.

getLocalPort **DatagramSocket** net

```
public int getLocalPort()
```

The `getLocalPort()` method returns the port on the local machine to which this socket is bound.

 An integer value containing the port value to which this socket is bound.

close **DatagramSocket** net

```
public synchronized void close()
```

The `close()` method closes the `DatagramSocket`.

↵ none

 InetAddress `net`

 Object

The class hierarchy for the InetAddress class derives from class java.lang.Object. (See Listing 33.4.) The InetAddress class is used to represent Internet addresses. InetAddress's overall derivation can be seen in Figure 33.1.

Listing 33.4. Public members of java.net.InetAddress.
```
public final class InetAddress {
  public String getHostName()
  public byte[] getAddress()
  public String getHostAddress()
  public int hashCode()
  public boolean equals(Object obj)
  public String toString()
  public static synchronized InetAddress getByName(String host) throws
  ➥ UnknownHostException
  public static synchronized InetAddress getAllByName(String host)[] throws
  ➥ UnknownHostException
  public static InetAddress getLocalHost() throws UnknownHostException
}
```

getHostName InetAddress `net`

`public String getHostName()`

The getHostName() method returns the name of the host for this InetAddress. If the host is null, the returned string will contain any of the local machine's available network addresses.

↵ A String object containing the name of the host for this InetAddress.

getAddress InetAddress `net`

`public byte[] getAddress()`

The getAddress() method returns an array of bytes containing the raw IP address in network byte order.

↵ A byte array containing the raw IP address of this InetAddress in network byte order.

getHostAddress InetAddress `net`

`public String getHostAddress()`

The getHostAddress() method returns the IP address string %d.%d.%d.%d.

↵ A String value containing the raw IP address using the standard IP address format (%d.%d.%d.%d).

hashCode   InetAddress   net

```
public int hashCode()
```

The hashCode() method returns a hash code for this InetAddress.

↵   An integer value representing this InetAddress's hash code.

equals   InetAddress   net

```
public boolean equals(Object obj)
```

The equals() method is used to compare this InetAddress object to the specified object.

▶   obj is the object to be compared with the InetAddress.

↵   A Boolean value that will be true if the objects are equal, false if not.

toString   InetAddress   net

```
public String toString()
```

The toString() method is used to return a string representation of the InetAddress.

↵   A String value containing information about the InetAddress.

getByName   InetAddress   net

```
public static synchronized InetAddress getByName(String host) throws
➥ UnknownHostException
```

The getByName() method returns an InetAddress object based on the specified hostname.

▶   host is a string object specifying the name of the host.

↵   An InetAddress object containing the internet address information for the specified host.

☞   An UnknownHostException if the specified host is invalid or unknown.

getAllByName   InetAddress   net

```
public static synchronized InetAddress getAllByName(String host)[] throws
➥ UnknownHostException
```

The getAllByName() method returns an array of InetAddress objects representing all of the addresses for the specified host.

▶   host is a String object specifying the name of the host.

↵   An array of all corresponding InetAddresses for the specified host.

☞   An UnknownHostException if the specified host is invalid or unknown.

getLocalHost InetAddress /net/

```
public static InetAddress getLocalHost() throws UnknownHostException
```

The getLocalHost() returns an InetAddress object representing the address of the local host.

↵ An InetAddress object containing the Internet address information for the local host.

ServerSocket /net/

+ Object

The class hierarchy for the ServerSocket class derives from class java.lang.Object. (See Listing 33.5.) The ServerSocket class is used to encapsulate a server socket. The setSocketFactory() method is used to change the ServerSocket's implementation based on specific firewalls. ServerSocket's overall derivation can be seen in Figure 33.1.

Listing 33.5. Public members of java.net.ServerSocket.

```
public final class ServerSocket {
   public ServerSocket(int port) throws IOException
   public ServerSocket(int port, int backlog) throws IOException
   public InetAddress getInetAddress()
   public int getLocalPort()
   public Socket accept() throws IOException
   public void close() throws IOException
   public String toString()
   public static synchronized void setSocketFactory(SocketImplFactory fac) throws
   ➥ IOException
}
```

 ServerSocket ServerSocket /net/

```
public ServerSocket(int port) throws IOException
```

The ServerSocket() constructor creates a server socket on the specified port.

▶ port is an integer value specifying the port to create the socket on.

⟋• An IOException if an I/O exception has occurred.

 ServerSocket ServerSocket /net/

```
public ServerSocket(int port, int backlog) throws IOException
```

This ServerSocket() constructor creates a server socket on the specified port and listens to it for a specified time.

 port is an integer value specifying the port to create the socket on.

▶ `backlog` is used to specify the amount of time to listen to a connection.

🐾 An `IOException` if an I/O exception has occurred.

getInetAddress ServerSocket net

```
public InetAddress getInetAddress()
```

The `getInetAddress()` method returns an `InetAddress` object specifying the address to which this socket is connected. For more information on the `InetAddress` class, see the documentation earlier in this chapter.

↩ An `InetAddress` object containing the address information to which the socket is connected.

getLocalPort ServerSocket net

```
public int getLocalPort()
```

The `getLocalPort()` method returns the local port on which the socket is currently listening.

↩ An integer value representing the port on the local machine to which the `ServerSocket` is listening.

accept ServerSocket net

```
public Socket accept() throws IOException
```

The `accept()` method is used to accept a connection. This method will block all others until a connection is made.

↩ A `Socket` object after the connection has been accepted.

🐾 An `IOException` if an I/O error occurred while waiting for the connection.

close ServerSocket net

```
public void close() throws IOException
```

The `close()` method closes the socket's connection.

🐾 An `IOException` if an I/O error occurred while closing the server socket.

toString ServerSocket net

```
public String toString()
```

The `toString()` method returns a string representation of the `ServerSocket`.

↩ A `String` object containing the implementation address and implementation port of the `ServerSocket`.

setSocketFactory ServerSocket net

```
public static synchronized void setSocketFactory(SocketImplFactory fac) throws
➥ IOException, SocketException
```

The `setSocketFactory()` method sets the server `SocketImplFactory` for use by this `ServerSocket`. This factory can only be set once. For more information on the `SocketImplFactory` interface, see the documentation later in this chapter.

▶ `fac` is a `SocketImplFactory` interface to be used by this `ServerSocket`.

An `IOException` if there was an I/O error when setting the `SocketImplFactory`.

A `SocketException` if the `SocketImplFactory` has already been set.

Socket net

 Object

The class hierarchy for the `Socket` class derives from class `java.lang.Object`. (See Listing 33.6.) The `Socket` class is used to implement socket functionality. The `setSocketImplFactory()` method is used to change the `Socket`'s implementation based on specific firewalls. `Socket`'s overall derivation can be seen in Figure 33.1.

Listing 33.6. Public members of `java.net.Socket`.
```
public final class Socket {
  public Socket(String host, int port) throws UnknownHostException, IOException
  public Socket(String host, int port, boolean stream) throws IOException
  public Socket(InetAddress address, int port) throws IOException
  public Socket(InetAddress address, int port, boolean stream) throws
  ➥ IOException
  public InetAddress getInetAddress()
  public int getPort()
  public int getLocalPort()
  public InputStream getInputStream() throws IOException
  public OutputStream getOutputStream() throws IOException
  public synchronized void close() throws IOException
  public String toString()
  public static synchronized void setSocketImplFactory(SocketImplFactory fac)
  ➥ throws IOException
}
```

 Socket Socket net

```
public Socket(String host, int port) throws UnknownHostException, IOException
```

This `Socket()` constructor creates a stream socket to the specified port on the specified host.

▶ `host` is a `String` object containing the host name to create the socket on.

▶ port is an integer value representing the port to create the socket on.

🐾 An UnknownHostException if the host name is unrecognized or invalid.

🐾 An IOException if an I/O error occurred while creating the socket.

Socket  Socket | net

```
public Socket(String host, int port, boolean stream) throws IOException
```

This Socket() constructor creates a stream socket to the specified port on the specified host. The Boolean stream value can be used to specify a stream socket or a datagram socket.

▶ host is a String object containing the host name to create the socket on.

▶ port is an integer value representing the port to create the socket on.

▶ stream is a Boolean value that is true if a stream socket is to be created, false if a datagram socket is to be created.

🐾 An IOException if an I/O error occurred while creating the socket.

Socket  Socket | net

```
public Socket(InetAddress address, int port) throws IOException
```

This Socket() constructor creates a stream socket to the specified port at the specified InetAddress. For more information on the InetAddress class, see the documentation earlier in this chapter.

▶ address is an InetAddress specifying the address at which to create the socket.

▶ port is an integer value representing the port on which to create the socket.

🐾 An IOException if an I/O error occurred while creating the socket.

Socket Socket | net

```
public Socket(InetAddress address, int port, boolean stream) throws IOException
```

This Socket() constructor creates a stream socket to the specified port at the specified address. The Boolean stream value can be used to specify a stream socket or a datagram socket. For more information on the InetAddress class, see the documentation earlier in this chapter.

▶ address is an InetAddress specifying the address at which to create the socket.

▶ port is an integer value representing the port on which to create the socket.

▶ stream is a Boolean value that is true if a stream socket is to be created, false if a datagram socket is to be created.

🐾 An IOException if an I/O error occurred while creating the socket.

getInetAddress Socket net

```
public InetAddress getInetAddress()
```

The `getInetAddress()` method is used to return the address to which the socket is connected. For more information on the `InetAddress` class, see the documentation earlier in this chapter.

 An `InetAddress` object containing information about the address to which the socket is connected.

 ## getPort Socket net

```
public int getPort()
```

The `getPort()` method returns the remote port to which the socket is connected.

 An integer value representing the remote port number to which the socket is connected.

 ## getLocalPort Socket net

```
public int getLocalPort()
```

The `getLocalPort()` method returns the local port to which the socket is connected.

An integer value representing the local port number to which the socket is connected.

 ## getInputStream Socket net

```
public InputStream getInputStream() throws IOException
```

The `getInputStream()` method returns an `InputStream` for this socket. For more information on the `InputStream` class, see the documentation in Chapter 31, "Package `java.io`."

An `InputStream` object to be used as the socket's input stream.

An `IOException` if an I/O error occurred while retrieving the input stream.

 ## getOutputStream Socket net

```
public OutputStream getOutputStream() throws IOException
```

The `getOutputStream()` method returns an `OutputStream` for this socket. For more information on the `OutputStream` class, see the documentation in Chapter 31.

An `OutputStream` object to be used as the socket's output stream.

An `IOException` if an I/O error occurred while retrieving the output stream.

close Socket

```
public synchronized void close() throws IOException
```

The `close()` method closes the socket's connection.

 An `IOException` if an I/O error occurred while closing the socket.

 toString Socket net

```
public String toString()
```

The `toString()` method returns a `String` representation of the socket.

A `String` object containing the `Socket` information.

 setSocketImplFactory Socket net

```
public static synchronized void setSocketImplFactory(SocketImplFactory fac)
➥ throws IOException
```

The `setSocketImplFactory()` method sets the `SocketImplFactory` interface for this socket. The factory can only be specified once. For more information on the `SocketImplFactory` interface, see the documentation later in this chapter.

▶ `fac` is a `SocketImplFactory` interface to be used by this `Socket`.

 An `IOException` if an I/O error occurred while setting the `SocketImplFactory`.

SocketImpl

 Object

The class hierarchy for the `SocketImpl` class derives from class `java.lang.Object`. (See Listing 33.7.) The `SocketImpl` class is an abstract base class provided as a template for socket implementations. `SocketImpl`'s overall derivation can be seen in Figure 33.1.

Listing 33.7. Public members of `java.net.SocketImpl`.
```
public abstract class SocketImpl {
  public String toString()
}
```

toString SocketImpl net

```
public String toString()
```

The toString() method returns a String representation of the SocketImpl class.

↵   A String object containing the port and address of this socket.

 # URL net

 Object

The class hierarchy for the URL class derives from class java.lang.Object. (See Listing 33.8.) The URL class is used to represent a Uniform Resource Locator. A URL is a reference to an object on the Web such as an FTP site, an e-mail address, or an HTML page on a Web server. URL's overall derivation can be seen in Figure 33.1.

Listing 33.8. Public members of java.net.URL.

```
public final class URL {
  public URL(String protocol, String host, int port, String file) throws
  ➡ MalformedURLException
  public URL(String protocol, String host, String file) throws
  ➡ MalformedURLException
  public URL(String spec) throws MalformedURLException
  public URL(URL context, String spec) throws MalformedURLException
  public int getPort()
  public String getProtocol()
  public String getHost()
  public String getFile()
  public String getRef()
  public boolean equals(Object obj)
  public int hashCode()
  public boolean sameFile(URL other)
  public String toString()
  public String toExternalForm()
  public URLConnection openConnection() throws java.io.IOException
  public final InputStream openStream() throws java.io.IOException
  public final Object getContent() throws java.io.IOException
  public static synchronized void
  ➡ setURLStreamHandlerFactory(URLStreamHandlerFactory fac)
}
```

 URL URL net

```
public URL(String protocol, String host, int port, String file) throws
➡ MalformedURLException
```

This URL() constructor creates a URL using the specified protocol, host, port, and host filename.

▶   protocol is a String object specifying the protocol to be used.

▶ host is a String object specifying the host name.

▶ port is an integer value specifying the port.

▶ file is a String object specifying the filename on the host.

🐾 A MalformedURLException if the protocol was unknown or invalid.

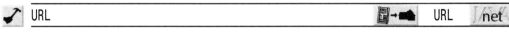

```
public URL(String protocol, String host, String file) throws
➥ MalformedURLException
```

This URL() constructor creates a URL using the specified protocol, host, and host filename. The port number will be the default port used for the specified protocol.

▶ protocol is a String object specifying the protocol to be used.

▶ host is a String object specifying the host name.

▶ file is a String object specifying the filename on the host.

🐾 A MalformedURLException if the protocol was unknown or invalid.

```
public URL(String spec) throws MalformedURLException
```

This URL() constructor creates a URL using the specified unparsed URL.

▶ spec is a String object containing an unparsed URL string.

🐾 A MalformedURLException if the specified unparsed URL was invalid.

```
public URL(URL context, String spec) throws MalformedURLException
```

This URL() constructor creates a URL using the specified context and unparsed URL. If the unparsed URL is an absolute URL, it is used as is; otherwise, it is used in combination with the specified context. The context may be null.

▶ context is a URL object specifying the context to be used in combination with the unparsed URL string (spec parameter).

▶ spec is a String object containing an unparsed URL string.

🐾 A MalformedURLException if the specified unparsed URL was invalid.

getPort

```
public int getPort()
```

The getPort() method returns the port number for this URL.

An integer value representing the port number for this URL. This will be –1 if the port has not been set.

getProtocol

```
public String getProtocol()
```

The getProtocol()method returns a string representing the protocol used by this URL.

A String object containing the protocol name.

getHost

```
public String getHost()
```

The getHost() method returns a string containing the host name.

A String object containing the host name.

getFile

```
public String getFile()
```

The getFile() method returns a string containing the host filename.

A String object containing the name of the file on the host.

getRef

```
public String getRef()
```

The getRef() method returns the ref (if any) that was specified in the unparsed string used to create this URL.

A String object containing the URL's ref.

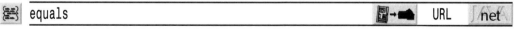

equals

```
public boolean equals(Object obj)
```

The equals() method can be used to compare this URL to another object.

▶ obj is an Object object that will be compared with this URL.

A Boolean value that will be true if the objects are equals, false if not.

hashCode  URL   net

```
public int hashCode()
```

The hashCode() method will return a hash code value for the URL.

↵ An integer value representing the hash code value of this URL.

sameFile  URL   net

```
public boolean sameFile(URL other)
```

The sameFile() method can be used to determine if the specified file is the same file used to create this URL.

▶ other is a URL object specifying the location of another file.

↵ A Boolean value that will be true if the files are equals, false if not.

toString  URL   net

```
public String toString()
```

The toString() method returns a string representation of the URL.

↵ A String object containing a textual representation of the URL including the protocol, host, port, and filename.

toExternalForm  URL   net

```
public String toExternalForm()
```

↵ The toExternalForm() method is used to reverse the parsing of the URL.

A String object containing the textual representation of the fully qualified URL (after it has been unparsed).

openConnection  URL   net

```
public URLConnection openConnection() throws java.io.IOException
```

The openConnection() method will open a URLConnection to the object specified by the URL. For more information on the URLConnection class, see the documentation later in this chapter.

↵ A URLConnection object that represents a connection to the URL.

☛ An IOException if an I/O error occurred while creating the URLConnection.

openStream URL net

```
public final InputStream openStream() throws java.io.IOException
```

The openStream() method opens an InputStream. For more information on the InputStream class, see the documentation in Chapter 31.

↵ An InputStream representing an input stream for the URL.

↗ An IOException if an I/O error occurred while creating the input stream.

 getContent URL net

```
public final Object getContent() throws java.io.IOException
```

The getContent() method retrieves the contents from the opened connection.

↵ An Object object representing the contents that are retrieved from the connection.

↗ An IOException if an I/O error occurred while retrieving the content.

 setURLStreamHandlerFactory URL net

```
public static synchronized void
➡ setURLStreamHandlerFactory(URLStreamHandlerFactory fac)
```

The setURLStreamHandlerFactory() method sets the URLStreamHandlerFactory interface for this URL. The factory can only be specified once. For more information on the URLStreamHandlerFactory interface, see the documentation later in this chapter.

▶ fac is a URLStreamHandlerFactory interface to be used by this URL.

↗ An Error if this factory has already been specified.

 URLConnection net

✚ Object

The class hierarchy for the URLConnection class derives from class java.lang.Object. (See Listing 33.9.) The URLConnection class is an abstract base class used to represent a URL connection. It must be subclassed in order to provide true functionality. URLConnection's overall derivation can be seen in Figure 33.1.

Listing 33.9. Public members of java.net.URLConnection.
```
abstract public class URLConnection {
  abstract public void connect() throws IOException
  public URL getURL()
```

continues

Listing 33.9. continued

```
    public int getContentLength()
    public String getContentType()
    public String getContentEncoding()
    public long getExpiration()
    public long getDate()
    public long getLastModified()
    public String getHeaderField(String name)
    public int getHeaderFieldInt(String name, int Default)
    public long getHeaderFieldDate(String name, long Default)
    public String getHeaderFieldKey(int n)
    public String getHeaderField(int n)
    public Object getContent() throws IOException
    public InputStream getInputStream() throws IOException
    public OutputStream getOutputStream() throws IOException
    public String toString()
    public void setDoInput(boolean doinput)
    public void setDoOutput(boolean dooutput)
    public boolean getDoOutput()
    public void setAllowUserInteraction(boolean allowuserinteraction)
    public boolean getAllowUserInteraction()
    public static void
  ➥ setDefaultAllowUserInteraction(boolean defaultallowuserinteraction)
    public static boolean getDefaultAllowUserInteraction()
    public void setUseCaches(boolean usecaches)
    public boolean getUseCaches()
    public void setIfModifiedSince(long ifmodifiedsince)
    public long getIfModifiedSince()
    public boolean getDefaultUseCaches()
    public void setDefaultUseCaches(boolean defaultusecaches)
    public void setRequestProperty(String key, String value)
    public String getRequestProperty(String key)
    public static void setDefaultRequestProperty(String key, String value)
    public static String getDefaultRequestProperty(String key)
    public static synchronized void
  ➥ setContentHandlerFactory(ContentHandlerFactory fac)
}
```

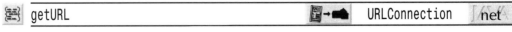

connect   URLConnection   net

```
abstract public void connect() throws IOException
```

The connect() method is used to connect the URLConnection after it has been created. Operations that depend on being connected will call this method to automatically connect. Calling this method after the connection has already been made does nothing.

 An IOException if an I/O error occurred while the connection was attempted.

getURL   URLConnection   net

```
public URL getURL()
```

The getURL() method returns the URL for this URLConnection.

A URL object. For more information on the URL class, see the documentation earlier in this chapter.

getContentLength URLConnection net

```
public int getContentLength()
```

The getContentLength() method returns the length of the content.

An integer value containing the length of the content. This value will be –1 if the length is not known.

getContentType URLConnection net

```
public String getContentType()
```

The getContentType() method returns the type of the content.

A String object containing the type of the content. This value will be null if the type is not known.

getContentEncoding URLConnection net

```
public String getContentEncoding()
```

The getContentEncoding() method returns the encoding of the content.

A String object containing the encoding of the content. This value will be null if the encoding is not known.

getExpiration URLConnection net

```
public long getExpiration()
```

The getExpiration() method will return the expiration of the object.

A long value containing the expiration of the object. This value will be 0 if the expiration is not known.

getDate URLConnection net

```
public long getDate()
```

The getDate() method will return the date of the object.

A long value containing the date of the object. This value will be 0 if the date is not known.

getLastModified   URLConnection   net

```
public long getLastModified()
```

The getLastModified() will return the last modified date of the object.

↵ A long value containing the last modified date of the object. This value will be 0 if the last modified date is not known.

getHeaderField   URLConnection   net

```
public String getHeaderField(String name)
```

The getHeaderField() method returns the contents of the header field based on the specified field name.

▶ name is a String object specifying the name of the header field to be returned.

↵ A String object containing the contents of the specified header field. This value will be null if the contents are not known.

getHeaderFieldInt   URLConnection   net

```
public int getHeaderFieldInt(String name, int Default)
```

The getHeaderFieldInt() method returns the preparsed contents of the specified header field.

▶ name is a String object specifying the name of the header field to be returned.

▶ Default is an integer value containing the value to be returned if the field is missing.

↵ An integer value containing the preparsed header field value.

getHeaderFieldDate   URLConnection   net

```
public long getHeaderFieldDate(String name, long Default)
```

The getHeaderFieldDate() method returns the contents of the specified header field parsed as a date.

▶ name is a String object specifying the name of the header field to be returned.

▶ Default is an integer value containing the value to be returned if the field is missing.

↵ A long value containing the header field value parsed as a date.

getHeaderFieldKey   URLConnection   net

```
public String getHeaderFieldKey(int n)
```

The getHeaderFieldKey() method returns the key for the specified header field.

▶ n is the position of the header field to be returned.

↵ A `String` object containing the key for the specified header field. This value will be `null` if there are fewer than *n* header fields.

getHeaderField  URLConnection `net`

```
public String getHeaderField(int n)
```

The `getHeaderField()` method returns the specified header field value.

▶ n is the position of the header field to be returned.

↵ A `String` object containing the contents of the specified header field. This value will be `null` if there are fewer than *n* header fields.

getContent ▦→◆ URLConnection `net`

```
public Object getContent() throws IOException
```

The `getContent()` method returns the object referred to by this `URLConnection`.

↵ An `Object` object that was referred to by this URL.

➤ An `IOException` if an I/O error occurred while retrieving the content.

getInputStream ▦→◆ URLConnection `net`

```
public InputStream getInputStream() throws IOException
```

The `getInputStream()` method returns an `InputStream` object to be used as an input stream to read from the object. For more information on the `InputStream` class, see the documentation in Chapter 31.

↵ An `InputStream` object to be used to read from the object.

➤ An `IOException` if an I/O error occurred while creating the input stream.

getOutputStream ▦→◆ URLConnection `net`

```
public OutputStream getOutputStream() throws IOException
```

The `getOutputStream()` method returns an `OutputStream` object to be used as an output stream to write to the object. For more information on the `OutputStream` class, see the documentation in Chapter 31.

↵ An `OutputStream` object to be used to write to the object.

➤ An `IOException` if an I/O error occurred while creating the output stream.

toString   URLConnection   net

```
public String toString()
```

The toString() method returns a string representation of the URLConnection.

 A String object containing a textual representation of the URLConnection object.

 ### setDoInput   URLConnection   net

```
public void setDoInput(boolean doinput)
```

The setDoInput() method sets the functionality of the URLConnection. If the parameter is true, the URLConnection will be used for input. If it is false, it will be used for output. (The default functionality is input.)

▶ doinput is a Boolean value that will be true if the URLConnection is to be used for input, false if for output.

 ### setDoOutput   URLConnection   net

```
public void setDoOutput(boolean dooutput)
```

The setDoOutput() method sets the functionality of the URLConnection. If the parameter is true, the URLConnection will be used for output. If it is false, it will be used for input. (The default functionality is input.)

▶ dooutput is a Boolean value that will be true if the URLConnection is to be used for output, false if for input.

 ### getDoOutput   URLConnection   net

```
public boolean getDoOutput()
```

The getDoOutput() method returns the input/output functionality of the URLConnection.

 A Boolean value that will be true if the URLConnection is used for output, false if it is used for input.

 ### setAllowUserInteraction   URLConnection   net

```
public void setAllowUserInteraction(boolean allowuserinteraction)
```

The setAllowUserInteraction() method allows the protocol to interact with the user. For example, a dialog box may need to be displayed to the user.

▶ allowuserinteraction is a Boolean value that should be true if user interaction is allowed, false if not.

getAllowUserInteraction URLConnection

```
public boolean getAllowUserInteraction()
```

The `getAllowUserInteraction()` method can be called to determine if user interaction is allowed (see `setAllowUserInteraction()`).

A Boolean value that will be `true` if user interaction is allowed, `false` if not.

setDefaultAllowUserInteraction URLConnection net

```
public static void
    setDefaultAllowUserInteraction(boolean defaultallowuserinteraction)
```

The `setDefaultAllowUserInteraction()` method allows the default user interaction value to be set for all `URLConnections` because it is a static method.

`defaultallowuserinteraction` is a Boolean value that should be `true` if user interaction is allowed, `false` if not.

getDefaultAllowUserInteraction URLConnection net

```
public static boolean getDefaultAllowUserInteraction()
```

The `getDefaultAllowUserInteraction()` static method returns the default user interaction value.

A Boolean value that will be `true` if user interaction is allowed, `false` if not.

setUseCaches URLConnection net

```
public void setUseCaches(boolean usecaches)
```

The `setUseCaches()` method is used to control the use of caching by the protocol. Some protocols allow files to be cached.

`usecaches` is a Boolean value that will be `true` if caching is to be used by the protocol, `false` if not.

getUseCaches URLConnection net

```
public boolean getUseCaches()
```

The `getUseCaches()` method can be called to determine if caching is to be used by the protocol.

A Boolean value that will be `true` if caching is to be used by the protocol, `false` if not.

setIfModifiedSince   URLConnection net

```
public void setIfModifiedSince(long ifmodifiedsince)
```

The `setIfModifiedSince()`method is provided to set the internal `ifmodifiedsince` variable of the `URLConnection` class. Because some protocols allow caching of files, if the file to be retrieved is newer than `ifmodifiedsince`, it will need to be retrieved from the URL (rather than the cache).

▶ `ifmodifiedsince` is a long value used to represent the `ifmodifiedsince` date.

 getIfModifiedSince   URLConnection net

```
public long getIfModifiedSince()
```

The `getIfModifiedSince()` method returns the internal `ifmodifiedsince` date value. See the `setIfModifiedSince()` method documentation.

↵ A long value representing the `ifmodifiedsince` date value.

 getDefaultUseCaches URLConnection net

```
public boolean getDefaultUseCaches()
```

The `getDefaultUseCaches()` method can be called to determine if caches are used by default. Because this value is static, it will apply to all current and future `URLConnections`.

↵ A Boolean value that will be `true` if caches are used by default, `false` if not.

setDefaultUseCaches URLConnection net

```
public void setDefaultUseCaches(boolean defaultusecaches)
```

The `setDefaultUseCaches()` method can be used to force all `URLConnections` to use caching by default because it is a static value.

▶ `defaultusecaches` is a Boolean value that should be `true` if caches are to be used by default, `false` if not.

 setRequestProperty   URLConnection net

```
public void setRequestProperty(String key, String value)
```

The `setRequestProperty()` method is used to set `URLConnection` properties.

▶ `key` is a `String` object containing the key by which the property is known.

▶ `value` is a `String` object containing the property value.

getRequestProperty   URLConnection   net

```
public String getRequestProperty(String key)
```

The getRequestProperty() method returns the value for the specified property key.

▶   key is a String object containing the key by which the property is known.

↵   A String object containing the specified property's value.

 setDefaultRequestProperty   URLConnection   net

```
public static void setDefaultRequestProperty(String key, String value)
```

The setDefaultRequestProperty() method sets the default value of a specified property. All current and future URLConnections will be initialized with these properties.

▶   key is a String object containing the key by which the property is known.

▶   value is a String object containing the specified property's value.

getDefaultRequestProperty   URLConnection   net

```
public static String getDefaultRequestProperty(String key)
```

The getDefaultRequestProperty() method gets the default value of a specified property.

▶   key is a String object containing the key by which the property is known.

↵   A String object containing the specified property's value.

 setContentHandlerFactory   URLConnection   net

```
public static synchronized void
➥ setContentHandlerFactory(ContentHandlerFactory fac)
```

The setContentHandlerFactory()method is used to set the ContentHandlerFactory interface for this URLConnection. The factory may only be set once. For more information on the ContentHandlerFactory interface, see the documentation later in this chapter.

▶   fac is a ContentHandlerFactory interface.

↰   An error if the ContentHandlerFactory has already been defined.

URLEncoder   net

➕ Object

The class hierarchy for the URLEncoder class derives from class java.lang.Object. (See Listing 33.10.) The URLEncoder class is used to encode text into x-www-form-urlencoded format. URLEncoder's overall derivation can be seen in Figure 33.1.

> **Listing 33.10. Public members of `java.net.URLEncoder`.**
> ```
> public class URLEncoder {
>   public static String encode(String s)
> }
> ```

 encode URLEncoder net

```
public static String encode(String s)
```

The `encode()` method is used to translate a string into x-www-form-urlencoded format.

 s is a `String` object that will be translated by the `encode()` method.

 A `String` object in x-www-form-urlencoded format.

URLStreamHandler net

 Object

The class hierarchy for the `URLStreamHandler` class derives from class `java.lang.Object`. The `URLStreamHandler` class is an abstract base class used to open URL connection streams. It must be subclassed in order to provide true functionality. `URLStreamHandler`'s overall derivation can be seen in Figure 33.1.

Listing 33.11 shows the declarations for all of the methods included in the class `java.awt.net.URLStreamHandler`.

> **Listing 33.11. Public members of `java.awt.net.URLStreamHandler`.**
> ```
> public class URLStreamHandler extends Object {
>   public URLStreamHandler()
>   protected abstract URLConnection openConnection(URL u) throws IOException
>   protected void parseURL(URL u, String spec, int start, int limit)
>   protected String toExternalForm(URL u)
>   protected void setURL(URL u, String protocol, String host, int port,
>   ➥ String file, String ref)
> }
> ```

 URLStreamHandler net

```
public URLStreamHandler()
```

This `URLStreamHandler()` method constructs a `URLStreamHandler`. After this object has been constructed, the `openConnection()` or `setURL()` methods are commonly called to perform operations with the URL connection stream.

▶ none

↵ none

OpenConnection   URLStreamHandler   net

```
protected abstract URLConnection openConnection(URL u) throws IOException
```

The openConnection() method is to be overridden by a subclass of URLStreamHandler. This method should open an input stream to the referenced URL.

▶ u references the URL stream to be opened.

↵ A URLConnection class that represents an active connection. For more information on the URLConnection class, see the documentation earlier in this chapter.

---

parseURL   URLStreamHandler   net

```
protected void parseURL(URL u, String spec, int start, int limit)
```

The parseURL() method is to be overridden by a subclass of URLStreamHandler. This method should parse the spec string into the URL u using the specified start and limit characters of the string.

▶ u references the URL referenced by the spec string.

▶ spec is a String containing a URL to be parsed.

▶ start references the character position in spec to start parsing at.

▶ limit is the character position in spec to stop parsing at.

---

toExternalForm   URLStreamHandler   net

```
protected String toExternalForm(URL u)
```

The toExternalForm() method is to be overridden by a subclass of URLStreamHandler. This method should "unparse" the specified URL and return a String.

▶ u references the URL stream to be unparsed.

↵ A String object containing the unparsed contents of the URL object.

---

setURL   URLStreamHandler   net

```
protected void setURL(URL u, String protocol, String host, int port,
➥ String file, String ref)
```

The setURL() method is to be overridden by a subclass of URLStreamHandler. This method should call the set() method of the specified URL u to set the fields of the URL. For more information on the set() method of the URL class, see the documentation earlier in this chapter.

▶ u references the URL whose fields will be set by this method.

▶ protocol is a String containing the protocol to use for the URL.

▶ host references the host machine pointed to by the URL.

▶ port is the protocol port that will be connected to by the URL.

▶ file is a String containing the file that is located on the host.

▶ ref is the reference value used by the URL.

MalformedURLException   net

 IOException

The class hierarchy for the MalformedURLException class derives from class java.io.IOException. (See Listing 33.12.) The MalformedURLException class is a class used to signal a malformed URL. MalformedURLException's overall derivation can be seen in Figure 33.1.

Listing 33.12. Public members of java.net.MalformedURLException.

```
public class MalformedURLException extends IOException {
  public MalformedURLException()
  public MalformedURLException(String msg)
}
```

MalformedURLException   MalformedURLException   net

```
public MalformedURLException()
```

This MalformedURLException() method constructs a MalformedURLException with no detail message to describe the exception.

 none

↵ none

MalformedURLException   MalformedURLException   net

```
public MalformedURLException(String msg)
```

This MalformedURLException() method constructs a MalformedURLException using the specified detail message to describe the exception.

 msg is a String object containing the detail message.

 **ProtocolException** net

 IOException

The class hierarchy for the ProtocolException class derives from class java.io.IOException. (See Listing 33.13.) This exception signals when a connect receives an EPROTO message. This exception is used by the Socket class. ProtocolException's overall derivation can be seen in Figure 33.1.

Listing 33.13. Public members of java.net.ProtocolException.
```
public class ProtocolException extends IOException {
  public ProtocolException(String host)
  public ProtocolException()
}
```

 ProtocolException ProtocolException net

```
public ProtocolException()
```

This ProtocolException() method constructs a ProtocolException with no detail message to describe the exception.

▶ none

↵ none

 ProtocolException ProtocolException net

```
public ProtocolException(String host)
```

This ProtocolException() method constructs a ProtocolException using the specified detail message to describe the exception.

▶ host is a String object containing the detail message.

 SocketException net

 IOException

The class hierarchy for the SocketException class derives from class java.io.IOException. (See Listing 33.14.) This exception signals when an error has occurred while trying to use a socket.

This exception is used by the `Socket` class. `SocketException`'s overall derivation can be seen in Figure 33.1.

Listing 33.14. Public members of `java.net.SocketException`.

```
public class SocketException extends IOException {
  public SocketException(String host)
  public SocketException()
}
```

 SocketException   SocketException   net

```
public SocketException()
```

This `SocketException()` method constructs a `SocketException` with no detail message to describe the exception.

   none

   none

 SocketException   SocketException   net

```
public SocketException(String host)
```

This `SocketException()` method constructs a `SocketException` using the specified detail message to describe the exception.

   `msg` is a `String` object containing the detail message.

UnknownHostException   net

➕ IOException

The class hierarchy for the `UnknownHostException` class derives from class `java.io.IOException`. (See Listing 33.15.) This exception signals that the host address specified by the client cannot be resolved. `UnknownHostException`'s overall derivation can be seen in Figure 33.1.

Listing 33.15. Public members of `java.net.UnknownHostException`.

```
public class UnknownHostException extends IOException {
  public UnknownHostException(String host)
  public UnknownHostException()
}
```

UnknownHostException   UnknownHostException   net

```
public UnknownHostException()
```

This `UnknownHostException()` method constructs an `UnknownHostException` with no detail message to describe the exception.

 none

 none

 UnknownHostException   UnknownHostException   net

```
public UnknownHostException(String host)
```

This `UnknownHostException()` method constructs a `UnknownHostException` using the specified detail message to describe the exception.

▶ `host` is a `String` object containing the detail message.

⊞→! UnknownServiceException   net

➕ IOException

The class hierarchy for the `UnknownServiceException` class derives from class `java.io.IOException`. (See Listing 33.16.) This exception signals when an unknown service exception has occurred. `UnknownServiceException`'s overall derivation can be seen in Figure 33.1.

> **Listing 33.16. Public members of `java.net.UnknownServiceException`.**
> ```
> public class UnknownServiceException extends IOException {
>   public UnknownServiceException()
>   public UnknownServiceException(String msg)
> }
> ```

 UnknownServiceException   UnknownServiceException   net

```
public UnknownServiceException()
```

This `UnknownServiceException()` method constructs an `UnknownServiceException` with no detail message to describe the exception.

 none

UnknownServiceException   UnknownServiceException   net

```
public UnknownServiceException(String host)
```

This `UnknownServiceException()` method constructs an `UnknownServiceException` using the specified detail message to describe the exception.

▶   host is a `String` object containing the detail message.

ContentHandlerFactory   net

The class hierarchy for the `ContentHandlerFactory` interface derives from class `java.lang.Object`. (See Listing 33.17.) This interface is used to create `ContentHandlers` for usage by various streams. `ContentHandlerFactory`'s overall derivation can be seen in Figure 33.1.

Listing 33.17. Public members of `java.net.ContentHandlerFactory`.

```
public interface ContentHandlerFactory{
  public abstract ContentHandler createContentHandler(String mimetype)
}
```

 createContentHandler   ContentHandlerFactory   net

```
public abstract ContentHandler createContentHandler(String mimetype)
```

The `createContentHandler()` method creates a new content handler to read the content from a `URLStreamHandler` using the specified mime type. For more information on the `URLStreamHandler` class, see the documentation later in this chapter.

▶   mimetype is a `String` object containing the mime type of the content.

↵   A `ContentHandler` object that will read data from a `URLConnection` and construct an object. For more information on the `ContentHandler` class, see the documentation earlier in this chapter.

SocketImplFactory   net

The class hierarchy for the `SocketImplFactory` interface derives from class `java.lang.Object`. (See Listing 33.18.) This interface is used by the socket class to specific socket implementations. `SocketImplFactory`'s overall derivation can be seen in Figure 33.1.

Listing 33.18. Public members of `java.net.SocketImplFactory`.

```
public interface SocketImplFactory {
   SocketImpl createSocketImpl()
}
```

---

 createSocketImpl   SocketImplFactory

SocketImpl createSocketImpl()

The `createSocketImpl()` method creates a `SocketImpl` instance that is an implementation of a socket. For more information on the `SocketImpl` class, see the documentation earlier in this chapter.

  A `SocketImpl` object that provides a socket implementation.

 URLStreamHandlerFactory

The class hierarchy for the `URLStreamHandlerFactory` interface derives from class `java.lang.Object`. (See Listing 33.19.) This interface is used by the `URL` class to create stream handlers for various stream types. `URLStreamHandlerFactory`'s overall derivation can be seen in Figure 33.1.

Listing 33.19. Public members of `java.net.URLStreamHandlerFactory`.

```
public interface URLStreamHandlerFactory {
   URLStreamHandler createURLStreamHandler(String protocol)
}
```

---

 createURLStreamHandler   URLStreamHandlerFactory

URLStreamHandler createURLStreamHandler(String protocol)

The `createURLStreamHandler()` method creates a `URLStreamHandler` instance for use by the `URL` class based on the specified protocol. For more information on the `URLStreamHandler` class, see the documentation earlier in this chapter.

▶ `protocol` is a `String` object that specifies the protocol to be used by the `URLStreamHandler` class.

  A `URLStreamHandler` class that is created with the protocol specified in the input parameter.

34

Package java.util

by Mike Cohn

In this chapter you learn about the util package. This package provides some of the most useful Java classes that you will come to rely on. It introduces ten classes, two exception classes, and two interfaces, as shown in Table 34.1. Figure 34.1 provides a graphical representation of the hierarchy of these contents.

Table 34.1. Contents of package `java.util`.

Class Index	*Interface Index*	*Exception Index*
BitSet	Enumeration	EmptyStackException
Date	Observer	NoSuchElementException
Dictionary		
Hashtable		
Observable		
Properties		
Random		
Stack		
StringTokenizer		
Vector		

FIGURE 34.1.
Contents of package
`java.util`.

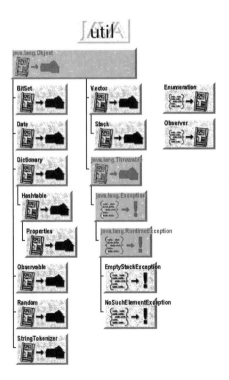

The `BitSet` class is useful for storing and manipulating arbitrarily long sets of bits. The `Date` class can be used to represent dates and times and provides methods for converting dates to and from `String`s. The abstract class `Dictionary` is a superclass of `Hashtable`. The `Hashtable` class can be used for creating an array of keys and values and allowing elements to be looked up by either key or value. The `Properties` class extends `Hashtable` in a couple of significant ways, most notably by allowing elements to be streamed into or out of the class. The `Observable` class can be extended and allows you to create new classes that notify other classes when they change. The `Random` class is a pseudo-random number generator that can return integer, floating-point or Gaussian-distributed values. The `Stack` class is an extension of `Vector` and supplies a last-in, first-out data structure. The `Vector` class can be used for storing any objects and can store objects of more than one type in the same vector. The `StringTokenizer` class provides a very flexible mechanism for parsing `String`s.

In addition to these classes the `util` package also includes two interfaces: `Enumeration` and `Observer`. The `Enumeration` interface provides two methods that allow for easy traversal through a set of items. The `Observer` interface can be implemented by any class that needs to observe a subclass of `Observable`.

 # BitSet

 Object

 Cloneable

The class `java.util.BitSet` is derived directly from `Object` but also implements the `Cloneable` interface, as shown in Listing 34.1.

Listing 34.1. The `BitSet` class.

```
public class BitSet extends Object implements Cloneable {
  // public constructors
    public BitSet();
    public BitSet(int nbits);
  // public instance methods
    public void and(BitSet set);
    public void clear(int bit);
    public Object clone();
    public boolean equals(Object obj);
    public boolean get(int bit);
    public int hashCode();
    public void or(BitSet set);
    public void set(int bit);
    public int size();
    public String toString();
    public void xor(BitSet set);
}
```

This class represents a dynamically sized set of bits. Two constructors are provided: one that creates an empty set of unspecified size and one that creates a set of a specified size. The `set` method can be used to set an individual bit or `clear` can be used to clear an individual bit. The first bit in a `BitSet` is the zero bit so that `myBitset.set(0)` is a valid statement.

The logical functions `and`, `or`, and `xor` are all supported and will combine the `BitSet` with another set. `BitSet`s can be compared for equality using `equals` and can be converted to strings using `toString`. For the purpose of converting a `BitSet` to a `String`, a set bit is represented by the value `1` and a clear bit is represented by `0`.

 BitSet BitSet util

```
public BitSet()
```

This constructor creates an empty bit set.

 BitSet BitSet util

```
public BitSet(int nbits)
```

This constructor creates an empty bit set with the specified number of bits.

 ▶ nbits is the number of bits in the set.

 and BitSet util

```
public void and(BitSet set)
```

This method logically ANDs the `BitSet` with another `BitSet`. For example, the following code results in only bit 4 being set in `bits1`:

```
BitSet bits1 = new BitSet(10);
bits1.set(1);
bits1.set(4);

BitSet bits2 = new BitSet(10);
bits2.set(4);
bits2.set(5);

bits1.and(bits2);
```

 ▶ set is the bit set to AND with the current set.

 clear BitSet util

```
public void clear(int bit)
```

Clears the specified bit.

 ▶ bit is the bit to clear.

clone BitSet util

```
public Object clone()
```

This method overrides the `clone` method in `Object`. It can be used to clone the bit set. For example, the following code creates a duplicate copy of `bits` in `clonedBits`:

```
BitSet bits = new BitSet(10);
bits.set(0);
bits.set(1);
bits.set(5);
BitSet clonedBits = (BitSet)bits.clone();
```

 equals BitSet util

```
public boolean equals(Object obj)
```

This method can be used to compare the contents of two `BitSets`. If the same bits are set in the two `BitSets`, they are considered equal. Consider the following code sample:

```
BitSet bits1 = new BitSet(10);
bits1.set(0);
bits1.set(1);
bits1.set(4);

BitSet bits2 = new BitSet(10);
bits2.set(0);
bits2.set(1);
bits2.set(4);

BitSet bits3 = new BitSet(10);
bits3.set(0);
bits3.set(1);
bits3.set(5);

Graphics g = getGraphics();
if (bits1.equals(bits2))
    g.drawString("bits1 equals! bits2", 15, 15);
if (bits1.equals(bits3))
    g.drawString("bits1 equals! bits3", 15, 30);
```

In this case, `bits1` will equal `bits2` because the same bits are set; however, `bits1` will not equal `bits3`.

 `obj` is a bit set to compare against.

 `true` if the set bits are the same; `false`, otherwise.

 get BitSet util

```
public boolean get(int bit)
```

Gets the value of a specified bit in the set.

bit is the bit to get.

 true if the bit is set; false if it is clear.

 ## hashCode BitSet util

```
public int hashCode()
```

This method overrides the hashCode method in Object and can be used to get a hash code for the instance.

 A hash code for the instance.

 ## or BitSet util

```
public void or(BitSet set)
```

This method logically ORs the BitSet with another. For example, the following code results in bits 1, 4, and 5 being set in bits1:

```
BitSet bits1 = new BitSet(10);
bits1.set(1);
bits1.set(4);

BitSet bits2 = new BitSet(10);
bits2.set(4);
bits2.set(5);

bits1.or(bits2);
```

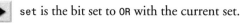 set is the bit set to OR with the current set.

set BitSet util

```
public void set(int bit)
```

Sets the specified bit.

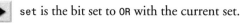 bit is the bit to set.

size BitSet util

```
public int size()
```

This method returns the amount of space, in bits, used to store the set. Space for a bit set is allocated in 64-bit increments, so the following example will indicate that len1 equals 64 and len2 equals 128:

```
BitSet bits1 = new BitSet();
bits1.set(0);
bits1.set(1);
bits1.set(4);
```

```
BitSet bits2 = new BitSet(65);
bits2.set(0);
bits2.set(1);
bits2.set(5);

int len1 = bits1.size();      // will equal 64
int len2 = bits2.size();      // will equal 128
```

↵ The amount of space, in bits, used to store the bit set.

 toString **BitSet** util

```
public String toString()
```

This method formats the `BitSet` as a `String`. The `String` will consist of an opening curly brace, comma-separated values representing each set bit, and a closing curly brace. For example, the following code places {0, 1, 4} in the variable `str`:

```
BitSet bits1 = new BitSet();
bits1.set(0);
bits1.set(1);
bits1.set(4);
String str = bits1.toString();
```

↵ A string representing the bits in the bit set that are set.

xor **BitSet** util

```
public void xor(BitSet set)
```

This method logically XORs the `BitSet` with another `BitSet`. For example, the following code results in bits 4 and 5 being set in `bits1`:

```
BitSet bits1 = new BitSet(10);
bits1.set(0);
bits1.set(1);
bits1.set(4);

BitSet bits2 = new BitSet(10);
bits2.set(0);
bits2.set(1);
bits2.set(5);

bits1.xor(bits2);
```

▶ set is the bit set to XOR with the current set.

 # Date util

 Object

The class java.util.Date extends Object. The Date class stores a representation of a date and time and provides methods for manipulating the date and time components. A new Date instance may be constructed using any of the following:

■ The current date and time as expressed in the UNIX-standard milliseconds since midnight January 1, 1970;

■ A String;

■ Integers representing the year, month, day, hours, minutes, and seconds.

Dates can be compared with the before, after, and equals methods. Methods are also provided for converting a date into various formatted Strings. The non-private interface of the Date class is shown in Listing 34.2.

Listing 34.2. The Date class.

```
public class Date extends Object {
  // public constructors
    public Date();
    public Date(long date);
    public Date (int year, int month, int date);
    public Date (int year, int month, int date,int hrs,int min);
    public Date (int year, int month, int date, int hrs,
            int min, int sec);
    public Date (String s);
  // static methods
    public static long UTC(int year, int month, int date,
            int hrs, int min, int sec);
    public static long parse(String s);
  // public instance methods
    public int getYear();
    public void setYear(int year);
    public int getMonth();
    public void setMonth(int month);
    public int getDate();
    public void setDate(int date);
    public int getDay();
    public int getHours();
    public void setHours(int hours);
    public int getMinutes();
    public void setMinutes(int minutes);
    public int getSeconds();
    public void setSeconds(int seconds);
    public long getTime();
    public void setTime(long time);
    public boolean before(Date when);
    public boolean after(Date when);
    public boolean equals(Object obj);
    public int hashCode();
    public native String toString();
    public native String toLocaleString();
    public native String toGMTString();
    public int getTimezoneOffset();
}
```

Date Date util

```
public Date()
```

This method creates a new Date object using today's date. For example, to display today's date you could write the following:

```
Date today = new Date();
Graphics g = getGraphics();
g.drawString("Today is " + today, 15, 15);
```

 Date Date util

```
public Date(long date)
```

This method creates a Date from a long that represents the number of milliseconds since January 1, 1970.

▶ date is the number of milliseconds since January 1, 1970.

 Date Date util

```
public Date(int year, int month, int date)
```

This method creates a new Date object that corresponds to the year, month, and day passed to it. The first month of the year is month zero. The day of the month is normalized so that impossible dates become real dates. For example, you'd think badDate in the following code would be equal to November 33, 1996.

```
Date goodDate = new Date(95, 10, 14);   // November 14, 1995
Date badDate = new Date(96, 10, 33);    // December 3, 1996
```

However, badDate is adjusted to be December 3, 1996 instead. The value in goodDate will correctly be November 14, 1995.

▶ year is the number of years since 1900.

▶ month is the zero-based month, from 0–11.

▶ date is the day of the month.

 Date Date util

```
public Date(int year, int month, int date, int hrs, int min)
```

This method creates a new Date object that corresponds to the year, month, day, hours, and minutes passed to it. As with the prior constructor, the day of the month is normalized so that impossible dates become real dates. For example, to create a variable named birthday that holds November 14, 1995 at 1:16 PM (13:16 in military time), you would use the following:

```
Date birthday = new Date(95, 10, 14, 13, 16);
```

▶ year is the number of years since 1900.

▶ month is the zero-based month, from 0–11.

▶ date is the day of the month.

▶ hrs is the zero-based number of hours (0–23).

▶ min is the zero-based number of minutes (0–59).

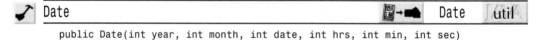

Date   Date   util

```
public Date(int year, int month, int date, int hrs, int min, int sec)
```

This method creates a new Date object that corresponds to the year, month, day, hour, minute, and seconds passed to it. As with the other constructors, the day of the month is normalized so that impossible dates become real dates.

▶ year is the number of years since 1900.

▶ month is the zero-based month, from 0–11.

▶ date is the day of the month.

▶ hrs is the zero-based number of hours (0–23).

▶ min is the zero-based number of minutes (0–59).

▶ sec is the zero-based number of seconds (0–59).

Date   Date   util

```
public Date(String s)
```

This method creates a new date based on the date string passed to it. For example, to create a variable that represents August 31, 1996, you could use the following:

```
Date aDate = new Date("August 31 1996");
```

▶ s is a time string in the format passed to java.util.Date.Parse, as described later in this chapter.

UTC   Date   util

```
public static long UTC(int year, int month, int date, int hrs, int min, int sec)
```

This method calculates the time in UTC (Coordinated Universal Time) format based on the specified parameters. Parameters are expected to be given in UTC values, not the time in the local time zone.

▶ `year` is the number of years since 1900.

▶ `month` is the zero-based month, from 0–11.

▶ `date` is the day of the month.

▶ `hrs` is the zero-based number of hours (0–23).

▶ `min` is the zero-based number of minutes (0–59).

▶ `sec` is the zero-based number of seconds (0–59).

↵ A UTC time value.

 parse   Date ⌐util⌐

```
public static long parse(String s)
```

This method calculates the time in UTC format based on the string passed to it.

▶ s is a formatted time string such as `"Mon, 8 Apr 1996 21:32:PM PST"`. To specify the time zone, you can use any of the continental United States time zone abbreviations (`est`, `edt`, `cst`, `cdt`, `mst`, `mdt`, `pst`, `pdt`) or you can use `"GMT"` with an offset, such as the following:

```
Mon, 8 Apr 1996 21:32:PM GMT+0800
```

This calculates GMT plus eight hours. This method considers GMT and UTC to be equivalent and does not make adjustments for the periodic "leap seconds."

↵ A UTC time value.

 after   Date ⌐util⌐

```
public boolean after(Date when)
```

Determines whether the `Date` occurs after the specified date. For example, to determine if the United States Independence Day (July 4) is after the French Bastille Day (July 14), use the following code:

```
Date independenceDay = new Date(96, 6, 4);
Date bastilleDay = new Date(96, 6, 14);

Graphics g = getGraphics();
if (independenceDay.after(bastilleDay))
    g.drawString("Independence Day is after Bastille Day",15,15);
else
    g.drawString("Independence Day is before Bastille Day",15,15);
```

▶ when is the date to compare against.

↵ `true` if the object's date occurs after the specified date; `false`, otherwise.

before   Date *util*

```
public boolean before(Date when)
```

Determines whether the date occurs before the specified date.

▶ `when` is the date to compare against.

↵ `true` if the object's date occurs before the specified date; `false`, otherwise.

 equals   Date *util*

```
public boolean equals(Object obj)
```

This method determines whether two date objects are the same by comparing the dates represented by each object. For example, the following code will verify that Independence Day and the Fourth of July are the same date:

```
Date independenceDay = new Date(96, 6, 4);
Date fourthOfJuly = new Date(96, 6, 4);

Graphics g = getGraphics();
if (independenceDay.equals(fourthOfJuly))
    g.drawString("They're equal", 15, 15);
else
    g.drawString("They're not equal", 15, 15);
```

▶ `obj` is the object to compare against.

↵ `true` if the dates are the same; `false`, otherwise.

 getDate   Date *util*

```
public int getDate()
```

This method returns the day (or date) portion of a date object.

↵ The day of the month from 1 to 31.

 getDay   Date *util*

```
public int getDay()
```

This method returns the day of the week. Sunday is assigned a value of 0.

↵ The day of the week from 0 (Sunday) to 6 (Saturday).

 getHours   Date *util*

```
public int getHours()
```

This method returns the hours.

↵ The hours from 0 to 23.

getMinutes 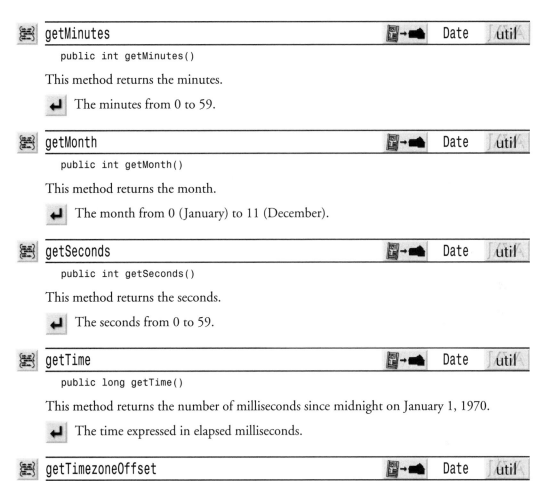 Date util

```
public int getMinutes()
```

This method returns the minutes.

↵ The minutes from 0 to 59.

getMonth Date util

```
public int getMonth()
```

This method returns the month.

↵ The month from 0 (January) to 11 (December).

getSeconds Date util

```
public int getSeconds()
```

This method returns the seconds.

↵ The seconds from 0 to 59.

getTime Date util

```
public long getTime()
```

This method returns the number of milliseconds since midnight on January 1, 1970.

↵ The time expressed in elapsed milliseconds.

getTimezoneOffset Date util

```
public int getTimezoneOffset()
```

This method returns the offset in minutes of the current time zone from the UTC. For example, California is in the Pacific time zone and during Pacific Standard Time the following will display that it is 480 minutes (8 hours) different from UTC:

```
Date date1 = new Date(96, 11, 14);

Graphics g = getGraphics();
g.drawString("Timezone Offset: " + date1.getTimezoneOffset()
        + " minutes from UTC", 15, 15);
```

↵ The number of minutes difference between the time zone of the object and UTC.

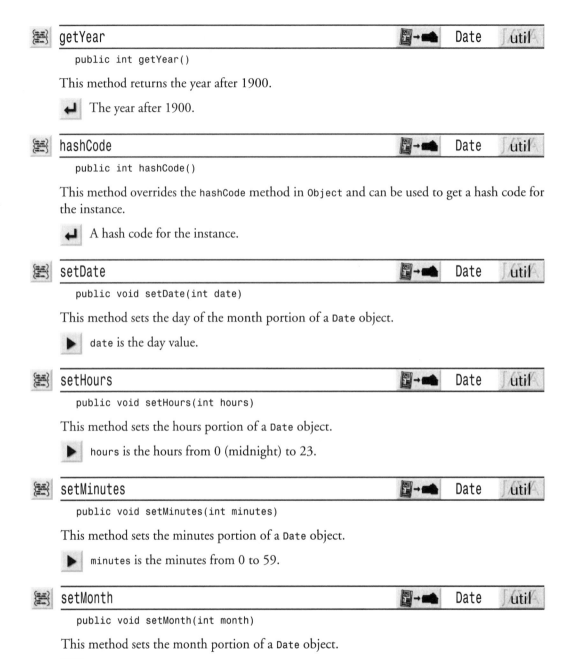

getYear — Date — util

```
public int getYear()
```

This method returns the year after 1900.

↵ The year after 1900.

hashCode — Date — util

```
public int hashCode()
```

This method overrides the hashCode method in Object and can be used to get a hash code for the instance.

↵ A hash code for the instance.

setDate — Date — util

```
public void setDate(int date)
```

This method sets the day of the month portion of a Date object.

▶ date is the day value.

setHours — Date — util

```
public void setHours(int hours)
```

This method sets the hours portion of a Date object.

▶ hours is the hours from 0 (midnight) to 23.

setMinutes — Date — util

```
public void setMinutes(int minutes)
```

This method sets the minutes portion of a Date object.

▶ minutes is the minutes from 0 to 59.

setMonth — Date — util

```
public void setMonth(int month)
```

This method sets the month portion of a Date object.

▶ month is the zero-based month from 0 (January) to 11 (December).

setSeconds Date *util*

```
public void setSeconds(int seconds)
```

This method sets the seconds portion of a Date object.

 seconds is the seconds from 0 to 59.

 setTime Date *util*

```
public void setTime(long time)
```

This method sets the time to the time represented by the number of milliseconds in the `time` parameter. It is frequently used in conjunction with the `getTime` method, which returns a number of milliseconds. An example of using `setTime` in conjunction with `getTime` is as follows:

```
Date date1 = new Date(96, 11, 14);
long milliSeconds = date1.getTime();
Date date2 = new Date();
date2.setTime(milliSeconds);

if (date1.equals(date2)) {
    Graphics g = getGraphics();
    g.drawString("Dates are equal", 15, 15);
}
```

 time is the new time in milliseconds since January 1, 1970.

 setYear Date *util*

```
public void setYear(int year)
```

This method sets the year portion of a date instance. As an example, consider the following code:

```
Date birthday = new Date(95, 10, 14);
birthday.setYear(100);
int day = birthday.getDay();
switch (birthday.getDay()) {
    case 0: // Sunday
        g.drawString("It will be a Sunday", 15, 15);
        break;
    case 1: // Monday
        g.drawString("It will be a Monday", 15, 15);
        break;
    case 2: // Tuesday
        g.drawString("It will be a Tuesday", 15, 15);
        break;
    case 3: // Wednesday
        g.drawString("It will be a Wednesday", 15, 15);
        break;
    case 4: // Thursday
        g.drawString("It will be a Thursday", 15, 15);
        break;
```

```
        case 5: // Friday
            g.drawString("It will be a Friday", 15, 15);
            break;
        case 6: // Saturday
            g.drawString("It will be a Saturday", 15, 15);
            break;
    }
```

This example shows how to plan a birthday party in the year 2000. First, the variable birthday is set to November 14, 1995. Then, setYear is used to change the year to 2000 (1900 + 100). Finally, a switch statement on getDay is used to determine the day of the week.

 year is the year after 1900. For 1996, use 96.

---

 toGMTString   Date   util

```
public String toGMTString()
```

This method creates a string that contains the date and time formatted according to GMT (Greenwich Mean Time) conventions. For example, if run on a machine set to Pacific Standard Time, the following code will display `"14 Nov 1995 08:00:00 GMT"`:

```
Date date1 = new Date(95, 10, 14);

Graphics g = getGraphics();
if (date1.equals(date1))
    g.drawString("GMT: " + date1.toGMTString(), 15, 15);
```

 A string representing the date in GMT format, such as `"14 Nov 1995 08:00:00 GMT"`.

---

 toLocaleString   Date   util

```
public String toLocaleString()
```

This method creates a string that contains the date and time in the format of the current locale. For example, the following code will display `"11/14/95 00:00:00"`:

```
Date date1 = new Date(95, 10, 14);

Graphics g = getGraphics();
if (date1.equals(date1))
    g.drawString("Locale: " + date1.toLocaleString(), 15, 15);
```

 A string representing the date as formatted for the locale of the instance, such as `"11/14/95 00:00:00"`.

---

 toString   Date   util

```
public String toString()
```

This method creates a string that contains the day of the week, the date, and the time. For example, the following code will display `"Tue Nov 14 00:00:00 1995"`:

```
Date date1 = new Date(95, 10, 14);

Graphics g = getGraphics();
if (date1.equals(date1))
    g.drawString("String: " + date1.toString(), 15, 15);
```

 A string representing the day of the week, date, and time of the instance, such as "Tue Nov 14 00:00:00 1995".

# Dictionary

 Object

The abstract class java.util.Dictionary extends Object. The non-private members of Dictionary are shown in Listing 34.3.

Listing 34.3. The Dictionary class.
```
public class Dictionary extends Object {
  // public constructors
    public Dictionary();
  // public instance methods
    public abstract Enumeration elements();
    public abstract Object get(Object key);
    public abstract boolean isEmpty();
    public abstract Enumeration keys();
    public abstract Object put(Object key, Object value);
    public abstract Object remove(Object key);
    public abstract int size();
}
```

The Dictionary class is an abstract class. Hashtable is derived directly from Dictionary, and Properties is derived from Hashtable. Although one of these classes will probably meet your needs, you could extend Dictionary in your own new class if necessary.

Each element in a Dictionary consists of a key and value. Elements are added to a Dictionary using put and are retrieved using get. Elements may be deleted with remove. The methods elements and keys each return an enumeration of the values and keys, respectively, stored in the Dictionary.

Dictionary   Dictionary | util

```
public Dictionary()
```

This is a default constructor that will create an empty Dictionary.

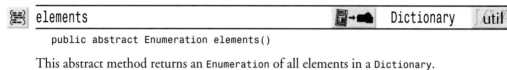

elements Dictionary util

```
public abstract Enumeration elements()
```

This abstract method returns an `Enumeration` of all elements in a `Dictionary`.

↵ An enumeration of each of the elements in the `Dictionary`. The methods of `Enumeration` can be used to iterate through the elements.

get Dictionary util

```
public abstract Object get(Object key)
```

This abstract method retrieves an object from a `Dictionary` based on its key.

▶ `key` is the key of the object to be retrieved.

↵ The value associated with the key, if found; `null`, if not.

isEmpty Dictionary util

```
public abstract boolean isEmpty()
```

This abstract method can be used to determine if the `Dictionary` is empty.

↵ `true` if the `Dictionary` is empty; `false`, if not.

keys Dictionary util

```
public abstract Enumeration keys()
```

This abstract method returns an `Enumeration` of all keys in a `Dictionary`.

↵ An enumeration of each of the keys in the `Dictionary`. The methods of `Enumeration` can be used to iterate through the keys.

put Dictionary util

```
public abstract Object put(Object key, Object value)
```

This abstract method inserts a new element into the `Dictionary`. To retrieve an element use the `get` method.

▶ `key` is the key to be added.

▶ `value` is the value associated with the key.

↵ If the key was already in the `Dictionary` the old value associated with it is returned. If not, `null` is returned.

↱ `NullPointerException` is thrown if the value to be put is `null`.

remove Dictionary util

```
public abstract Object remove(Object key)
```

This abstract method removes an object from a `Dictionary`.

▶ `key` is the key of the element to be removed.

↵ If the key is found, the value associated with it is returned; if not, `null` is returned.

 size Dictionary util

```
public abstract int size()
```

This abstract method returns the number of elements in the `Dictionary`.

↵ The number of items stored in the `Dictionary`.

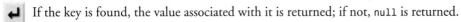 # Enumeration util

The interface `java.util.Enumeration` defines methods that can be used to iterate through a set of objects. The methods `hasMoreElements` and `nextElement` are typically used in a loop that visits each item in the set. For example, the following code will iterate through each item in a `Vector` calling the method `DoSomething` for each element:

```
for (Enumeration e = myVector.elements() ; e.hasMoreElements() ;)
    DoSomething(e.nextElement());
```

The `Enumeration` interface is shown in Listing 34.4.

Listing 34.4. The `Enumeration` interface.
```
public interface Enumeration {
  // public instance methods
    public abstract boolean hasMoreElements();
    public abstract Object nextElement();
}
```

 hasMoreElements Enumeration util

```
public abstract boolean hasMoreElements()
```

Can be used to determine if the enumeration has more elements.

↵ `true` if there are more elements; `false`, if not.

nextElement   Enumeration *util*

```
public abstract Object nextElement()
```

This method returns the next element in the enumeration. Calling it repeatedly will move through the enumeration.

 The next element in the enumeration.

 NoSuchElementException is thrown if there are no more elements in the enumeration.

 # Hashtable   *util*

+ Dictionary

The class java.util.Hashtable extends Dictionary. The non-private members of Hashtable are shown in Listing 34.5.

Listing 34.5. The Hashtable class.
```java
public class Hashtable extends Dictionary {
  // public constructors
    public Hashtable(int initialCapacity, float loadFactor);
    public Hashtable(int initialCapacity);
    public Hashtable();
  // public instance methods
    public synchronized void clear();
    public synchronized Object clone();
    public synchronized boolean contains(Object value);
    public synchronized boolean containsKey(Object key);
    public synchronized Enumeration elements();
    public synchronized Object get(Object key);
    public boolean isEmpty();
    public synchronized Enumeration keys();
    public synchronized Object put(Object key, Object value);
    public synchronized Object remove(Object key);
    public int size();
    public synchronized String toString();
  // protected instance methods
    protected void rehash();
}
```

A Hashtable is used for mapping keys to values. For example, it could be used to map names to ages, programmers to projects, job titles to salaries, and so on. The Properties class extends Hashtable and adds the ability to read and write a Hashtable to a stream.

Each element in a Hashtable consists of a key and value. Elements are added to a Hashtable using the put method and are retrieved using get. Elements may be deleted from a Hashtable with remove. A Hashtable expands in size as elements are added to it. When creating a new

`Hashtable`, you can specify an initial capacity and a load factor. The `Hashtable` increases in size whenever adding a new element would move the `Hashtable` past its threshold. A `Hashtable`'s threshold is its capacity multiplied by its load factor. For example, a `Hashtable` with a capacity of 100 and a load factor of 0.75 would have a threshold of 75 items.

 Hashtable Hashtable util

```
public Hashtable(int initialCapacity, float loadFactor)
```

This constructor creates a new instance of a `Hashtable` with the specified initial capacity and load factor. Although an initial capacity is specified, the `Hashtable` grows as needed when new items are added. The initial capacity specifies how many elements could be stored in the `Hashtable` if the load factor is 1.0. The load factor is a number between 0.0 and 1.0 and specifies the percent of the `Hashtable` that must be full before the size is automatically increased.

▶ `initialCapacity` is the initial capacity of the `Hashtable`.

▶ `loadFactor` is a value between 0.0 and 1.0 which specifies the percent of available hash slots that can be filled before the table is automatically rehashed into a larger `Hashtable`.

 Hashtable Hashtable util

```
public Hashtable(int initialCapacity)
```

This constructor creates a new `Hashtable` with the specified initial capacity and a default load factor of 0.75.

▶ `initialCapacity` is the initial capacity of the `Hashtable`.

 Hashtable Hashtable util

```
public Hashtable()
```

This constructor creates a new `Hashtable` using default values for the initial capacity and the load factor. A default of 101 is used for the initial capacity, and 0.75 is used for the load factor.

 clear Hashtable util

```
public synchronized void clear()
```

This method removes all elements from a `Hashtable`. The following example creates a `Hashtable`, inserts three items into it, and then removes all of them using `clear`:

```
Hashtable ages = new Hashtable();
ages.put("Mike", new Integer(33));
ages.put("Laura", new Integer(34));
ages.put("Savannah", new Integer(0));
ages.clear();
```

clone   Hashtable util

```
public synchronized Object clone()
```

This method clones the Hashtable into a new Hashtable. The keys and values themselves are not cloned. The following example results in the creation of two Hashtables, each with the same three elements:

```
Hashtable ages = new Hashtable();
ages.put("Mike", new Integer(33));
ages.put("Laura", new Integer(34));
ages.put("Savannah", new Integer(0));
Hashtable clonedAges = (Hashtable)ages.clone();
```

   A cloned Hashtable.

contains   Hashtable util

```
public synchronized boolean contains(Object value)
```

This method searches the Hashtable to determine if a specific value is stored. For example, consider the following example, which searches the ages Hashtable for anyone with an age of 0:

```
Hashtable ages = new Hashtable();
ages.put("Mike", new Integer(33));
ages.put("Laura", new Integer(34));
ages.put("Savannah", new Integer(0));

Graphics g = getGraphics();
if (ages.contains(new Integer(0)))
    g.drawString("Found a baby!", 15, 15);
else
    g.drawString("No babies found!", 15, 15);
```

▶   value is the value to search for.

   true if the value is found; false, if not.

   NullPointerException is thrown if the value is null.

containsKey   Hashtable util

```
public synchronized boolean containsKey(Object key)
```

This method searches the Hashtable to determine if a specific key occurs. As an example, consider the following code, which searches for the name Savannah:

```
Hashtable ages = new Hashtable();
ages.put("Mike", new Integer(33));
ages.put("Laura", new Integer(34));
ages.put("Savannah", new Integer(0));
```

```
Graphics g = getGraphics();
if (ages.containsKey("Savannah"))
    g.drawString("Savannah was found!", 15, 15);
else
    g.drawString("Savannah not found!", 15, 15);
```

▶ key is the key to search for.

↵ true if the key is found; `false`, if not.

 ## elements Hashtable util

```
public synchronized Enumeration elements()
```

This method returns an enumeration of all of the element values in the instance. For example, the following code will display the integers 33, 34, and 0:

```
Hashtable ages = new Hashtable();
ages.put("Mike", new Integer(33));
ages.put("Laura", new Integer(34));
ages.put("Savannah", new Integer(0));

Graphics g = getGraphics();
int count = 0;
for (Enumeration enum = ages.elements() ; enum.hasMoreElements() ;) {
    count++;
    g.drawString("Value = " + (Integer)enum.nextElement(), 15, 15*count);
}
```

↵ An enumeration of each of the keys in the `Hashtable`. The methods of `Enumeration` can be used to iterate through the keys.

 ## get Hashtable util

```
public synchronized Object get(Object key)
```

This function retrieves the object associated with the specified key. For example, the following code puts three objects into a `Hashtable` and then retrieves Laura's age:

```
Hashtable ages = new Hashtable();
ages.put("Mike", new Integer(33));
ages.put("Laura", new Integer(34));
ages.put("Savannah", new Integer(0));

Integer age = (Integer)ages.get("Laura");

Graphics g = getGraphics();
if (age != null)
    g.drawString("Laura is " + age, 15, 15);
```

▶ key is the key of the object to be retrieved.

↵ The value associated with the key, if found; `null`, if not.

isEmpty   Hashtable   util

```
public boolean isEmpty()
```

This method can be used to determine if the Hashtable is empty.

    true if the Hashtable is empty; false, if not.

 keys   Hashtable   util

```
public synchronized Enumeration keys()
```

This method returns an enumeration of all of the keys in the instance. For example, the following code will display the names Mike, Laura, and Savannah:

```
Hashtable ages = new Hashtable();
ages.put("Mike", new Integer(33));
ages.put("Laura", new Integer(34));
ages.put("Savannah", new Integer(0));

Graphics g = getGraphics();
int count = 0;
for (Enumeration enum = ages.keys() ; enum.hasMoreElements() ;) {
    count++;
    g.drawString((String)enum.nextElement(), 15, 15*count);
}
```

    An enumeration of each of the keys in the Hashtable. The methods of Enumeration can be used to iterate through the keys.

 put   Hashtable   util

```
public synchronized Object put(Object key, Object value)
```

This method inserts a new element into the Hashtable. To retrieve an element use the get method. The following sample code creates a new Hashtable and then puts three elements into it:

```
Hashtable ages = new Hashtable();
ages.put("Mike", new Integer(33));
ages.put("Laura", new Integer(34));
ages.put("Savannah", new Integer(0));
```

▶   key is the key to be added.

▶   value is the value associated with the key.

    If the key was already in the Hashtable, the old value associated with it is returned. If not, null is returned.

☞   NullPointerException is thrown if the value is null.

rehash   Hashtable util

```
protected void rehash()
```

This method rehashes the Hashtable into a larger Hashtable. It is not normally necessary to call this method directly because it is invoked automatically based on the capacity and load factor of the Hashtable.

 remove   Hashtable util

```
public synchronized Object remove(Object key)
```

This method removes an object from a Hashtable. The following code illustrates how to remove an element:

```
Hashtable ages = new Hashtable();
ages.put("Mike", new Integer(33));
ages.put("Laura", new Integer(34));
ages.put("Savannah", new Integer(0));
ages.remove("Laura");
```

▶ key is the key of the element to be removed.

↵ If the key is found, the value associated with it is returned; if not, null is returned.

 size   Hashtable util

```
public int size()
```

This method returns the number of elements in the Hashtable.

↵ The number of items stored in the Hashtable.

 toString   Hashtable util

```
public synchronized String toString()
```

This method overrides the toString method in Object and formats the contents of the Hashtable as a String. For example, the following code will display {Savannah=0, Laura=34, Mike=33}:

```
Hashtable ages = new Hashtable();
ages.put("Mike", new Integer(33));
ages.put("Laura", new Integer(34));
ages.put("Savannah", new Integer(0));
Graphics g = getGraphics();
g.drawString(ages.toString(), 15, 15);
```

↵ A String representation of the Hashtable.

Observable   util

 Object

The class java.util.Observable extends Object directly. An Observable class is a class that may be watched or monitored by another class that implements the Observer interface. Associated with an Observable instance is a list of Observers. Whenever the Observable instance changes, it can notify each of its Observers. By using Observable and Observer classes, you can achieve a better partitioning of your code by decreasing the reliance of one class on another.

The non-private members of Observable are shown in Listing 34.6.

Listing 34.6. The Observable class.

```
public class Observable extends Object {
  // public constructors
    public Observable();
  // public instance methods
    public synchronized void addObserver(Observer o);
    public synchronized int countObservers();
    public synchronized void deleteObserver(Observer o);
    public synchronized void deleteObservers();
    public synchronized boolean hasChanged();
    public void notifyObservers();
    public synchronized void notifyObservers(Object arg);
// protected instance methods
    protected synchronized void clearChanged();
    protected synchronized void setChanged();
}
```

As an example of how Observable can be used, consider the following declaration of a class that extends Observable:

```
class Obsable extends Observable {
    private int secretNumber;

    public Obsable(int x) {
        secretNumber = x;
    }
    public void setSecretNumber(int x) {
        secretNumber = x;
        setChanged();
        notifyObservers(new Integer(secretNumber));
    }
}
```

The `Obsable` class stores a secret number, and whenever that number changes, all `Observers` are notified. No `Observable` class is complete without an `Observer`, so here is the `Test` class that extends `Applet` and implements the `Observer` interface:

```java
public class Test extends Applet implements Observer {
    Integer secretNumber;

    public void update(Observable o, Object arg) {
        secretNumber = (Integer)arg;
    }

    public boolean mouseDown(Event e, int x, int y)    {
        Obsable obs = new Obsable(12);
        obs.addObserver(this);
        obs.setSecretNumber(23);

        Graphics g = getGraphics();
        g.drawString("Secret Number: " + secretNumber, 15, 35);
        return true;
    }

    public boolean handleEvent(Event event) {
        return super.handleEvent(event);
    }

    public void init() {
        super.init();
        setLayout(null);
        resize(230,190);
    }
}
```

The `Test` class contains an `update` method that is part of the `Observer` interface. This method is passed an `Observable` item and an `Object` as parameters. As shown in the declaration of `Obsable`, the `Object` is an `Integer`. Therefore, `update` casts the `Object` into an `Integer` and stores it in the instance variable `secretNumber`. The `mouseDown` method is used to test this code. When a mouse button is pressed, a new `Obsable` instance is created, the instance of `Test` is added as an `Observer` and the `setSecretNumber` method is called. This method in `Obsable` causes all `Observers` to be notified. Because `Test` is an `Observer`, its `update` method is invoked, and the new value for `secretNumber` (23) is stored. It is then displayed as evidence that `update` was called.

 Observable   Observable   util

```java
public Observable()
```

This is an empty, default constructor.

addObserver Observable util

```
public synchronized void addObserver(Observer o)
```

This method adds an Observer to the list of objects that are observing this instance. The observer must implement the Observer interface. Frequently, the Observer parameter passed to this method is the this implicit member variable, as shown in the following:

```
Obsable obs = new Obsable(12);
obs.addObserver(this);
```

 o is the observer to add.

 clearChanged Observable util

```
protected synchronized void clearChanged()
```

This method clears the internal flag that indicates an Observable instance has changed.

 countObservers Observable util

```
public synchronized int countObservers()
```

This method counts the number of Observers that are observing the instance.

 The number of Observers for the instance.

 deleteObserver Observable util

```
public synchronized void deleteObserver(Observer o)
```

This method deletes an Observer from the list of Observers that are monitoring an Observable object. The Observer must have been previously added with addObserver.

 o is the observer to delete.

deleteObservers Observable util

```
public synchronized void deleteObservers()
```

This method deletes all Observers of the Observable instance.

hasChanged Observable util

```
public synchronized boolean hasChanged()
```

This method can be used to query whether an Observable has changed.

true if an observable change has occurred; false, otherwise.

notifyObservers Observable util

```
public void notifyObservers()
```

This method notifies all Observers that a change has occurred in the Observable object. This results in a call to the update method in each Observer.

 notifyObservers Observable util

```
public synchronized void notifyObservers(Object arg)
```

This method notifies all Observers that a change has occurred in the Observable object. This results in a call to the update method in each Observer to which arg will be passed.

▶ arg is any object that can be used to convey information to the Observers.

 setChanged Observable util

```
protected synchronized void setChanged()
```

This method sets an internal flag to indicate that an observable change has occurred within the instance.

 # Observer util

The interface java.util.Observer defines an update method that is invoked by an Observable object whenever the Observable object has changed and wants to notify its Observers. The Observer interface is shown in Listing 34.7.

Listing 34.7. The Observer interface.
```
public interface Observer {
  // public instance methods
    public abstract void update(Observable o, Object arg);
}
```

For an example of how to use an Observer with an Observable class, see the discussion of the Observable class earlier in this chapter.

update   Observer util

```
public abstract void update(Observable o, Object arg)
```

This method is called whenever an `Observable` instance that is being observed invokes either of its `notifyObservers` methods.

▶ o—The `Observable` object that is generating this message.

▶ arg—Any additional information passed by the `Observable` object's `notifyObservers` method. This may be `null`.

 # Properties util

 Hashtable

The class `java.util.Properties` extends `Hashtable`, which extends `Dictionary`. The non-private members of `Properties` are shown in Listing 34.8.

Listing 34.8. The Properties class.

```
public class Properties extends Hashtable {
  // public constructors
    public Properties();
    public Properties(Properties defaults);
  // public instance methods
    public String getProperty(String key);
    public String getProperty(String key, String defaultValue);
    public void list(PrintStream out);
    public synchronized void load(InputStream in);
    public Enumeration propertyNames();
    public synchronized void save(OutputStream out, String header);
  // protected variables
    protected Properties defaults;
}
```

This class can be used to store keys and associated values. Through its `save` and `load` methods, `Properties` can be written to disk. This makes this class an excellent mechanism for storing configuration information between runs of a program. An example of a `Properties` file written by the save method is as follows:

```
#This is a header comment
#Sun Jun 02 15:01:48  1996
prop3=put three
prop2=put two
prop1=put one
```

Because `Properties` is a subclass of `Hashtable`, new key/value pairs are added by using the `put` method of `Hashtable`. The following example shows how to create an instance, put three properties into it, save it, and then reload the keys and values into a different instance:

```
// create a new instance
Properties props1 = new Properties();

// put three properties into it
props1.put("prop1", "put one");
props1.put("prop2", "put two");
props1.put("prop3", "put three");

// retrieve each of the three properties
String prop1 = props1.getProperty("prop1", "one");
String prop2 = props1.getProperty("prop2", "two");
String prop3 = props1.getProperty("prop3");

// save the properties to a file
props1.save(new FileOutputStream("test.ini"), "My header");

// create a new instance and read the file in from the file
Properties props2 = new Properties();
FileInputStream inStr = new FileInputStream("test.ini");
props2.load(inStr);

// retrieve a property from the second instance
String prop = props2.getProperty("prop2", "two");
```

Variable

protected Properties defaults

This member stores the default property values.

 ## Properties

```
public Properties()
```

This constructor is used to create an empty, new instance of `Properties` as follows:

```
Properties myProps = new Properties();
```

 ## Properties

```
public Properties(Properties defaults)
```

This constructor creates a new instance of `Properties` and will establish a set of default properties.

getProperty   Properties   util

```
public String getProperty(String key)
```

This method is used to retrieve a property based on its key. If no matching key is found, the defaults are searched. If no match is found there either, `null` is returned. It can be used as follows:

```
String prop1 = myProps.getProperty("prop1");
```

▶ key is the key of the property to retrieve.

↵ The property associated with the key or null if there is no matching key.

getProperty   Properties   util

```
public String getProperty(String key, String defaultValue)
```

This method is used to retrieve a property based on its key. If no match is found, the `defaultValue` is returned. It can be used as follows:

```
String prop1 = myProps.getProperty("prop1", "default");
```

▶ key is the key of the property to retrieve.

▶ defaultValue is the value to use if no matching key is found.

↵ The property associated with the key or the defaultValue if there is no matching key.

list   Properties   util

```
public void list(PrintStream out)
```

This method lists all of the properties to the specified `PrintStream`. It is useful mainly while debugging.

▶ out is the PrintStream where the properties are to be printed.

load   Properties   util

```
public synchronized void load(InputStream in) throws IOException
```

This method reads a set of properties from the specified `InputStream`. Used in conjunction with the save method, `Properties` can be written to disk at the end of a program run and then re-loaded at the start of the next run. The following example illustrates how to load a `Properties` instance from a file named TEST.INI:

```
Properties props = new Properties();
FileInputStream inStr = new FileInputStream("test.ini");
props.load(inStr);
```

▶ in is the InputStream from which the Properties are to be read.

☞ IOException is if the specified file is not found or cannot be read.

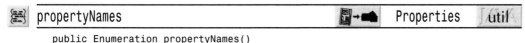

propertyNames — Properties — util

```
public Enumeration propertyNames()
```

This method returns an enumeration of all the property names in the instance. For example, the following code displays the names of each of the three properties:

```
Properties props1 = new Properties();
props1.put("prop1", "put one");
props1.put("prop2", "put two");
props1.put("prop3", "put three");

int count = 0;
Graphics g = getGraphics();
for (Enumeration enum = props1.propertyNames() ; enum.hasMoreElements() ;) {
    count++;
    g.drawString((String)enum.nextElement(), 15, 15*count);
}
```

↵ An enumeration of each of the property names. The methods of Enumeration can be used to iterate through the property names.

save — Properties — util

```
public synchronized void save(OutputStream out, String header)
```

This method saves the Properties to an OutputStream. Because FileOutputStream is a subclass of OutputStream, this method can be used to write to a file. As an example of writing Properties to a file, consider the following code:

```
Properties props1 = new Properties();
props1.put("prop1", "put one");
props1.put("prop2", "put two");
props1.put("prop3", "put three");
props1.save(new FileOutputStream("test.ini"), "My header");
```

This example creates a Properties set with three values and then writes them to a file named TEST.INI. The file is written with the header text My header. In this case, TEST.INI appears as follows:

```
#My header
#Sun Jun 02 15:01:48  1996
prop3=put three
prop2=put two
prop1=put one
```

▶ out is the OutputStream to which the Properties are to be written.

▶ header is a header that will be sent to the OutputStream before the properties.

 # Random

 Object

The class `java.util.Random` is derived directly from `Object`, as shown in Listing 34.9.

Listing. 34.9. The Random class.

```
public class Random extends Object {
  // public constructors
    public Random();
    public Random(long seed);
  // public instance methods
    public double nextDouble();
    public float nextFloat();
    public synchronized double nextGaussian();
    public int nextInt();
    public long nextLong();
    public synchronized void setSeed(long seed);
}
```

This class represents a pseudo-random number generator. Two constructors are provided: One takes a seed value as a parameter, and the other takes no parameters and uses the current time as a seed. Values can be retrieved from the generator using the following methods:

```
nextDouble
nextFloat
nextGaussian
nextInt
nextLong
```

 random Random util

```
public random()
```

This constructor creates a new random number generator that is seeded based on the current time.

 random Random util

```
public random(long seed)
```

This constructor creates a new random number generator based on the specified seed value. You should use this constructor rather than `random()` if a repeatable sequence of pseudo-random numbers is necessary. Even if a repeatable sequence of numbers is not necessary once a program is complete, it can frequently be useful during the debugging stages. A program that uses random numbers can be particularly difficult to debug. Because of this, you may want to consider providing a configuration setting that enables you to force a random number generator to a known seed.

A program can reset the seed of an already created instance by using the member method `setSeed`.

▶   `seed` is the seed value.

---

nextDouble 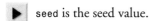 Random `util`

```
public double nextDouble()
```

This method retrieves the next number from the random number generator. The number will be a pseudo-random, uniformly distributed double between `0.0D` and `1.0D`.

↵   A randomly distributed double between `0.0D` and `1.0D`.

---

nextFloat 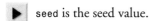 Random `util`

```
public float nextFloat()
```

This method retrieves the next number from the random number generator. The number will be a pseudo-random, uniformly distributed float between `0.0F` and `1.0F`.

↵   A randomly distributed float between `0.0F` and `1.0F`.

---

nextGaussian 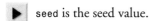 Random `util`

```
public synchronized double nextGaussian()
```

This method retrieves the next value from the pseudo-random number generator. The value will be returned as a Gaussian-distributed double that has a mean of `0` and a standard deviation of `1`.

↵   A Gaussian-distributed double.

---

nextInt 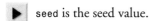 Random `util`

```
public int nextInt()
```

This method retrieves the next number from the random number generator. The number will be a pseudo-random `int` with a value that is uniformly distributed among all possible `int` values.

↵   A randomly distributed `int`.

nextLong Random

```
public long nextLong()
```

This method retrieves the next number from the random number generator. The number will be a pseudo-random `long` with a value that is uniformly distributed among all possible `long` values.

  A randomly distributed `long`.

 setSeed Random

```
public synchronized void setSeed(long seed)
```

This method sets a seed value for the pseudo-random number generator. The seed value is used to determine the values that are generated. By setting a specific seed value, the random number generator can be coerced into generating a specific sequence of values.

  `seed` is the seed value.

 # Stack

 Vector

The class `java.util.Stack` extends the class `java.util.Vector`, which is described later in this chapter. This class implements a simple last-in, first-out stack. An item is stored on a stack by "pushing" it onto the stack. An item may subsequently be "popped" off the stack and used. The item popped off a stack will always be the most recently pushed item. The non-private interface of the class is shown in Listing 34.10.

Listing 34.10. The Stack class.

```
public class Stack extends Vector {
  // public constructors
     public Stack();
  // public instance methods
     public empty();
     public peek();
     public pop();
     public push(Object item);
     public search(Object o);
}
```

Because `Stack` extends the `Vector` class, no size is associated with a `Stack` instance. The `Stack` continues to grow in size as new items are pushed onto it. In addition to methods to push and pop items, a `peek` method is provided for looking at the next item, a `search` method is provided for scanning the `Stack` for a specific item, and an `empty` method is provided for determining whether more items are stored in the `Stack`.

 Stack Stack util

```
public Stack()
```

There is no explicit constructor provided. To create a new `Stack`, use the default constructor as follows:

```
Stack myStack = new Stack();
```

 empty Stack util

```
public boolean empty()
```

This method can be used to determine whether the `Stack` contains items.

 `true` if the `Stack` is empty; `false`, otherwise.

 peek Stack util

```
public Object peek()
```

This method can be used to peek at the top item on the `Stack`. It is similar to `pop` but does not remove the item from the `Stack`.

 The item at the top of the `Stack`.

`EmptyStackException` is thrown if the `Stack` is empty.

pop Stack util

```
public Object pop()
```

This method retrieves the last item added to the `Stack`. To examine, but not remove, the top item in the `Stack` use the `peek` method.

The item at the top of the `Stack`.

`EmptyStackException` is thrown if the `Stack` is empty.

 push Stack util

```
public Object push(Object item)
```

This method adds a new item to the `Stack`.

▶ `item` is the item to push onto the `Stack`.

The item that was pushed onto the `Stack`.

search   **Stack**   util

```
public int search(Object o)
```

This method examines the `Stack` to see whether the specified object is in the `Stack`.

  o is the object of the search.

  The distance from the top of the `Stack`, or `-1` if the item is not in the `Stack`.

 # StringTokenizer   util

➕ Object

🔌 Enumeration

The class `java.util.StringTokenizer` extends `Object` and implements the `Enumeration` interface. A `StringTokenizer` can be used to parse a `String` into its constituent tokens. For example, each word in a sentence could be considered a token. However, the `StringTokenizer` class goes beyond the parsing of sentences. You can create a fully customized tokenizer by specifying the set of token delimiters when the `StringTokenizer` is created. For parsing text, the default whitespace delimiters are usually sufficient. However, you could use the set of arithmetic operators (+, *, /, and -) if parsing an expression.

Because `StringTokenizer` implements the `Enumeration` interface, it includes the `hasMoreElements` and `nextElement` methods. Additionally, the methods `hasMoreTokens` and `nextToken` are provided. The `hasMoreTokens` method is identical to `hasMoreElements`, except that you may prefer the method name. The same is true of `nextToken` and `nextElement`. The non-private interface of the class is shown in Listing 34.11.

Listing 34.11. The StringTokenizer class.

```
public class StringTokenizer extends Object implements Enumeration {
  // public constructors
    public StringTokenizer(String str, String delim, boolean returnTokens);
    public StringTokenizer(String str, String delim);
    public StringTokenizer(String str);
  // public instance methods
    public int countTokens();
    public boolean hasMoreElements();
    public boolean hasMoreTokens();
    public Object nextElement();
    public String nextToken();
    public String nextToken(String delim);
}
```

StringTokenizer   StringTokenizer   util

```
public StringTokenizer(String str, String delim, boolean returnTokens)
```

This constructor creates a new instance based on the String to be tokenized, the set of delimiters, and a flag indicating whether delimiters should be returned as tokens. The following example shows how to create a StringTokenizer for parsing simple math expressions:

```
String s = "4*3+2/4";
StringTokenizer st = new StringTokenizer(s, "*+/-", true);

Graphics g = getGraphics();
int tokenCount = 0;
while (st.hasMoreTokens()) {
    tokenCount++;
    g.drawString(st.nextToken(), 15, 15*tokenCount);
}
```

▶ str is the String to be tokenized.

▶ delim is a String containing the delimiters to use when tokenizing the String.

▶ returnTokens is true if the StringTokenizer should return delimiters as tokens; false, if not.

 StringTokenizer   StringTokenizer   util

```
public StringTokenizer(String str, String delim)
```

This constructor creates a new instance based on the String to be tokenized and a set of delimiters. The following example shows how to create a StringTokenizer, which can be used on a comma-delimited String:

```
String s = "field1,field2,field3,and field 4";
StringTokenizer st = new StringTokenizer(s,",",false);
int tokenCount = 0;

Graphics g = getGraphics();
while (st.hasMoreTokens()) {
    tokenCount++;
    g.drawString(st.nextToken(), 15, 15*tokenCount);
}
```

▶ str is the String to be tokenized.

▶ delim is a String containing the delimiters to use when tokenizing the String.

StringTokenizer StringTokenizer util

```
public StringTokenizer(String str)
```

This constructor creates a new instance based on the String to be tokenized and the default set of delimiters. The default delimiters are the space, tab, newline, and carriage return characters.

 countTokens StringTokenizer util

```
public int countTokens()
```

This method returns the number of remaining tokens.

 The quantity of tokens remaining in the String being tokenized.

 hasMoreElements StringTokenizer util

```
public boolean hasMoreElements()
```

This method can be used to determine whether the StringTokenizer contains more elements (tokens). This method is identical to hasMoreTokens and is a member of StringTokenizer because StringTokenizer implements the Enumeration interface.

 true if there are more elements; false, otherwise.

 hasMoreTokens StringTokenizer util

```
public boolean hasMoreTokens()
```

This method can be used to determine whether the StringTokenizer contains more tokens. It is identical to hasMoreElements.

 true if there are more tokens; false, otherwise.

 nextElement StringTokenizer util

```
public Object nextElement()
```

This method overrides nextElement in the Enumeration interface and exists because StringTokenizer implements that interface. It is identical to nextToken and returns the next token in the enumeration.

 The next token in the enumeration.

 NoSuchElementException is thrown if there are no more elements.

nextToken StringTokenizer util

```
public String nextToken()
```

This method returns the next token in the `String` that is being tokenized. Typically, it is used inside a loop that processes each token. For example, the following code uses whitespace delimiters to tokenize the string `"This has four tokens"` and displays each of the tokens:

```
String s = "This has four tokens";
StringTokenizer st = new StringTokenizer(s);

int tokenCount = 0;
Graphics g = getGraphics();
while (st.hasMoreTokens()) {
    tokenCount++;
    g.drawString(st.nextToken(), 15, 15*tokenCount);
}
```

↵ The next token in the string being tokenized.

☞ `NoSuchElementException` is thrown if there are no more tokens.

 nextToken StringTokenizer util

```
public String nextToken(String delim)
```

This method changes the set of delimiter characters and then returns the next token. The new delimiter set remains in effect after this method completes.

▶ `delim` is a `String` containing the new set of delimiters.

↵ The next token in the string being tokenized.

☞ `NoSuchElementException` is thrown if there are no more tokens.

Vector util

 Object

 Cloneable

The class `java.util.Vector` extends the class `java.util.Object` and implements the `Cloneable` interface. A `Vector` is analogous to a linked list in other languages or class libraries. A `Vector` stores items of type `Object`, so it can be used to store instances of any Java class. A single `Vector` may store different elements that are instances of different classes. The non-private interface of the class is shown in Listing 34.12.

Listing 34.12. The Vector class.

```
public class Vector extends Object {
  // public constructors
    public Vector(int initialCapacity, int capacityIncrement);
    public Vector(int initialCapacity);
    public Vector();
  // public instance methods
    public final synchronized void addElement(Object obj);
    public final int capacity();
    public synchronized Object clone();
    public final boolean contains(Object elem);
    public final synchronized void copyInto(Object anArray[]);
    public final synchronized Object elementAt(int index);
    public final synchronized Enumeration elements();
    public final synchronized void ensureCapacity(int minCapacity);
    public final synchronized Object firstElement();
    public final int indexOf(Object elem);
    public final synchronized int indexOf(Object elem, int index);
    public final synchronized void insertElementAt(Object obj, int index);
    public final boolean isEmpty();
    public final synchronized Object lastElement();
    public final int lastIndexOf(Object elem);
    public final synchronized int lastIndexOf(Object elem, int index);
    public final synchronized void removeAllElements();
    public final synchronized boolean removeElement(Object obj);
    public final synchronized void removeElementAt(int index);
    public final synchronized void setElementAt(Object obj, int index);
    public final synchronized void setSize(int newSize);
    public final int size();
    public final synchronized String toString();
    public final synchronized void trimToSize();
  // protected variables
    protected int capacityIncrement;
    protected int elementCount;
    protected Object elementData[];
}
```

 Vector Vector　util

```
public Vector(int initialCapacity, int capacityIncrement)
```

This constructor creates a new instance of a Vector with space for initialCapacity elements initially. Memory for additional elements is allocated in blocks that each hold capacityIncrement elements. For example, to allocate a Vector that will hold 100 elements initially and will allocate space for ten more at a time, use the following code:

```
Vector myVector = new Vector(100, 10);
```

 initialCapacity is the number of elements for which to allocate space when the object is created.

▶ capacityIncrement is the number of additional elements for which to allocate space whenever additional space is needed.

 ## Vector Vector util

```
public Vector(int initialCapacity)
```

This constructor creates a new instance of a Vector with space for initialCapacity elements. Whenever a new element that would exceed this capacity is added, the size of the vector is doubled.

▶ initialCapacity is the number of elements for which to allocate space when the object is created.

 ## Vector Vector util

```
public Vector()
```

This constructor creates a new instance of a Vector. Initially, the Vector has room for storing ten elements, but this increases automatically to accommodate new elements. Whenever a new element is added that exceeds this capacity, the size of the vector is doubled.

Variables

protected int capacityIncrement

This member stores the amount by which the Vector will be incremented each time it needs to grow. If capacityIncrement is 0, then the buffer does not grow by a fixed amount but instead, doubles whenever it needs to grow.

protected int elementCount

This member stores the number of elements in the Vector.

protected Object elementData[]

This member is the array where the Vector elements are stored.

 ## addElement Vector util

```
public final synchronized void addElement(Object obj)
```

This method is used to insert new elements into the Vector. A Vector can store objects of different types. For example, to create a Vector holding three Dates and a Stack with three items pushed onto it, use the following code:

```
Vector myVector = new Vector();

myVector.addElement(new Date(95, 10, 14));
myVector.addElement(new Date(96, 10, 14));
myVector.addElement(new Date(97, 10, 14));
```

```
Stack s = new Stack();
s.push(new Integer(0));
s.push(new Integer(10));
s.push(new Integer(20));

myVector.addElement(s);
```

▶   obj is the object to add to the vector.

capacity   Vector   util

```
public final int capacity()
```

The method returns the number of elements that will fit in the Vector before more space is allocated. For example, the variable qty in the following code will equal 15:

```
Vector myVector = new Vector(10, 5);
myVector.addElement(new Integer(1));
myVector.addElement(new Integer(2));
myVector.addElement(new Integer(3));
myVector.addElement(new Integer(4));
myVector.addElement(new Integer(5));
myVector.addElement(new Integer(6));
myVector.addElement(new Integer(7));
myVector.addElement(new Integer(8));
myVector.addElement(new Integer(9));
myVector.addElement(new Integer(10));
myVector.addElement(new Integer(11));
int qty = myVector.capacity();
```

In this example, qty equals 15 because of the 10 allocated by the constructor and the additional 5 allocated when the size of the Vector exceeded its initial capacity.

↵   The number of elements that will fit in the currently allocated portion of the Vector.

clone   Vector   util

```
public synchronized Object clone()
```

This method overrides clone in Object and will clone the Vector. Only the Vector itself is cloned; the elements of the Vector are not cloned. The following example creates two duplicate Vectors, each containing the same three strings:

```
Vector vector1 = new Vector();
vector1.addElement(new String("first string"));
vector1.addElement(new String("second string"));
vector1.addElement(new String("third string"));

Vector vector2 = (Vector)vector1.clone();
```

↵   A cloned copy of the Vector.

contains Vector util

```
public final boolean contains(Object elem)
```

This method determines whether an object is stored in a Vector. In the following example, 2 is contained in the vector but 12 is not:

```
Vector myVector = new Vector();
myVector.addElement(new Integer(1));
myVector.addElement(new Integer(2));
myVector.addElement(new Integer(3));

Graphics g = getGraphics();
if (myVector.contains(new Integer(2)))
    g.drawString("it contains 2", 15, 15);
if (myVector.contains(new Integer(12)))
    g.drawString("it contains 12", 15, 30);
```

 true if the object is stored in the Vector; false, otherwise.

 copyInto Vector util

```
public final synchronized void copyInto(Object anArray[])
```

This method copies the elements of the Vector into an array. The following example copies the Vector into the array strArray and then displays the second string ("second string"):

```
String strArray[];

Vector vector1 = new Vector();
vector1.addElement(new String("first string"));
vector1.addElement(new String("second string"));
vector1.addElement(new String("third string"));

strArray = new String[vector1.size()];
vector1.copyInto(strArray);

Graphics g = getGraphics();
g.drawString("second array element is " + strArray[1], 15, 15);
```

▶ anArray is the array into which the Vector elements will be copied.

 elementAt Vector util

```
public final synchronized Object elementAt(int index)
```

This method retrieves the element located at the specified index within the Vector. The index into a Vector is zero-based, so the following example will display "second string":

```
Vector myVector = new Vector();
myVector.addElement(new String("first string"));
myVector.addElement(new String("second string"));
myVector.addElement(new String("third string"));
```

```
Graphics g = getGraphics();
g.drawString((String)myVector.elementAt(1), 15, 15);
```

▶ index is the zero-based index number of the element to retrieve.

↵ The element at the specified zero-based index.

➹ ArrayIndexOutOfBoundsException is thrown if an invalid index is specified.

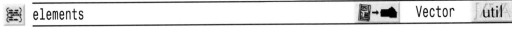

elements   Vector   util

```
public final synchronized Enumeration elements()
```

This method returns an Enumeration of the elements in the Vector, making it easy to iterate through the elements. As an example, consider the following code, which creates a Vector and then steps through an enumeration of the Vector displaying each item:

```
Vector vector1 = new Vector(5);
vector1.addElement(new String("Mike"));
vector1.addElement(new String("Laura"));
vector1.addElement(new String("Savannah"));

int count = 0;
Graphics g = getGraphics();
for (Enumeration enum = vector1.elements() ; enum.hasMoreElements() ;) {
    count++;
    g.drawString((String)enum.nextElement(), 15, 15*count);
}
```

↵ An Enumeration consisting of all the elements in the Vector.

ensureCapacity   Vector   util

```
public final synchronized void ensureCapacity(int minCapacity)
```

This method ensures that the Vector has at least the specified minimum capacity. If the current capacity of the Vector is less than minCapacity, the size of the Vector is increased to hold at least minCapacity.

▶ minCapacity is the desired minimum capacity of the Vector.

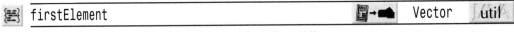

firstElement   Vector   util

```
public final synchronized Object firstElement()
```

This method retrieves the first element in the Vector. If the Vector is empty, an exception is thrown. It performs the same function as elementAt(0). As an example of its use, the following displays "first string":

```
Vector myVector = new Vector();
myVector.addElement(new String("first string"));
myVector.addElement(new String("second string"));
myVector.addElement(new String("third string"));
```

```
Graphics g = getGraphics();
g.drawString((String)myVector.firstElement(), 15, 15);
```

↵ The element at the specified zero-based index.

☞ `NoSuchElementException` is thrown if the `Vector` is empty.

 ## indexOf 📖→🔺 Vector util

```
public final int indexOf(Object elem)
```

This method searches the `Vector` and returns the zero-based index number of the first matching object. The following example creates a `Vector` and then finds the element number (1) that matches the `Integer` 21 element:

```
Vector vector1 = new Vector();
vector1.addElement(new Integer(11));
vector1.addElement(new Integer(21));
vector1.addElement(new Integer(31));
vector1.addElement(new Integer(11));

int index = vector1.indexOf(new Integer(21));

Graphics g = getGraphics();
g.drawString("Item found at index " + index, 15, 15);
```

Because this method always starts searching from the first element in the `Vector`, it can be used only to find the first matching index number. To find subsequent matching index numbers, use `indexOf(Object elem, int index)`. Similarly, the methods `lastIndexOf(Object elem)` and `indexOf(Object elem, int index)` can be used for backward traversal of a `Vector`.

▶ `elem` is the element for which you want to find the index.

↵ The element number of the first element that matches `elem`; if no match is found, `-1` is returned.

 ## indexOf 📖→🔺 Vector util

```
public final synchronized int indexOf(Object elem, int index)
```

This method finds the first element in the `Vector` that matches `elem` starting at the element given by `index`. It is very useful for traversing a `Vector` searching for all elements matching a specific object. The following example demonstrates this by searching for the three integer elements with a value of `11`:

```
Vector vector1 = new Vector();
vector1.addElement(new Integer(11));
vector1.addElement(new Integer(21));
vector1.addElement(new Integer(31));
vector1.addElement(new Integer(11));
vector1.addElement(new Integer(11));
vector1.addElement(new Integer(21));
```

```
int index = 0;
int itemsFound = 0;
Integer findMe = new Integer(11);
Graphics g = getGraphics();
while (index != -1) {
    index = vector1.indexOf(findMe, index);
    if (index != -1) {
        itemsFound++;
        g.drawString("Matched element " + index, 15, itemsFound * 15);
        index++;     // move to the next element and continue search
    }
}
g.drawString("Matching items: " + itemsFound, 15, itemsFound*15 + 15);
```

▶ elem is the element for which you want to find the index.

▶ index is the index number at which to start the search.

↵ The element number of the first element that matches elem; if no match is found, -1 is returned.

---

insertElementAt 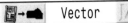 Vector util

```
public final synchronized void insertElementAt(Object obj, int index)
```

This method, like addElement, is used to add a new element to a Vector. However, this method can be used to specify where in the Vector the new element should be added. All Vector elements with index numbers greater than or equal to index are moved to make room for the new element. The following example builds a Vector of Integer values and uses insertElementAt to fill in a gap:

```
Vector vector1 = new Vector();
vector1.addElement(new Integer(10));
vector1.addElement(new Integer(11));
vector1.addElement(new Integer(12));
vector1.addElement(new Integer(14));
vector1.addElement(new Integer(15));

vector1.insertElementAt(new Integer(13), 3);

Graphics g = getGraphics();
g.drawString(vector1.toString(), 15, 15);
```

▶ obj is the object to add to the vector.

▶ index is the zero-based index at which the object is to be inserted.

↰ ArrayIndexOutOfBoundsException is thrown if the specified index is invalid.

---

 isEmpty Vector util

```
public final boolean isEmpty()
```

This method is used to determine whether the `Vector` contains any elements.

↵ `true` if the `Vector` has no elements; `false`, otherwise.

 lastElement  Vector util

```
public final synchronized Object lastElement()
```

This method retrieves the last element in the `Vector`. If the `Vector` is empty, an exception is thrown. As an example of `lastElement`, the following will display `"third string"`:

```
Vector myVector = new Vector();
myVector.addElement(new String("first string"));
myVector.addElement(new String("second string"));
myVector.addElement(new String("third string"));

Graphics g = getGraphics();
g.drawString((String)myVector.lastElement(), 15, 15);
```

↵ The element at the specified zero-based index.

↵ `NoSuchElementException` is thrown if the `Vector` is empty.

lastIndexOf  Vector util

```
public final int lastIndexOf(Object elem)
```

This method searches the `Vector` and returns the zero-based index number of the last matching object. The following example creates a vector and then finds the last element number (4) that matches the `Integer` 11 element:

```
Vector vector1 = new Vector();
vector1.addElement(new Integer(11));
vector1.addElement(new Integer(21));
vector1.addElement(new Integer(31));
vector1.addElement(new Integer(11));
vector1.addElement(new Integer(11));
vector1.addElement(new Integer(21));

int index = vector1.lastIndexOf(new Integer(11));

Graphics g = getGraphics();
g.drawString("Item found at index " + index, 15, 15);
```

Because this method always starts searching from the last element in the `Vector`, it can be used only to find the last matching index number. For other methods that can be used to find items, see `indexOf(Object elem, int index)`, `lastIndexOf(Object elem)`, and `indexOf(Object elem, int index)`.

▶ `elem` is the element for which you want to find the index.

↵ The element number of the last element that matches `elem`; if no match is found, `-1` is returned.

lastIndexOf Vector util

```
public final synchronized int lastIndexOf(Object elem, int index)
```

This method finds the last element in the Vector that matches elem starting at the element given by index. It is very useful for traversing a Vector backward, searching for all elements matching a specific object. The following example demonstrates this by searching from the end of the Vector to the front:

```
Vector vector1 = new Vector();
vector1.addElement(new Integer(11));
vector1.addElement(new Integer(21));
vector1.addElement(new Integer(31));
vector1.addElement(new Integer(11));
vector1.addElement(new Integer(11));
vector1.addElement(new Integer(21));

int index = vector1.size() - 1; // start on last element
int itemsFound = 0;
Integer findMe = new Integer(11);
Graphics g = getGraphics();
while (index != -1) {
    index = vector1.lastIndexOf(findMe, index);
    if (index != -1) {
        itemsFound++;
        g.drawString("Matched element " + index, 15, itemsFound * 15);
    }
}
g.drawString("Matching items: " + itemsFound, 15, itemsFound*15 + 15);
```

▶ elem is the element for which you want to find the index.

▶ index is the index number at which to start the search.

↵ The element number of the last element that matches elem; if no match is found, -1 is returned.

removeAllElements Vector util

```
public final synchronized void removeAllElements()
```

This method can be used to remove all elements from the Vector.

removeElement Vector util

```
public final synchronized boolean removeElement(Object obj)
```

This method can be used to remove a specific element from the Vector. Only the first element that matches obj is removed. In order to remove all matching elements, create a loop as shown in the following code:

```
Vector vector1 = new Vector();
vector1.addElement(new String("Jay"));
```

```
vector1.addElement(new String("Mark"));
vector1.addElement(new String("Ted"));
vector1.addElement(new String("Ron"));
vector1.addElement(new String("Ted"));

int removed = 0;
while (vector1.removeElement(new String("Ted")))
    removed++;
```

▶ `obj` is the object to remove.

↵ `true` if the element was found and deleted; `false`, otherwise.

---

removeElementAt  Vector   util

```
public final synchronized void removeElementAt(int index)
```

This method removes the element at the specified zero-based index. For example, the following code inserts duplicate elements with a value of `13`. To remove the one stored in index `3`, you would use the following:

```
Vector vector1 = new Vector();
vector1.addElement(new Integer(10));
vector1.addElement(new Integer(11));
vector1.addElement(new Integer(12));
vector1.addElement(new Integer(13));
vector1.addElement(new Integer(13));
vector1.addElement(new Integer(14));
vector1.addElement(new Integer(15));

vector1.removeElementAt(3);

Graphics g = getGraphics();
g.drawString(vector1.toString(), 15, 15);
```

▶ `index` is the index number of the element to remove from the vector.

☞ `ArrayIndexOutOfBoundsException` is thrown if the specified index is invalid.

---

setElementAt  Vector   util

```
public final synchronized void setElementAt(Object obj, int index)
```

This method replaces an element in the `Vector` with another element. The following example replaces the element at index `3` with the `Integer` `13`:

```
Vector vector1 = new Vector();
vector1.addElement(new Integer(10));
vector1.addElement(new Integer(11));
vector1.addElement(new Integer(12));
vector1.addElement(new Integer(23));
vector1.addElement(new Integer(14));
vector1.addElement(new Integer(15));

vector1.setElementAt(new Integer(13), 3);
```

► obj is the object to be placed in the Vector.

► index is the index number of the element to be replaced.

✦ ArrayIndexOutOfBoundsException is thrown if the specified index is invalid.

---

setSize  Vector util

```
public final synchronized void setSize(int newSize)
```

This method sets the size of the Vector. If the specified size makes the Vector too small to hold its current elements, elements from the end of the Vector are removed. If the new size is larger than the current size, empty elements are added at the end of the Vector. For example, the following code sets the Vector to a size of three and removes two elements from the end of the Vector:

```
Vector vector1 = new Vector(5);
vector1.addElement(new Integer(10));
vector1.addElement(new Integer(11));
vector1.addElement(new Integer(12));
vector1.addElement(new Integer(13));
vector1.addElement(new Integer(14));

// vector = [10, 11, 12, 13, 14]
vector1.setSize(3);
// vector = [10, 11, 12]
```

► newSize is the desired size of the Vector.

---

size  Vector util

```
public final int size()
```

The method returns the number of elements currently in the Vector. For example, the variable qty in the following code will equal 3:

```
Vector myVector = new Vector(10);
myVector.addElement(new Integer(1));
myVector.addElement(new Integer(2));
myVector.addElement(new Integer(3));
int qty = myVector.size();              // will equal 3
```

↵ The number of elements in the Vector.

---

toString  Vector util

```
public final synchronized String toString()
```

This method overrides the toString method in Object and formats the contents of the Vector as a string. For example, the following code will display [10, 11, 12, 13]:

```
Vector vector1 = new Vector(5);
vector1.addElement(new Integer(10));
vector1.addElement(new Integer(11));
vector1.addElement(new Integer(12));
vector1.addElement(new Integer(13));

Graphics g = getGraphics();
g.drawString("Contents are "+ vector1.toString(), 15, 15);
```

 A string representation of the `Vector`.

---

 trimToSize Vector   util

```
public final synchronized void trimToSize()
```

This method removes any excess capacity from the `Vector` by resizing it to hold only the quantity of elements it currently holds. If new items are added, the size of the `Vector` will be increased. In the following example, `originalCapacity` will equal `10`, and `newCapacity` will equal `4`:

```
Vector vector1 = new Vector(10);
vector1.addElement(new Integer(10));
vector1.addElement(new Integer(11));
vector1.addElement(new Integer(12));
vector1.addElement(new Integer(13));

int originalCapacity = vector1.capacity();
vector1.trimToSize();
int newCapacity = vector1.capacity();
```

EmptyStackException   util

➕ RuntimeException

The class `java.util.EmptyStackException` is thrown to indicate that a `Stack` is empty. It can be thrown by the following methods:

- ■ `Stack.peek`
- ■ `Stack.pop`

The non-private interface of the class is shown in Listing 34.13.

Listing 34.13. The exception `EmptyStackException`.

```
public class EmptyStackException extends RuntimeException {
  // public constructors
     public EmptyStackException();
}
```

EmptyStackException   EmptyStackException   util

```
public EmptyStackException();
```

This constructor creates a new instance of the exception without a detail message.

NoSuchElementException   util

RuntimeException

The class `java.util.NoSuchElementException` is thrown to indicate either of the following conditions:

■ A collection object (such as `Enumeration`, `StringTokenizer`, or `Vector`) has no more elements.

■ There are no more elements beyond the current one when iterating through a set, as with `Enumeration.nextElement`.

This exception can be thrown by the following methods:

■ `Enumeration.nextElement`

■ `StringTokenizer.nextElement`

■ `StringTokenizer.nextToken`

■ `Vector.firstElement`

■ `Vector.lastElement`

The non-private interface of the class is shown in Listing 34.14.

Listing 34.14. The exception NoSuchElementException.
```
public class NoSuchElementException() extends RuntimeException {
  // public constructors
     public NoSuchElementException();
}
```

 NoSuchElementException   NoSuchElementException   util

```
public NoSuchElementException();
```

This constructor creates a new instance of the exception without a detail message.

NoSuchElementException   ⬚→!   NoSuchElementException   util

```
public NoSuchElementException(String  s);
```

This constructor creates a new instance of the exception using the specified detail message. To retrieve the contents of the detail after an exception occurs, use code similar to the following:

```
try {
    // exception producing code
}
catch (NoSuchElementException e) {
    System.out.println("Exception: " + e.getMessage());
}
```

35

Package
sun.tools.debug

by Bryan Morgan

The sun.tools.debug package contains the classes used for Java debugging and object inspection tools. The sun.tools.debug package's classes and interfaces are described in detail throughout the remainder of this chapter. Table 35.1 contains all the classes and interfaces that have public members. Figure 35.1 shows graphically the hierarchy of the contents of this package. The remainder of the chapter shows the member variables and methods of each class, interface, and exception in the sun.tools.debug package.

Table 35.1. Contents of package sun.tools.debug.

Class Index	Interface Index	Exception Index
RemoteArray	DebuggerCallback	NoSessionException
RemoteBoolean		NoSuchFieldException
RemoteByte		NoSuchLineNumberException
RemoteChar		
RemoteClass		
RemoteDebugger		
RemoteDouble		
RemoteField		
RemoteFloat		
RemoteInt		
RemoteLong		
RemoteObject		
RemoteShort		
RemoteStackFrame		
RemoteStackVariable		
RemoteString		
RemoteThread		
RemoteThreadGroup		
RemoteValue		
StackFrame		

FIGURE 35.1.

Contents of package
`sun.tools.debug.`

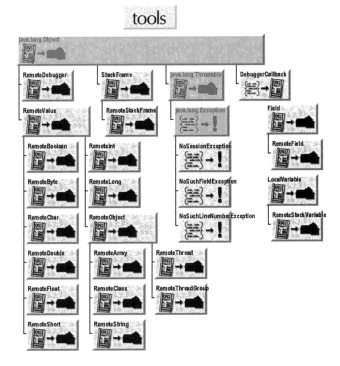

RemoteArray   tools

The class hierarchy for the `RemoteArray` class derives from class `sun.tools.debug.RemoteObject`. The `RemoteArray` class is provided to allow remote debugging of arrays. `RemoteArray`'s overall derivation is shown in Figure 35.1 and its public members are shown in Listing 35.1.

Listing 35.1. Public members of `sun.tools.debug.RemoteArray`.

```
public class RemoteArray {
  public final int getSize()
  public String typeName()
  public String arrayTypeName(int type)
  public final int getElementType() throws Exception
  public final RemoteValue getElement(int index)
  ➥ throws ArrayIndexOutOfBoundsException
  public final RemoteValue[] getElements()
  ➥ throws ArrayIndexOutOfBoundsException
  public final RemoteValue[] getElements(int beginIndex, int endIndex)
  ➥ throws Exception
  public String description()
  public String toString()
}
```

getSize

```
public final int getSize()
```

The `getSize()` method is used to return the number of elements in the remote array.

↵ An integer value representing the number of elements in the array.

typeName

```
public String typeName()
```

The `typeName()` method returns this `RemoteValue` object's type ("Array").

↵ `typeName()` produces a `String` object corresponding to the `RemoteValue` object's type.

arrayTypeName

```
public String arrayTypeName(int type)
```

The `arrayTypeName()` method returns the element type as a string based on the specified integer type.

▶ type is an integer value representing the element type (`TC_CHAR`, for instance).

↵ `arrayTypeName()` retrieves a `String` representation of the element type.

getElementType

```
public final int getElementType() throws Exception
```

The `getElementType()` method returns the integer constant for the element type.

↵ `getElementType()` returns an integer value representing the element type.

↗ An `Exception` if the element type is not determinable.

getElement

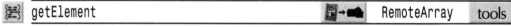

```
public final RemoteValue getElement(int index)
➡ throws ArrayIndexOutOfBoundsException
```

The `getElement()` method returns the `RemoteValue` at the array's specified index. For more information on the `RemoteValue` class, see the documentation later in this chapter.

▶ Index is an integer value representing the index into the array.

↵ `getElement()` retrieves a `RemoteValue` object at the specified index of the array.

↗ An `ArrayIndexOutOfBoundsException` if the specified index is greater than the number of elements in the array.

 getElements RemoteArray tools

```
public final RemoteValue[] getElements() throws ArrayIndexOutOfBoundsException
```

The `getElements()` method returns the contents of the array as an array of `RemoteValue` objects. For more information on the `RemoteValue` class, see the documentation later in this chapter.

↵ `getElements()` creates an array of `RemoteValue` objects.

➤ An `Exception` if the operation could not be completed.

getElements RemoteArray tools

```
public final RemoteValue[] getElements(int beginIndex, int endIndex)
➥ throws ArrayIndexOutOfBoundsException
```

The `getElements()` method returns a subset of the contents of the array as an array of `RemoteValue` objects. For more information on the `RemoteValue` class, see the documentation later in this chapter.

▶ `beginIndex` is an integer value representing the beginning element of the array to copy to the `RemoteValue` array.

▶ `endIndex` is an integer value representing the ending element of the array to copy to the `RemoteValue` array.

↵ `getElements()` creates an array of `RemoteValue` objects.

➤ An `ArrayIndexOutOfBoundsException` if the specified indexes are greater than the number of elements in the array.

description RemoteArray tools

```
public String description()
```

The `description()` method returns a string description of the array.

↵ `description()` produces a `String` object containing a description of the array.

toString RemoteArray tools

```
public String toString()
```

The `toString()` method returns a string version of the array's contents.

↵ `toString()` returns a `String` object containing a textual version of the array.

RemoteBoolean   tools

The class hierarchy for the RemoteBoolean class derives from class sun.tools.debug.RemoteValue. The RemoteBoolean class is provided to allow remote debugging of Boolean values. RemoteBoolean's overall derivation is shown in Figure 35.1, and its public members appear in Listing 35.2.

> **Listing 35.2. Public members of sun.tools.debug.RemoteBoolean.**
> ```
> public class RemoteBoolean {
>   public boolean get()
>   public String typeName()
>   public String toString()
> }
> ```

 get   RemoteBoolean   tools

```
public boolean get()
```

The get() method returns the Boolean value of the RemoteBoolean object.

 get() produces a Boolean value representing the value of the RemoteBoolean object.

 typeName   RemoteBoolean   tools

```
public String typeName()
```

The typeName() method returns a String object containing the type name of the remote object.

typeName() produces a String object containing this RemoteValue's type.

 toString   RemoteBoolean   tools

```
public String toString()
```

The toString() method returns a string representation of this RemoteValue.

toString() creates a String object containing a textual representation of this RemoteValue.

RemoteByte   tools

The class hierarchy for the RemoteByte class derives from class sun.tools.debug.RemoteValue. The RemoteByte class is provided to allow remote debugging of byte values. RemoteByte's overall derivation is shown in Figure 35.1. Listing 35.3 shows its public members.

Listing 35.3. Public members of sun.tools.debug.RemoteByte.

```
public class RemoteByte {
  public byte get()
  public String typeName()
  public String toString()
  }
```

 get RemoteByte tools

```
public byte get()
```

The get() method returns the byte value of the RemoteByte object.

↵ get() produces a byte value representing the value of the RemoteByte object.

 typeName RemoteByte tools

```
public String typeName()
```

The typeName() method returns a String object containing the type name of the remote object.

↵ typeName() produces a String object containing this RemoteValue's type.

 toString RemoteByte tools

```
public String toString()
```

The toString() method returns a string representation of this RemoteValue.

↵ toString() creates a String object containing a textual representation of this RemoteValue.

RemoteChar tools

The class hierarchy for the RemoteChar class derives from class sun.tools.debug.RemoteValue. The RemoteBoolean class enables remote debugging of character values. RemoteChar's overall derivation is shown in Figure 35.1. Listing 35.4 shows its public members.

Listing 35.4. Public members of sun.tools.debug.RemoteChar.

```
public class RemoteChar {
  public char get()
  public String typeName()
  public String toString()
  }
```

```
public char get()
```

The `get()` method returns the character value of the `RemoteChar` object.

↵   `get()` retrieves a `char` value representing the value of the `RemoteChar` object.

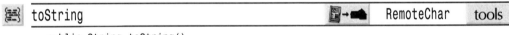

```
public String typeName()
```

The `typeName()` method returns a `String` object containing the type name of the remote object.

↵   `typeName()` produces a `String` object containing this `RemoteValue`'s type.

🔳 **toString**   📠→🔨 **RemoteChar**   tools

```
public String toString()
```

The `toString()` method returns a string representation of this `RemoteValue`.

↵   `toString()` creates a `String` object containing a textual representation of this `RemoteValue`.

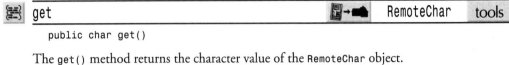

RemoteClass   tools

The class hierarchy for the `RemoteClass` class derives from class `sun.tools.debug.RemoteObject`. The `RemoteClass` class enables remote debugging of class objects. `RemoteClass`'s overall derivation is shown in Figure 35.1. Listing 35.5 shows its public members.

Listing 35.5. Public members of `sun.tools.debug.RemoteClass`.

```
public class RemoteClass {
  public String getName() throws Exception
  public String typeName() throws Exception
  public boolean isInterface() throws Exception
  public RemoteClass getSuperclass() throws Exception
  public RemoteObject getClassLoader() throws Exception
  public RemoteClass[] getInterfaces() throws Exception
  public String getSourceFileName()
  public InputStream getSourceFile() throws Exception
  public RemoteField[] getFields() throws Exception
  public RemoteField[] getStaticFields() throws Exception
  public RemoteField[] getInstanceFields() throws Exception
  public RemoteField getField(int n) throws ArrayIndexOutOfBoundsException
  public RemoteField getField(String name) throws Exception
  public RemoteField getInstanceField(int n)
  ➥ throws ArrayIndexOutOfBoundsException
  public RemoteValue getFieldValue(int n) throws Exception
```

```
public RemoteValue getFieldValue(String name) throws Exception
public RemoteField getMethod(String name) throws Exception
public RemoteField[] getMethods() throws Exception
public String[] getMethodNames() throws Exception
public String setBreakpointLine(int lineno) throws Exception
public String setBreakpointMethod(RemoteField method) throws Exception
public String clearBreakpoint(int pc) throws Exception
public String clearBreakpointLine(int lineno) throws Exception
public String clearBreakpointMethod(RemoteField method) throws Exception
public void catchExceptions() throws Exception
public void ignoreExceptions() throws ClassCastException
public String description()
public String toString()
}
```

---

 getName RemoteClass tools

`public String getName() throws Exception`

The `getName()` method returns the name of the remote class.

 `getName()` produces a `String` object containing the name of the class.

An `Exception` if the class name could not be determined.

---

typeName RemoteClass tools

`public String typeName() throws Exception`

The `typeName()` method returns the name of the class as its type.

`typeName()`produces a `String` object containing the type of the class.

An `Exception` if the class type could not be determined.

---

 isInterface RemoteClass tools

`public boolean isInterface() throws Exception`

The `isInterface()` method is used to determine if the remote class is an interface.

`isInterface()` returns a Boolean value that is `true` if the class is an interface, `false` if not.

An `Exception` if it could not be determined if the class was or was not an interface.

---

 getSuperclass RemoteClass tools

`public RemoteClass getSuperclass() throws Exception`

The `getSuperclass()` method returns the superclass of the `RemoteClass` as a `RemoteClass` object.

↵ getSuperclass() produces a RemoteClass object representing this RemoteClass's superclass.

↗• An Exception if the superclass could not be determined.

getClassLoader   RemoteClass   tools

```
public RemoteObject getClassLoader() throws Exception
```

The getClassLoader() method returns the classloader of the RemoteClass as a RemoteObject object.

↵ getClassLoader() retrieves a RemoteObject object representing this RemoteClass's classloader.

↗• An Exception if the classloader could not be determined.

getInterfaces   RemoteClass   tools

```
public RemoteClass[] getInterfaces() throws Exception
```

The getInterfaces() method returns the interfaces of this RemoteClass as an array of RemoteClass objects.

↵ getInterfaces() creates an array of RemoteClass objects representing this RemoteClass's interfaces.

↗• An Exception if the interfaces could not be determined.

getSourceFileName   RemoteClass   tools

```
public String getSourceFileName()
```

The getSourceFileName() method returns the name of the source file referenced by this RemoteClass object.

↵ getSourceFileName() produces a String object representing the name of the source file referenced by this RemoteClass object.

getSourceFile   RemoteClass   tools

```
public InputStream getSourceFile() throws Exception
```

The getSourceFile() method returns the source file referenced by this RemoteClass object as an InputStream. For more information on the InputStream class, see the documentation in Chapter 31, "Package java.io."

↵ getSourceFile() returns an InputStream representing this RemoteClass's source file.

↗• An Exception if the source file could not be retrieved.

getFields RemoteClass | tools

```
public RemoteField[] getFields() throws Exception
```

The `getFields()` method returns all of the static fields of this object as an array of `RemoteField` objects. For more information on the `RemoteField` class, see the documentation later in this chapter.

 `getFields()` creates an array of `RemoteField` objects representing the fields of this `RemoteClass` object.

An `Exception` if the fields could not be returned.

 getStaticFields RemoteClass | tools

```
public RemoteField[] getStaticFields() throws Exception
```

The `getStaticFields()` method returns all the static fields of this object as an array of `RemoteField` objects. For more information on the `RemoteField` class, see the documentation later in this chapter.

 `getStaticFields()` creates an array of `RemoteField` objects representing the fields of this `RemoteClass` object.

 An `Exception` if the fields could not be returned.

 getInstanceFields RemoteClass | tools

```
public RemoteField[] getInstanceFields() throws Exception
```

The `getInstanceFields()` method returns all of the instance fields of this object as an array of `RemoteField` objects. Because this is a `RemoteClass` method, only the name and type methods will be valid (not the data). For more information on the `RemoteField` class, see the documentation later in this chapter.

 `getInstanceFields()` creates an array of `RemoteField` objects representing the instance fields of this `RemoteClass` object.

 An `Exception` if the instance fields could not be returned.

 getField RemoteClass | tools

```
public RemoteField getField(int n) throws ArrayIndexOutOfBoundsException
```

The `getField()` method returns the static field at the specified index of the `RemoteClass`. For more information on the `RemoteField` class, see the documentation later in this chapter.

▶ n is an integer value representing the index of the field to be returned.

↵ getField() produces a RemoteField object representing the static field at the specified index.

☞ An Exception if the field at the specified index could not be returned.

getField   RemoteClass   tools

```
public RemoteField getField(String name) throws Exception
```

The getField() method returns the static field using the specified field name. For more information on the RemoteField class, see the documentation later in this chapter.

▶ name is a String object containing the name of the static field to be returned.

↵ getField() returns a RemoteField object specified by the field name.

☞ An Exception if the field with the specified name could not be returned.

getInstanceField   RemoteClass   tools

```
public RemoteField getInstanceField(int n) throws ArrayIndexOutOfBoundsException
```

The getInstanceField() method returns the instance field at the specified index of the RemoteClass. For more information on the RemoteField class, see the documentation later in this chapter.

▶ n is an integer value representing the index of the field to be returned.

↵ getInstanceField() produces a RemoteField object representing the instance field at the specified index.

☞ An Exception if the field at the specified index could not be returned.

getFieldValue   RemoteClass   tools

```
public RemoteValue getFieldValue(int n) throws Exception
```

The getFieldValue() method returns the RemoteValue of the static field at the specified index. For more information on the RemoteValue class, see the documentation later in this chapter.

▶ n is an integer value representing the index of the field to be returned.

↵ getFieldValue() retrieves a RemoteValue object representing the value of the field at the specified index.

☞ An Exception if the field's value could not be returned.

getFieldValue  RemoteClass tools

```
public RemoteValue getFieldValue(String name) throws Exception
```

The getFieldValue() method returns the RemoteValue of the static field using the specified name. For more information on the RemoteValue class, see the documentation later in this chapter.

▶ name is a String object representing the name of the static field whose value will be returned.

↵ getFieldValue() produces a RemoteValue object containing the value of the field.

☞ An Exception if the field's value could not be returned.

getMethod 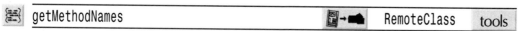 RemoteClass tools

```
public RemoteField getMethod(String name) throws Exception
```

The getMethod() method returns the method using the specified method name. For more information on the RemoteField class, see the documentation later in this chapter.

▶ name is a String object representing the name of the method to be returned.

↵ getMethod() produces a RemoteField object representing the specified method.

☞ An Exception if the specified method could not be returned.

getMethods RemoteClass tools

```
public RemoteField[] getMethods() throws Exception
```

The getMethods() method returns all of a class's methods in an array of RemoteField objects. For more information on the RemoteField class, see the documentation later in this chapter.

↵ getMethods() produces an array of RemoteField objects representing all of the RemoteClass's methods.

☞ An Exception if all of the methods could not be returned.

getMethodNames RemoteClass tools

```
public String[] getMethodNames() throws Exception
```

The getMethodNames() returns an array containing the names of the RemoteClass's methods.

↵ getMethodNames() creates an array of String objects containing the name of the RemoteClass's methods.

☞ An Exception if the names of the RemoteClass's methods could not be returned.

setBreakpointLine RemoteClass tools

```
public String setBreakpointLine(int lineno) throws Exception
```

The `setBreakpointLine()` method sets a breakpoint at the specified line number of the `RemoteClass`.

▶ `lineno` is an integer value representing the line number at which to set the breakpoint.

↵ `setBreakpointLine()` produces a `String` object that is empty if the method was successful or contains an error message if it was unsuccessful.

☛ An `Exception` if the breakpoint was unable to be set.

setBreakpointMethod RemoteClass tools

```
public String setBreakpointMethod(RemoteField method) throws Exception
```

The `setBreakpointMethod()` method sets the breakpoint at the first line of a class method specified by the `RemoteField` parameter. For more information on the `RemoteField` class, see the documentation later in this chapter.

▶ `method` is a `RemoteField` object specifying the method at which to set the breakpoint.

↵ `setBreakpointMethod()` produces an empty `String` object if the method was successful or an error message if it was unsuccessful.

☛ An `Exception` if the `setBreakpointMethod()` method failed.

clearBreakpoint RemoteClass tools

```
public String clearBreakpoint(int pc) throws Exception
```

The `clearBreakpoint()` method clears the breakpoint at the specified class address.

▶ `pc` is an integer value representing the class address at which to clear the breakpoint.

↵ `clearBreakpoint()` produces an empty `String` object if the method was successful or an error message if it was unsuccessful.

☛ An `Exception` if the `clearBreakpoint()` method failed.

clearBreakpointLine   RemoteClass tools

```
public String clearBreakpointLine(int lineno) throws Exception
```

The `clearBreakpointLine()` method clears the breakpoint at the specified line number.

▶ `lineno` is an integer value representing the line number at which to clear the breakpoint.

↵ `clearBreakpointLine()` produces an empty `String` object if the method was successful, or an error message if it was unsuccessful.

An Exception if the `clearBreakpointLine()` method failed.

clearBreakpointMethod RemoteClass tools

```
public String clearBreakpointMethod(RemoteField method) throws Exception
```

The `clearBreakpointMethod()` method is used to clear a breakpoint for a specified method. For more information on the `RemoteField` class, see the documentation later in this chapter.

▶ `method` is a `RemoteField` object specifying the method at which to clear the breakpoint.

 `clearBreakpointMethod()` produces an empty `String` object if the method was successful, or an error message if it was unsuccessful.

 An Exception if the `clearBreakpointMethod()` method failed.

catchExceptions RemoteClass tools

```
public void catchExceptions() throws ClassCastException
```

The `catchExceptions()` method enters the debugger when an instance of this class is thrown.

 A `ClassCastException` if this `RemoteClass` isn't an exception class.

ignoreExceptions RemoteClass tools

```
public void ignoreExceptions() throws ClassCastException
```

The `ignoreExceptions()` method prevents the entering of the debugger when an instance of this class is thrown.

 A `ClassCastException` if this `RemoteClass` isn't an exception class.

description RemoteClass tools

```
public String description()
```

The `description()` method returns a `String` description of the class. This method overrides the `description()` method in class `RemoteObject`.

 `description()` produces a `String` object that describes the remote class.

toString RemoteClass tools

```
public String toString()
```

The `toString()` method returns a `String` description of the class.

 A `String` object that describes the remote class.

RemoteDebugger   tools

The class hierarchy for the `RemoteDebugger` class derives from class `java.lang.Object`. The `RemoteDebugger` class is provided to define a client interface to the Java debugging classes. `RemoteDebugger`'s overall derivation is shown in Figure 35.1, and its members appear in Listing 35.6.

Listing 35.6. Public members of `sun.tools.debug.RemoteDebugger`.

```
public class RemoteDebugger {
    public RemoteDebugger(String host, String password, DebuggerCallback client,
    ➥ boolean verbose) throws Exception
    public RemoteDebugger(String javaArgs, DebuggerCallback client,
    ➥ boolean verbose) throws Exception
    public void close()
    public RemoteObject get(Integer id)
    public RemoteClass[] listClasses() throws Exception
    public RemoteClass findClass(String name) throws Exception
    public RemoteThreadGroup[] listThreadGroups(RemoteThreadGroup tg)
    ➥ throws Exception
    public void gc(RemoteObject save_list[]) throws Exception
    public void trace(boolean traceOn) throws Exception
    public void itrace(boolean traceOn) throws Exception
    public int totalMemory() throws Exception
    public int freeMemory() throws Exception
    public RemoteThreadGroup run(int argc, String argv[]) throws Exception
    public String[] listBreakpoints() throws Exception
    public String[] getExceptionCatchList() throws Exception
    public String getSourcePath() throws Exception
    public void setSourcePath(String pathList) throws Exception
}
```

 RemoteDebugger   RemoteDebugger   tools

```
public RemoteDebugger(String host, String password, DebuggerCallback client,
➥ boolean verbose) throws Exception
```

This `RemoteDebugger()` constructor creates a `RemoteDebugger` object using the Java interpreter and the specified host, password, and client method.

▶   `host` is a `String` object that contains the name of the host where the debuggable Java instance is running.

▶   `password` is the password reported by the debuggable Java instance.

▶   `client` is a `DebuggerCallback` interface to which the notification messages are sent. For more information on the `DebuggerCallback` interface, see the documentation later in this chapter.

▶ verbose is a Boolean value that should be `true` if internal debugger message text is to be turned on, `false` if not.

An `Exception` if creating the `RemoteDebugger` caused an error.

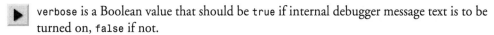

RemoteDebugger — RemoteDebugger — tools

```
public RemoteDebugger(String javaArgs, DebuggerCallback client,
➥ boolean verbose) throws Exception
```

This `RemoteDebugger()` constructor is used to create a `RemoteDebugger` object using a new client interpreter.

▶ javaArgs is a `String` object containing optional Java command-line parameters.

▶ client is a `DebuggerCallback` interface to which the notification messages are sent. For more information on the `DebuggerCallback` interface, see the documentation later in this chapter.

▶ verbose is a Boolean value that should be `true` if internal debugger message text is to be turned on, `false` if not.

An `Exception` if creating the `RemoteDebugger` caused an error.

---

close — RemoteDebugger — tools

```
public void close()
```

The `close()` method closes the connection to the remote debugging tool.

▶ None.

↵ None.

---

get — RemoteDebugger — tools

```
public RemoteObject get(Integer id)
```

The `get()` method retrieves an object from the remote debugging object store.

▶ id is the remote object's identification number.

↵ A `RemoteObject` object, or `null` if no corresponding object is cached.

---

listClasses — RemoteDebugger — tools

```
public RemoteClass[] listClasses() throws Exception
```

The `listClasses()` method lists the currently known classes.

An array of RemoteClass objects. For more information on the RemoteClass class, see the documentation earlier in this chapter.

An Exception if an error occurred while retrieving classes.

findClass RemoteDebugger tools

```
public RemoteClass findClass(String name) throws Exception
```

The findClass() method returns the specified RemoteClass. For more information on the RemoteClass class, see the documentation earlier in this chapter.

▶ name is a String object specifying the name of the remote class to be returned.

The specified RemoteClass object or null if not found.

An Exception if an error occurred while retrieving the class.

listThreadGroups RemoteDebugger tools

```
public RemoteThreadGroup[] listThreadGroups(RemoteThreadGroup tg)
➡ throws Exception
```

The listThreadGroups() method returns either part or all of the RemoteThreadGroup objects available.

▶ tg is the thread group that holds the groups to be listed or null for all of the thread groups.

An array of RemoteThreadGroup objects. For more information on the RemoteThreadGroup class, see the documentation later in this chapter.

An Exception if an error occurred while listing the thread groups.

gc RemoteDebugger tools

```
public void gc(RemoteObject save_list[]) throws Exception
```

The gc() method frees all objects referenced by the debugger except for those objects specified to save.

▶ save_list is an array of RemoteObject objects that are not to be deleted by the gc() method. For more information on the RemoteObject class, see the documentation later in this chapter.

An Exception if an error occurred while freeing the objects.

trace RemoteDebugger tools

```
public void trace(boolean traceOn) throws Exception
```

The trace() method allows call tracing to be turned on or off.

▶ traceOn is a Boolean value that is `true` if tracing is to be turned on, `false` if tracing is to be turned off.

🖝 An `Exception` if this method caused an error.

itrace  RemoteDebugger tools

```
public void itrace(boolean traceOn) throws Exception
```

The `itrace()` method allows instruction tracing to be turned on or off.

▶ traceOn is a Boolean value that is `true` if tracing is to be turned on, `false` if it is to be turned off.

🖝 An `Exception` if this method caused an error.

totalMemory  RemoteDebugger tools

```
public int totalMemory() throws Exception
```

The `totalMemory()` returns the total memory usage of the Java interpreter being debugged.

↵ An integer value representing the total number of bytes being used by the Java interpreter.

🖝 An exception if the total memory cannot be determined.

freeMemory RemoteDebugger tools

```
public int freeMemory() throws Exception
```

The `freeMemory()` method returns the free memory that is available to the Java interpreter being debugged.

↵ An integer value representing the number of free memory bytes available to the Java interpreter being debugged.

🖝 An `Exception` if the free memory available cannot be determined.

run RemoteDebugger tools

```
public RemoteThreadGroup run(int argc, String argv[]) throws Exception
```

The `run()` method loads and runs a Java class using the specified parameters. The Java interpreter being debugged creates a new thread group to run the class inside.

▶ argc is an integer value representing the number of arguments passed to the interpreter.

▶ argv is an array of `String` objects containing the arguments passed to the interpreter.

↵ A `RemoteThreadGroup` object that the class will be run inside. For more information on the `RemoteThreadGroup` class, see the documentation later in this chapter.

An Exception if the class could not be run.

---

listBreakpoints — RemoteDebugger — tools

```
public String[] listBreakpoints() throws Exception
```

The listBreakpoints() method returns a list of the breakpoints that are currently set.

An array of String objects containing the class and line number for each breakpoint that is currently set.

An Exception if the list of breakpoints cannot be retrieved.

---

getExceptionCatchList — RemoteDebugger — tools

```
public String[] getExceptionCatchList() throws Exception
```

The getExceptionCatchList() method returns the list of exceptions that the debugger will halt on.

An array of String objects that represent exception class names.

An Exception if the list of exceptions could not be returned.

---

getSourcePath — RemoteDebugger — tools

```
public String getSourcePath() throws Exception
```

The getSourcePath() method returns a String object containing the source file path that the debugging agent is currently using.

A String object containing the source file path.

An Exception if the source file path could not be returned.

---

setSourcePath — RemoteDebugger — tools

```
public void setSourcePath(String pathList) throws Exception
```

The setSourcePath() method uses the specified pathList to set the source file path used by the debugging agent.

pathList is a String object containing a list of colon-delimited paths for use by the debugging agent.

An Exception if the source path could not be set.

 ## RemoteDouble   tools

The class hierarchy for the RemoteDouble class derives from class sun.tools.debug.RemoteValue. The RemoteDouble class enables remote debugging of double values. RemoteDouble's overall derivation is shown in Figure 35.1. Listing 35.7 shows its public members.

> **Listing 35.7. Public members of sun.tools.debug.RemoteDouble.**
> ```
> public class RemoteDouble {
>   public double get()
>   public String typeName()
>   public String toString()
> }
> ```

 ### get   RemoteDouble   tools

```
public double get()
```

The get() method returns the double value of the RemoteDouble object.

 A double value representing the value of the RemoteDouble object.

typeName   RemoteDouble   tools

```
public String typeName()
```

The typeName() method returns a String object containing the type name of the remote object.

 A String object containing this RemoteValue's type.

toString   RemoteDouble   tools

```
public String toString()
```

The toString() method returns a string representation of this RemoteValue.

A String object containing a textual representation of this RemoteValue.

RemoteField   tools

The class hierarchy for the RemoteField class derives from class sun.tools.debug.Field. The RemoteField class enables remote debugging of field values of an object in a Java interpreter. RemoteField's overall derivation is shown in Figure 35.1. Listing 35.8 shows its public members.

Listing 35.8. Public members of `sun.tools.debug.RemoteField`.

```
public class RemoteField {
  public String getName()
  public String getType()
  public String getModifiers()
  public boolean isStatic()
  public String toString()
  }
```

getName RemoteField   tools

```
public String getName()
```

The `getName()` method returns a string containing the field's name.

↵ A `String` object that contains the field's name.

getType RemoteField   tools

```
public String getType()
```

The `getType()` method returns a `String` object containing information about the field's type.

↵ A `String` object that describes the field.

getModifiers RemoteField   tools

```
public String getModifiers()
```

The `getModifiers()` method returns a string containing information about the field.

↵ A `String` object that contains the field's modifiers.

isStatic RemoteField   tools

```
public boolean isStatic()
```

The `isStatic()` method can be called to determine whether or not the field is static.

↵ A Boolean value that is `true` if the field is static, `false` if not.

toString RemoteField   tools

```
public String toString()
```

The `toString()` method returns a textual representation of the field.

↵ A `String` object that represents the value of this `RemoteField`.

 # RemoteFloat tools

The class hierarchy for the RemoteFloat class derives from class sun.tools.debug.RemoteValue. The RemoteFloat class allows remote debugging of float values. RemoteFloat's overall derivation appears in Figure 35.1 and its public members in Listing 35.9.

> **Listing 35.9. Public members of sun.tools.debug.RemoteFloat.**
> ```
> public class RemoteFloat {
>   public float get()
>   public String typeName()
>   public String toString()
> }
> ```

 ## get   RemoteFloat tools

```
public float get()
```

The get() method returns the float value of the RemoteFloat object.

↵ A float value representing the value of the RemoteFloat object.

 ## typeName   RemoteFloat tools

```
public String typeName()
```

The typeName() method returns a String object containing the type name of the remote object.

↵ A String object containing this RemoteValue's type.

 ## toString   RemoteFloat tools

```
public String toString()
```

The toString() method returns a string representation of this RemoteValue.

↵ A String object containing a textual representation of this RemoteValue.

RemoteInt tools

The class hierarchy for the RemoteInt class derives from class sun.tools.debug.RemoteValue. The RemoteInt class allows remote debugging of int values. RemoteInt's overall derivation appears in Figure 35.1. Listing 35.10 shows its public members.

> **Listing 35.10. Public members of `sun.tools.debug.RemoteInt`.**
>
> ```
> public class RemoteInt {
>   public int get()
>   public String typeName()
>   public String toString()
> }
> ```

 get   RemoteInt   tools

```
public int get()
```

The `get()` method returns the `int` value of the `RemoteInt` object.

↵   An `int` value representing the value of the `RemoteInt` object.

 typeName   RemoteInt   tools

```
public String typeName()
```

The `typeName()` method returns a `String` object containing the type name of the remote object.

↵   A `String` object that contains this `RemoteValue`'s type.

 toString   RemoteInt   tools

```
public String toString()
```

The `toString()` method returns a string representation of this `RemoteValue`.

↵   A `String` object that contains a textual representation of this `RemoteValue`.

RemoteLong   tools

The class hierarchy for the `RemoteLong` class derives from class `sun.tools.debug.RemoteValue`. The `RemoteLong` class allows remote debugging of `long` values. `RemoteLong`'s overall derivation is shown in Figure 35.1. Listing 35.11 shows its public members.

> **Listing 35.11. Public members of `sun.tools.debug.RemoteLong`.**
>
> ```
> public class RemoteLong {
>   public long get()
>   public String typeName()
>   public String toString()
> }
> ```

get RemoteLong   tools

```
public long get()
```

The get() method returns the long value of the RemoteLong object.

↵ A long value representing the value of the RemoteLong object.

 typeName RemoteLong   tools

```
public String typeName()
```

The typeName() method returns a String object that contains the type name of the remote object.

↵ A String object containing this RemoteValue's type.

 toString RemoteLong   tools

```
public String toString()
```

The toString() method returns a string representation of this RemoteValue.

↵ A String object that contains a textual representation of this RemoteValue.

RemoteObject   tools

The class hierarchy for the RemoteObject class derives from class sun.tools.debug.RemoteValue. The RemoteObject class enables remote debugging of objects. RemoteObject's overall derivation appears in Figure 35.1. Listing 35.12 shows its public members.

Listing 35.12. Public members of sun.tools.debug.RemoteObject.

```
public class RemoteObject {
  public String typeName() throws Exception
  public final int getId()
  public final RemoteClass getClazz()
  public RemoteValue getFieldValue(int n) throws Exception
  public RemoteValue getFieldValue(String name) throws Exception
  public RemoteField[] getFields() throws Exception
  public RemoteField getField(int n) throws Exception
  public RemoteField getField(String name) throws Exception
  public String description()
  public String toString()
  }
```

typeName 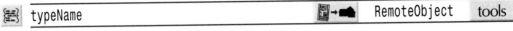 RemoteObject   tools

```
public String typeName() throws Exception
```

The `typeName()` method returns the `RemoteObject`'s type name.

↵   A `String` value that contains the `RemoteObject`'s type name ("`Object`").

➤   An `Exception` if the `RemoteObject`'s type name was unable to be determined.

getId   RemoteObject   tools

```
public final int getId()
```

The `getId()` method returns the ID of the `RemoteObject`.

↵   An integer value that represents the ID of the `RemoteObject`.

getClazz   RemoteObject   tools

```
public final RemoteClass getClazz()
```

The `getClazz()` returns the object's class as a `RemoteClass` object. For more information on the `RemoteClass` class, see the documentation earlier in this chapter.

↵   A `RemoteClass` object that represents this object's class.

getFieldValue   RemoteObject   tools

```
public RemoteValue getFieldValue(int n) throws Exception
```

The `getFieldValue()` method returns the value of the specified object as a `RemoteValue` object. For more information on the `RemoteValue` class, see the documentation later in this chapter.

▶   n is an integer value that represents the ID of the variable to be returned.

↵   A `RemoteValue` class.

➤   An `Exception` if this field's value could not be determined.

getFieldValue   RemoteObject   tools

```
public RemoteValue getFieldValue(String name) throws Exception
```

The `getFieldValue()` method returns the value of the specified field as a `RemoteValue` object. For more information on the `RemoteValue` class, see the documentation later in this chapter.

▶   name is a `String` object that specifies the field's name.

↵   A `RemoteValue` object that represents the field's value.

➤   An `Exception` if the specified field could not be returned.

getFields   RemoteObject   tools

```
public RemoteField[] getFields() throws Exception
```

The `getFields()` method is used to return all of the non-static fields of a `RemoteObject`.

An array of `RemoteField` objects. For more information on the `RemoteField` class, see the documentation earlier in this chapter.

An `Exception` if the fields could not be returned.

getField   RemoteObject   tools

```
public RemoteField getField(int n) throws Exception
```

The `getField()` method is used to return the field at the specified index.

n is an integer value representing the slot number of the field.

A `RemoteField` object that corresponds to the specified field index. For more information on the `RemoteField` class, see the documentation earlier in this chapter.

An `Exception` if the specified field could not be retrieved.

getField   RemoteObject   tools

```
public RemoteField getField(String name) throws Exception
```

The `getField()` method returns a `RemoteField` object based on the specified field name.

name is a `String` object containing the name of the field to be returned.

A `RemoteField` object that corresponds to the specified field name. For more information on the `RemoteField` class, see the documentation earlier in this chapter.

An `Exception` if the field could not be retrieved.

description   RemoteObject   tools

```
public String description()
```

The `description()` method returns a string description of the `RemoteObject`.

A `String` object containing a description of the object.

toString   RemoteObject   tools

```
public String toString()
```

The `toString()` method returns a textual representation of the `RemoteObject`.

`toString()` The `RemoteObject` as a `String`.

RemoteShort   tools

The class hierarchy for the RemoteShort class derives from class sun.tools.debug.RemoteValue. The RemoteShort class enables remote debugging of short values. RemoteShort's overall derivation is shown in Figure 35.1. Listing 35.13 shows its public members.

> **Listing 35.13. Public members of sun.tools.debug.RemoteShort.**
>
> ```
> public class RemoteShort {
>   public short get()
>   public String typeName()
>   public String toString()
> }
> ```

get   RemoteShort   tools

```
public short get()
```

The get() method returns the short value of the RemoteShort object.

↵ A short value representing the value of the RemoteShort object.

typeName   RemoteShort   tools

```
public String typeName()
```

The typeName() method returns a String object containing the type name of the remote object.

↵ A String object containing this RemoteValue's type.

toString   RemoteShort   tools

```
public String toString()
```

The toString() method returns a string representation of this RemoteValue.

↵ A String object containing a textual representation of this RemoteValue.

RemoteStackFrame   tools

The class hierarchy for the RemoteStackFrame class derives from class sun.tools.debug.StackFrame. The RemoteStackFrame provides access to a stack frame of a suspended thread. RemoteStackFrame's overall derivation is shown in Figure 35.1. Listing 35.14 shows its public members.

> **Listing 35.14. Public members of `sun.tools.debug.RemoteStackFrame`.**
> ```
> public class RemoteStackFrame {
>   public RemoteStackVariable getLocalVariable(String name) throws Exception
>   public RemoteStackVariable[] getLocalVariables() throws Exception
>   public int getLineNumber()
>   public String getMethodName()
>   public int getPC()
>   public RemoteClass getRemoteClass()
> }
> ```

getLocalVariable RemoteStackFrame   tools

```
public RemoteStackVariable getLocalVariable(String name) throws Exception
```

The `getLocalVariable()` method returns the specified stack variable.

▶ `name` is a `String` object specifying the name of the stack variable.

↵ A `RemoteStackVariable` object. For more information on the `RemoteStackVariable` class, see the information later in this chapter.

☛ An `Exception` if the variable could not be retrieved.

getLocalVariables RemoteStackFrame   tools

```
public RemoteStackVariable[] getLocalVariables() throws Exception
```

The `getLocalVariables()` method returns all valid local variables and method arguments for this `RemoteStackFrame`.

↵ An array of `RemoteStackVariable` objects. For more information on the class `RemoteStackVariable`, see the documentation later in this chapter.

☛ An `Exception` if the local variables could not be retrieved.

getLineNumber RemoteStackFrame   tools

```
public int getLineNumber()
```

The `getLineNumber()` method returns the current source file line number.

↵ An integer value representing the source file line number.

getMethodName RemoteStackFrame   tools

```
public String getMethodName()
```

The `getMethodName()` method returns the name of the method referenced by this `RemoteStackFrame`.

↵ A `String` object that contains the name of the method referenced by this `RemoteStackFrame`.

---

getPC RemoteStackFrame tools

```
public int getPC()
```

The `getPC()` method retrieves this `RemoteStackFrame`'s program counter.

↵ An integer value representing the program counter referenced by this `RemoteStackFrame`.

---

getRemoteClass RemoteStackFrame tools

```
public RemoteClass getRemoteClass()
```

The `getRemoteClass()` method returns the class referenced by this `RemoteStackFrame`.

↵ A `RemoteClass` object. For more information on the `RemoteClass` class, see the documentation earlier in this chapter.

RemoteStackVariable tools

The class hierarchy for the `RemoteStackVariable` class derives from class `sun.tools.debug.LocalVariable`. The `RemoteStackVariable` class enables remote debugging of method arguments or local variables. `RemoteStackVariable`'s overall derivation is shown in Figure 35.1. Listing 35.15 shows its public members.

> **Listing 35.15. Public members of `sun.tools.debug.RemoteStackVariable`.**
> ```
> public class RemoteStackVariable {
>   public String getName()
>   public RemoteValue getValue()
>   public boolean inScope()
> }
> ```

---

getName RemoteStackVariable tools

```
public String getName()
```

The `getName()` method returns the name of this `RemoteStackVariable`.

↵ A `String` object that contains the name of the stack variable.

---

getValue RemoteStackVariable tools

```
public RemoteValue getValue()
```

The getValue() method returns the value of the stack variable.

 A RemoteValue object. For more information on the RemoteValue class, see the documentation later in this chapter.

---

 inScope   RemoteStackVariable   tools

```
public boolean inScope()
```

The inScope() method is used to determine if this stack variable is in scope.

 A Boolean value that will be true if the variable is in scope, false if not.

RemoteString   tools

The class hierarchy for the RemoteString class derives from class sun.tools.debug.RemoteObject. The RemoteString class enables remote debugging of string objects. RemoteString's overall derivation is shown in Figure 35.1. Listing 35.16 shows its public members.

Listing 35.16. Public members of sun.tools.debug.RemoteString.

```
public class RemoteString {
  public String typeName()
  public String description()
  public String toString()
}
```

---

 typeName   RemoteString   tools

```
public String typeName()
```

The typeName() method prints this object's type.

 A String object containing the type of this object ("String").

---

 description   RemoteString   tools

```
public String description()
```

The description() method returns the string value of this RemoteString (or null).

 A String object containing the value of the RemoteString.

---

 toString   RemoteString   tools

```
public String toString()
```

The toString() method returns the string representation of this RemoteString (or null).

↵   A String object that contains the contents of the RemoteString.

 # RemoteThread   tools

The class hierarchy for the RemoteThread class derives from class sun.tools.debug.RemoteObject. The RemoteThread class enables remote debugging of threads in a Java interpreter. RemoteThread's overall derivation appears in Figure 35.1. Listing 35.17 shows its public members.

Listing 35.17. Public members of sun.tools.debug.RemoteThread.

```
public class RemoteThread {
  public String getName() throws Exception
  public int getCurrentFrameIndex()
  public void setCurrentFrameIndex(int iFrame)
  public void resetCurrentFrameIndex()
  public void up(int nFrames) throws Exception
  public void down(int nFrames) throws Exception
  public String getStatus() throws Exception
  public RemoteStackFrame[] dumpStack() throws Exception
  public RemoteStackFrame getCurrentFrame() throws Exception
  public void suspend() throws Exception
  public void resume() throws Exception
  public void step(boolean skipLine) throws Exception
  public void next() throws Exception
  public boolean isSuspended()
  public void cont() throws Exception
  public void stop() throws Exception
  public RemoteStackVariable getStackVariable(String name) throws Exception
  public RemoteStackVariable[] getStackVariables() throws Exception
}
```

 getName   RemoteThread   tools

```
public String getName() throws Exception
```

The getName() method returns the name of the RemoteThread.

↵   A String object that contains the name of the thread.

☞   An Exception if the name could not be returned.

 getCurrentFrameIndex   RemoteThread   tools

```
public int getCurrentFrameIndex()
```

The getCurrentFrameIndex() returns the index of the current stack frame.

↵ An integer value containing the index number.

setCurrentFrameIndex   🖳→🪨   RemoteThread   tools

```
public void setCurrentFrameIndex(int iFrame)
```

The `setCurrentFrameIndex()` method is used to set the current stack frame index.

▶ `iFrame` is an integer value specifying the index.

resetCurrentFrameIndex   🖳→🪨   RemoteThread   tools

```
public void resetCurrentFrameIndex()
```

The `resetCurrentFrameIndex()` method resets the current stack frame.

▶ None.

↵ None.

up   🖳→🪨   RemoteThread   tools

```
public void up(int nFrames) throws IllegalAccessError,
➥ ArrayIndexOutOfBoundsException
```

The `up()` method increments the current stack frame to a higher stack frame (`nFrames` higher).

▶ `nFrames` is an integer value representing the number of stack frames to increment.

☛ An `IllegalAccessError` if the thread isn't suspended or waiting.

☛ An `ArrayIndexOutOfBoundsException` if the requested frame is beyond the stack boundary.

down   🖳→🪨   RemoteThread   tools

```
public void down(int nFrames) throws IllegalAccessError,
➥ ArrayIndexOutOfBoundsException
```

The `down()` method decrements the current stack frame to a lower stack frame (`nFrames` lower).

▶ `nFrames` is an integer value representing the number of stack frames to decrement.

☛ An `IllegalAccessError` if the thread isn't suspended or waiting.

☛ An `ArrayIndexOutOfBoundsException` if the requested frame is beyond the stack boundary.

getStatus   🖳→🪨   RemoteThread   tools

```
public String getStatus() throws Exception
```

The getStatus() method returns a string description of the thread's status.

↵ A String object that contains the thread's status.

☞ An Exception if the status could not be returned.

---

dumpStack 　　　　　　　　　　　　　 RemoteThread 　 tools

```
public RemoteStackFrame[] dumpStack() throws Exception
```

The dumpStack() method is used to dump the stack contents.

↵ An array of RemoteStackFrame objects. For more information on the RemoteStackFrame class, see the documentation earlier in this chapter.

☞ An Exception if the RemoteStackFrames could not be retrieved.

---

getCurrentFrame 　　　　　　　　　　　 RemoteThread 　 tools

```
public RemoteStackFrame getCurrentFrame() throws IllegalAccessError
```

The getCurrentFrame() method retrieves the current stack frame.

↵ A RemoteStackFrame object. For more information on the RemoteStackFrame class, see the documentation earlier in this chapter.

☞ An IllegalAccessError if the RemoteStackFrame could not be retrieved.

---

suspend 　　　　　　　　　　　　　　　 RemoteThread 　 tools

```
public void suspend() throws Exception
```

The suspend() method suspends execution of the thread.

☞ An Exception if the thread cannot be suspended.

---

resume 　　　　　　　　　　　　　　　　 RemoteThread 　 tools

```
public void resume() throws Exception
```

The resume() method resumes execution of the thread.

☞ An Exception if the thread's execution cannot be resumed.

---

step 　　　　　　　　　　　　　　　　　 RemoteThread 　 tools

```
public void step(boolean skipLine) throws IllegalAccessError
```

The step() method steps the execution of this thread to the next line.

▶ skipLine is a Boolean value that is true to skip to the next line, false to skip to the next instruction.

An `IllegalAccessError` if the thread isn't suspended or waiting.

next ![icon] RemoteThread tools

```
public void next() throws IllegalAccessError
```

The `next()` method advances the execution of this thread to the next line, but won't step into a method call.

An `IllegalAccessError` if the thread isn't suspended or waiting.

isSuspended ![icon] RemoteThread tools

```
public boolean isSuspended()
```

The `isSuspended()` method is used to determine whether or not the thread is suspended.

A Boolean value that is `true` if the thread is suspended, `false` if not.

cont ![icon] RemoteThread tools

```
public void cont() throws Exception
```

The `cont()` method resumes execution of the thread from a breakpoint unless it has been previously suspended.

An `Exception` if the thread cannot continue.

stop ![icon] RemoteThread tools

```
public void stop() throws Exception
```

The `stop()` method stops the execution of the remote thread.

An `Exception` if the thread cannot be stopped.

getStackVariable ![icon] RemoteThread tools

```
public RemoteStackVariable getStackVariable(String name) throws Exception
```

The `getStackVariable()` method retrieves the specified variable from the stack frame.

name is a `String` object containing the name of the variable to be retrieved.

A `RemoteStackVariable` object. For more information on the `RemoteStackVariable` class, see the documentation earlier in this chapter.

An `Exception` if the remote variable could not be returned.

getStackVariables   RemoteThread   tools

```
public RemoteStackVariable[] getStackVariables() throws Exception
```

The getStackVariables() method returns all of the remote stack variables of the current stack frame.

    An array of RemoteStackVariable objects. For more information on the class RemoteStackVariable, see the documentation earlier in this chapter.

    An Exception if the remote variables could not be returned.

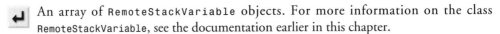

RemoteThreadGroup   tools

The class hierarchy for the RemoteThreadGroup class derives from class sun.tools.debug.RemoteObject. The RemoteThreadGroup class enables remote debugging of a thread group in a Java debugger. RemoteThreadGroup's overall derivation is shown in Figure 35.1. Listing 35.18 shows its public members.

Listing 35.18. Public members of sun.tools.debug.RemoteThreadGroup.

```
public class RemoteThreadGroup {
    public String getName() throws Exception
    public void stop() throws Exception
    public RemoteThread[] listThreads(boolean recurse) throws Exception
}
```

 getName   RemoteThreadGroup   tools

```
public String getName() throws Exception
```

The getName() method returns the name of the RemoteThreadGroup as a string.

    A String object containing the name of the RemoteThreadGroup.

    An Exception if the name could not be returned.

 stop   RemoteThreadGroup   tools

```
public void stop() throws Exception
```

The stop() method is used to stop the execution of the RemoteThreadGroup.

    An Exception if the stop operation fails.

listThreads RemoteThreadGroup tools

```
public RemoteThread[] listThreads(boolean recurse) throws Exception
```

The `listThreads()` method returns a list of all of the `RemoteThreadGroup`'s threads based on the specified recursive option.

▶ `recurse` is a Boolean value that will be `true` if the threads are to be returned recursively, `false` if not. If `recurse` is true, any thread groups contained in this thread group will have their contents returned also, and so on.

↵ An array of `RemoteThread` objects. For more information on the `RemoteThread` class, see the documentation earlier in this chapter.

↵ An `Exception` if the contents of the `RemoteThreadGroup` could not be retrieved.

RemoteValue tools

The class hierarchy for the `RemoteValue` class derives from class `java.lang.Object`. The `RemoteValue` class enables remote debugging of values. `RemoteValue`'s overall derivation is shown in Figure 35.1. Listing 35.19 shows its public members.

> ### Listing 35.19. Public members of `sun.tools.debug.RemoteValue`.
> ```
> public class RemoteValue {
>   public final int getType()
>   public final boolean isObject()
>   public abstract String typeName() throws Exception
>   public String description()
>   public static String toHex(int n)
>   public static int fromHex(String hexStr)
> }
> ```

 getType RemoteValue tools

```
public final int getType()
```

The `getType()` method returns an integer value representing the type of the object.

↵ An integer value used to specify the remote value's type.

 isObject RemoteValue tools

```
public final boolean isObject()
```

The `isObject()` method is used to determine if the remote value is an `Object` (descended from the `Object` class) or is a primitive type such as `int`.

A Boolean value that will be true if the RemoteValue is an Object, false if not.

typeName   RemoteValue   tools

```
public abstract String typeName() throws Exception
```

The typeName() method returns the type of the RemoteValue object as a string.

 A String object containing the type of the RemoteValue.

An Exception if the object's type could not be retrieved.

description   RemoteValue   tools

```
public String description()
```

The description() method is used to return a string description of the RemoteValue.

 A String object containing a description of the RemoteValue.

toHex   RemoteValue   tools

```
public static String toHex(int n)
```

The toHex() method converts the specified integer value into a hexadecimal string.

▶ n is an integer value to be converted.

 A String object containing a hexadecimal representation of the specified integer value.

fromHex   RemoteValue   tools

```
public static int fromHex(String hexStr)
```

The fromHex() method converts the specified hexadecimal string into an integer value.

▶ hexStr is a hexadecimal string value.

 An integer value containing an integer representation of the specified hexadecimal string.

StackFrame   tools

The class hierarchy for the StackFrame class derives from class java.lang.Object. The StackFrame class represents the stack frame of a suspended thread. StackFrame's overall derivation is shown in Figure 35.1. Listing 35.20 shows its public members.

```
public class StackFrame {
  public StackFrame()
  public String toString()
}
```

 StackFrame StackFrame tools

```
public StackFrame()
```

The StackFrame() method creates a default StackFrame object.

▶ None.

↵ None.

 toString StackFrame tools

```
public String toString()
```

The toString() method is used to return a string representation of the StackFrame object.

↵ A String object containing the value of this StackFrame.

 DebuggerCallback tools

The class hierarchy for the DebuggerCallback interface derives from class java.lang.Object. The DebuggerCallback interface allows asynchronous communication between a client and a debugger. DebuggerCallback's overall derivation appears in Figure 35.1. Listing 35.21 shows its public members.

Listing 35.21. Public members of sun.tools.debug.DebuggerCallback.

```
public class DebuggerCallback {
  public abstract void printToConsole(String text) throws Exception
  public abstract void breakpointEvent(RemoteThread t) throws Exception
  public abstract void exceptionEvent(RemoteThread t, String errorText)
  ➡ throws Exception
  public abstract void threadDeathEvent(RemoteThread t) throws Exception
  public abstract void quitEvent() throws Exception
}
```

printToConsole DebuggerCallback | tools

```
public abstract void printToConsole(String text) throws Exception
```

The `printToConsole()` method prints the specified text to the console window of the debugger.

▶ `text` is a `String` object containing the text to be printed in the debugger console window.

✦ An `Exception` if the string could not be printed.

breakpointEvent DebuggerCallback | tools

```
public abstract void breakpointEvent(RemoteThread t) throws Exception
```

The `breakpointEvent()` method is an event method that notifies when a breakpoint has been hit in the specified thread.

▶ `t` is a `RemoteThread` object. For more information on the `RemoteThread` class, see the documentation earlier in this chapter.

✦ An `Exception` if this method fails.

exceptionEvent DebuggerCallback | tools

```
public abstract void exceptionEvent(RemoteThread t, String errorText)
    ➥ throws Exception
```

The `exceptionEvent()` method is used to notify when an exception has occurred.

▶ `t` is a `RemoteThread` object. For more information on the `RemoteThread` class, see the documentation earlier in this chapter.

▶ `errorText` is a `String` value containing the error that occurred.

✦ An `Exception` if this method fails.

threadDeathEvent DebuggerCallback | tools

```
public abstract void threadDeathEvent(RemoteThread t) throws Exception
```

The `threadDeathEvent()` method is used to notify when a thread dies.

▶ `t` is the `RemoteThread` that has died. For more information on the `RemoteThread` class, see the documentation earlier in this chapter.

✦ An `Exception` if this method fails.

quitEvent DebuggerCallback tools

```
public abstract void quitEvent() throws Exception
```

The `quitEvent()` method notifies when the interpreter has exited, either by returning from the main thread or by calling `System.exit()`.

An `Exception` if this method fails.

→! NoSessionException tools

The hierarchy for the `NoSessionException` exception derives from class `java.lang.Exception`. `NoSessionException` signals that the remote session has been closed. `NoSessionException`'s overall derivation is shown in Figure 35.1. Listing 35.22 shows its public members.

Listing 35.22. Public members of `sun.tools.debug.NoSessionException`.

```
public class NoSessionException extends Exception{
  public NoSessionException()
  public NoSessionException(String s)
}
```

 NoSessionException NoSessionException tools

```
public NoSessionException()
```

The `NoSessionException()` constructor creates a new `NoSessionException` exception object with no default message string.

 NoSessionException NoSessionException tools

```
public NoSessionException(String s)
```

This `NoSessionException()` constructor creates a new `NoSessionException` exception object with a detail message string.

```
public NoSessionException(String s)
```

 `s` is a `String` value containing the detail message associated with this exception.

NoSuchFieldException   tools

The hierarchy for the NoSuchFieldException exception derives from class java.lang.Exception. NoSessionException signals that the class does not have a field of the specified name. NoSuchFieldException's overall derivation is shown in Figure 35.1. Listing 35.23 shows its public members.

Listing 35.23. Public members of sun.tools.debug.NoSuchFieldException.

```
public class NoSuchFieldException extends Exception{
  public NoSuchFieldException()
  public NoSuchFieldException(String s)
}
```

NoSuchFieldException   NoSuchFieldException   tools

```
public NoSuchFieldException()
```

The NoSuchFieldException() constructor creates a new NoSuchFieldException exception object with no default message string.

NoSuchFieldException   NoSuchFieldException   tools

```
public NoSuchFieldException(String s)
```

This NoSuchFieldException() constructor creates a new NoSuchFieldException exception object with a detail message string.

```
public NoSuchFieldException(String s)
```

 s is a String value containing the detail message associated with this exception.

NoSuchLineNumberException   tools

The hierarchy for the NoSuchLineNumberException exception derives from class java.lang.Exception. The NoSuchLineNumberException signals that no code is associated with a specified line number within a Java source file. NoSuchLineNumberException's overall derivation is shown in Figure 35.1. Listing 35.24 shows its public members.

Listing 35.24. Public members of sun.tools.debug.NoSuchLineNumberException.

```
public class NoSuchLineNumberException extends Exception{
    public NoSuchLineNumberException()
    public NoSuchLineNumberException(String s)
}
```

 NoSuchLineNumberException NoSuchLineNumberException   tools

```
public NoSuchLineNumberException()
```

The NoSuchLineNumberException() constructor creates a new NoSuchLineNumberException exception object with no default message string.

 NoSuchLineNumberException NoSuchLineNumberException   tools

```
public NoSuchLineNumberException(String s)
```

This NoSuchLineNumberException() constructor creates a new NoSuchLineNumberException exception object with a detail message string.

▶ s is a String value containing the detail message associated with this exception.

Index

Symbols

" (double quotes)
arguments, 157
string literals, 43
' (single quotes), character literals, 42
<!> HTML tag, 200
!! (exclamation points), jdb option, 246
/* comment delimiter, 34
/ comment delimiter, 34**
// comment delimiter, 34
? (question mark), jdb option, 246
@ (at symbol), JavaDoc documentation tags, 252
[ ] (square brackets), arrays, 43, 78
{ } (curly braces), block statements, 49, 91
3D rectangles drawing, 291, 294

A

a filter that uses data from a pixel's local data, (listing), 357-359
<A> HTML tag, 201
abs( ) method, Math class, 932-933
absbottom value (<APPLET> HTML tag ALIGN attribute), 191
absmiddle value (<APPLET> HTML tag ALIGN attribute), 191
Abstract Windowing Toolkit, *see* **AWT**
abstract
classes, 10, 70-71, 84
compared to Delphi, 103
declaring, 70

methods
compared to Delphi, 103
declaring, 70
abstract keyword, 84, 103
AbstractMethodError
constant, 1013
error, 1012-1013
accept( ) method
FilenameFilter interface, 809
ServerSocket class, 1034
ports, 535
access controls, native methods, 399
access modifiers, classes compared to Delphi, 100
security, 127
accessing
arrays, 44-45, 80
compared to Delphi, 98
class variables, native methods, 415-416
classes, 61
instance variables, native methods, 414-415
structures, macros, 419
vector elements, 508
accessing FontMetrics information (listing), 285-286
acos( ) method, Math class, 933
ACTION EVENT event type, 447
action( ) method
Component class, 300, 613
events, 138-139
activeCount( ) method
Thread class, 987
ThreadGroup class, 994
activeGroupCount( ) method, ThreadGroup class, 994

ActiveX, 220
controls compared to classes, 110-111
Add Current To Places Menu command, Places menu (HotJava), 217
add( ) method
Container class, 304, 617-618
Menu class, 691
MenuBar class, 693
MenuComponent class, 369-370
Rectangle class, 279, 706-707
addConsumer( ) method
FilteredmageSource class, 741
ImageProducer interface, 767
MemoryImageSource class, 753
addElement( ) method, Vector class, 1103
addHelpMenu( ) method, MenuBarPeer interface, 788
addImage( ) method, MediaTracker class, 350, 685
adding to the Truck class (listing), 110
addItem( ) method
Choice class, 316, 591
ChoicePeer interface, 774
List class, 319, 679
ListPeer interface, 786
MenuPeer interface, 791
addLayoutComponent( ) method
BorderLayout class, 578
CardLayout class, 583
FlowLayout class, 636
GridBagLayout class, 668
GridLayout class, 670

X-Y-Z

SAVINGS On Nutmeg and CinnaMoney

http://www.thoughtinc.com

Join the growing number of Java Developers who use Thought Inc. Class Libraries to make the Creation of Advanced Java Applications EASIER.

Special Offer!

Benefits of Nutmeg	Benefits of CinnaMoney
Manage Lists of Objects Easily	Handle complex calculations accurately
Programmer defined sorting criteria	Convert from native Java data types
User created Subclasses	You determine precision & printing
Programmer defined error handling	Precision redefined on the fly
Chose from many advanced list classes	Works with Nutmeg

The special Thought Inc. price for purchasers of this book is $435 for one order of the Nutmeg binary and $735 for one order of the CinnaMoney binary. This is a savings of **$60** off of each of the classes.

Pricing:	**http://www.thoughtinc.com**	Save up to
Orders:	**orders@thoughtinc.com**	**$120**
Information:	**http://www.thoughtinc.com**	On commercial orders

---

Order Form   Thought, Inc. ◆ 415-928-4229

Company _____   ❑ Nutmeg / $435.   Quantity: ____

Name _____   ❑ CinnaMoney / $735   Quantity: ____

Address _____

City _____ State _____

Zip _____ Phone _____

email _____

Payment Method: ❑ Visa   ❑ MasterCard   ❑ Check

Card# _____   Exp. Date ___/___/___

Signature _____

Send To:
Thought Inc. ◆ 2222 Leavenworth St., Suite 304 ◆ San Francisco, CA 94115

Order Code: **jdr0696**   *Expires November 30, 1996*

Don't Forget to subscribe to our email list on our home page to learn about more advanced Java Classes:
http://www.thoughtinc.com

Teach Yourself Java in 21 Days

—Laura Lemay, et al.

Introducing the first, best, and most detailed guide to developing applications with the hot new Java language from Sun Microsystems. *Teach Yourself Java in 21 Days* provides detailed coverage of the hottest new technology on the World Wide Web by showing readers how to develop applications using the Java language. *Teach Yourself Java in 21 Days* includes coverage of browsing Java applications with Netscape and other popular Web browsers, and the accompanying CD-ROM includes the Java Developer's Kit. Covers Java.

Price: $39.99 USA/$53.99 CDN   User Level: Casual–Accomplished–Expert
ISBN: 1-57521-030-4   500 pages

Java Developer's Guide

—Jamie Jaworski and Carie Jardean

Java is one of the major growth areas for developers on the World Wide Web; it brings with it the capability to download and run small applications, called *applets*, from a Web server. *Java Developer's Guide* teaches developers everything they need to know to effectively develop Java applications. It covers the Java interface, VRML extensions, and security, as well as explores new technology and future trends of Java development. The CD-ROM includes source code from the book and valuable utilities. Covers Java 1.1.

Price: $49.99 USA/$67.99 CDN   User Level: Accomplished–Expert
ISBN: 1-57521-069-X   768 pages

Peter Norton's Guide to Java Programming

—William Stanek and Sams DeWolfe

Peter Norton's Guide to Java Programming is a programmer's guide for Web developers. The highly qualified authors dispense their knowledge of Web programming with Java in an easy-to-understand format that will have you programming Java applets in no time. *Peter Norton's Guide to Java Programming* teaches you about threads and exceptions, Java tools, the Java API, applet reuse, as well as provides the most extensive coverage available on how to enhance Java. A CD-ROM is included. Covers Java.

Price: $39.99 USA/$56.95 CDN   User Level: Casual–Accomplished
ISBN: 1-57521-088-6   800 pages

Teach Yourself SunSoft Java WorkShop in 21 Days

—Rogers Cadenhead, Laura Lemay, and Charles E. Perkins

Written in Java itself, the Java WorkShop included with *Teach Yourself SunSoft Java WorkShop in 21 Days* works as a cross-platform tool that provides a rich set of tools for the beginner or professional Java programmer. The workshop combines with the book to provide the most comprehensive way to learn SunSoft Java WorkShop. This book teaches you how to quickly create Java applets with easy-to-use visual development tools, as well as explores the advanced features of the Java WorkShop. Covers Java WorkShop. The accompanying CD-ROM includes source code from the book as well as powerful utilities.

Price: $39.99 USA/$56.95 CDN   User Level: Casual–Accomplished
ISBN: 1-57521-159-9   600 pages

HTML, JAVA, CGI, VRML, SGML
Web Publishing Unleashed

—William Stanek

HTML, JAVA, CGI, VRML, SGML Web Publishing Unleashed teaches you how to convey information on the Web using the latest technology—including Java. Included are sections on how to organize and plan your information, design pages, and become familiar with hypertext and hypermedia. Also, you'll learn how to integrate multimedia and interactivity into Web publications. You can choose from a range of applications and technologies, including Java, SGML, VRML, and the newest HTML and Netscape extensions. This book's CD-ROM contains software, templates, and examples to help you become a successful Web publisher. Covers the World Wide Web.

Price: $49.99 USA/$67.99 CDN   User Level: Casual–Expert
ISBN: 1-57521-051-7   960 pages

Netscape 3 Unleashed, Second Edition

—Dick Oliver

Readers of *Netscape 3 Unleashed, Second Edition* will learn how to fully exploit the new features of this latest version of Netscape—the most popular Web browser in use today. This book teaches you how to install, configure, and use Netscape Navigator™ 3 and also covers how to add interactivity to Web pages with Netscape. The CD-ROM includes Netscape Navigator™ 3, source code from the book, and powerful utilities. Covers Netscape 3.

Price: $49.99 USA/$70.95 CDN   User Level: Accomplished–Expert
ISBN: 1-57521-164-5   1,000 pages

Netscape Server Survival Guide

—David Gulbransen Jr.

With the recent reduction in the price of its server technology, Netscape's marketability is increasing. Both current and migrating Netscape administrators alike will need the comprehensive coverage found in *Netscape Server Survival Guide*. This book teaches you how to install, configure, and maintain a Netscape server, as well as discusses third-party products and commonly used Netscape utilities. An extensive troubleshooting guide is also included. This book's CD-ROM contains software demonstrations, sample configuration files, and exotic logon scripts.

Price: $59.99 USA/$84.95 CDN   User Level: Accomplished–Expert
ISBN: 1-57521-111-4   800 pages

Teach Yourself Web Publishing with HTML 3.2 in a Week, Third Edition

—Laura Lemay

This is the updated edition of Lemay's previous bestseller, *Teach Yourself Web Publishing with HTML in 14 Days, Premier Edition*. In it, you'll find all the advanced topics and updates, such as adding audio, video, and animation and Web page creation. This book explores the use of CGI scripts, tables, HTML 3.0, the Netscape and Internet Explorer extensions, Java applets and JavaScript, and VRML. Covers HTML 3.2.

Price: $29.99 USA/$42.95 CDN   User Level: New–Casual–Accomplished
ISBN: 1-57521-192-0   600 pages

Add to Your Sams.net Library Today
with the Best Books for Internet Technologies

ISBN	Quantity	Description of Item	Unit Cost	Total Cost
1-57521-030-4		Teach Yourself Java in 21 Days (Book/CD-ROM)	$39.99	
1-57521-069-X		Java Developer's Guide (Book/CD-ROM)	$49.99	
1-57521-088-6		Peter Norton's Guide to Java Programming (Book/CD-ROM)	$39.99	
1-57521-159-9		Teach Yourself SunSoft Java WorkShop in 21 Days (Book/CD-ROM)	$39.99	
1-57521-051-7		Web Publishing Unleashed (Book/CD-ROM)	$49.99	
1-57521-164-5		Netscape 3 Unleashed, Second Edition (Book/CD-ROM)	$49.99	
1-57521-111-4		Netscape Server Survival Guide (Book/CD-ROM)	$55.00	
1-57521-192-0		Teach Yourself Web Publishing with HTML 3.2 in a Week, Third Edition (Book/CD-ROM)	$29.99	
		Shipping and Handling: See information below.		
		TOTAL		

Shipping and Handling: $4.00 for the first book, and $1.75 for each additional book. If you need to have it NOW, we can ship product to you in 24 hours for an additional charge of approximately $18.00, and you will receive your item overnight or in two days. Overseas shipping and handling adds $2.00. Prices subject to change. Call between 9:00 a.m. and 5:00 p.m. EST for availability and pricing information on latest editions.

201 W. 103rd Street, Indianapolis, Indiana 46290

1-800-428-5331 — Orders   1-800-835-3202 — FAX   1-800-858-7674 — Customer Service

Installing the CD-ROM

The companion CD-ROM contains all of the authors' source code and sample projects from the book; plus, Sun's JDK, Kawa, Jpad, and many other useful tools.

Windows 95/NT 4 Installation Instructions

1. Insert the CD-ROM disc into your CD-ROM drive.
2. From the Windows desktop, double-click on the My Computer icon.
3. Double-click on the icon representing your CD-ROM drive.
4. Double-click on the icon titled `CDSETUP.EXE` to run the installation program.
5. Installation creates a program group named "Java Developers Ref." This group will contain icons to browse the CD-ROM.

NOTE

If Windows 95/NT is installed on your computer and you have the AutoPlay feature enabled, the `CDSETUP.EXE` program starts automatically whenever you insert the disc into your CD-ROM drive.

Windows 3.1 Installation Instructions

1. Insert the CD-ROM disc into your CD-ROM drive.
2. From File Manager or Program Manager, choose Run from the File menu.
3. Type `<drive>\CDSETUP.EXE` and press Enter, where `<drive>` corresponds to the drive letter of your CD-ROM. For example, if your CD-ROM is drive D:, type `D:\CDSETUP.EXE` and press Enter.
4. Installation creates a program group named "Java Developers Ref." This group will contain icons to browse the CD-ROM.

Macintosh Installation Instructions

1. Insert the CD-ROM disc into your CD-ROM drive.
2. When an icon for the CD appears on your desktop, open the disc by double-clicking on its icon.
3. Double-click on the icon named Guide to the CD-ROM and follow the directions that appear.